RAVENS & RED LIPSTICK

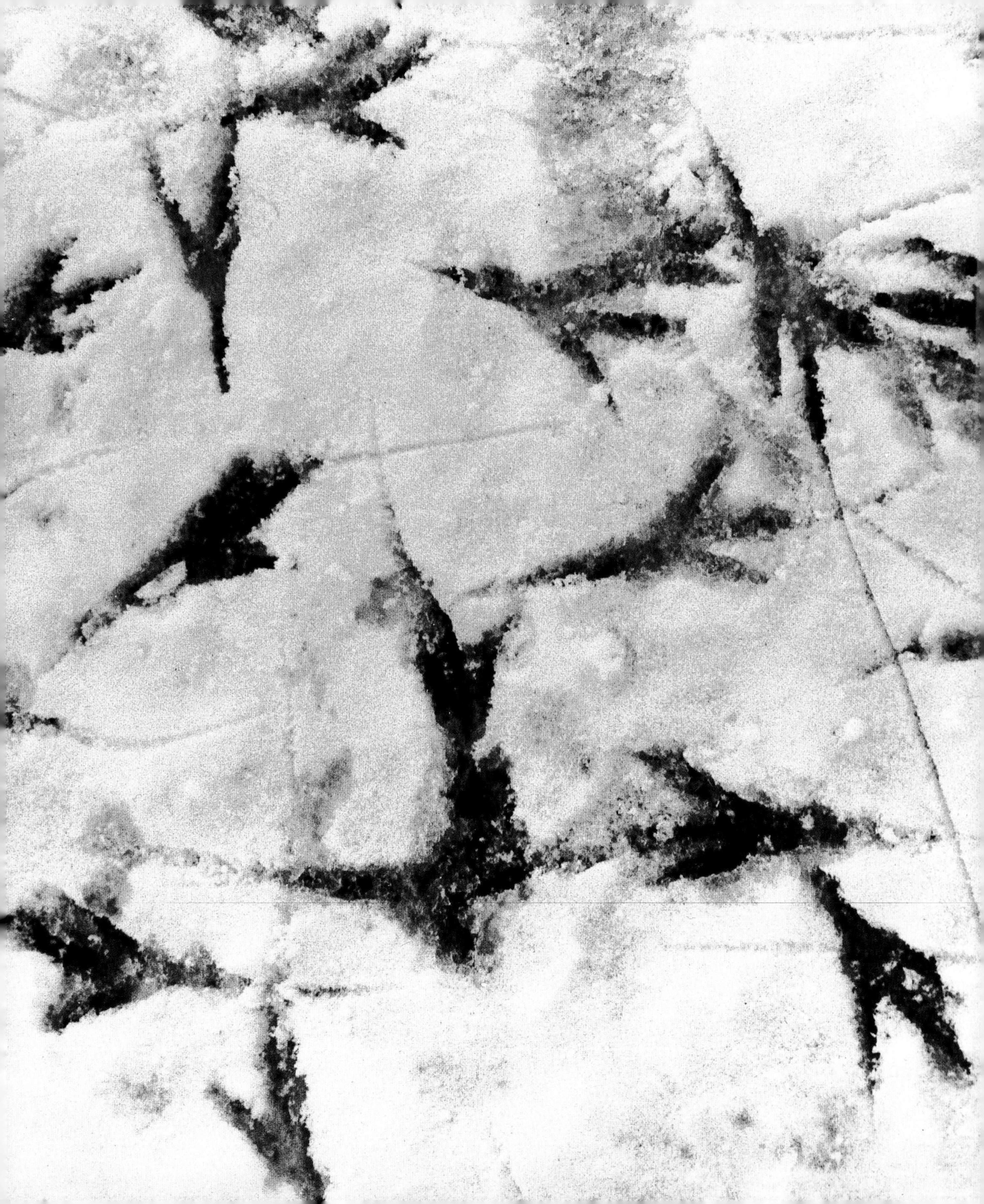

RAVENS &
RED LIPSTICK

JAPANESE
PHOTOGRAPHY
SINCE 1945

LENA FRITSCH

T&H

page 2:
detail from Fukase Masahisa, *Wakkanai,*
1975, *Ravens* series.

First published in the United Kingdom in 2018 by
Thames & Hudson Ltd, 181A High Holborn, London WC1V 7QX

This compact paperback edition published in 2024

Ravens & Red Lipstick: Japanese Photography Since 1945
© 2018 and 2024 Thames & Hudson Ltd, London

Text © 2018 and 2024 Lena Fritsch

Designed by Sarah Boris

British Library Cataloguing-in-Publication Data
A catalogue record for this book is available from the
British Library

ISBN 978-0-500-29762-9

Printed and bound in China by Toppan Leefung Printing Limited

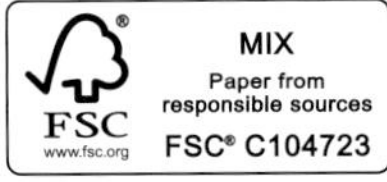

CONTENTS

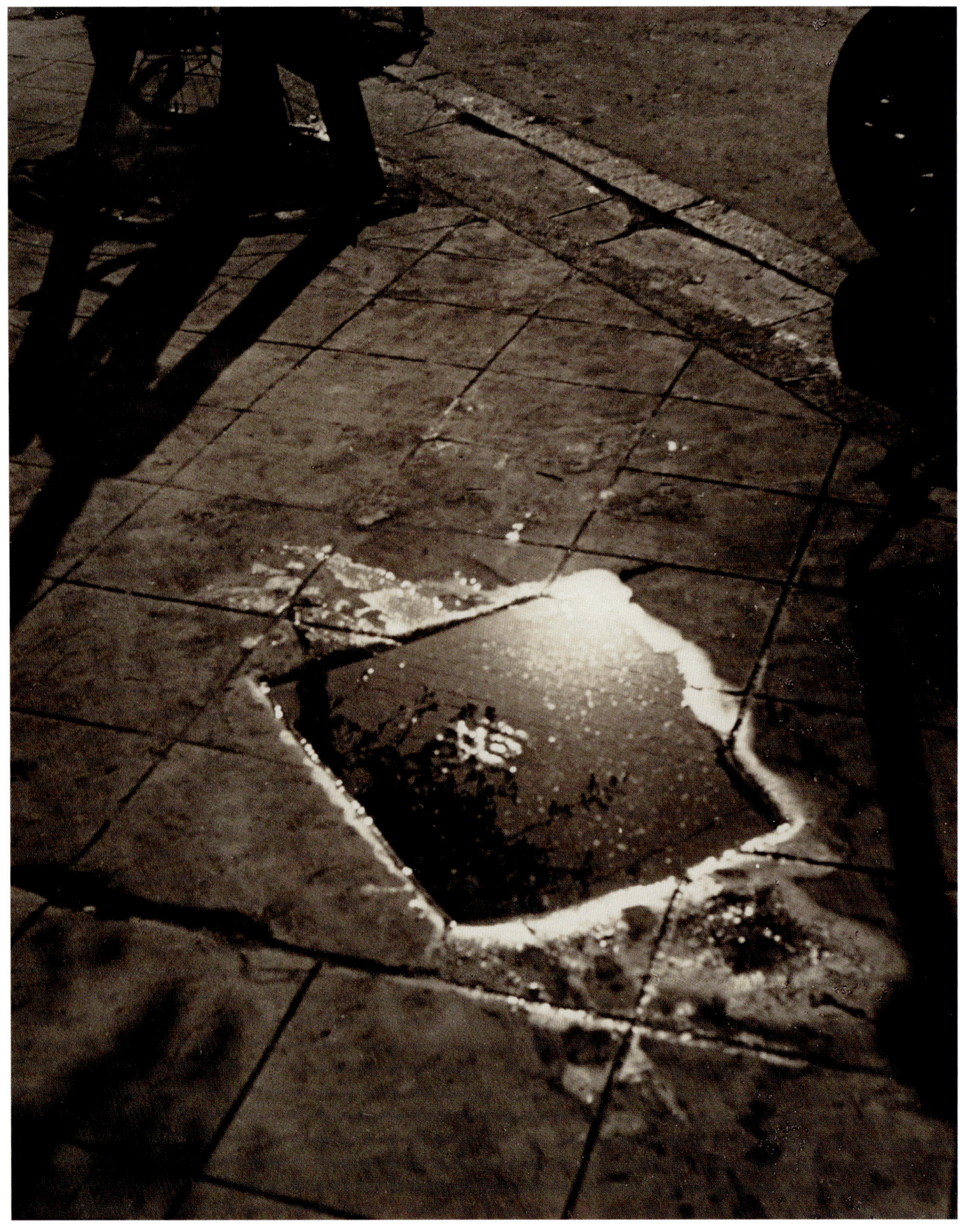

Yagaki Shikanosuke, untitled, 1930s.

Since the 1990s, there has been a growing interest in Japanese photography both within and outside of Japan, resulting in a number of major gallery and museum exhibitions.[1] Japanese photobooks have also become more popular on the 'Western'[2] market; however, there are few publications in English that provide an introduction to Japanese photography. This publication presents a chronological overview of Japanese photography since 1945. It does not set out to be an exhaustive thesis or a unified theory of Japanese photography. It does, however, aim to display the richness of the medium by featuring a selection of photographs. Any photograph is a cultural product that says as much about the world it reflects as it does about the photographer and the world that produced it; this book also, therefore, necessarily investigates the socio-cultural and historical contexts of the photographs. After a brief introduction to the history of photography in Japan before the Second World War and its social contexts today, the chapters are organized broadly chronologically, highlighting movements, influential individuals and iconic photographs.

Why 'Japanese photography'? It can be problematic to view photography through the lens of nationality; the sheer number and diversity of photographs taken in Japan defy categorization by any 'national aesthetic'. However, photography in Japan has grown into an unparalleled industry and socio-cultural world, with camera companies, photography clubs, journals, photo galleries and competitions, and this 'photography world' has produced a vast number of interesting images. 'Japanese photography' in this book is an umbrella term for photographs taken by Japanese photographers and artists, mostly in Japan.

'Photography' and 'photographic art' have long existed in two separate socio-cultural systems, but their differences are often independent of the images themselves. This book is concerned with both. The selection of images is based on their photo-historical relevance as well as my subjective taste. I am interested in photography in a broad sense, but have excluded photographs that were taken solely for documentary purposes. The book title, *Ravens & Red Lipstick*, is inspired by Fukase Masahisa's melancholic black and white photographs of ravens and Ishiuchi Miyako's photographs of the lipsticks that her mother left behind after her death. These projects exemplify the diversity of Japanese photography: black and white as well as colour, photobooks as well as large prints, symbolic stories as well as personal documentations.

'Western' authors have persistently oversimplified Japanese photography. Heinz Spielmann's book *Die japanische Photografie* (1984), for example, presents a great selection of photographs but is filled with stereotypes. Spielmann writes about the 'naturalness' of the Japanese aesthetic,[3] and explains that 'the Japanese man understands more with his eyes than with his mind, his intelligence is connected to looking', assuming that the photographic medium suits 'the Japanese character'.[4] Such expressions are precarious generalizations. Another example is the curator David Streiff's comments on Ishiuchi Miyako's photographs in a 1993 exhibition catalogue. In the series *1·9·4·7*, Streiff sees a 'Japanese' and 'more natural relationship with the feet than in "the West" where feet are put in shoes all day.'[5] Ishiuchi has explained that 'showing women's bare feet is rather considered a disgrace in Japan. It is the absolute opposite of a natural relationship – when I took photographs of women's feet, the husbands of two of the photographed women protested.'[6] Art historian Sawaragi Noi has compared such misinterpretations with statements by the American art historian and educator Ernest Fenollosa (1853–1908), who was an important figure during Japan's modernization but 'projected his own desire onto "Japan as Other" and prescribed the representation of "Japan" to Japanese people'.[7] At the same time, some 'Western' art criticism has offered profound insights into Japanese art. Morimura Yasumasa is a good example of an artist whose work has met with different interpretations in the Euro-American and Japanese art worlds. In Japan, his photography has been interpreted in the context of the entertainment culture of his hometown, Osaka,[8] whereas Euro-American critics have interpreted his works in a political, postcolonial light.[9] The complexity of Morimura's art can only be understood when both perspectives are considered.

I make no claims to methodological originality in this book, but as both a European art historian and somebody who has lived in Japan, whose personal history has been intertwined with Japanese culture and language since an early age, I have attempted to interpret Japanese photography from a perspective that avoids clichés. Over the last ten years,

I have developed my own scholarship and viewpoint – a viewpoint that is constantly shifting between a 'Western' distant position, and a 'Japanese' proximal perspective. Two principles have been paramount: an awareness of my own cultural perspective, and continuous interaction with photography specialists and photographers in Japan. A major part of this publication is the dialogue with photographers, some of whom have sadly passed away since the first edition of this book was published. I conducted 25 interviews in 2016 and 2017, mostly face-to-face in Japan. They represent the photographers' voices, complementing my texts and the images (which also speak for themselves). My interviews were structured with a fixed set of questions, but I often added new questions in reaction to the interviewees' answers, with the aim of hearing more about people's views and experiences.

All unattributed translations are my own. Since Japanese syntax, semantics and style differ so much from the English, compromises were inevitable in the translation process. Where the original passage is linguistically central to the argument, translations tend to be more literal; where it concerns narration, the translation is often freer. Japanese words are italicized; their spelling follows the Hepburn system. Japanese names are written in Japanese order: the surname followed by the personal name.

Shashin: Photography in Japan Until 1945

The Japanese term for photography, *shashin*, is composed of the characters *sha*, meaning 'to reproduce' or 'to copy', and *shin* for 'truth'. Artists Shiba Kōkan and Satake Shōzan used the word to describe the realism of 'Western' art, but in the late 1860s it became associated with photography.[10] The characters illustrate the way photography was viewed: as the process of 'making a copy' of a 'true' subject.

Photography was introduced to Japan in the late 1850s. One of the first Japanese professional photographers, Ueno Hikoma, opened a photo atelier in Nagasaki in 1862. One year later, photojournalist Felice Beato and Charles Wirgman, a correspondent for the *Illustrated London News*, opened a studio in Yokohama. Beato took a great number of journalistic photographs, but it was his introduction of studio photography to Japan that made him influential. Photographers began to take photographs of models staging 'traditional' scenes, mostly for European and American tourists. The photographs were often taken with stereotypical landscape backdrops, such as Mount Fuji. The production and export of these souvenir pictures mainly took place in Yokohama and Nagasaki, which is why this early commercial photography is referred to as 'Yokohama *shashin*' or 'École de Yokohama'.

In the 1880s, the introduction of the simpler dry plate process meant that photography was no longer exclusively the preserve of professionals. In 1889, the amateur club Japan Photographic Society (Nihon Shashinkai) was founded, proclaiming that photography should not only be used for practical purposes but also as an art medium.[11] Photography

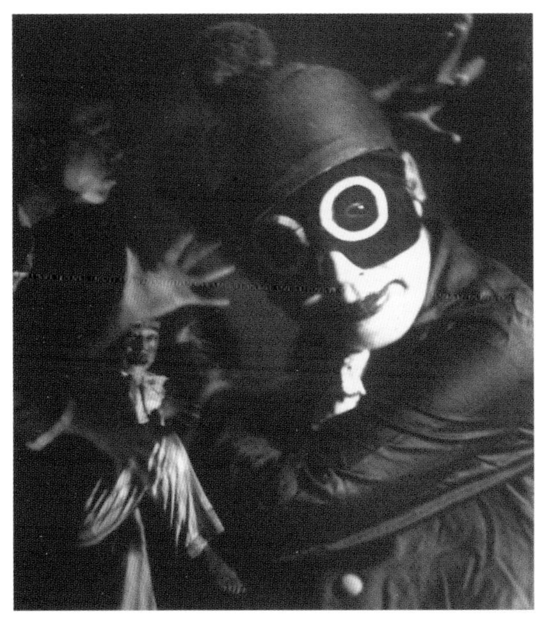

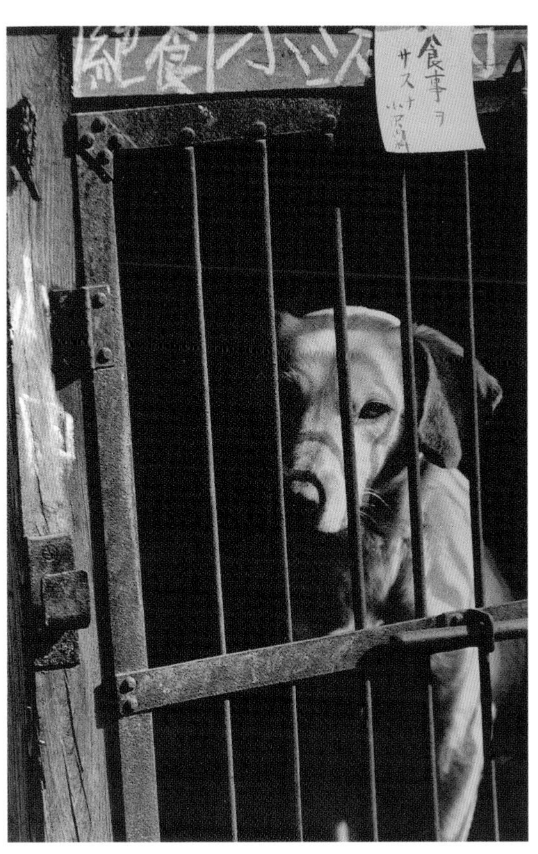

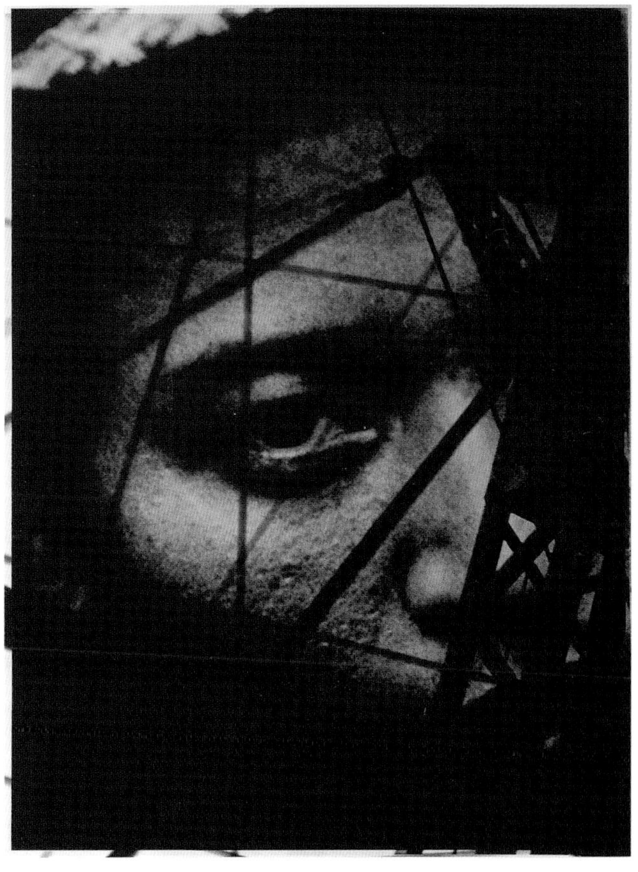

Top left: Nakayama Iwata , · · · ·, 1933.
Above: Yasui Nakaji, *Gaze*, 1931.
Left: Yasui Nakaji, *Dog*, 1935.

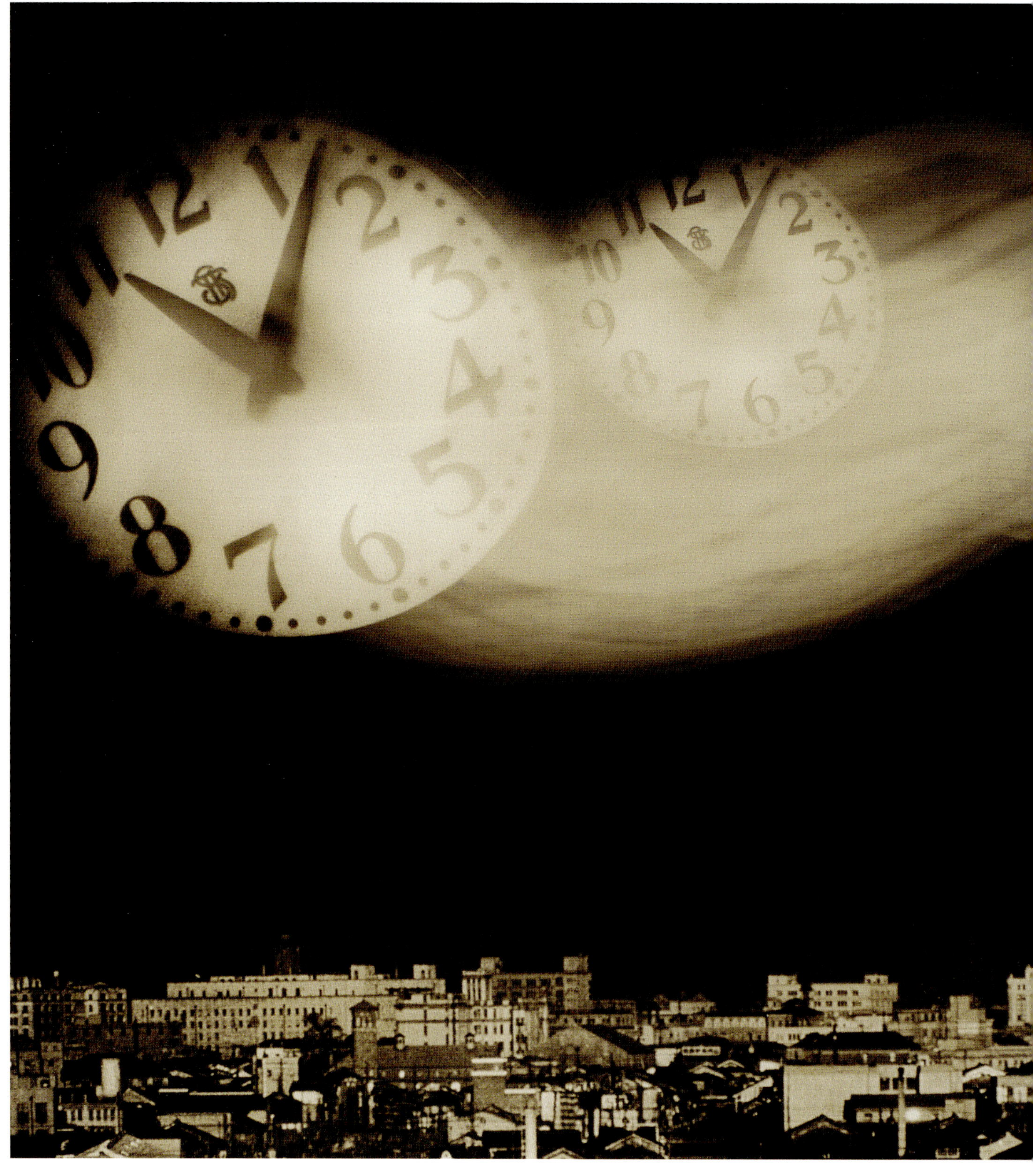

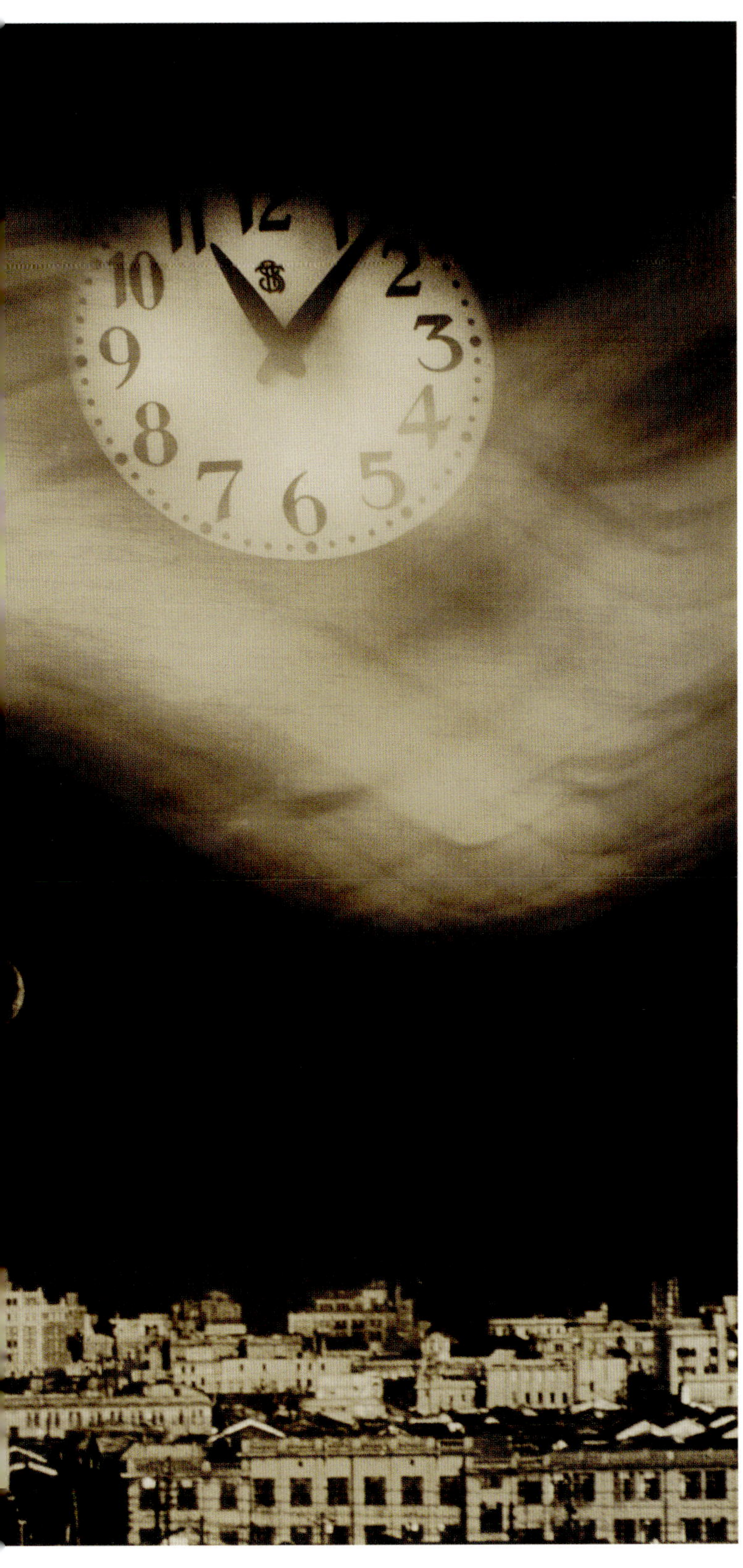

Koishi Kiyoshi, *Fatigue*, 1936, *Drunken Dream* series.

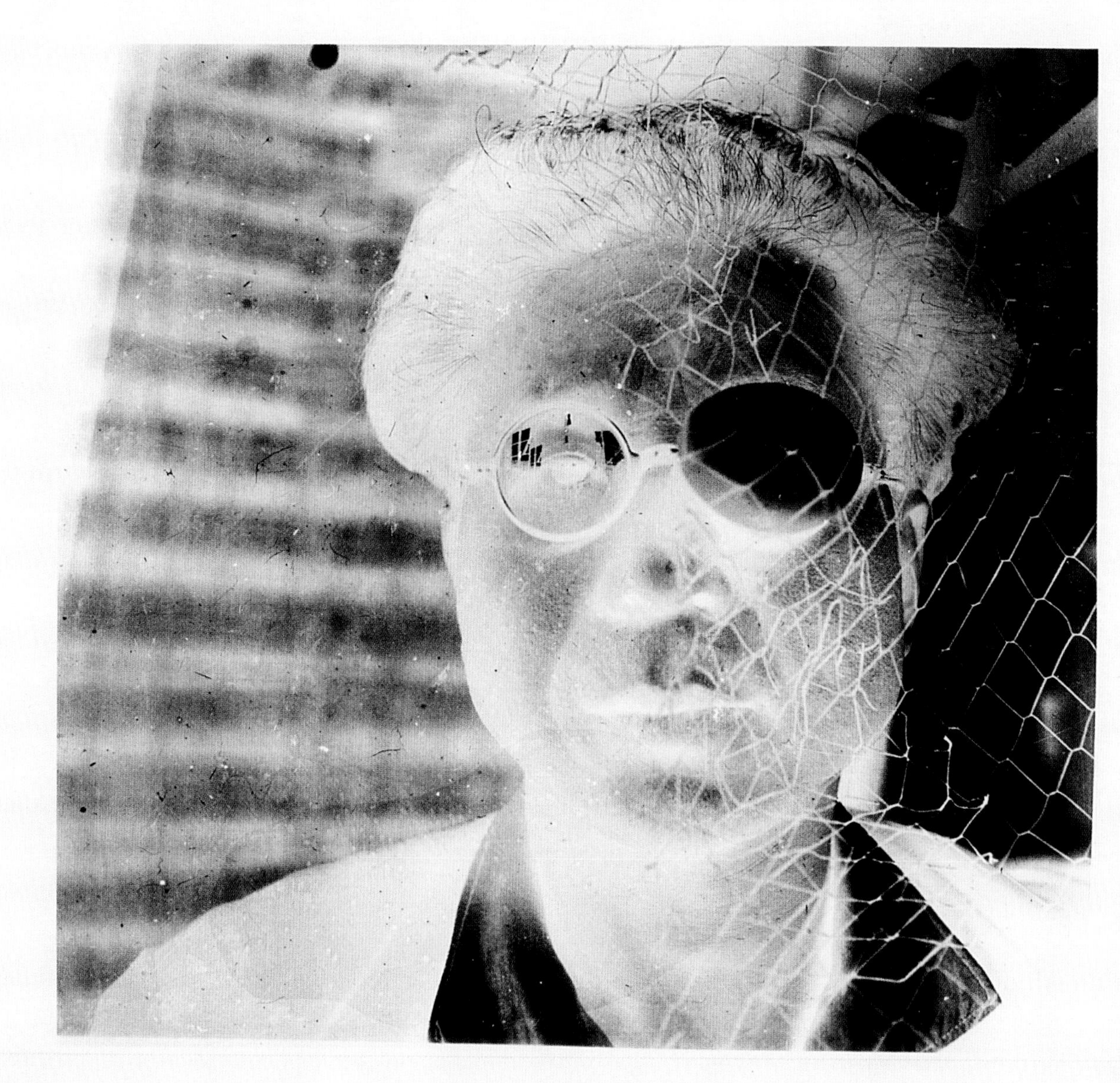

Shiihara Osamu, *Self-portrait*, 1930s.

magazines, which often also served as instruction manuals, promoted amateur photography; but it was not until the introduction of the lower-priced Eastman Kodak Vest Pocket compact camera, in the middle of the Taishō era (1912–25), that photography truly became more accessible.

Modern photography in Japan began to develop by adapting new ideas from Europe. The *Asahi Camera* magazine, first published in 1926, introduced the work of László Moholy-Nagy, Man Ray and El Lissitzky. A group of young photographers founded the collective New Photography Research Society (Shinkō Shashin Kenkyūkai), pursuing a vision that was unique to photography and experimenting with special perspectives, camera angles and photograms. This photography was called 'new photography' (*shinkō shashin*), and became dominant in 1931, when the touring photography section of the 'Internationale Ausstellung, "Film und Foto"', organized by Deutscher Werkbund, was exhibited in Tokyo and Osaka. Not only did it present photographic trends, including works by Moholy-Nagy, T. Lux Feininger and Marianne Brandt, but examples of new photographic techniques too. Works by amateur photographer Yagaki Shikanosuke (1897–1966) exemplify the exhibition's influence on photographers: his works employ unusual vantage points and focus on finding beauty in everyday life (p. 6). Various photo clubs emerged during the late 1920s and 1930s, in the Kantō region around Tokyo and the Kansai region around Osaka.

An important contributor to the *shinkō shashin* movement was Nakayama Iwata (1895–1949), who studied and worked in California, New York and Paris, before returning to Japan in 1927. His work uses a vivid artistic language, and in a 1928 essay he emphasized that it is wrong to think of painting or sculpture as a higher art form than photography: 'of course there are photographs that could be called "pure art".'[12] In the 1930s, photography began to promote surrealism and abstraction. Avant-garde photography became popular, with collectives like the Avant-Garde Image Group (Avant-Garde Zōei Shūdan) and the Avant-Garde Photography Association (Zen'ei Shashin Kyōkai). Influential photographers in the Kansai region included Yasui Nakaji (1903–42) (p. 9), Koishi Kiyoshi (1908–57), who created surrealist photomontages (pp. 10–11) and Shiihara Osamu (1905–74), who experimented with multiple exposure or solarization techniques (opposite). Yamawaki Iwao (1898–1987) studied architecture at the Tokyo School of Fine Arts. He moved to Berlin in 1930, and later attended the Bauhaus in Dessau. Yamawaki's photographs were strongly influenced by the Neues Sehen movement. *Reflection in Mirrored Ball* (1932) exemplifies this influence, showing an ordinary room from an unfamiliar, round, mirrored perspective (p. 15).

Photographers also drew attention to the social responsibilities of the medium. In 1932, Natori Yōnosuke (1910–62), who had practised journalistic photography in Germany, came back to Japan. In 1933, together with Kimura Ihei (1901–74), Ina Nobuo (1898–1978) and the graphic designer Hara Hiromu (1903–86), he co-founded the Japan Studio (Nippon Kōbō), promoting a new ideology and technique of photography in Japan. The magazine *Nippon*, which was launched in 1934 by Nippon Kōbō, publicized Japanese culture to other countries, and typifies Natori's photojournalism.

Photography developed into two separate strands in the 1930s: avant-garde photography and journalistic photography. However, both were increasingly suppressed during the Second World War, when photography was used primarily for propaganda.

The 'Photography World' in Japan

Since 1962, Japan has led the world in camera manufacturing, with companies like Canon, Fuji Film, Nikon, Olympus, Pentax (previously Asahi) and Sony creating some of the best cameras, lenses and films. These companies support numerous photo galleries, such as Fuji Salon or Canon Salon, which present short-term exhibitions. There are also many amateur photography clubs in Japan, such as the Photographic Society of Japan (Nihon Shashin Kyōkai), which was founded in 1952 to support competitions, exhibitions and the publication of periodicals. The Japan Professional Photographers' Society (Nihon Shashinka Kyōkai) is its counterpart for professional photographers. The All-Japan Association of Photographic Societies (AJAPS, Zennihon Shashin Renmei), founded in 1926, is supported by the Asahi Newspaper Company and sponsors photography competitions.

Asahi Camera, founded in 1926 by the Asahi Newspaper Company as the voice of the AJAPS, is the oldest surviving photography magazine in Japan. It publishes photographs by professionals and amateurs, as well as equipment and exhibition reviews. Another popular monthly magazine, *Nippon Camera*, has existed since 1951. It features photographs by a mixture of established and promising photographers, and runs a monthly photography contest. It is impossible to overestimate the role of magazines and photobooks in the evolution of Japanese photography. Today, the internet provides easy access to photographs and information; however, until the 1990s, magazines were an important source for information on photography, including works from overseas. For many Japanese photographers, the photobook is the ultimate format in which to present their works. Numerous masterpieces have been published, including Hosoe Eikoh's *Ordeal by Roses (Barakei)* in 1961, Kawada Kikuji's *The Map (Chizu)* in 1965, Araki Nobuyoshi's *Sentimental Journey* in 1971 and Fukase Masahisa's *Ravens* in 1986.

Photography in Japan has become a web of camera companies, clubs, galleries, publishers and magazines. It is not only an important industry, but also a large community of amateur photographers and camera fans. This 'photography world' exists parallel to the 'art world', which has also produced photographic works.

Photography Education

Although modern art education in Japan began in 1876,
the first photography course was only established in 1915,
at the Tokyo School of Fine Arts. The course was cancelled
after twelve years, on the grounds that 'photography and
print departments belong in a craft school which is neither
a purely fine arts school nor a purely industrial arts school'.[13]
In 1923, the photo company Konishi founded the Konishi
Professional School of Photography (Konishi Shashin Senmon
Gakkō), which became part of Tokyo Polytechnic University,
and has remained one of the most popular schools for
photography. Other schools to offer photography courses
included the Japan Photographic Academy (Nihon Shashin
Gakuen), which closed in 2005, and the Tokyo College of
Photography (Tōkyō Sōgō Shashin Senmon Gakkō), whose
curriculum focuses mainly on techniques and industrial
viewpoints. Nihon University is also renowned for photography,
having produced famous practitioners such as Dōmon Ken
(1909–90). It was only in recent years that photography was
introduced to other art academies, so it is not surprising that
a number of the people whose work is featured in this book
studied art or design instead, or are self-taught.

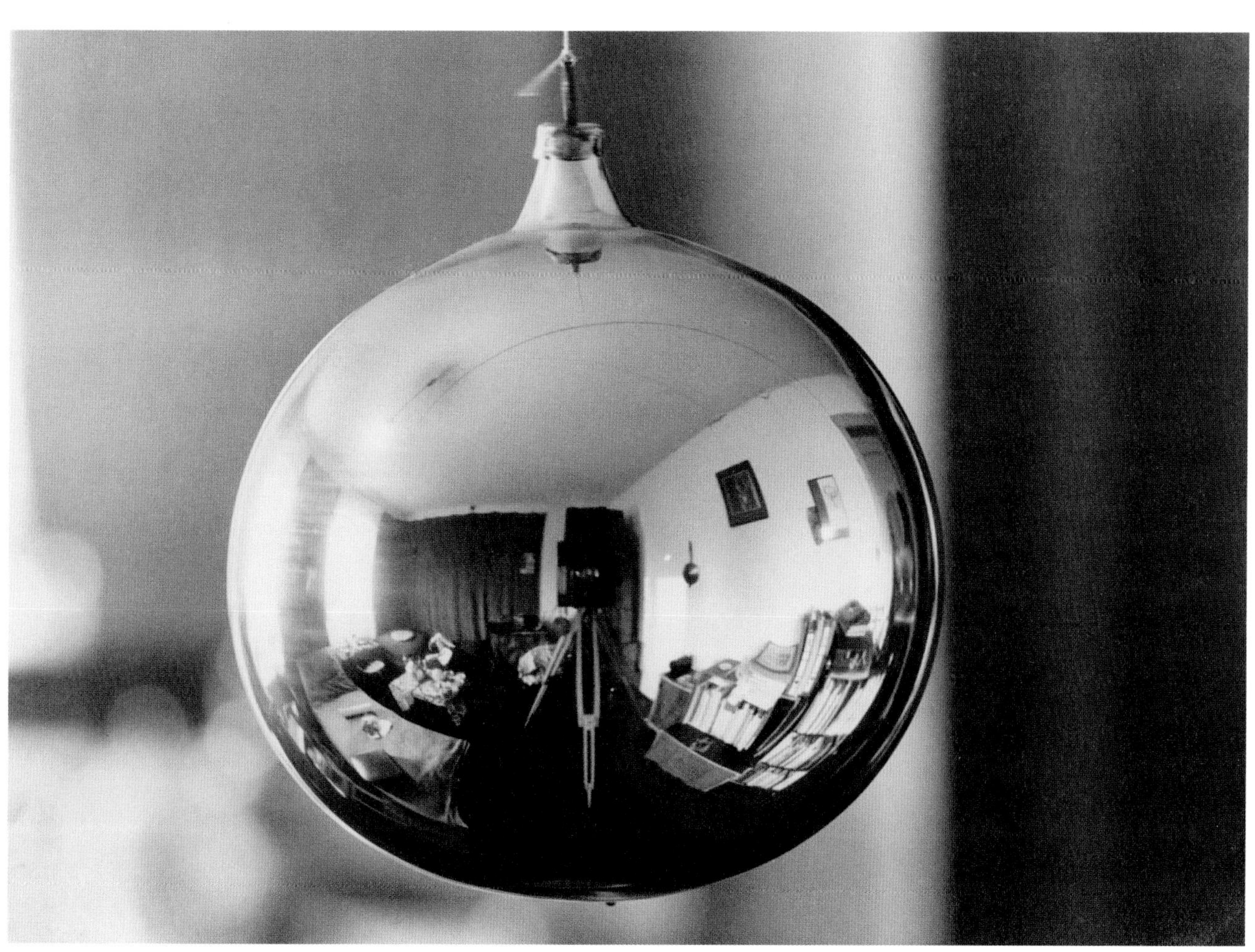

Yamawaki Iwao, *Reflection in Mirrored Ball,* 1932.

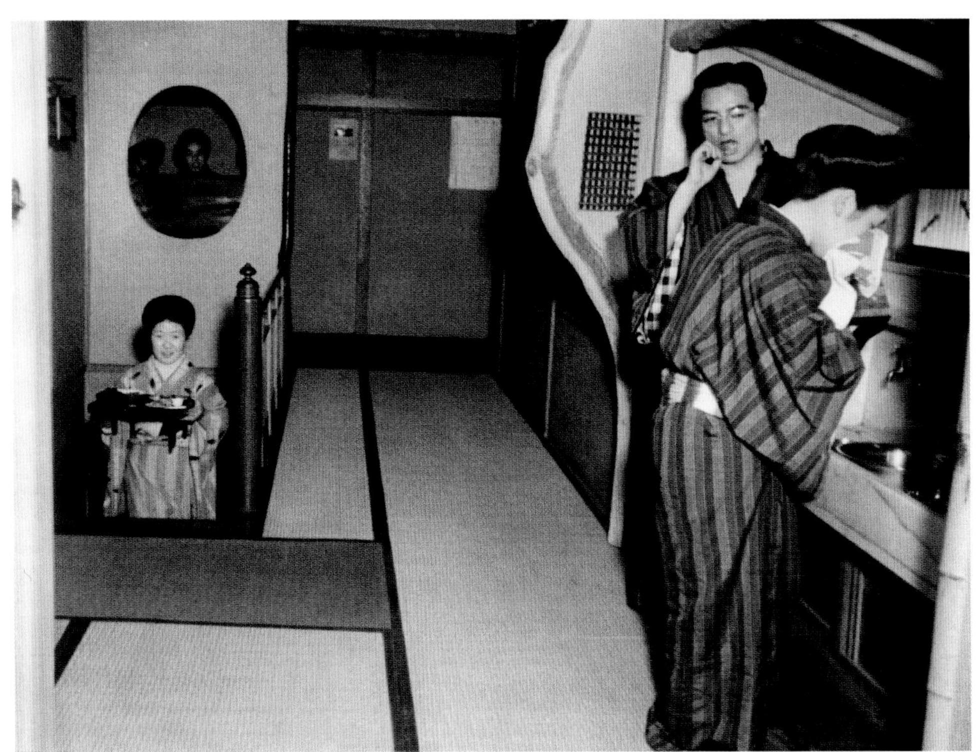

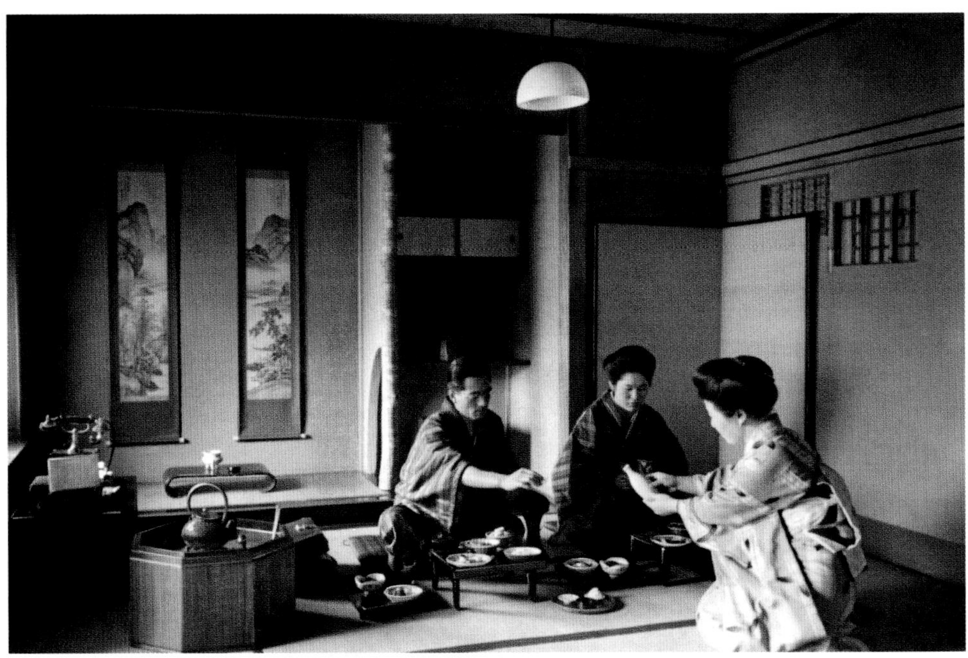

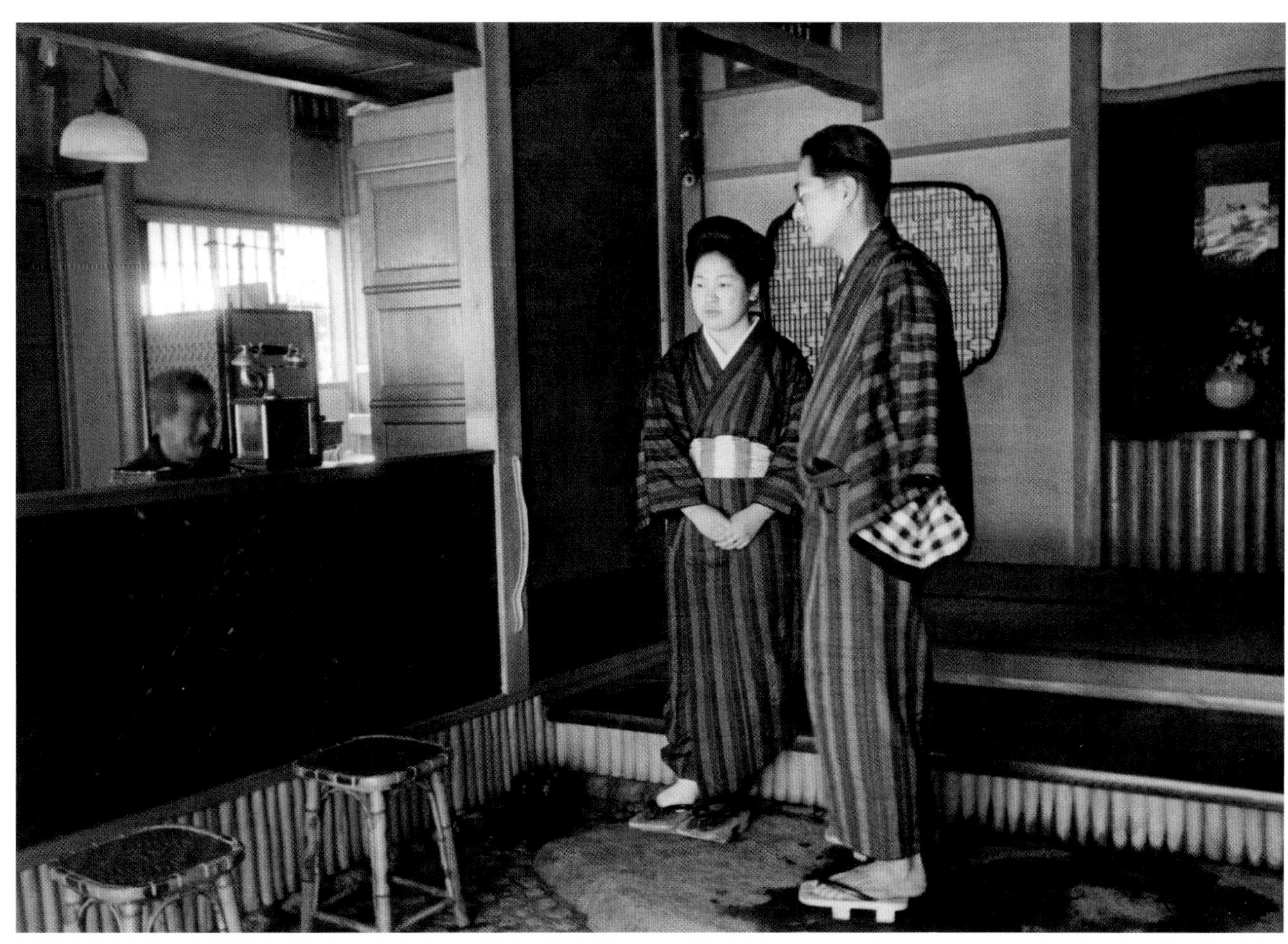

Opposite and above: Natori Yōnosuke, *Hotels in Japan* series, 1932.

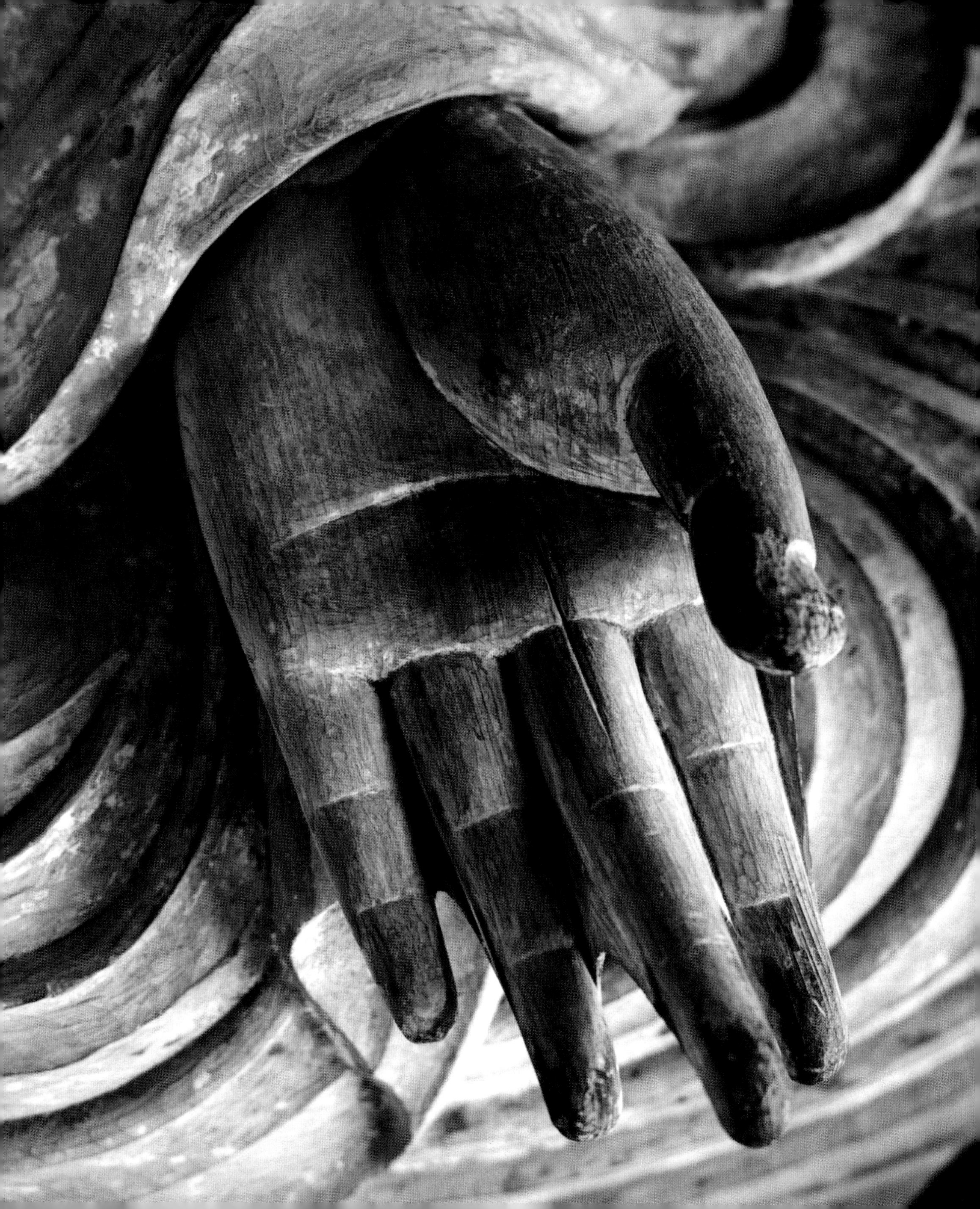

I

POST-WAR TRAUMA

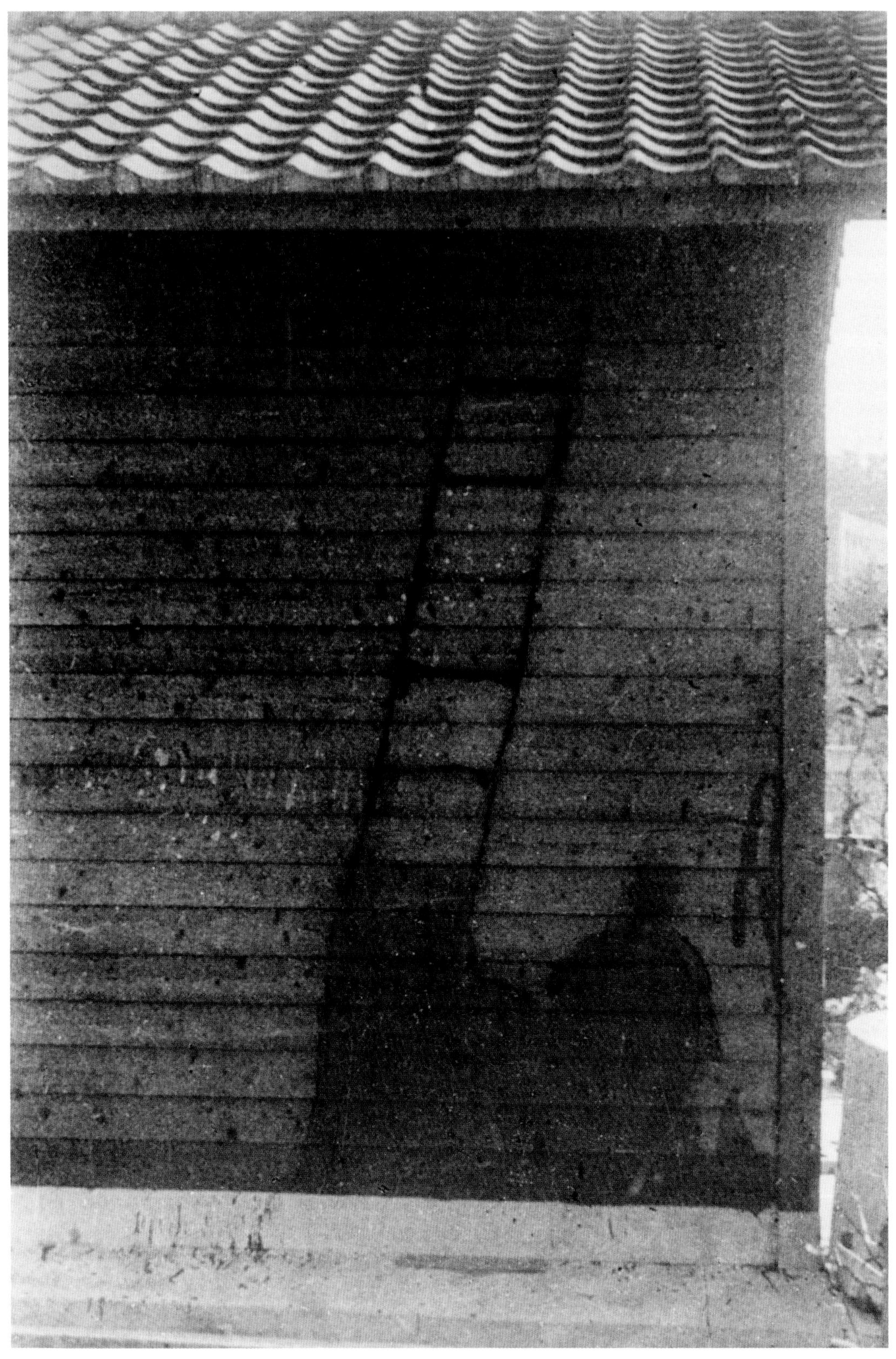

Previous spread:
detail from Dōmon Ken,
*Left hand of the sitting
image of Buddha
Shakyamuni in the
Hall of Mroku, Muro-ji,
Nara, c.* 1943.
Left: Matsumoto Eiichi,
*Shadow of a Soldier
remaining on the
wooden wall of
the Nagasaki military
headquarters,* 1945.

The atomic bombing of Hiroshima on 6 August 1945 killed approximately 150,000 people, either instantly or gradually over the following months. The bombing of Nagasaki three days later killed over 75,000 people. Almost all buildings were destroyed or heavily damaged, turning the cities into atomic wastelands. Matsumoto Eiichi (1915–2004) visited Hiroshima and Nagasaki for the *Asahi Newspaper*. His photograph of a soldier's shadow imprinted on a wall in Nagasaki (opposite) exemplifies the way that photography was able to show traces of the tragedy, but failed to convey its reality. The American occupying forces imposed censorship on Japan, prohibiting pictures of the bombed cities. Although the names 'Hiroshima' and 'Nagasaki' were incised into people's memories, there were few pictures to accompany them. On 15 August, the Japanese people heard Emperor Hirohito's voice and difficult, antiquated language for the first time, when he announced the country's unconditional surrender on the radio. The war was over. In Niigata, Hamaya Hiroshi (1915–99) lifted his camera towards the sky and took a photograph of the bright sun. His *The sun on the day of defeat* is an abstract image: the sun is a grainy white sphere, contrasting with the pitch-black surrounding of the sky (p. 23).[14] It symbolizes great change, evoking an inverted image of the Japanese flag.

A key image representing Japan's defeat was published in newspapers just over a month later: it shows Emperor Hirohito next to General MacArthur (p. 24). The emperor, who had traditionally been seen as a descendant of the sun goddess Amaterasu, is shown as a short mortal man standing stiffly next to the tall general, who is posing in a relaxed manner. The superiority of the United States was emphasized both physically and symbolically, leaving Hirohito emasculated. Japan's national identity was altered with a single photograph.[15]

Realism and *Kumi Shashin*

In the late 1940s and early 1950s, photography was dominated by two similar approaches: realism and 'grouped photographs' (*kumi shashin*), a photojournalistic trend of creating narrative series. One of the most important photographers to embrace a realist style was Kimura Ihei (1901–74). He had taken photojournalistic works with his Leica camera throughout the 1930s and the war years, and now portrayed daily life in post-war Japan. His photograph of a soldier returning to the ruins of his home documents the destruction of Japan's cities, and the harsh realities that people faced after the war (p. 25). Kimura's most celebrated photographs include a series of snapshot-like images documenting rural life in Akita Prefecture, in northern Japan (pp. 29–30). Rural Japan and its people became a popular photographic motif among amateur photographers who wanted to escape the destroyed cities. Photographs by Midorikawa Yōichi (1915–2001) focus on Japan's landscapes. His images of the Seto Inland Sea, with bright lights reflected on the surface of the water, convey the captivating beauty of nature (p. 32).

Dōmon Ken (1909–90) was an important proponent of the realism movement. He took lively photographs of children, showing their improvised plays in Tokyo and their daily lives in the impoverished town of Chikuhō, where a coal mine had shut down (pp. 33–35). He celebrated the directness of photography and its ability to reflect reality in an un-dramatized, un-staged style. Dōmon also had a passion for traditional culture, and photographed Buddhist temples and statues throughout Japan for decades. He focused on the faces or hands of the Buddha statues, revealing stunning details (pp. 18, 33). In the late 1950s, when the American occupation had officially ended, photographs of Hiroshima and Nagasaki from 1945 were finally published. Photographers also began to draw attention to the after-effects of the bombing. Dōmon's photobook *Hiroshima* documents, unflinchingly, the lives of the explosion victims (*hibakusha*) and the bombing's atrocities (p. 36).

Made popular by magazines such as *Camera*, the realism movement grew. It reflected the desire of many amateur photographers to confront the severe realities of the post-war period, as well as their distrust of the 'closed, salon-like character of the pre-war photography world'.[16] Kimura, Dōmon, Hamaya, Hayashi Tadahiko (1918–90), Tanuma Takeyoshi (b. 1929) and others sought to show social circumstances as objectively as possible, criticizing staged photography. Kimura was instrumental in founding the Japan Professional Photographers' Society (Nihon Shashinka Kyōkai) in 1950, and became its first president. The Kimura Ihei Award, established in 1975 after Kimura's death, has become the most prestigious photography award in Japan. A Dōmon Ken Award was established in 1981 and a museum followed in 1983; it is Japan's first museum of photography. It is reflective of the medium's long-standing association with realism that Kimura and Dōmon became such celebrated photographers in Japan.

The *kumi shashin* approach was established by Natori Yōnosuke (1919–62), the founder of modern photojournalism in Japan. He compared grouped photographs with words in a sentence: the individual photographs in his works became signs subordinated to a wider topic and functioned as illustrations (pp. 16–17).[17] Realism and *kumi shashin* were regarded as opposites: one highlighted the meaning of the photographic subject, while the other focused on the choice of images to create a particular context. However, as photo critic and curator Fukagawa Masafumi has emphasized, 'regarding the relationship between photograph and photographic subject, both movements are in step with each other: they both assume a simple subject-object dualism, presupposing that there exists a meaning, attached to the subject, which can then be understood'.[18] This dualism was soon to be questioned by a new generation of photographers.

Ueda Shōji

Far from the realism and *kumi shashin* movements, there was a photographer working remotely in Tottori Prefecture, at the Japan Sea coast: Ueda Shōji (1913–2000). He took photographs in a unique language that he had begun to create in the 1930s, combining a modernist focus on composition with his subjective viewpoints. His *Tottori Sand Dunes* series presents his family members in the dunes in a dreamy, surreal style, contrasting with the documentary photographs of his contemporaries (pp. 38–39). Ueda received numerous awards, and a museum dedicated to his work opened in Tottori in 1995. His photography has inspired many younger photographers, including Hosoe Eikoh.

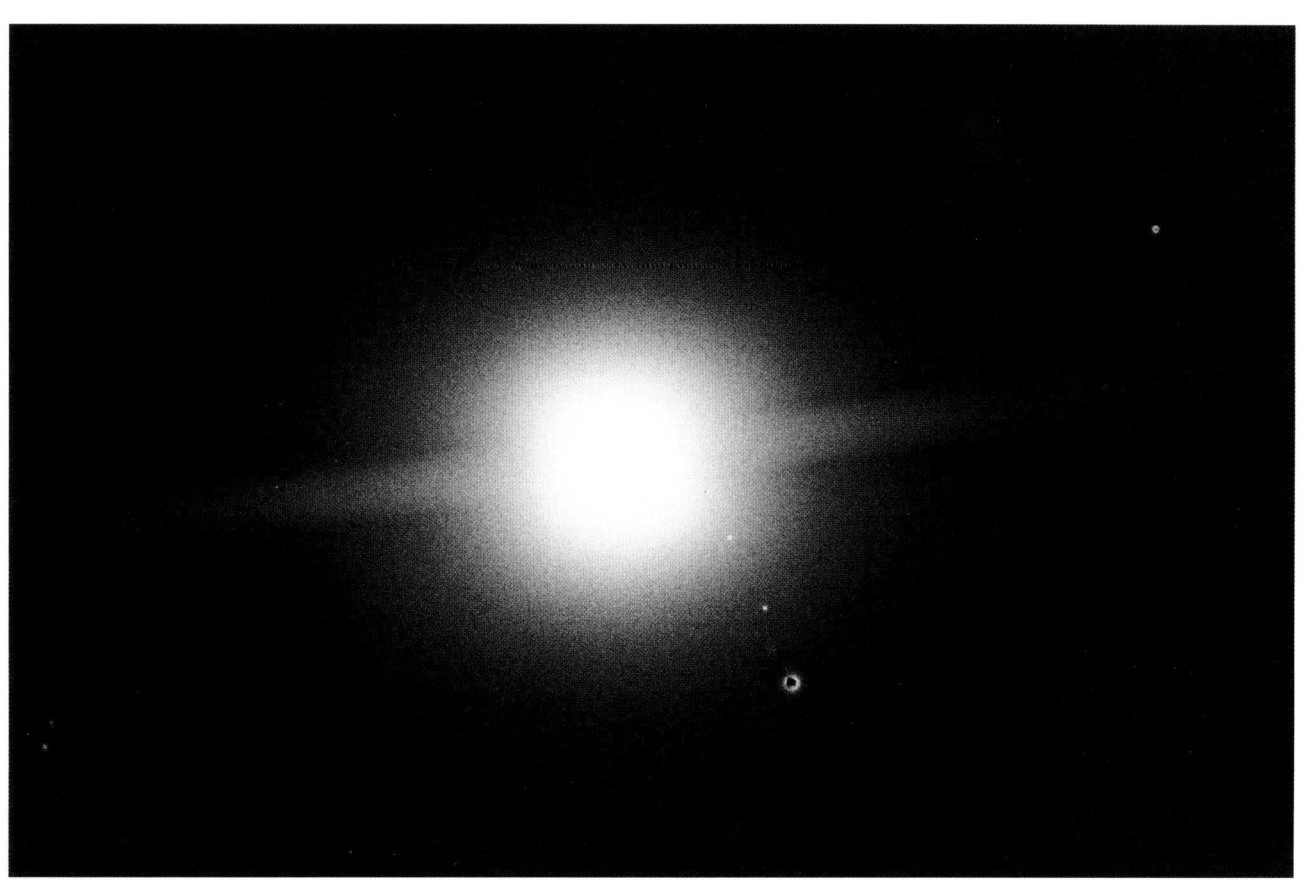

Hamaya Hiroshi, *The sun on the day of defeat*, 1945.

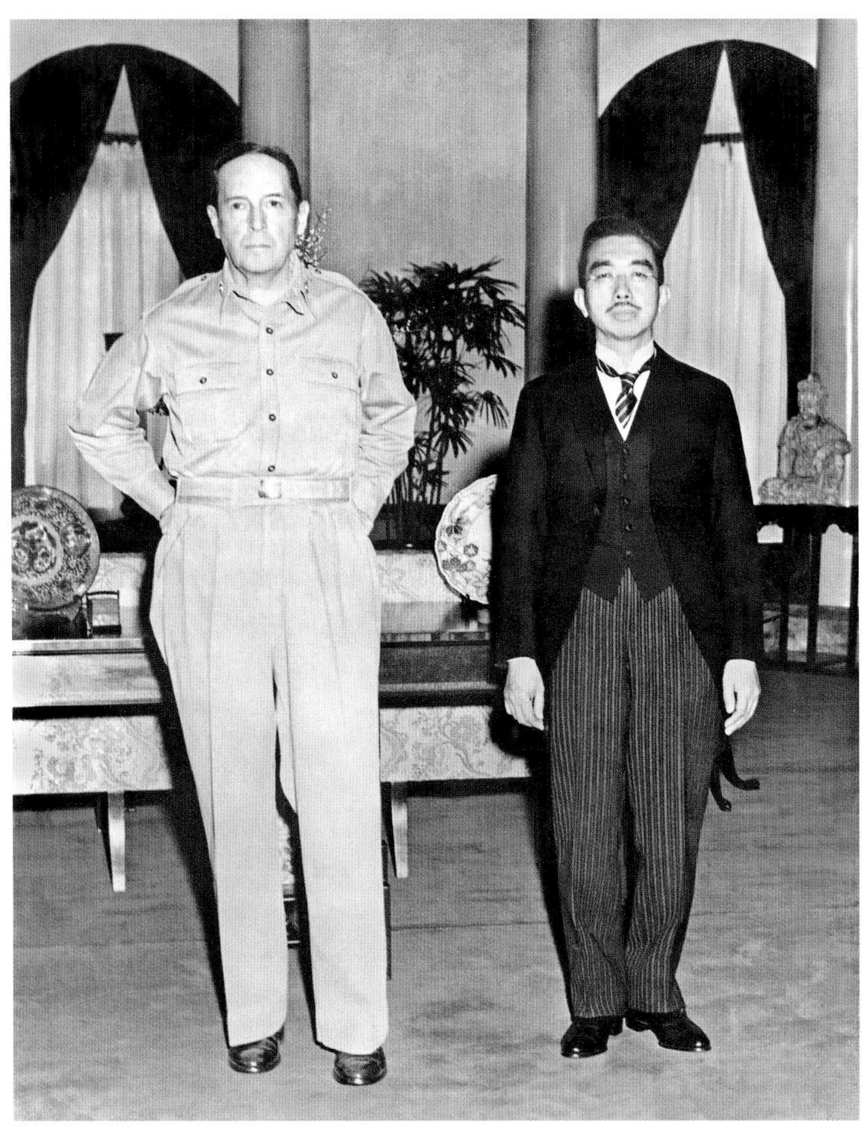

Above: Lt Gaetano Faillace (US Army photographer),
*Emperor Hirohito and General MacArthur at their
first meeting*, 1945.
Opposite: Kimura Ihei, *Discharged soldier returning
to his home in ruins*, 1948.

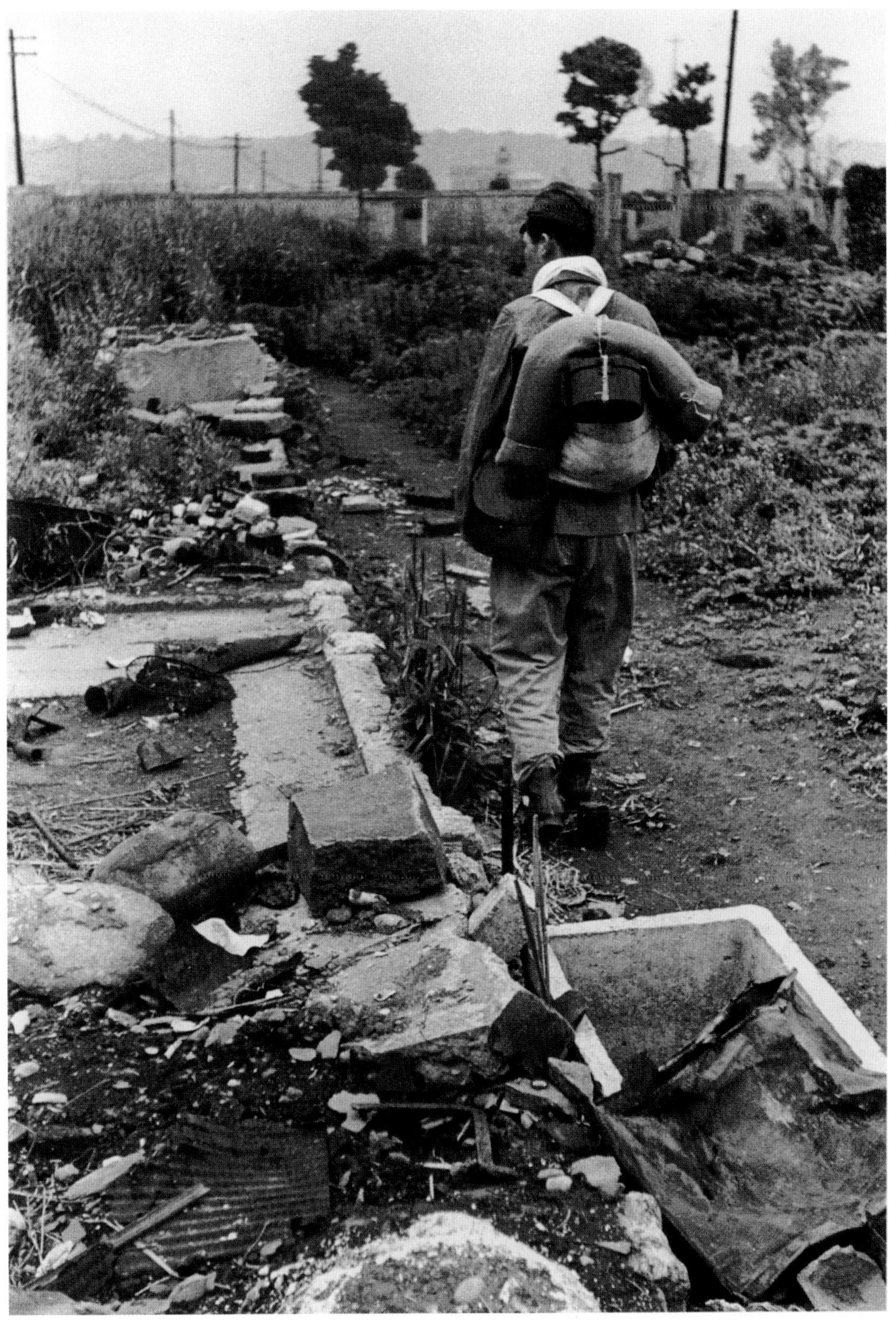

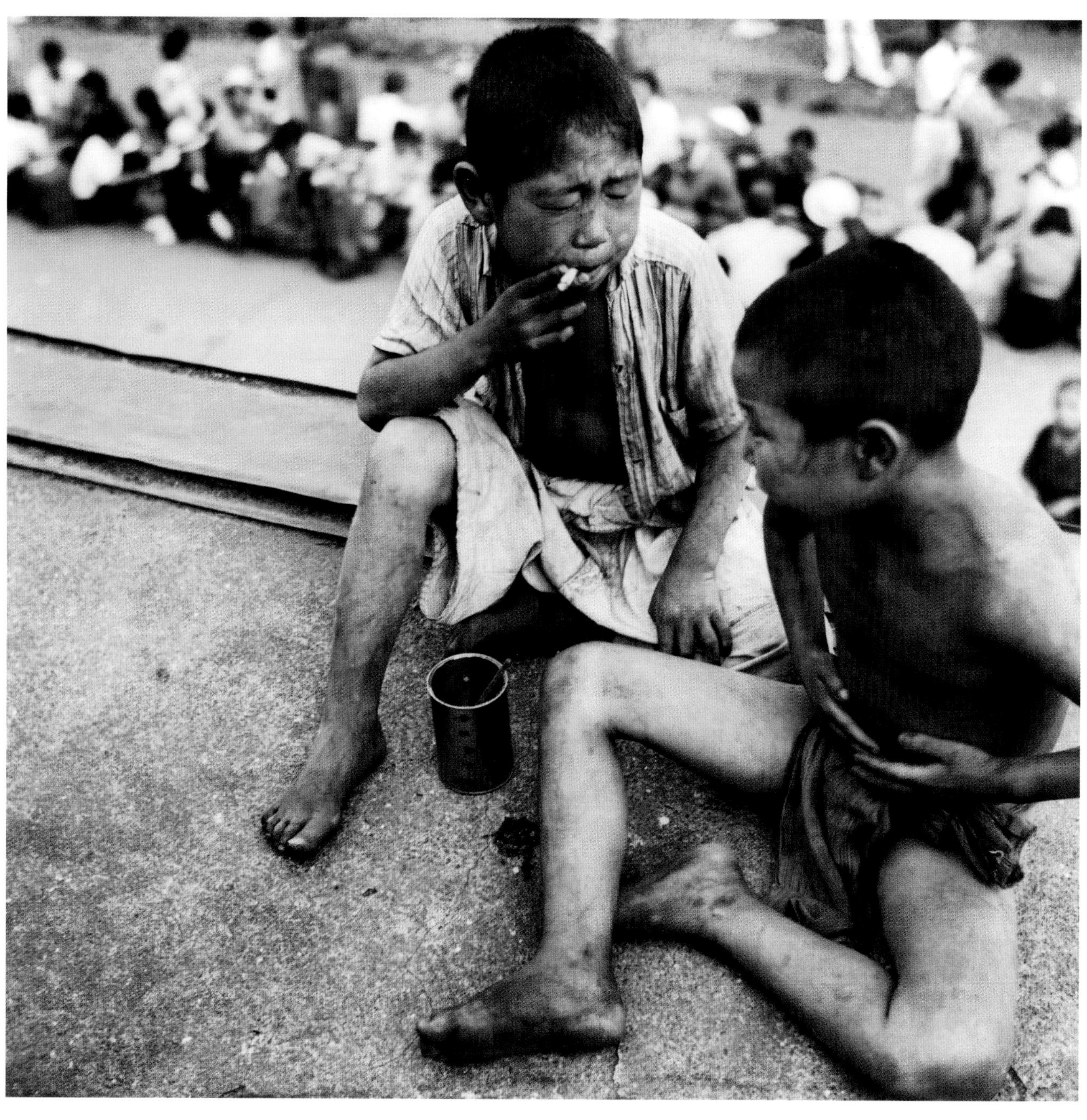

Hayashi Tadahiko, *Orphaned street children smoking*, 1946, *Days in the Dregs* series.

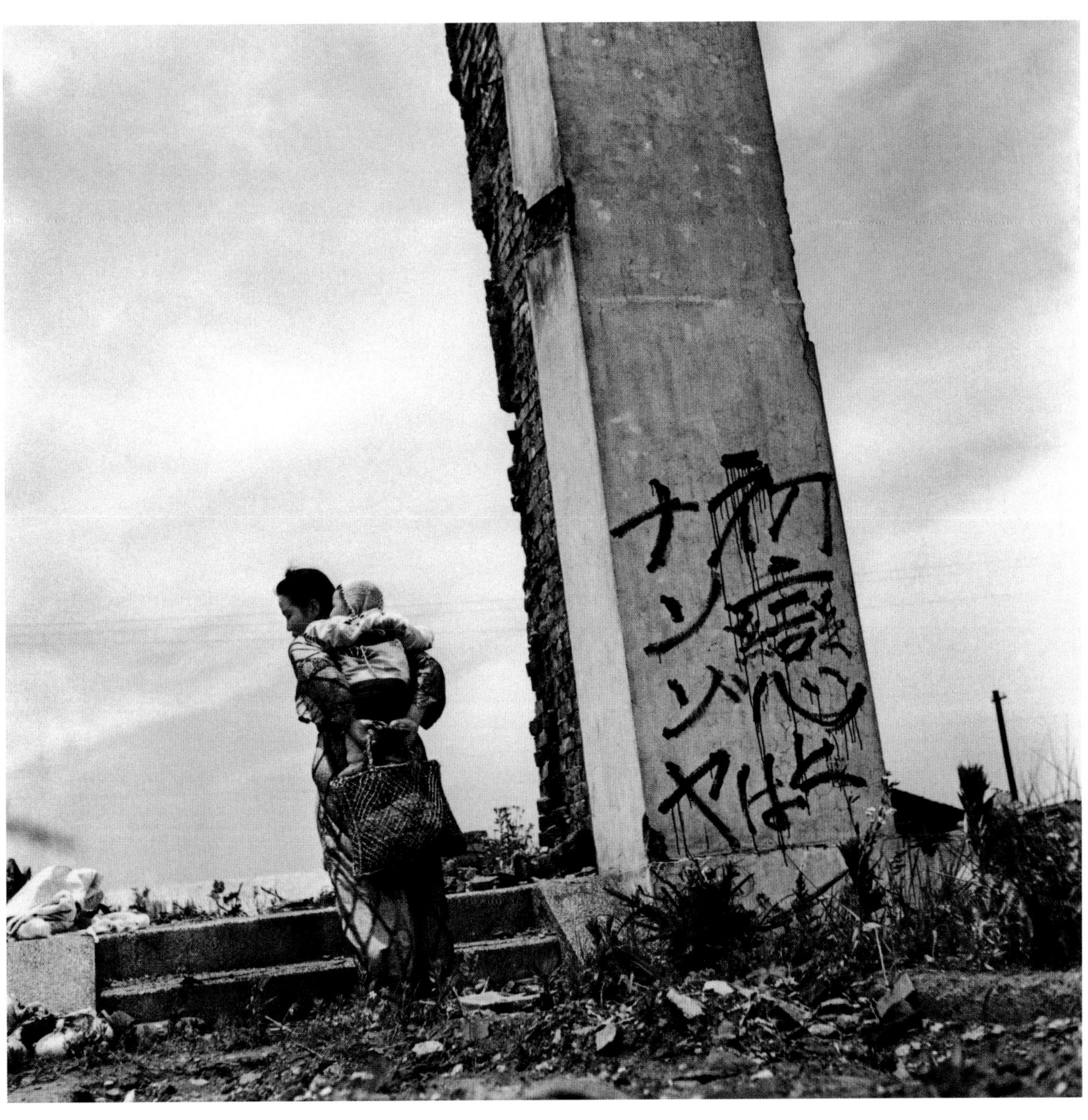

Hayashi Tadahiko, *Mother and child in
a wasteland burned out by the war*, 1947.

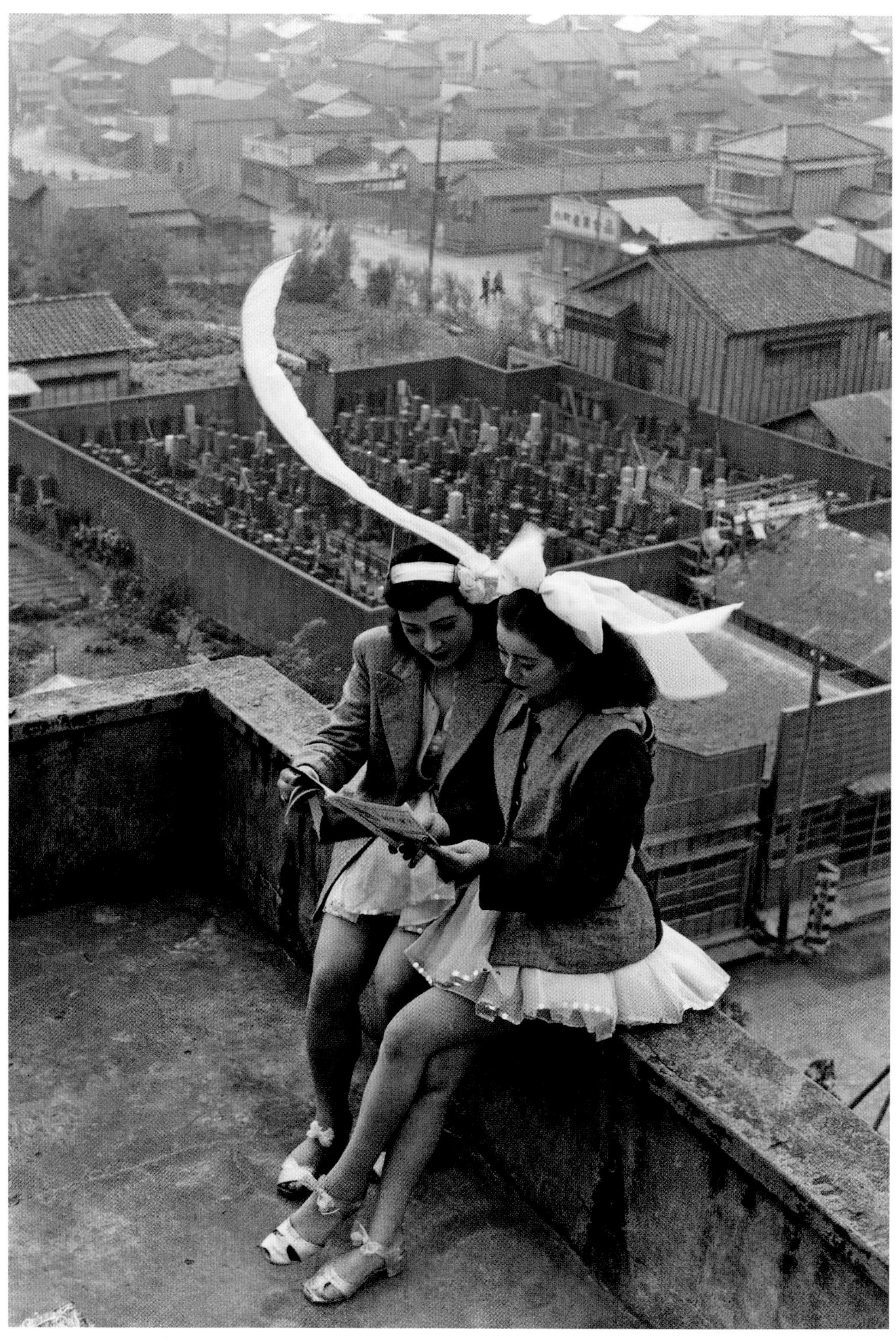

Tanuma Takeyoshi, *Dancers resting
on the rooftop of the SKD Theatre,* 1949.

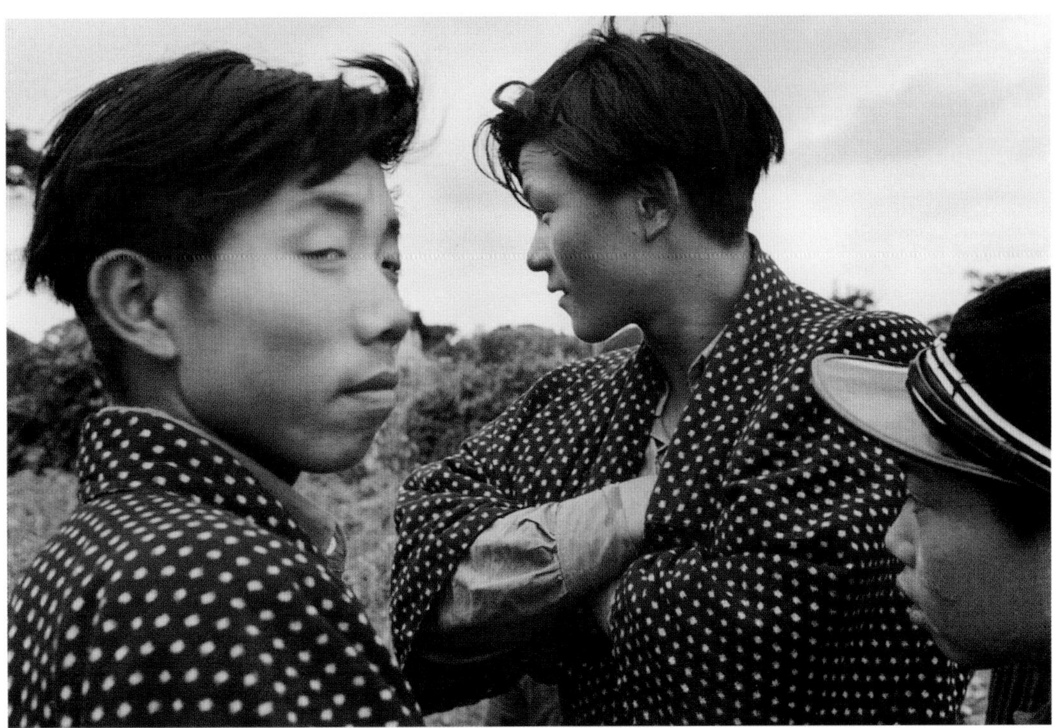

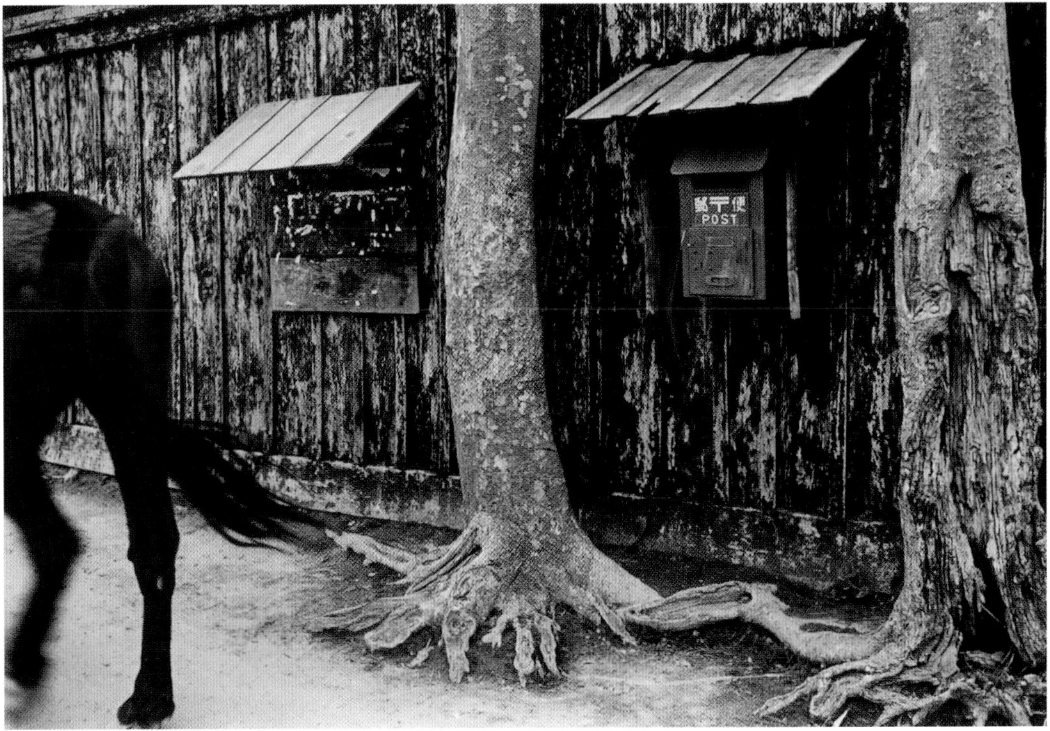

Above: Kimura Ihei, *Young Men*, 1952.
Below: Kimura Ihei, *Wooden Fence*, 1953.

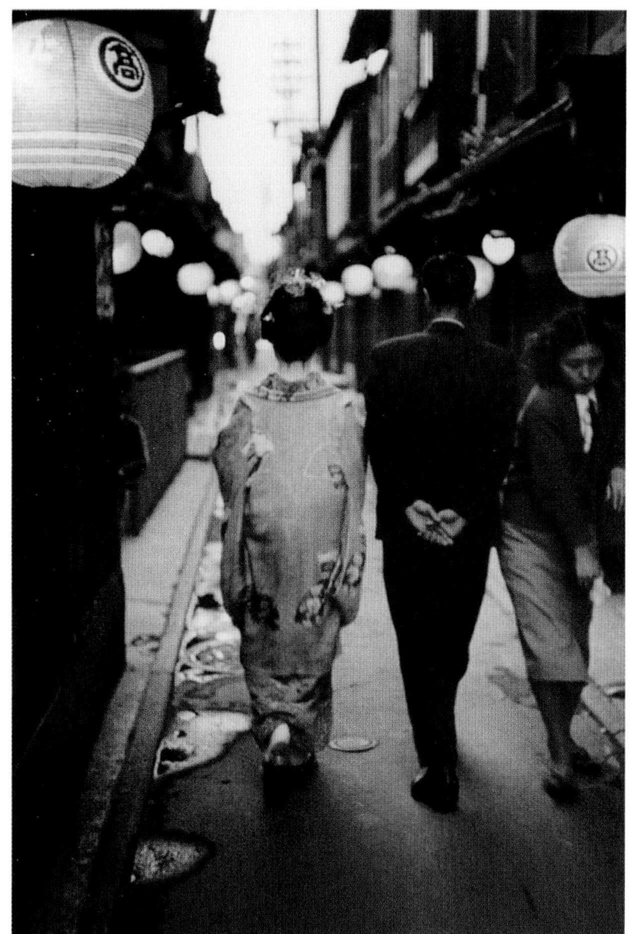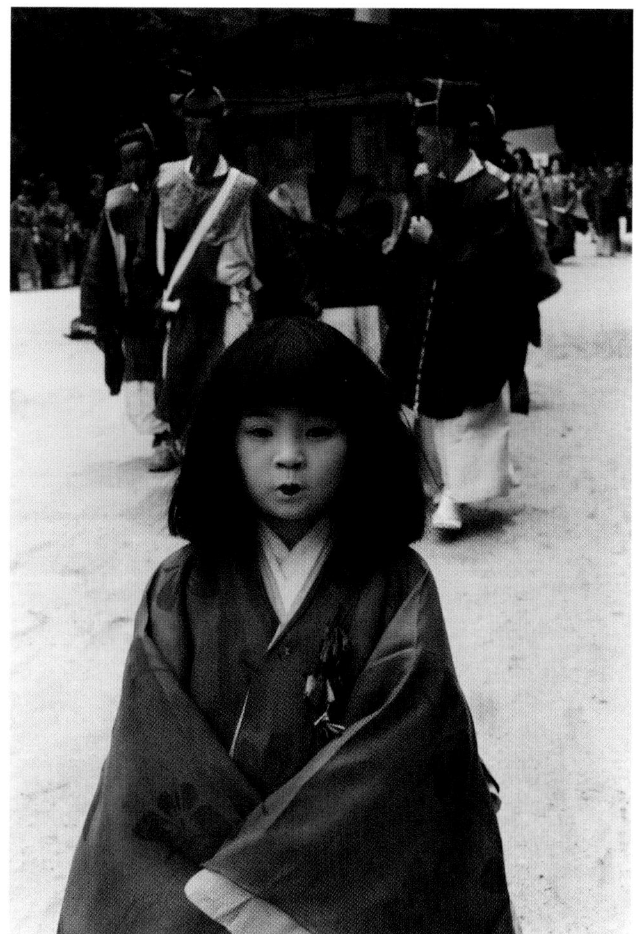

Above left: Kimura Ihei, untitled, 1956.
Above right: Kimura Ihei, *Aoi festival*, 1959.
Opposite: Hamaya Hiroshi, *Kannenbutsu prayers marching on the snowy streets,* 1955.

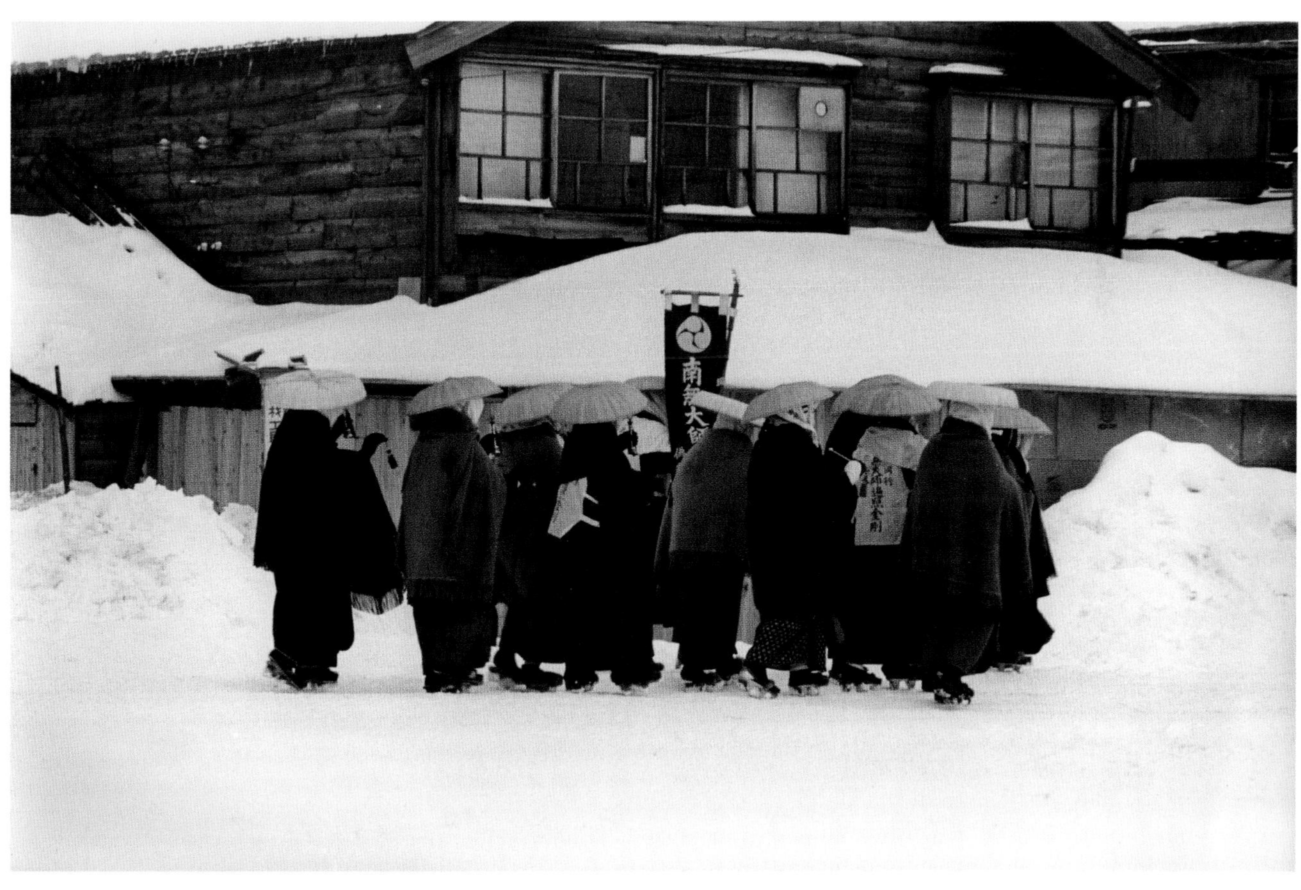

南智大命

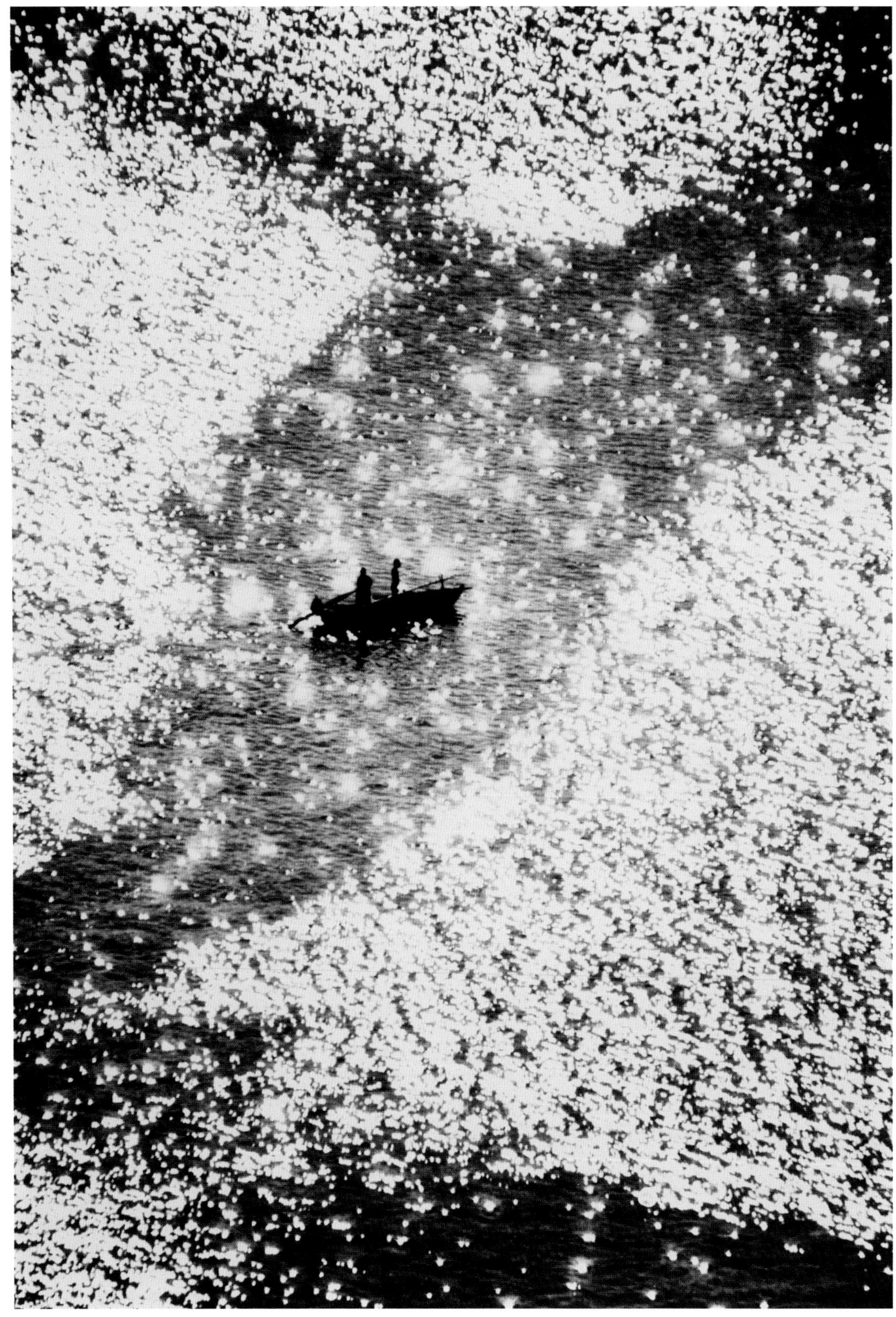

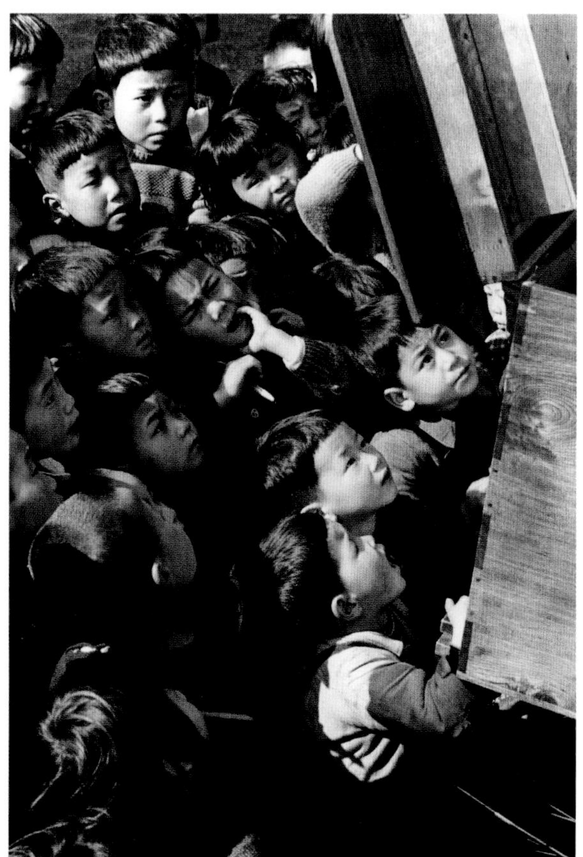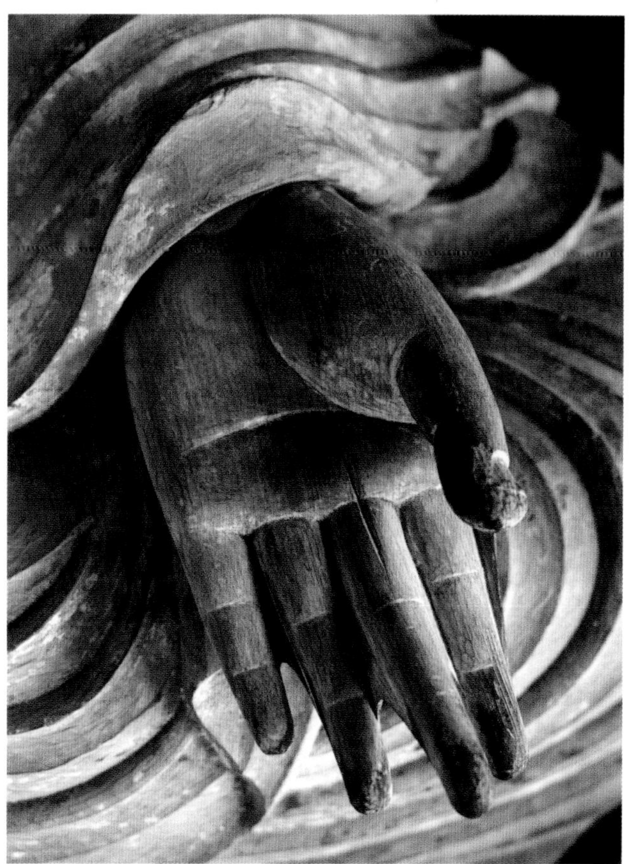

Opposite: Midorikawa Yōichi, untitled, 1955,
Seto Inland Sea and its Circumference series.
Above left: Dōmon Ken, *Children looking
at a picture-card show*, Tokyo, 1953.
Above right: Dōmon Ken, *Left hand of the
sitting image of Buddha Shakyamuni in
the Hall of Miroku, Muro-ji, Nara*, c. 1943.

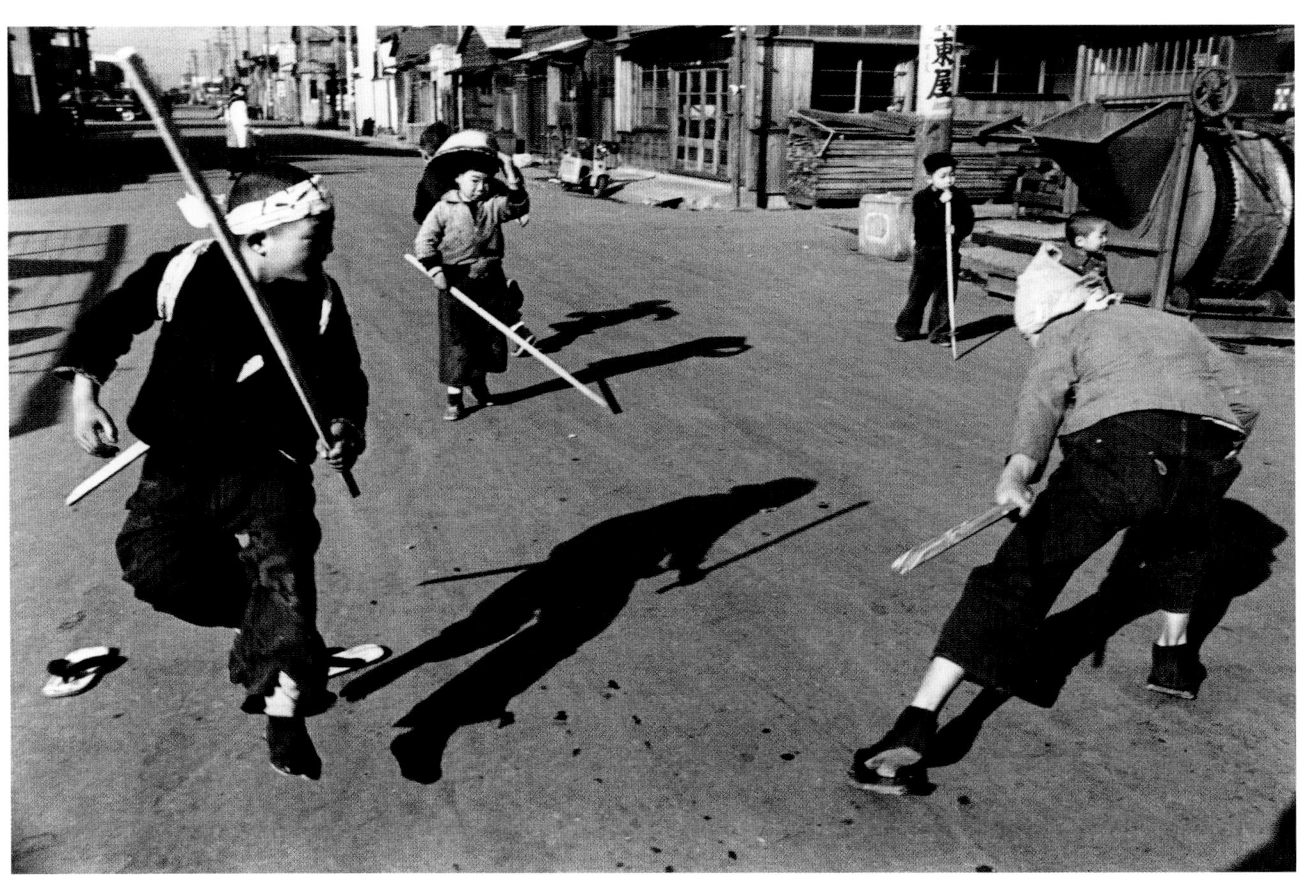

Dōmon Ken, *Kondo Isami and Kurama Tengu,* 1955.

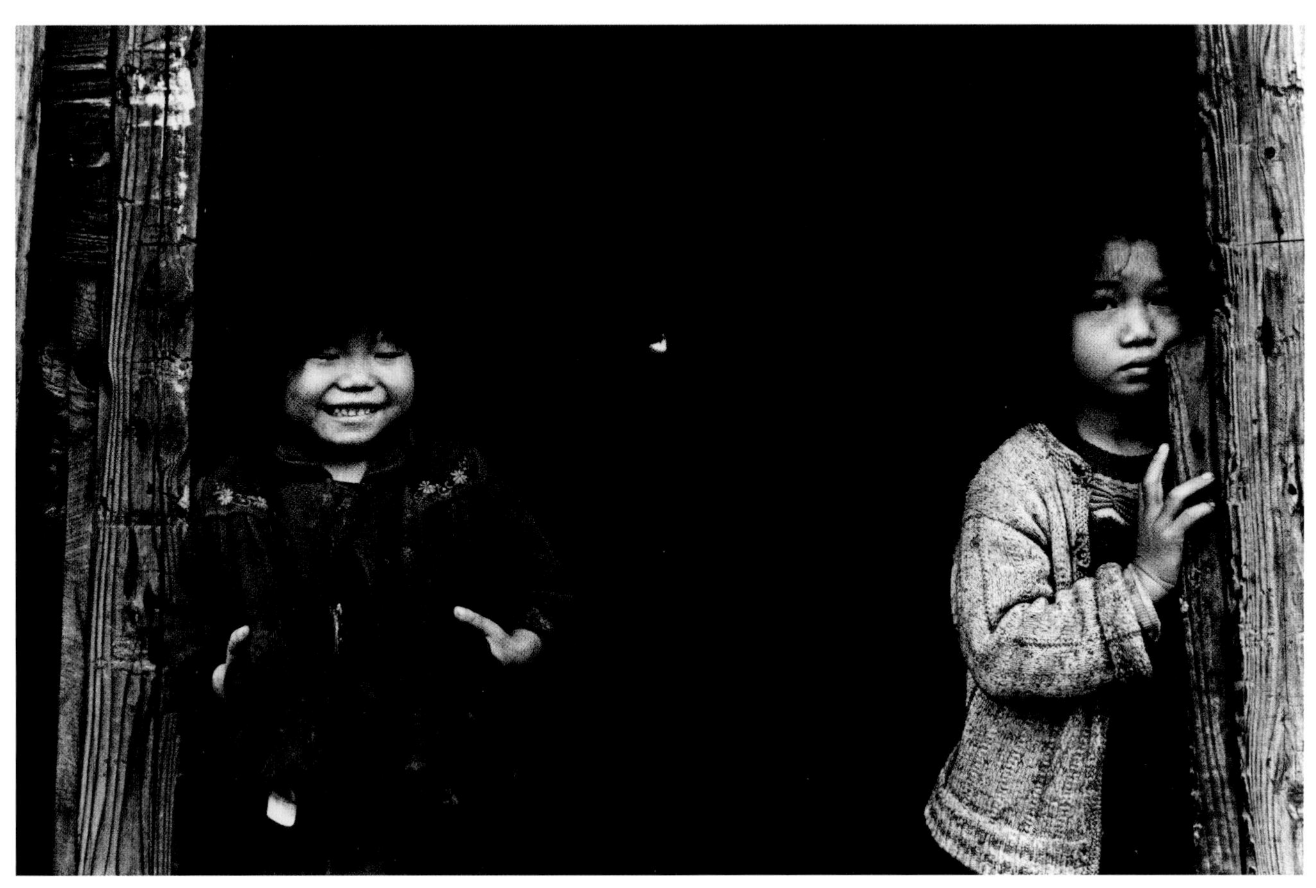

Dōmon Ken, *Rumie-chan and Sayuri-chan*,
1959, *The Children of Chikuho* series.

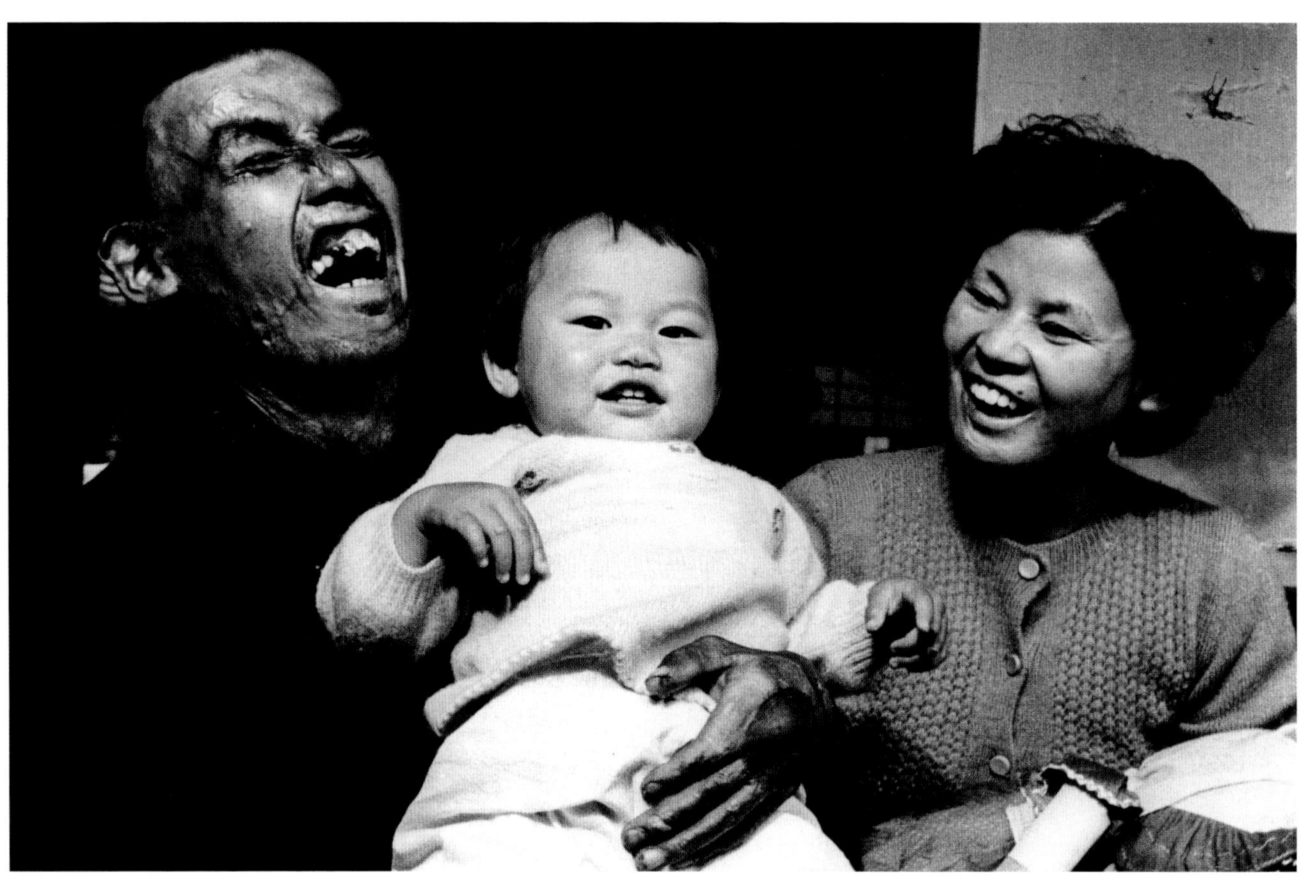

Above: Dōmon Ken, *Mr and Mrs Kotani: survivors of the atomic bomb*, 1957, *Hiroshima* series.
Opposite: Tanuma Takeyoshi, *Dressed up to go shopping*, 1955.

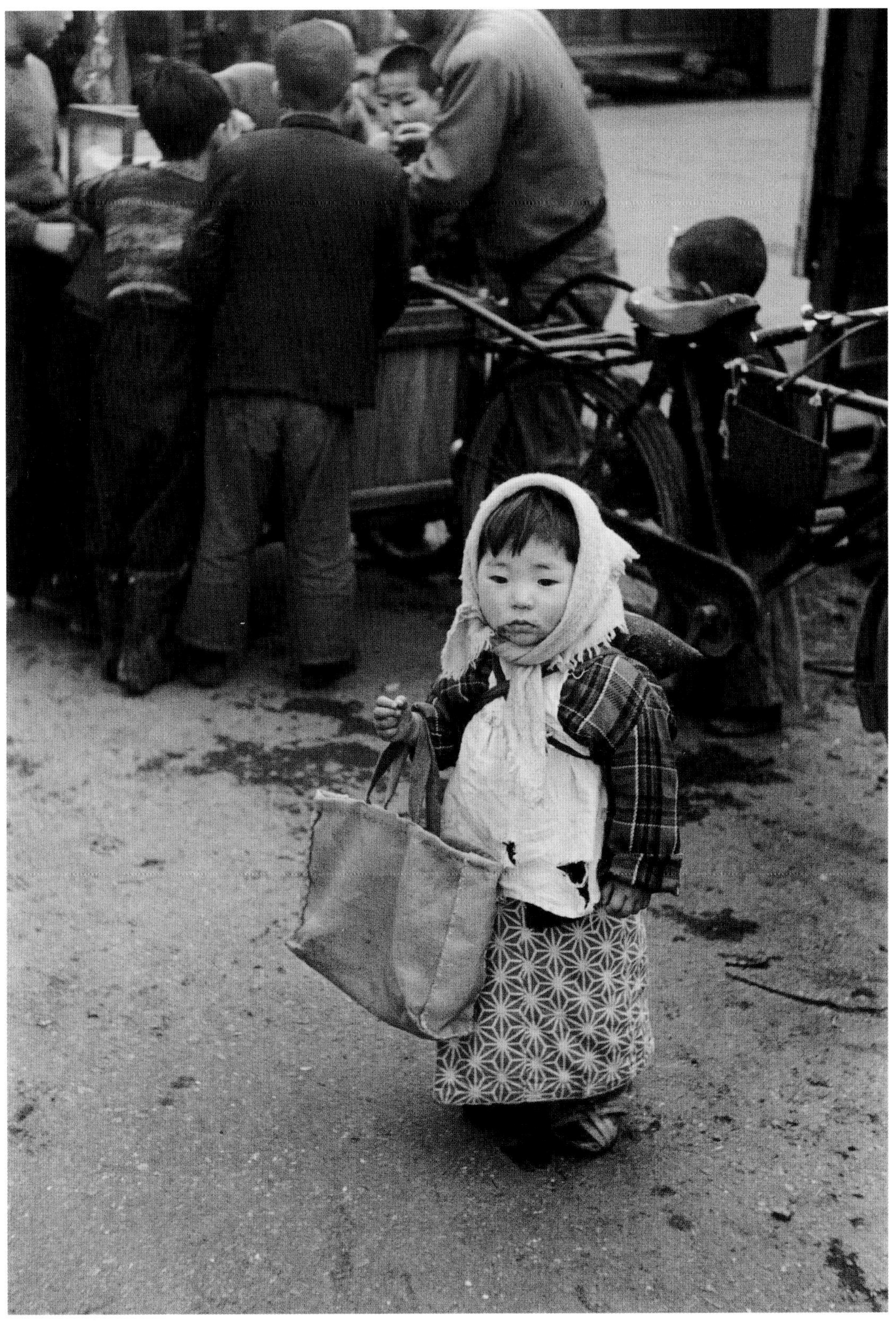

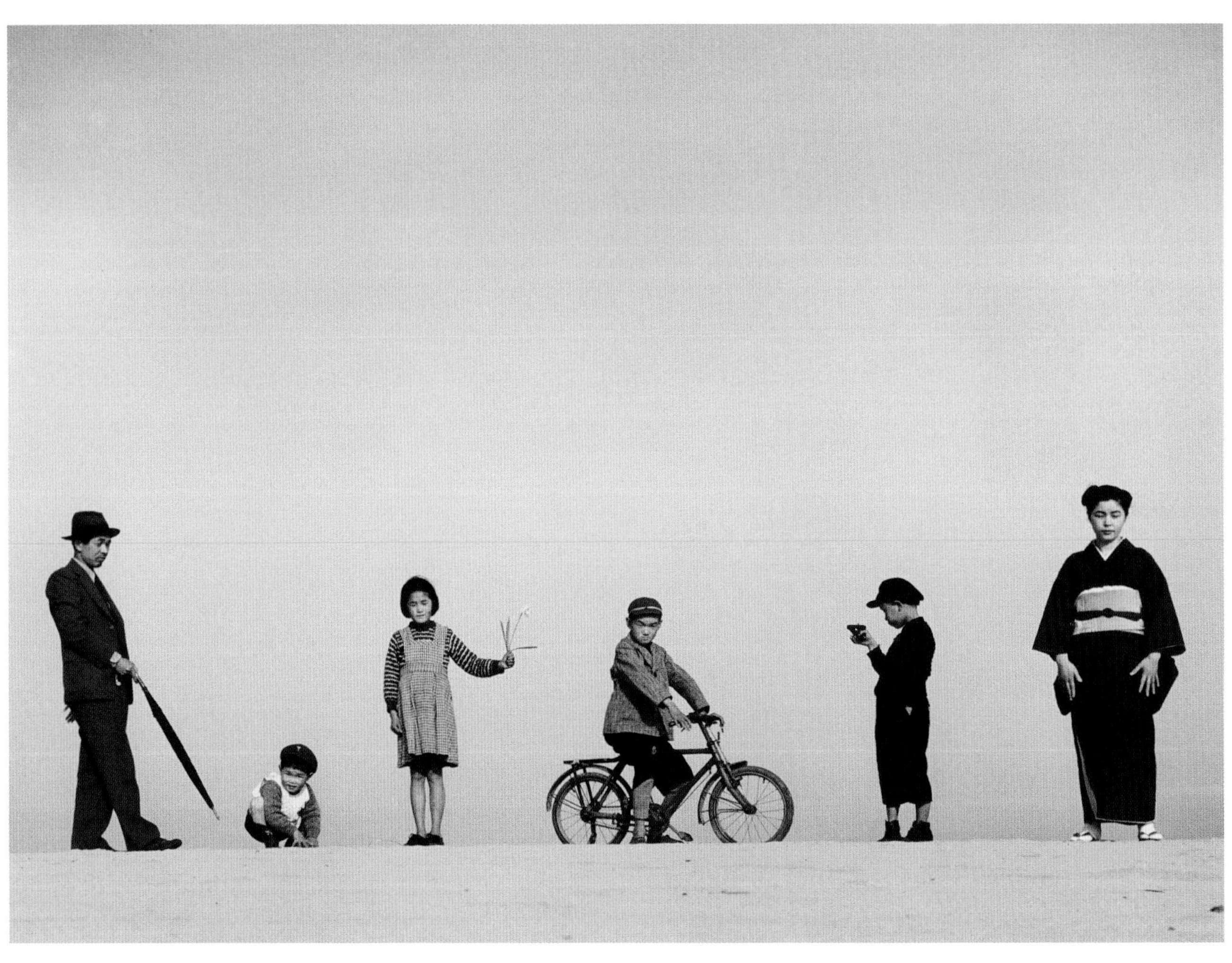

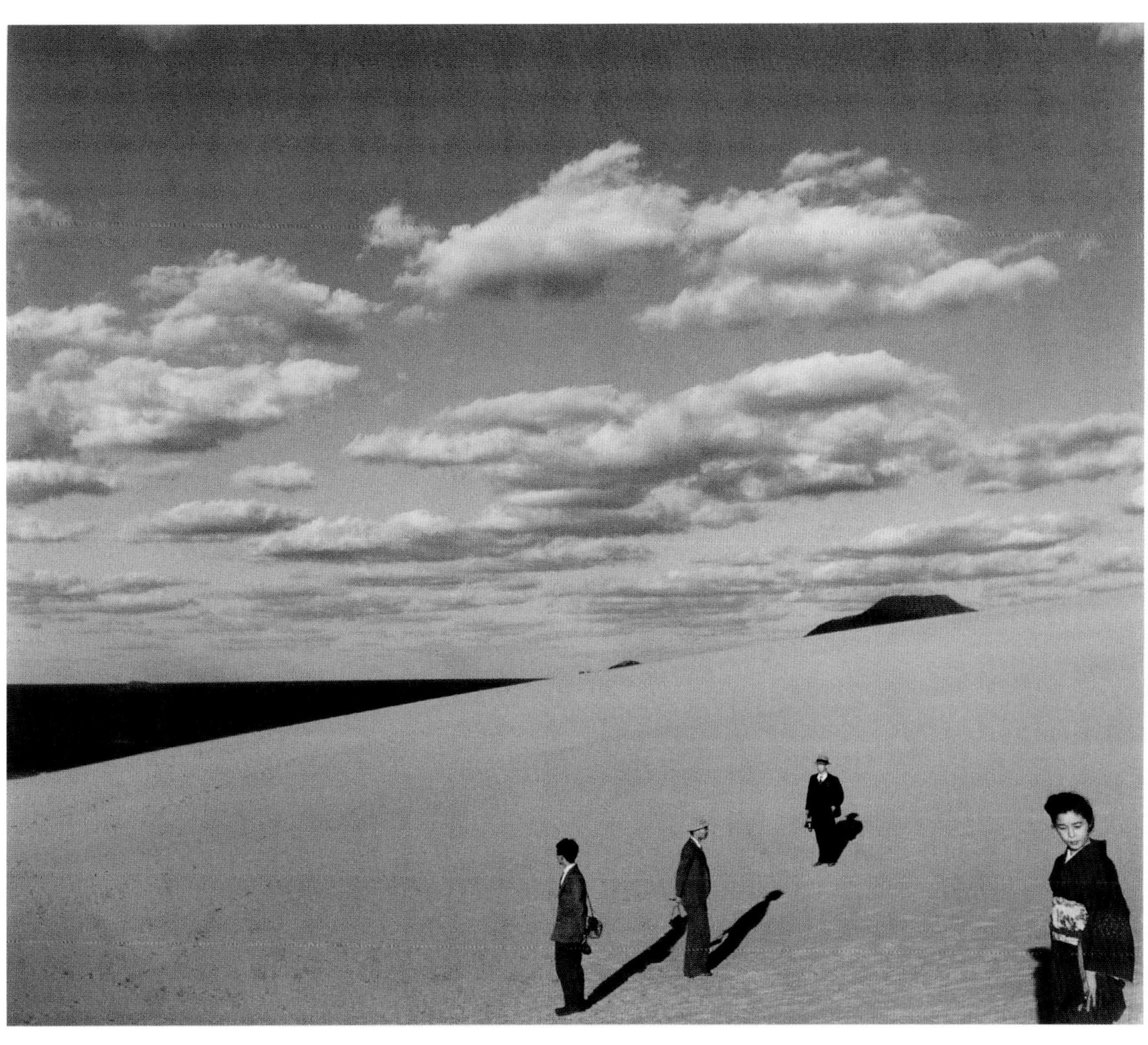

Opposite: Ueda Shōji, *Papa, Mama and Children*, 1950.
Above: Ueda Shōji, *My Wife in the Dunes*, 1950s.

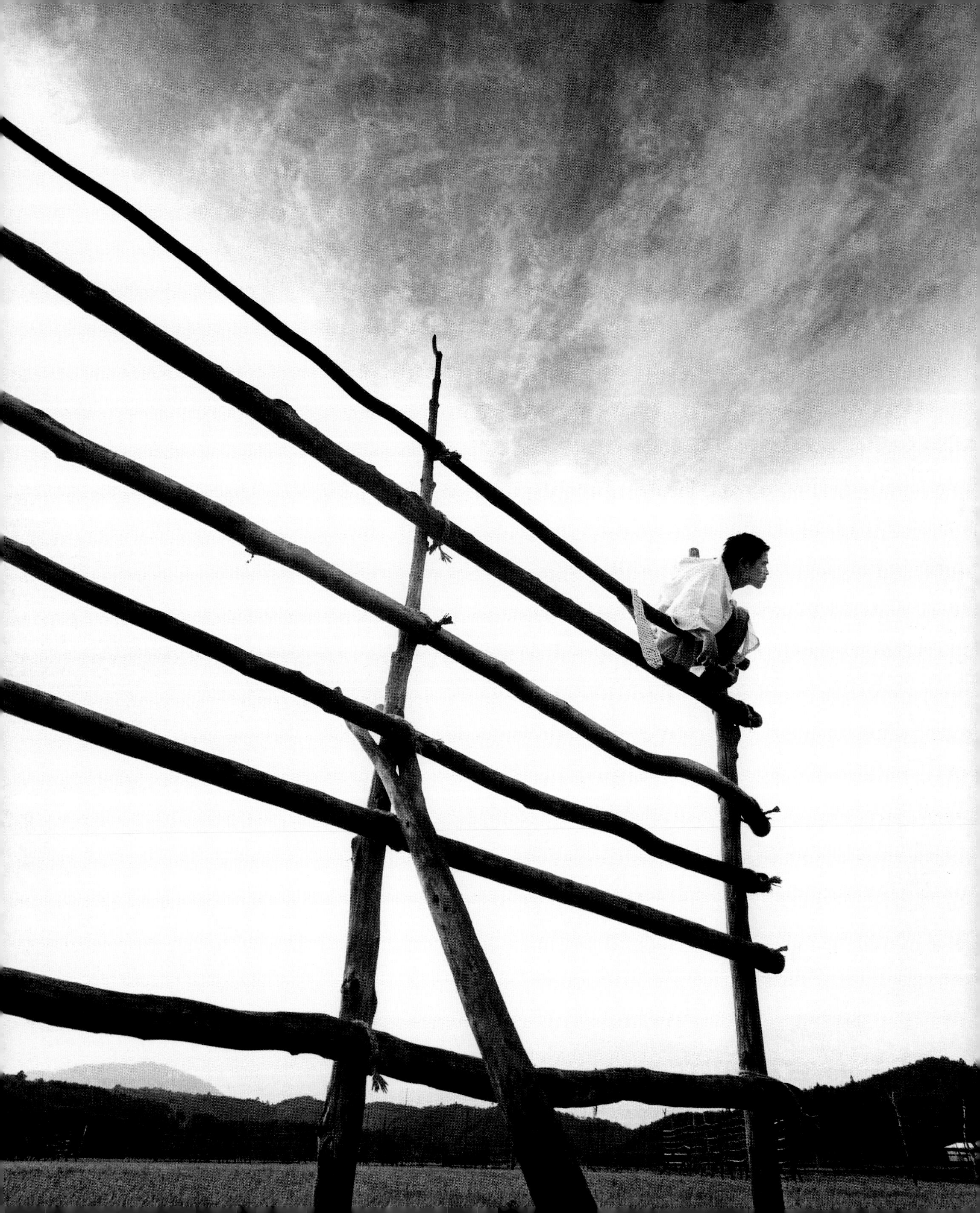

THE IMAGE GENERATION

II

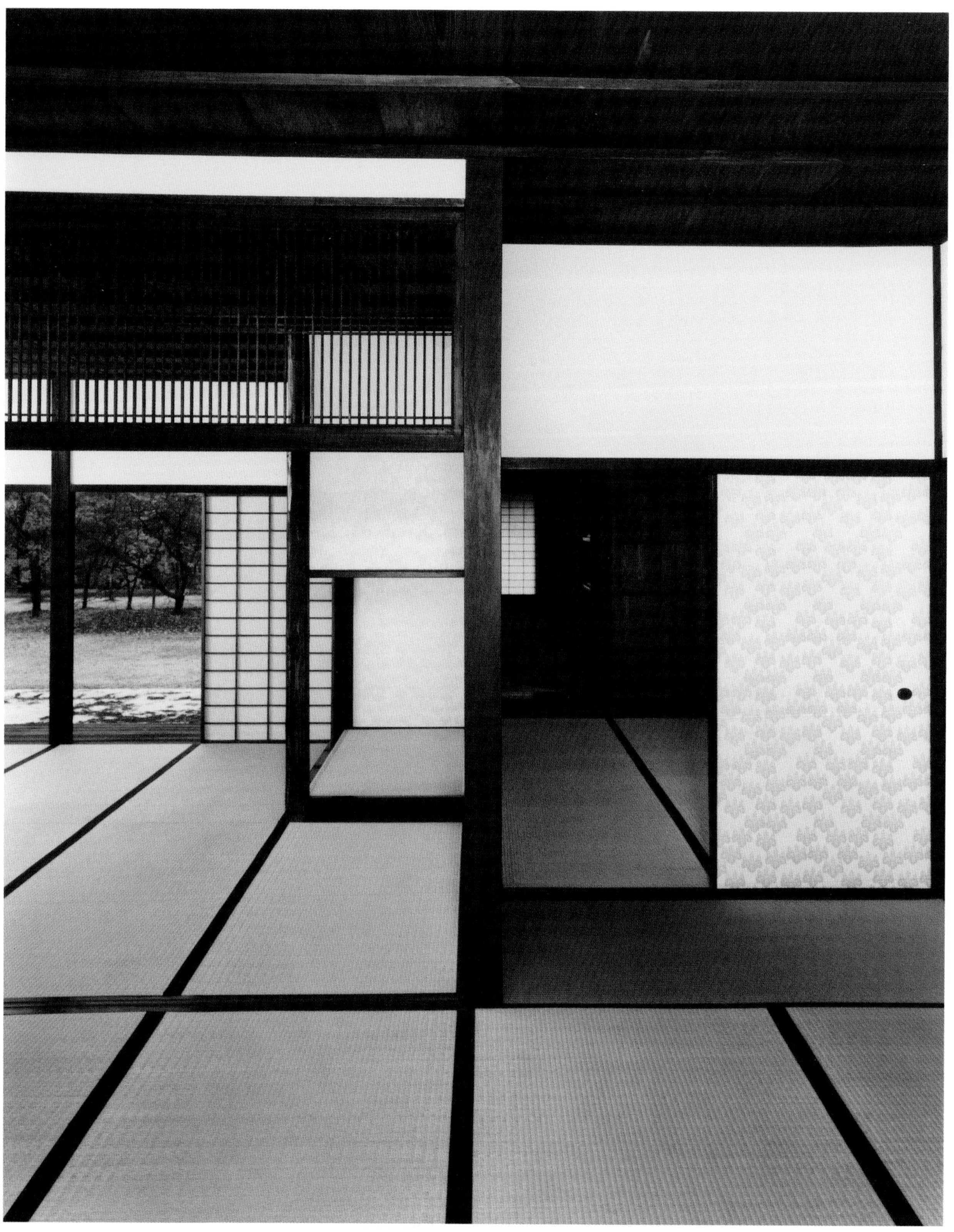

Previous spread: detail from Hosoe Eikoh, *Kamaitachi #8*, 1968.
Above: Ishimoto Yasuhiro, *Katsura Imperial Villa*, 1981–82.

In post-war Japan, photography was dominated by realism and photojournalism. But in the mid-1950s this gradually began to change: a new generation of photographers emerged, using photography creatively, for subjective expression rather than objective documentation.

One photographer whose work brought new inspiration to the scene was Ishimoto Yasuhiro (1921–2012). After studying at the Chicago Institute of Design with influential photographers Harry Callahan and Aaron Siskind, Ishimoto returned to Japan in 1953 and was commissioned to photograph the Katsura Imperial Villa in Kyoto. His photographs were published in a book about the building in 1960, together with texts by Bauhaus founder Walter Gropius and architect Tange Kenzō. Ishimoto returned to Katsura almost thirty years later, photographing the villa from the same angles and in similar compositions, this time in colour as well as black and white (opposite). His precise compositions and meticulous artistic approach contrasted with the language of realism.

Subjektive Fotografie, first advocated by German photographer Otto Steinert as a humanized and individual form of photography, was introduced to Japan in photo magazines such as *Camera*. In 1956, the Japan Subjective Photography League (Nihon Shūkanshugi Shashin Renmei) was established, with around forty members. Later in the same year, the Takashimaya department store in Nihonbashi, Tokyo, presented the 'First International Subjective Photography Exhibition' with works by eighty photographers from different countries, including Ōtsuji Kiyoji (1923–2001). Ōtsuji was an important member of the avant-garde collective Experimental Workshop (Jikken Kōbō), which comprised artists, photographers, designers and composers.

A New Hunger for Expression

Jikken Kōbō was based around the fusion of different disciplines. It existed from 1951 to 1957 and resulted not only in experimental artworks but also audiovisual events, performances and publications. Ōtsuji's conceptual photographs (p. 130) and writings about photography were to influence many younger practitioners, and he became a mentor for Takanashi Yutaka (b. 1935), Gochō Shigeo (1946–83) and Hatakeyama Naoya (b. 1958). As a movement, subjective photography declined soon after the exhibition in 1956. However, the hunger for a subjective and more experimental form of photography remained.

The photographers' group Vivo, named after the Esperanto word for 'life' and founded in Tokyo in 1959, is a manifestation of this hunger. Its six members, Hosoe Eikoh (b. 1933), Kawada Kikuji (b. 1933), Narahara Ikkō (b. 1931), Satō Akira (1930–2002), Tanno Akira (1925–2015) and Tōmatsu Shōmei (1930–2012) had all participated in a group exhibition titled 'Eyes of Ten' (*Jūnin no me*) at Konishiroku Photo Gallery two years earlier, organized by the photography critic Fukushima Tatsuo. After the show, Fukushima helped the young men to join forces as a cooperative. The group shared an office with a manager and a darkroom in East Ginza, Tokyo. Kawada remembered that there was 'this collaborative atmosphere',[19] and photo historian Iizawa Kōtarō described the group's office as the 'epicentre' of the new 'image generation's photographic expression'.[20]

Political Unrest and National Identity

In 1960, Japan experienced massive protests over the passage of a revised security treaty with the United States. The new Treaty of Mutual Cooperation and Security (*Sōgo Kyōryoku oyobi Anzen Hoshō Jōyaku*, abbreviated as *Anpo*) was signed in Washington in January 1960, and became the subject of heated debate when it was submitted for ratification. One of the main issues was that it would allow US military bases to remain on Japanese soil. When the House of Representatives approved the treaty in a session populated by members of the conservative Liberal Democratic Party (LDP), the protests increased and millions of people participated in demonstrations and strikes. The Vivo members led the Japanese Photographers' Association to join the protests.

Tōmatsu Shōmei, who had started photography while studying economics at Aichi University, was a key member of Vivo and became one of the most influential photographers in 20th-century Japan. After moving to Tokyo in 1954 and working for Iwanami Publishing House for two years, he began his freelance career. One of his best-known photographs, *Nagasaki, Bottle Melted and Deformed* (1961), from his *Nagasaki 11:02* series, depicts a relic from the atomic bomb (p. 67). It is a grainy, unsettling 'portrait' of a bottle that has been mutated by the intense heat and radiation to resemble a surreal creature. Tōmatsu also took photographs of the students' barricades at Tama School of Art, where he used to work as a lecturer, and wrote about these experiences in his photobook *I Am a King* (1972) (p. 66).[21] These works exemplify Tōmatsu's dynamic style, pioneering extreme subjectivity while addressing post-war traumas. His series *Chewing Gum and Chocolate*, begun in the late 1950s and continued for over twenty years, is a defining portrait of Japan's difficult relationship with the United States. It includes an iconic photograph of a small girl making a large chewing gum bubble (p. 66), and photographs of American military bases with the soldiers, for example, entertaining themselves with Japanese women. The series mirrors Tōmatsu's ambivalence towards the continuing American 'occupation' of Japan, and the country's struggle with its national identity.

In his legendary photobook *The Map* (*Chizu*) (1965), Kawada Kikuji was also concerned with the scars in Japan's post-war identity. The series features dark, grainy photographs of dumped American products such as Coca-Cola bottles (p. 48, above) and a Lucky Strike cigarette packet (p. 53, below), and a Japanese flag on the ground after demonstrations (p. 53, above). It also includes intensely tactile photographs of stains in the Atomic Bomb Dome in Hiroshima. Kawada had previously visited Hiroshima with Dōmon Ken, assisting the established photographer. He recalled standing inside the only structure left near the bomb's epicentre: 'A dozen years after the atomic bomb was dropped on Hiroshima, out of nowhere a giant black "stain" appeared above the basement ceiling…Each night the "stain" – which I had seen myself – filled my dreams with horror'.[22] The close-up photographs of the Atomic Bomb Dome show how Kawada turned away from the conventions of post-war documentation towards a uniquely abstract language, mirroring his horror. They contrast with previous works about Hiroshima, such as Dōmon's 1958 photobook, *Hiroshima*. Though they both documented major events in Japan in the late 1950s and 1960s, Tōmatsu and Kawada were not objective observers; they communicated their own realities.

Hosoe Eikoh gained attention with his 1960 solo show 'Man and Woman', at the Konishiroku Photo Gallery. The stylized compositions (p. 59) reflect Hosoe's career-long interest in the human body, his most important subject. His best-known series is probably *Ordeal by Roses (Barakei)* (1961), which features the writer, actor, nationalist and 'bodybuilder' Mishima Yukio (1925–70). Mishima was a tireless promoter of his body and celebrity image, and Hosoe's photographs emphasize his erotic expressiveness (p. 58).[23] For his equally striking series *Kamaitachi* (1965), Hosoe collaborated with *butoh* dancer Hijikata Tatsumi.[24] The work is linked to the photographer's teenage memories of the war, when he was evacuated to the rural Tōhoku region. Hijikata, who grew up there, embodies the *kamaitachi*, a weasel-like spirit of folk culture said to haunt the rice fields. The staged scenes show the dancer running on the fields, dramatically jumping, hiding and 'stealing' a village baby (pp. 56, 68). Today, fifty years later, Hosoe still vividly remembers the photoshoot and

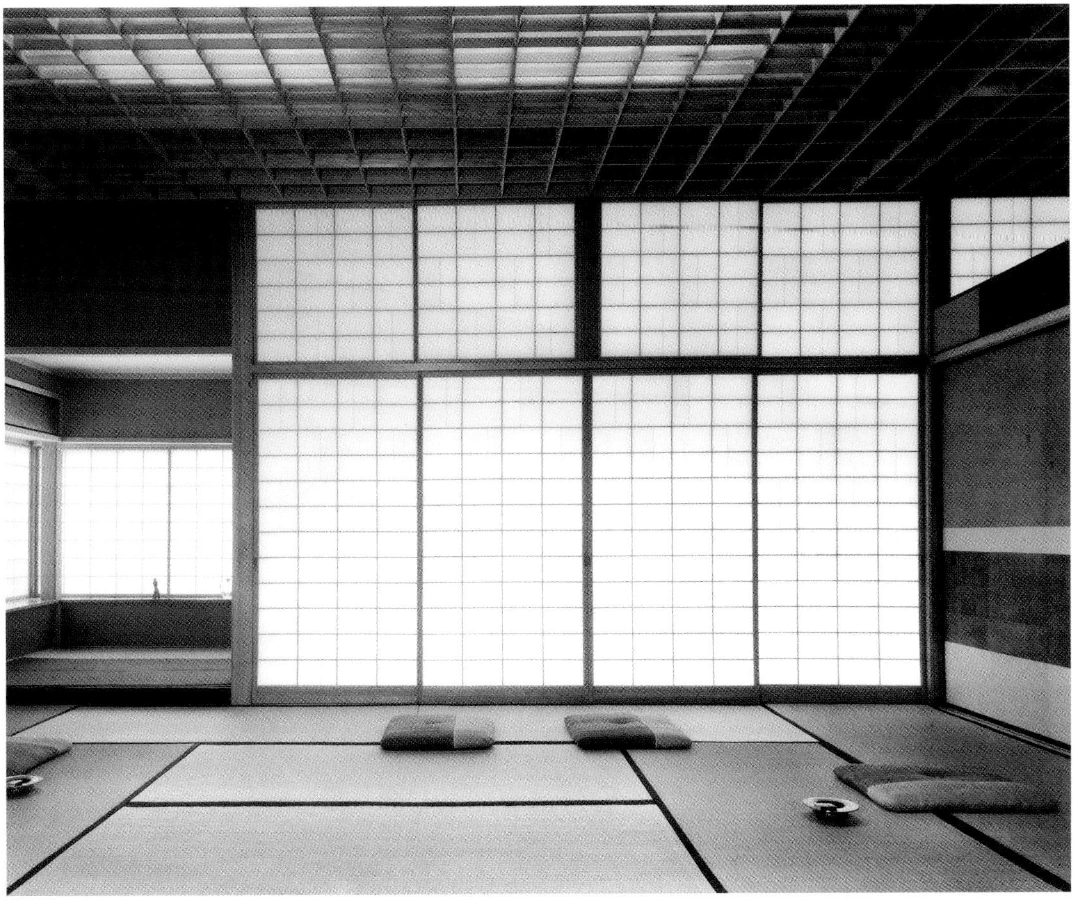

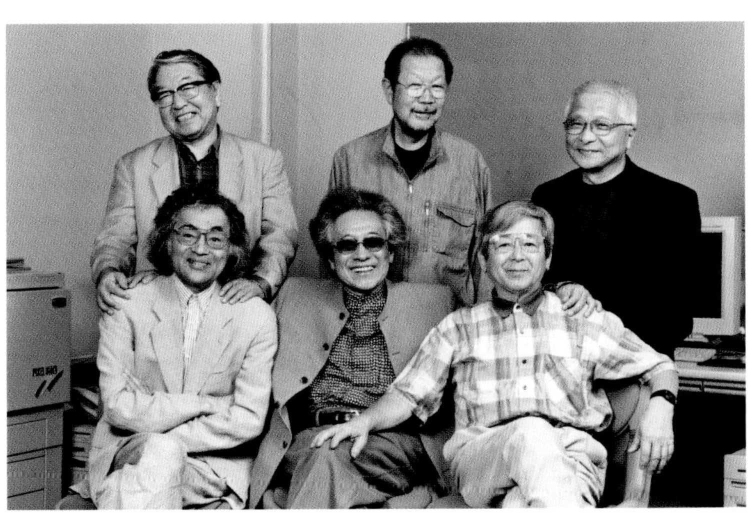

Above: Watanabe Yoshio, *Japanese Architecture, Room (A)*, c. 1950.
Left: Sakurai Shū, *The Vivo group*, 2001; from left to right: Hosoe Eikoh, Tōmatsu Shōmei, Kawada Kikuji (back row); Tanno Akira, Narahara Ikkō, Satō Akira (front row).

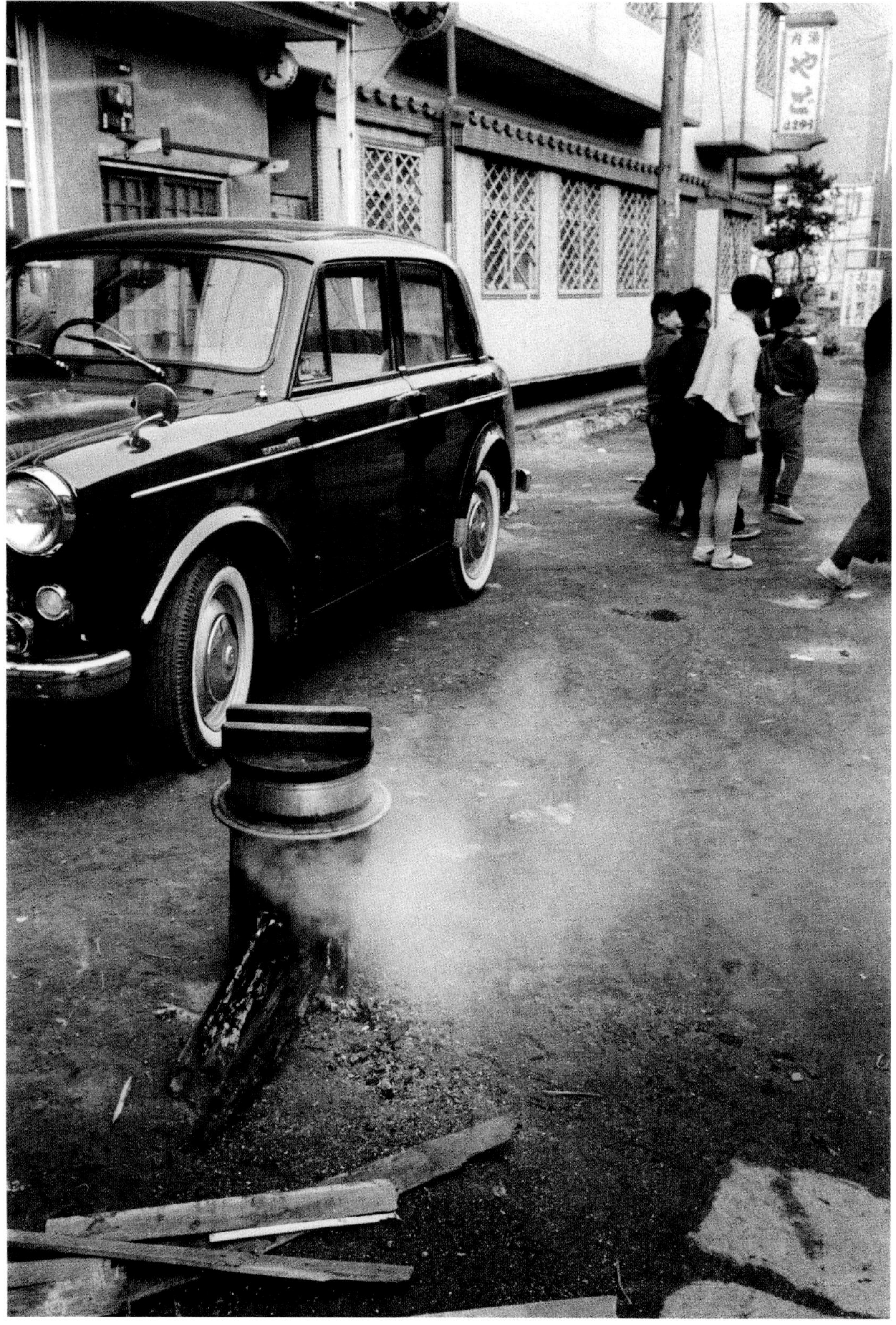

Inoue Seiryu, untitled, *c.* 1958–63, *Kamagasaki* series.

the spontaneous performances by Hijikata. The photographs represent his cinematic aesthetic, his interest in the moving human body and his collaborative practices, which often linked dance or acting with photography. As curator Simon Baker has pointed out, Hosoe accepted 'more completely and honestly than any other artist of his generation the absolute equilibrium at the heart of the relationship between photography and performance.'[25] Through his friendship with Hijikata, Hosoe also began to work with Ohno Kazuo, the other founding figure of *butoh* dance, culminating in *The Butterfly Dream* series of photographs from over forty years (p. 57). With his unrivalled theatrical language, Hosoe is one of the most important photographers of 20th-century Japan. As curator Marc Feustel has written, 'his openness and his innovation have greatly enriched the global language of photography.'[26]

Narahara Ikkō came to photography after studying law and art history. In 1955 he joined the artists' collective Real Existence (Jitsuzaisha), together with avant-garde artists Ikeda Masuo (1934–97) and Ay-O (b. 1931). He was still a graduate student when he had his first solo exhibition at the Matsushima Gallery in Tokyo in 1956. The show was titled 'Human Land', and featured photographs of Sakuraijima Island and an artificial concrete island built for mining coal. The show made Narahara's name on the photography scene. In his series *Man and His Land/Domains* (1958) (p. 70), which features photographs of a monastery juxtaposed with images of a women's prison, and in *Japanesque/Zen* (1969) (p. 71), Narahara presented evocative photographs that convey a fascination with the spiritual and otherworldly. His first photobook, *Europe: Where Time Has Stopped* (1967), is a poetic anthology of images from his travels in Europe (p. 70). They suggest a melancholic photographer indulging in his thoughts; the book earned Narahara numerous awards, including the Photographer of the Year Award from the Japan Photo Critics Association.

Lesser-known Vivo photographers Satō Akira and Tanno Akira also made interesting works. Satō took dynamic photographs of women that go beyond fashion photography (p. 64), and Tanno made a lively series entitled *Circus of Showa Japan*, focusing on the dynamics of circus performances (pp. 62–63).

The Vivo photographers all had individual styles, themes and approaches, but their photographs share a more personal, expressive and symbolically charged aesthetic than the works of their predecessors. It is not surprising that their confident rejection of conventions challenged older generations of photographers, including Natori Yōnosuke. In a now legendary open discussion published in *Asahi Camera* in 1960, Natori contrasted Tōmatsu's photographs with orthodox journalistic works, criticizing one of Tōmatsu's works as 'no more than an impression. There is no effort to make it readable to others.'[27] The dispute was triggered by an essay by critic Watanabe Tsutomu, 'New Tendencies in Photographic Expression', that had been published in the previous issue of the magazine. Watanabe had praised the work of young photographers including Tōmatsu, Narahara and Hosoe, highlighting their interest in the 'image' (*eizō*) itself. The debate ended with a statement by Tōmatsu in the following issue of *Asahi Camera*: 'to prevent the hardening of photography's arteries, I believe we should drive off the evil spirits that haunt "photojournalism" and destroy the existing concepts carried by those words.'[28] His declaration reflects the new generation's urge to re-invent photography. In Iizawa Kōtarō's words, photographers like Tōmatsu 'gave the image its independence'.[29] In Japan, they are referred to as the 'image generation'.

The Vivo members became more independent and the group was dissolved after two years, in 1961. Many of them became major photographers, and had an important impact on subsequent artists.

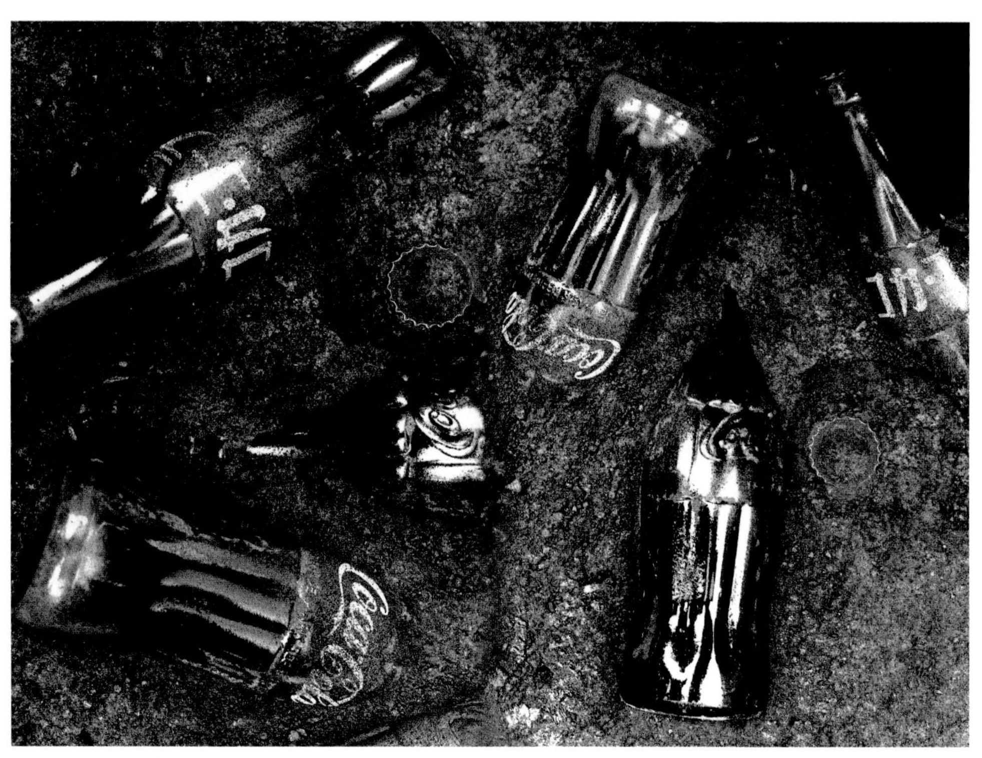

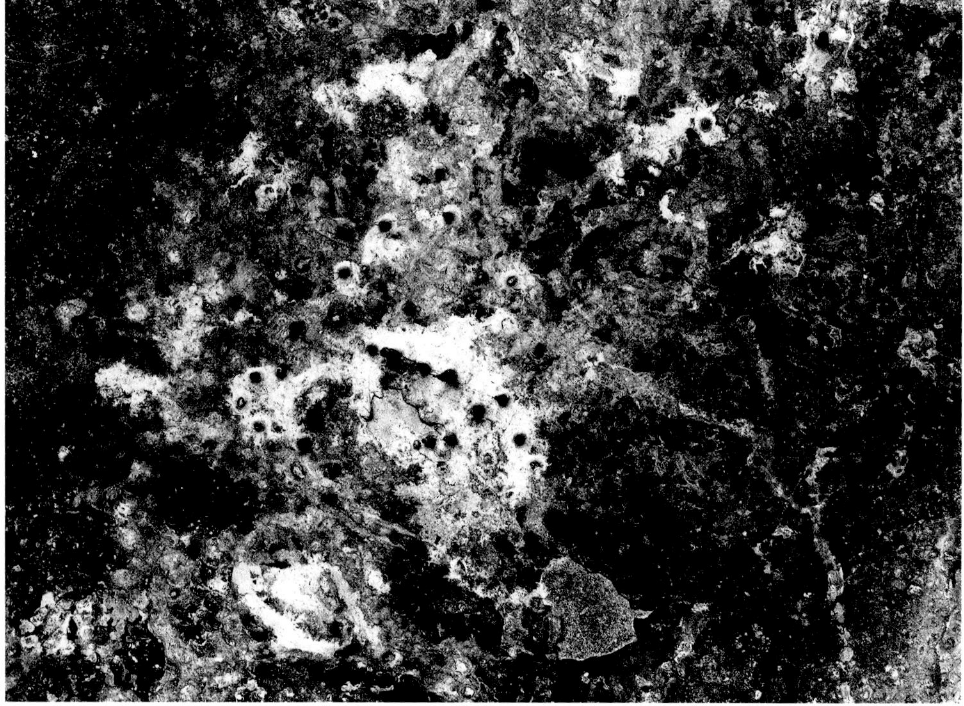

Top and above: Kawada Kikuji, *The Map* (*Chizu*) series, 1965.

Lena Fritsch: Let's start at the beginning – what inspired you to take up photography?

Kawada Kikuji: I must have been around 15 or 16 years old. At the time, cameras were really valuable and children usually could not afford them. There were two or three kids at my high school showing off their cameras, and this made me want to own a machine as cool as that, too. If they had had pistols, I might have gone for that [laughs]. Well, I convinced my father to buy me a camera.

What kind of photographs did you take as a teenager?

First I took a portrait of my father, and then one of my mother. I had these photos until recently, but they seem to have disappeared somewhere. I probably continued taking photographs because there was nothing else to do [laughs]. I took photographs during school trips, for example, but I did not see this as creating any form of art. Then I enrolled in university. In Japan at the time, there were hardly any opportunities to exhibit photographs. Deep down I sought to express myself and present something artistic, so I submitted a photograph to the monthly contest organized by *Ars Camera* – at the time, the best-known photo magazine. Dōmon Ken and Kimura Ihei chose my work. I knew about the contest because I was interested in the magazine's explanations of camera techniques, but it never crossed my mind to go to photography school.

At the time, were you interested in or inspired by any photographers?

Yes, Dōmon Ken and Kimura Ihei. Hamaya Hiroshi was important too. I was particularly interested in photography that starts from a documentary stance and develops into something artistic. I looked at all kinds of photographs in magazines. At the time, photographs from overseas were not yet well known in Japan. I remember seeing photographs by *LIFE* photographers, such as Margaret Bourke-White and Alfred Eisenstaedt, and I researched some earlier works that had come to Japan, like *Point Lobos* by Edward Weston. I thought I needed a bigger camera and had to travel a lot to be a good photographer. I was still a student, and was not able to do that [laughs].

After participating in the exhibition 'The Eyes of Ten' in 1957 you became a member of the photographers' group Vivo. Could you tell me about Vivo?

We were all around the same age and had in common that we wanted to create a new form of photography. There was this collaborative atmosphere of wanting to do something together. I was the only member of the group who was employed, I think; the others were all independent photographers. The photo critic Fukushima Tatsuo was a kind of organizer, but it developed in a very natural way. It was good to do the administrative and business side of things together. We had our office in East Ginza, next to the Sumida river. The photographer Satō Akira, working for Fuji Film, needed a large studio and chose this space, a bit outside of the centre. It was ideal for our meetings. I was employed by the publisher Shinchōsha for their weekly journal *Shūkanshichō* and could not always participate in the meetings. Shinchōsha actually asked me if I could recommend another good photographer, and I suggested Narahara Ikkō, but he was not interested. He said he would not want to do such hard work – I was really working all day and night, without sleeping [laughs].

Vivo did not exist for long – why?

There comes a time when you need to move on. We never planned on staying together as a group for long. Even from a financial viewpoint, it was not meant to last: some people were not bringing in a lot of income, and they had to face the other members who brought money in [laughs]. We 'head-hunted' a business manager, Mr Ījima. We convinced him to work for us, arguing that we were the Vivo group: a group of photographers that would soon become famous! [laughs] However, we only lasted for two years.

Poor man.

Yes, Mr Ījima had to find a new job. He spoke English, and was therefore able to help us with business overseas. One of the most memorable visits during our Vivo years was by William Klein, together with his wife, carrying all his films. He came to our studio and developed the photographs that he took in Tokyo, making selections in our office. However, our office was of course full of photographers looking at his work and I think he realized that he had chosen a weird place to come to [laughs]. So he quickly found himself another, more professional photo studio. At the time, we had Sakurai Shū working in our darkroom and then later Moriyama Daidō. Sakurai developed Klein's photos. We were six people and all had different requests: some of us wanted the photographs a bit darker, others wanted them lighter. It was not easy for the darkroom assistants. Even from a technical viewpoint the group could not last forever.

It was a group of individuals with individual styles after all.

We received some big jobs, for example from a beer company, and to create a calendar. But we became too busy: doing

Vivo while also trying to find photography jobs for us as individuals was too much.

Just before the group dissolved in 1961, you began taking photographs for your best-known series: *The Map (Chizu)* **[pp. 48, 53]. It is one of the best photobooks of the last century.**
I started the series in 1960. I was not sure what it would become, and began presenting some of the photographs in journals and small solo exhibitions. The first exhibition therefore differed quite a lot from the photobook *The Map*, published in 1965. I tend to find my photographic themes during the process of taking photographs, and I like to take my time.

You tend to take photographs over a long period of time indeed – not only for *The Map* **but also other series'.**
Yes. For *The Map*, I took photographs of different things over a period of five years. Japan changed greatly during those years, and I am interested in this temporality. I tend to do one project over a period of five or ten years. If you look at the work of Kimura Ihei or Dōmon Ken, they usually have fixed themes and projects, such as Dōmon's photographs of different Buddha statues, followed by a trip overseas to the Silk Road. Unfortunately, he passed away before the Silk Road trip. But for us, or at least for me, the theme is less fixed. Even today, my projects usually develop over time.

But you decided on the title *The Map* **quite early on, and exhibited works under this title in 1961 – long before finishing the project in 1965.**
Yes, I had decided on the title. But it was a wide title. I could have also chosen 'the universe' as a title [laughs].

The same probably applies to your series *The Last Cosmology* **(1979–97) [pp. 54–55].**
That series is the one that took the longest. I don't know why I take such a long time over my projects. They develop naturally that way. At the moment, I am working on a photobook with works that I actually took before *The Map*, from 1951 to 1961 – I was not able to produce this photobook at the time. I take other photographs as well; I don't only focus on one project. And I'm old enough now to take just the photographs that I like to take.

Do you take photographs every day?
Yes, more or less. Until last year, I took photographs every day; now I am a bit too busy with other things. I always have my camera and even if I see something interesting on TV, I take a photograph. Photography suits me and helps me to express myself. I like paintings too – looking at them – but my medium is photography.

What do you like best about photography?
I probably like the fact that photography is new, compared to painting or literature. I find that fascinating. I also like the paradoxical character of photography: you can take photographs of reality and they become a lie, but you can also take photographs of lies and they become real. Photographic expressions can change dramatically over time – it is a fascinating genre in many ways.

*	This is a shortened version of an interview conducted in Japanese on 30 August 2016, at PGI, Tokyo.

Lena Fritsch: Let's start at the beginning – what inspired you to take up photography?

Hosoe Eikoh: I borrowed my father's camera, ended up taking good photographs and participated in the very first Fuji Photo Contest in 1951. As the winner of the students' section for Tokyo/Kanagawa, I received ¥5,000. Then I came first in the national contest and received ¥50,000. I was very young and thought, 'wow, with photography you can make a lot of money' [laughs]. I was brought up in a Shinto shrine. My father was a priest who became a photographer. During the war, the shrine was busy and soldiers would be seen off there, but after the war, the shrine became quiet and was not bringing in enough money. My father liked photography and although he was not trained professionally, he was good. He decided to turn it into a business, taking photographs at shrine festivals such as *shichigosan*.[1] Later, he also took photographs externally, for example at graduation ceremonies.

So you were surrounded by your father's photographic practice from a young age.

Yes, my father often asked me to help. A friend then introduced me to an American army base, where I went to improve my English with a book called *Jack and Betty*, asking random people to read it out for me. I became interested in the people and started taking my camera with me, for example photographing children. I would give the photos to the families and they would treat me to some coffee. Coffee was special during those post-war years, and I began to like it! [laughs] After winning the Fuji Photo Contest, I went to the Tokyo College of Photography.[2]

At the time, were you interested in or inspired by any photographers in particular?

Dōmon Ken was probably the most important influence. But there were others too, for example Ueda Shōji. I was interested in the work of many photographers, not really inspired by a particular person. The US magazine *LIFE* came to Japan as well; while I never thought I would be able to take photographs that great, I still decided to turn photography into my profession. The Tokyo College of Photography had a long history and most professional photographers studied there.

After graduating in 1954 you worked as an independent photographer right away. Could you tell me about your work at that time?

Well, 'independent' basically means that you don't have any work. I was 'free' [laughs]. I went to different magazines showing them my photographs, and they gradually became interested in me.

I learned a lot by working, for example, for women's magazines. After a while I became interested in taking more photographs for myself and exhibiting them. There were photo company galleries, like Konishiroku Photo Gallery and Fuji Photo Salon. Konishiroku Photo Gallery let me do an exhibition for free, and photo journal representatives became interested in my work – it was a business chance. I had become a photographer. It was the post-war era: a chaotic time when nothing and everything was possible. In Japan, this small country, there were two big film companies: Konishiroku and Fuji Film. In other words, there was film to spare.

After participating in the exhibition 'The Eyes of Ten' organized by Fukushima Tatsuo in 1957, you co-founded the photographers' group Vivo, referencing the Esperanto word for 'life' in the group's name. Could you tell me more about this time and Vivo? Who came up with this great name?

I bought an Esperanto dictionary and we all looked at it together. Why Esperanto? Well, it's international – not English, not German, not French but truly international. A friend's wife was an Esperanto specialist. And *LIFE* was the most important journal in the field of photojournalism – 'vivo' is another word for 'life'. But it is also a term that combines the essential with everyday reality: 'life' stands for a person's life as well as daily life. Vivo is a good word.

It is a very good word!

We had a great time and felt so alive. We competed with each other and also decided to share a darkroom and office. Together, it was affordable to hire a manager. He was a businessman with an interest in photography and would get us work. As photographers we were not good with money talk, and he helped us focus on photography. It was also easier for the people commissioning us to talk to a manager rather than to us directly. A great business model.

But it did not last long…Why did the group dissolve after two years?

We all wanted to become more independent and do our own thing, like going to Paris or New York. We had become famous enough and were able to get jobs by ourselves. Oh, we were all so young back then [laughs].

In 1960 you made a beautiful series: *Man and Woman* [p. 59]. How did this series come about?

I really liked nude photography. I grew up in a shrine, and you would think that there is no connection between a shrine and nudes, but there were *ukiyoe* woodblock prints and it was actually a free environment. Coming from this free background, I was interested in the nude

– both female and male – in a pure form. In photography, it was the time of realism – street scenes and such – but I was more interested in the human body. There were no professional nude models in Japan, but I asked models from art school and then modern dancers to get naked. Dancers have great bodies, and they know how to move. At the same time, strobes became more accessible, even in rental studios. Without strobes the photos that I took would not have been possible. In the 1960s, there was a parallel development of camera techniques and lighting, and my own photography; both became more advanced at the same time. As Japan's economy grew, money came in and photography began to flourish. Good times.

It was also in the early 1960s that you made a well-known series: *Ordeal by Roses (Barakei)*, with Mishima Yukio [p. 58]. How was this collaboration with the writer?
Mishima approached me through a publishing company, because he had seen my photographs. I was surprised: 'THAT Mishima Yukio'? He confirmed that he wanted me to take photographs of him and I could do whatever I wanted. I asked him if he would get naked for me and he said 'ok, fine', telling his wife to leave the house for a few hours and to go to her parents' [laughs].

That's funny. I did not know that the photographs were taken at Mishima's house.
First I photographed him at his house and later we took photographs in the studio. Mishima's wife complained [speaking with a high-pitched voice]: 'because of you, Mr Hosoe, I have to leave our own house!' [laughs] But his wife was the daughter of a famous painter, Sugiyama Yasushi. She was therefore quite understanding and liked the photographs, saying 'oh this is beautiful!' Of course, her husband was handsome, but a wife who says 'oh this is beautiful' about a photograph is rare. She looked at them from an artistic viewpoint and thanked me. In this way, I was able to continue photographing Mishima freely.

How many photo sessions were there?
We had five or six photo sessions. I exhibited the photographs and then decided to make a book. Mishima was embarrassed at first, but then he agreed. And he really liked it. Apparently he bought 100 copies of the book – without telling me, as he was embarrassed [laughs]. Even outside Japan, people became aware of the photographs. The series made me famous and I started to work with Light Gallery in New York. In Japan, photographs were hardly ever sold as prints. The *Ordeal by Roses* series brought me more work and enabled me to live a good life and get married. Mishima came to my wedding, and

gave a rather ironic speech. I was shocked when he died; we got along well during the photoshoots.

Your next big series was *Kamaitachi* in 1965.
My friend, the dancer Hijikata Tatsumi, wanted to go back to his hometown in Akita Prefecture and I had the idea to take photographs of him there. So we went. There were rice fields and children playing, who agreed to do what we told them to do: 'this uncle will now jump really high, so stay there and just look.' And then 'boing!' Hijikata came flying [p. 68]. It all became very natural and spontaneous, and we enjoyed it. There is a photograph in which Hijikata sits on a fence-like structure on the rice field [p. 68]: these were used for the rice to dry [laughs].

It is a fantastic series.
I went back recently, for the first time after fifty years. There was an elderly woman who was one of the little girls in the photos, and she remembered us. We are famous in that village. People come and ask if this is where my *Kamaitachi* photo series was made. The people in the village even call me Hosoe-sensei, offering me sake [laughs]!

It sounds like the photoshoot was very spontaneous. You probably did not take a large number of photographs. How often did you go to the village?
The photos were all taken very quickly and we only went once. You can't take a photo like the one of Hijikata jumping twice. He jumped once and I took one photograph. Or the photo with the baby: 'Can we quickly borrow your baby? Ok, thank you', and 'whoosh!' Hijikata would run! [p. 56] Then he returned quickly, and gave the baby back to the still-surprised mother. The area has actually not changed much – there are no concrete buildings and the prefecture tries to preserve local traditions. I feel that our photo series was good for the region. At the time, people there thought that we were [imitating the local accent]: 'weird people, doing weird things, jumping and running and photographing it.' But now I'm 'Hosoe-sensei', it is funny. I was even interviewed by the local newspaper [laughs].

Looking at your best-known photographic series', the collaboration with your photographic subjects is an important part of your practice. This is obvious in the series with Mishima Yukio or Hijikata Tatsumi but also in your long-standing work with another *butoh* dancer, Ohno Kazuo [p. 57].[3] How did the collaboration with Ohno Kazuo come about?
Yes, collaborations became a major part of my work. Ohno-sensei was famous and Hijikata Tatsumi respected him very much as a dancer. Hijikata also knew his son, Ohno Yoshito; they sometimes practised together. Here is a nice story: Ohno-sensei

was actually a sports teacher at a famous elementary school in Yokohama. When my works were exhibited in Bulgaria, I met the ambassador's wife and it turned out that she was taught by Ohno-sensei. She was nostalgic, seeing her old teacher in my photographs. He was a dancer and used the sports lessons to teach dance to the children as well – he combined sports and art.

Your collaboration with Ohno-san lasted a long time – you photographed him for over forty years.
Yes. Ohno-sensei was very intelligent, and a free character. He was truly respected by his pupils. It was a fun collaboration for both of us. While trying out new movements for the camera, Ohno-sensei would get inspiration for his dance. And I would ask myself why certain movements and forms looked good or not and even try them myself, suggesting them to him. 'Let's move the leg a little bit further down. Oh, this looks good' – like that. It is very interesting to look at the photographs as a viewer afterwards. It really was a good collaboration.

You even photographed Ohno-san just before he passed away.
Yes, he was in bed and many people came to see him. It was nice to see his reactions when children sat on his bed. The mother would tell the kids to get off – I also took photographs of that. Until the very end, Ohno-sensei truly understood what my photography is about, and he trusted me. That is why I was able to take such photographs of him. It is good that we have these photographic documents – for him, too.

What do you like best about photography?
To me, the most interesting and attractive aspect of photography is the simple joy of the people who are photographed. I have always liked human relationships, making people happy – the reactions of people being photographed are great. Another reason why I have continued photography is my endless interest in discovering new photographic moments and expressions.

*   This is a shortened version of an interview conducted in Japanese on 8 April 2017, at Eikoh Hosoe Laboratory of Photographic Arts, Tokyo.
1   *Shichigosan* literally means 'seven-five-three' and is a religious rite of passage day on 15 November, celebrating the growth and wellbeing of seven-, five- and three-year old children.
2   Tokyo College of Photography (Tōkyō Sōgō Shashin Senmon Gakkō) is known for its technical education. See also Introduction, Photography Education, pp. 14–15.
3   *Butoh* is an expressive contemporary dance form, founded by Hijikata Tatsumi and Ohno Kazuo in 1959 as a reaction against the rigid contemporary dance scene in Japan. Incorporating both 'Western' and traditional Japanese elements, it is traditionally performed in white body make-up. It often features grotesque imagery, controlled slow motion, and taboo topics.

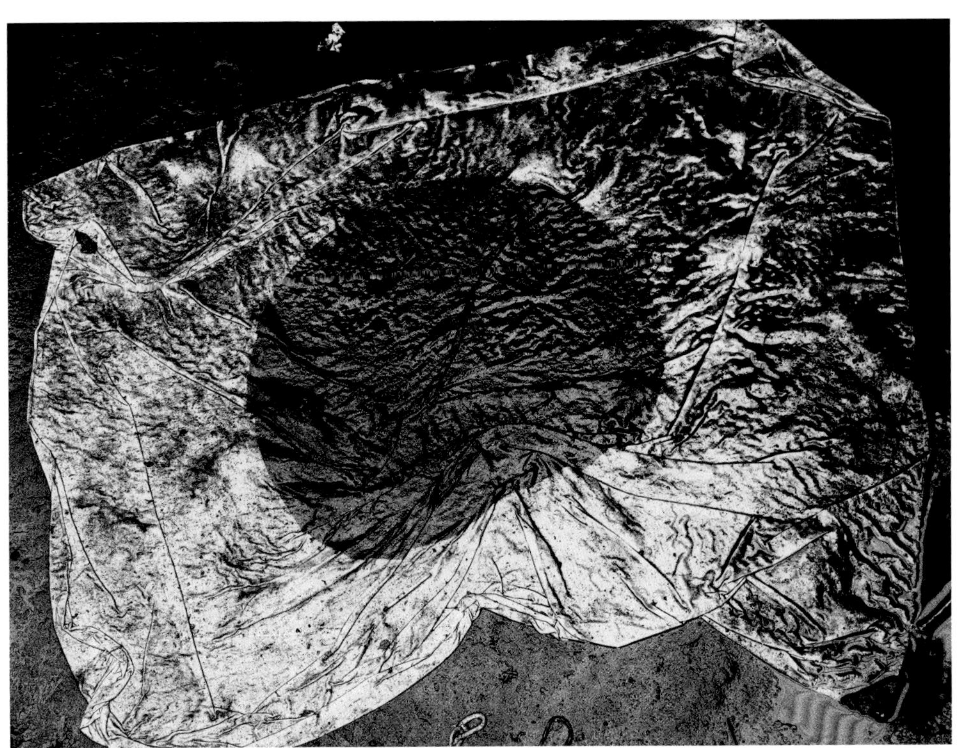

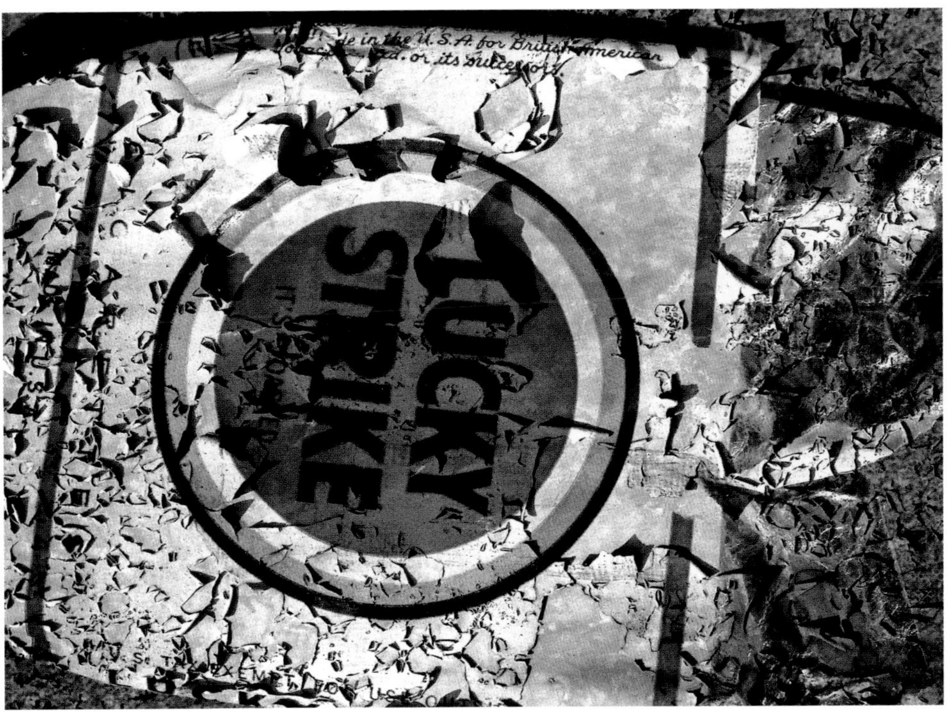

Top and above: Kawada Kikuji, *The Map (Chizu)* series, 1965.

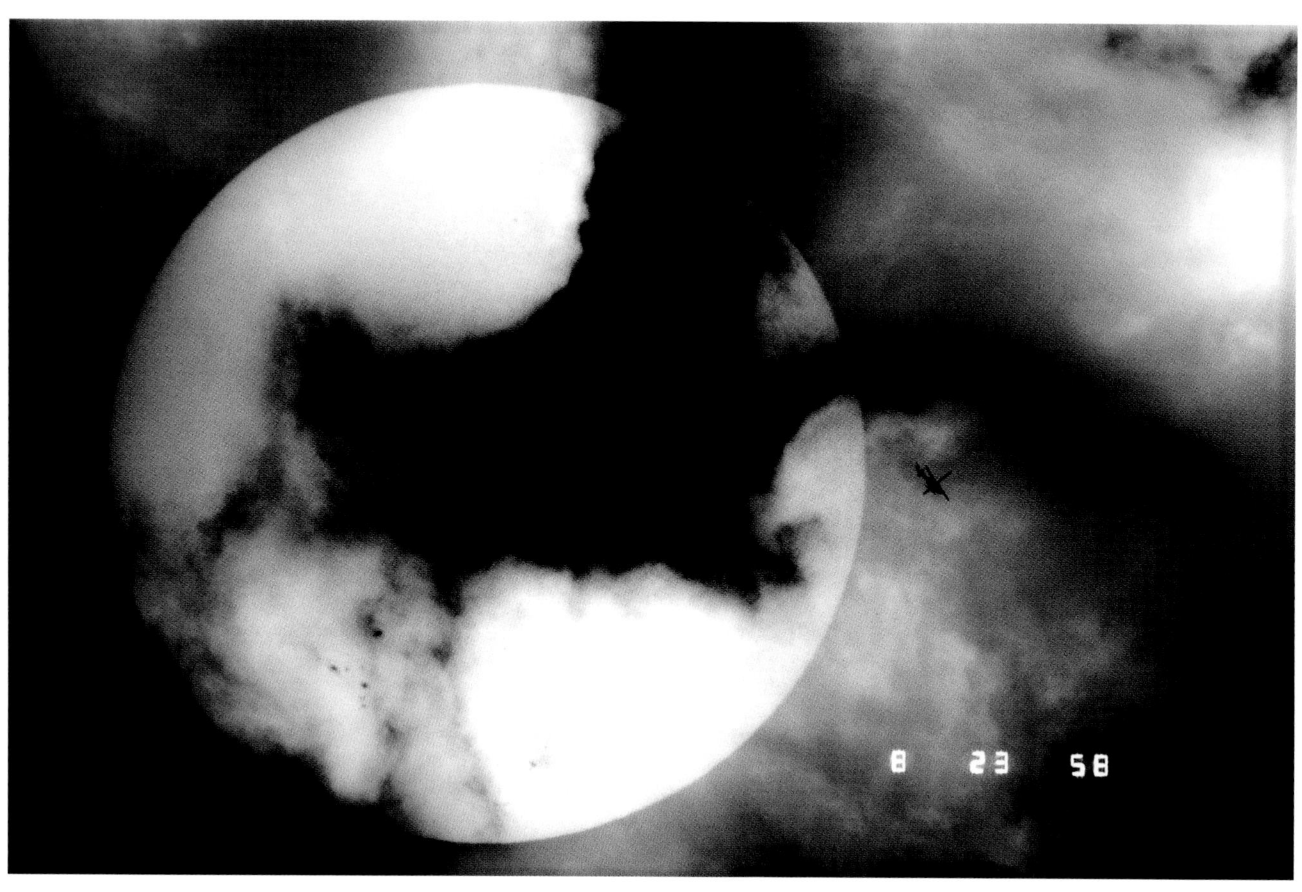

Kawada Kikuji, 1990,
The Last Cosmology series.

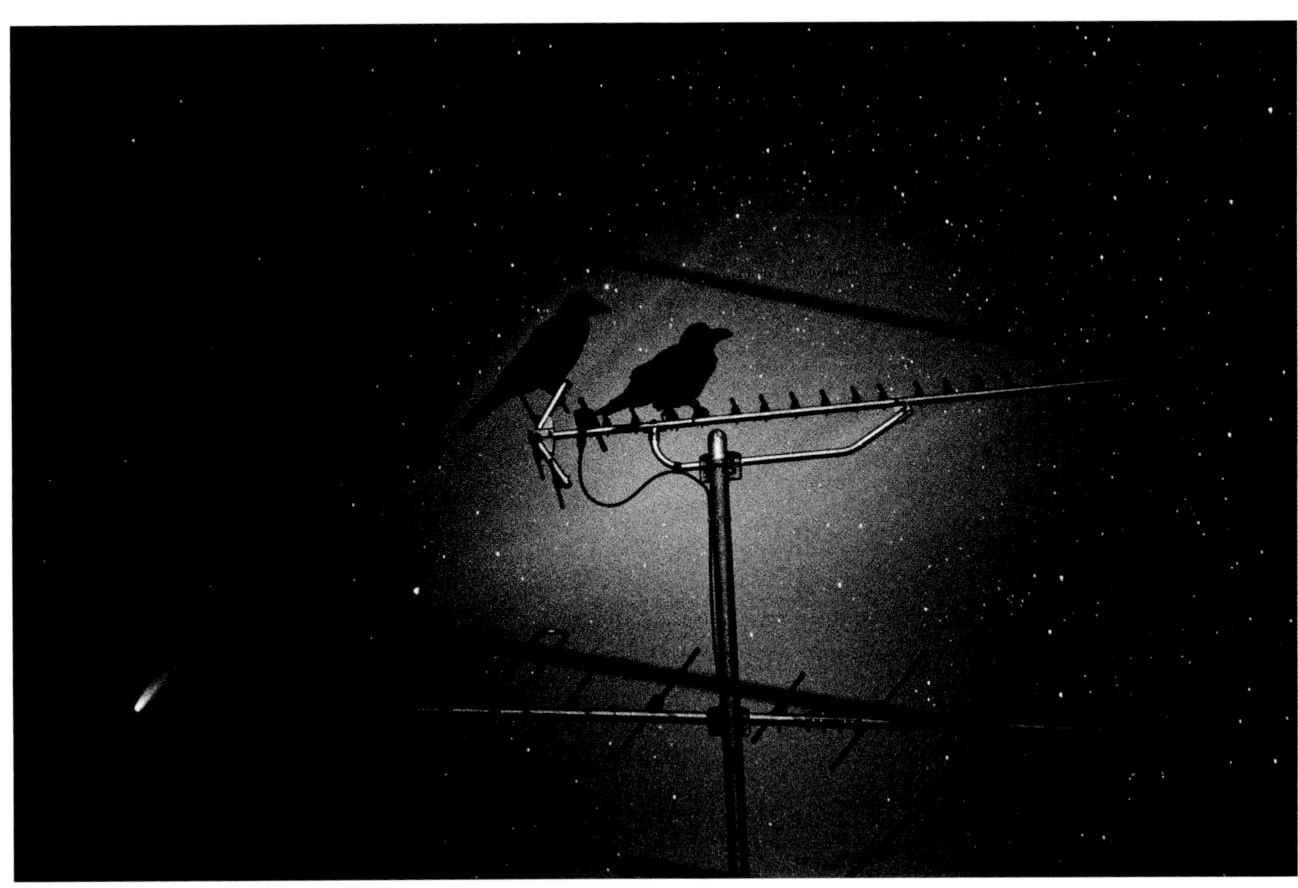

Kawada Kikuji, 1995,
The Last Cosmology series.

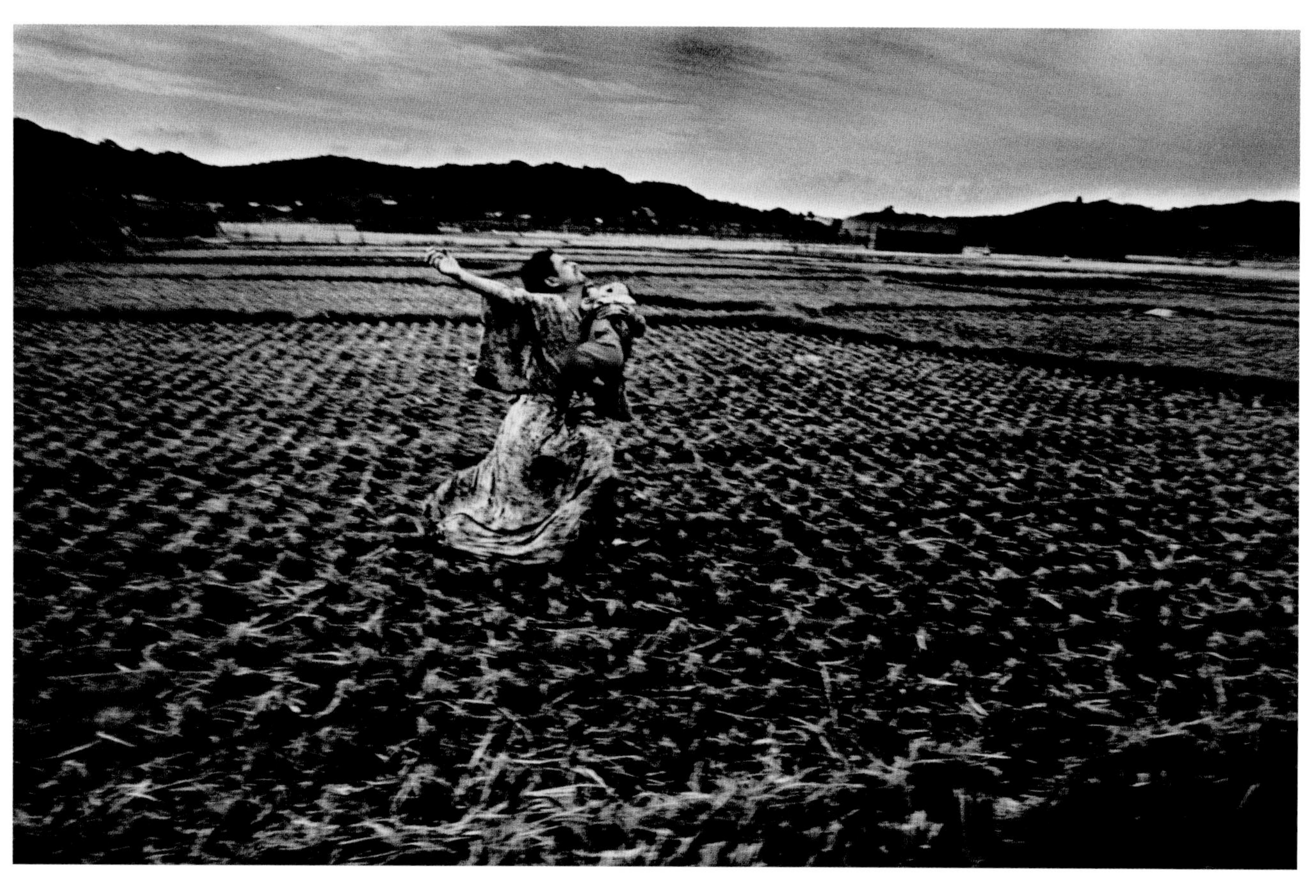

Above: Hosoe Eikoh, *Kamaitachi #37*, 1965.
Opposite: Hosoe Eikoh, *Dancing in Kushiro Marsh*, 1994, *The Butterfly Dream* series.

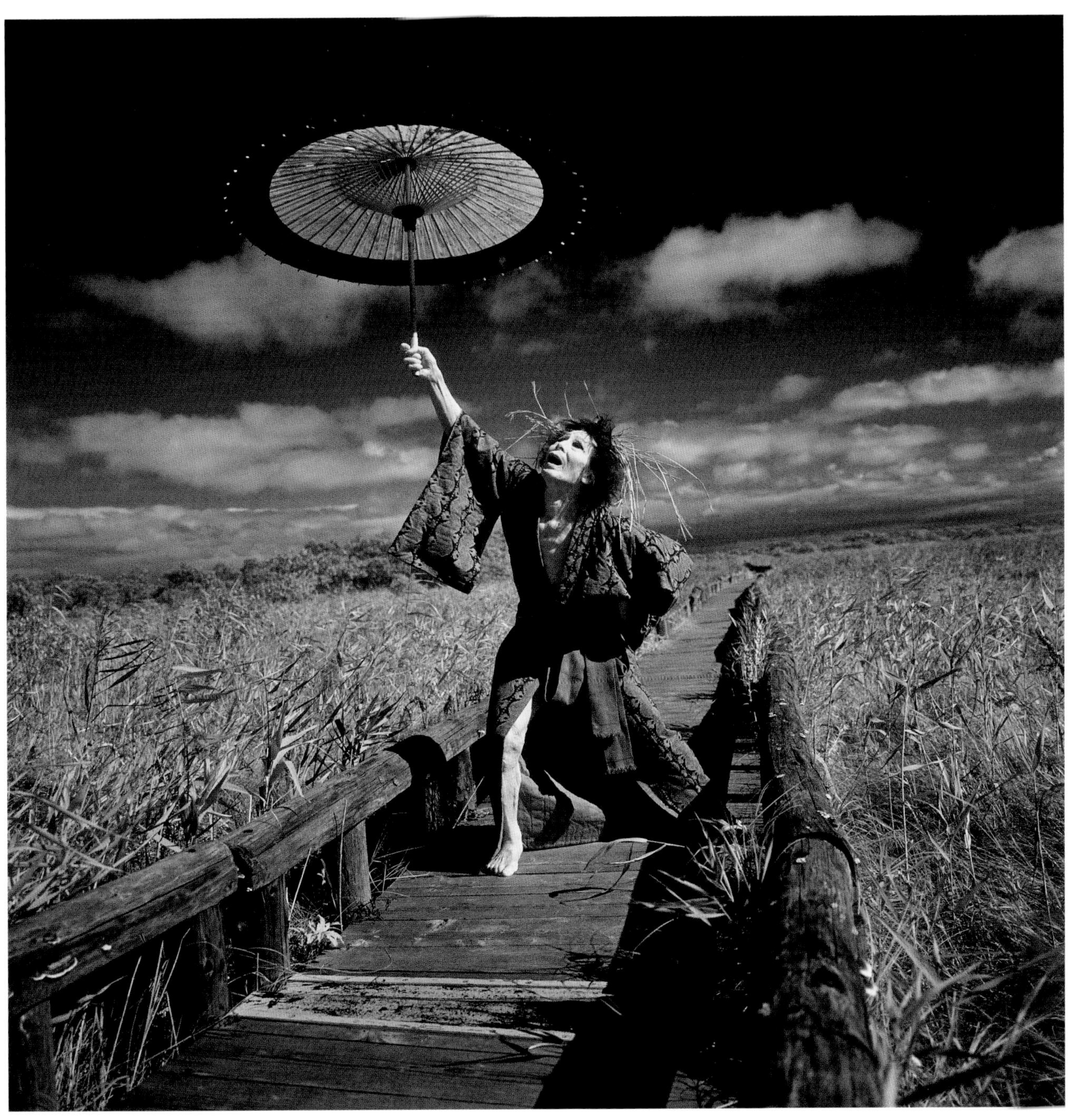

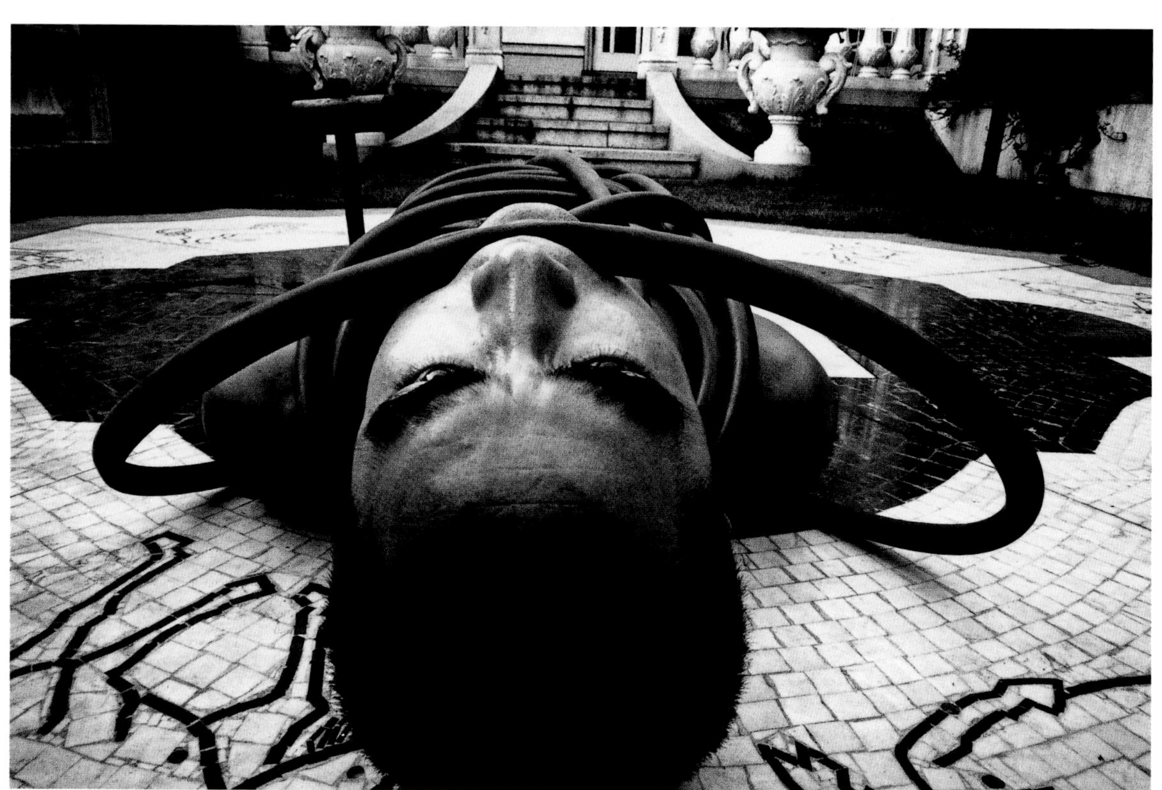

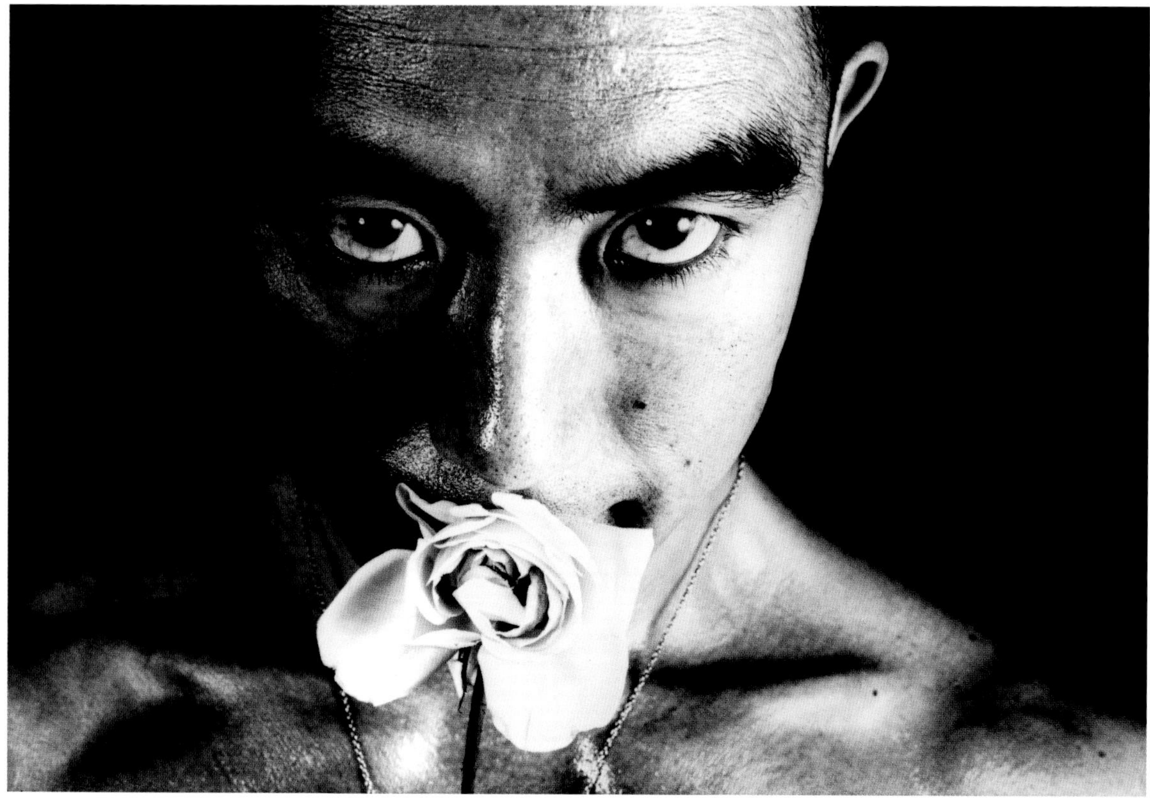

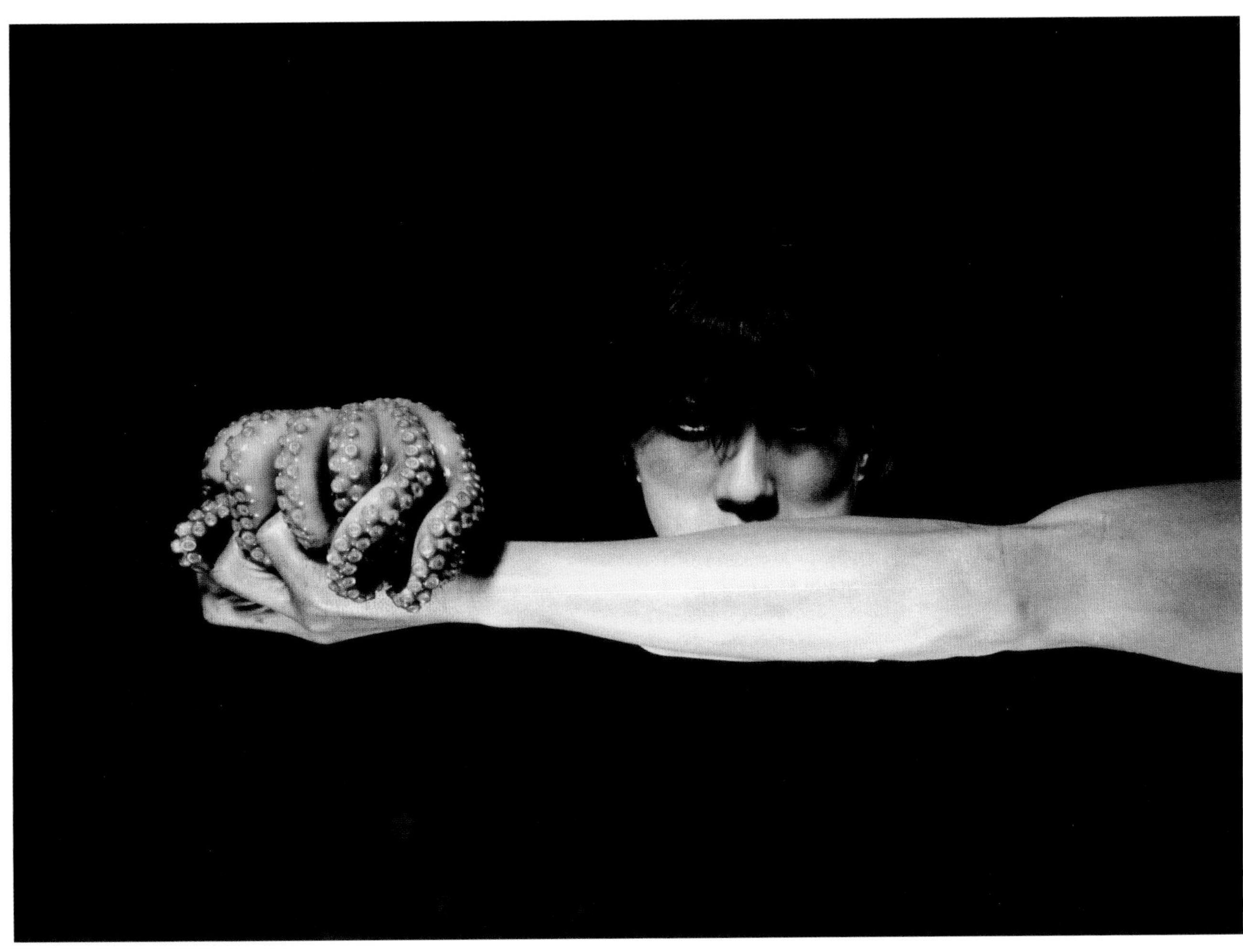

Opposite above: Hosoe Eikoh, *Ordeal by Roses (Barakei) #6*, 1961.
Opposite below: Hosoe Eikoh, *Ordeal by Roses (Barakei) #32*, 1961.
Above: Hosoe Eikoh, *Man and Woman #31*, 1960.

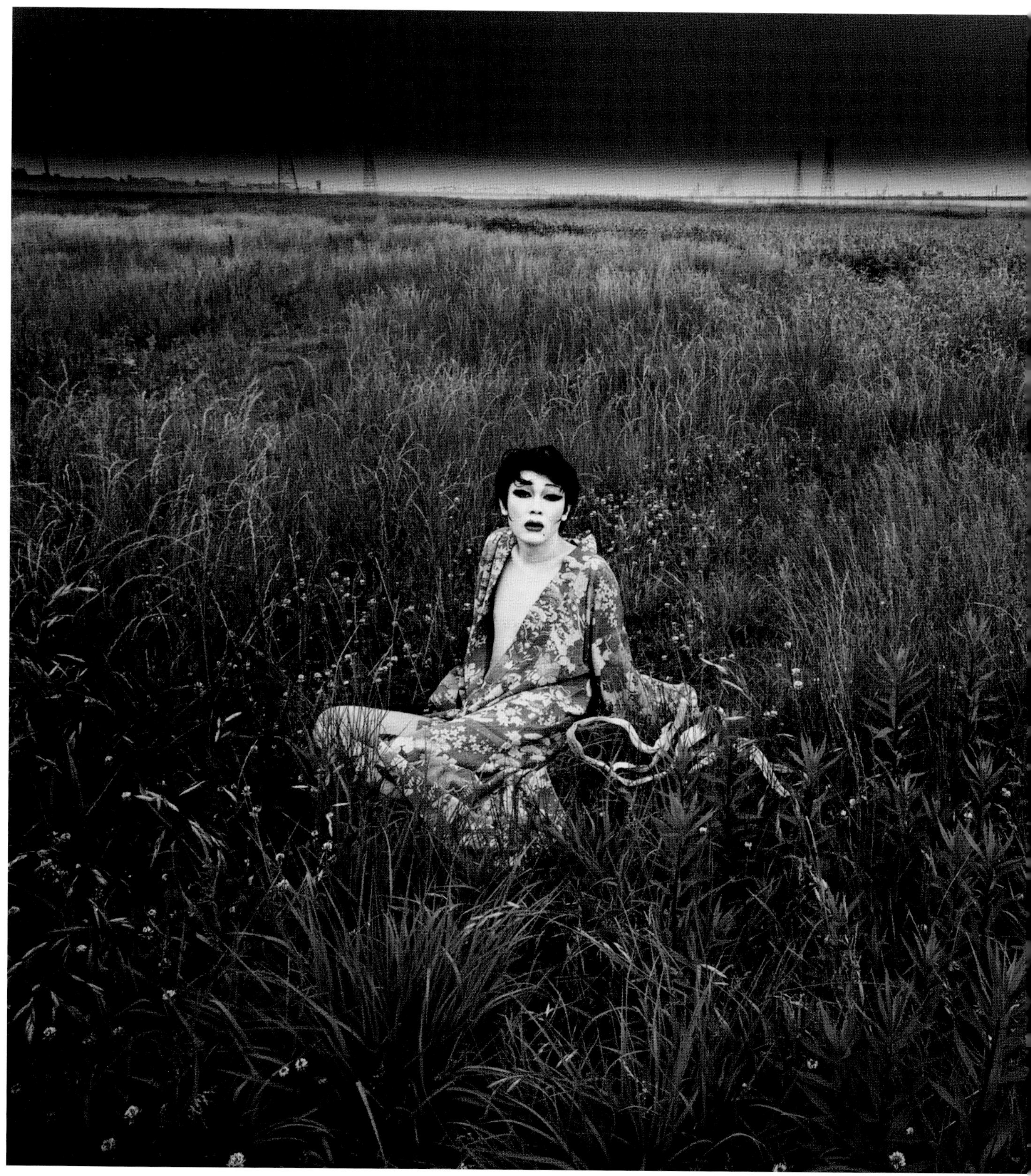

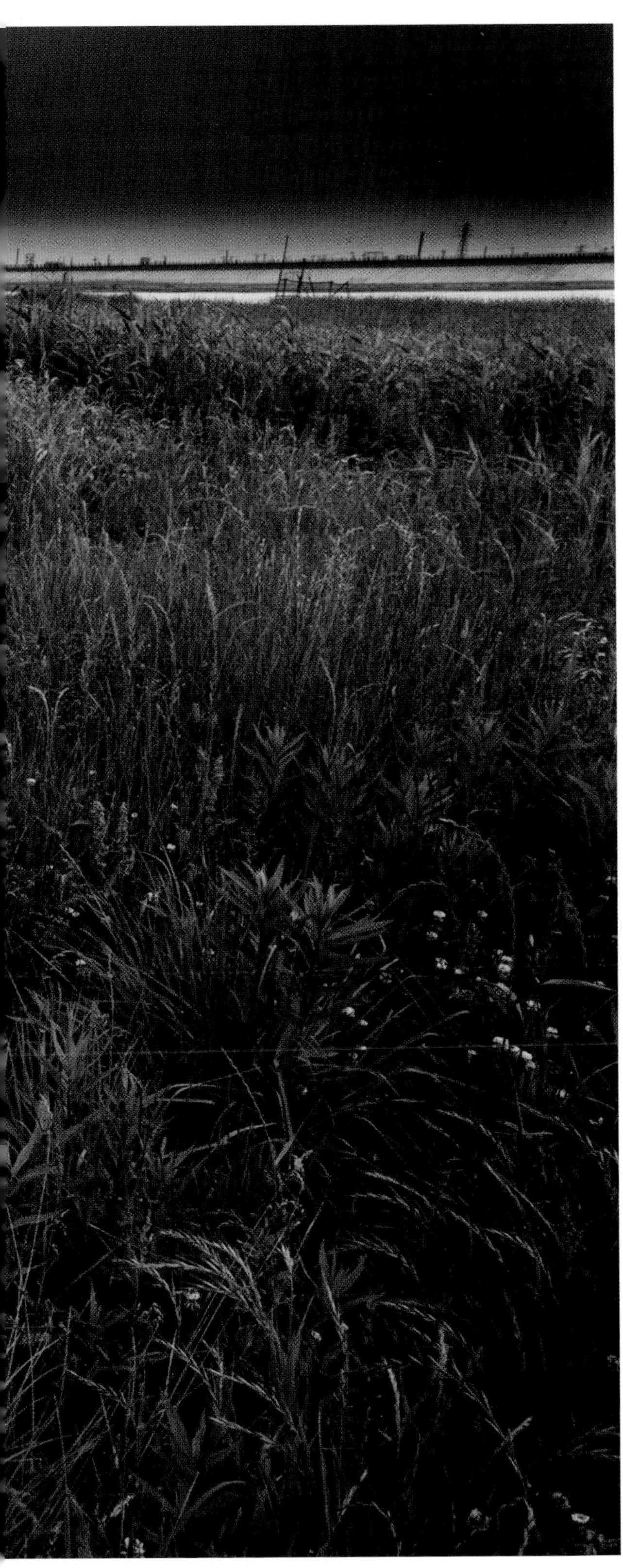

Hosoe Eikoh, *Near the Arakawa River*, 1971,
Simmon: A Private Landscape series.

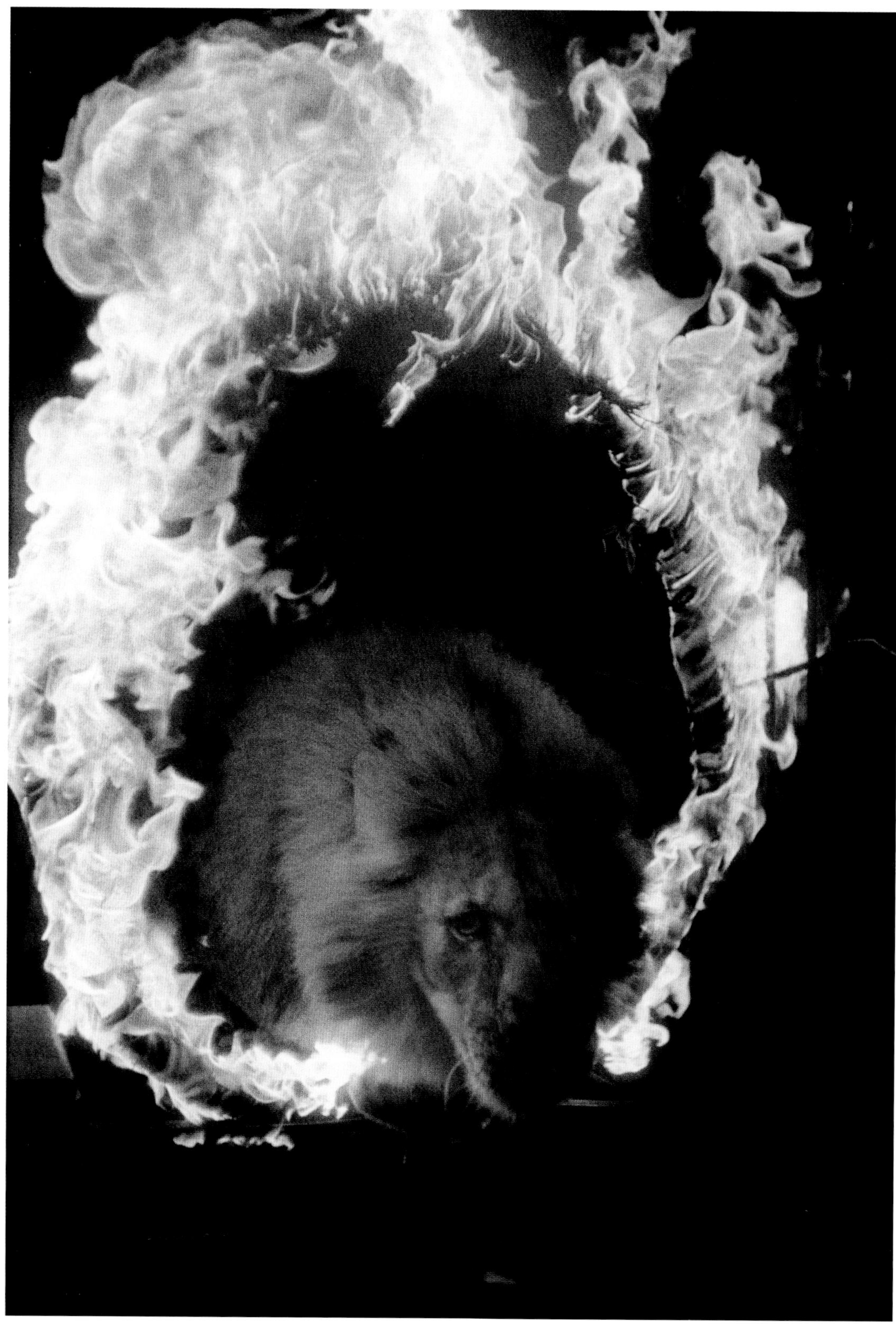

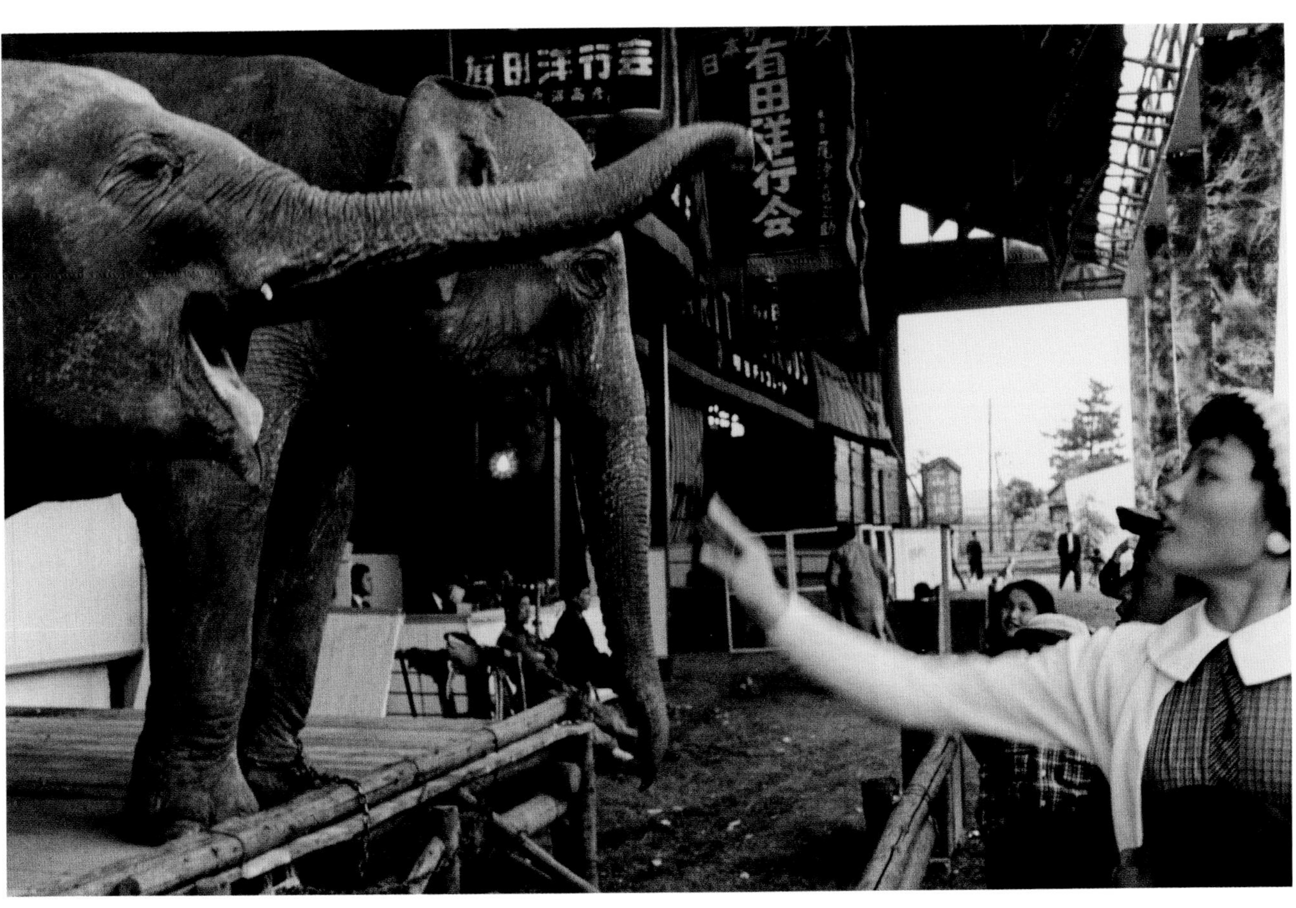

Opposite and above: Tanno Akira,
Circus of Showa Japan series, 1956–57.

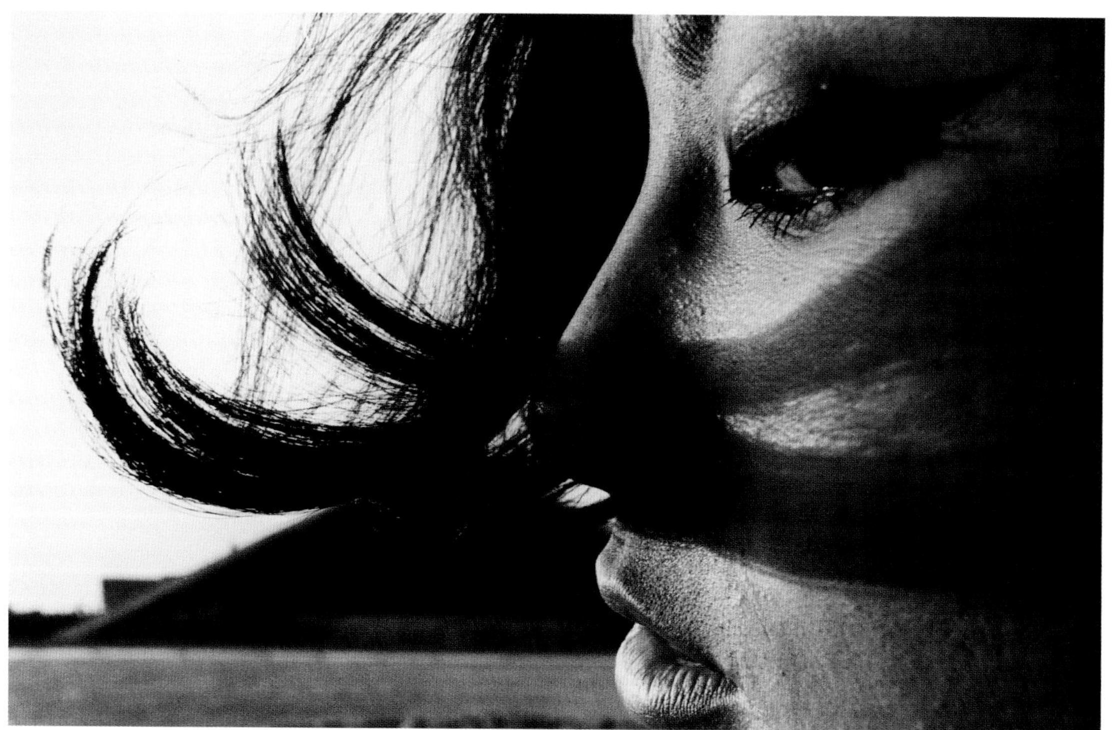

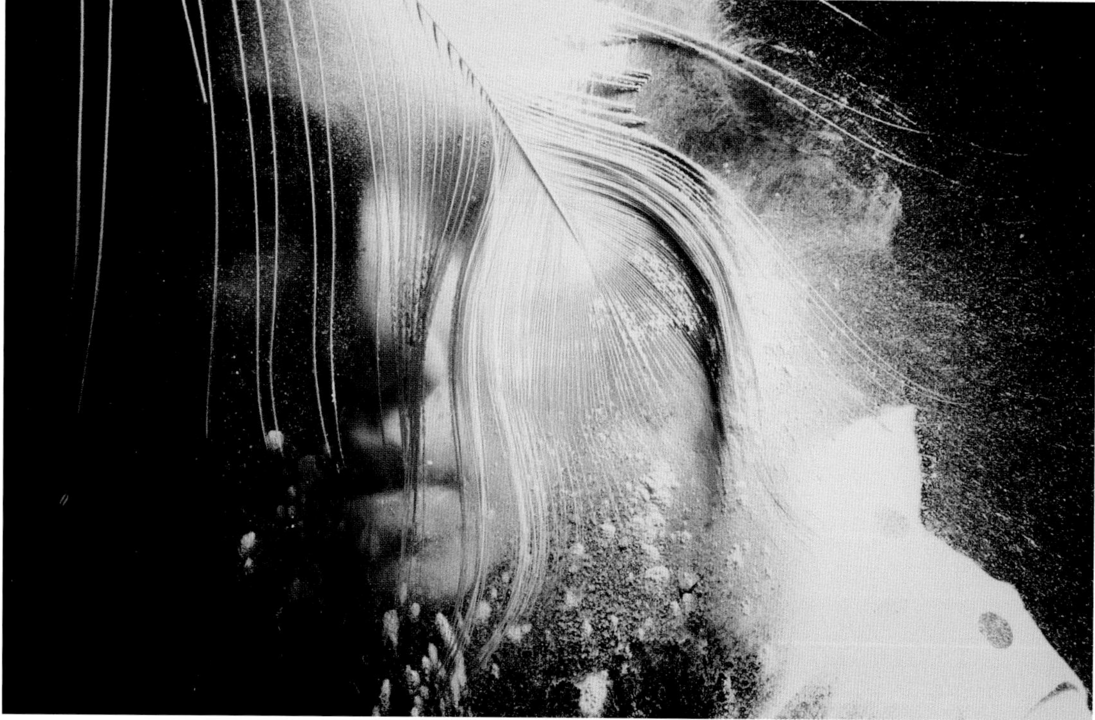

Top: Satō Akira, *Takashima Mieko (Cold Sunset)*, 1960.
Above: Satō Akira, *Enami Kyoko (Cyclopean)*, 1962.
Opposite: Tōmatsu Shōmei, *Prostitute, Nagoya*, 1958.

64

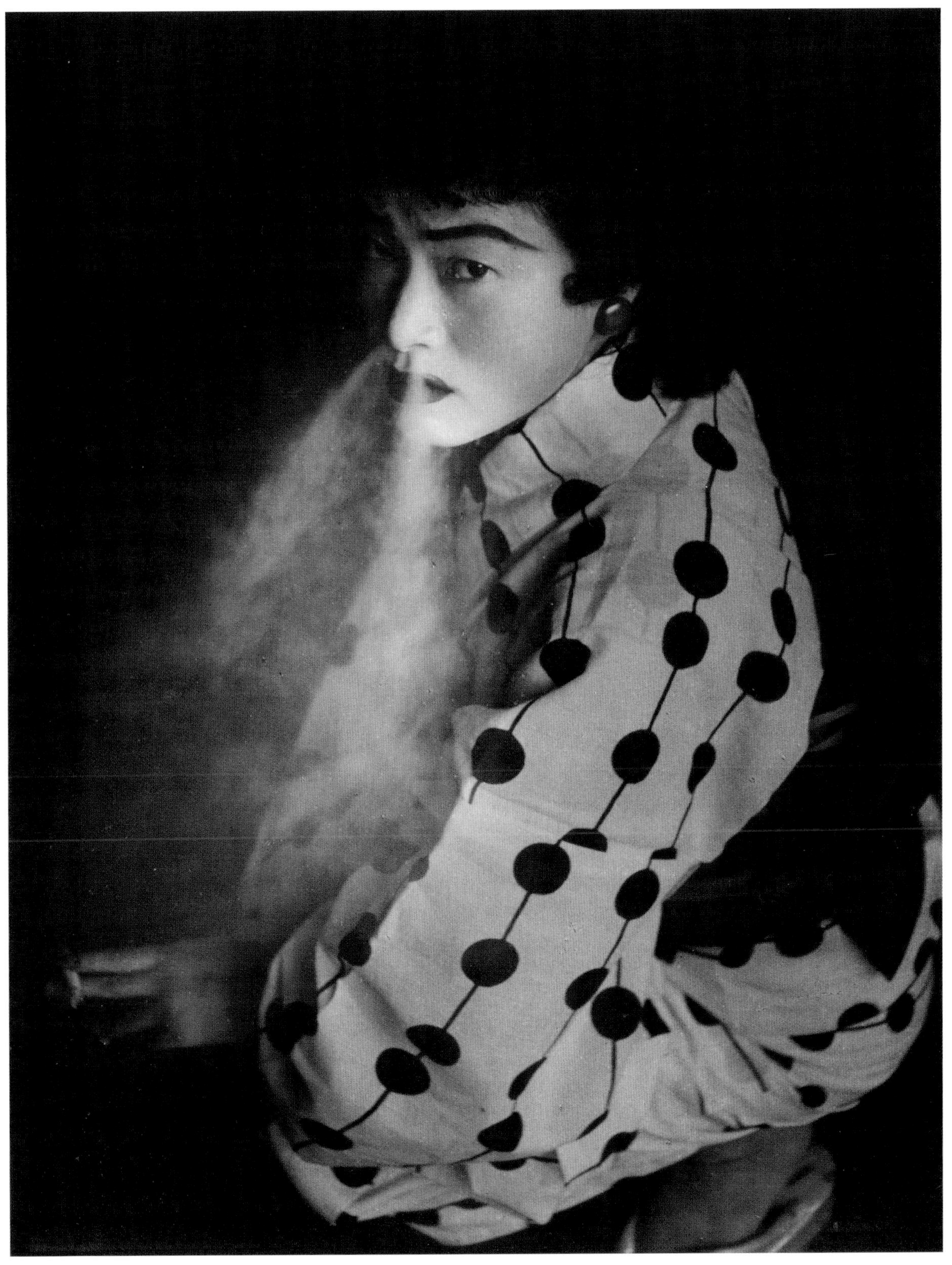

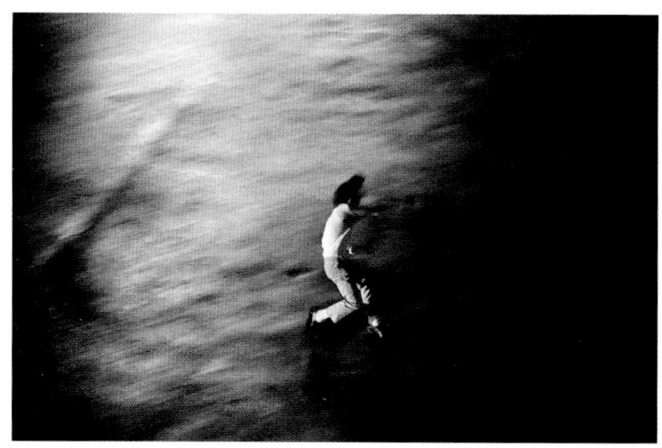

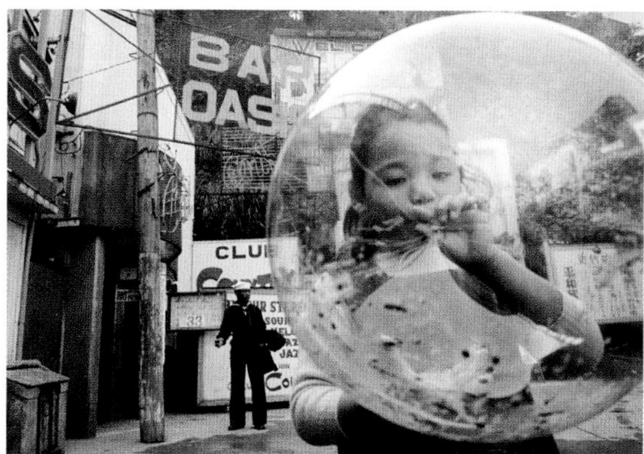

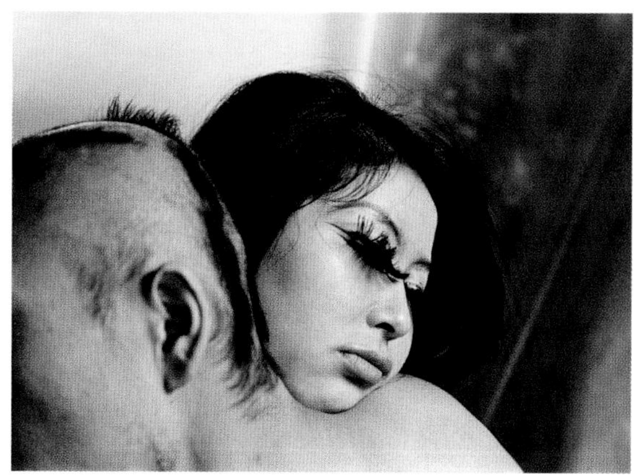

Top: Tōmatsu Shōmei, *Protest, Tokyo*, 1969, *I am a King* series.
Centre: Tōmatsu Shōmei, 1959, *Chewing Gum and Chocolate* series.
Above: Tōmatsu Shōmei, *Blood and Rose*, 1969.

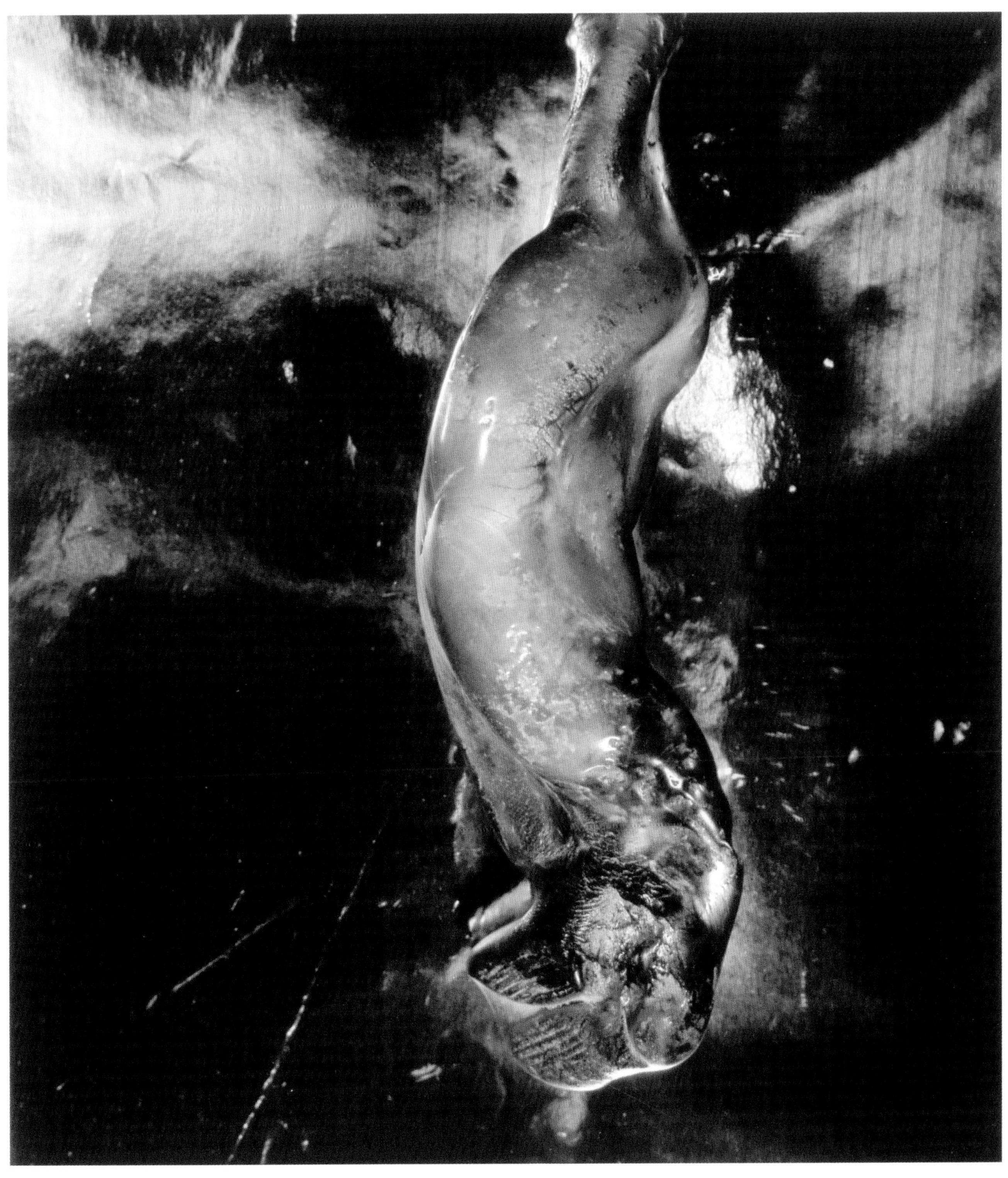

Tōmatsu Shōmei, *Nagasaki, Bottle Melted and Deformed*, 1961.

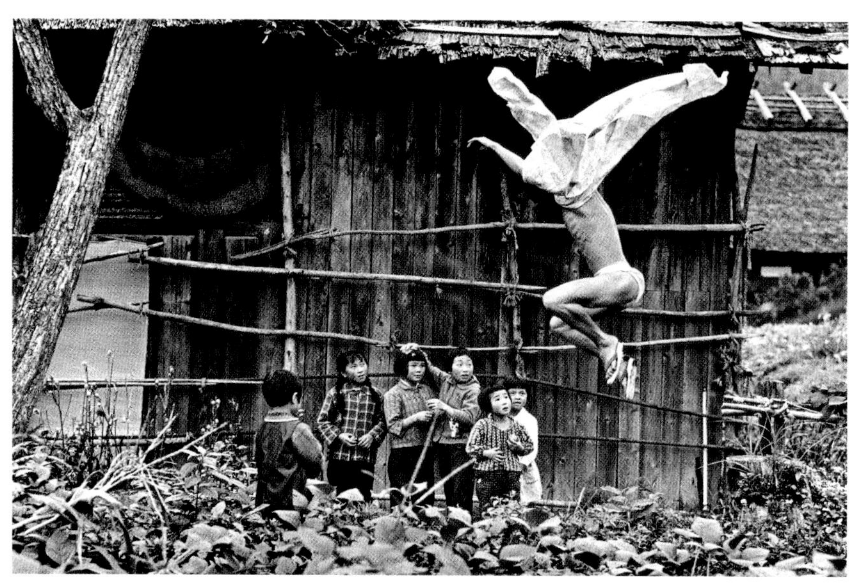

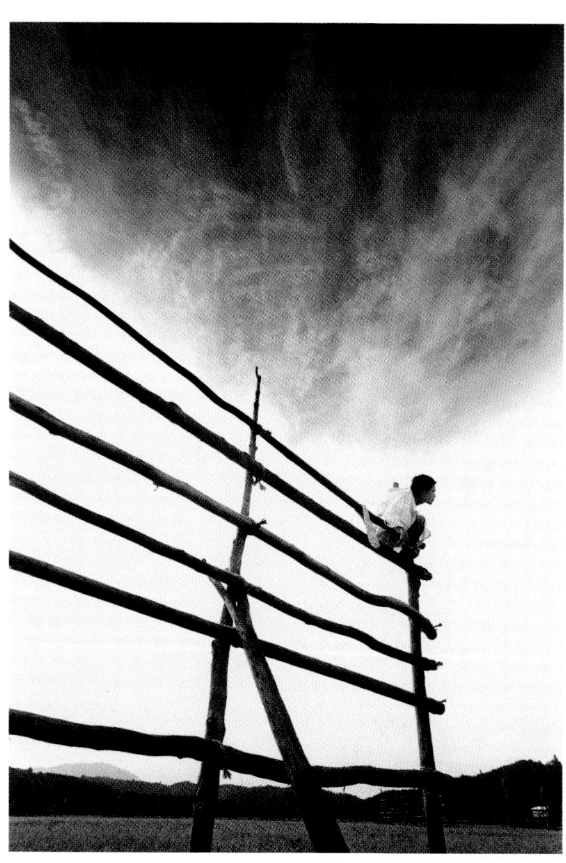

Above: Hosoe Eikoh, *Kamaitachi #17*, 1965.
Left: Hosoe Eikoh, *Kamaitachi #8*, 1965.
Opposite: Narahara Ikkō, untitled,
c. 1954–58, *Tokyo, the 50s* series.

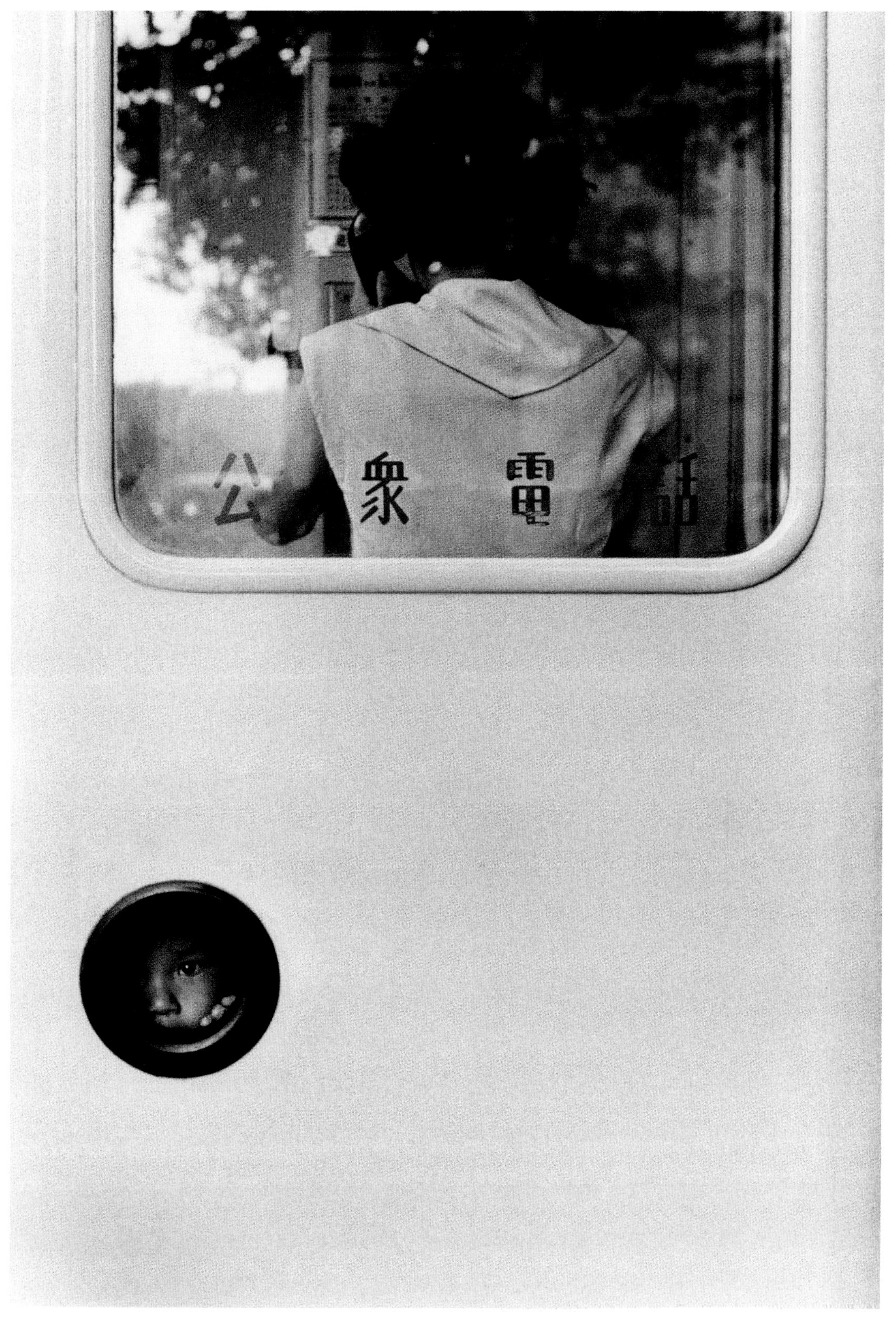

公衆電話

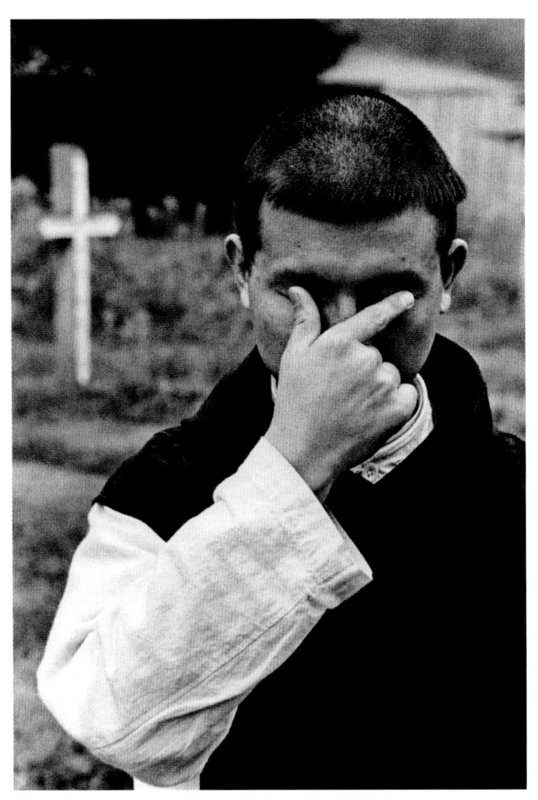

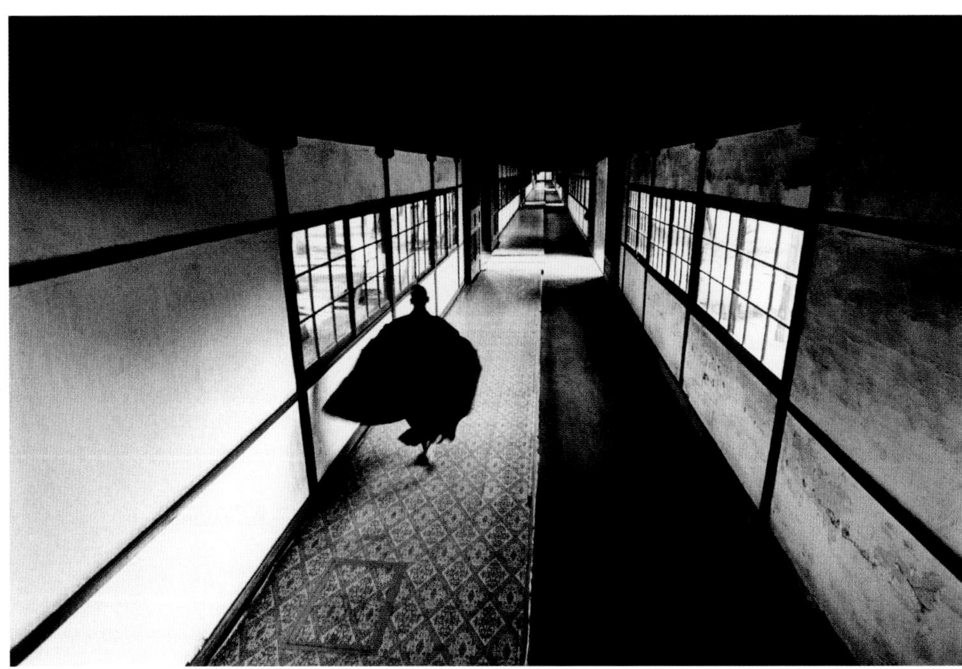

Above: Narahara Ikkō, *Man and His Land/Domains*, 1958.
Right: Narahara Ikkō, untitled, 1969, *Japanesque/Zen* series.
Opposite: Narahara Ikkō, untitled, 1963, *Europe: Where Time Has Stopped* series.

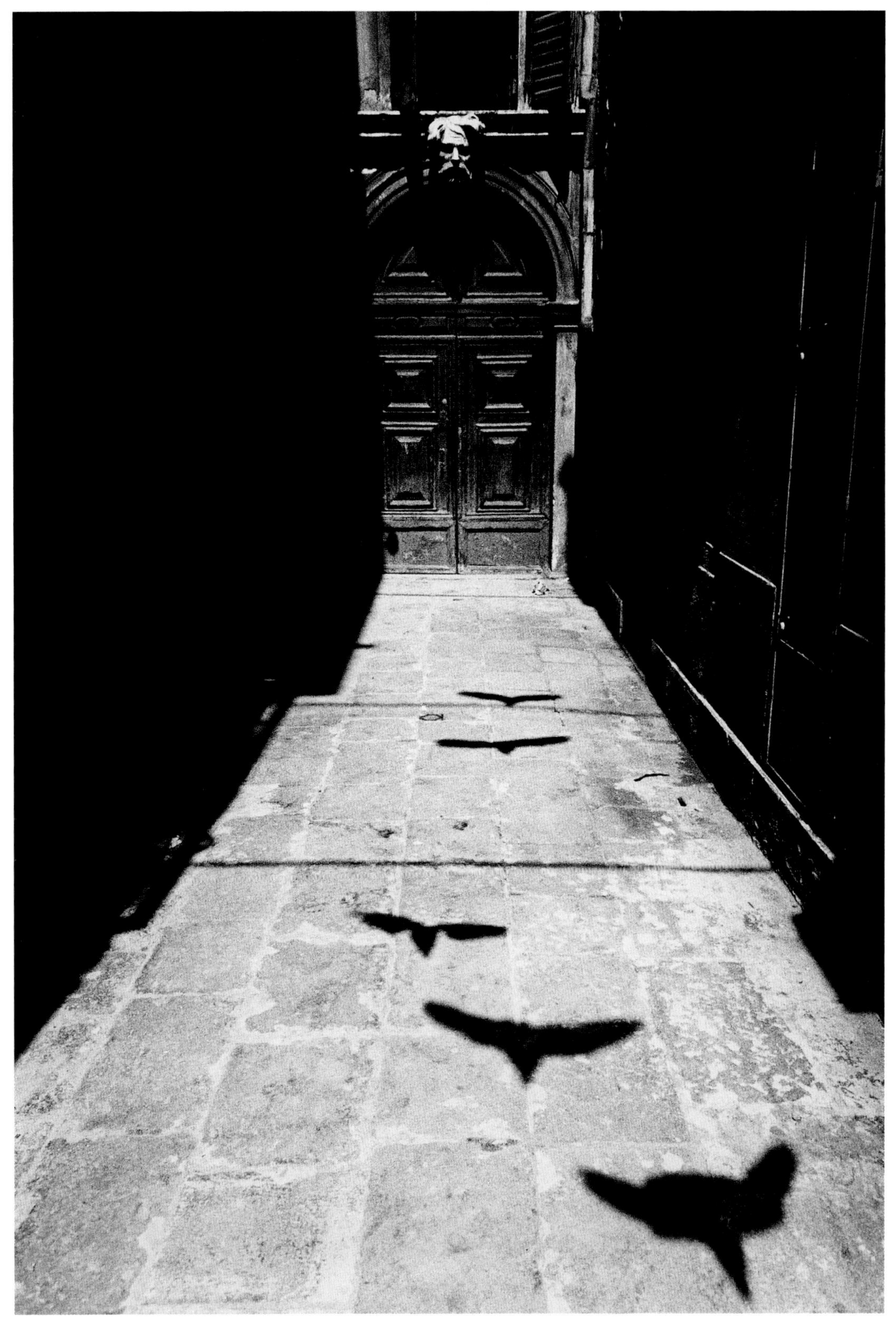

III

NEW PHOTOGRAPHIC FREEDOM

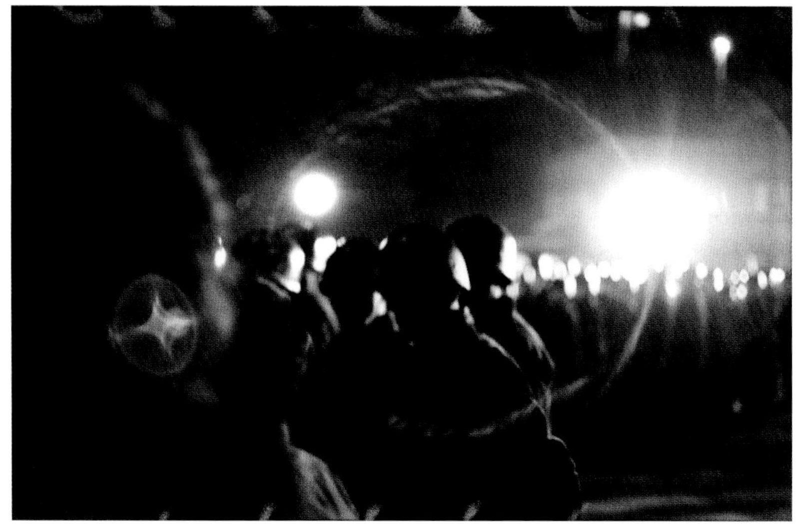

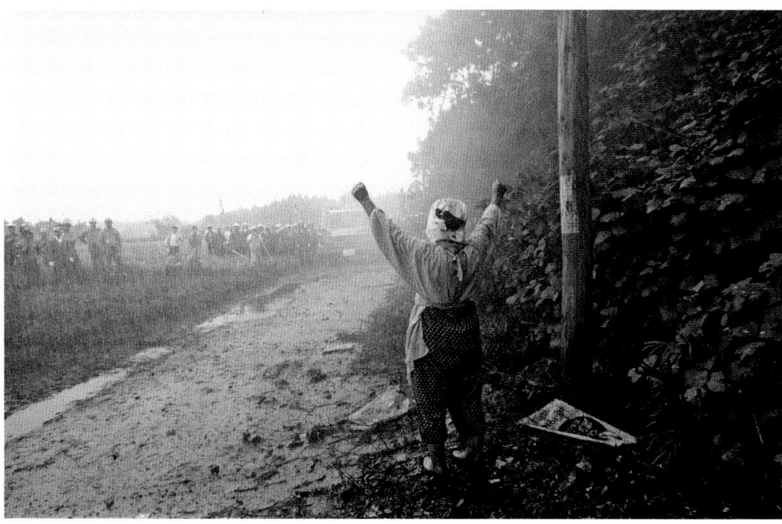

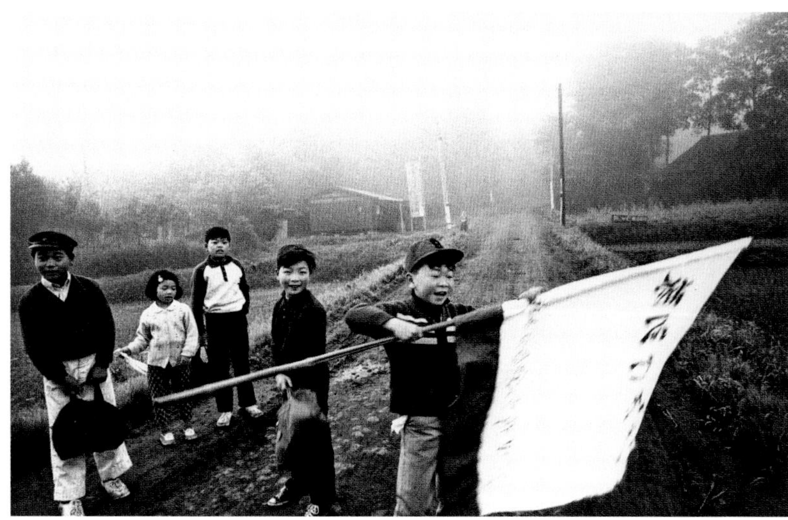

Previous spread: detail from Nakahira Takuma, untitled, 1970, *For a Language to Come* series.
Top: Kitai Kazuo, *"Riot Squad" Yokosuka, Kanagawa*, 1964, *Teikou/Resistance* series.
Centre: Kitai Kazuo, *Old lady faces the water cannon*, 1970, *Sanrizuka* series.
Left: Kitai Kazuo, *Children's Resistance Corps*, 1970, *Sanrizuka* series.

In the late 1960s, a range of different approaches emerged to change the face of Japanese photography. The photographs in this chapter differ in style and tone, but share an impulse to break with the photography of the past.

A number of photographers documented the protests and demonstrations of the turbulent 1960s. Kitai Kazuo (b. 1944) was still a student when he photographed the barricades at Nihon University from inside, and published his work in *Asahi Graph* magazine. He also presented his protest photographs in the now iconic photobook *Teikou/Resistance* (1965) (opposite, top). Kitai has emphasized that he took a clear political side, representing the same viewpoint as the photographic subjects.[30] He continued to convey a socio-political message in his next series, supporting the farmers in Sanrizuka against the building of Narita airport (opposite, centre and below). The photographs vividly show their daily lives and peaceful demonstrations.

A radical new definition of photography can be found in photographs by Moriyama Daidō (b. 1938) (pp. 81–84), Nakahira Takuma (1938–2015) (pp. 90–91) and Takanashi Yutaka (b. 1935) (p. 77), all of whom were associated with *Provoke* magazine.

After working as a graphic design assistant and joining a photography studio in Osaka, Moriyama moved to Tokyo in 1961. He began working in the Vivo office, and became Hosoe Eikoh's personal assistant when the group disbanded. Three years later he became independent, working for magazines. In 1968, he joined Nakahira, Takanashi, Okada Takahiko (b. 1939) and Taki Kōji (1928–2011), who had just founded the quarterly magazine *Provoke*. It was subtitled 'provocative materials for thought', and sought to give experimental photography and photo theory a platform, overriding the conventions of modern photography. Each issue was published in a small edition of 1,000 copies.

Provoke and the 1960s–1970s

Provoke was discontinued in 1969 but by then, to the photographers' annoyance, its name had already become associated with them as a collective.[31]

Moriyama was awarded the Newcomer's Award by the Japan Photo Critics Association in 1967 for a series of black-saturated, often grainy photographs published in *Camera Mainichi*, some of which were close-ups of folklore entertainment in Shinjuku. Critics began to define his style with the catchy description *are bure boke* (grainy, blurry, out-of-focus). An important inspiration for Moriyama was the 1956 photobook *Life is Good & Good for You in New York,* by William Klein. Klein used different angles and out-of-focus shots to convey the vitality of New York. Nakahira described his photographic gaze in 1967: 'It is not the static perspective of "me and the world", but endlessly moving and supported by an infinite number of viewpoints.'[32] Although Klein's work influenced Moriyama, photo critic Shimizu Minoru has convincingly contrasted the reasons for their 'grainy, blurry, out-of-focus' techniques. Klein chose this aesthetic to capture dynamic urban life straightforwardly: 'it is a pictorial technique used to create a straight (accurate) account of New York'.[33] Moriyama did not aim to tell any documentary stories. When presenting him with the Newcomer's Award in 1967, the jury argued that his work engaged specifically, and impressively, with Japanese minorities' post-war life.[34] His style was evaluated in a similar way to Klein's: a straightforward technique for documenting the entertainers.

Moriyama felt misunderstood; he was more concerned with the pictures themselves. He reacted by creating a photobook: 'Deep down in myself, there was…a strong feeling of "It's not like that"…I thoroughly segmented my own flesh and as part of my method of successively presenting these fragments, I created a photography book.'[35] This now legendary book, *Japan: A Photo Theater* (*Nippon Gekijōshashinchō*), was published in 1968. It features a blend of urban shots, portraits, everyday scenes and performance documentation, with texts by avant-garde writer and film director Terayama Shūji (p. 84). Instead of explaining where the photographs were taken or who the subjects are, Moriyama invites the viewer to focus on the decontextualized images and the relationships between them. By declaring 'a war against the general concept of traditional photography based on topics', he ushered in a new form of photography.[36] The idea of 'equivalence' is central to his work: photography does not aim to represent a coherent context, but rather exists in its own right.

The irrelevance of themes is partly why Moriyama was able to have a more positive relationship with 'the West' than for example Tōmatsu Shōmei. Moriyama read Albert Camus and Jack Kerouac, admired the work of Klein and Warhol, travelled to New York and took photographs of American products in Japan (p. 81, below) without any negative undertones. Real scenes and reproduced reality are also of equal value in his photographs. Moriyama has explained that he treats all motifs in the same way: 'To me, reality and the images on posters and TV are equivalent, all existing as things of the outside world.'[37] This becomes obvious in his *Accidents* photographs, which were serialized in *Asahi Camera* throughout 1969. *Accident #6* consists of images depicting the immediate aftermath of a car accident (p. 81, above), but Moriyama did not take any photographs at the real scene. He photographed a traffic safety poster that he saw at the exit of an underground station; the seven pages in *Asahi Camera* consist of one photograph of the complete image, as well as cropped versions and close-up shots. Moriyama also takes photographs using a 'no finder' technique, or from a moving car (p. 82) to avoid any deliberate choice of motif. Created by pressing the shutter fast and repeatedly, his photography follows his physical and intuitive actions.

The *Provoke* members sought to encounter an unexplored world rather than looking at people, objects and landscapes as already articulated by language and culture. This becomes obvious in Takanashi's photobook *Towards the City* (*Toshi-e*) (1969) (opposite). It consists of cityscape imagery and fragments of architectural details or people, often photographed from a car window – blurred and grainy, with tilted horizons. Takanashi has described his mutually antagonistic approaches: 'Two conflicting creatures settled into my body. One is a "hunter of images", aiming exclusively to shoot down the invisible, and the other is a "scrap picker" who can only believe in what is visible.'[38] He recognises the tension inherent in his practice, between a more traditional approach and a new, experimental viewpoint.

Moriyama, Nakahira and Takanashi were concerned with the 'bare photograph', and interested in light, materiality and printing techniques. In his legendary book *For a Language to Come* (1970), Nakahira searched for a new photographic language, often shooting into the light (p. 90). In his photobook *Farewell Photography* (*Shashin yo Sayōnara*) (1972), Moriyama strove to reach the limits of the medium, presenting starkly cropped photographs, blurs and abstracted grains (p. 91). In the end, he did not bid photography 'farewell', but has remained incredibly active. He continues to challenge photography as a medium and to take as many photographs as possible.[39]

Personal Life/Photographic Practice

The Vivo artists questioned their realist predecessors by emphasizing subjectivity and self-expression. The *Provoke* photographers took this emphasis even further, aiming for a new photography so subjective that there was no differentiation between the photographer and his works. In Moriyama's words from 1967, 'I and photography are one'.[40] This statement also applies to another 'big name' in Japanese photography: Araki Nobuyoshi (b. 1940). Araki studied at Chiba University and joined the advertising agency Dentsu, before working as an independent photographer from 1972 onwards. He highlighted the influence *Provoke* had on him: 'I was very inspired by *Provoke*. Although *Provoke* is not usually discussed in the history of Japanese photography, it was like a giant bomb, made underground and thrown by the radicals. That era

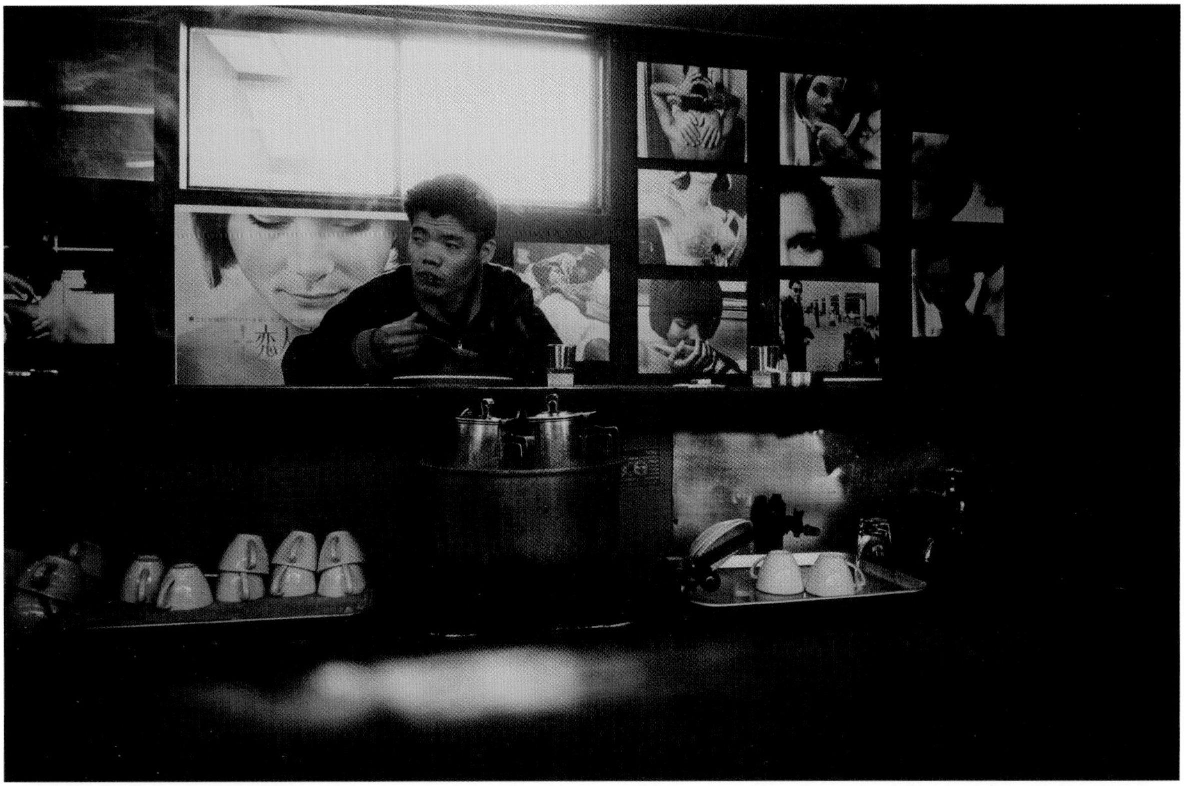

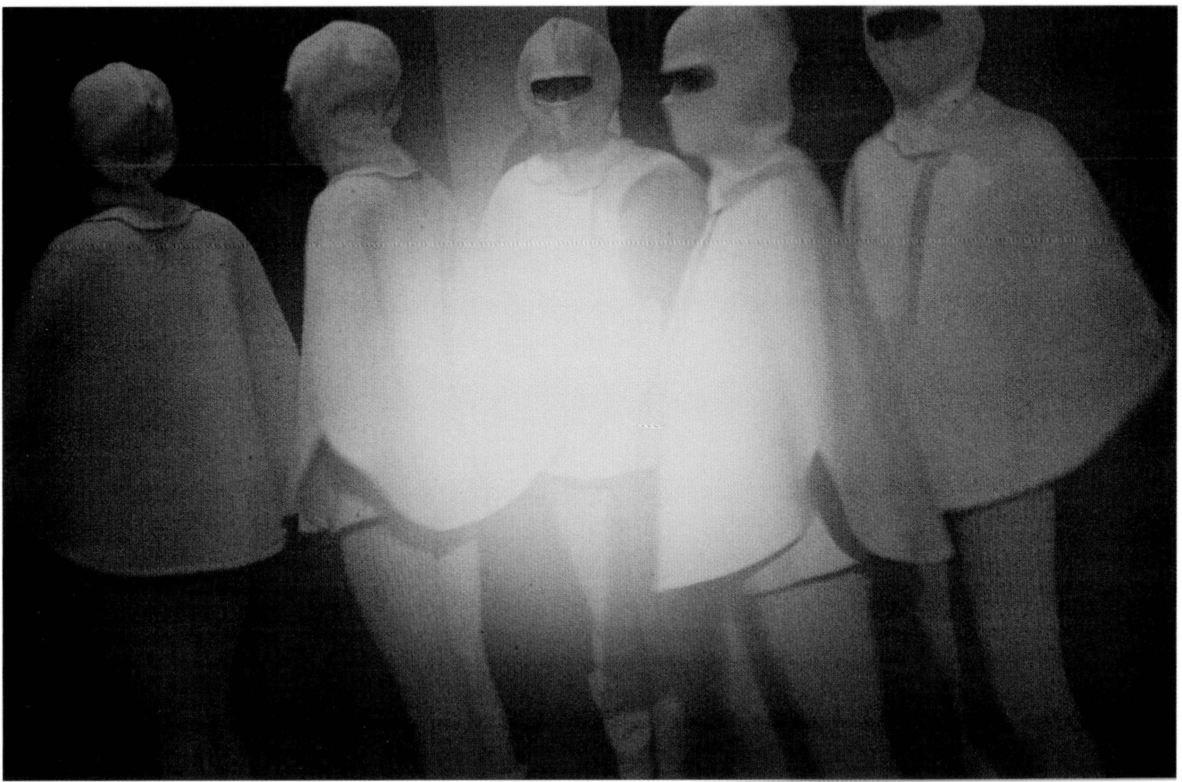

Top: Takanashi Yutaka, *Bar Toyota, Shinjuku*, 1965.
Above: Takanashi Yutaka, untitled, 1969, *Towards the City* (*Toshi-e*) series.

was also a very exciting period.'[41] Araki first received attention for photographs of a young boy named Sachin and his friends, portraying the children's lives in a run-down apartment block not far from his home in Tokyo. *Sachin and his brother Mabo* (1964) is an image of two boys aiming with small catapults at the lens (p. 101). The constructed close-up shot exemplifies Araki's subjective viewpoint, and references his fascination with Neo-Realist films. His diaristic, idiosyncratic approach has defined his photography since the 1970s, and becomes obvious in the intimate photobook *Sentimental Journey* (1971), which records his honeymoon with his wife Yōko (pp. 94–95). In *Winter Journey* (1991), the viewer witnesses Araki's last days with his beloved, terminally ill wife before she died, her funeral and his lonely return home, where only their cat Chiro awaited him (p. 96). Having published over 500 photobooks and exhibited his works worldwide, Araki's photographic practice is inextricably intertwined with his personal life; he has explained that photography feels 'like breathing in and out'.[42] Blurring the boundaries between the private and public, and challenging taboos surrounding sexuality and death, he has been a prominent figure in international photography for decades.

Another photographer whose work was intertwined with his personal life is Fukase Masahisa (1934–2012). His family had a photo studio in Hokkaido, and he studied at Nihon University before becoming a freelance photographer in Tokyo in 1968. Six years later, together with Tōmatsu, Moriyama and other contemporaries, he set up a photographic school named The Workshop. Like Araki, he often photographed his wife, whose name was also Yōko. In *From Window* (1974) he stood at the window of his apartment and took photographs of her outside, leaving the house to go to work (pp. 116–17). She posed for the camera, smiling or making a face and striking a dynamic pose. In the wake of their divorce (partly due to his alcoholism), Fukase created the series *Ravens* (pp. 118–19). Although interspersed with other subjects, such as a cat in the snow or a nude, corpulent masseuse, it is the recurrent presence of ravens – alone or in groups, dead or alive – that sets the dark, melancholic tone of this personal series. The lonely photographer identified with the animals, writing that he had 'become a raven with a camera'.[43] *Ravens* was published in 1986 and has since met with international acclaim.

One of the few women photographers whose works were exhibited in the 1970s is Ishiuchi Miyako (b. 1947), who studied textile design before trying a friend's photographic equipment. Her first major series, *Yokosuka Story* (1977), cannot be separated from her memories of growing up in Yokosuka. Ishiuchi disliked the city on the Tokyo Bay, which became a United States Naval base after the Second World War. She revisited the city that she 'hated the most' to begin her photographic career with a personal theme.[44] The Yokosuka of her photographs is a dark place, full of stains and scars. *Yokosuka Story #98* shows a girl running on the street, and can be interpreted as a self-portrait of the photographer remembering her childhood (p. 114). In her second series,

Apartment (1977–78), Ishiuchi revisited her memories of living in a small apartment. In the 1960s and 1970s, the area around Tokyo became increasingly urbanized, and many buildings were erected rapidly and cheaply. *Apartment* documents the simple, provisional living conditions of that period. The room in *Apartment #50* is sparsely furnished, and its walls are cracked (p. 115). A pair of gloves, two umbrellas and a kettle are attached to a laundry line strung across the room. Ishiuchi recalled: 'Every corner and every wall is permeated by a mix of different body smells...These apartments are small, dark, and somewhat dirty, and nobody wants to live in them. But I sense a certain kind of reality in them – they are places that feel very human.'[45] Ishiuchi received the Kimura Ihei Award in 1978 for the series. In her next project, she continued revisiting areas associated with memories of her childhood: *Endless Night* (1978–80) featured former brothels and the red-light district that she was told to avoid as a child.

Yoshiyuki Kōhei (1946–2022) created a series that was more directly concerned with sexual activity: *The Park (Kōen)* (1972–80) documents couples in public parks in Tokyo at night, often with spectators around them (pp. 102–3). Yoshiyuki visited the park for months, befriending the voyeurs who went regularly, before taking his photographs using handheld infrared cameras.[46] The series attracted much attention in *Camera Mainichi* and in an exhibition at Komai Gallery. It raises questions about the relationships between the couples, voyeurs and the viewers of the photographs, while documenting a phenomenon of 1970s Tokyo that Yoshiyuki was surprised to discover not far from his neighbourhood.

Folk Culture

In the late 1960s, greater prosperity and an increase in people's leisure time saw a broad interest in Japanese folklore and rural life begin to emerge. The challenges of enormous economic growth and internationalization, as well as the radical demonstrations taking place, made nostalgic ideas of a 'traditional' Japan particularly attractive. Many photographers began to point their cameras at rural areas and local traditions. Yanagisawa Shin (1936–2008), who studied at Tokyo College of Art, took vivid photographs of people's lives in Aomori and Hokkaido (p. 106), and of his personal erotic encounters there (pp. 104–5). In 1975, Kitai Kazuo earned the first Kimura Ihei Award for his work *To the Village (Mura-e)*, a year-long documentation of life in rural Japan. Suda Issei (1940–2019), who began his career in 1967 as a photographer for Terayama Shūji's avant-garde film company Tenjō Sajiki, photographed festivals across the country for his series *Fūshi Kaden* (1978) (p.113). Suda's work often combines images of folklore or everyday life with a mysterious, dark atmosphere. Naitō Masatoshi (b. 1938), who came to photography through his interest in ethnological traditions, portrayed female shamans in his seminal series *Grandma Explosion (Baba Bakuhatsu)* (1969). The old women in the Tōhoku region mourn the dead and invoke their spirits by performing rituals and dancing at night. Naitō photographed

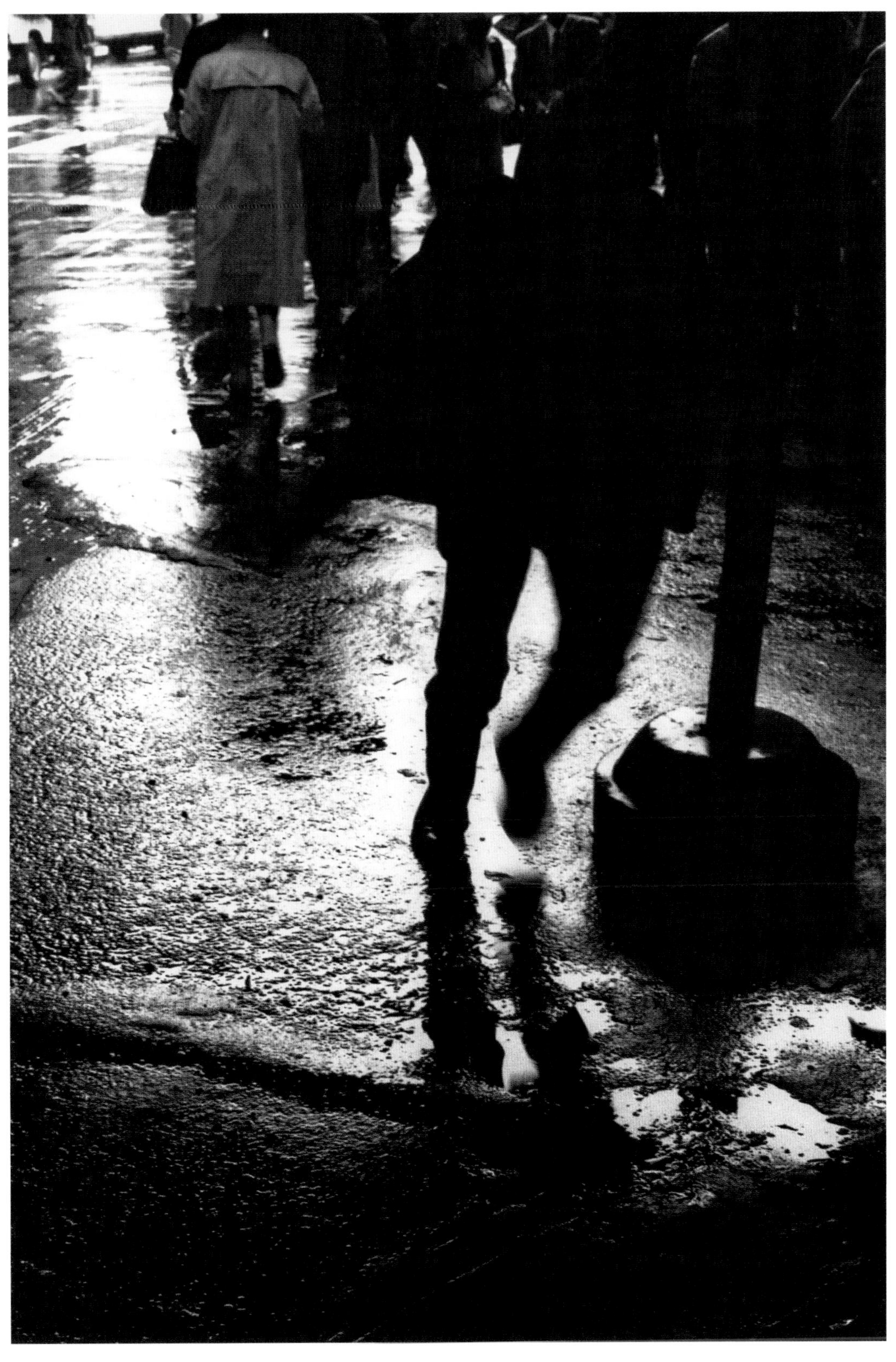

Yanagisawa Shin, *Sketches, Tokyo,* 1964.

New Photographic Freedom

the women in the dark with a bright flash, often in close-up,
conveying a strong sense of the otherworldly (p. 92). In his
long-term project *Tokyo, A vision of its other side* (1970–85)
(pp. 92–93), Naitō presented an alternative Tokyo, featuring
homeless people and those outcast by society.

An interest in Japanese rural folklore can also be found
in *Zokushin* (p. 125), an early series by Tsuchida Hiromi
(b. 1939) in which he searched for his 'cultural roots'.[47] In 1979,
Tsuchida pointed his camera at Hiroshima, photographing
the *hibakusha,* the cityscapes and buildings, publishing
them in his book *Hiroshima 1945–1979.* A few years later, he
created a series documenting the objects at the Hiroshima
Peace Memorial Museum, titled *Hiroshima Collection* (p. 126).
Tsuchida has emphasized that he tried to 'disappear' from the
photographs instead of using a personal language.[48] His work
draws on the capacity of photography to bear witness even
decades after the catastrophic event, while raising questions
about the relationship between the visible and invisible.

Conceptual Art
Photography also emerged as a tool for conceptual art.
Ōtsuji Kiyoji (1923–2001) (p. 130), Takamatsu Jirō (1936–98),
Wakae Kanji (b. 1944) (p. 131), Katase Kazuo (b. 1947) and Uematsu
Keiji (b. 1947) (pp. 128–29) all used photography to realize their
artistic concepts and ideas of perception and recognition.
They sought to exclude any emotions, creating an aesthetic
that contrasted with the personal atmosphere of works by
Moriyama, Araki or Ishiuchi.

In 1970, the 10th Tokyo Biennale 'Between Man and Matter',
at the Tokyo Metropolitan Art Museum, introduced conceptual,
post-minimal and performance art to a wider audience. The
curator, Nakahara Yūsuke, invited forty artists, approximately
two-thirds of whom came from overseas. For the Japanese
artists, the Biennale provided a rare opportunity to exchange
ideas and experiences with their 'Western' contemporaries.
Self-taught photographer Anzaï Shigeo (1939–2020) began his
artistic practice as a painter, moving towards photography in
the late 1960s. Nakahara asked him to support several of the
exhibiting artists, including Richard Serra and Daniel Buren,
in the production of site-specific works. While assisting them,
Anzaï began photographing the production process and the
works themselves. His photographs of the Biennale mark the
beginning of his concern with avant-garde art (p. 120). They
record a landmark exhibition, and are also extraordinary works
of art in their own right, evoking the experimental atmosphere
of the 1970s.

Many of the photographers mentioned in the last two
chapters – Dōmon, Hosoe, Ishimoto, Fukase, Kawada, Moriyama,
Naitō, Narahara, Tōmatsu, Tsuchida – were among the fifteen
whose works were shown in the seminal 1974 'New Japanese
Photography' exhibition at the Museum of Modern Art, New
York. It was co-curated by John Szarkowski and Yamagishi Shōji,
editor of *Camera Mainichi,* and included 187 photographs dated
from 1940 to 1973. This was the first exhibition dedicated to
contemporary Japanese photography outside Japan.

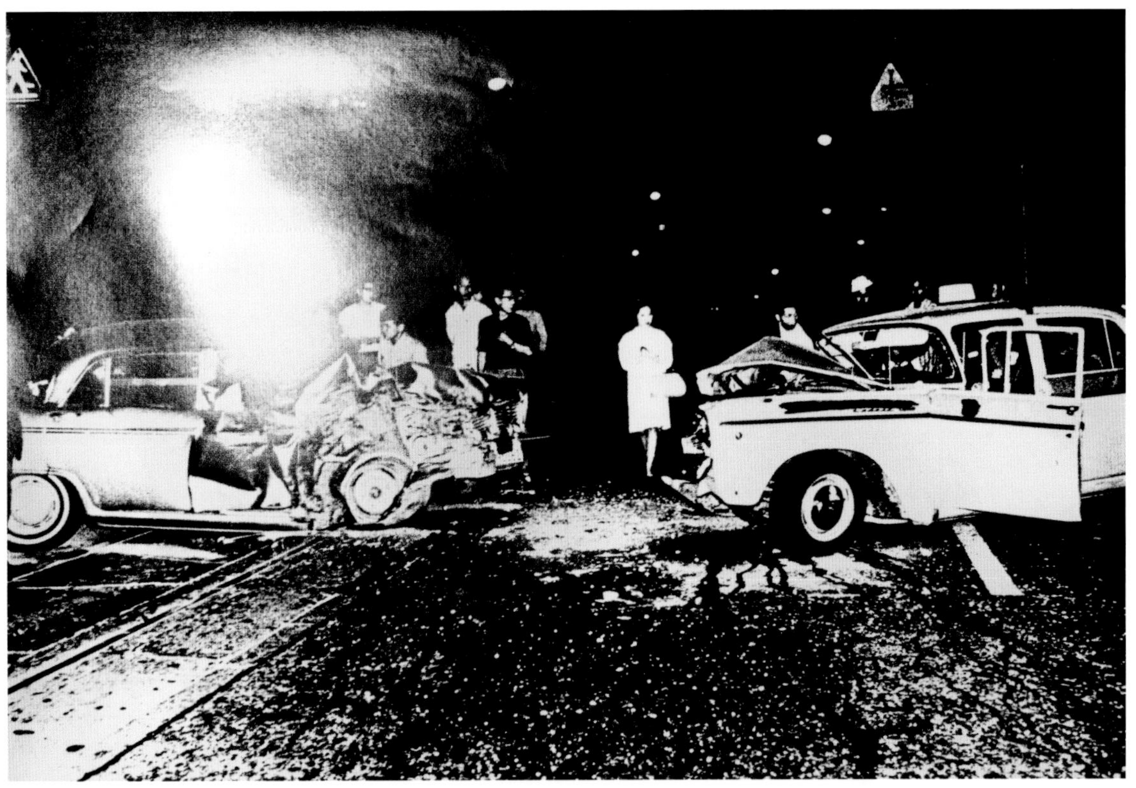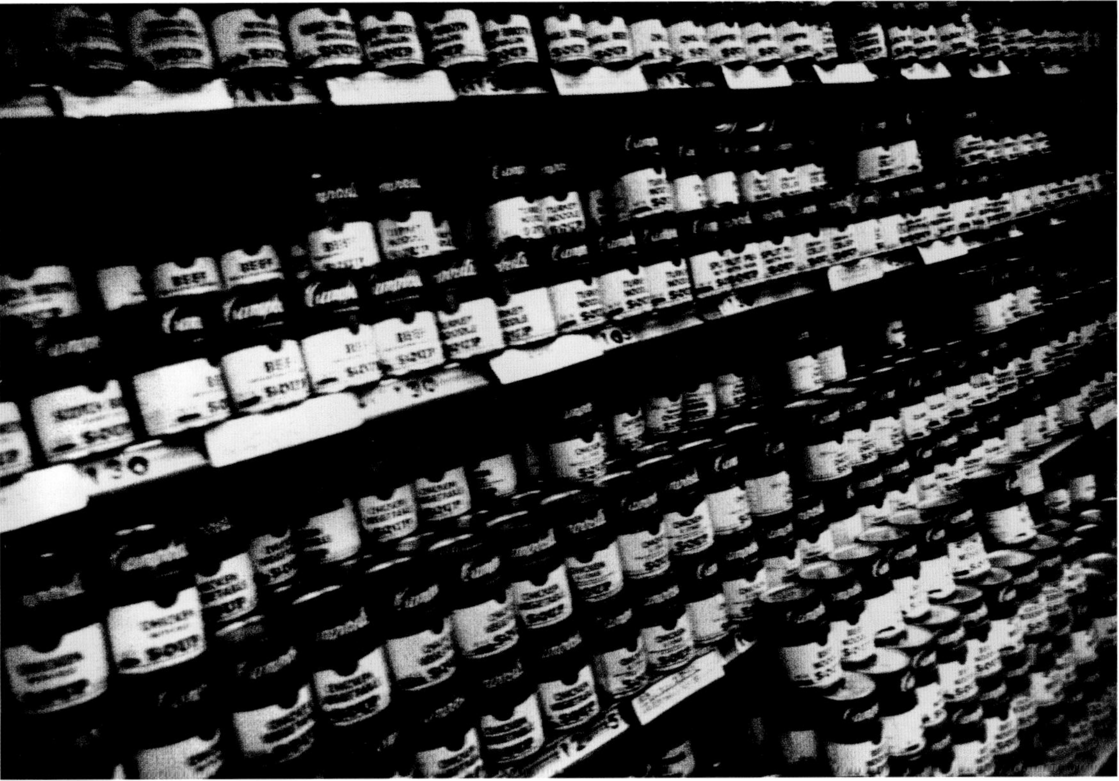

Top: Moriyama Daidō, *Accident #6*, 1969.
Above: Moriyama Daidō, untitled, 1969, *Provoke no. 3*.

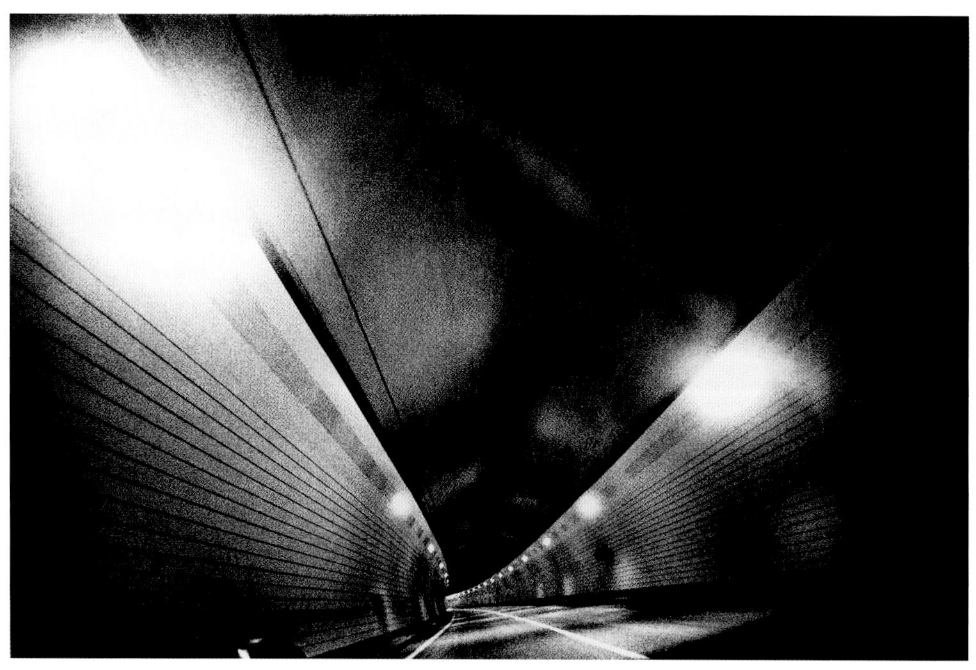

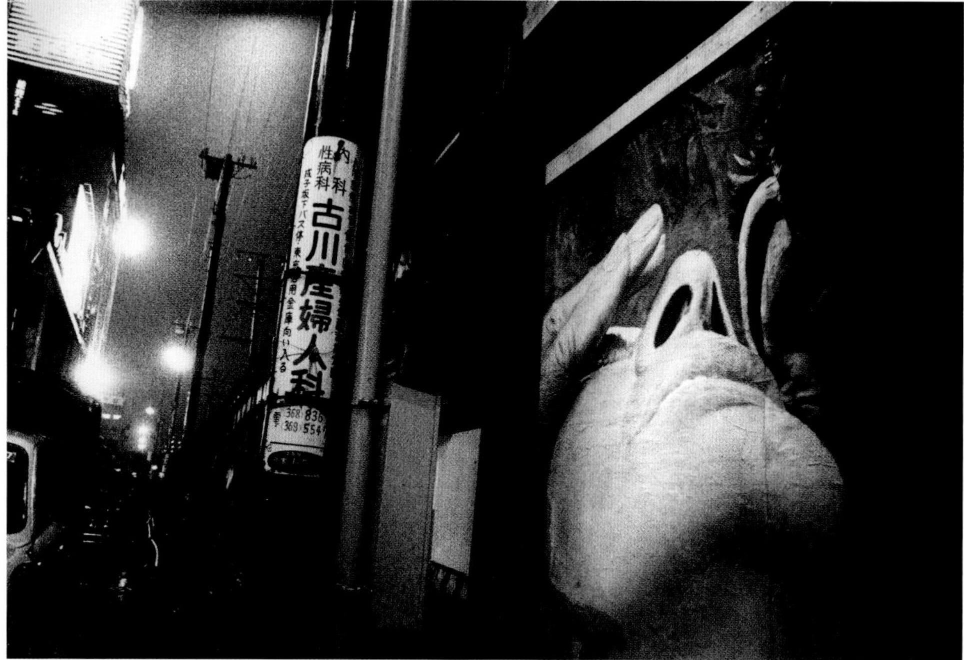

Top and above: Moriyama Daidō, *Hunter* series, 1972.

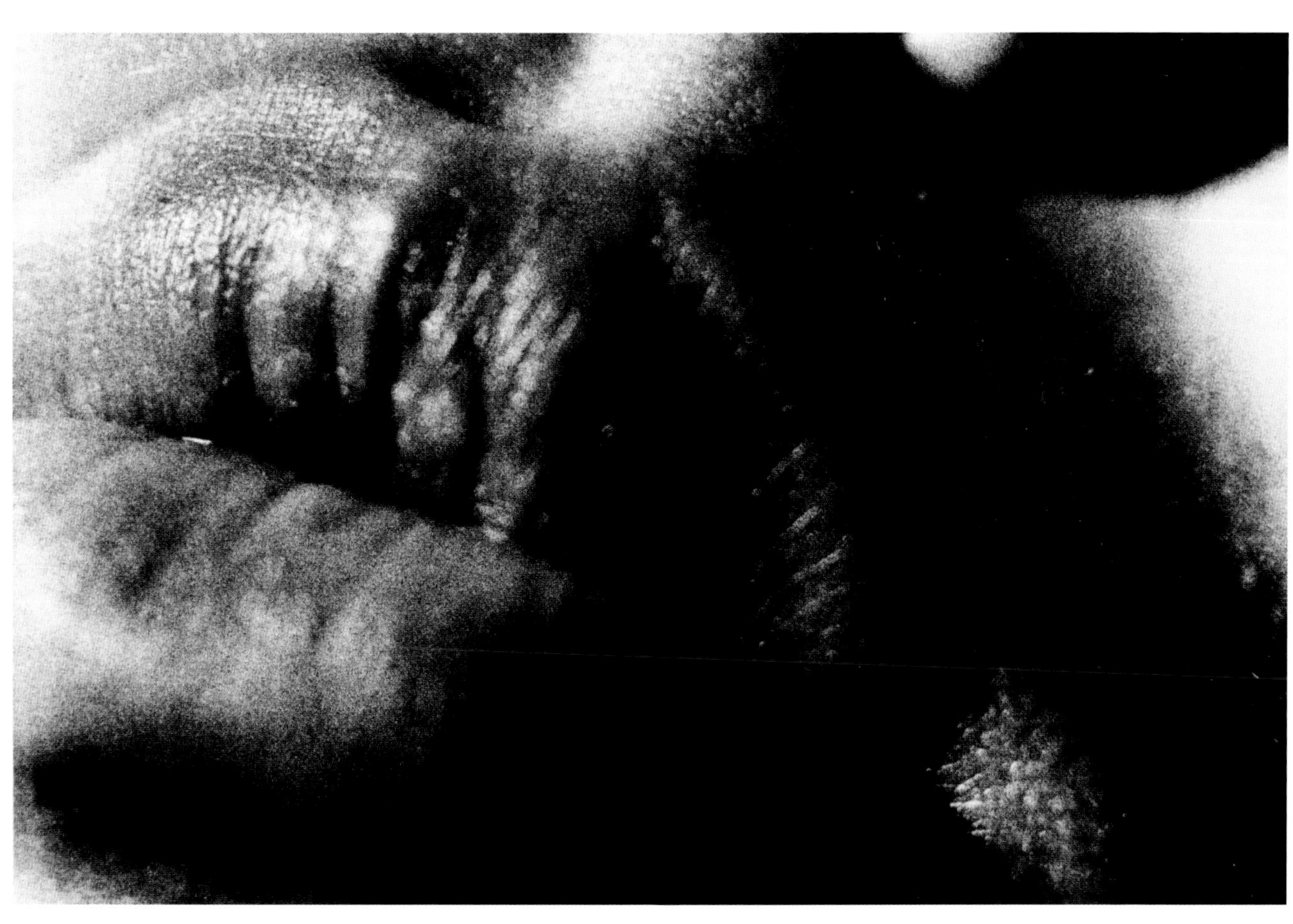

Moriyama Daidō, untitled, 1972,
Farewell Photography series.

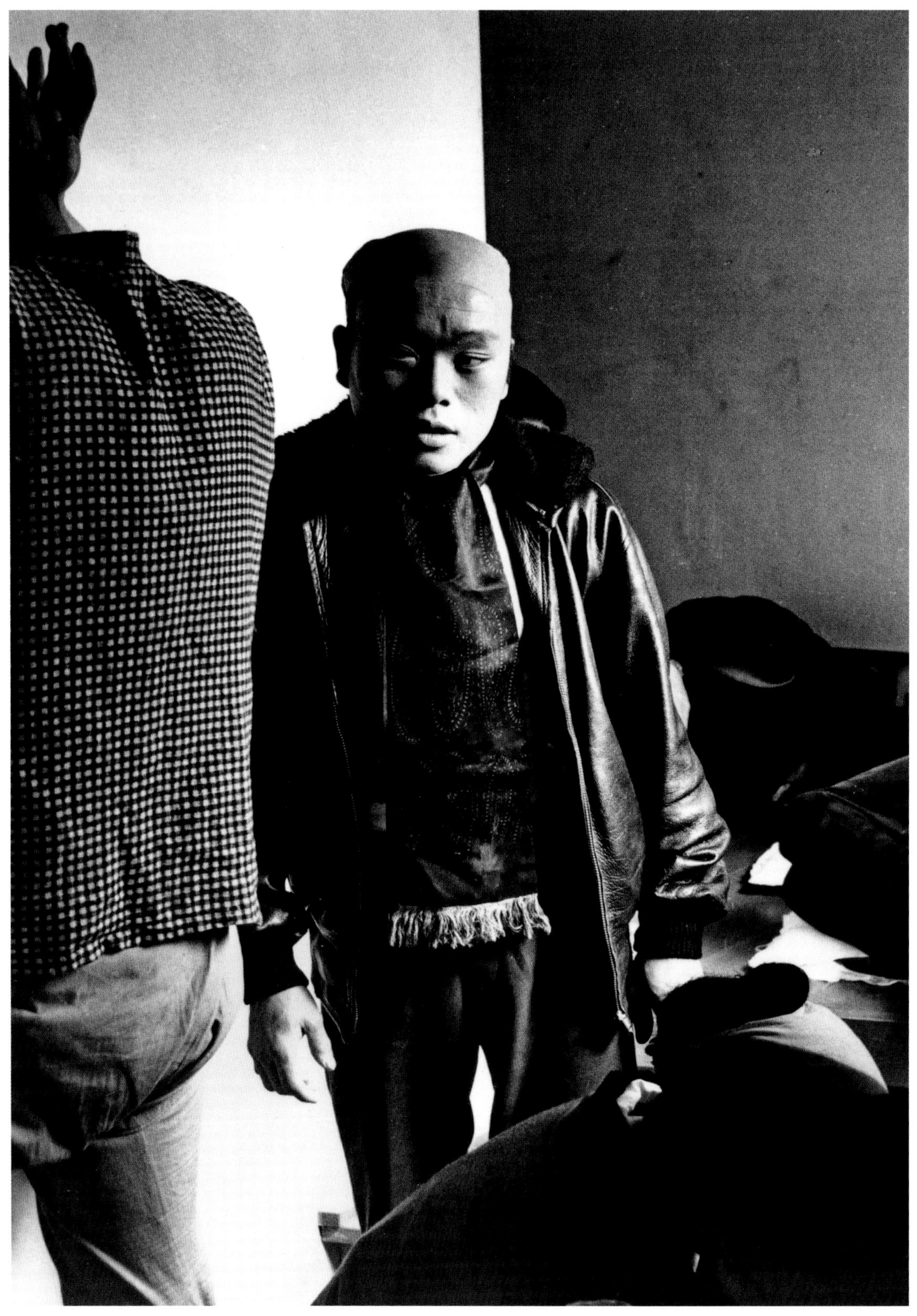

 Moriyama Daidō, untitled, 1968, *Japan: A Photo Theater* series.

Lena Fritsch: Let's start at the beginning – what inspired you to take up photography?
Moriyama Daidō: I worked as a graphic design assistant in Osaka. One day, as part of my job, I went to the studio of a famous photographer, Iwamiya Takeji, to ask if he could do a commercial photography job for us. Of course, he was a top photographer and too busy, but he had many good assistants. It was the first time that I encountered the 'world of photography', and met photographers. Until then, I had not been particularly interested; it had never crossed my mind to become a photographer. I was just over twenty-one years old when I met these photographers and encountered this new world. Commercial design (particularly at the time) was manual work at a desk, and it had begun to annoy me. I liked design, but the concrete work that I was doing was unpleasant. It was as if 'a mummy-hunter gets lost and becomes a mummy'.[1] Meeting these photographers made me want to change the environment that I worked in and 'poof!' I quit design and asked Iwamiya-sensei if I could work in his studio. When I began in his studio I did not know anything about photography; nothing about the aperture or shutter speed, and I gradually had to learn it all. Then I left for Tokyo and became Hosoe Eikoh's assistant.

Were you interested in or inspired by any photographers in particular?
At the beginning I was just hanging out and experiencing the world of photography, but then I started to look at camera magazines and photobooks. I came across William Klein's photobook *New York*, which had a great, shocking impact on me. In Japan, Tōmatsu Shōmei also had a strong impact. Those two were the key photographers for me. Inoue Seiryu had a great effect on me too – like me, he had learned with Iwamiya Takeji. When I started working there he was already an independent photographer, but he still sometimes came to Iwamiya's studio and used the darkroom to print his photographs. Sometimes he took me with him when he was going out to take streetlight and snapshot photographs. When I met him, he was taking the photographs for his famous photobook, *Kamagasaki* [p. 46]. Even today, I still wander around and take photographs of the streets and streetlights – it all started with Inoue-san. He was very cool and the first photographer that I saw taking such photographs; I was fascinated by it. My first real experiences of street and snapshot photography were with Inoue-san.

There has been a lot of interest in *Provoke* and Japanese photography of the 1960s and 1970s recently, with exhibitions and new publications. How do you view your early works when you see them now?
When I see my photographs from that time and also the work by other *Provoke* members I feel nostalgic. These photographs are from such a long time ago. The period between around 1965 and 1970 brought a lot of change for different artistic genres, not only for photography. People started to do new things. *Provoke* connects with that larger picture. Tokyo was quite intense at the time, with student protests and demonstrations. The city was violent, but also very lively.

You joined *Provoke* with the second issue of the journal.
Yes, Nakahira Takuma asked me if I wanted to join. At the time, Terayama Shūji and I had been thinking about creating a new magazine: *Scandal*. At first, I was not sure about *Provoke*. But Nakahira was my best friend and also rival, and very special to me – and he asked me to join. So I did – I was not too interested in the political slogans.

provoke as a journal was a lot about using photography in a new, free way...**
Exactly. I put the political part aside and just focused on what I, as a photographer, wanted to do.

One photographic project that you created around the same time was the *Accident* series, including a photograph of a photograph, namely a photograph of a traffic warden poster, in 1969 [p. 81].
The world that I lived in appeared very 'incidental' and 'accidental' to me. I always felt a bit nervous and rushed around; I was young. Deep down I had a constant feeling of uneasiness and frustration. Therefore, when it was decided that I would get a photographic series in *Asahi Camera* magazine for the first time, I called it *Accident*. It was the most extreme point in the Vietnam War, and you saw violent images on TV all the time. Then, Robert Kennedy was assassinated. When Kennedy was assassinated, 'boom!' there were all these newspaper supplements everywhere at Shinjuku station and the city around. When I saw that scene, it really shocked me. What I found most shocking was not the factual reality of the assassination but finding out about it like that, in such a scene. That was an important moment for me personally, and led to the *Accident* series and its title.

That is very interesting. And where did you take the photograph of the traffic warden poster – did you just find it somewhere here in Tokyo?
Yes, when I was thinking about these things I came across the poster by coincidence; it

was hanging on a wall at Roppongi station, when you go up and exit the station. It was a very intense image. I told the people from Asahi right away and then went to get permission to take a photograph of the poster.

Oh, so you went and got proper permission?
Yes. Well, I did take a photograph of it right away but then I thought it would be better to receive a poster and get permission to photograph it.

That is a very correct approach [laughs].
It was for a series published by *Asahi Newspaper*, and if you do these kinds of things secretly they complain. Nowadays I don't need to worry about such complaints but at the time, for a series in *Asahi Camera*, I wanted to do it correctly. So, I did it the correct way [laughs]. Why are you laughing? I'm a correct guy...

This photograph of the poster made me think about photography: every photograph is a copy anyway, and a camera is a photocopy machine. Realizing this was important for my work. Rather than viewing myself as an artist who creates works of art, I see myself as a photographer who photocopies things from the external world. Ever since *Japan: A Photo Theater* I have continued to photocopy: other people's photographs, posters, billboards, film images, as well as all kinds of other things in the world.

Including the city. Cities and urban landscapes are an important motif in your work, Tokyo and particularly Shinjuku [pp. 132–33]. Could you tell me what you like best about the city in photography, what is 'the city' to you?
The city really fascinates me. It comes into existence through so many things, not just people. It is a place that carries and shows the desires of many people, and of particular times. For me, as a photographer, it is something that just needs to be photographed. As a child, I did not enjoy going to school or to study, and I was not good at making friends either. But I have always enjoyed wandering around the city by myself. So I have always liked the city. Even now, I find it fascinating to wander around various cities. In a city, there is always something going on. It is alive. Tokyo – and Shinjuku in particular – is an urban stadium of human desires. A city is a theatre, school, everything. And with my work, I think I create my own city: a city of my own interests, desires and memories.

Speaking of photographs of the city, do you go out and take photographs almost every day?
I'm very busy with various pieces of work, so it is difficult to take a large number of photographs every day. But I try to take photographs for one or two hours every day, if possible.

Photography is really part of your everyday life.
I just try to take as many photographs as possible of the time in which I have lived, since I was born. Photographs become records of my time and perhaps they connect with the time of the world as well. I don't want to overemphasize the word, but personal 'records' can at times link with world 'records' as well. I seek to take as many photographs as possible, so each additional photograph counts. There is no time to be thinking about meanings and to be making selections. The basics of my photography have not changed; people often say that they can't tell if my photographs were taken a long time ago or just yesterday.

That shows that you really have your own particular photography – it is great!
I want to think that I have taken photographs of everywhere that I have been to and that I have seen; every place and every corner of the city, even if it is not really possible.

When you create a photobook, how do you select the works and compile them?
When I make a new photobook, I basically let the editor decide. There is no story and I don't take my photographs according to any strict concept. It does not matter how my books begin and how they end. If I did all this work myself, my own style would come through. When I was young I wanted to do it all myself, but then I realized that it does not make any sense – it is better to let many eyes work on it. I just make the final adjustments.

When looking at my photobooks, I see what I thought about photography at the time, what I paid attention to and what attracted me. That is interesting. My photobooks usually show the works that I have taken over a particular period of time, six months or so. I like to present my photographs right after I have taken them, when they are still contemporary. Whether the photographs are good or bad is a different question but in the end, my photobooks will represent my life. Photography as a 'life line' – I find that an interesting thought.

What do you like best about the medium of photography?
I like the fact that photography can create photocopies. No other medium has such great potential as a thorough photocopy machine. Film might also be a world of photocopying, but it is different... Also, photography has the potential to disconnect time. To me these two factors are its most attractive characteristics.

* This is a shortened version of an interview conducted in Japanese on 1 September 2016, at the Moriyama Daidō Photo Foundation, Tokyo.
1 'A mummy-hunter gets lost and becomes a mummy' is a Japanese saying that Moriyama uses here to express that he went out to get photographs taken but ended up becoming a photographer himself.

Lena Fritsch: Let's start at the beginning – what inspired you to take up photography?

Kitai Kazuo: At senior high school I wanted to become a painter, and painted abstract images. This was in the early 1960s, when I lived in Kobe. At the time, close to Umeda station in Osaka, a Gutai art exhibition space opened.[1] I liked it and went to see the works a number of times. I painted similar, abstract works, and did not learn how to draw or sketch. The entrance exams at most art schools included drawing, so this was not an option for me. Then I found out that Nihon University College of Art had a photography department and I thought, 'why not photography?' A painting is something that you create on your own. I found it interesting that in photography you take a camera, walk around and take a photograph when you see something interesting – the other side, the photographic subject, is extremely important. I never enjoyed sitting still at school and was quite rebellious from my childhood, not liking whatever the teacher would tell me [laughs]. I quit university early and began to take photographs by myself.

The first photographs that I took were published in my *Teikou/Resistance* photobook [pp. 74, 89]. I wanted to take photos that were nothing like what they taught us at university; not like Cartier-Bresson or Ansel Adams. That is how I started taking photographs of the student protests.

At the time, were you interested in or inspired by any photographers?

At university I liked Eugène Atget. His work does not have anything to do with my photographs but I thought it was great. At senior high school I also liked Jasper Johns' Pop Art, and the way he included everyday life objects such as an iron or coat hanger in his works.

I took photographs of the student demonstrations in black and white and decided to publish them as a photobook, but I also took colour photographs in Yokosuka [p. 89]. I really liked films. There were films in colour at the time, for example erotic *pink eiga* films; most scenes would be in black and white but then the bed scene would be in colour [laughs]! It was too expensive at the time to show everything in colour. I found it interesting that the films were partly in colour, and planned to include some city images in colour in my photobook.

It is interesting to see your Yokosuka photographs in colour. Looking at the Yokosuka photographs by Ishiuchi Miyako, for example, or all the student demonstration photographs, I have always had monochrome images in my mind.

When I was asked by Diane Dufour from Le Bal last year about my colour photographs from *Teikou/Resistance,* I realized that I had never seen them myself. When publishing the book in 1965, I had been told right away that colour prints would not be possible financially.

So you had the colour negatives all these years and never printed them in colour?

Yes, I had the colour negatives and used them to print the photographs in black and white. So I became interested in finally printing them in colour and talked to a printer. The images had faded, but they managed. I self-published the book secretly and was surprised that it sold very quickly. It is a weird book [laughs].

When I first published *Teikou/Resistance,* it did not sell well at all, and did not receive much attention. It cost me around ¥600,000 to publish it and I basically forced my parents to give me the money for it [laughs]. After this book, I felt that now I had to be a photographer, it couldn't just end like that. Also, I enjoyed working on the book, and thought 'this is something that I can see myself continuing to do'.

How did you create the photobook?

I had taken around seven or eight rolls of film, including two with the city photographs in colour. I picked the good ones out of these and organized the photographs into their order myself. I enjoyed that structuring process. I trimmed maybe two photographs, but in general I don't do image enlargements in the darkroom, it does not make much sense to me. I decide on the composition when taking the photograph; that feels more natural to me.

From 1969 until 1971 you took the photographs for the *Sanrizuka* series [p. 74]. Could you tell me about the photographic process?

After taking photographs of the student demonstrations for a while, I was asked to take more radical photos, or photos that showed the aggressive side of the demonstrations. I did not want to take such photos; I felt that in doing so I would have become estranged from being a photographer. Thinking of photographers like Atget, I felt I should start taking photographs of everyday life instead. Sanrizuka was a typical Japanese agricultural village, and because they wanted to build the airport there, there were fights. I decided to take photographs with a focus on the farmers' lives instead of the fights. I went with the documentary filmmaker Ogawa Shinsuke. He said that he was going with his staff and that there was enough space for me as well, so it was easy for me to go. He was a bit of a dictator – I think many documentary film directors are [laughs].

So you went a number of times to Sanrizuka, regularly returning home?
Yes, I was married and our child had just been born. Ogawa said I should stay in Sanrizuka and not go home so often. 'As a documentarist you should not leave the place', he said. The world of films is strict [laughs]! I learned the basics of documentaries from Ogawa – for example, that it is about recording one's own relationship with the people. I think documentary photographers are often more ambiguous, not taking a clear side, like at the student demonstrations. I took a clear side – probably because of Ogawa's influence. He told me to think about the position from which I'm taking photographs: am I against building the airport or do I support the airport? I had to make my position clear. Photojournalists in Japan often said that they were neutral, and photographers who published photobooks also often took this viewpoint. But I think it is important to make it clear which side you are on; I don't think neutrality exists. Going to Sanrizuka, of course I was against the airport. I took my new Canon 25mm camera with a wide-angle lens with me and took photographs of the people in very close quarters. I wanted to express my position clearly.

The photographs convey a natural and familiar atmosphere – I think one can tell that the people were happy with you taking the photographs.
Yes – I can't take photographs of people and look at them in a negative way. I wanted to take the photographs on the basis of understanding each other; I viewed the photographic subjects with positive eyes. Going to Sanrizuka, I realized that peoples' lives were to become my life-long photography theme. In that sense, the series' that I took afterwards, *Somehow Familiar Places* and *To the Village*, are continuations of *Sanrizuka*.

You received the Kimura Ihei Award in 1976 for *To the Village*. Your works are always series', I think – do you decide on a theme and then go out to take photographs?
Yes. I have never been employed by a publisher or newspaper; I was independent from the beginning. In other words, nobody wanted to hire me [laughs]. I decided on a theme, took the photographs and then sold them to a magazine. When taking photographs of the student demonstrations, *Asahi Graph* asked me to take photographs for them for the first time. I must have been twenty-three years old. I wondered why Nakamura Yutaka, who was their editorial director, had

asked me. My photographs of the Nihon University barricades, taken from the inside, were published on six or so pages and the magazine sold well. According to Nakamura, when there are strikes or barricades, the photographs taken from the outside are not convincing to the readers – they need to be taken from the inside. They had therefore decided to ask young photographers at the university, and I was one of them. They liked my work and continued to ask me. At the end of 1968, I decided to stop photographing the student protests and go to Sanrizuka, suggesting to *Asahi Graph* that I did a series for them. They agreed and gave me quite a few pages. I realized then that I could survive with photography [laughs]. So, I decide on a theme myself. Sometimes I'm commissioned, but I usually find that boring.

I now earn money by selling vintage prints, but originally I took photographs for magazines or photobooks, not to create original prints. Until the late 1970s, magazines were very important and there were many good ones. Then, gradually, they didn't sell anymore – today you can't survive as a photographer just working for magazines.

The digital world is getting stronger – what do you think about that?
I think I have taken so many photographs with film, and done everything that I wanted to do. Therefore, this year, I have begun to take digital photographs. It is not easy [laughs]. But I thought it might be a good change of mood.

Most of your series – aside from the new colour prints of *Teikou/Resistance* – are monochrome photographs.
Yes, I just prefer monochrome photography. I started taking colour photographs for magazines in the late 1970s, but I did not include them in my photobooks. I sometimes took two cameras with me and took colour photographs for magazine work, and black and white photographs for myself [laughs].

We have already talked about the photographic process a bit – how do you usually approach your subjects? You mentioned that you try to get close to them and understand them.
When I went to Sanrizuka, Ogawa Shinsuke was strict and said that 'if you want to take photographs of the muddy rice fields you need to enter them, together with the farmers. You can't stand outside and look at them without getting muddy yourself.' I take my photographs in that way, entering the mud. My photographs are not objective works that explain something from the outside. I think it is better to take them from

the same position as the photographic subjects; one should not look down on them. I think that the photographer should see his position as the lowest.

The farmers in Sanrizuka probably know your photographs, then?
Yes, they have seen the series and like its peacefulness. When I go back, they invite me for dinner. I actually went back two years ago: Ōtsu Kōshirō, a famous cameraman who had been to Sanrizuka with Ogawa Shinsuke once at the very beginning was already over eighty years old. He wanted to film Sanrizuka again, as his last film, and went together with a young film director. Unexpectedly, he gave me a phone call, asking for my help. I thought he wanted me to take photographs, for posters or something, but it turned out that he wanted me to interview the farmers – all the other people who could do this had passed away [laughs]. So I went, for Ōtsu-san. The title of the film is *Sanrizuka ni ikiru* (*Living in Sanrizuka*). I was moved that Ōtsu-san wanted to go there for his last film. But the people of Sanrizuka have left a strong impression on me also: they were fighting for their lives and we fought together.

What do you like best about photography?
I've been taking photographs for over fifty years now, and I never thought I would continue anything for such a long time. In hindsight, I have enjoyed seeing different lives by taking photographs. I decided to take photographs because I wanted to show people's lives and hear their stories. I feel I have probably lived four or five times more than many other people – photography is really a treasure to me [laughs]. I'm glad I chose photography.

*   This is a shortened version of an interview conducted in Japanese on 5 April 2017, at Yumiko Chiba Associates, Tokyo.
1   The Gutai Art Association originated in Ashiya (Kansai region) in 1954 and continued until 1972, when the artist and founder of the group, Yoshihara Jirō, passed away. Gutai means 'concrete' or 'concreteness' and represents the artists' direct engagement with materials. Gutai artists sought to break down the barriers between art and everyday life, experimenting with new art materials, performance and theatrical events.

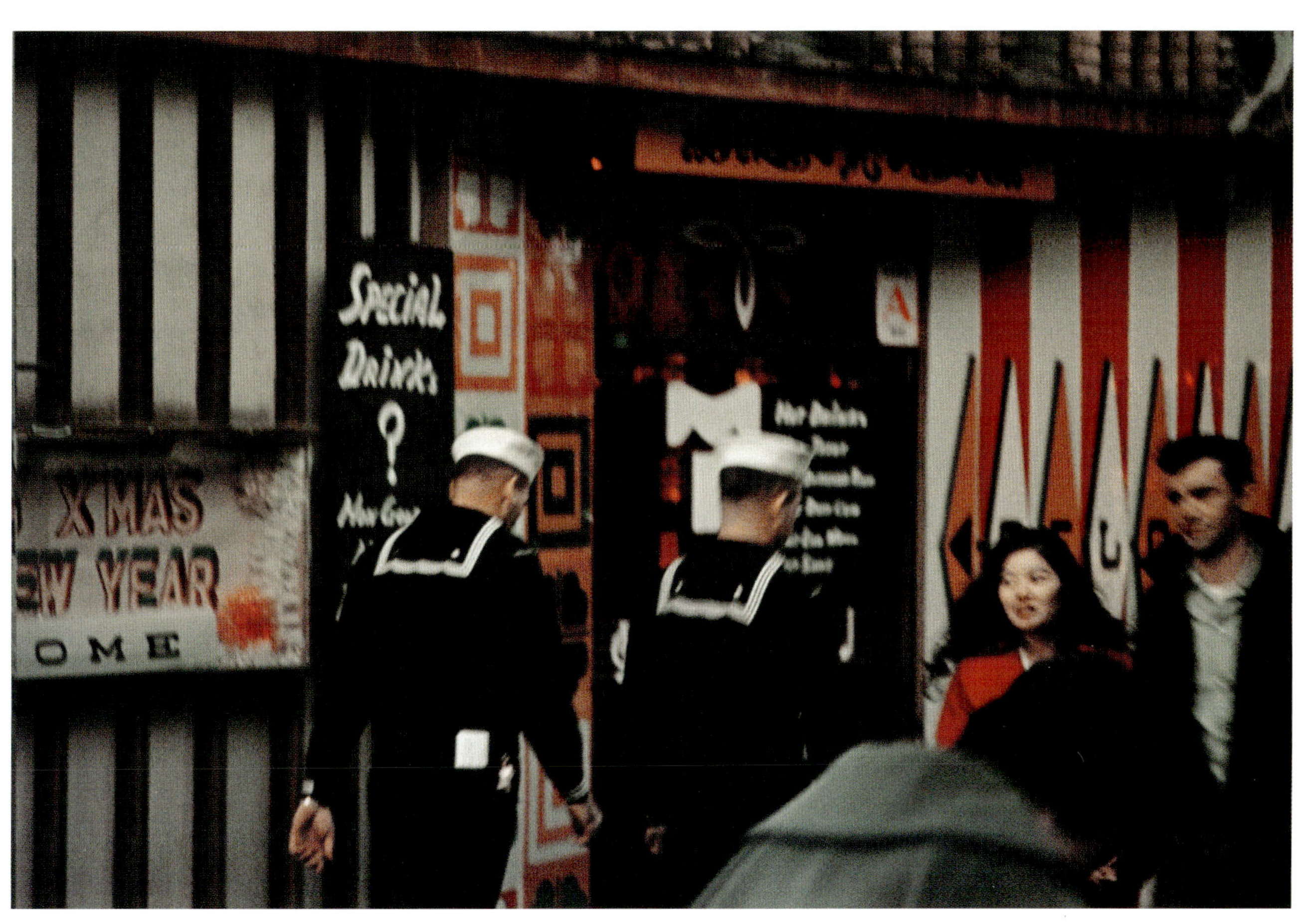

Kitai Kazuo, untitled, 1964/2015,
Teikou/Resistance (Colour) series.

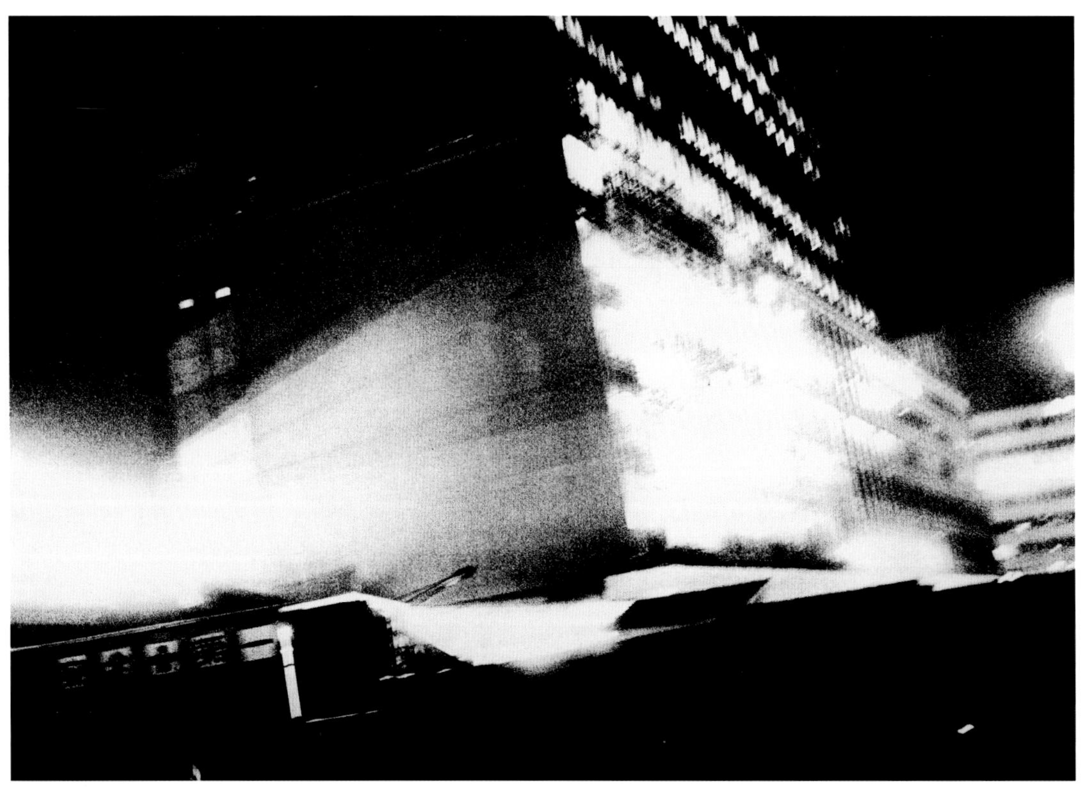

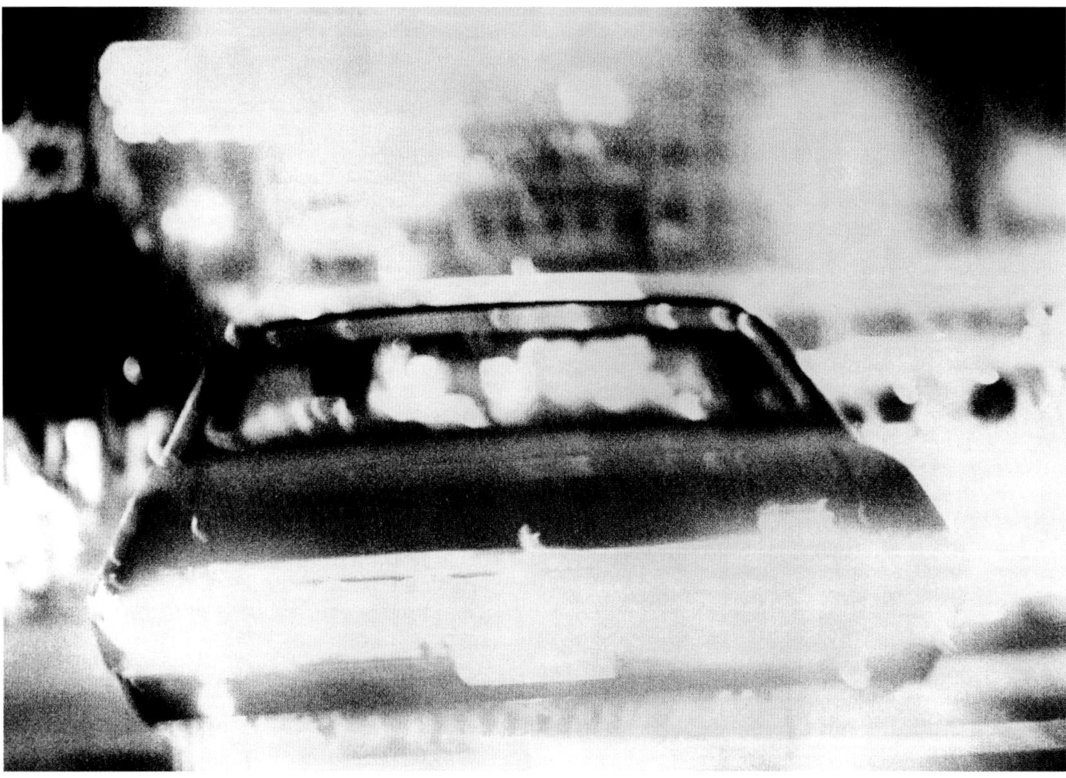

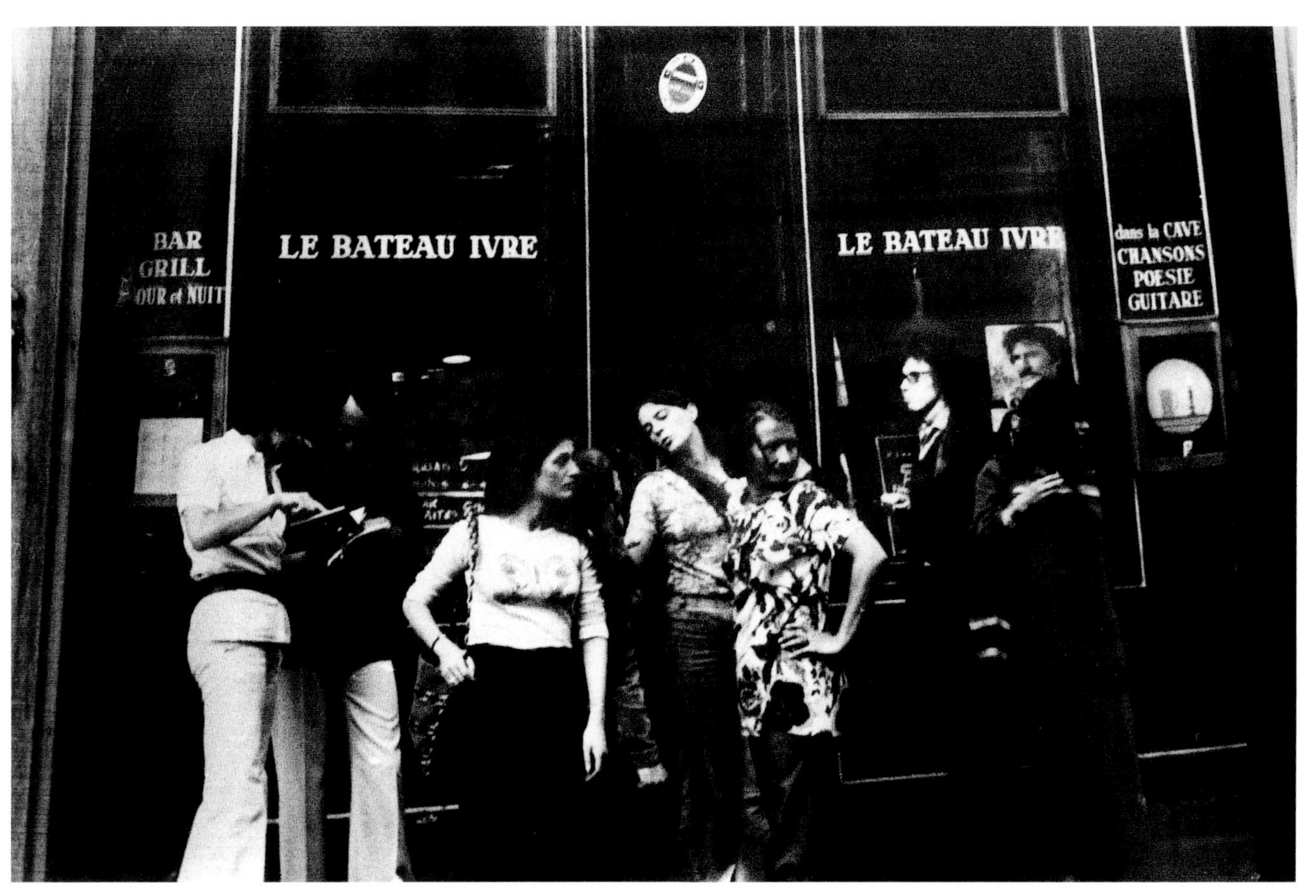

Opposite: Nakahira Takuma, *For a Language to Come* series, 1970.
Above: Nakahira Takuma, untitled, 1971, *Circulation: Date, Place, Events* series.

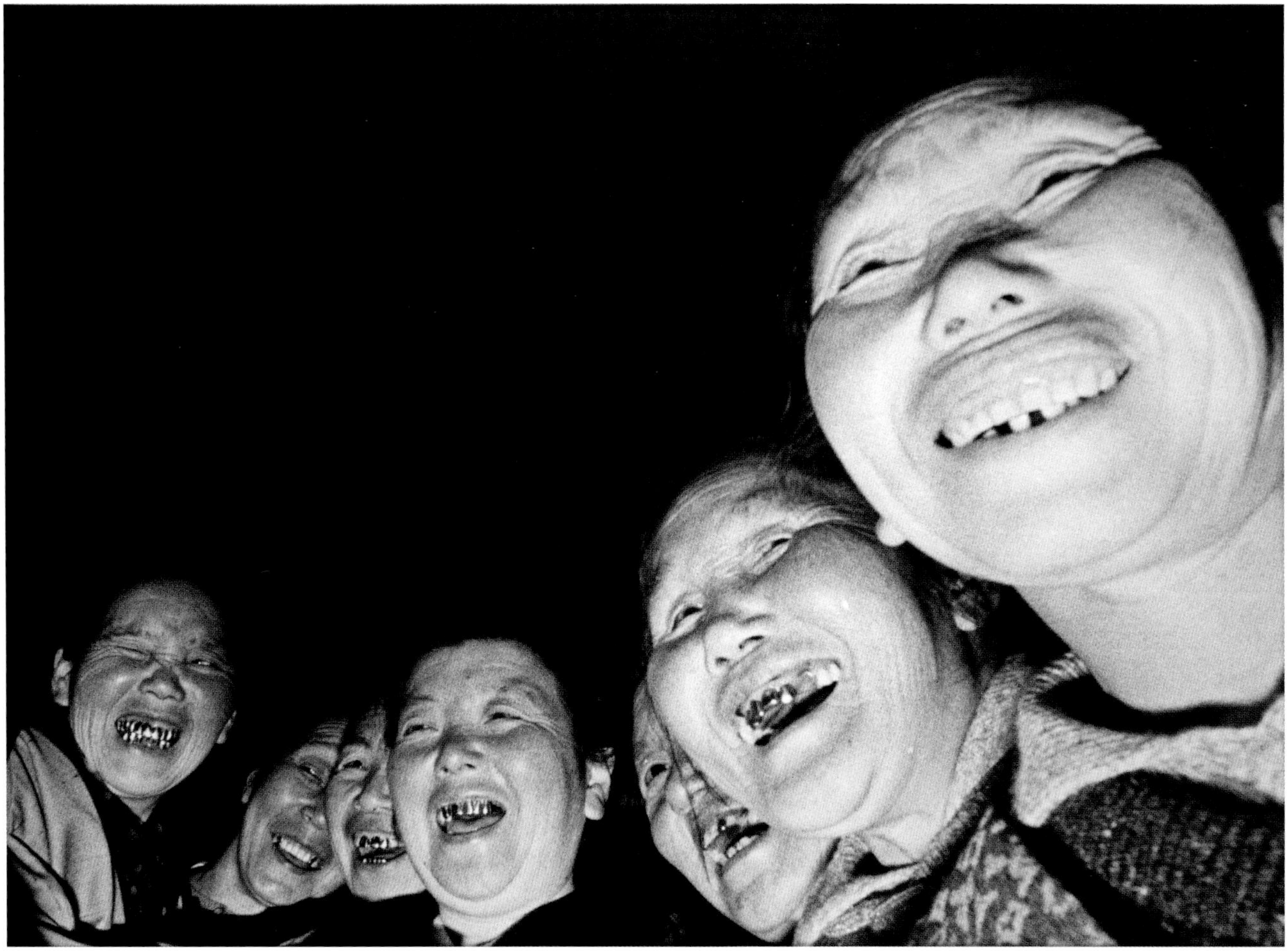

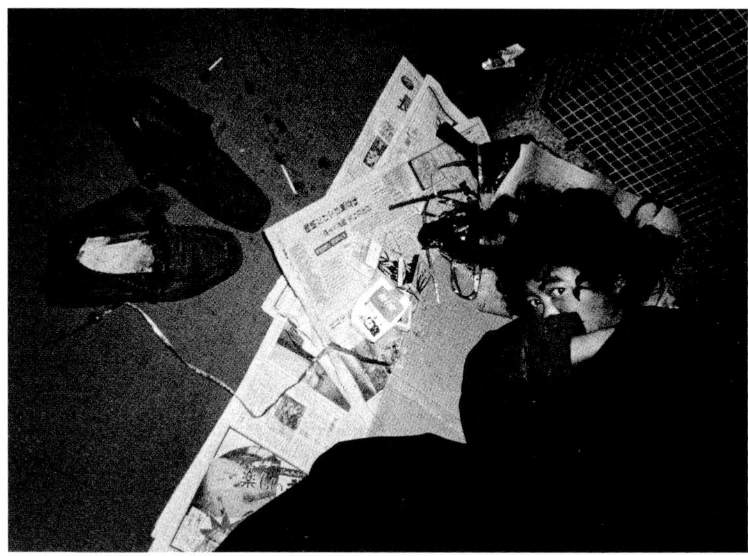

Above: Naitō Masatoshi, untitled, 1969,
Grandma Explosion (Baba Bakuhatsu).
Right: Naitō Masatoshi, *Homeless Woman*, 1970,
Tokyo, a vision of its other side series.
Opposite: Naitō Masatoshi, *Billboard for a Striptease*,
1971, *Tokyo, a vision of its other side* series.

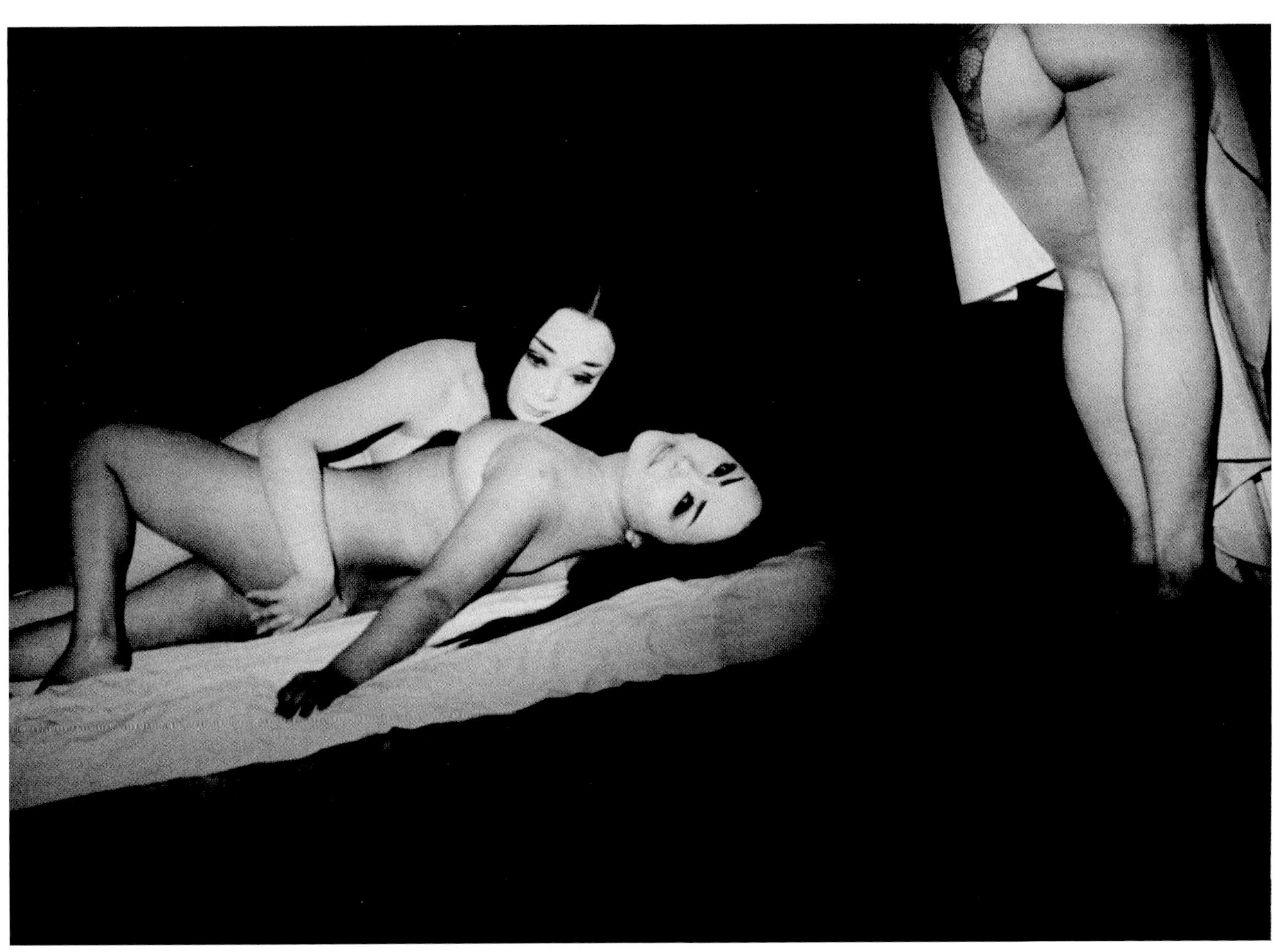

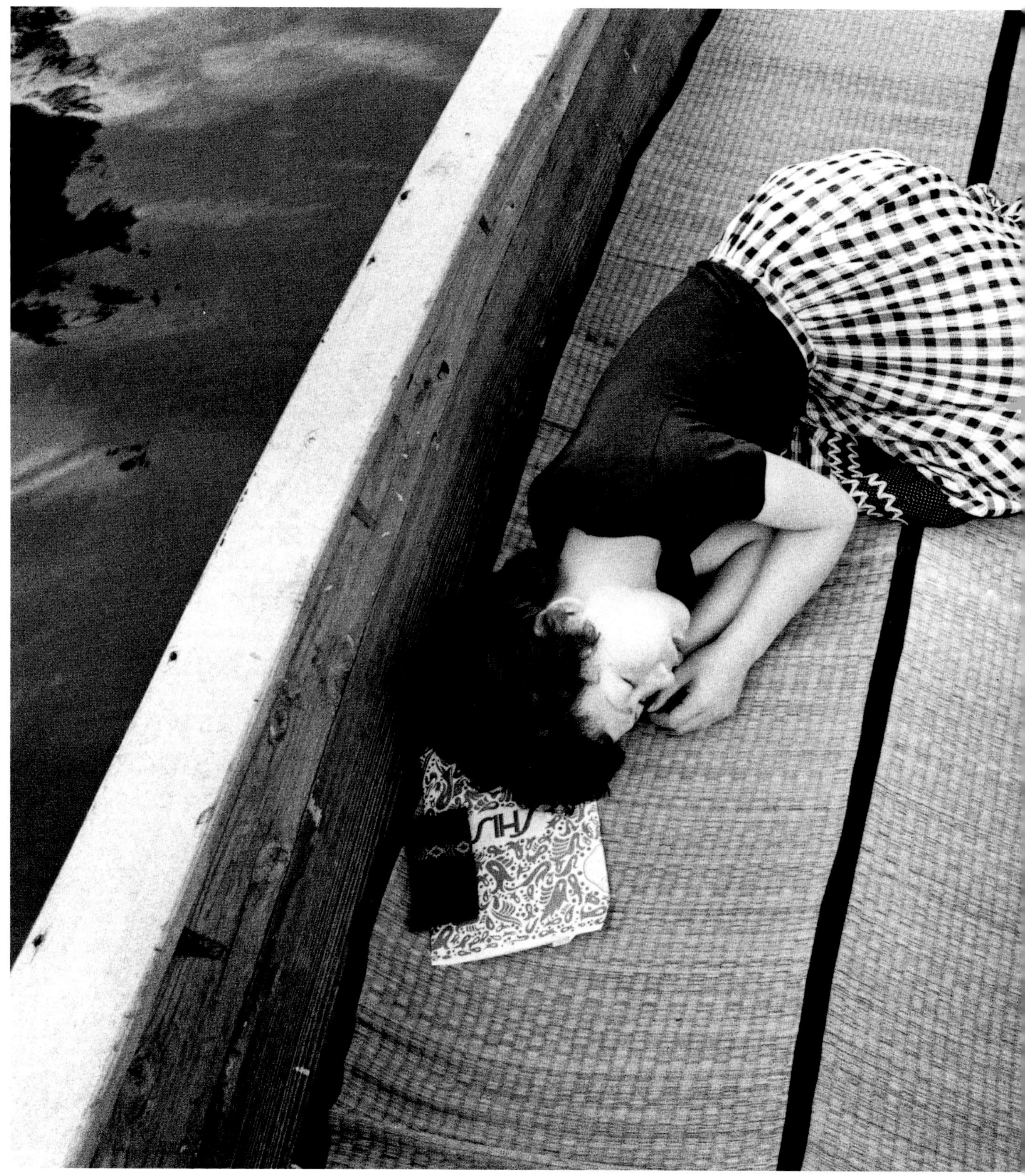

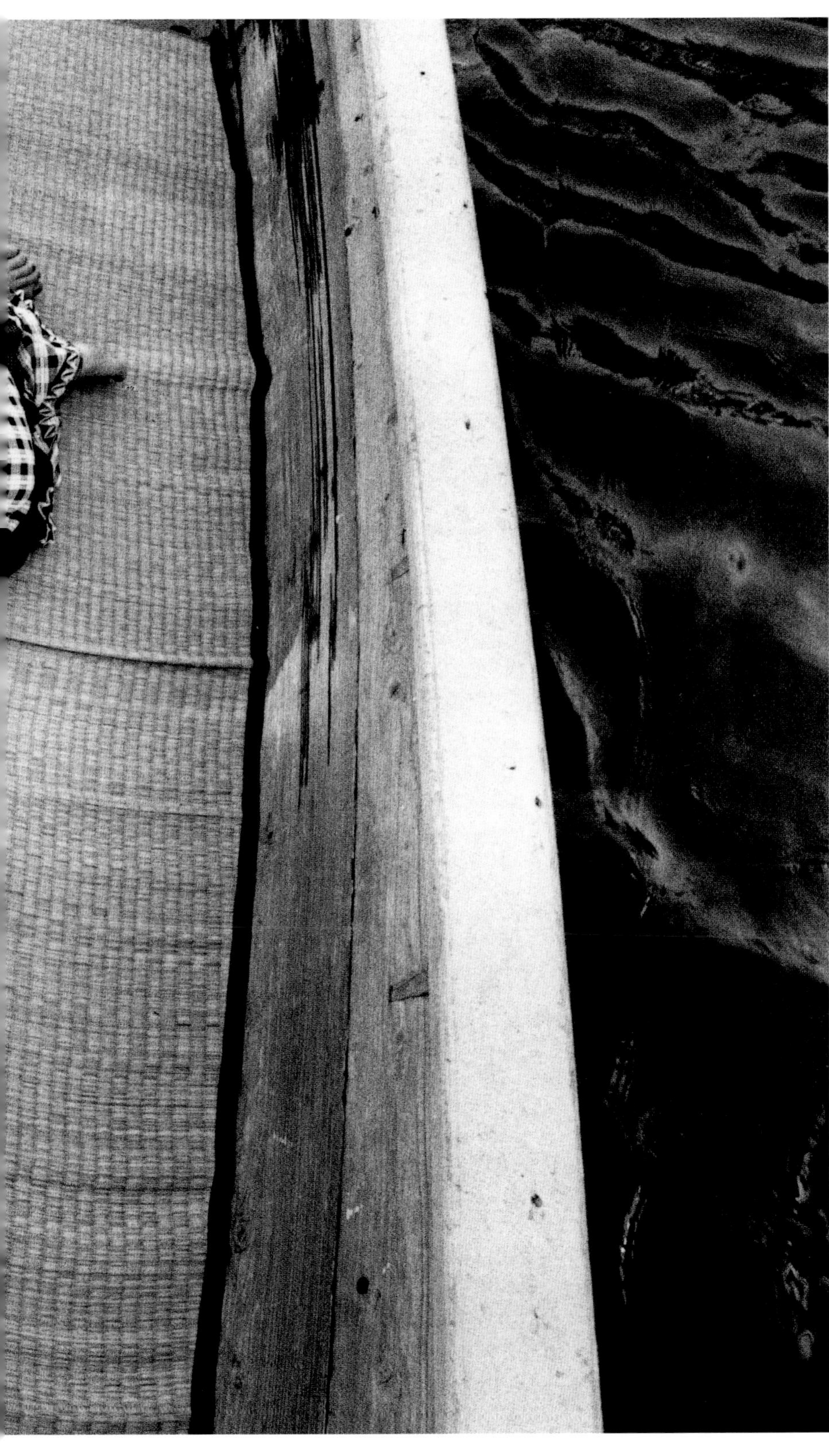

Araki Nobuyoshi, untitled, 1971,
Sentimental Journey series.

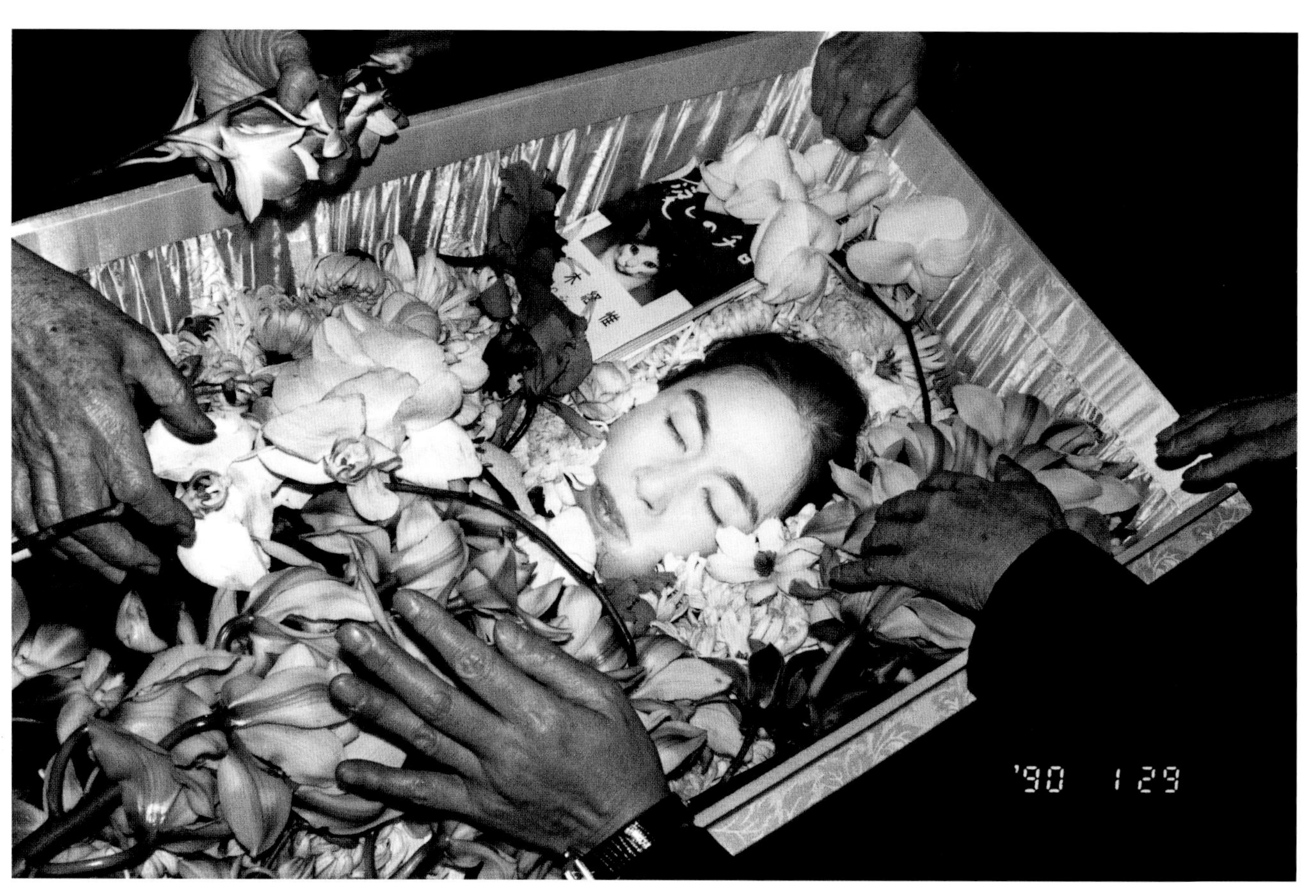

Araki Nobuyoshi, untitled, 1991,
Winter Journey series.

96

Lena Fritsch: Let's start at the beginning – what inspired you to take up photography?
Araki Nobuyoshi: My father was an amateur photographer, and I sometimes spent time with him when he took photographs. But I never aspired to become a photographer, it just happened. I don't aspire to anything and I don't have any photographic aims – taking photographs is like breathing. There was a time when photographers had a particular role (for example the photographers that worked for *LIFE* magazine), but I don't feel like that at all.

What kind of photographs did your father take?
He would be asked by neighbours to take photographs at special events, such as the *shichigosan* festival,[1] school and kindergarten festivals or graduation ceremonies. The camera had to be assembled and I helped my father. When he left the camera, I would stay next to it and make sure that it didn't fall over. I remember making myself a bit taller to reach the camera and then seeing the photographic image upside down. That was fascinating. Perhaps I also noticed (in an intuitive way) that you can create your own world with photography. I remember being with my father in the small darkroom and seeing how the photographs gradually developed. It was like a scientific game. That is how photography began for me – it was fun rather than any form of purposeful learning.

How old were you?
I was in elementary school. My father was the first to recognize my skills in photography. My father made *geta* shoes, and we lived in a poor downtown part of town. Of course, he did not know anything about *LIFE* magazine or similar. We had the *Yomiuri* newspaper at home and my father subscribed to one other newspaper: *San Shashinshinbun*. Now, in hindsight, I think that perhaps he subscribed to this to make me look at the photographs.

Odate Natsuko, Araki's manager: What kinds of photographs were featured in this?
Journalistic photographs, news photographs of the world. It was a tabloid newspaper with more images than text. It was like Natori Yōnosuke's photojournalism, but the tabloid version. Why didn't he show me any erotic photographs [laughs]? He recognized my skills and showed me various other photos too; our neighbourhood used to be a place where criminals were beheaded, and my father showed me those photographs. I think that has probably influenced my photography. I saw these photos of heads on rods. We looked at them in a secretive manner, similar to the way you would look at erotic photographs. That is why I like throats now [laughs].

Sometimes my father went away for a whole day, carrying the camera on the back of his bicycle. I also remember that he met up with the neighbours and amateur photographers from the area and showed the photographs he had taken that month – such gatherings were quite common in Japan at the time. When I was a child, he impressed me with a photograph of Mount Fuji: normally you would include a cherry blossom branch or something to the side, in the photographic foreground. But in his photograph the tree trunk went through the photo: 'boom', right over Mount Fuji. 'Wow', I thought. I have always been good at viewing…I was already avant-garde [laughs]! I do not think my father was influenced much by *ukiyoe* woodblock prints.

A woodblock print would certainly not have the cherry tree trunk right in the middle, in front of Mount Fuji.
Not even Van Gogh would do that [laughs]! My father was a good craftsman as well, making *geta* shoes out of wood from scratch, and wooden billboards for his shop and so on. Ha, I grew up in an artistic environment – he was a 'sculptor' [laughs]!

In 1964, you made the photographic series *Sachin* [p. 101] and were awarded the very first Taiyō Award. What was the trigger for this series?
I studied at Chiba University – there were not many universities or schools that taught photography at all, and it was one of the few places that I could afford. I loved films, particularly French films and Neo-Realism. I liked Robert Bresson: his films *Pickpocket* and *A Man Escaped. The Trial of Joan of Arc* shows his typical sequences of minimal, close-up scenes. One day, walking around downtown Tokyo, I discovered some run-down concrete apartment blocks that had been there since before the war. The children that ran around looked like a scene from Vittorio De Sica's film *Bicycle Thieves*, and also reminded me of myself when I was a child. I began filming the children with a Bolex camera as well as photographing them. I went there regularly over a period of two to three years. It was just a thirty-minute walk from where I lived.

At the time, there were many photo contests. When the new Taiyō Award for documentary photographs was established, I already knew what kind of photos people would submit: of war veterans, victims of the Minamata disease,[2] protests in Sanrizuka. I was confident that I would get the award by submitting photographs that were not as much like *LIFE* photographs. My work documented something close to people's everyday life, something that people were familiar with. I knew I was going to win [laughs]! In the jury, there were only a few photography-related people: Kimura Ihei, Watanabe Yoshio and Ina Nobuo. The other jurors came from other cultural fields.

What happened to the Bolex film?
It was a three-minute film – unfortunately,
I don't know where it is. Somewhere in that
lower drawer...it probably doesn't exist
anymore, it's a shame. The Bolex camera
influenced my photography a lot: it is all
about the moment and I can't help but
continuously press the shutter even when
I already have a good shot. It is like sex
[laughs].

**Odate Natsuko, Araki's manager:
Good that the Taiyō contest was a
photography contest. Imagine you had
submitted your film to a film contest –
your life and career could have taken a
very different turn [laughs].**
That's true [laughs]. Even before going to
university I went to film festivals all the
time. When people ask me about my first
'camera', I always say it was a tattered
manual Bolex camera [laughs].
   With *Sachin* and the award, I noticed
something that has not changed until
today: if I take photographs over a period
of one year or so, the photographs that
get selected are always the ones that
I took during the last months or weeks
before the deadline. Somehow, the works
that were taken just yesterday seem most
contemporary and have the best energy.

**Does that apply to your photobooks
as well?**
Yes, the percentage of new photographs
is always larger. I often include a few
old photos though, to add some salt and
pepper to the mix. When looking at old
photographs like those from *Sachin* now,
I think that they are great. I can also see
myself as a young man in them.

**How do you compile your photographs?
You take so many photographs, do you
have a kind of archive?**
Yes, but I just try to publish my
photographs as soon as possible. Showing
the photographs to people is part of
photography, and it is extremely important
to me. It is a collaboration with the viewers.
Photography, *shashin*, means *sha* for
'reflection' and *shin* for 'truth' and 'God'.
Objectivity in that sense is part of my
photography – despite all the personal
photographs that I take.

**How many photobooks have you
published now?**
Over 500. Some of them are not known
overseas. There are many ways to show
photographs, and they can change
according to their presentation and
the way they are viewed. I would never
tell people how they should look at
photographs; it's completely free.
But for me personally, the photobook –
not too big – is still the best way to
show them.

**Your photographic focus on familiar
things, things around you, in a diaristic
way, has not changed since your first
photobooks.**
That is what photography is about. To put
a camera into a rocket and send it out into
the universe is not photography. Things
like 'the truth' or 'great things' are close to
you; they are part of your own life, you can
always reach them with your hands. There
is no need to go to London or to climb on
top of a mountain [laughs].

**But perhaps you can say that because
you live in Tokyo, a great city! If you lived
on top of a mountain, there would not be
so many interesting photographic motifs
directly around you...**
Oh, I'm not sure about that. Some
mushrooms look great, like holy penises
[laughs]...Your art is always connected to
the place that you were born, I think. There
is no need to travel far.

**Do you still take photographs
every day?**
Yes – it is like breathing in and out to me.
Although I sometimes get an irregular
pulse these days [laughs]. Since I got
cancer, around five things in my body are
broken. Half of my time I'm now busy with
clinic appointments, going to different
specialists and check-ups for the eyes,
the heart and so on. I need to put these
appointments in my diary first. But these
things can inspire your work and become
a starting point for something new.

**You have continued to work really hard,
and have produced a lot of work over
the last years.**
Yes. When I was diagnosed with prostate
cancer, I saw it as a chance and made
a photobook about it. As of yesterday,
I have my calligraphy works displayed in
an exhibition at Isetan department store.
One work is a bit different: it shows the
characters for 'The Cries of the Mother'.
I remember being a child and lying in bed
at night, hearing my mother cry in the other
room. That had a shocking impact – again,
it was something close to me. When I went
to London for my exhibition at the Barbican,
I thought it was a great city, but I felt like a
stranger and didn't really take any photos.
They were photos I took 'in London' but they
are not photos 'of London'. Tokyo and Japan
are more familiar to me. I also like traditional
Japanese art and aesthetics, but when they
are too beautiful – for example paintings by
Ogata Kōrin – they make me want to add
small dirty things. When looking closely
you suddenly see a small dog peeing at
the side or something [laughs].

**I imagine that some things about you
have not changed much since you were
a boy...your photographs of nude women
that feature a small dinosaur or other
toys represent that playful side of
you as well! And your puns.**
I love puns – I want the title for my next
photobook to be *Kōkikōreisha*, as in 'the
elderly, who are over 75 years old' (an
insurance category in Japan). But I will
replace the *sha* at the end for 'people'
with the character *sha* for 'photography'
[laughs]! In literature, I prefer the satirical
senryū to *haiku* poems, and the satirical
kyōka to *waka* poems. They are more fun!

**When did you start to overpaint some
of your nude photographs [p. 269]?**
I think I got the idea in a bar, under the
influence of alcohol. I have previously said
things like 'monochrome photographs are
death' and 'colour is life' and 'I wanted
to mix death and life' [laughs]. But there
is also a feeling of wanting to paint over:
looking at the monochrome photographs
on a concrete wall, I just had to add some
paint. It has also been a good way to hide
certain parts and avoid censorship. I still
enjoy doing that – 'splash!', adding colour
[laughs]. But the basis of my photography is
always documentary. It is not an expression
but rather a reflection of the photographic
subject.

**You have taken many photographs of
flowers – sometimes combined with
small dolls [pp. 152, 268]. Where do
you get them from?**
I take photographs of the flowers that
I receive at exhibition openings, or
at flower shops, all kinds of places.
[Pointing at the flowers in the bar] I also
took some photos of these, before you
arrived. The toys and dolls are usually
presents and I have all kinds of different
ones, from different women. It is a game –
I also include small devils sometimes,
representing myself.

**What do you like best about the
medium of photography?**
I can't help it, I really like it [laughs]. The
other day someone told me about a text
in a collection of essays written by my
wife. I had never read it and it included
a description of us having sex. My hand
was moving around, looking for the
camera [laughs]. She thought that I loved
the camera more than her. That's how
irresistible photography is to me. I'm still
pretty lively – this year I'm seventy-seven
years old and recently I'm feeling quite
confident that I should be able to somehow
continue until I'm eighty [laughs].

*   This is a shortened version of an interview
conducted in Japanese on 6 April 2017, at Bar
Rouge, Tokyo.
1   *Shichigosan* literally means 'seven-five-
three' and is a religious rite of passage day
on 15 November, celebrating the growth and
well-being of seven-, five- and three-year-old
children.

Lena Fritsch: Let's start at the beginning – what inspired you to take up photography?
Yoshiyuki Kōhei: When I was in senior high school I came across photographic series by photographers like Yamagishi Shōji and Shinoyama Kishin in *Camera Mainichi* magazine, as special features. If you get a special feature in *Camera Mainichi*, your ranking – also for commercial photography – goes up quite a lot. I saw all these works by people who were around five years older than me, and became interested in becoming a photographer myself. Until then I painted and wrote calligraphy.

Did you participate in a photography club at senior high school?
I worked during the day and went to an evening school. There was nothing fancy like a photography club – so I founded a photography club myself, just before graduating. After graduating, I came to Tokyo and worked for a photography shop in Shinjuku, printing monochrome photographs. The owner provided me with a room to live in as well. There were photo contests and I came second in the *Camera Mainichi* Year Award. To my surprise, the juror for the *kumi shashin* photo story section for amateurs was Yamagishi Shōji. When I told him that I was aiming to become a professional photographer, he did not take me very seriously [laughs]. There is a big difference between photographs taken by amateurs and photographs taken by professionals. Three years later, I took the photographs for *The Park* series [pp. 102–3].

How long did it take you to compile these photographs?
It took me around one and a half years. At the beginning, I brought my camera but took no photographs: there are people who look at the couples in the park, so if I had suddenly turned up and taken photographs, they would probably have beaten me up. I had to become one of them first.

Were there many 'regulars' who would come to the park to watch?
There were many people that I got to know, and I even made friends.

An interesting place to make new friends...[laughs]
Yes [laughs]. I always brought my camera, but did not use it for around six months. The photographs were then taken over a period of one year. After presenting them in the weekly news magazine *Shūkan Shinchō* in 1972, I received a message from Yamagishi Shōji, who asked me to include the photographs in *Camera Mainichi*. I was using my pseudonym, but another member of *Camera Mainichi* recognized me from a

previous job and my identity was revealed [laughs].

How did you become interested in the park and the couples as a photographic motif?
I had read about the parks in an article, but there were no photographs or any other illustrations accompanying the text. One day, I wanted to take photographs of a new building in Shinjuku at sunset. I was an amateur photographer at the time and went there with a friend. We found an elevated spot from which I could take good photographs of the building. Looking down, we noticed some model houses and behind them, there were couples and voyeurs in the park. So we went there right away. That's when I decided to take photographs of it. At the time, Kodak produced high-speed infrared films – they don't exist anymore. To begin with I used Konica films, which were less sensitive, and took the photographs from a bit further away, but then I became friends with the voyeurs and stopped hiding my camera. So I changed to Kodak, which was easier to use. I also gradually went closer. The 'senior voyeurs' would give me advice on how to get closer to the couples [laughs]. Some would even go closer to a couple so I could take my photographs more easily, without getting noticed.

Are the couples usually aware of the people around them?
It depends – some people tried to touch them before they got noticed.

At the time, were you interested in or inspired by any photographers in particular?
Not really – I focused more on the fact that if I wanted to become a professional photographer, I had to find something that was unique. There were so many people in photography schools or photo studios who all wanted to become professional photographers. I wanted to find a special theme, and when I came across the park, I knew that would be it. It was a difficult theme, and the photographic process and relationship with the photographic subjects became big parts of the series. They were more important than how well the individual photographs were taken or not taken.

The majority of the photos were taken at a slightly remote park in Shinjuku that is now called Chūō Kōen. It was close to pubs and bars, and after drinking some men would suggest to the women they had a date with that they go for a little walk. It was conveniently located. In the photographs you can see that some of the trees were only just planted, and had these supports around them. The park itself was still new and not completed

2   Minamata disease is a neurological illness caused by mercury poisoning. It was discovered in 1956 in Minamata, Kumamoto Prefecture, where industrial wastewater was released into the sea, and as a result, highly toxic fish and shellfish were eaten by the local populace.

Later I also went to Yoyogi Park, but I lived in Shinjuku so the park there was close to home. My photography is about the area where I live; I want to record what is close to me. I was really surprised: close to where I live there are these couples having sex in the park, and there are people looking!

You published the photographs as a photobook a few years later. How did you compile the photographs?
When I was thirty years old, I became independent and published the book. I had not taken a large number of photographs, so I did not have many photographs to choose from. I made another series, focusing on homosexuals who met in another park. They were taken over a period of around one or two months, just for the photobook [p. 103]. For those photos, I had to hide my camera – I had it inside my bag and the bag had a hole. Both the couples and the people who are looking at them are homosexual men.

The atmosphere was probably quite different.
Very different. People were more scared to be discovered.

When I was over sixty years old, Martin Parr kindly wrote about my photographs, emphasizing that the series is social documentation: he values that they document how Tokyo has grown into a gigantic metropolis. However, for many years in Japan my photographs have been viewed in the context of sex entertainment [laughs]. When working for the journal *Focus*, for example, I took commercial photographs for the sex industry section. I accepted these jobs because I had to survive as a commercial photographer. But the main reason I took the park photographs was that I wanted to show and prove what was happening very close to where I lived. In Japan, the photographs have even been viewed as *tōsatzu*: secret photographs that you take illegally. But I took photos in a park, not secretly in someone's house...

Which is a public place, as the Japanese characters for 'park' nicely show.
Exactly – and the people all remained anonymous. In the United States there are around seven museums that have photographs of my *Park* series in their collection. They see the works as interesting documents of a specific phenomenon. I'm also interested in the social context: for example, there was a couple in China who were arrested for having sex in a park. It turned out that they were a married couple and had sex outside as their apartment was too small and didn't provide any privacy. Such contexts are interesting.

What do you like best about the medium of photography?
At the beginning, I particularly liked the camera itself. I also enjoyed developing the photos in the darkroom; I have always had an interest in photographic mechanisms. In addition, I'm interested in the way you can express yourself through photography. In painting or calligraphy works come into existence through your own imagination, but with photography you borrow a different place or environment in order to express yourself. Photographs are not things that you create only by yourself – which sometimes makes it difficult, but also particularly interesting. It is hard to survive as a photographer, though. Young people in Japan seem to understand that, and there are fewer people now who want to become professional photographers.

*   This is a shortened version of an interview conducted in Japanese on 8 April 2017, at Akio Nagasawa Gallery, Tokyo.

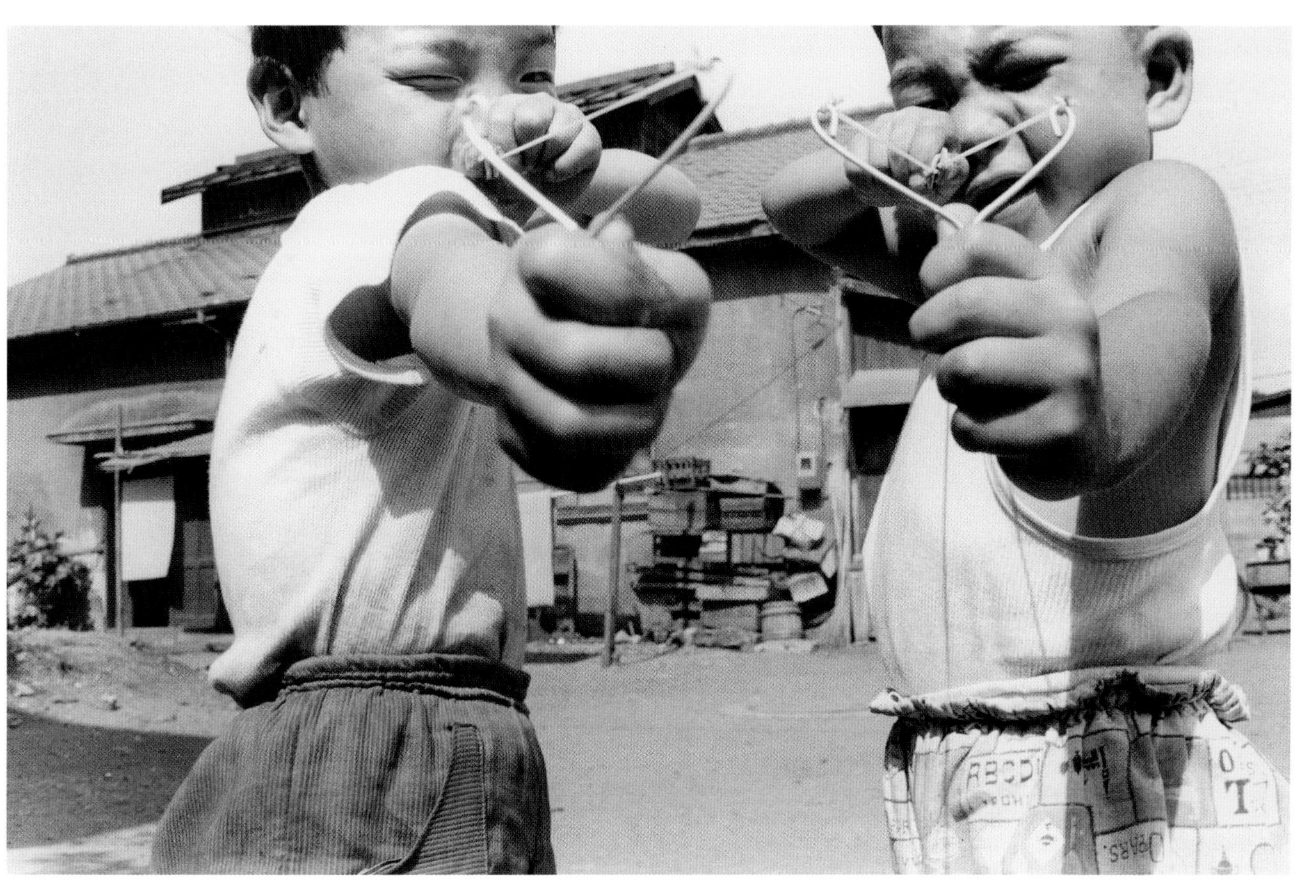

Araki Nobuyoshi, *Sachin and his brother Mabo*, 1964.

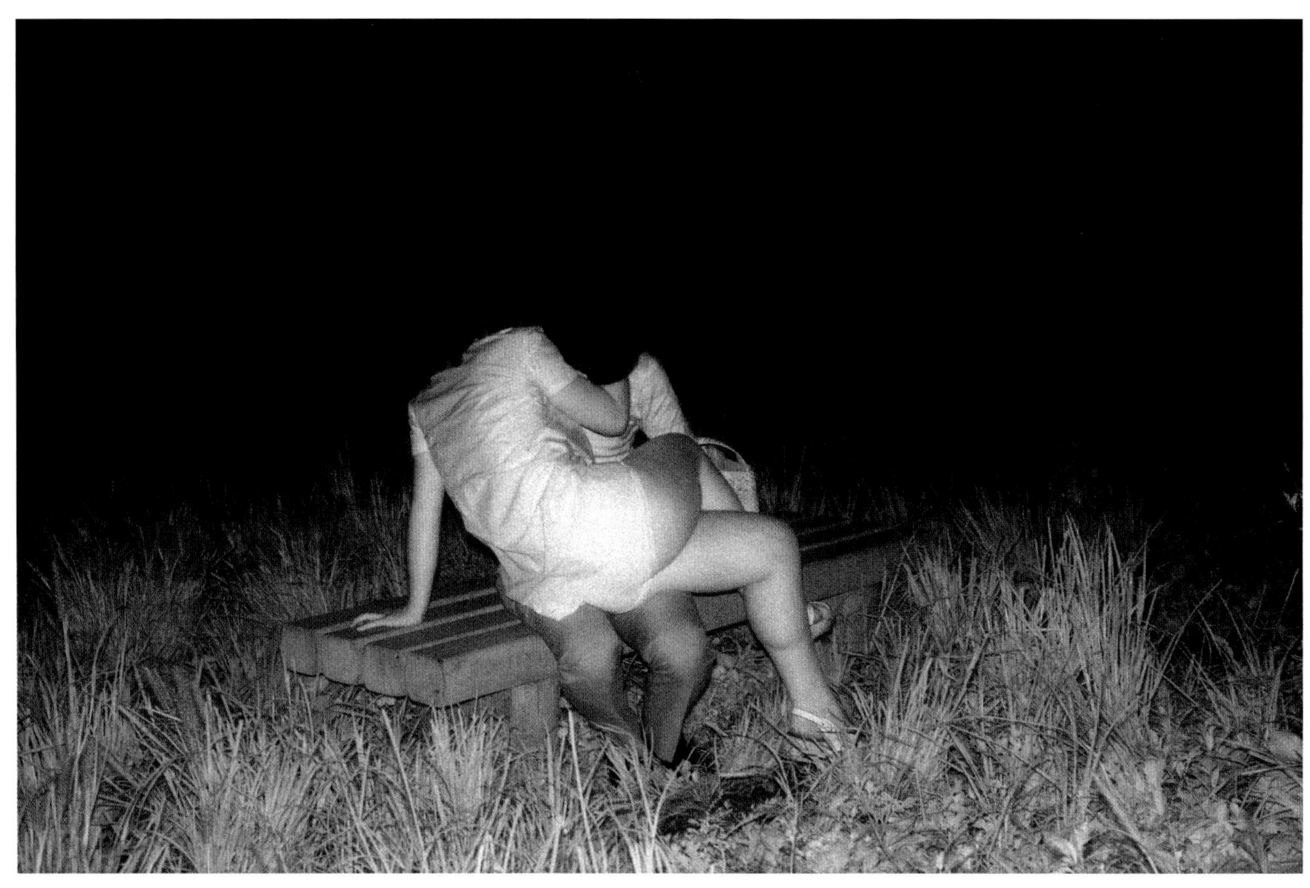

Above: Yoshiyuki Kōhei, 1972,
The Park (Kōen) series.
Opposite, above: Yoshiyuki Kōhei,
1972, *The Park (Kōen)* series.
Opposite, below: Yoshiyuki Kōhei,
1979, *The Park (Kōen)* series.

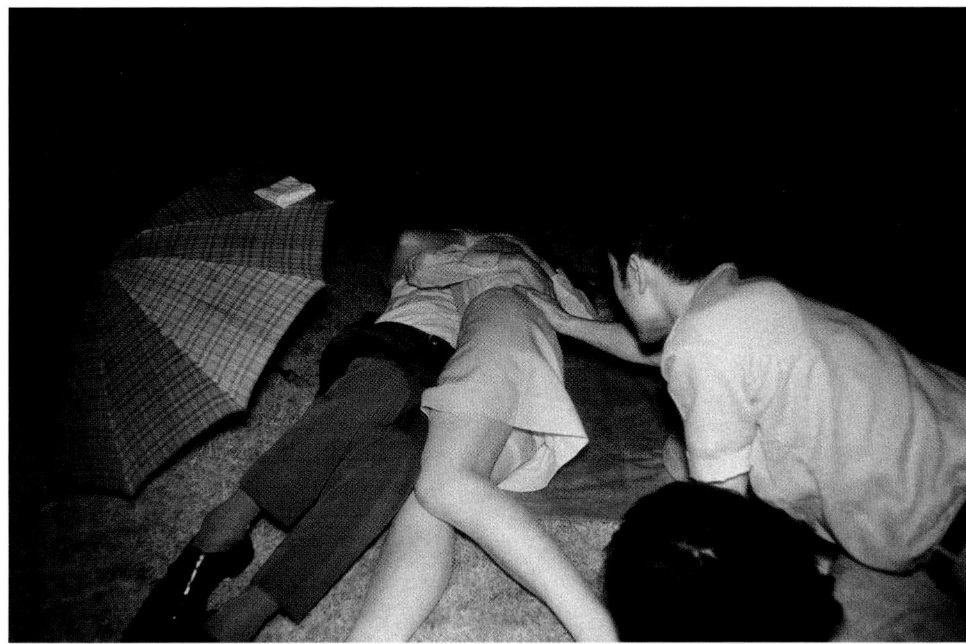

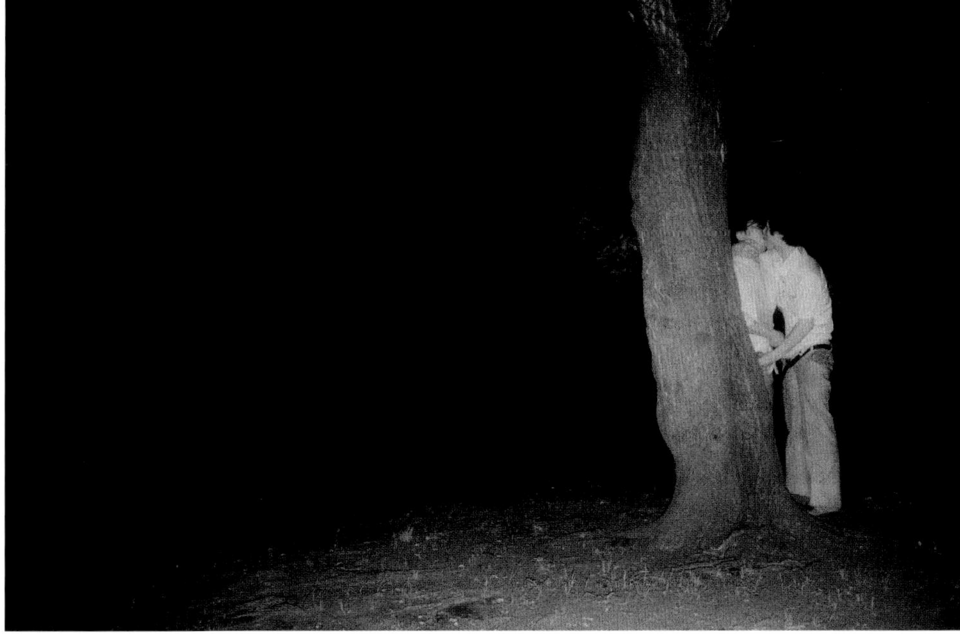

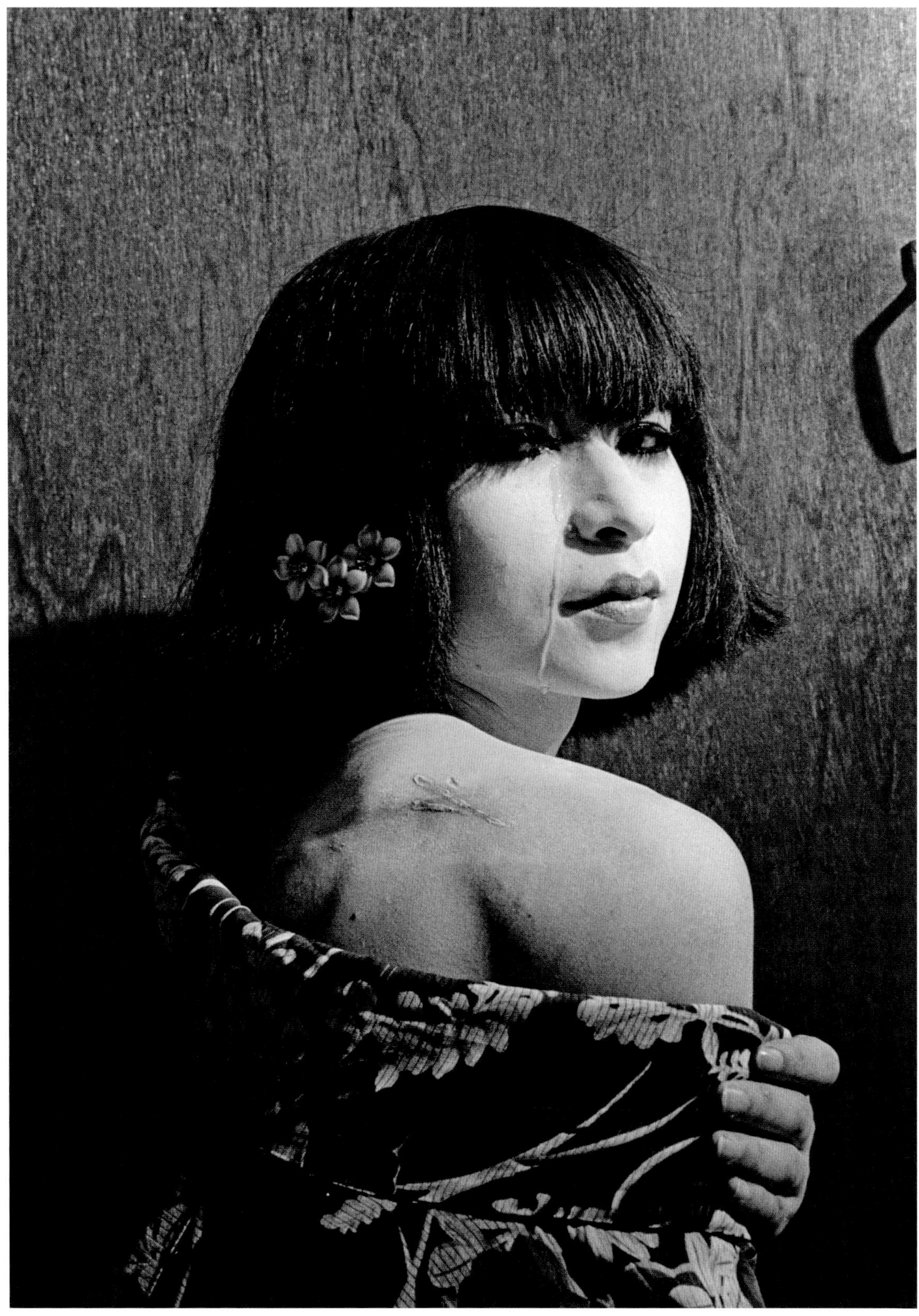

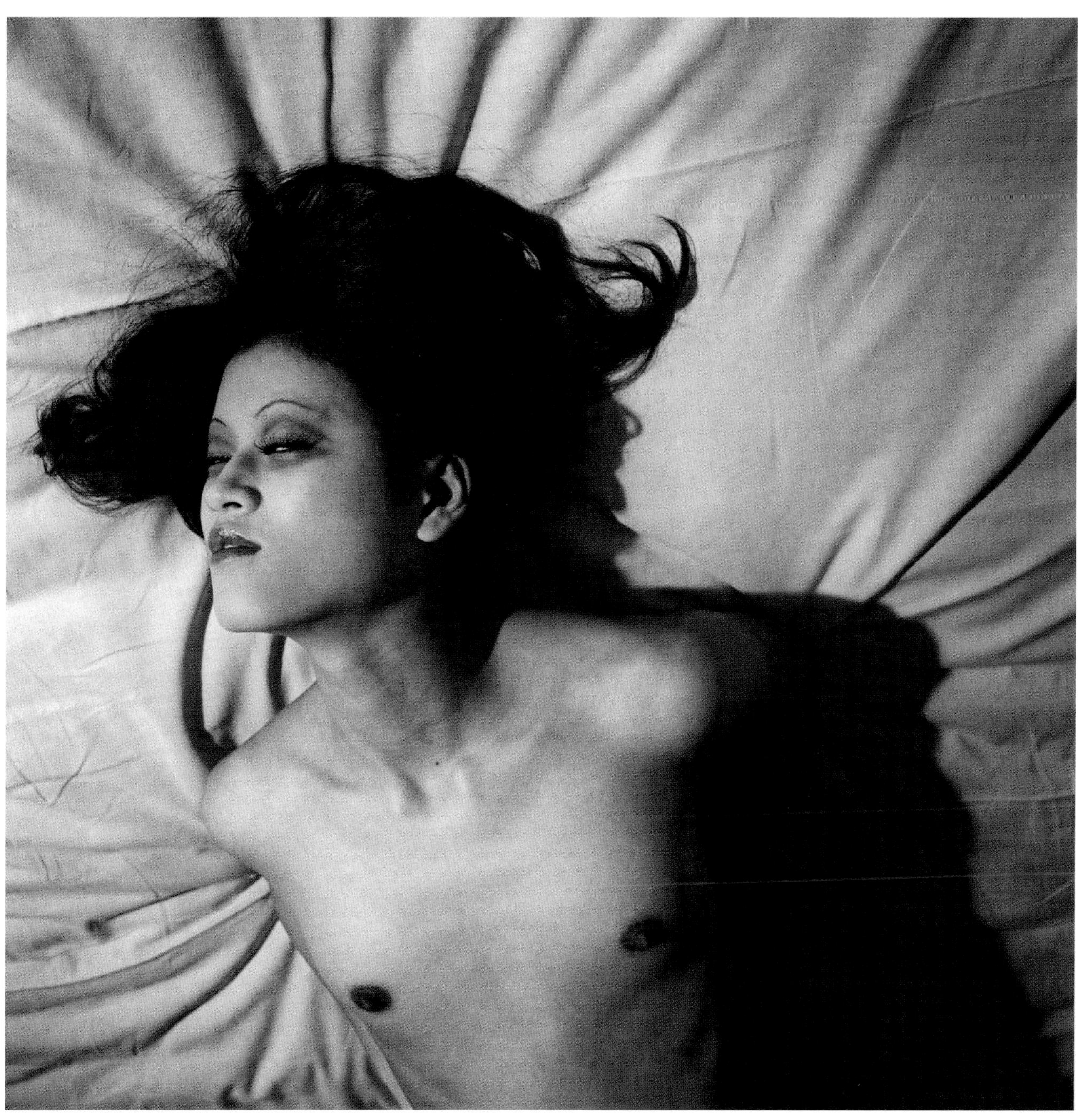

Opposite: Yanagisawa Shin, *Scorpio, Tokyo,* 1970.
Above: Yanagisawa Shin, *Hard Winter, Otaru,* 1973.

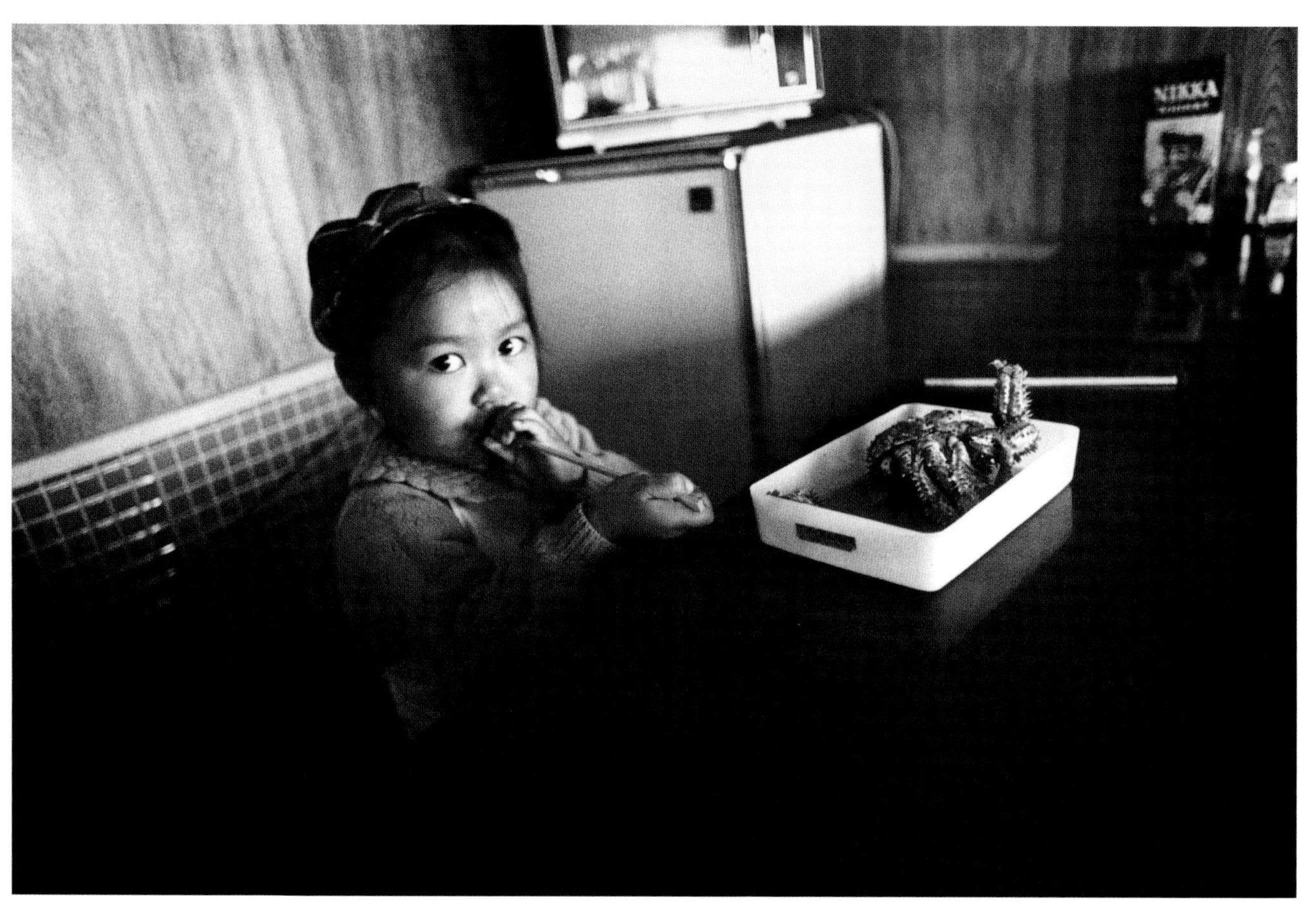

Above: Yanagisawa Shin, *Hokkaido Wilderness*, 1970.
Opposite: Suda Issei, *Nagatoro, Saitama*, 1974, *Scarlet Bloom* series.

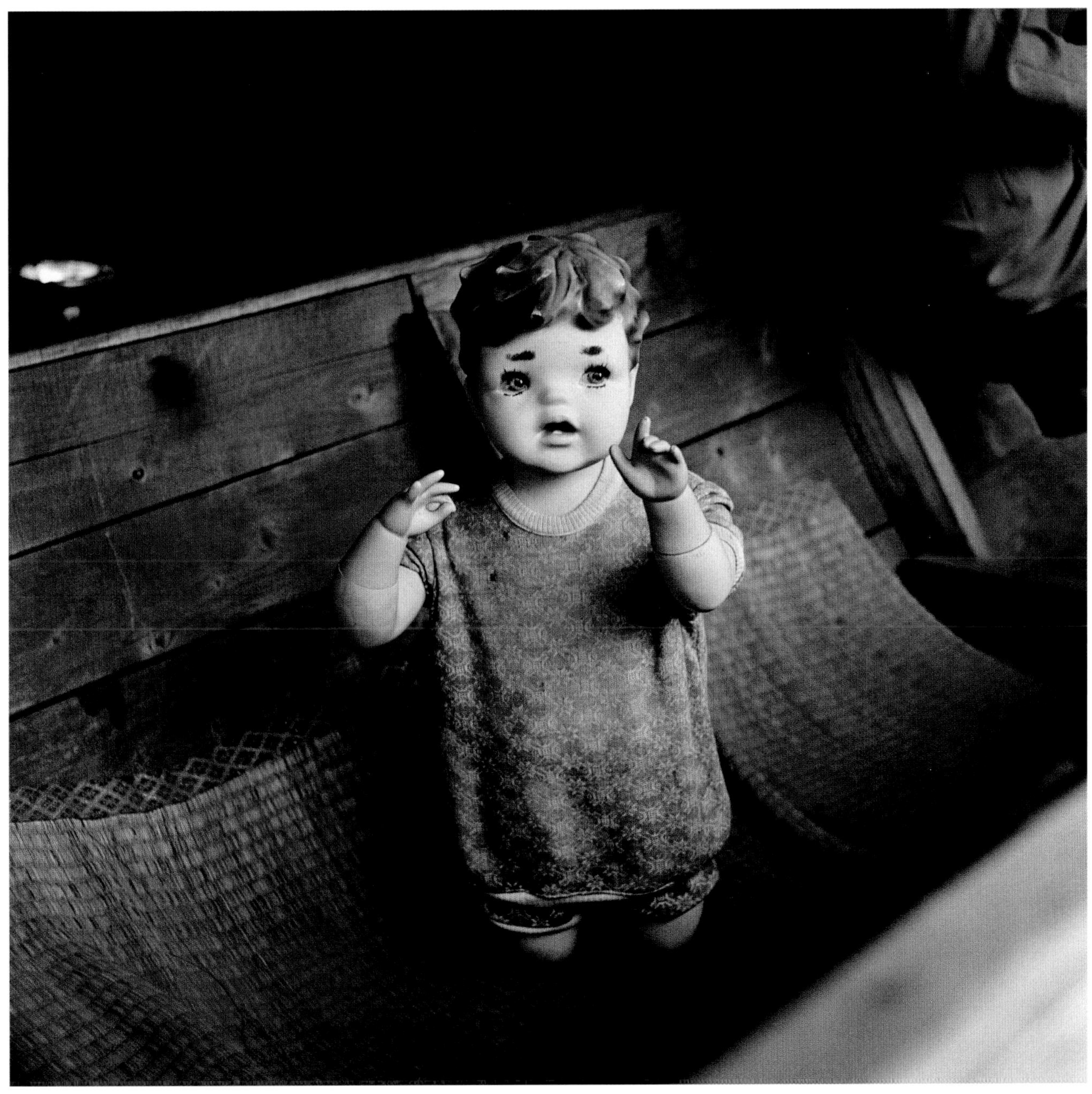

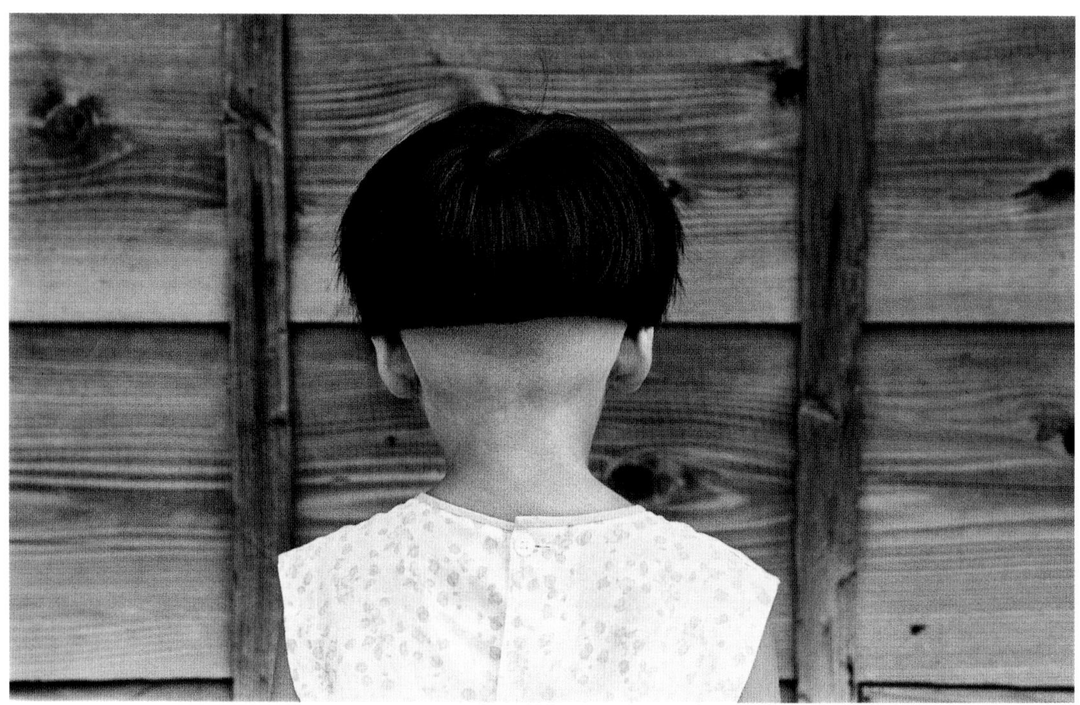

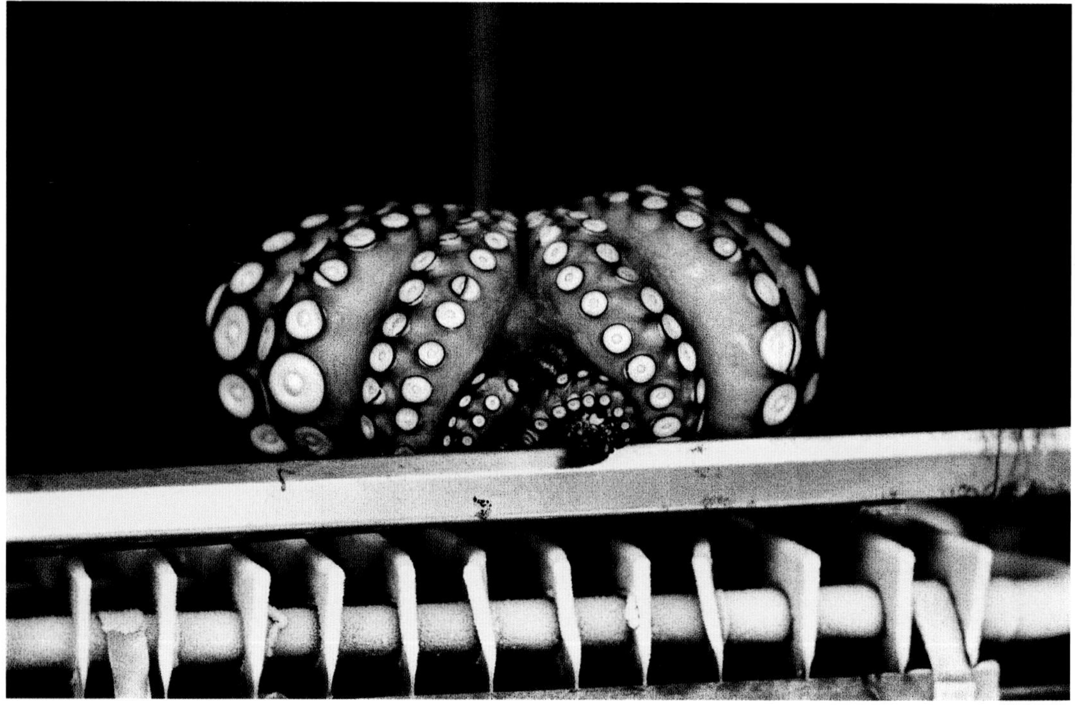

Top: Suda Issei, *Sawara Chiba*, 1972, *Clipped* series.
Above: Suda Issei, *Moka Tochigi*, 1974, *Memory* series.

108

Lena Fritsch: Let's start at the beginning – what inspired you to take up photography?
Suda Issei: I started later than most photographers. After graduating, I first had to work in my father's company. Before the war, he had a bar here in Kanda and then a wholesale company selling building materials. I never thought of becoming his successor, though. Since my school years, I had always liked the cinema, and I watched many films by myself, thinking that I would like to work in that field one day.

Were there any films in particular that you liked?
In the post-war years not many films from overseas made it to Japan, but there were a few Hollywood films that I liked. Dramas from the West were fascinating and so straightforward; they made us children feel better. I also liked Japanese historical dramas, *jidaigeki*. I remember seeing the 1951 film *Kurama Tengu* [Goblin of Mount Kurama] with Misora Hibari, in which she plays the role of a boy, Tsugisaku [laughs]. I still enjoy watching films today.

So film inspired you to start photography?
It was all about seeing. My interest did not begin with *taking* photographs but with *looking* at them. I enjoyed looking at images in camera magazines and photobooks, such as William Klein's *New York*.

To start photography by looking – that is interesting. There are also quite a few people in Japan whose starting point was their camera.
Yes, that was most common: students would have a camera and bring it to school trips, or take photos of their cat and their friends. In my case, it was different: I started by looking at films and images. There was a bookshop in Jimbōchō, which was not far from me, where I went quite often to check out their American comics (such as *Blondie*), American film magazines and later also films. I enjoyed going there.

At the back of Jimbōchō there was a local photo studio, Mori Photo Studio, where they took photographs and developed them. I often went there to look at the photographs, and one day they invited me: 'why don't you come in, sit on the chair, and you can take your time and look through the photographs'. I began to look at photographs more regularly, and then they said, 'if you like photography that much, come and join us upstairs where we meet as a photography group.' There were about five seniors, studying at Tokyo College of Photography, a famous school. I decided to enrol there as well, and began to learn all the basics about photography. My parents agreed to buy me a camera and when they asked me which camera I wanted, I said 'Rollei', which many of them used. Well, it was an expensive camera [laughs]. That's when I actually started taking photographs. So I was quite late, compared to many others, who joined photo clubs at school.

Suda Issei's wife, Suda Yoshiko: During school, he did not take any photographs, and until he enrolled at the Tokyo College of Photography he did not really know much about photography. This was unusual. At college, apparently he was hiding from other people and caused a mess in the darkroom. He just owned a proper camera [laughs].

In 1967 you became a photographer for the avant-garde theatre group Tenjō Sajiki, working for Terayama Shūji. How did this come about?
I liked Terayama's novels. And when I found out that they were recruiting actors and other staff for the Tenjō Sajiki group it seemed like the right job at the right time. I had won the annual award from the *Nippon Camera* magazine and gained some confidence that I was perhaps able to take photographs that differed from other people's work. So I joined the avant-garde group – it was exciting.

Suda Yoshiko: At the time, Suda was still expected to take over from his father to continue the family business. He was twenty-seven years old when he saw the job advertisement, and he had just won the special monthly commendation by *Nippon Camera* for his series *Mount Osorezan*. Terayama had also written folktale dramas about *Osorezan*. Well, and then Suda joined the group for three years.

A few years later, you decided against your father's company and to make a living as a photographer. You opened your own photo studio and began to take photographs, which you published in 1978 in your photobook *Fūshi Kaden* [p. 113]. Could you tell me about this book?
The basis of my work is not so much Zeami's treatise *Fūshikaden*, but that I was interested in showing a different, everyday side to Kanda, in Tokyo – basically the downtown area (*shitamachi*). For example, I was interested in people's facial expressions. Downtown people have a particular sense of community. There are many photographs of festivals in the book, like the Kanda and Asakusa festivals, where people come together. I went there and walked around and looked. I was interested in photographing the community vibe of people getting together, laughing and enjoying themselves. They all work towards the same goal. At the time, it was still easy

to portray random people without any copyright issues.

The title of the photobook is a direct reference to Zeami's *noh* theatre treatise *Fūshikaden (The Transmission of the Flower of Acting)*. Why did you choose this title?
I was never good at sports – I could not even jump over a vaulting box at school [laughs]! But my publisher invited me to go skiing with him. Well, on the first day when waiting at the lift, I fell into a hole. I went back home to Tokyo without skiing at all and had to go to hospital right away [laughs].

It seems you really are not lucky with sports [laughs]!
After this accident, my foot took time to heal and for over two months I was mostly resting at home. I became bored and started to print the photographs that I had taken so far. That became the *Fūshi Kaden* photobook. I was reading Zeami's book at the time, as a paperback.

Suda Yoshiko: It is a book about *noh* theatre, but he interpreted it in relation to photography. He likes doing that – before you arrived he said that even this text here [points at a coffee advertisement on the café table] can be read in connection to photography. This part here about intensity and flavour...

Suda Issei: Yes, it can be applied to photography as well [laughs]! In *Fūshi Kaden* I thought that 'with concealment a flower blooms, without concealment there is no flower' fit the concept of photography as well as *noh*.

In your photography, the everyday is an important aspect, but there is also often a somewhat mysterious aesthetic, it is difficult to describe...
If you say so, that makes me actually very happy. I myself find it difficult to describe what I want to photograph...I aim to take photographs that can't be described with words. Recently, I have felt that I would like to strengthen my photography and its accuracy; I think there is a very individual ideal, something like an 'individual 100%'. I think I should search for that. But I also know that it can't be found; it is my own, very personal feeling.

In 2015, you published a series titled *Rei*, portraying mannequins [p. 259]. Could you tell me more about this work?
I have a bit of a foot fetish. The photographs of the mannequins were taken at department stores at Ginza. If you go there during the day it is crowded, so I went in the early mornings, around 5am. The shops are still closed but the mannequins in the windows are visible.

I took the photographs from a distance of approximately 1 m, or maybe 80 cm. It took me around a year, and I returned to the same shops a number of times when they wore new clothes and shoes, focusing on their perfect feet. I am a bit weird like that [laughs]. There are mannequins in other parts of Tokyo too, but the Ginza ones are the best.

You mostly take monochrome, analogue photographs, correct?
I take colour photographs as well but I don't do digital photography. I use different cameras though, ranging from a 6x9 Fuji camera to a small, subtle Minox camera.

Why did you choose photography and what do you like best about photography?
When I look back now, I think it has something to do with the power of photographic images to stay in your memory. It is like a magic charm: a photograph that you have seen at some point in the past can stay in your mind forever. Yes, that is it: 'the magic charm of photography' – that sounds good, doesn't it? [laughs]

It does indeed.
Suda Yoshiko: This man's photography and private life are one, you can't separate them from each other!

*   This is a shortened version of an interview conducted in Japanese on 6 September 2016, at Kanda-Coffee-En, Tokyo.

Lena Fritsch: Let's start at the beginning – what inspired you to take up photography?
Ishiuchi Miyako: A friend did not need his darkroom equipment any more and I agreed to store it for him. He had all the equipment required: camera, enlarger, tray, tweezers. I also went to see various friends' photography exhibitions. One day I bought films, papers and chemicals and gave it a try. I had studied textile design at university, including fabric dyeing, and in the darkroom I recognized the smell of the chemicals. The fixatives for photography and for colouring fabrics were the same – photographs are like dyed fabrics, I thought [laughs]. I really enjoyed the work in the darkroom. That moment when the dark and light grains appear and the photographic image comes together...it is just beautiful! I did not know what to photograph but I liked working in the darkroom.

Gradually, I began to think about photographic motifs. The first time I went somewhere to take photographs, I went to Miyako, on the Sanriku Coast. When I arrived, I did not know what to photograph [laughs]. I thought, 'why did I travel so far – I don't want to take photographs at all. Where should I take photographs instead, which town feels most far away to me personally?' I realized that it had to be Yokosuka, where I grew up. Soon after, I went to the town that felt most alien to me and that I hated the most. I wanted to see Yokosuka again. I bought a map and walked around.

Was that the map included in the recent catalogue accompanying your exhibition at the J. Paul Getty Museum? You marked all the places that you went to.
Yes, I put little star stamps on the places that I had photographed. That became the *Yokosuka* series – my first real photographs, my 'debut' [p. 114]. Soon after, I made the *Apartment* series [p. 115]. I wanted to return to all the places that I associated with bad memories. I received the Kimura Ihei Award [for *Apartment*], which surprised me. Following this, I made *Endless Night*, which was also connected to my memories. As a high-school pupil, I passed by the red-light district every morning and afternoon, feeling its weird atmosphere.

For the *Apartment* series, you entered other people's apartments, which is quite a private thing in Japan?
Yes, I just knocked on their doors. Some of them were friends of friends. I was a woman and carried a camera, so people let me in, particularly young people. The same with *Endless Night*: the fact that I was a woman made it easier. I did not mention the 'red-light district', but always said that I had

come to take photographs of 'old buildings' [laughs]. I took photographs as a way of revisiting my old memories.

Being a woman made it easier for you to photograph some places. But how was it for you in general, as a female photographer in the 1970s and 1980s male-dominated photography world?
I didn't have much to do with the photography world. But over the years, I got to know some individual photographers quite well: Araki-san, Moriyama-san, Fukase-san, Tōmatsu-san. Tōmatsu-san did not respect women very much. His photographs are good but as a person...some of these photographers are still alive but one day when they are dead, I might publish a book... [laughs]

'Photography and Photographic Relations in Japan – the Real Story'! [laughs]
Yes [laughs]. Overall, the fact that I was a woman didn't really matter. I was able to communicate with these photographers freely because I was not a disciple of any master. When I was still practising, and exhibited my earliest photographs in a group show, people said my photos looked a bit like Moriyama's work. I did not even know his photographs but when I saw them, I liked them – our photographs are quite different, though. When I had my first solo show with *Yokosuka Story*, I gave Moriyama a call, saying: 'my name is Ishiuchi Miyako and people think that I'm your disciple. Therefore, if you like, please come to my exhibition.' And he came!

That was nice of him.
He wore pitch-black sunglasses, but he kindly took them off because it is difficult to see my dark photographs through sunglasses! He looked at my photographs [laughs]. That was the first time I met Moriyama-san; he was very nice. He liked my photographs and when I published *Yokosuka Story* as a book, I asked him to write a text for it.

How cool – calling Moriyama as a young woman who had just begun taking photographs.
I was quite direct as a young woman. Whenever there was someone I wanted to meet, I would just go and meet him. I would go to parties even if I was not invited [laughs].

Araki-san was nice too: he came to an early group show and told me that if I wanted a solo exhibition at Ginza Nikon Salon, he would be able to help. Miki Jun led the gallery committee at the time. I wanted to have a solo show, just once, and Nikon Salon was the biggest gallery with the most visitors. So I showed Araki-san my photos. He liked them and gave Miki-san a call right away. We met Miki-san together, and that is how my *Yokosuka Story* was exhibited at Nikon Salon. I met a few nice people at the very beginning, before my 'debut'. I'm good at choosing the right people and I was not interested in any of these photographers as men – that helped [laughs].

Let me make a temporal jump to your ひろしま/*hiroshima* series [p. 262]. I remember that a publisher had seen your *Mother's* series and commissioned you to take photographs of the objects in the Hiroshima Peace Memorial Museum. Could you tell me more about the series?
I always thought that there was no need for me to go to Hiroshima – many photographers had taken photos there, so I felt there was nothing left for me to photograph. But then the publisher suggested I go to Hiroshima and take new photographs, as 'works of art'. I had never been, and I accepted. Over a period of around one year I went four or five times.

Normally you would create a photobook and that would be the end of it. However, the museum receives new objects every year, so I continue this project. This month, they have received new objects again, and I will go and photograph them. I have been working on ひろしま/*hiroshima* for ten years now. ひろしま/*hiroshima* and *Frida* both started as commissions, but they have become personal projects, and have had a big impact on my life.

ひろしま/*hiroshima*, *Frida* and your series *Silken Dreams* (2009–10) are all concerned with fabrics. Could you tell me about *Silken Dreams* [p. 263]?
My interest in fabrics is linked with my studies in weaving at university – I still have the weaving machine here.

Do you still use it?
It is in parts, and I don't use it but I can't throw it away. My interest in silk began with ひろしま/*hiroshima*. Many of the fabrics in Hiroshima that have survived are made of silk or cotton. Summer kimonos are made of silk. So I began thinking about silk and the town where I was born, Kiryu, which was once a busy silk-production region. From Hiroshima I went to Kiryu and started taking photographs. I always thought that I was born in the same town as my mother, in Kasagakemura. But a journalist working for the *Kiryu Times* found out that my birthplace was in a town nearby, in Kiryu.

How long did you live in Kiryu as a child?
I lived there until I was six years old, before moving to Yokosuka. I still have relatives there but it felt like an unknown place.

Kiryu used to be famous for silk, but there is hardly any production there today.
Most of the factories have closed; kimonos are expensive and people don't often buy them. But there are still a few places. I went to a textile school in Kiryu, where they teach silk weaving. At the Getty Museum exhibition opening I wore a *kimono* made of textiles from there. Kiryu is an interesting town, it has a unique character and history to it. It used to be a rich town, with its thriving silk industry, so there were many banks. Today, there are a few local banks such as the Kiryu bank or Gunma bank, and just one external bank remains: Yokohama bank. I went to Kiryu from Yokohama and when I saw that bank it made me happy. Somehow, without looking for them, I tend to find these fateful connections through my photography. It happens in a natural way, and I find that very interesting. I'm thankful to photography for that, maybe photography suits me...[laughs]

Of course it suits you!
I don't take so many photographs, though – I don't wander around and take photographs all the time. Recently, I accept commissions more often; sometimes they show me the way. When I was younger, just after receiving the Kimura Ihei Award, I received so many offers from magazines to take photographs. But I only accepted one job, and it made me bored and exhausted. It even made me consider stopping taking photographs altogether.

You didn't take photographs for quite a while in the 1980s.
Yes, and for twenty-five years I didn't accept any work from outside. But that time was probably important. With ひろしま/*hiroshima* and *Frida* it changed: these projects began as external work, but I made them my own.

They are projects that suit your photography. People now commission you because they have seen your previous work and only want you, no other photographer.
That's true. After receiving the Kimura Ihei Award, people just offered me jobs because I was the first woman who had received the award. The photography world was a 'boys' club' [laughs] – there were hardly any women photographers at the time. But I didn't want to accept those jobs; they were too simple, boring and didn't suit me. Even today, I hardly ever interact with the 'photography world'. I also don't like hanging out with people who are older than me; only younger. It is more fun and more relaxed! [laughs] I have decided that I'm old enough to just do what I want.

Since your first exhibition of *Yokosuka Story* in 1977, forty years have passed and you have taken different photographs and used different motifs. Do you think your approach to photography has changed?
In general, I take more photographs than I used to. And I take colour photographs now. The change from monochrome to colour was quite a big one. I developed the monochrome photographs myself and really enjoyed it, but now I give the films away and the printing process is out of my hands. However, the basics have not changed.

You don't take that many photographs – it is not part of your everyday life.
It is September now and I have not taken any photographs yet this year – I'm going to Kumamoto and Hiroshima soon though. Yes, I photograph in a focused way [laughs]. I have a mini camera though, and I take photographs of the area here, just as records. The area is changing so much, for example, around the train station. I also enjoy writing essays. My next deadline is next week, so I'm quite busy writing.

When you create a photobook, how do you proceed?
I think every photobook has a beginning, middle and end. Therefore, the first thing I think about is the story with its beginning and end. I then line up the photographs in a certain order and leave them for a while, looking at them every morning, gradually changing the order. If I look at them for long enough, I start seeing the best dynamic.

What do you like best about the medium of photography?
I like the ability of photography to lie – it not only reflects reality but your own thoughts, and you can even tell lies with it. At the same time, I like how photographs are based in technology. They can be created quickly and are not a continuation of your body – unlike, for example, paintings. And a photograph exists on a piece of paper and can be torn very easily.

*   This is a shortened version of an interview conducted in Japanese on 3 September 2016, at Ishiuchi Miyako's home in Kanazawa.

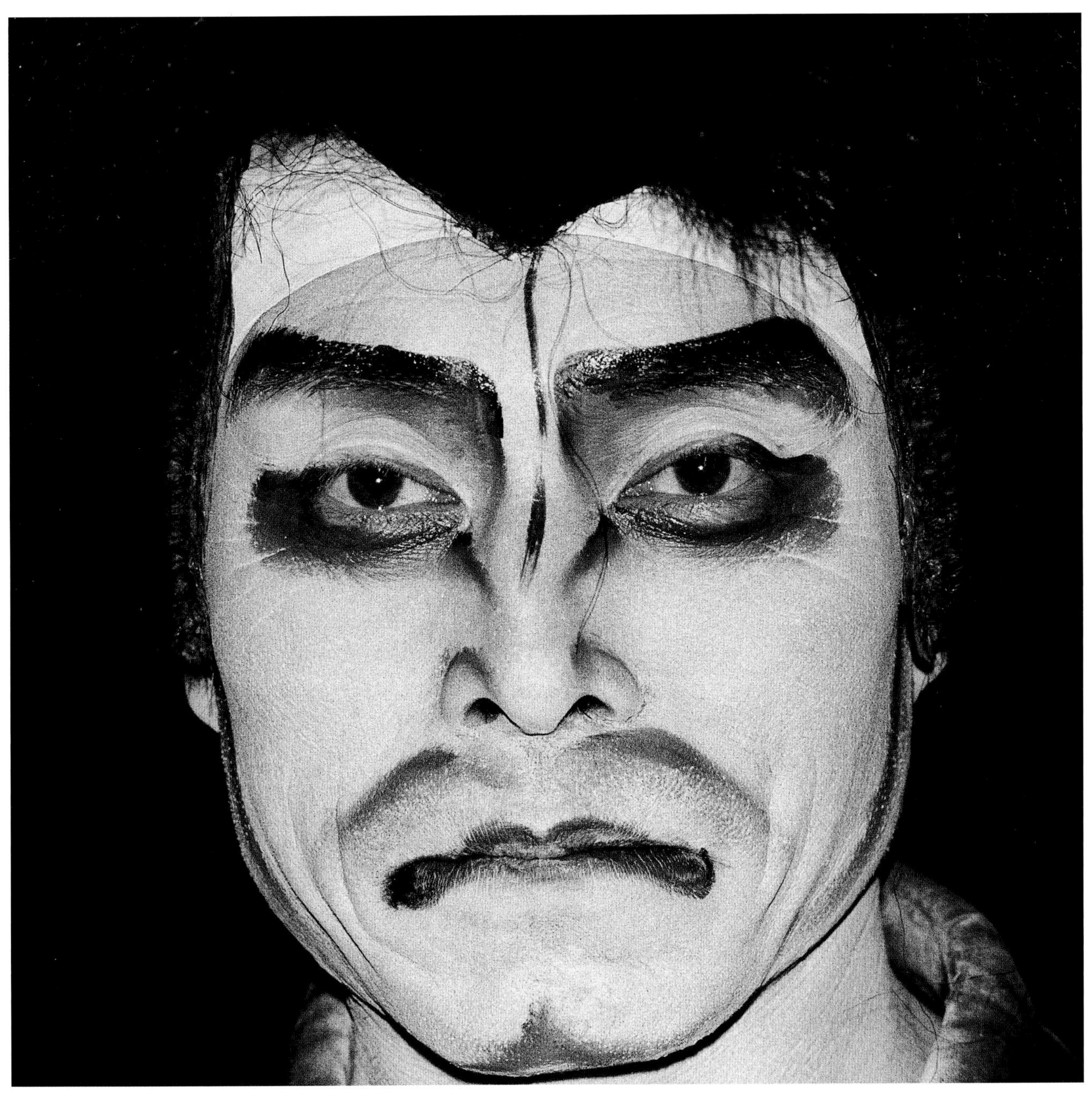

Suda Issei, *Teppo-matsuri Ogano Chichibu,*
Suitama, 1976, *Fūshi Kaden* series.

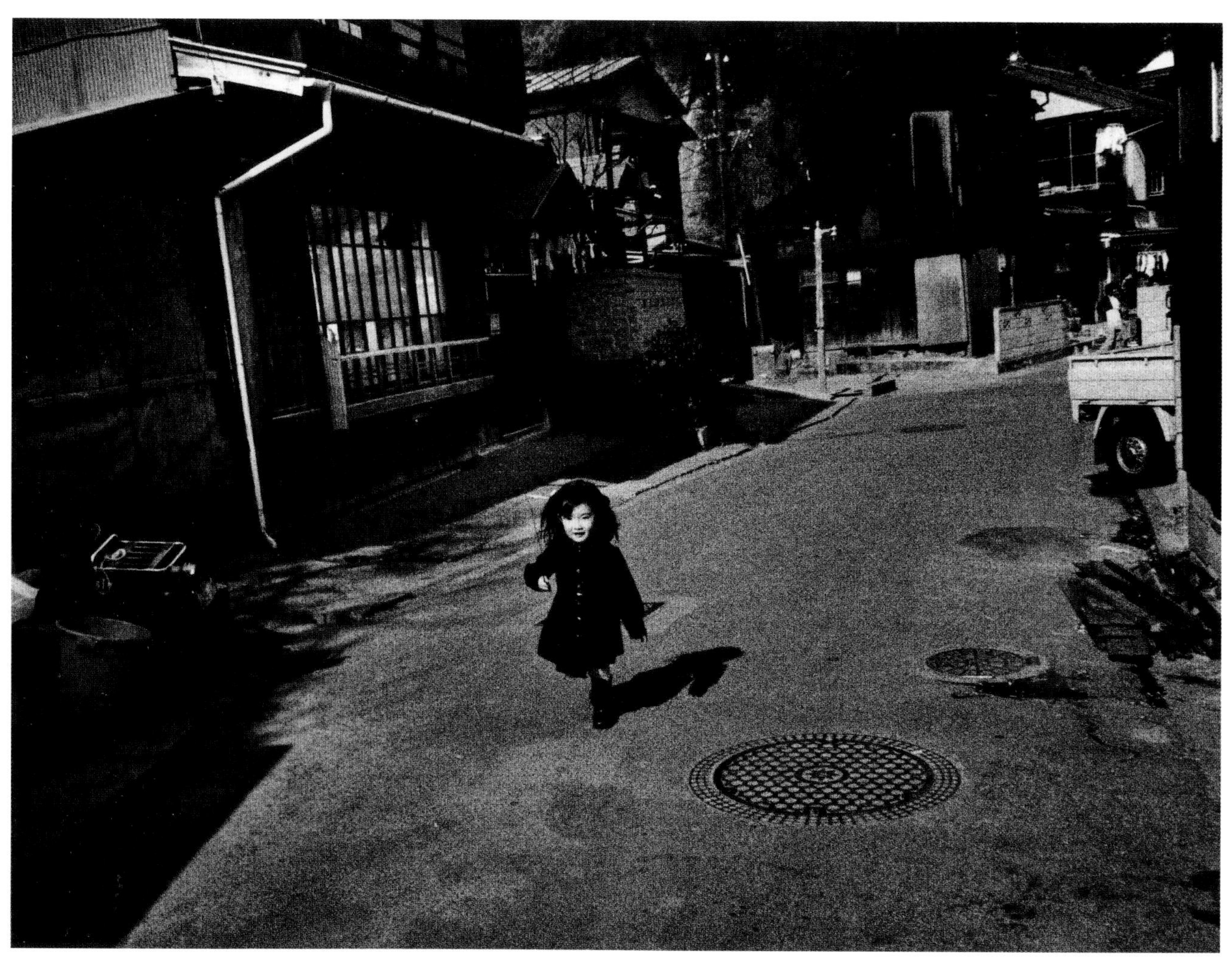

Ishiuchi Miyako, *Yokosuka Story #98*, 1977.

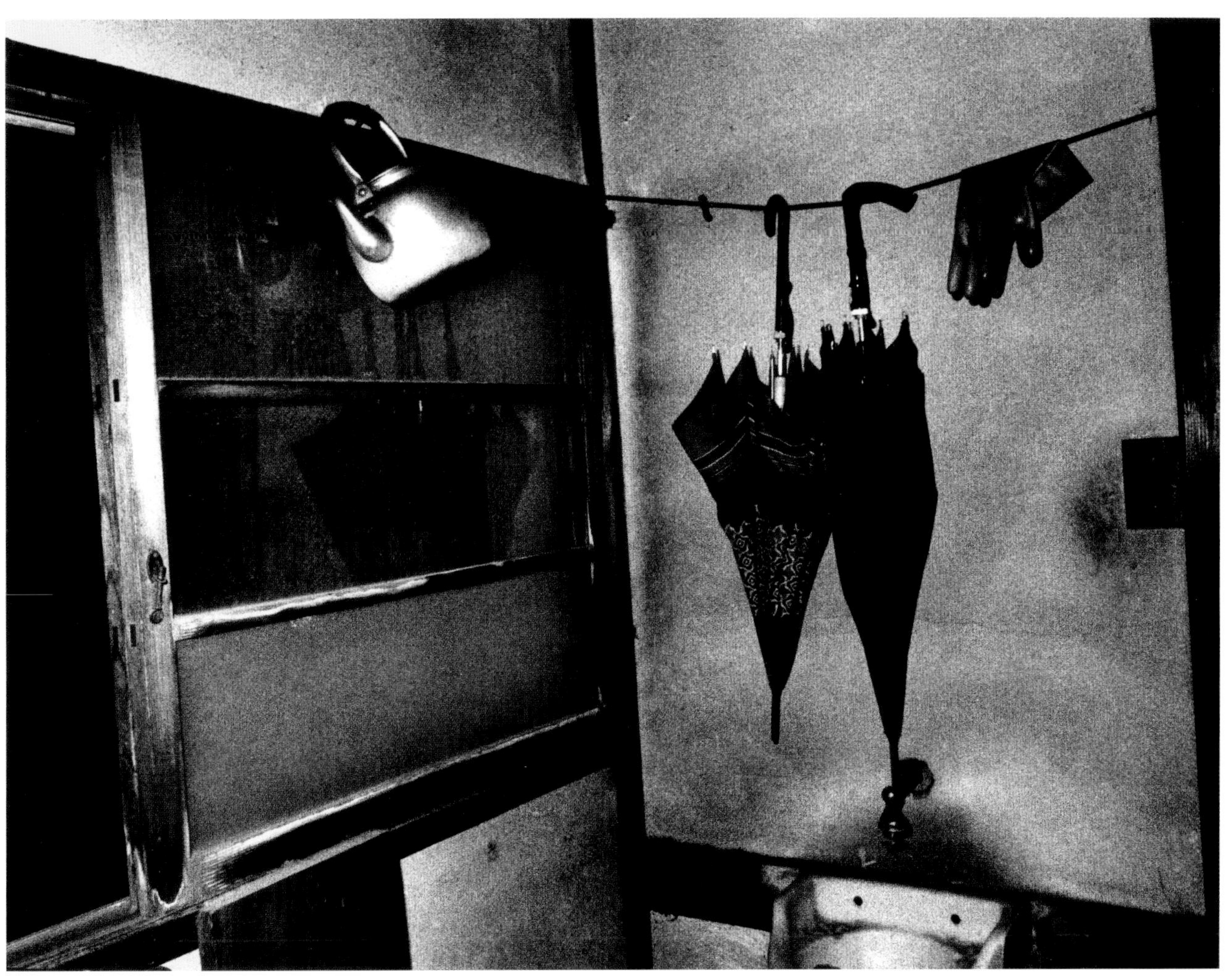

Ishiuchi Miyako. *Apartment #50*, 1977–78.

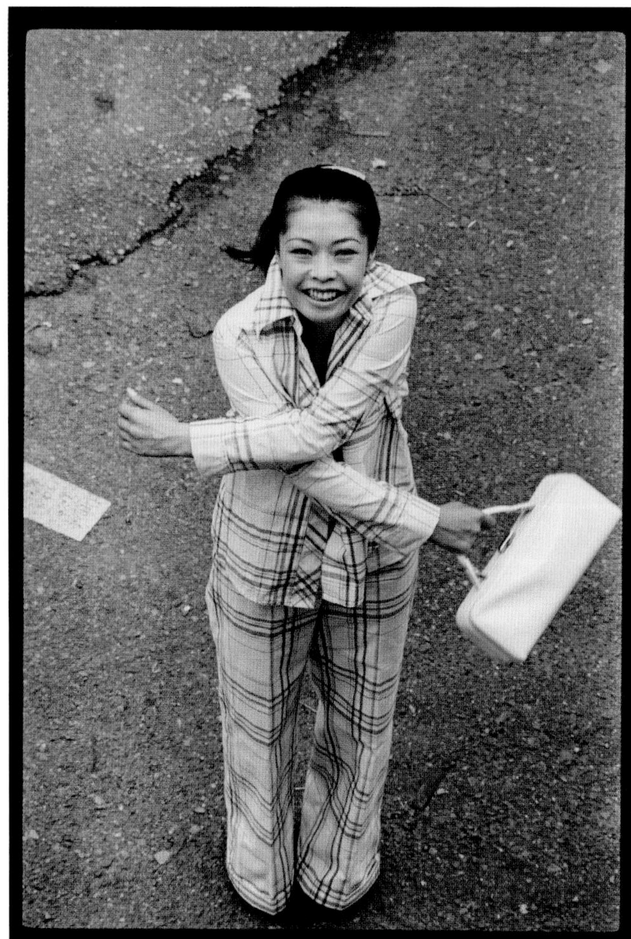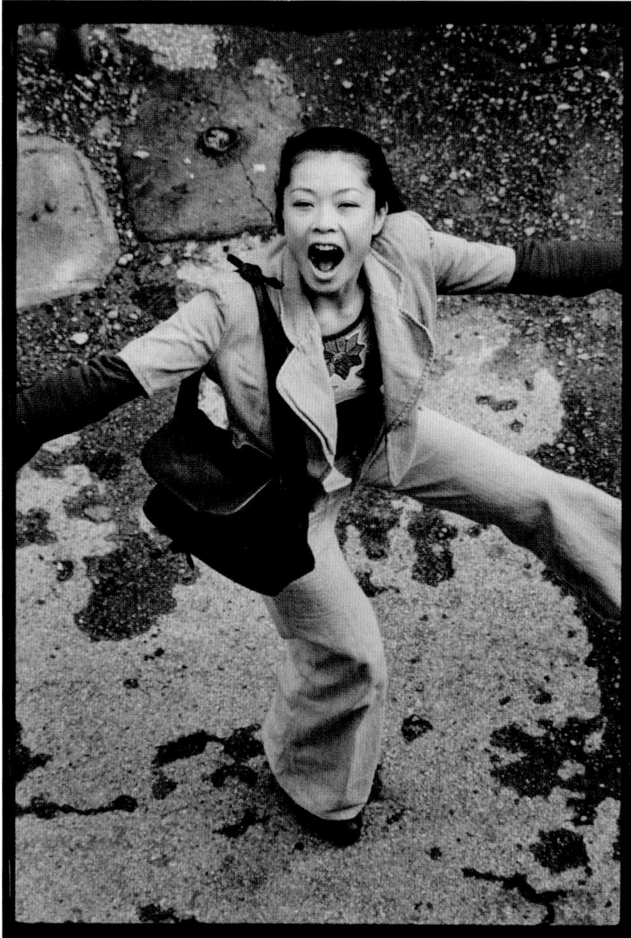

Above and opposite: Fukase Masahisa,
From Window series, 1974.

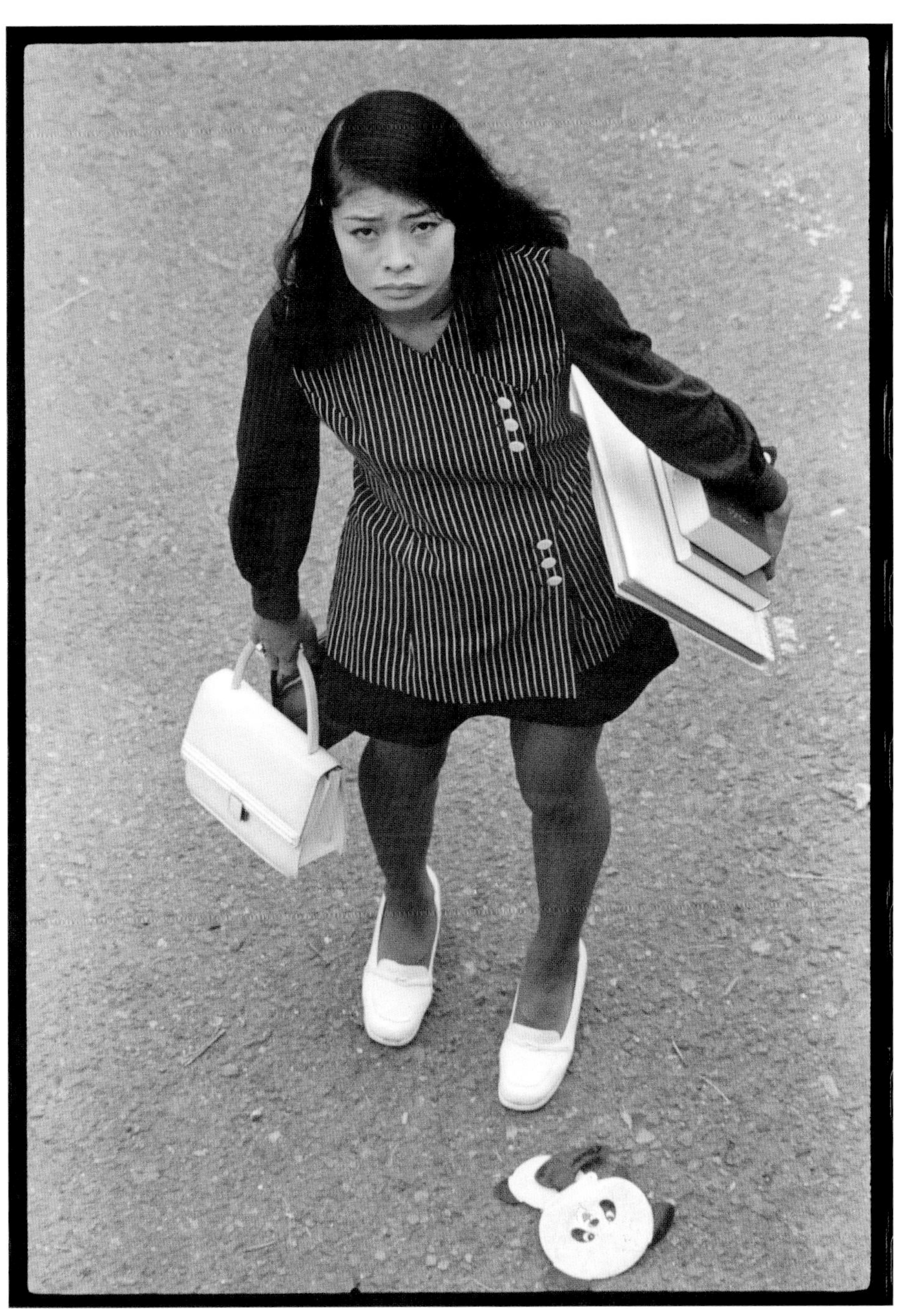

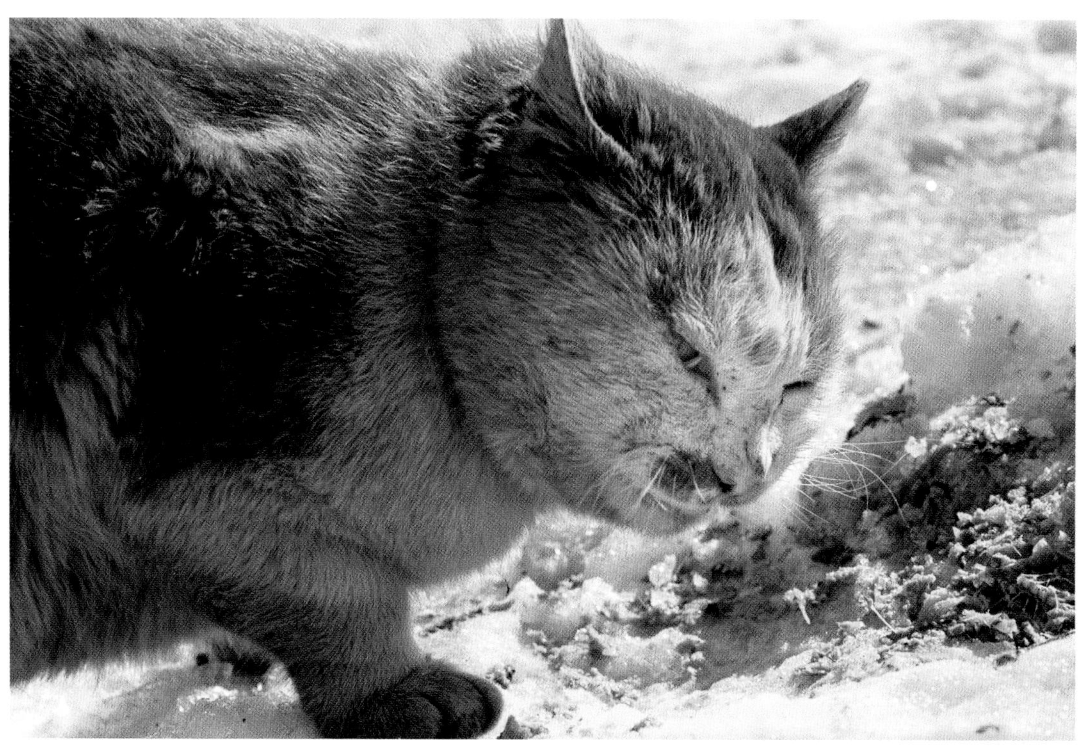

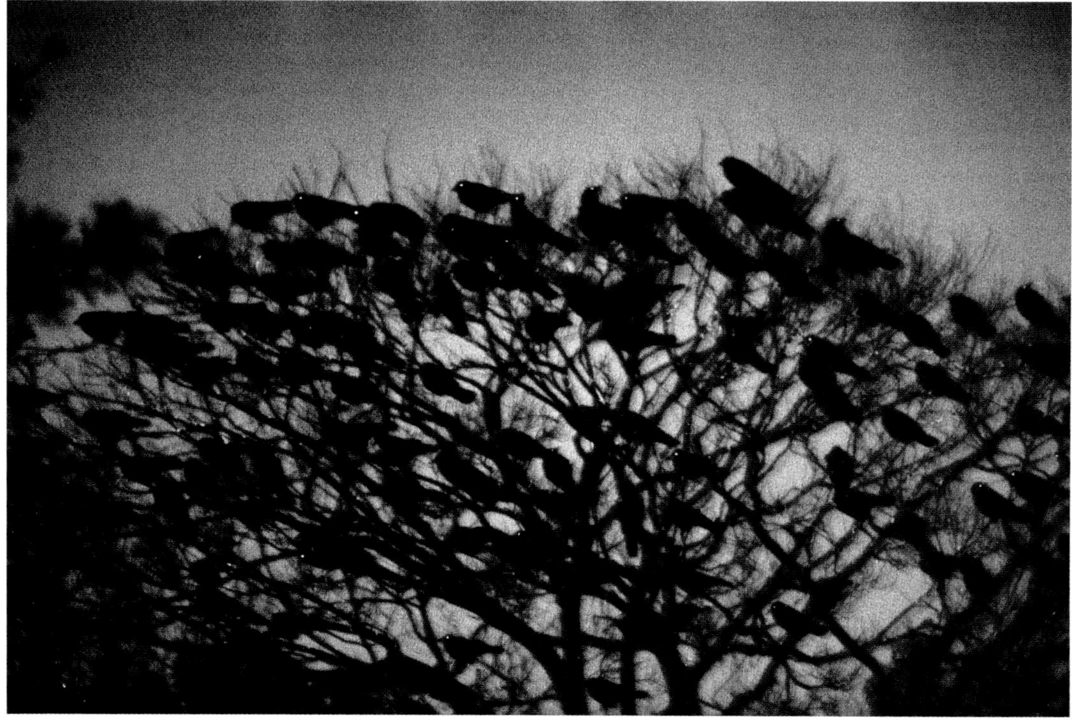

Top: Fukase Masahisa, *Hakodate*, 1975, *Ravens* series.
Above: Fukase Masahisa, *Kanazawa*, 1977, *Ravens* series.

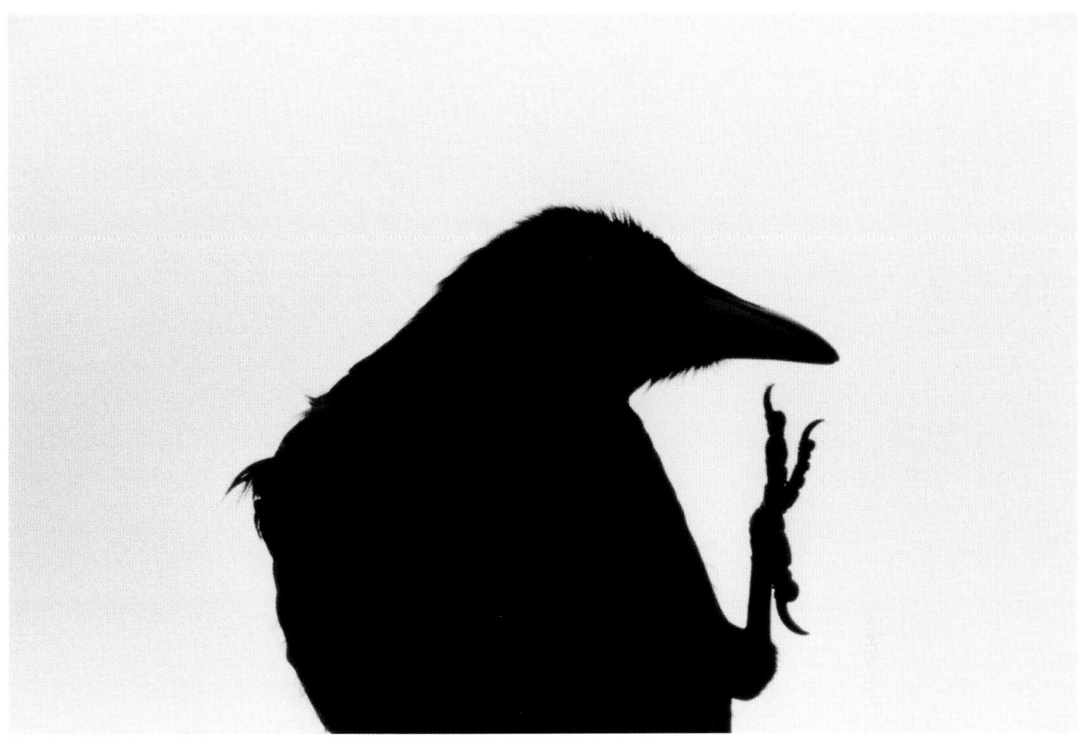

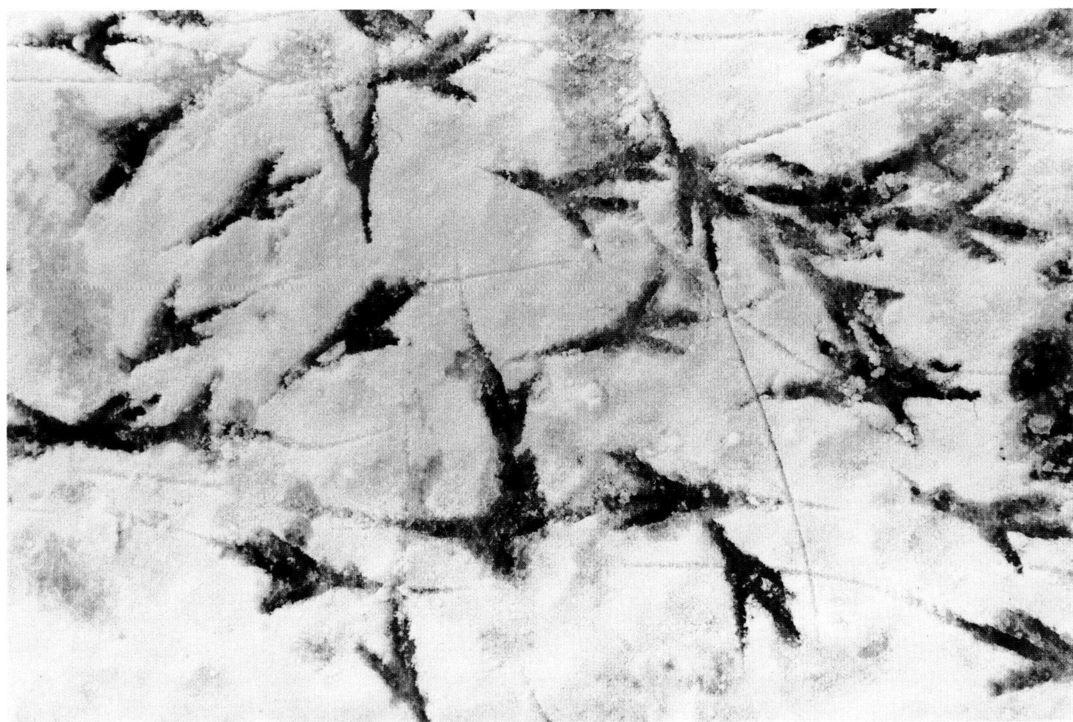

Top: Fukase Masahisa, *Erimo Cape*, 1976, *Ravens* series.
Above: Fukase Masahisa, *Wakkanai*, 1975, *Ravens* series.

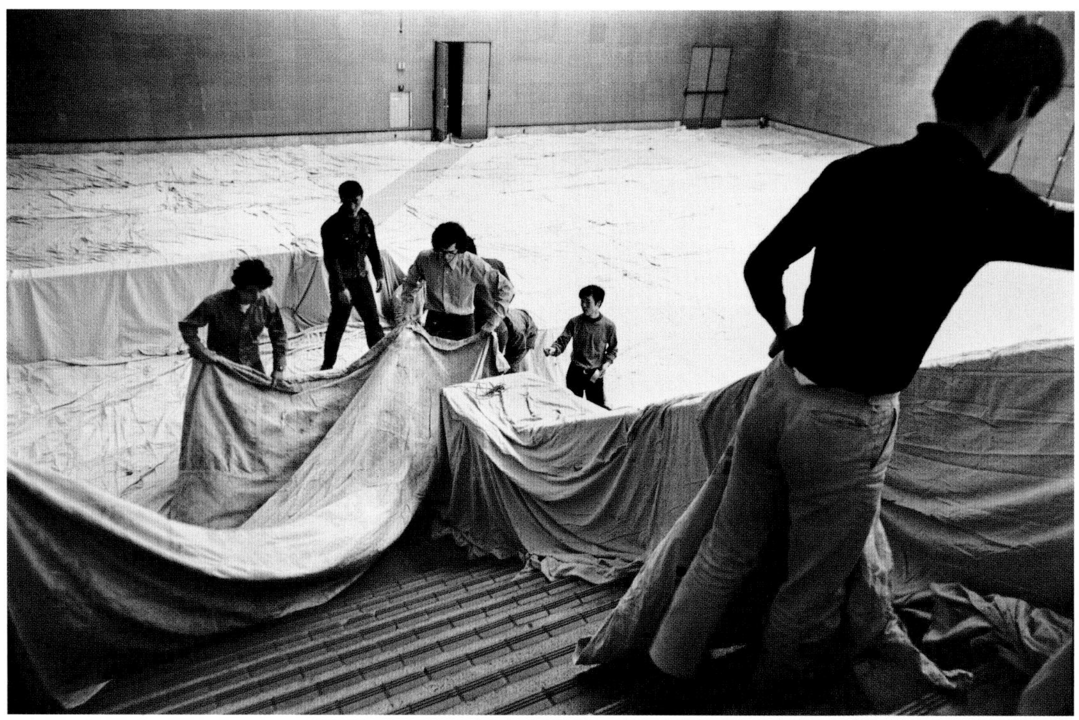

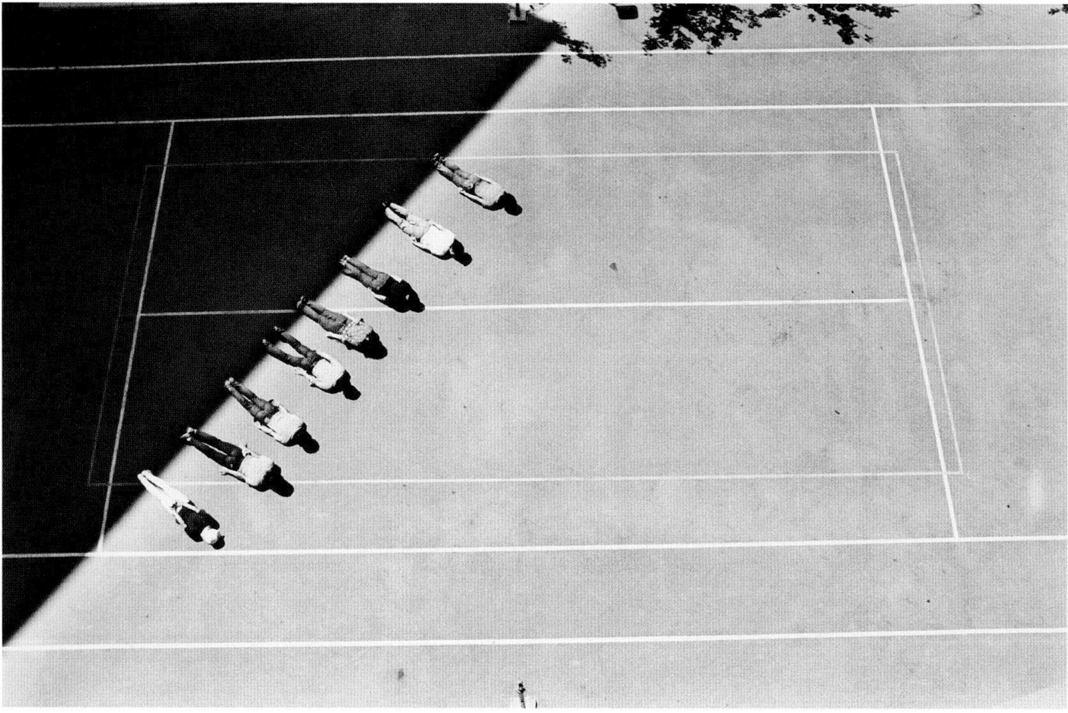

Top: Anzaï Shigeo, *Christo, The 10th Toyko Biennale ' 70 – Between Man and Matter*, 1970.
Above: Anzaï Shigeo, *Group 361°*, 1970.

Lena Fritsch: Let's start at the beginning – what inspired you to take up photography?
Anzaï Shigeo: I was never that interested in the photographs themselves. I am much more interested in the situation in which a photograph was taken. When I began my career I had a deep desire to paint, to produce fine art. I gradually switched over to fine art while holding down a regular job. In those days, the 1960s, the influence of American, British and foreign Pop Art was pretty strong, and that is what young people in Japan were interested in. I was really interested in dadaism, because as a movement it allowed people's preconceptions to change. I produced a number of pieces inspired by Dada; they were not installations back then, but paintings. I entered them into competitions and showed them in exhibitions.

Towards the end of the 1960s, Harald Szeemann held his big exhibition 'When Attitudes Become Form' in Bern, in Switzerland. It was big news among my friends and I. We started thinking that it was important to find a uniquely Japanese form of expression, independent of American Pop Art. I did not know much about Arte Povera at that point. From the end of the 1960s and into the early 1970s, the move towards so-called experimental art, art that took place outside – in spaces other than art galleries – gained a lot of momentum. I got involved in that, and it was exciting, but then an art event would be over and it was very hard to explain to someone in words what happened and what people did. So if, for example, I was with Lee Ufan, he would ask me to take pictures, even if they were just snapshots.

That must have been just before the 1970 Tokyo Biennale?
Yes, maybe in 1969. And then, Japan held the Osaka Expo. For me, 1970 was a year of going around with my camera, with all these exciting people taking part in new experimental work all over the place. In May, Nakahara Yūsuke said that he wanted to hire the Metropolitan Art Museum, in collaboration with the *Mainichi Shinbun* newspaper, to hold an exhibition. Nakahara based quite a lot on Szeemann's exhibition list; I believe most of the same artists were selected, apart from Joseph Beuys. Then there were Japanese artists who suited that form of expression: On Kawara, Matsuzawa Yutaka, Enokura Kōji, Koshimizu Susumu, Narita Katsuhiko and so on. But no one was familiar with the format; Japanese people had no experience of that kind of work being referred to as art. As a result, people did not come to see it. For the newspaper, it was a huge failure.

I used to work in an oil company laboratory, and it just so happened that opposite the laboratory there was another laboratory belonging to an American base, which carried out oil-related tests. I got to talk to the staff there at lunchtimes. That is where I learned to speak English. Nakahara knew about that. He said, 'You have got a camera, and can more or less speak English'. He said that he could not pay much, but would I work for him part time? I knew that there were going to be a lot of people travelling to Tokyo for the Biennale, and I had a feeling that something really interesting was bound to happen, so I agreed. I can see now that the photos I took back then were actually really important photographs, because most of them are photographs of the preparations, or the hunt for materials.

Of course, the Arte Povera artists came, and I met people like Mario Merz and Jannis Kounellis, Giuseppe Penone and Gilberto Zorio. I was able to understand and appreciate their way of looking and of expressing things because of my awareness of young Japanese artists like Koshimizu, Narita and Takamatsu Jiro, and because I had been through a certain amount of training myself. That made for smooth communication.

That really comes across in the photos.
If you want to know why I am still going, it is because I still find it exciting. Maybe it is curiosity.

Three or four years after the Tokyo Biennale, I wondered what all those people were up to, and it just so happened that in 1974 there was a Japanese exhibition at the Louisiana Museum of Modern Art in Denmark. I went to see it with Sekine Nobuo. After the exhibition, I crossed to Dover and went to London to visit Barry Flanagan. That is when I met all the young British artists like Michael Craig-Martin and Bruce McLean, the Nice Style group, as well as Gilbert and George.

What I find interesting is that those first photographs from the Biennale were often of preparation and performance, but looking at photos like of the ones of the Gordon Matta-Clark project, it looks like you put a lot of thought into the best way to take them. They are beautiful photographic compositions, not just documents.
The amount of information provided by a photograph depends on the framing. I instantaneously decide what information in front of the camera is the most important. Then I think really hard about which lens I should use and where I should stand in order to get the maximum amount of information into a single photograph. It is similar to painting a picture. When I make a print in the darkroom, I never do any cropping. But I was originally a chemist, so I do not find the darkroom as boring as some people; printing photographs brings the same joy as painting a picture.

The 9th Paris Youth Biennale took place the year after I came back from the UK. Quite a few people went from Japan, like Nomura Hitoshi. The Japan Foundation spent a lot of money on it, so they asked me to go over and take photos as proof of how that money was being used. They paid me for one month, and covered a one-way flight. That was as much as they had. I managed somehow, and was there for almost three months.

At that time Gordon Matta-Clark was doing really showy, event-type work involving architecture. In Paris, he cut into old buildings with a chainsaw. I met him one day at an art gallery. He had a chainsaw and said he was looking for a building to cut. I said he would not be able to do it [laughs]. Then, two or three days later, I got a call: he said that he had found a good location and would I bring my camera over if he gave me the address? When I got there I could hear the noise, but I did not know where he was. There was a building being demolished next to where the Pompidou Centre was being built, and that was what he was cutting. As I was taking photos a Parisian lady came along and asked what I was doing in such a dirty place. I did my best to explain that it was an art event, but she did not get it. Three years later, in 1978, Matta-Clark died of cancer, but he is popular again today.

What do you like best about the medium of photography?
I have a lot of experience now, so when I find myself in a situation I instinctively know how far away and where to stand. Some artists are nervous, and it is rude to stand too close. It is not about the technical ability to take the photo; it is about understanding the subject. It is a question of sensibility. You need to make a constant effort to select, in your own way, from among the bizarre, the strange and the great. What I tell students is to look at lots of things. Keep looking. You need to train your eyes, your heart and your feelings.

What makes me happiest is when I meet an artist after three years, and even though three years have passed we can just carry on as if nothing has changed. I'm lucky.

That is interesting: the importance of the human side to your photography.
Ultimately, I think that at some level you need to make an effort to think about how you can make yourself a more attractive human being. Unless you think about the personality you were born with, and how to live the life you were made for, you will find it hard to find work. That is the most important thing; that, and the fact that you have to really love your work.

It is clear from your work that you love taking photographs, as well as encountering people and their work.
Yes. When I started taking photographs I often felt that my photos, in terms of sharpness and quality, lagged behind other people's – that they were immature. But that did not bother Lee Ufan. He said that he preferred a blurry photo taken from the right angle to a sharper one taken from the wrong angle. That is what was important to him as an artist.

Sometimes I get invited to photography schools. The students ask how they can get into this kind of work, and I say that I cannot answer that. Because even if I tell you what to do, and you do it, there is no guarantee that it will suit you.

*   This is a shortened version of an interview conducted in Japanese on 3 September 2016, Zeit-Foto Salon, Tokyo. It was translated by Bethan Jones and first published as a Tate Research Resource (8 November 2016) ‹http:// www.tate.org.uk/research/research-centres/ asia/research-resource/interview-shigeo-Anzaï-and-lena-fritsch›

Lena Fritsch: Let's start at the beginning – what inspired you to take up photography?
Tsuchida Hiromi: I was around thirty years old, so I started photography properly quite late. Before, I worked as a normal *sararīman* ('salaryman'). After studying chemistry at university I worked with synthetic dye and pigments at a make-up company, developing new products for around eight years. I had begun to take photographs at university, and joined a photography club. I went to photography school while working at the make-up company. When I turned thirty, I quit my work at the company and started photography full time.

From an early age I liked two-dimensional images, and was quite good at drawing and painting. At university I also participated in a contemporary art club – we looked at paintings by Pollock and painted ourselves; it was the 1960s, so it had to be abstract art, otherwise it was not considered an image [laughs]. So the aspiration to do something to express myself was already there – it seems to be part of me as a person.

At the time were you interested in or inspired by any photographers?
I was around twenty-five years old when I went to the photography school, and I really liked Robert Frank's work, particularly *The Americans*. It is such a strong work. A little later, I saw Hosoe Eikoh's *Ordeal by Roses (Barakei)* [p. 58].

Oh, I like that series too.
It is a wonder, isn't it? Hosoe created it when he was only thirty years old; there are not many wonderful works like that. Of course, Mishima Yukio's directing played an important part in the series as well. I was definitely fascinated by that work.

In 1976 you published your first photobook: *Zokushin* [p. 125]. Could you tell me about these photographs?
The term *zokushin* does not exist in Japanese, you would not find it in any dictionary: 'common' combined with 'God'. When I turned thirty and became an independent photographer, I felt I should look more closely at my cultural roots. I grew up in the countryside: my mother farmed and my father worked for the national railways. I helped out at the farm and we had goats, chicken, cats [laughs]. It was a small village, and there were small local festivals; that is how I grew up, and these local folklore customs are part of my roots. Photography is a very temporal medium, and I felt that when starting it, I should first look back at my own local culture properly. Japanese culture is ultimately based on farming, and I wanted to look at all the local festivals in different parts of the country, for example in places that are seen as holy, such as at the Ise Shrine. I photographed the people who came to the festivals to enjoy themselves. One day, a friend suggested I published the photographs in a book. I compiled them and titled the book *Zokushin*, but I could have also titled it 'common people', who simply live their lives.

A main theme in your work is Hiroshima [pp. 126–27]. You have made different photographic series concerned with traces of the atomic bombing of Hiroshima since the late 1970s. What was the first trigger to do something about Hiroshima?
The war ended when I was five years old and although I don't remember hearing about Hiroshima at the time – perhaps because we were far away in the countryside – I do remember hearing that something terrible had happened and the war had ended. I also remember the air raids, and from the top of a mountain I once saw a town burning – the sky was bright red and I was scared. That is my generation. Hiroshima was such a big incident of the 20th century, showing how 20th-century technology was misused, how humans decided to extinguish other humans. It affected my generation; I wanted to document it and felt I *had* to document it.

I was in my late thirties, and it was more than thirty years after the end of the Second World War – both Japan and Hiroshima were well restored. Even if you go to Hiroshima, you don't see any traces – to me as a photographer, this aspect of not seeing anything (a very non-photographic element) was of great interest. How should I show this in photographs? I found that stimulating.

I find this aspect of non-visibility interesting, particularly in the photo-historical context of Hiroshima, as there was already a history of (quite different) Hiroshima photos when you began your series.
Yes, for example the photographs by Dōmon Ken [p. 36]. There were a number of different, reportage-like works – however, the reality did not really come across. There was a problem of discrimination against the *hibakusha* (explosion victims) and many did not want to be recognized in photographs. To me, it was an important fact that they were still discriminated against, thirty years after the end of the war. I took photographs of their backs, or the area around their house, or the chair that the person sat on in a café. I personally feel sad that they are discriminated against, and that we can't share their sadness; I did not want to create a reportage that gave the impression that I felt what they feel. I therefore chose not to show them

in a dramatic way. I also did not want to include myself as a photographer in the photographs, and wondered how I could avoid showing my personality. This was very important to me. In *Zokushin* I express myself, and I started to work on *Hiroshima* right after – I really had to do something completely different.

The photographs of the families in Hiroshima, inside the houses, convey an everyday atmosphere; they are very different to the dynamic in the *Zokushin* series.
I tried to exclude any artistic consciousness when taking the Hiroshima photographs: in these early photographs of the *hibakusha*, in the city photographs and also later, in the *Hiroshima Collection* photographs of the museum objects. I did not want the photographs to become 'the Hiroshima photos that Tsuchida Hiromi took'. I wanted to hide myself and that applies to all of my Hiroshima series.

I remember you once told me that for the *Hiroshima Collection* photographs [p. 126], you wanted to create images that are reminiscent of supermarket pamphlets, placing the objects on a neutral white background, linking the images to an everyday life aesthetic that the viewers are familiar with.
Yes, I wanted to create basic images that don't recall any other images.

Your *Zokushin* and Hiroshima photographs are all monochrome series. When did you begin to take colour photographs? Your Berlin photos are partly in colour.
That must have been in the early 1990s. Until then, in the 1960s, 1970s or 1980s, if you wanted to show a serious reality, you would not use colour photography. It was more associated with family album photos or travel photos. But then, as of the late 1980s and early 1990s, monochrome photography began to feel more restricted, narrow. This might also be connected to TV: we all watch images in colour now, we all see the world in colour. I might do projects in black and white in the future – but at the moment, I take colour photographs: for example, my Israel photographs that I have been taking since 2005, or my Fukushima photographs.

In around 1983, I went to Berlin for the first time [p. 125] because I wanted to see the wall and take photographs of it once. A wall dividing the city – it felt like seeing politics, it was extreme. I wanted to go back regularly and take more photographs of the wall. I was still thinking about how to best approach the subject when, one day, the wall fell. It all happened very fast. In 1999, to celebrate the ten-year anniversary, there were festivals and I wondered what would still be visible. Therefore, I went back to Berlin.

In 1999, you could still see the differences between East and West Berlin quite strongly, I think. I also remember how the city felt like a big building site.
You could tell if a person was from East or West Berlin by looking at the clothes. Parts of the wall were also still visible. But I was also interested in the areas where it was not so obvious. In 2009, I went back to Berlin again to see how much less visible it has become – it almost felt like an illusion that there used to be a wall and such politics.

This aspect of invisibility is probably something that interests you in Fukushima as well?
Yes, definitely. In Fukushima as well as in Hiroshima. And I have taken photographs in Jerusalem: Hiroshima, Berlin, Jerusalem (with the wall there) could be interesting, I think.

Around two months after the tsunami, I started going to Fukushima. I didn't want to take any photogenic photographs; everybody already took those photographs. Everybody had seen images of the tsunami on TV as well, so instead I started taking photographs of a forest and the seasons there. For example, I saw a nice tree and took a photograph of it. When I returned the next time, the tree had died. I don't know if these photographs can predict Fukushima, but it feels as if humans have betrayed nature; nature and humans have become alienated. In Japanese culture, humans live within nature and carry nature inside of them. They used to have a balanced relationship with nature. However, if you look at Fukushima, humans now have to leave, withdraw...I think there is a serious problem in the relationship between nature and humans; that's what I want to express. Going to the forest is like a pilgrimage; I have gone a few times every year since 2011. I'm probably quite contaminated now [laughs].

By taking photographs of Fukushima, as well as of Hiroshima and Berlin, I continue to track places after a big incident. By showing how things are now, I seek to think about the problems of the past.

What do you like best about photography?
Photography is probably a good way to face the present. In order to see the present, you move your own body to a particular place: this physicality is interesting. At the same time, photography can expose the problems of the past. I think it provides us with useful material to think about the problems of the past and the present, and about the future. I'm interested in this present, wondering what times we live in, or who I am.

You will probably soon be able to take photographs without even going to the place, thinking about advances in the internet and digital images. Perhaps we are at a borderline: physicality and its relationship with photography might change a lot in the future. We have come from the 20th century to the 21st – there are many big changes, not just in photography...

*   This is a shortened version of an interview conducted in Japanese on 30 August 2016, at Tsuchida Hiromi's office, Tokyo.

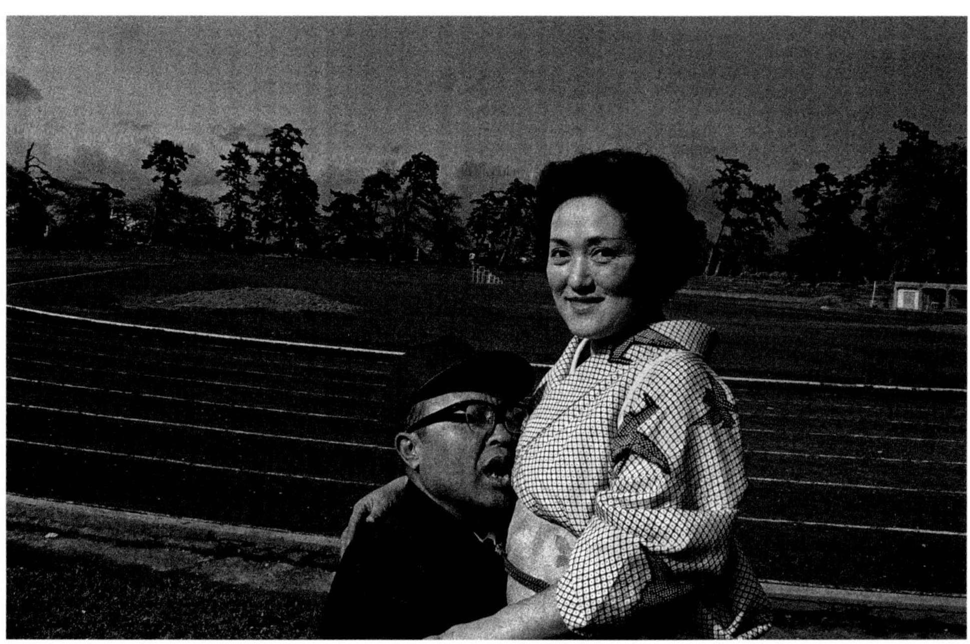

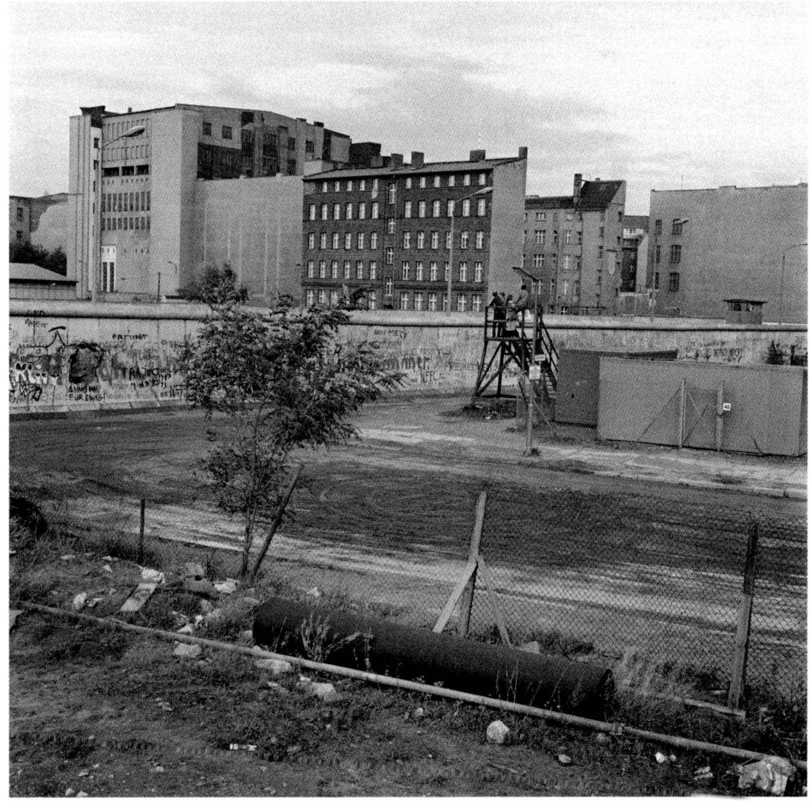

Above: Tsuchida Hiromi, *Hirosaki, Aomori Prefecture*, 1972, *Zokushin* series.
Right: Tsuchida Hiromi, *Berlin*, 1983.

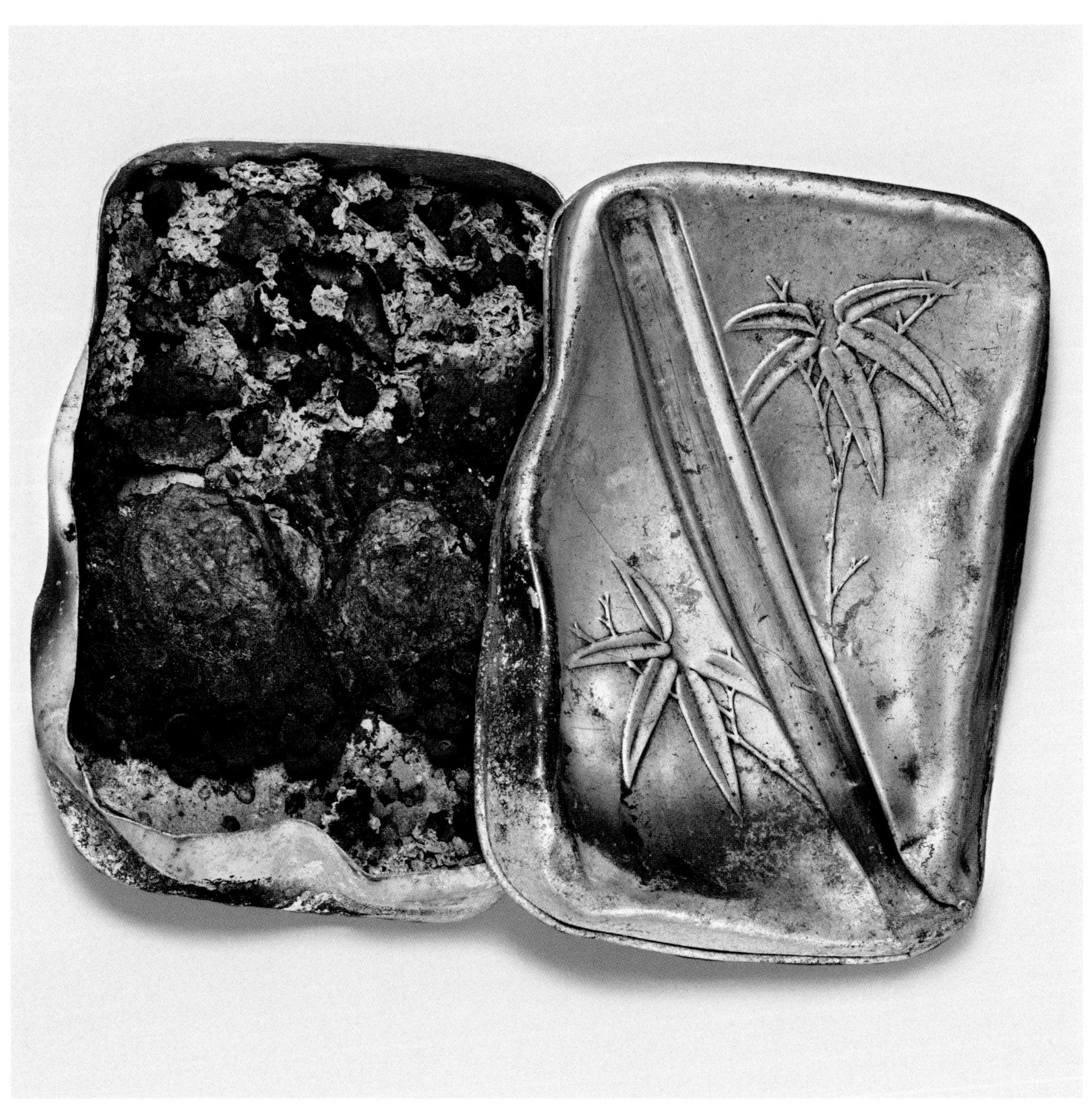

Tsuchida Hiromi, *Lunch Box*, 1982–95,
Hiroshima Collection series.

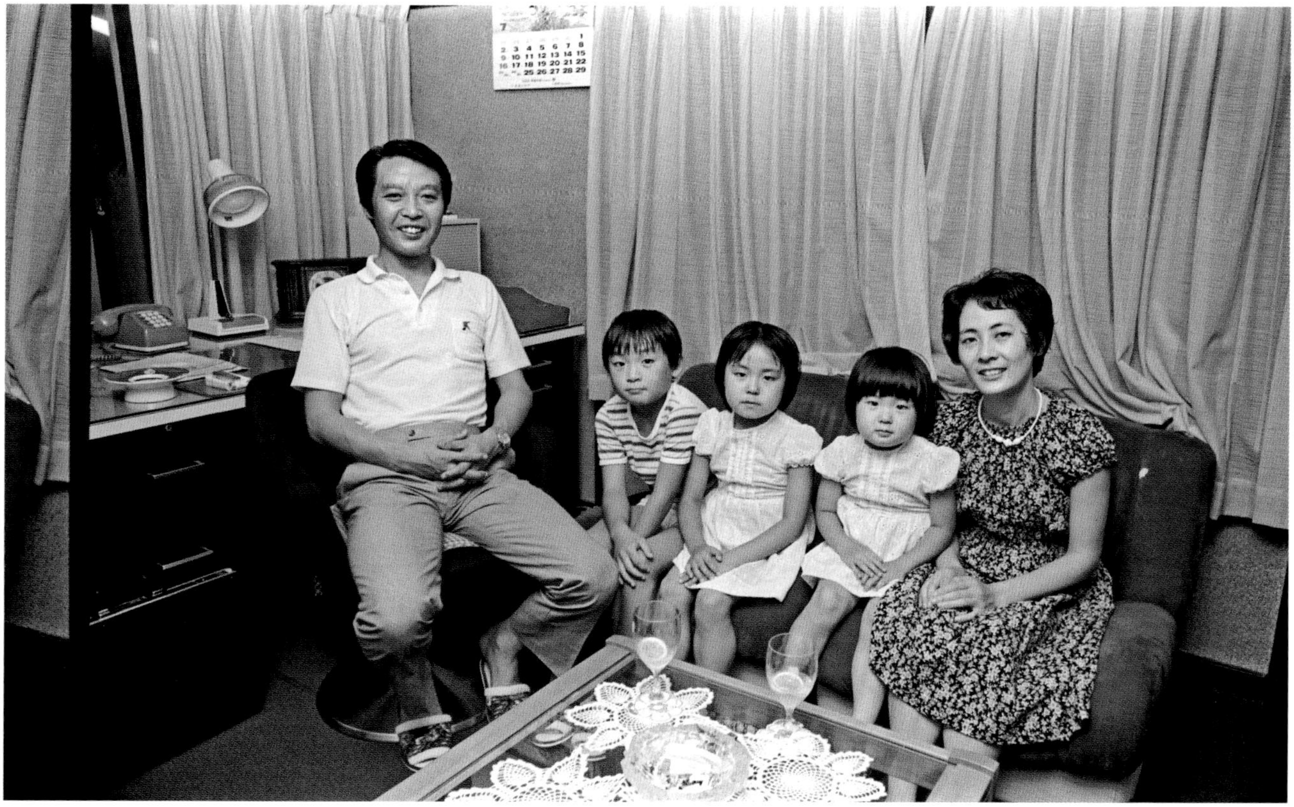

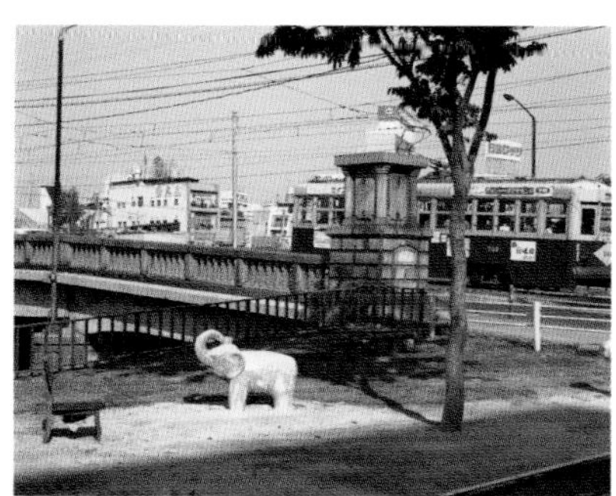
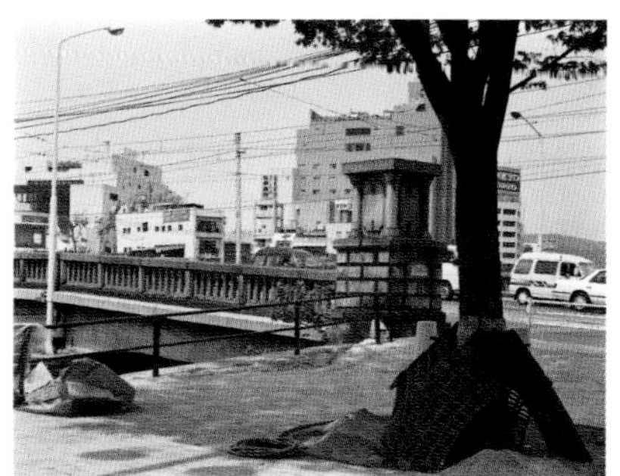
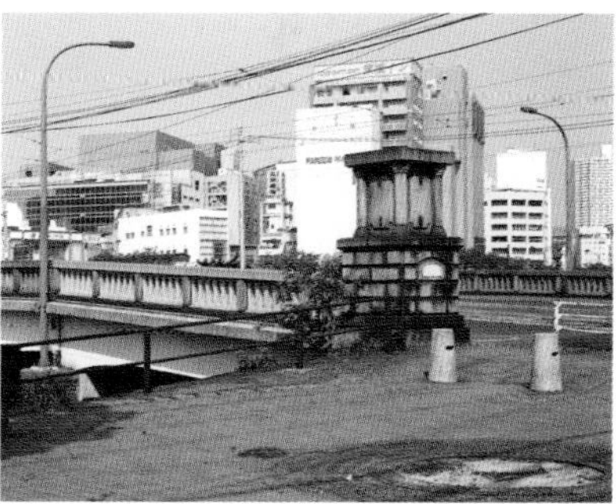

Top: Tsuchida Hiromi, *Mr. Yasuo Fujita, age: 38; occupation: manager; family: wife and three children, age: 5 (at the time); at home (1,500 meters from the hypocenter); elder sister and elder brother died; grandmother, parents, and older sister injured,* 1976, *Hiroshima* series.
Above: Tsuchida Hiromi, *Kojin Bridge 1,800 meters from the hypocenter,* 1979, *Hiroshima Monument* series.

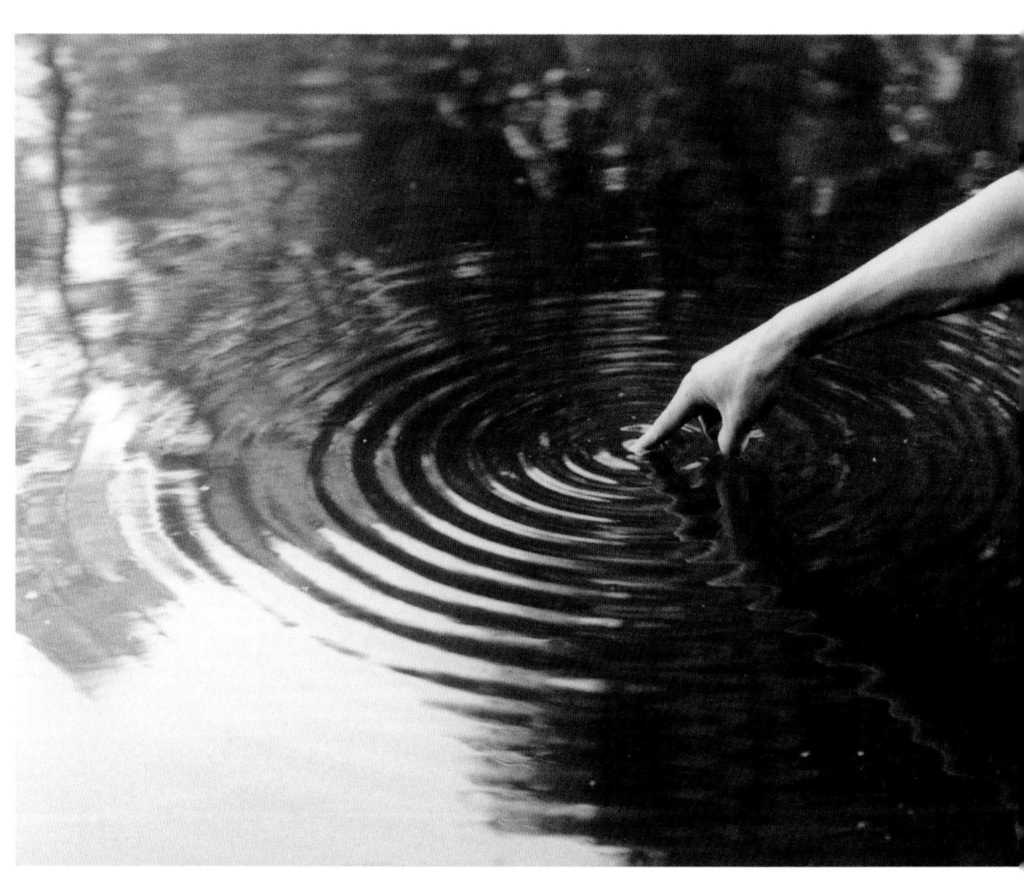

Uematsu Keiji, *Wave Motion I,* 1976.

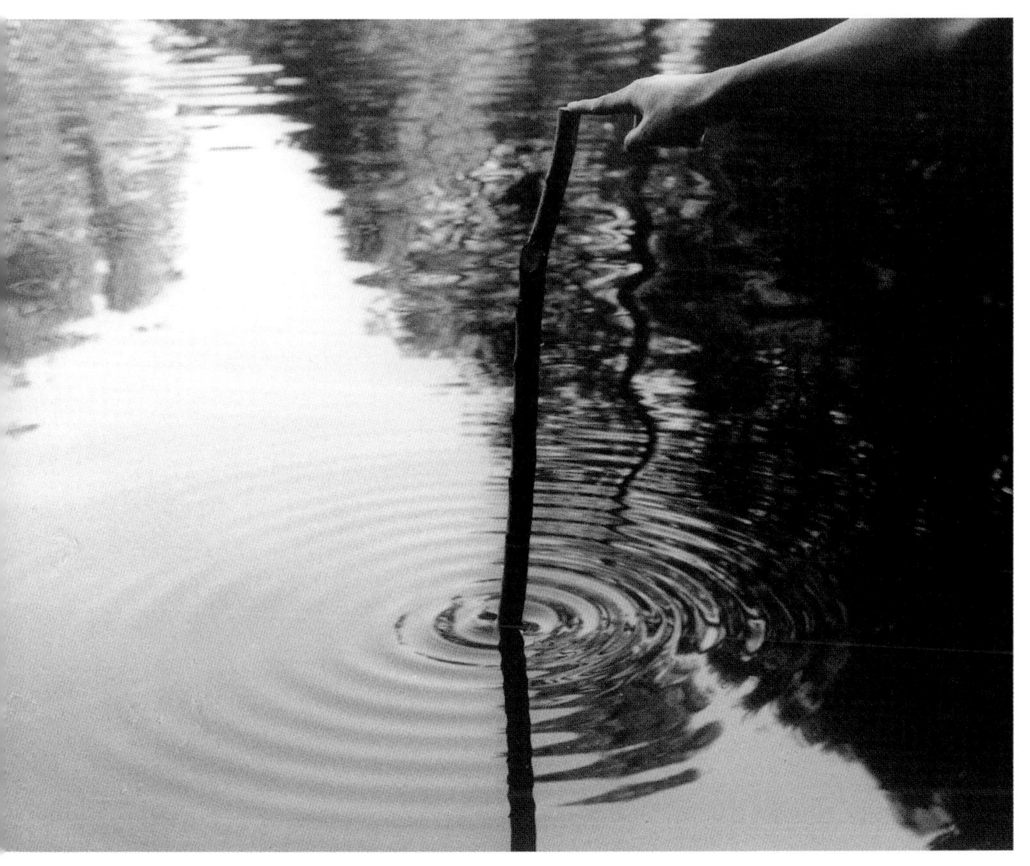

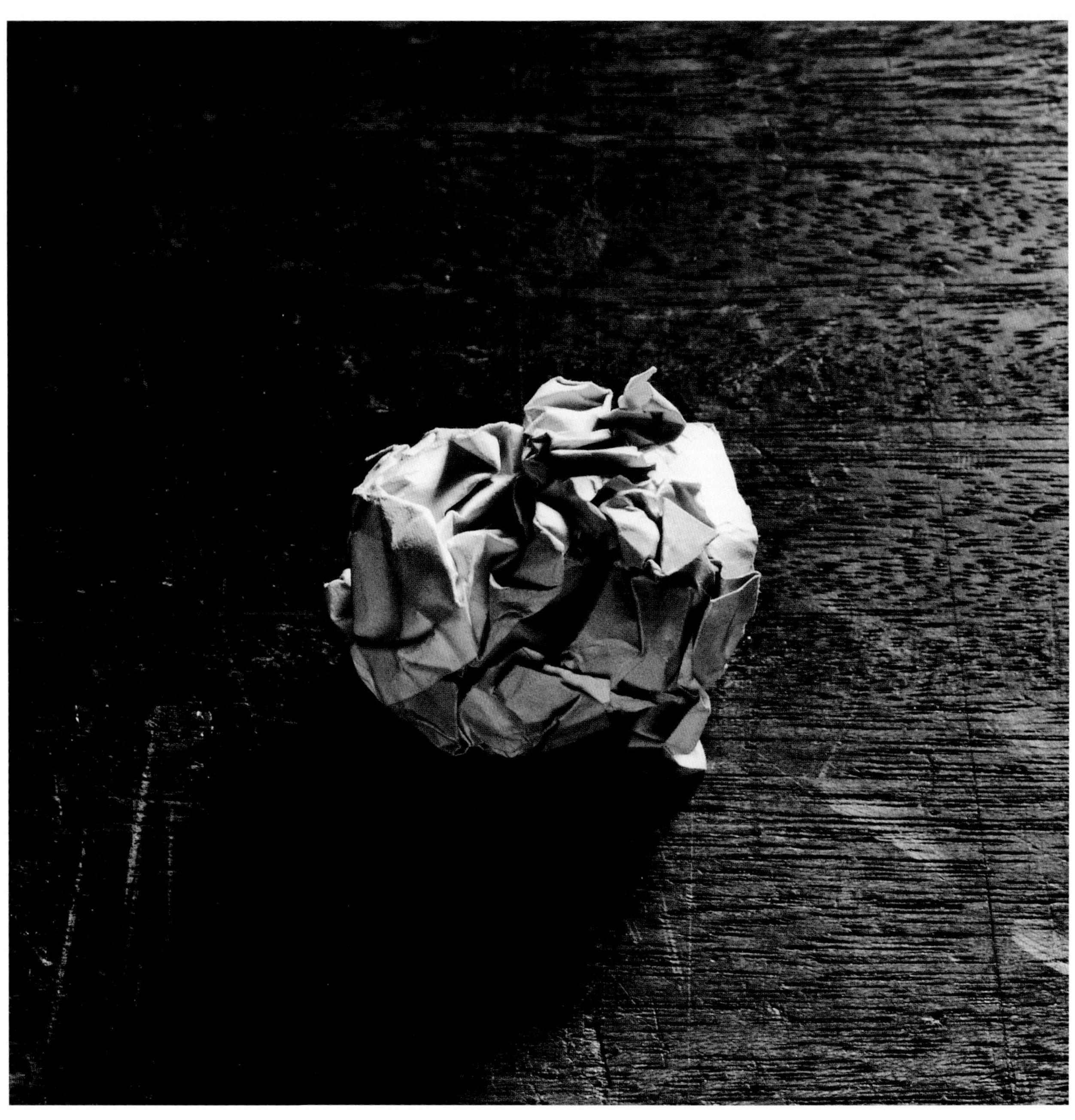

Ōtsuji Kiyoji, *Discarded Crumpled Paper*, 1975.

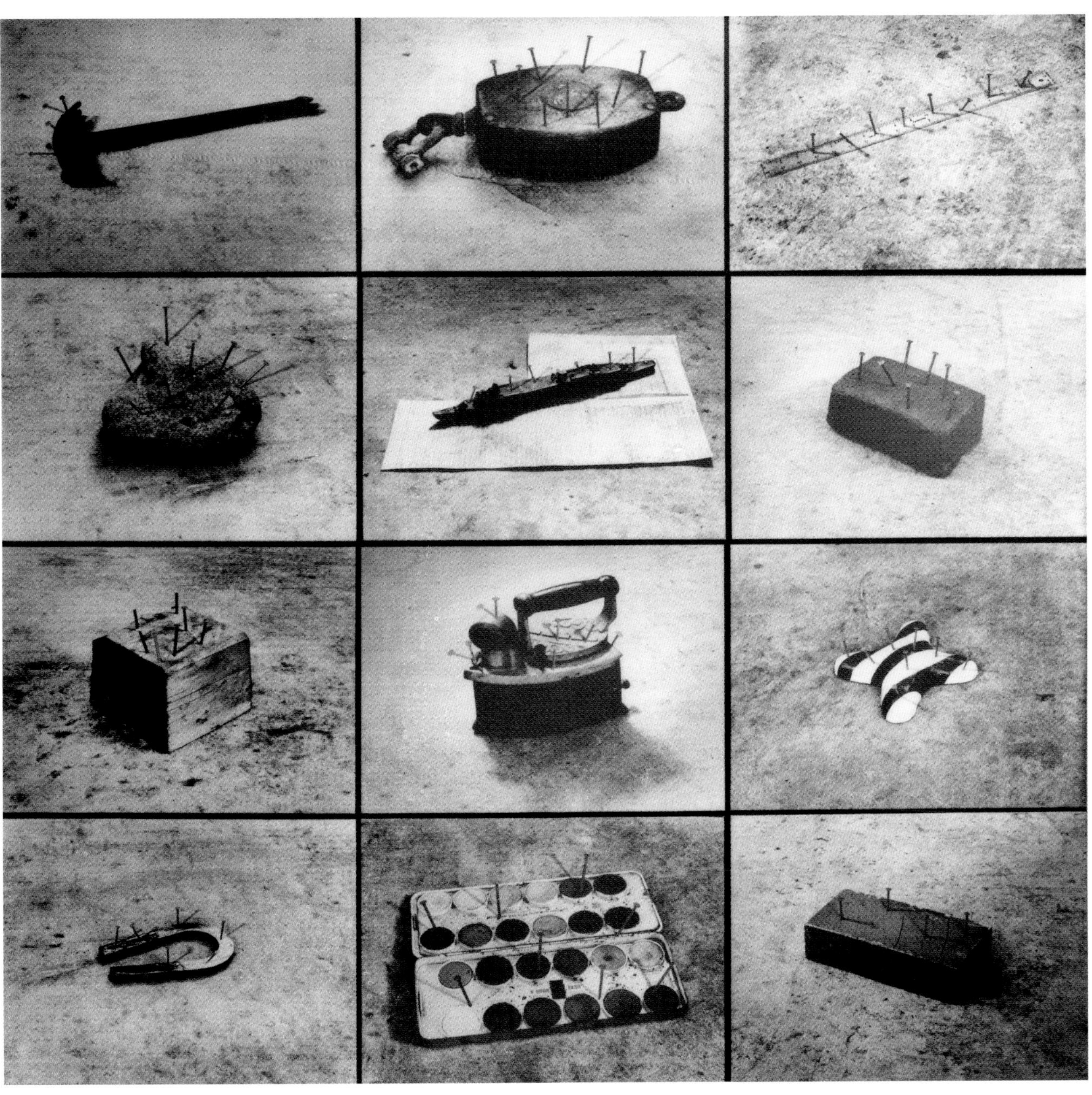

Wakae Kanji, *Seeing and Looking: Nails,* 1974.

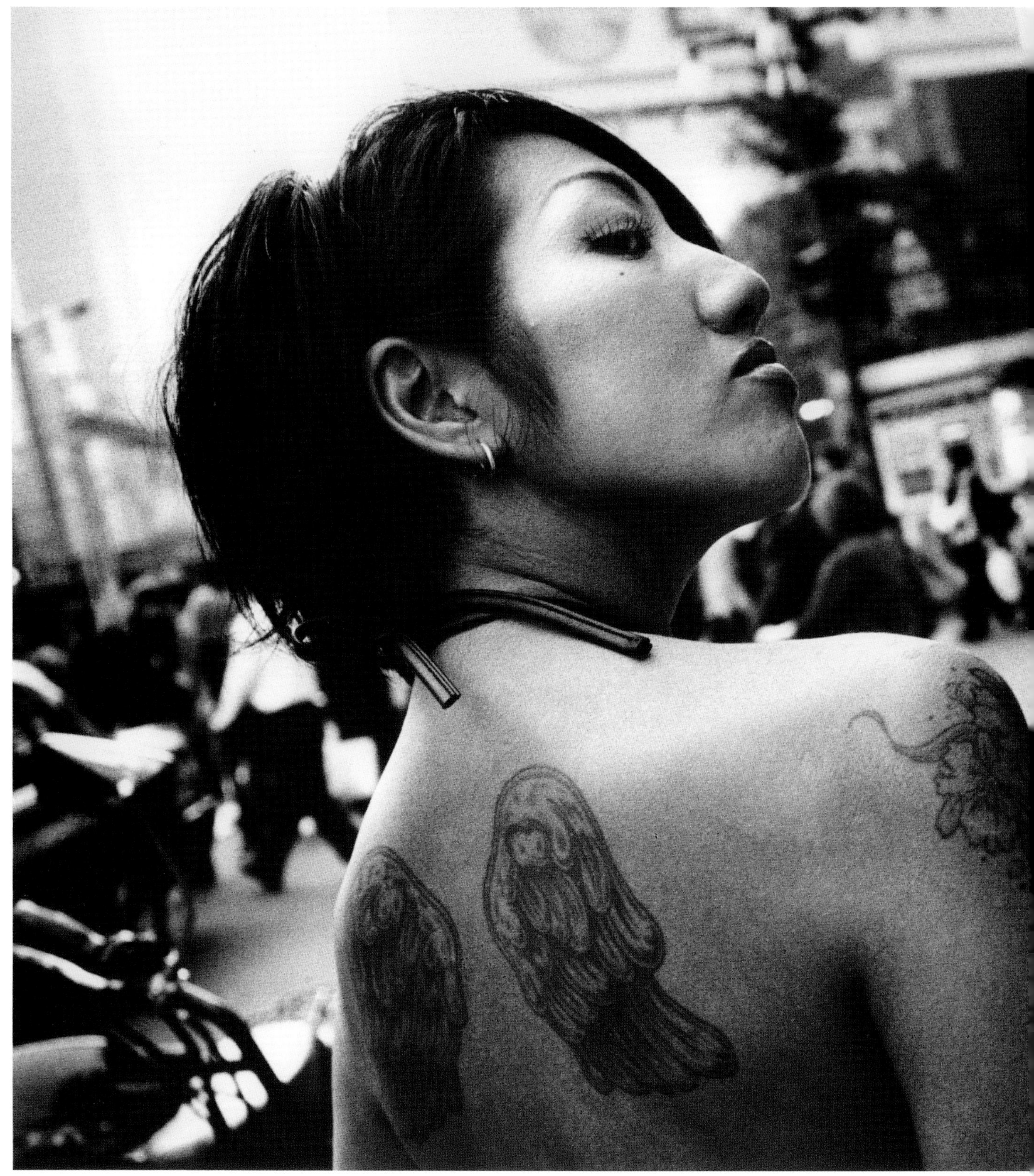

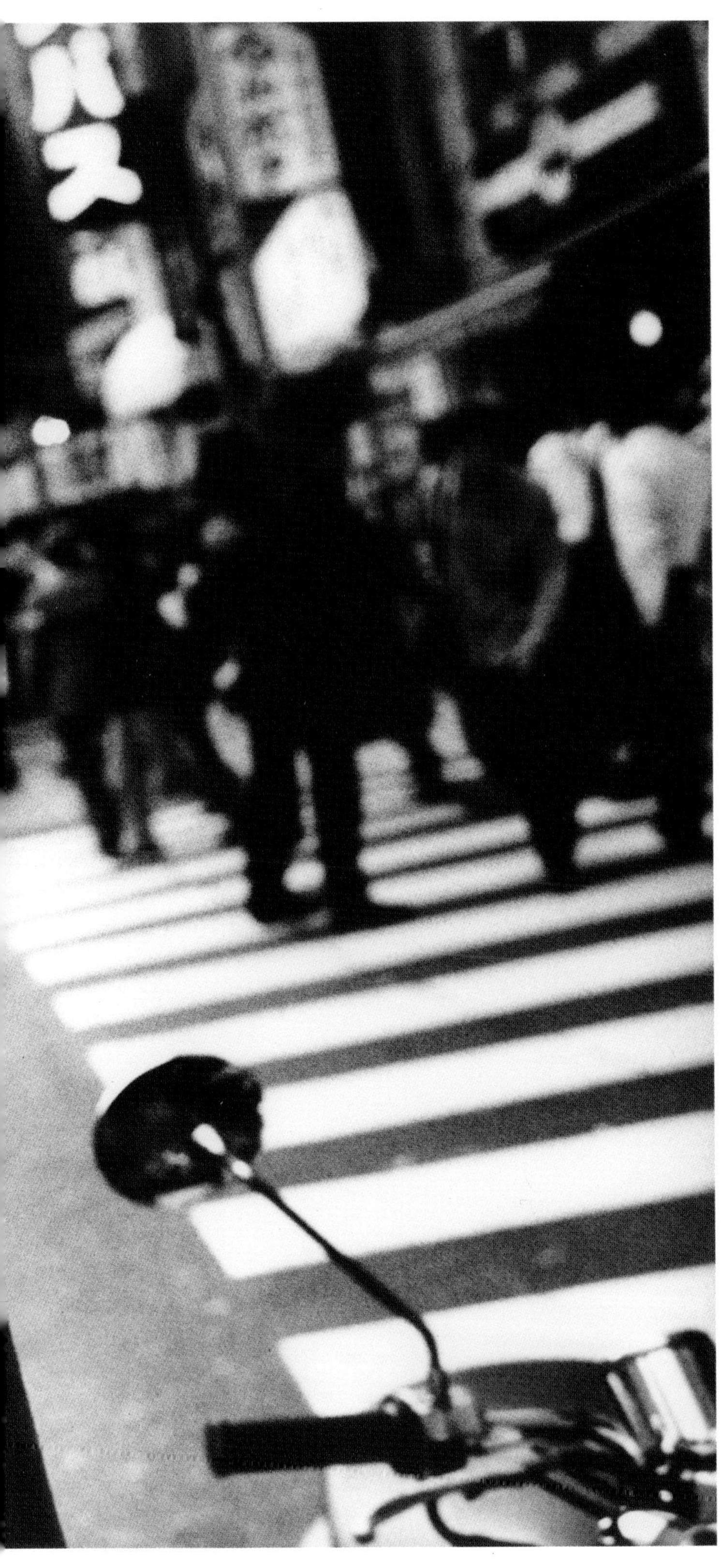

Moriyama Daidō, *Shinjuku*, 2002.

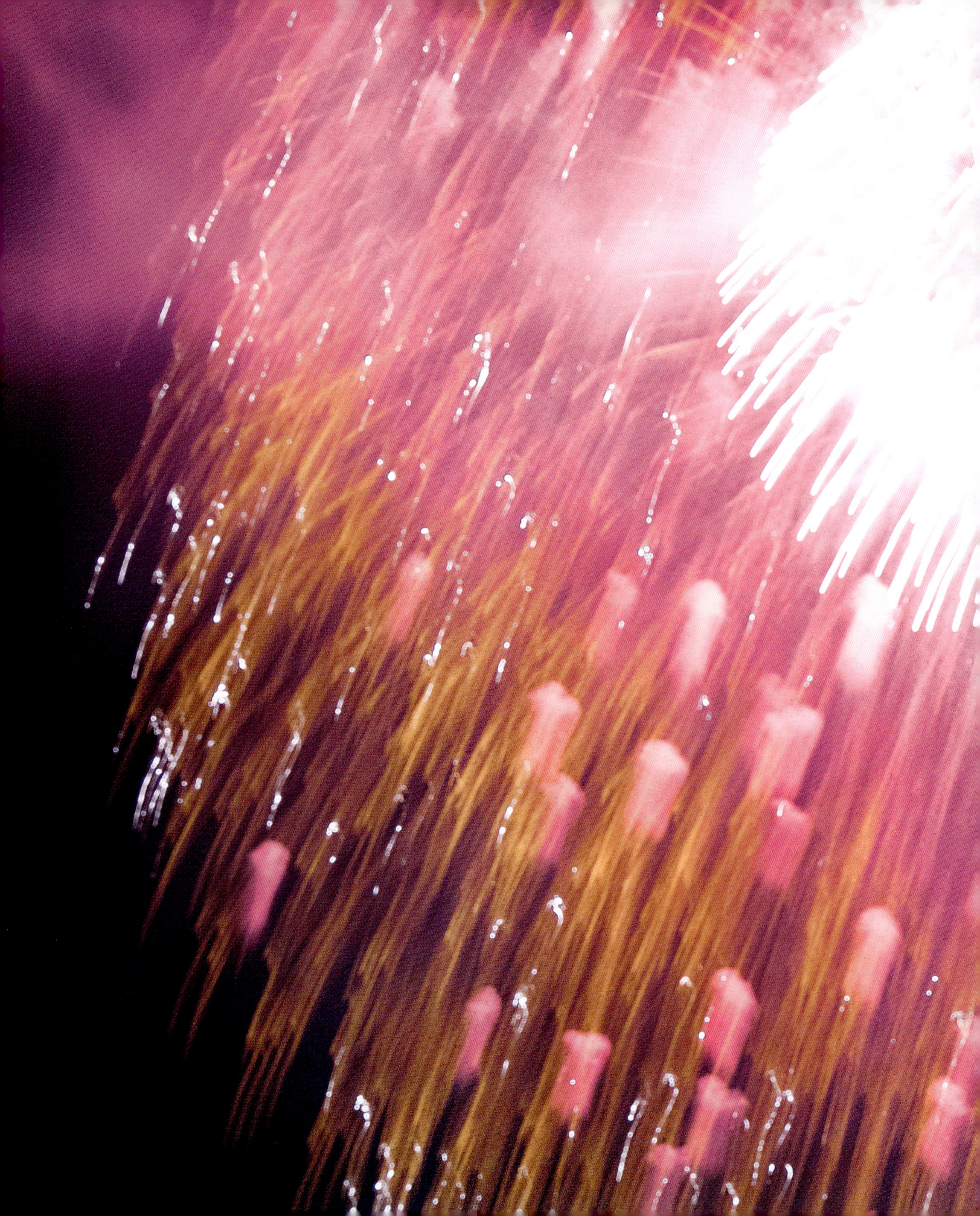

IV

GIRLS' PHOTOGRAPHY

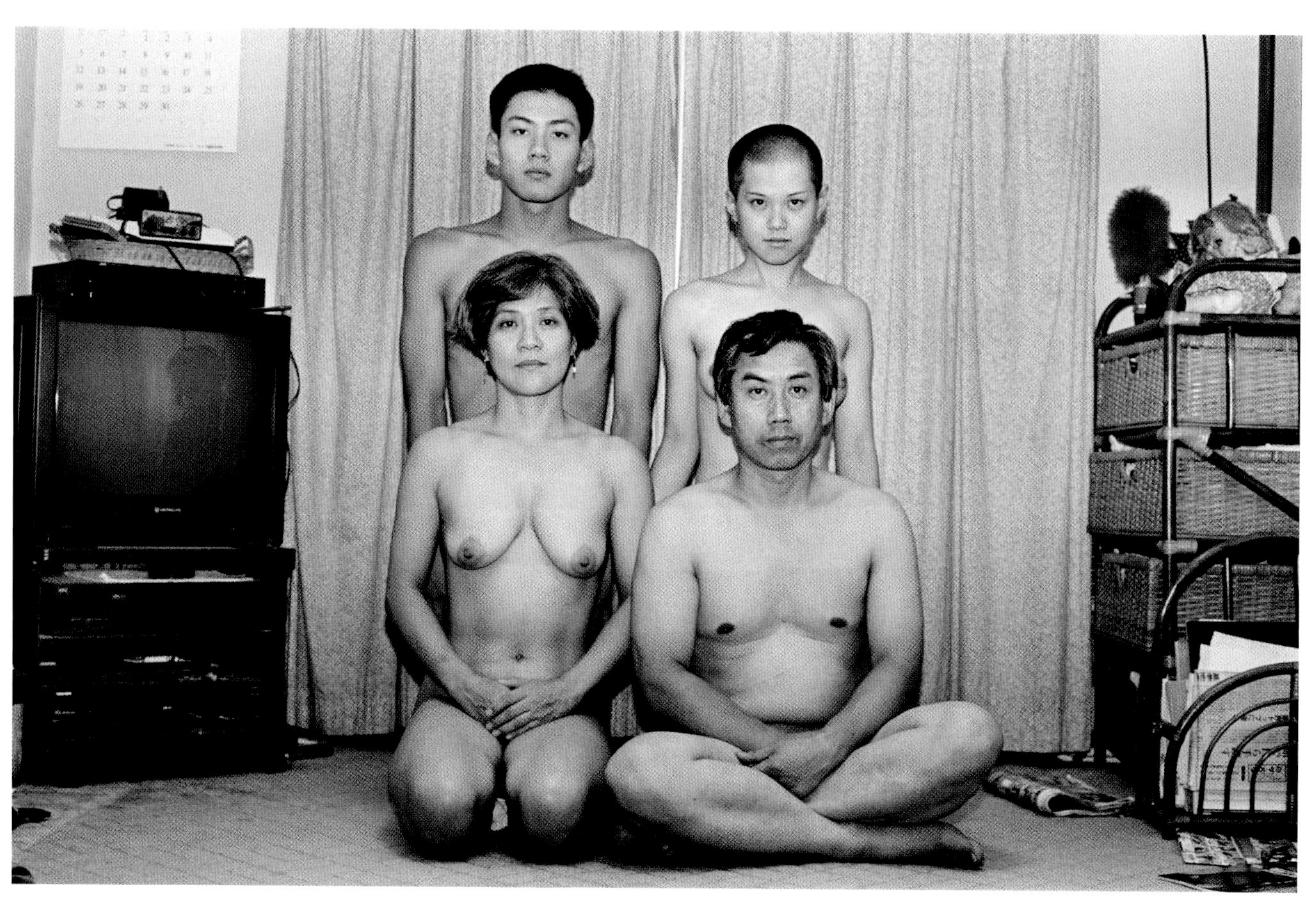

Previous spread: detail from Ninagawa
Mika, *Light of*, 2015.
Above: Nagashima Yurie, *Self-Portrait
(Family #26)*, 1993.

Photography in Japan was always male-dominated: male photographers, male camera fans, male gallerists, male critics. In the 1990s, it became a social activity among teenage girls. They began to document their lives with compact 35mm cameras, and to spend time in 'print club' (*purikura*) photo booths, decorating photographs of themselves with hearts, cute messages and stars, and collecting and swapping the sticker images. These teenage girls' focus on the cute (*kawaii*) and childlike has links with 1990s popular culture, exemplified by the Hello Kitty cat.

Against this background, young women photographers emerged to widespread public and critical attention, with self-portraits, snapshots of their everyday lives and intimate, domestic images. Iizawa Kōtarō has written about their use of photography 'for self-identification'.[49] Their work prompted the term 'girls' photographs' (*onnanoko shashin*). Similar to Nan Goldin or Araki Nobuyoshi, whose works were available in photobooks and exhibitions in the 1990s, the girls' photographs had a diaristic quality. Araki, whose photography has always been closely intertwined with his personal life, was a juror in various competitions and supported the trend. The best-known photographers associated with 'girls' photography' are Hiromix (b. 1976), Nagashima Yurie (b. 1973) and Ninagawa Mika (b. 1972). Their work was promoted by awards, magazines, exhibitions and TV programmes. In 2001, they shared the Kimura Ihei Award.

Nagashima Yurie first received attention when she was awarded the Parco Prize for emerging artists at the 1993 'Tokyo Urbanart 2' exhibition, for a series of black and white self-portraits that she took with her family, naked (opposite). The protagonists are comfortably naked, pursuing their daily routines, rather than 'nude'. The works are concerned with ideas of family, gender and the female body.

Nagashima's *Tank Girl* (1994) typifies her strong, direct photographic language: she faces the camera with a cigarette in her mouth and a provocative look, reflecting punk culture and questioning rigid ideas of femininity (p. 145).

Hiromix, one of Nagashima's contemporaries, rose to prominence in 1995 when she won the 11th New Cosmos of Photography contest, sponsored by Canon. Her photos, compiled in the *Seventeen Girl Days* album, offered a light-hearted look into her life as a photogenic schoolgirl who loved retro images and 1960s fashion. In 1996 she published the photobook *Girls Blue*, followed by *Hiromix* two years later. Her photographs presented a teenager's perspective, in contrast with the images that were published and exhibited by Japanese photographers at the time, who were mostly older men. Hiromix's self-portraits were often taken with her hand holding the camera outstretched in front of her (pp. 148–49); they can be seen as precursors of today's 'selfies'.

Ninagawa Mika's photographs present a dreamlike, theatrical world, characterized by a bright colour palette. She won the 13th New Cosmos of Photography contest. Her motifs have remained similar since the 1990s, featuring colourful flowers, young girls including her sister, self-portraits and goldfish (p. 134, pp. 146–77). Comparable to artist Murakami Takashi, Ninagawa has elevated an aesthetic associated with pop- and subculture to the world of art. She received the Kimura Ihei Award for two photobooks that she published on the same day, in 2001: *Sugar and Spice* was a compilation of her commercial work, including photographs of film and pop stars, and *Pink Rose Suite* showed her personal snapshots and art photographs. As the motif of artificially bred (and sometimes colour-injected) goldfish shows, Ninagawa is fascinated by beauty while also questioning its links with human desires.

The term 'girls' photography' is simplistic and controversial: it focuses on the photographers' gender and youth, and places a range of styles, photographic approaches and themes in the same category. Curator Dana Friis-Hansen has connected the 'girls' photography' label with 1990s Japanese society's views of 'the girl', that 'allowed for both an adoration of her as cute, fresh, pure, and playful and a dismissal of her as insipid, inane, and insignificant.'[50] It became obvious when speaking to Hiromix, Nagashima and Ninagawa that the photography and entertainment industries had commercialized the trend, treating the young women as marketing products.

They dealt with this in different ways: Hiromix became a media sensation, accepted modelling work and even appeared in TV commercials for mayonnaise. However, she struggled with the sudden fame and withdrew from the public eye and the photography world. She rarely shows her photographs today. Nagashima rejected all offers for film roles and modelling jobs, and left Japan in 1996 to continue her studies in the United States. She has always seen herself as a serious artist addressing gender issues, and was disappointed when she was misunderstood as a model,

subject to the male gaze. Ninagawa, whose parents were well known in the theatre and film industries, has emphasized that she made a conscious decision to use the 'girls' photography' trend to her advantage. For her, it became a stepping-stone to an extremely successful career in photography and film directing. Ninagawa is one of the best-known photographers in Japan today, and has published over a hundred photobooks. Her work is not only exhibited in museums but has remained popular among the Japanese youth – she is a 'star', and her homepage features a 'fan mail' button.

When the prestigious Kimura Ihei Award was presented to Hiromix, Nagashima and Ninagawa in 2001, it was only the fourth time since its establishment in 1975 that it had been given to women photographers. Despite the simplistic 'girls' photography' label, the attention and recognition that the young women photographers received for their work had a refreshing impact on the photography world. It helped empower the next generation of women, and provided them with more opportunities for exhibitions, photobooks and artistic careers. In the 1990s, Hiromix had – unsurprisingly – associated the image of a photographer with a 'middle-aged man'.[51] This has changed. The 1990s were the beginning of 'girl power photography' – using the term 'girl' in a strong, positive sense.

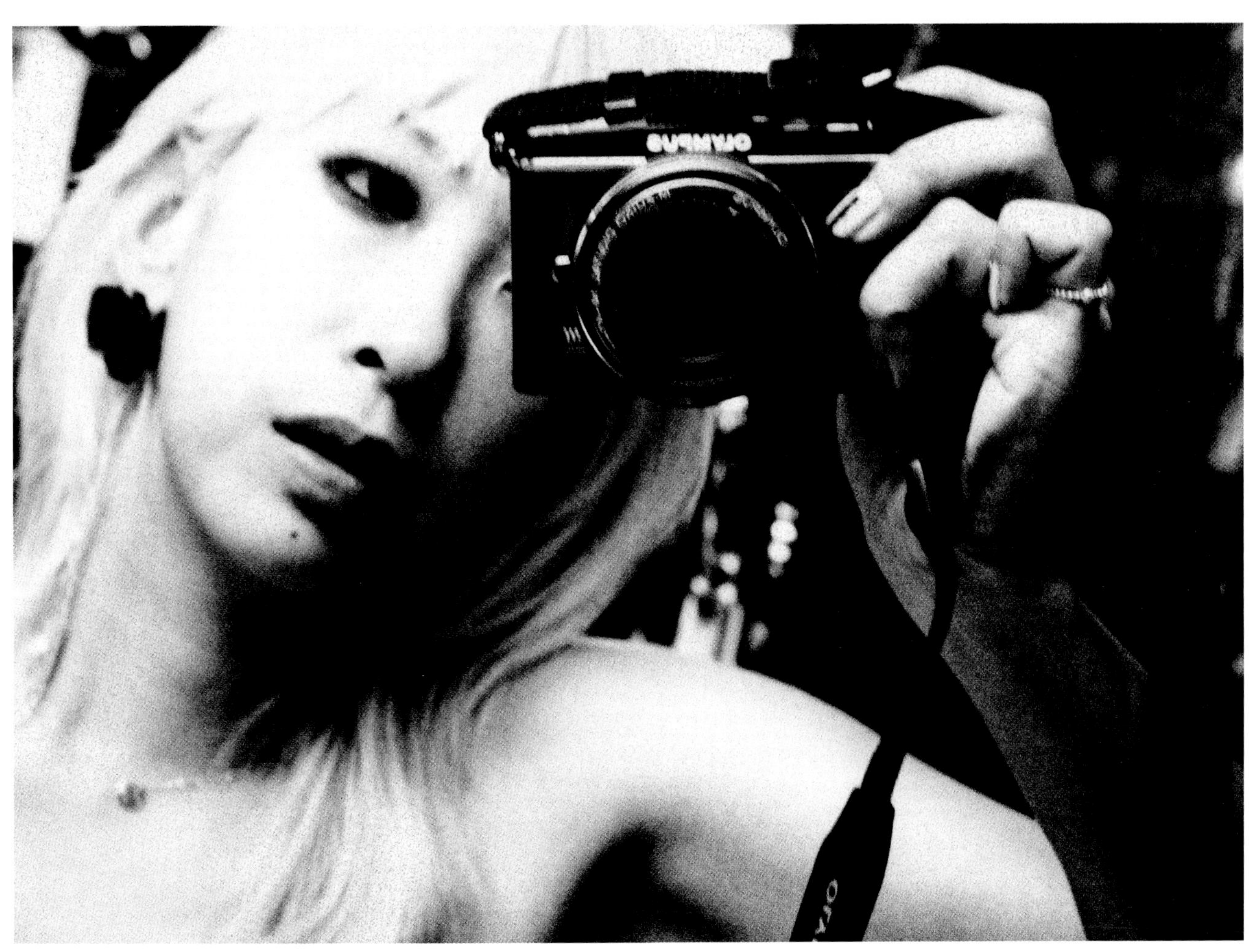

Ninagawa Mika, *Self-image*, 2013.

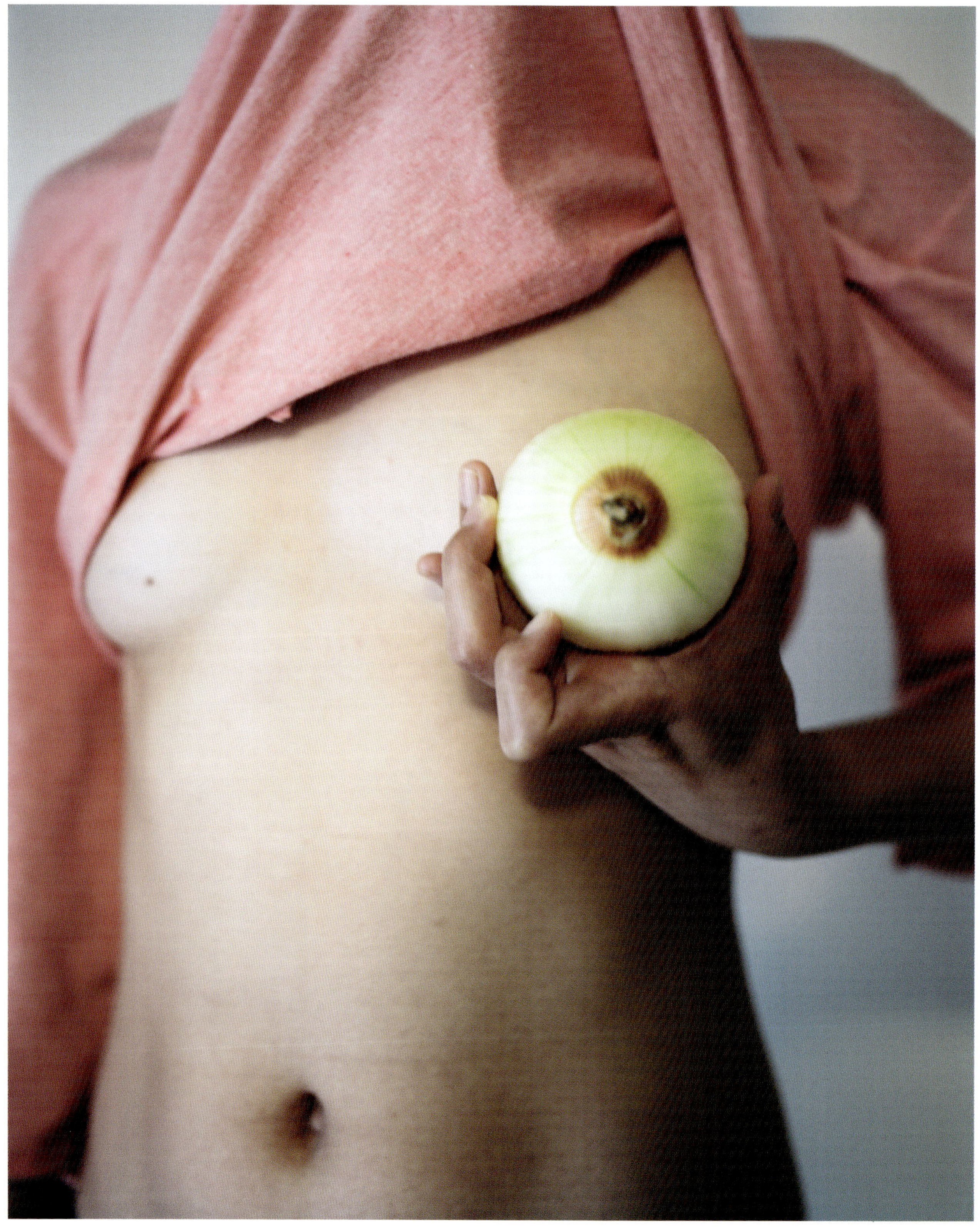

Nagashima Yurie, *Onion*, 2005.

Lena Fritsch: Let's start at the beginning – what inspired you to take up photography?

Nagashima Yurie: It is difficult to put a finger on 'the beginning'. On my mother's side of the family there was an uncle who was an amateur photographer and had an 8mm camera, and photography felt familiar. My grandmother took photographs of flowers using slide films, and I enjoyed looking at them hanging at the light windows. My first camera was a Quick Snap camera and I took photographs with friends; I went to a girls' school and we would dress up in weird clothes and take photos of ourselves.

At university I originally wanted to make films rather than take photographs, but the classes on film only began in my fourth year. It was during my first year, studying graphic design, that I first borrowed my uncle's camera for a photography course.

At the time, were there any photographers in particular that inspired or interested you?

At the beginning I was not interested in 'photography'. But I liked all kinds of films: ranging from Tarkovsky to Nouvelle Vague, and Italian Neo-Realism to American cult films. I also liked Western paintings from the late 19th and early 20th centuries, Viennese Fin de Siècle and so on, as well as contemporary art.

Could you tell me about the self-portrait photographs that you took in 1993 with your family, naked [p. 136]?

In my photographs I usually visualize what I want to say and express. When I took these photographs, I was wondering what 'family' really is.

I grew up in a free and open family environment, in quite a downtown (*shitamachi*) style: thinking about the relationship with the naked body, for example, my family would walk around half-naked with just a towel around their bodies after taking a bath. To me, nakedness is not necessarily something sexual. After graduating from a girls' school, when I was approached sexually by men more often, I felt as though my body was not my own but rather owned by men. In the contemporary photography scene in Japan in the 1990s, there were some famous 'hair nude' photobooks. One by Shinoyama Kishin, *Santa Fe*, caused a sensation: the model was Miyazawa Rie. I think over 1.5 million copies were sold. I was her age, and was shocked because it appeared to me that these women had been 'consumed' by men and by society. She [Miyazawa] was only seventeen years old when the photographs were taken. Since then, questions around the body have interested me. At the time, we received a task at school to take portraits and I began to take self-portraits instead. Then I started posing nude, with and without my family, creating works that presented a different

meaning to the naked body, in opposition to the 'hair nude' photographs.

Could you talk about your photographic practice in the 1990s? There were hardly any women in the Japanese 'photography world' and it must have been difficult.

I was in America to study art from 1995 to 1999 so I don't really know. I think it was more difficult for Hiromix, who I met before she became well known. After I left, female photographers were all referred to as 'girls' photographers' and the trend really took off. I never thought that this absurd term would become so established. There were quite a few young women photographers in the 1990s, but they all had their own styles. There were also numerous women artists who took nude self-portraits, but looking at their works closely, I think their nude photographs were much more complex and diverse than those taken by men. It was a shame that many adults could only see these 'girls' as models whose historic role was to be the photographic subject, not as photographers. When I was offered a film role or a job as a nude model for a famous photographer, these offers did not make any sense to me.

I think the perspective in your photographs is strong, and shows clearly that you are not only the photographic subject but also the photographer.

I was offered nude modelling jobs by photographers like Araki and Shinoyama. But there is a concept to my work, namely that my body is mine and not a product for men. I took photographs of my body myself; if a man had taken photographs of me, they would have meant something very different. I declined all offers.

In 2001, you received the Kimura Ihei Award – together with Hiromix and Ninagawa Mika. Could you tell me about your experiences at the time and how you felt, receiving this traditional photography award and sharing it with the other two girls?

Ninagawa used the 'girls' photography' trend; according to her in an honest interview, part of her did not like it but made a conscious decision to use it. I went to the US, so I did not have to face such situations, but if I had been in Japan for the second half of the 1990s it would have been difficult for me. I received the award about a year and a half after I came back from the US.

In hindsight, looking at the history of the Kimura Ihei Award – in twenty-five years it had only been given to three women – it was a really big thing that in the year 2000 it was given to three women, doubling the number overall. In the 2000s, the number of female awardees increased and actually

exceeded the number of men; without Shinoyama on the jury I personally think that this would not have been possible.

Since your 'debut' in the 1990s, more than twenty years have passed. You have created different works and used different artistic media, not only photography. However, in regards to your photography, how do you think your works have changed?

Some themes have not changed: for example questions about being a woman, focusing on small communities and the idea that the personal is political. In Japan, once you become a high-school student the uniform for girls is always skirts rather than trousers, and school books are full of stories about men. When I think about my teenage struggles now, I realize that they were mostly not related to puberty but rather to the social roles of 'women' that society is pushing onto us. Such gender issues have become an important theme in my work. I think the photographs of my family and the *empty white room* series are influenced by second wave feminism's principle that 'the personal is political'. To face issues relating to women, I first used my own body. Recently, I have focused more on other people; for example, I made a work focused on my partner's mother's life history. What has not changed is that I start with an individual problem while creating a work about 'relations'. I have never seen myself particularly as a photographer, I just want to express something by making art. This can also be done by using written text, and if necessary I would study new things. In 2015, I received a Master's degree in Sociology. After I received the Kimura Ihei Award I had a phase when I thought I should be a photographer. But now I just do what I like.

Do you think your recent studies in Sociology have influenced your photography?

Yes, I think so. The way I read photographs has changed and I have also found out more about my works of art, that I was not able to put into words before.

What do you like best about the medium of photography?

Perhaps I like that you can't have full control. I still use films, and sometimes I accidentally open the camera when there is a film inside. Even these kinds of mistakes can result in something interesting. And I think photography suits me. The way my brain memorizes and recalls a moment is quite similar to how photography and film function – and also, I hate sitting still. I write at the dining table so I can get up every forty-five minutes and make myself coffee [laughs]. Photography is fun: it leads me to see different people, and I really like the working process – maybe even more than the final image.

*   This is a shortened version of an interview with Nagashima Yurie, conducted in Japanese on 2 September 2016, at Nomu café, Tokyo.

Lena Fritsch: Let's start at the beginning – what inspired you to take up photography?
Ninagawa Mika: My father was a theatre director and my mother was an actress, so I grew up in a creative home. When I was around five years old, I already knew that I wanted to do something creative, maybe become a painter or an actress. I painted a lot and of course we also had a camera at home. In my fourth year of elementary school I took self-portraits, and in my sixth year I took photographs of a Barbie with volcanic rocks at a park in Karuizawa. I really liked the lava rocks: how they looked, and also the idea that the red lava had hardened and turned into rocks.

Do you still have these photographs?
Unfortunately, the 'volcanic rocks and Barbie' photographs do not exist anymore. They showed an encounter between Barbie and a curious landscape [laughs]. The things that I like have not changed much since then. When entering senior high school, I bought a single-lens reflex camera. At home we had a compact camera with an autofocus, and you could not take a photograph unless it was focused. It frustrated me that I could not press the shutter when I wanted, for example to create a blurred photograph. With the single-lens reflex camera this became possible and I became obsessed with taking photographs. At university, I studied graphic design. It was not so much about becoming a photographer but more about doing something creative.

At the time, were you interested in or inspired by any photographers?
Not really. People like Araki, Shinoyama and Moriyama were very active, and of course I saw their photographs, but I did not want to become a photographer and was not influenced by their photography. I just really wanted to create something – and that ended up being photographs.

In 1998 you published your first photobook, *17 9 '97*. Could you tell me more about the photographs?
[Pointing at the photo on the cover of the book, p. 146, and her sister, sitting next to her] This is my little sister when she was young, twenty years ago [laughs]! When I look at these photographs now, it is interesting that all my main themes are already there: self-portraits, flowers, goldfish, glowing young girls (like my sister), landscapes (for example, taken during my travels). At the time, I took photographs of the things that I liked, which were directly around me. Even when travelling, I took photographs of the things that were

close to me. The keyword was 'I', my own viewpoint. That has not changed to this day. In the 1990s, there was this girls' photography boom and taking photographs became a trendy, exciting thing. It was a fun decade.

The 1990s and this 'girls' photography' trend changed the role of women in the Japanese photography world quite considerably, I think.
Yes. But I was a student, and did not really understand why being a young woman was suddenly valued so much. Girls' photography was a trend. I was thinking to myself: 'should I use this and participate or not? Maybe I should.' So it was my conscious decision. I knew that there were risks, but I was confident enough to think that I would be able to continue my work after this trend. It really was a big wave, and the fact that Yurie-chan [Nagashima Yurie] went overseas and Hiromix stopped taking photographs for a while surely had something to do with it. When the trend was over, people lost interest and it was not easy to stay.

The trend was not 'womens' photography' but 'girl's photography'. And girls grow up at some point...
Exactly. Although it never felt like 'girls' photography' – of course we were young, but not all of us were cute and glowing. I guess it was easier to sell the photographs in this simple 'girls' category. Traditionally there were very few women in Japanese photography. But the other day, there was a big photoshoot here in Tokyo with Ryan Gosling, for his film *La La Land*. There were around ten photographers and out of ten, nine were female. It is great that things have changed; I was surprised!

In 2001, you received the Kimura Ihei Award for two photobooks: *Pink Rose Suite*, and *Sugar and Spice*.
These two early books are quite symbolic for my practice. The fact that I received an award for them is important to me. *Sugar and Spice* features my commercial work (magazine work, CD covers and so on), and *Pink Rose Suite* shows the photographs that I took as artworks and snapshots. I published these two books simultaneously, in the same size; they came out on the same day, because I wanted people to know that I do both. Today, I am represented by a gallery and exhibit my works in art museums, but I still do commercial work as well, and I enjoy it. It is probably a very Japanese thing to do, and rather unusual. The commercial work is fun and fast-paced and it complements my artistic practice, for which I can take my time. My private work benefits from

my commercial work; I learn a lot. Therefore, these two books are important to me, even today.

The bright colours that you use in the two books are also typical of your photography. Could you tell me more about the colours in your work?
You have come to our office today so you can see the colours here: I really like bright colours [laughs]. There was a time when I painted, and I used similar colours then. When I started photography, it was with analogue films and the colours were not manipulated at all. I just chose things that are colourful. My mother works with fabrics and makes patchwork quilts – interestingly, she uses similar colours. She started making these quilts around the same time that I started photography. Our house was not particularly colourful, but the colours of our works are similar – it must be in our DNA [laughs]. Even in my photographs today, I usually don't change the colours. I just pick up on the things in the world that have bright colours.

Like flowers.
Yes. When I think about my basic reasons for taking photographs, there is this feeling that 'I want to keep this' and 'I want to show this to other people as well'. Flowers are beautiful and I want to photograph them before they wither; I want to stop something that I can't stop. I just can't help it, and feel an urge to photograph it. Right now, the cherry blossoms are beautiful and in full bloom – I took some photographs yesterday, and over the last two to three days I have taken around 1,800 photographs of cherry blossoms. The only reason is that they are in full bloom now, and I have to take photographs quickly to record this!

I assume you generally take a large number of photographs, and you select from what you have for your photobooks?
Yes, although 1,800 photographs is a lot, even by my standards [laughs]. I just really like cherry blossoms, and I am productive this year. I also have a new book coming out next month. My father passed away last year and this book features photographs that I took just before he died over a period of one month, and during the two weeks after he was gone. These photographs are different – everything appears very light. Thinking that my father was soon to part from this world, the whole world appeared very bright and beautifully radiant. Even I was surprised when I looked at these photographs.

How many photobooks have you published so far? Are photobooks the ultimate way to present your works?

I have published more than 100 books now. I exhibit my work a lot and have big solo shows, so photobooks and exhibitions are both important to me. When I take photographs, I don't have any particular concept. Like classic photographers such as Moriyama or Araki, I wander around the city and take photographs of whatever catches my eye. When looking at the photographs later I start seeing a concept, and compile them in a book.

Another motif of your work is the goldfish [p. 147].
The goldfish is an important symbolic motif in my work. People have continued to create various breeds in order for goldfish to become even more beautiful. They are not natural. As animals, they have inconvenient forms and their lives are short – the fish have been changed just to meet human desires and ideas of beauty. They are beautiful and cute and to people in Asia they are very familiar. Yet, they carry such a deep sadness. That seems symbolic to me, as the world is full of victims and absurd things. Human desires are a big theme in my photography, and also connect with works that I have made as a film director, such as *Helter Skelter* (2012). Beauty that has been artificially created interests me; it symbolizes human desires.

Where do you photograph goldfish?
I have taken photos of goldfish in Japan, but also in Hong Kong (at the goldfish market) and in Shanghai – different cities in Asia. In Hong Kong, there are so many. They put artificial colour into the fish, similar to blue roses. I have not changed the colour of these photographs, but the colours of the goldfish have been changed. It is really cruel – but it looks beautiful nevertheless.

The goldfish is a very 'Asian' motif. Are you interested in traditional Japanese motifs and beauty concepts? The cherry blossom is of course a very Japanese motif as well...
I don't want to show 'the beauty of Japan' to the world, but I do sometimes feel that I have a Japanese or Asian aesthetic intuition. However, it is not a conscious decision.

You create a large number of marketing products for your work. Why, and how much are you creatively involved in these?
[Pointing at her dress] This is one of my products as well. There are people who say that as a photographer I should not make all these products. But I don't want to follow any rules as to what a photographer or an artist should or should not do. That is important to me. There are no taboos, and I enjoy commercial work. My only rule is that I create things that I think are good. I take this seriously and only make things that I myself would want to have. Perhaps that is the reason why I work a bit differently, compared to other photographers.

Why did you choose photography and what do you like best about photography?
I did not become a photographer because I wanted to be a photographer. I did not particularly like cameras either. I wanted to become someone creative who expresses herself, an artist. Photography suited me best because things are reflected directly. My own feelings and my photographs have always been closely intertwined. In my photographs, what I think and feel is reflected right away – and I like expressing myself [laughs].

*   This is a shortened version of an interview conducted in Japanese on 4 April 2017, at Ninagawa Mika's studio Lucky Star, Tokyo.

Lena Fritsch: Let's start at the beginning – what inspired you to take up photography?

Hiromix: From a young age, people always praised my artistic talents. I had my first creative experiences when I was around three to five years old. By the time that I was ten years old, I was taking photographs with an automatic compact camera. I also engaged with oil painting, animation and food culture. At thirteen, I was interested in imported retro music, fashion and film, and was analysing and researching social issues (including ecology and organic food) by myself. That year, I selected optional club activities at school, participating in a photography club and an art club. I was the head of the art club, painting and sometimes printing black and white photographs, taken with an analogue camera. Almost every day after school, I strolled around several multicultural parts of town, and I looked at and bought a lot of inexpensive retro visual material from different cultures – imported images as well as ones from Japan. It was fun to find fancy retro visuals, and I enjoyed them in a pure way – their colours and atmosphere – simply because I thought they were cool. In hindsight, I think I learned photography by viewing a lot of copies of retro visual materials. It was an important learning experience. But I didn't really understand the logical structures of these visuals in the world; I only recently recognized the meaning of 'rock'. Thinking about those days, I was creative and took photos, but I think it was even more important for me to learn from retro images. If I had only learned about famous art photography, it would probably have been difficult for me to enjoy any photographic practice.

When you started taking photographs, were you interested in or inspired by any other photographers?

No, I was not inspired by any photographers. Basically, photographers appeared to be mostly middle-aged men; I was a girl and did not have any inte tions or hopes of becoming a photographer. At the time, art photography was not popular in Asia (including Japan) – probably less so than in England. After the 'girly photo' trend in Japan, since my debut in 1995, art photography has suddenly become popular. My favourite visuals were of swinging London, and retro rock snapshots from the UK. Both inspirations are reflected in the 1990s Tokyo 'girly photo' trend and *kawaii* culture.

Your first photobook, *Girls Blue*, was published in 1996. Could you tell me more about the background of this book? What kind of camera did you use?

After my photographic debut in 1995, I received endless offers for work and interview requests from the media. Journalists made statements such as 'sensational genius girl photographer appears from Japan'. Within just a few months my name had spread all around the world. I often rejected offers because I was too busy. I accepted the photobook offers because it seemed that many people expected my photobooks. Having read many art photobooks in the past, I already had a vision of my own photobooks. The photographs in the book were all taken with an automatic compact camera during my teenage years. Most photographs were taken at a fun independent retro music event with people who enjoyed retro cosplay, whose names I have mostly forgotten now.

In 2001, you, Ninagawa Mika and Nagashima Yurie all won the Kimura Ihei Award. How did you experience this as a young woman? What did you think about the popular 'girls photography' trend in the 1990s?

I was very surprised; I never expected this award. People had asked me about it before I received it, but I was too polite and humble, and never felt any greed (in traditional Asian culture, modesty is regarded as a virtue). At the time, I was already working a lot; I was tired of working too much.

I liked a style that was cool rather than cute (*kawaii*) then, and I felt strange when people described my photographs as *kawaii*. To be honest, I was not excited about being a pioneer of the 'girly photo' trend, because so many people copied my style. It was difficult to look at it objectively. Maybe I was too exhausted, becoming a pop star so quickly and unexpectedly. Everything seemed unreal. But fifteen years later I recognise and appreciate these trends of *kawaii* culture and 'girly photo' as an honour. So many people were surprised when I appeared: there was praise and admiration as well as jealousy, hate...there were pros and cons to so many people discussing my art photography. I was young, a girl, Asian – at the time, it was difficult to gain any advanced social status. I was not aware, but mine was a very innovative position. There might be links to 'feminism', and I might even have contributed to women's more advanced social status.

My 'girly photo' style features a child's mind with innocent expressions. I felt like becoming a 'transparent fairy', expressing feelings of happiness, dreamy or blue emotions and being full of love for everyone, creating a pleasant, cheerful atmosphere. Taking self-portraits was a very private time for me alone; I decided to take them to record myself growing up. The small, closed world of my self-portraits is similar to a girl's secret diary, written only for myself, with a key. In fact, I did not really take my photographs to show them to people. In interviews at the time, I often said: 'adults are always too busy and they seem to forget about the beauty of the sky. I am happy if my photographs remind adults that it is possible to find little beautiful things within everyday life.' At the time and to this day, I have always prayed for everyone's happiness. I have always hoped for the very best in human society. In the 1990s, in many advanced nations the economy stagnated. Perhaps people needed a child's innocence and the fresh, optimistic, bright energy of simplicity.

When you create a photobook, how do you choose your photographs and how do you work?

Mu is a familiar concept in Asia. It means 'nothing' or 'not too much thinking, keeping your concentration on the present', and is related to Zen mindfulness. I always take this kind of perspective when taking photos and editing them, without any particular meaning for the past or present, or the future.

You have not published any photobooks recently – do you still take photographs?

The social status and expectation to be innovative were a huge responsibility, a burden. I suffered badly. For a long time, ignorant people with bad intentions have put me in uncomfortable situations; it was chaotic, and I was too tired. I have received many offers to publish photobooks, but they are pending. I will make a book when I encounter the perfect male muse, and the right situation presents itself. I always appreciate people's support.

What do you like best about photography?

I never intended to become a photographer, but I think it fits my personality. It is similar to being a painter but requires good communication abilities; photographers could be called 'contemporary painters'. I have never thought about 'liking' or 'hating' photography. It simply exists.

Art photography is probably one of the newest art genres. Perhaps photography is even futuristic?

People have called my photography style 'diaristic', and I think what is great about photographs is the way that they help to record scenes and beautiful memories that would otherwise be forgotten.

* This interview was conducted by email in Japanese and English, from May to November 2017.

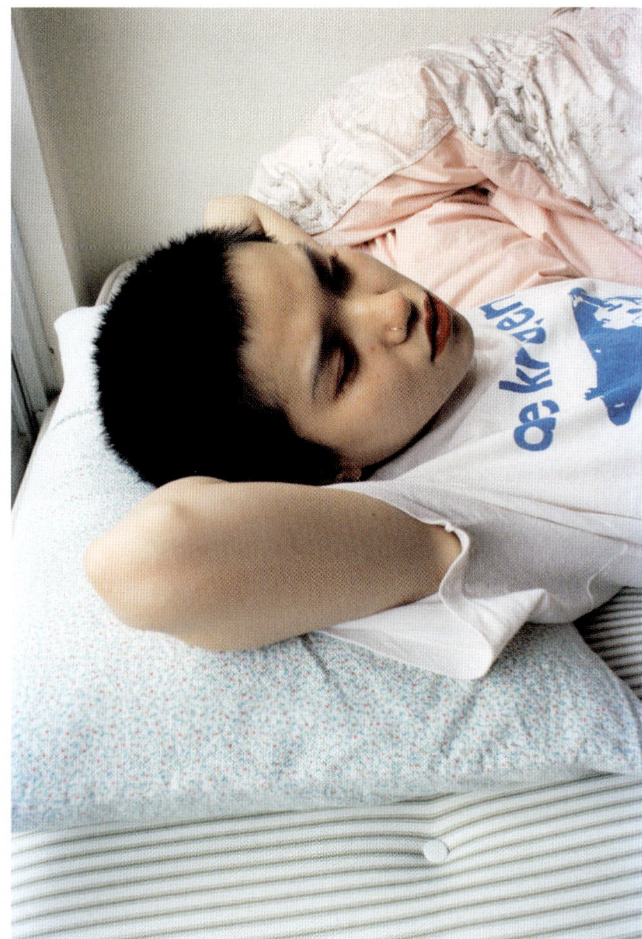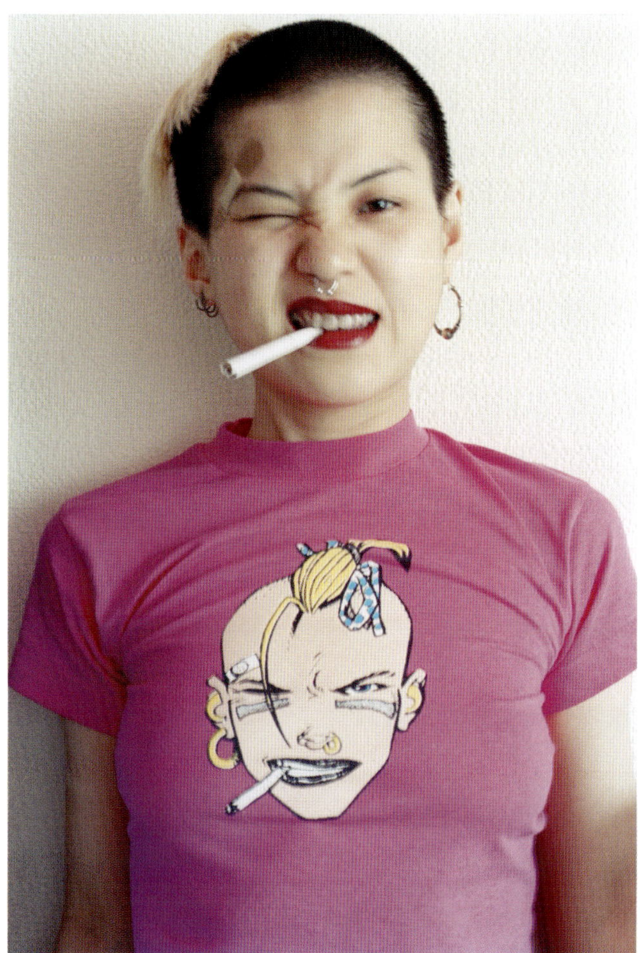

Above left: Nagashima Yurie, untitled, 1994,
Serious Worries series.
Above right: Nagashima Yurie, *Tank Girl*, 1994.

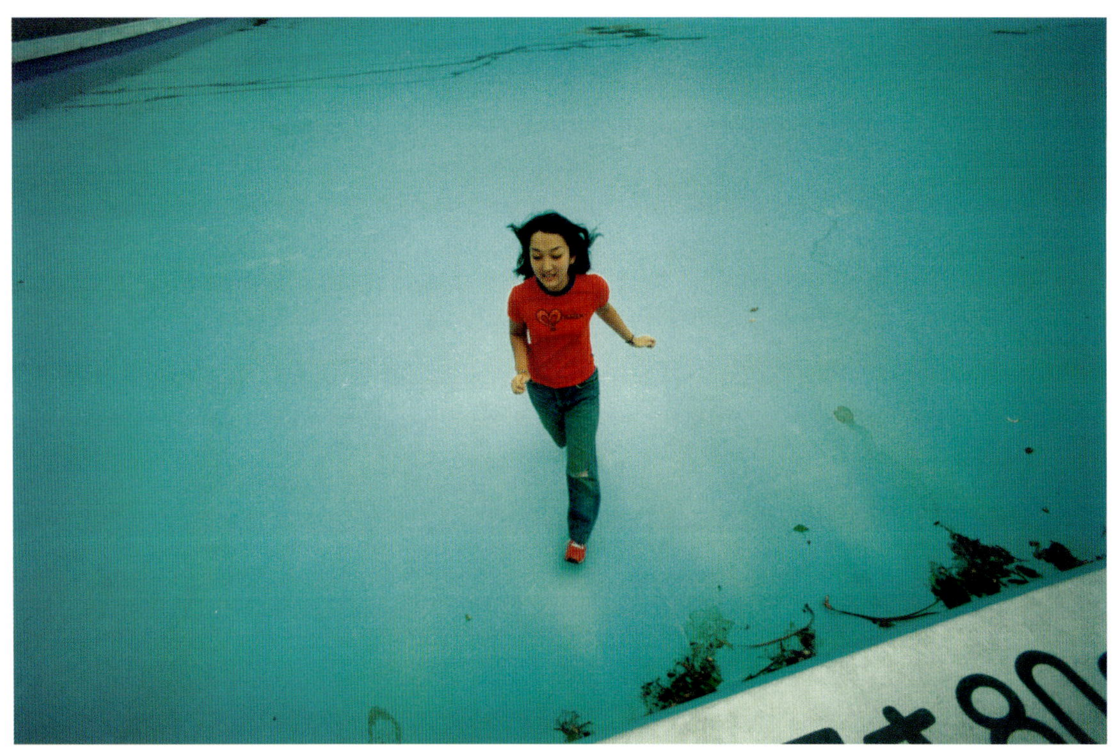

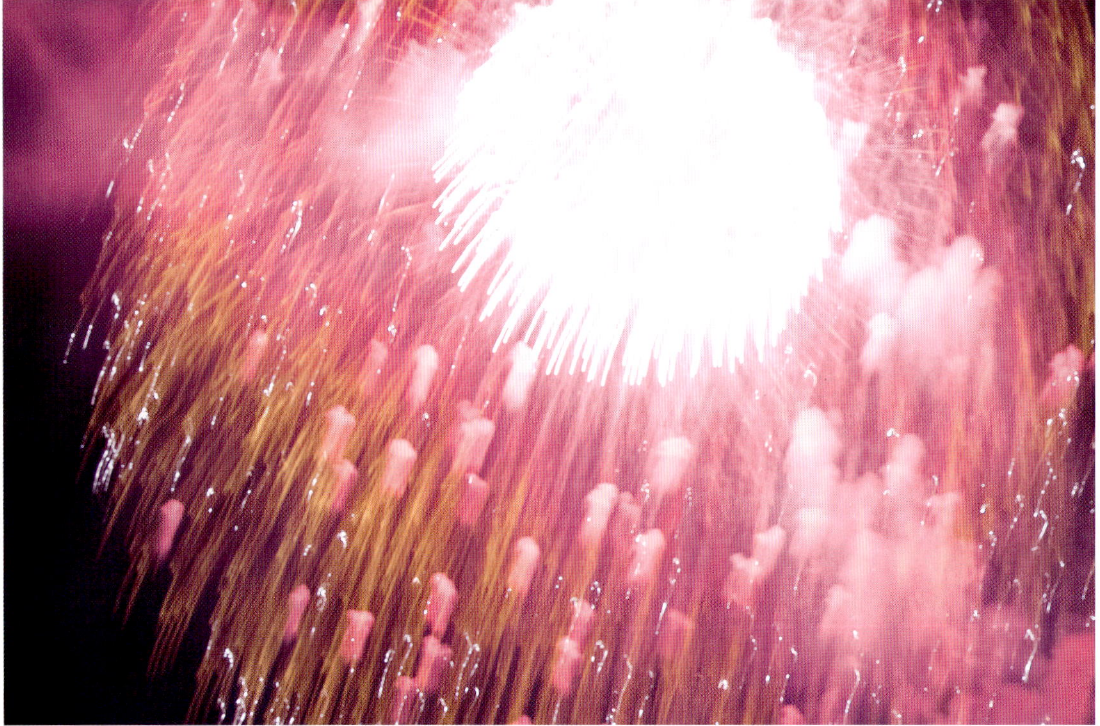

Top: Ninagawa Mika, *17 9 '97*, 1998.
Above: Ninagawa Mika, *Light of*, 2015.

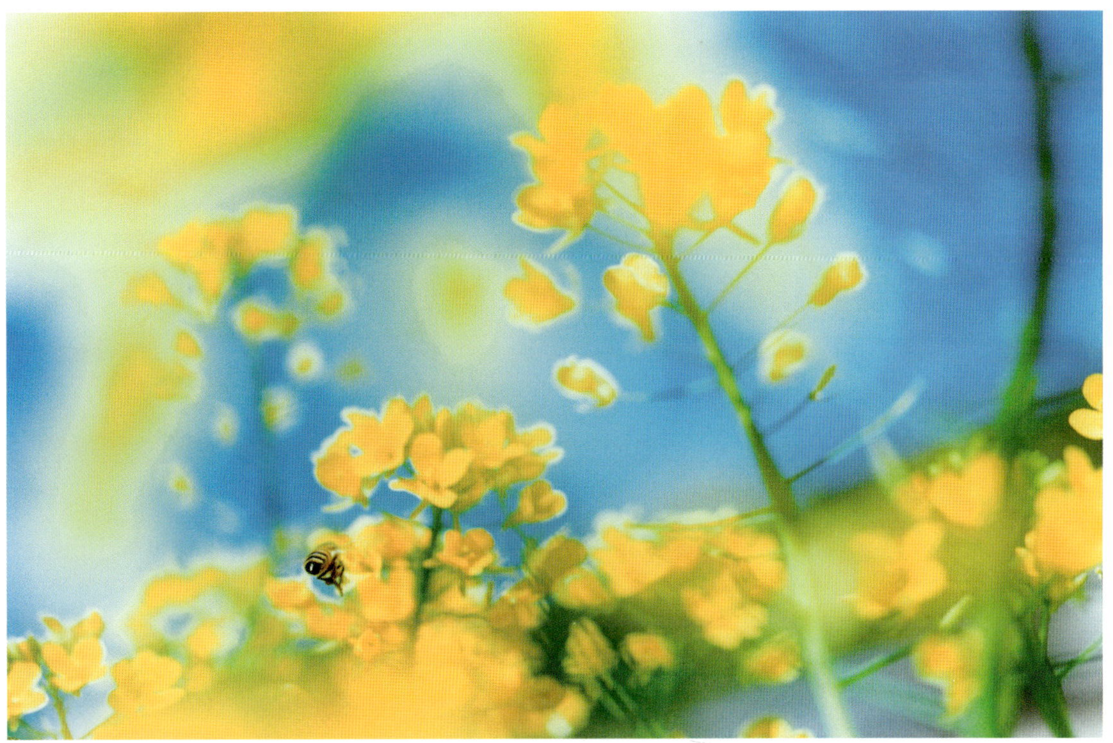

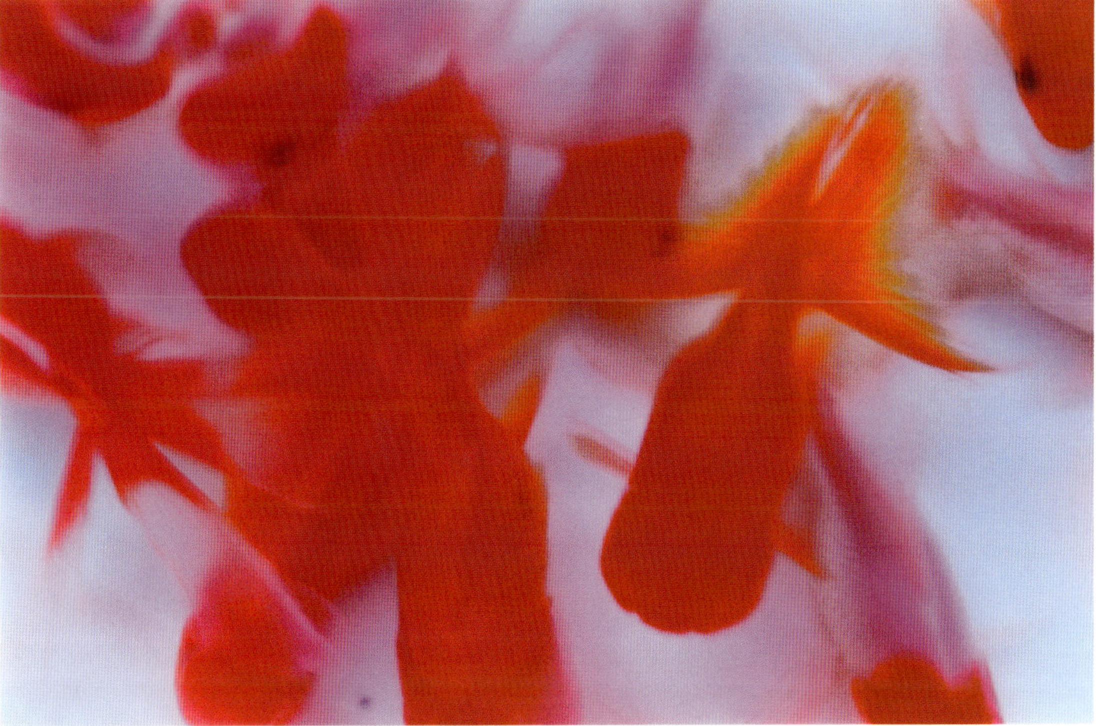

Top: Ninagawa Mika, *a piece of heaven*, 2002.
Above: Ninagawa Mika, *Liquid Dreams*, 2003.

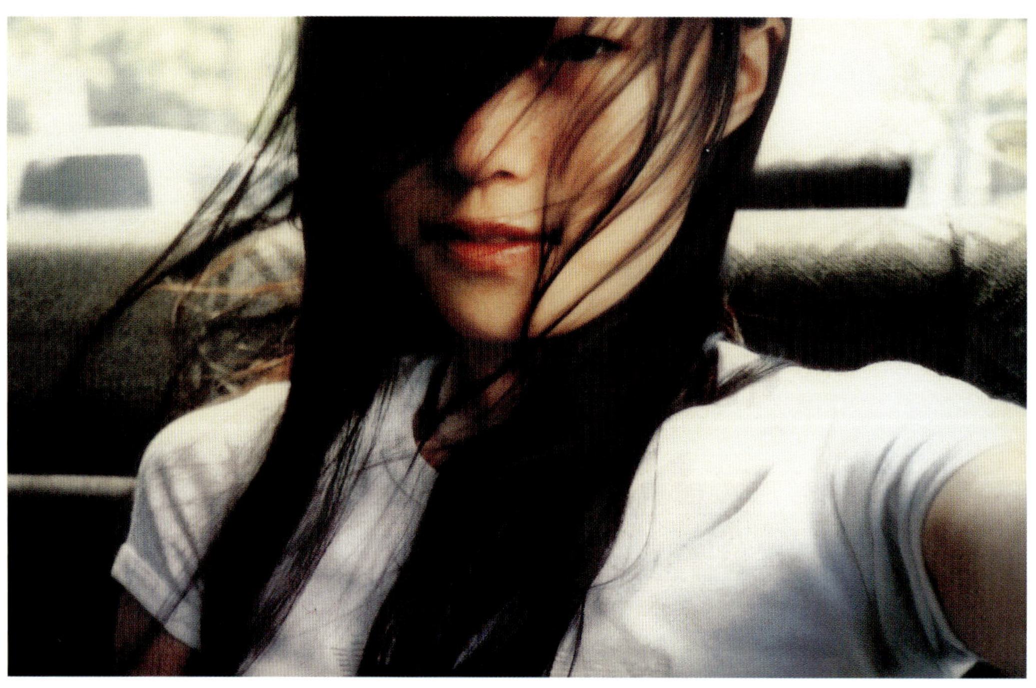

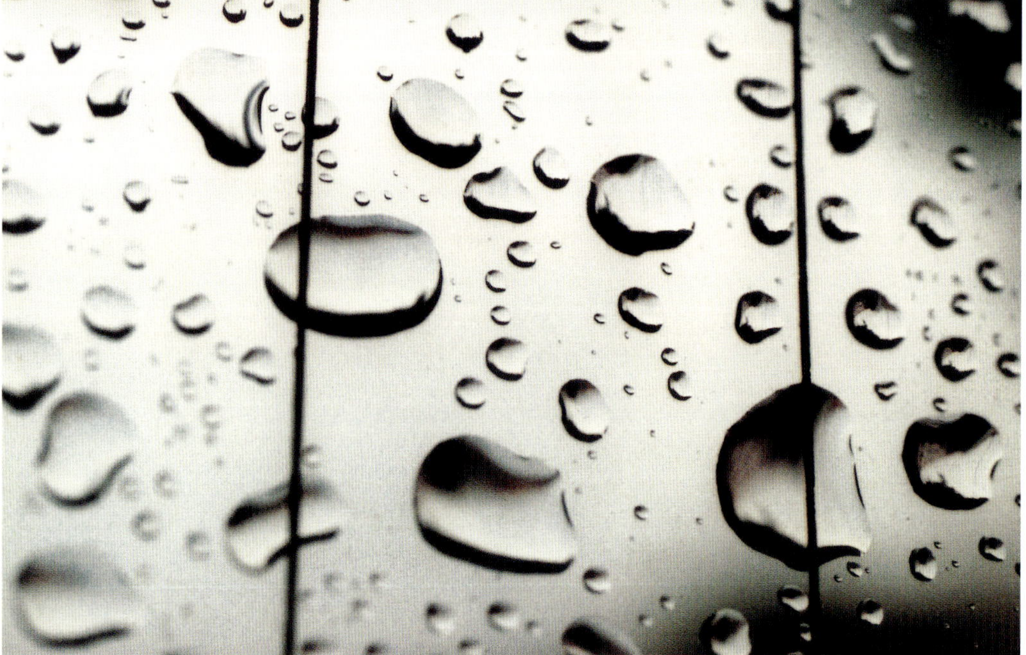

Top: Hiromix, *Self-portrait*, 1998.
Above: Hiromix, untitled, 1998.

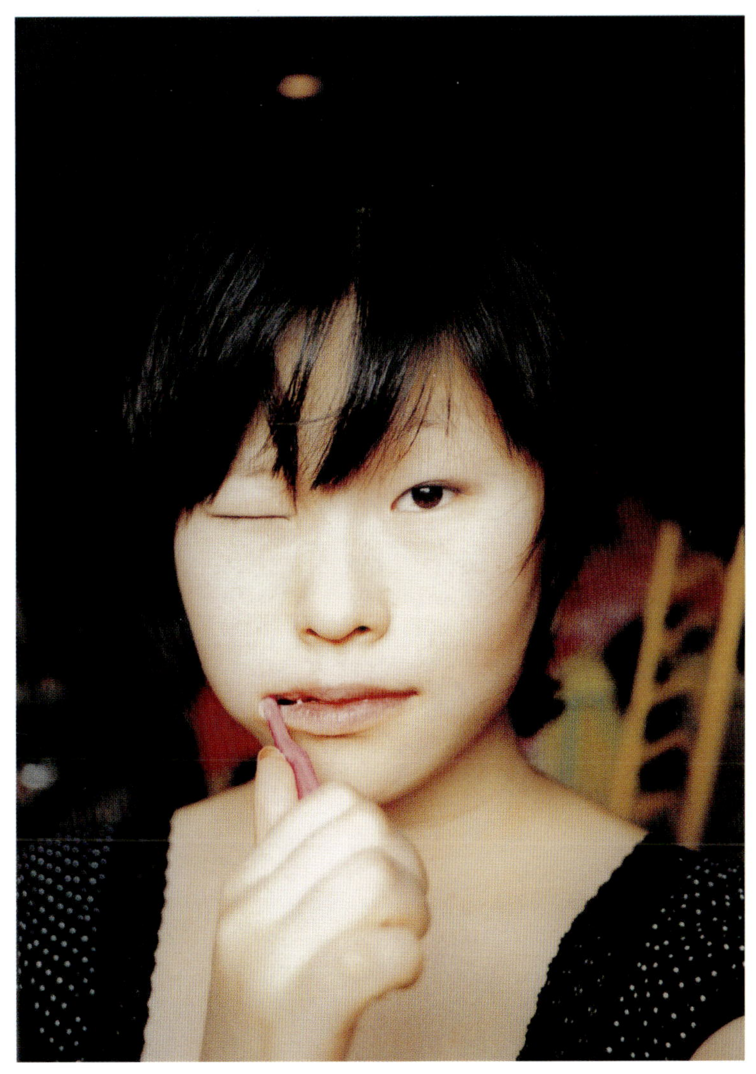

Hiromix, *Self-portrait*, 1999.

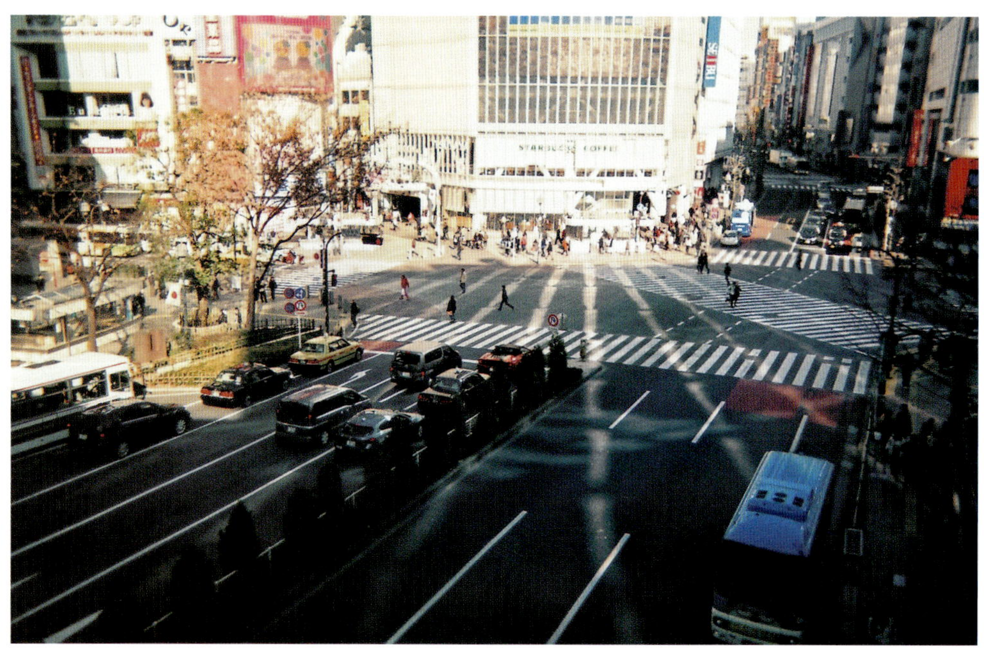

Hiromix, *Shibuya*, 2014.

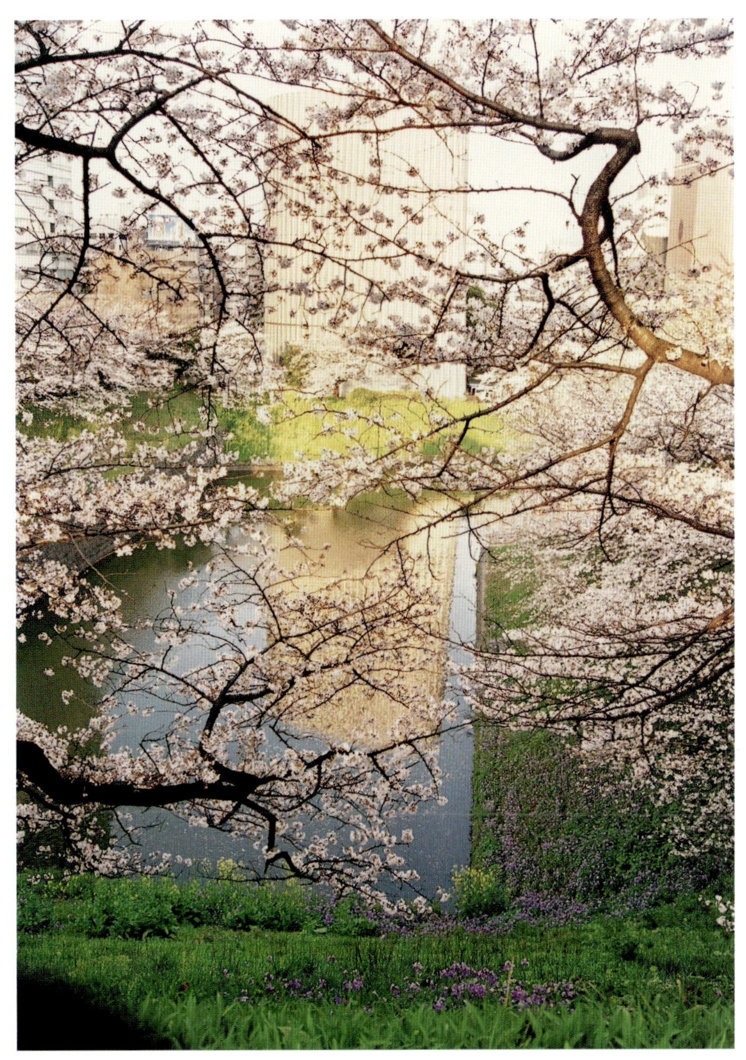

Hiromix, *Cherry Blossoms*, 2009.

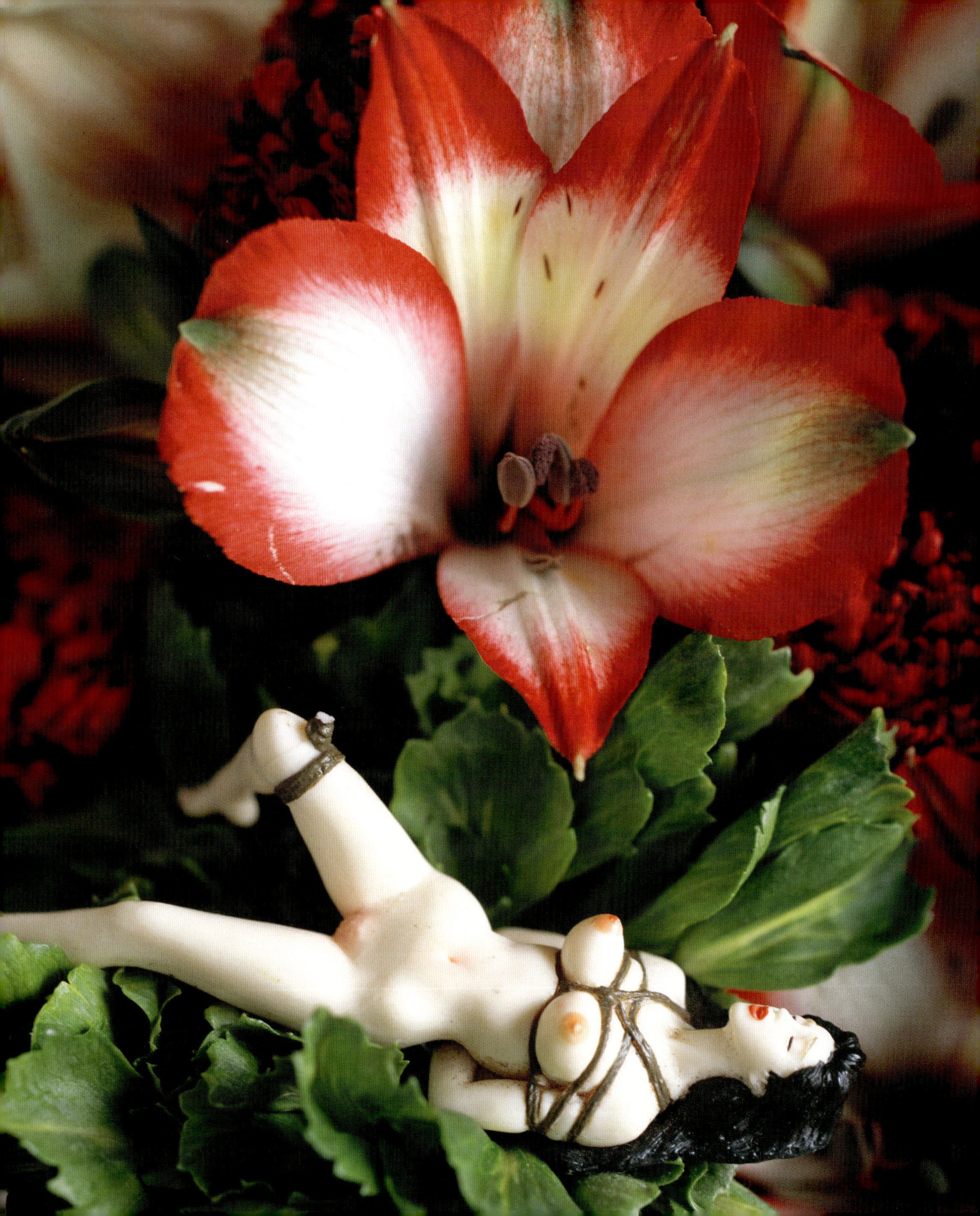

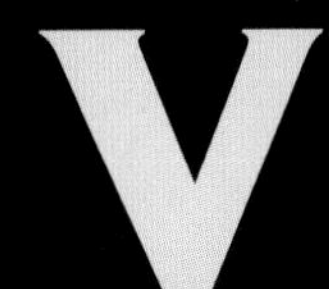

V

CONTEMPORARY JAPANESE PHOTOGRAPHY

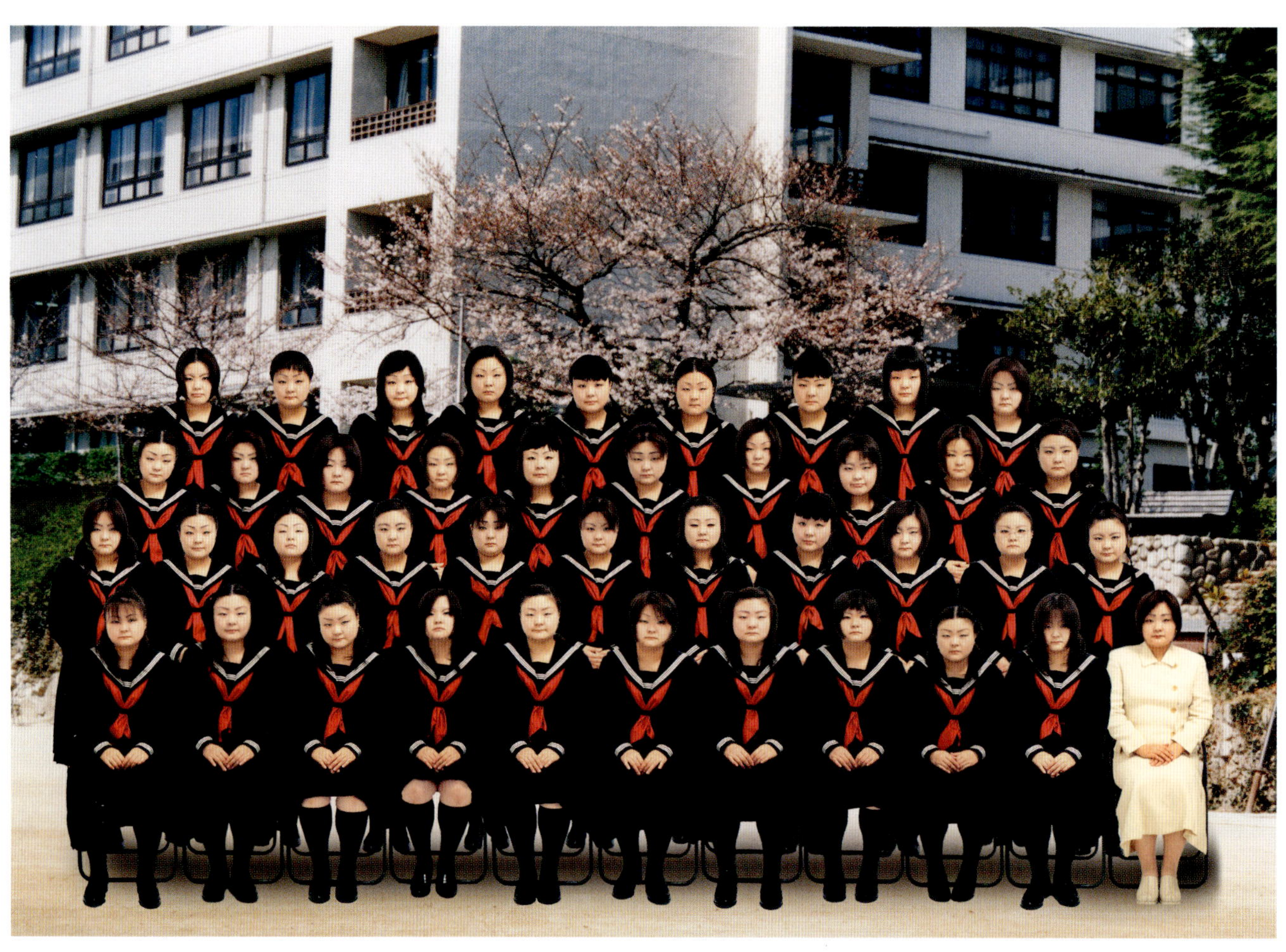

Previous spread: detail from Araki
Nobuyoshi, untitled, 2017, *Imshun* series.
Above: Sawada Tomoko, *School Days*, 2004.

The 1990s in Japan are referred to as the 'lost decade': the economic bubble had burst and the 1989 financial crisis had halted growth. In the worlds of art and photography, however, this was a time of change and internationalization. New museums and contemporary art galleries were established, and the infrastructure around photographic art was strengthened. In 1987, curator Yamamoto Kazuhiro wrote that 'the environment surrounding photography begins to show faint but definite signs of life, and communication between the fields of art and photography is starting to grow.'[52] This included international exhibitions that introduced photographic practice to the public. National, municipal and private museums began to found photography collections. In 1988, the Kawasaki City Museum opened a photography collection. The Yokohama Museum of Art followed one year later, and in 1995 the Tokyo Metropolitan Museum of Photography, now the Tokyo Museum of Photographic Art, inaugurated its permanent building in Ebisu. Acceptance of photography as art was 'finally starting to take root.'[53] As photography was recognised more regularly by art museums, the interaction between Japanese museums and overseas institutions increased. Japanese museums and galleries started to pay attention to photographers who had become popular in Europe and North America, like Araki Nobuyoshi and Morimura Yasumasa.

The recipient of the 2004 Kimura Ihei Award reflects the influence of the art world's newfound recognition of photography: Sawada Tomoko (b. 1977) was presented with the award for her self-portraits in costumes (pp. 217–19). Fukagawa Masafumi has emphasized the symbolic meaning of this for the photography community: 'Sawada Tomoko getting the Kimura Ihei Award was a big thing. Only those who release the shutter used to be viewed as photographers. They represented the award. But that concept broke down.'[54] For the jury, artistic concepts had become as important as photojournalistic values, blurring the boundaries between 'photography' and 'art photography'.

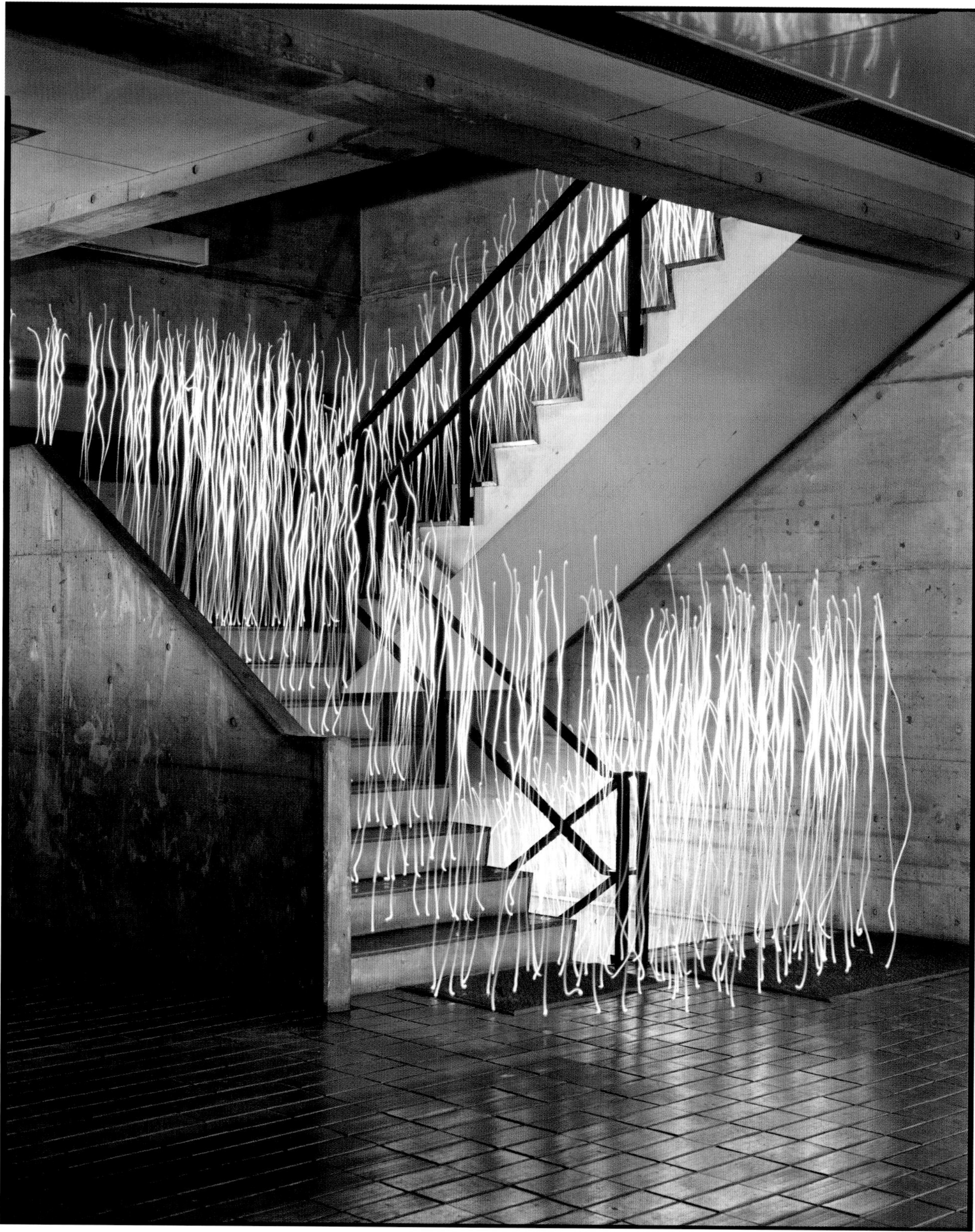

Satō Tokihiro, *Photo-Respiration #22*, 1988.

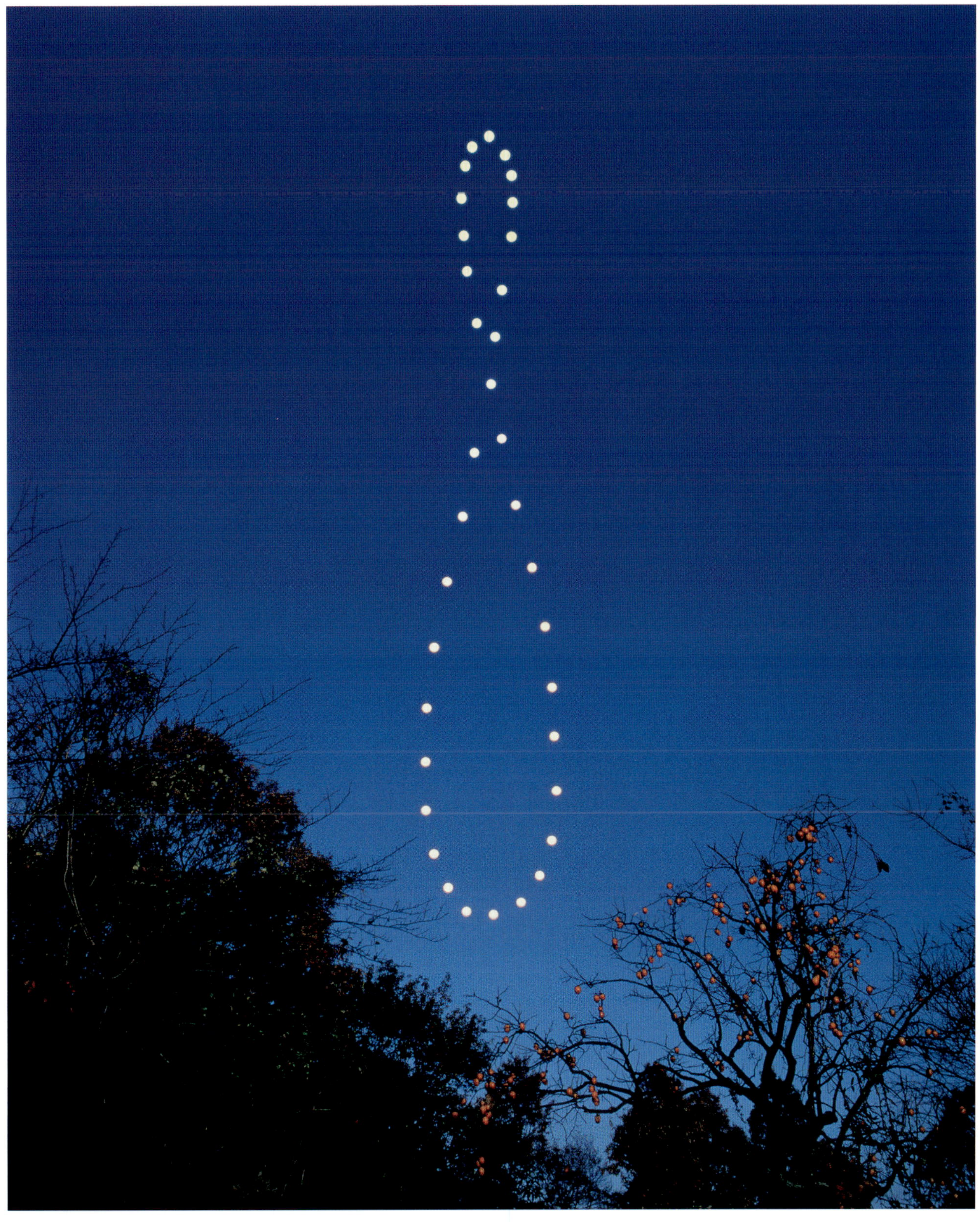

Nomura Hitoshi, *The Analemma '91 – Noon,* 1991.

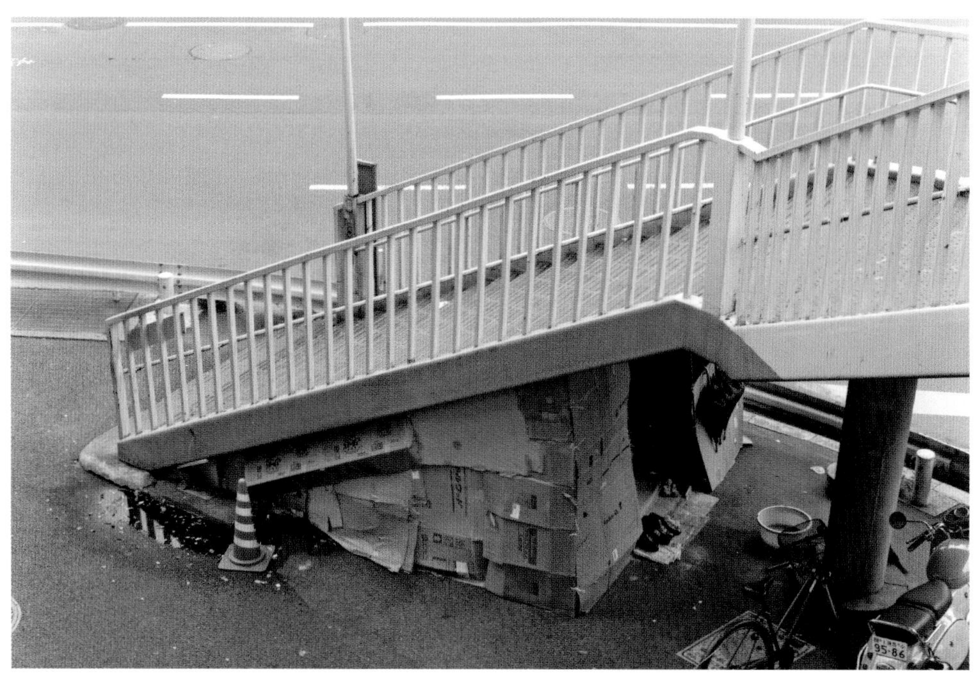

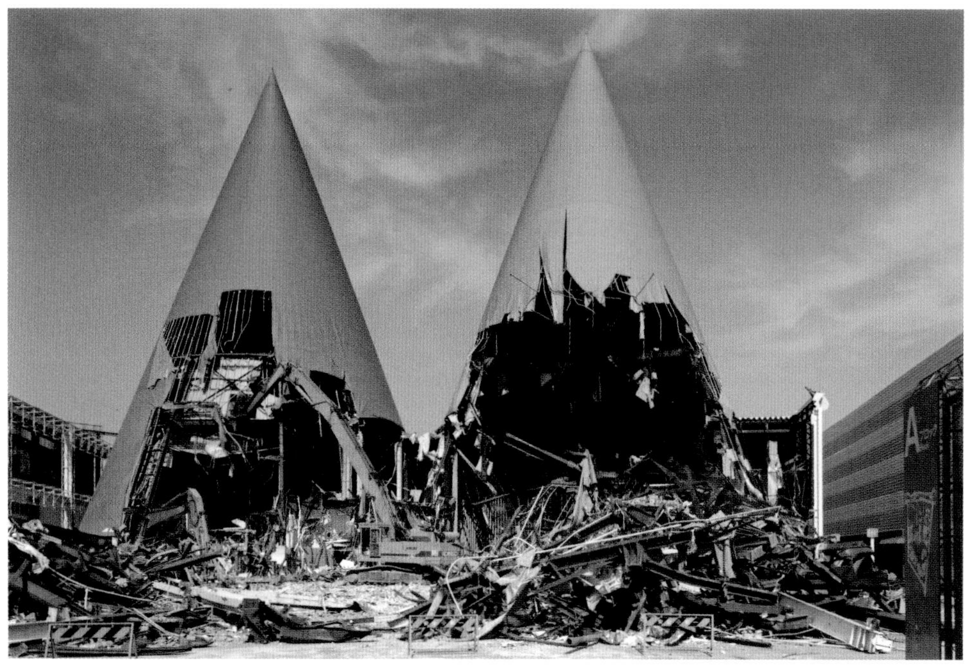

Top: Miyamoto Ryūji, *Cardboard Houses*, 1994.
Above: Miyamoto Ryūji, *Pavilions of Tsukuba
Expo '85*, 1985, *Architectural Apocalypse* series.

In the 1980s, some of the magazines that had played a leading role in the Japanese photography world were discontinued, including *Camera Mainichi*. Photographers have since turned to books as a way of disseminating their work, and the number of photographic prints on the art market has also increased greatly.

Contemporary photography is incredibly diverse and difficult to categorize. This chapter features a selection of photographs taken since the 1980s in three sections: The City/Landscapes/Interiors, Still Life and The Human. These provide a thematic focus, but there are still numerous overlaps between photographers, their approaches and individual works.

Cityscapes, Landscapes and Interiors

The city – particularly Tokyo – has been a popular photographic motif for decades, ranging from post-war photographs by Kimura Ihei and Tanuma Takeyoshi, to Moriyama Daidō's countless snapshots of Shinjuku. Some photographers have presented alternative cityscapes, focusing on details or structures that others might not pay attention to. Miyamoto Ryūji (b. 1947), who has worked as a photographer since graduating in graphic design from Tama Art University in 1973, turns his camera on ruins and the destruction of architecture. His motifs include abandoned houses and demolished buildings, like those in his *Architectural Apocalypse* series, for which he received the Kimura Ihei Award in 1989. *Pavilions of Tsukuba Expo '85* shows the dismantling of an exhibition site, and exemplifies the careful composition of his photographs (opposite). Miyamoto also drew attention to homelessness in big cities by making the *Cardboard Houses* series – in some areas, it is impossible to imagine the urban landscape without the makeshift dwellings he photographed (opposite).

Shibata Toshio (b. 1949) and Hatakeyama Naoya (b. 1958) have also concerned themselves with the city in unique ways. Shibata learned oil painting, before switching to photography during his studies at The Royal Academy in Ghent. When he returned to Japan, he focused on quiet streets, empty petrol stations and other deserted scenes at night, creating images that could exist in almost any international city. His carefully composed photographs, such as *Nakai Parking Area, Tomei Expressway* (1986) (p. 251), convey a tranquil atmosphere and mirror his interest in painting.[55] Shibata has continued to photograph cityscapes without any people, and in 1992 he received the Kimura Ihei Award. Hatakeyama also came to photography from painting: he was inspired by a course at Tsukuba University, led by conceptual photographer Ōtsuji Kiyoji. For his *Rivers* series, he entered the manmade rivers in Shibuya, showing the city from an unusual, low viewpoint. Subsequently, in his *Underground* series he turned his camera on the tunnels under Tokyo, presenting painterly photographs of a hidden world in the metropolis (p. 181). Narahashi Asako (b. 1959) has also taken photographs from the water, offering an unexpected view of the land. In contrast to Hatakeyama's work, her photographs are taken in coastal areas. Using a waterproof camera, Narahashi submerges the camera halfway, filling the frame with water below and the shoreline above, and creating quiet compositions that are concerned with the relationship between water, land and the sky (p. 163).

Many photographers have presented personal perspectives on the cities that they live in. Homma Takashi (b. 1962) focused on suburban buildings, car parks, chain restaurants and children in his photobook *Tokyo Suburbia* (1998) (p. 187). He received the Kimura Ihei Award for the book, and has continued to look at the architecture, urban environments and people around him. The Tokyo of his photography is an unglamorous place, contrasting with the bustling city centre which is usually photographed. In *Tokyo and My Daughter* (1999–2010) Homma combined cityscapes and interiors with portraits of a friend's daughter from her first months to elementary school age, telling an individual story of his Tokyo life (p. 187). In 2014, Hiromix captured one of the most photographed locations in Tokyo, the crowded pentagon-shaped crossing in Shibuya. It is known as the world's largest pedestrian scramble, and is surrounded by neon billboards, shops and restaurants. Her photograph shows the rather empty crossing from an elevated perspective. Reflected in a large glass building, the sunlight creates a star-shaped sunray pattern that overlaps with the crossing stripes. Hiromix's Shibuya appears quiet and peaceful – a moment of calm before the traffic lights turn green again (p. 150).

Takano Ryūdai (b. 1963), best known for his photographs of nude men, has also photographed the common environments and 'shabby' urban details that he encounters in his daily life. In 2016, he presented an elegant series of black and white photographs of the shadows of anonymous passersby in the city, *When the absence of light touches the ground, Distance is lost and distance created* (p. 258). They exemplify Takano's interest in light and shadow, while raising questions about the relationship between people and the cities they live in. Kawauchi Rinko (b. 1972), one of the most popular contemporary Japanese photographers, also creates work that reflects an interest in the motifs of her personal environment. Her images of fireworks, *Hanabi* (2001) (p. 198), and her series *Illuminance* (2011) (p. 197) exemplify her serenely poetic style, which finds a fascinating beauty in daily life. Her focus on light, and round, organic forms creates a natural, glowing aesthetic that can be linked with traditional Japanese concepts such as *mono no aware* (literally 'a sensitivity/empathy towards things'), an appreciation of the transience of all things in life.

Shibata Toshio is one of Japan's most important landscape photographers. Instead of depicting conventional motifs such as Mount Fuji, cherry blossoms or autumn leaves, his work draws attention to human interventions across the country, showing dams, bridges and other constructions as part of the landscape. Using a large-format camera and black and white film, his works of the 1980s and 1990s focused on the forms and shapes of the landscape, conveying an almost abstract aesthetic (pp. 184–85).

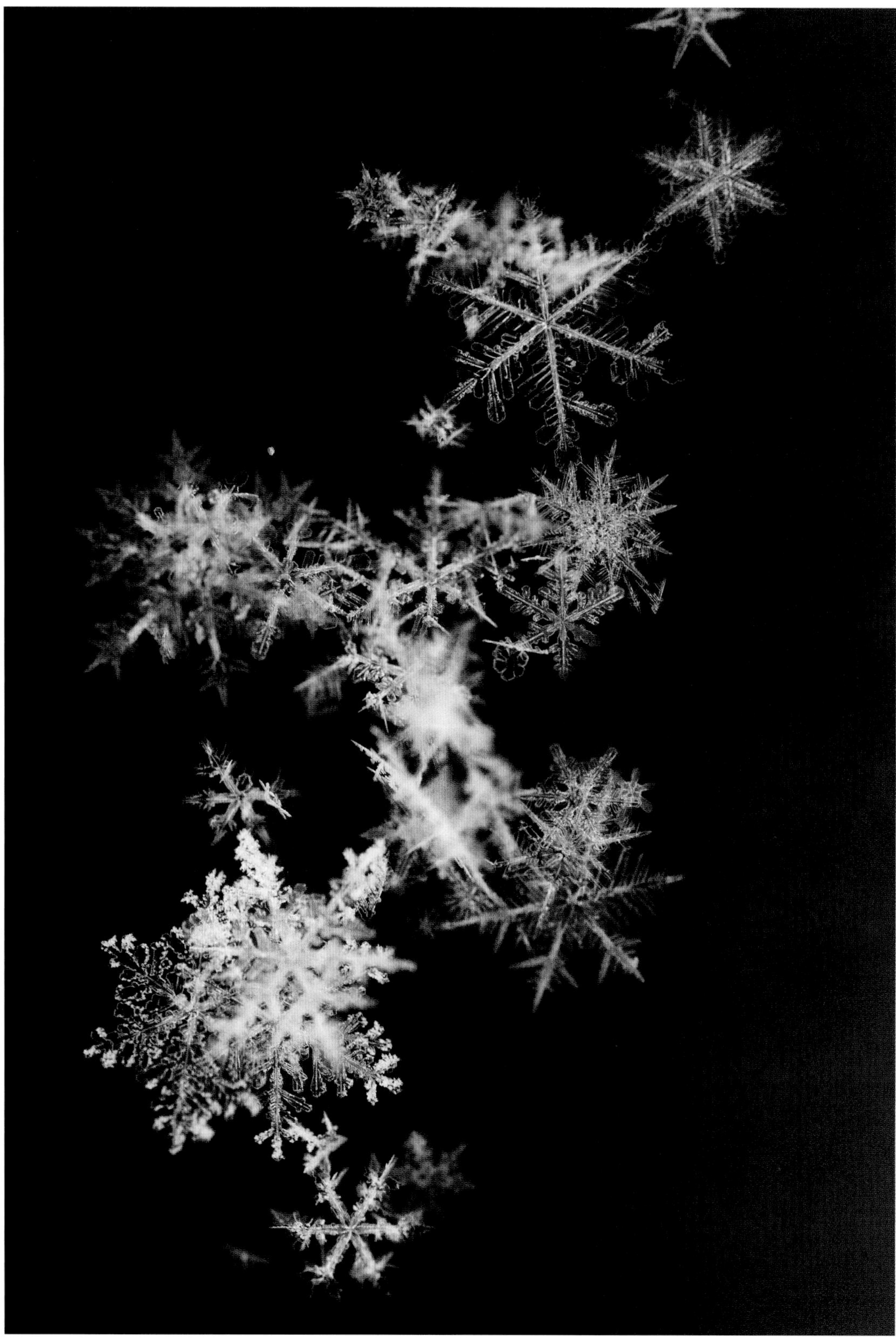

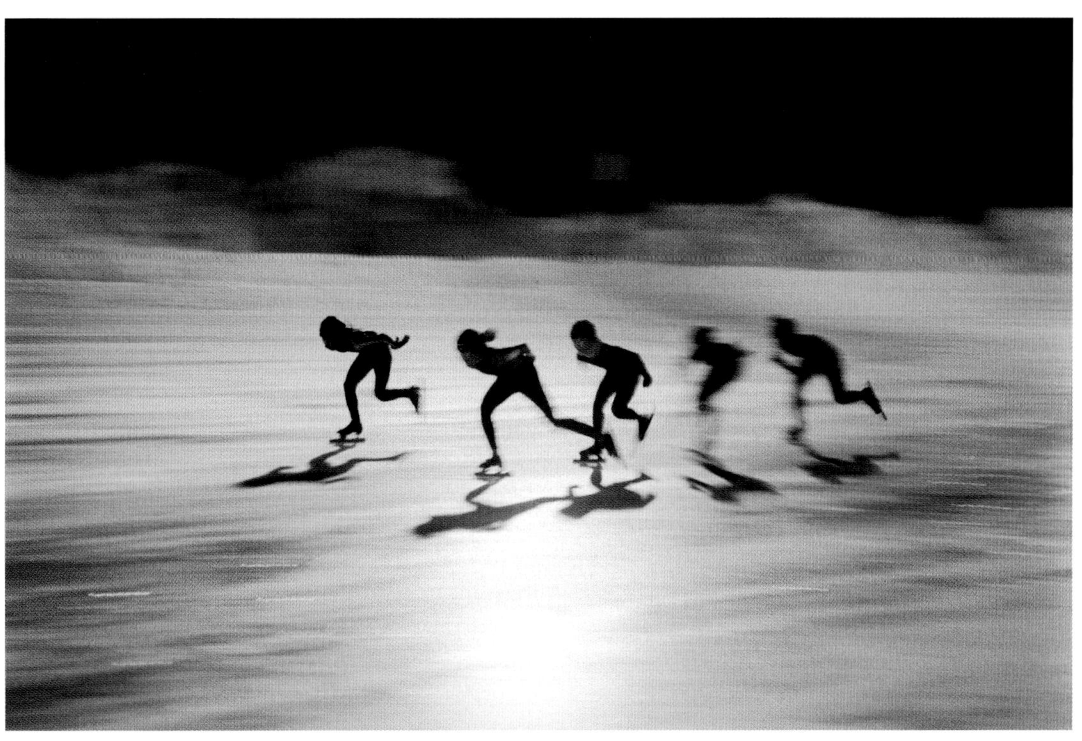

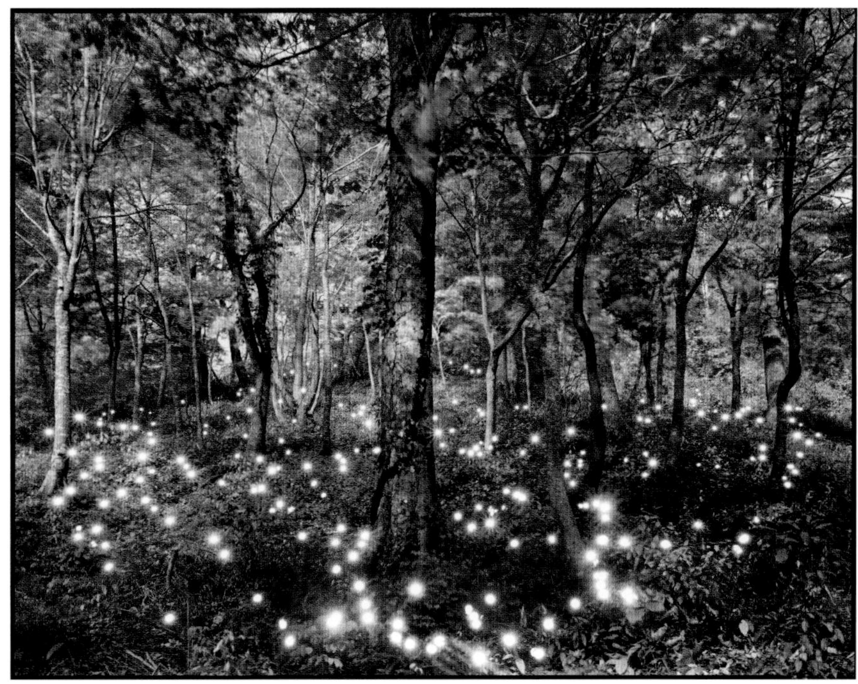

Opposite: Obata Yūji, *Tokachidake*, 2007,
Wintertale series.
Above: Satō Tokihiro, *Shirakami #10*, 2008.
Right: Obata Yūji, *Bekkai*, 2004,
Wintertale series.

Sugimoto Hiroshi, *Sea of Japan, Oki,* 1987.

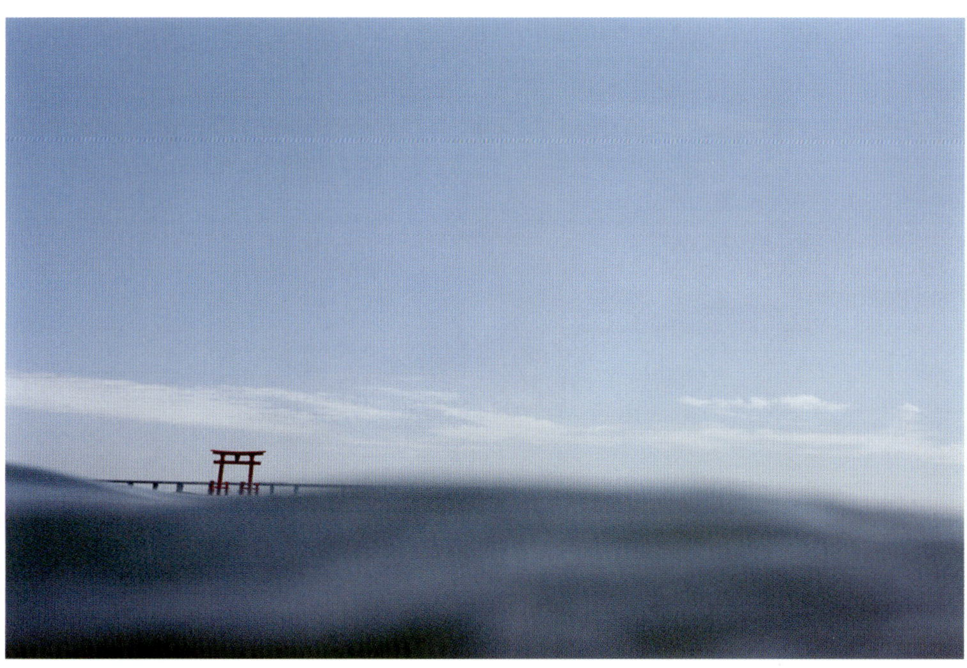

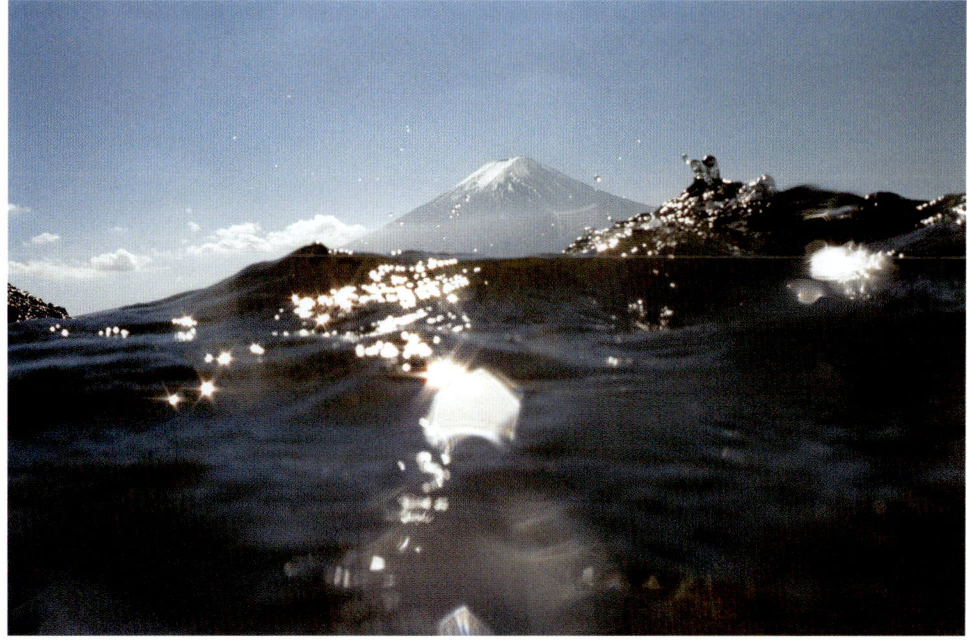

Top: Narahashi Asako, *Bentenjima*, 2001.
Above: Narahashi Asako, *Kawaguchiko #2*, 2003.

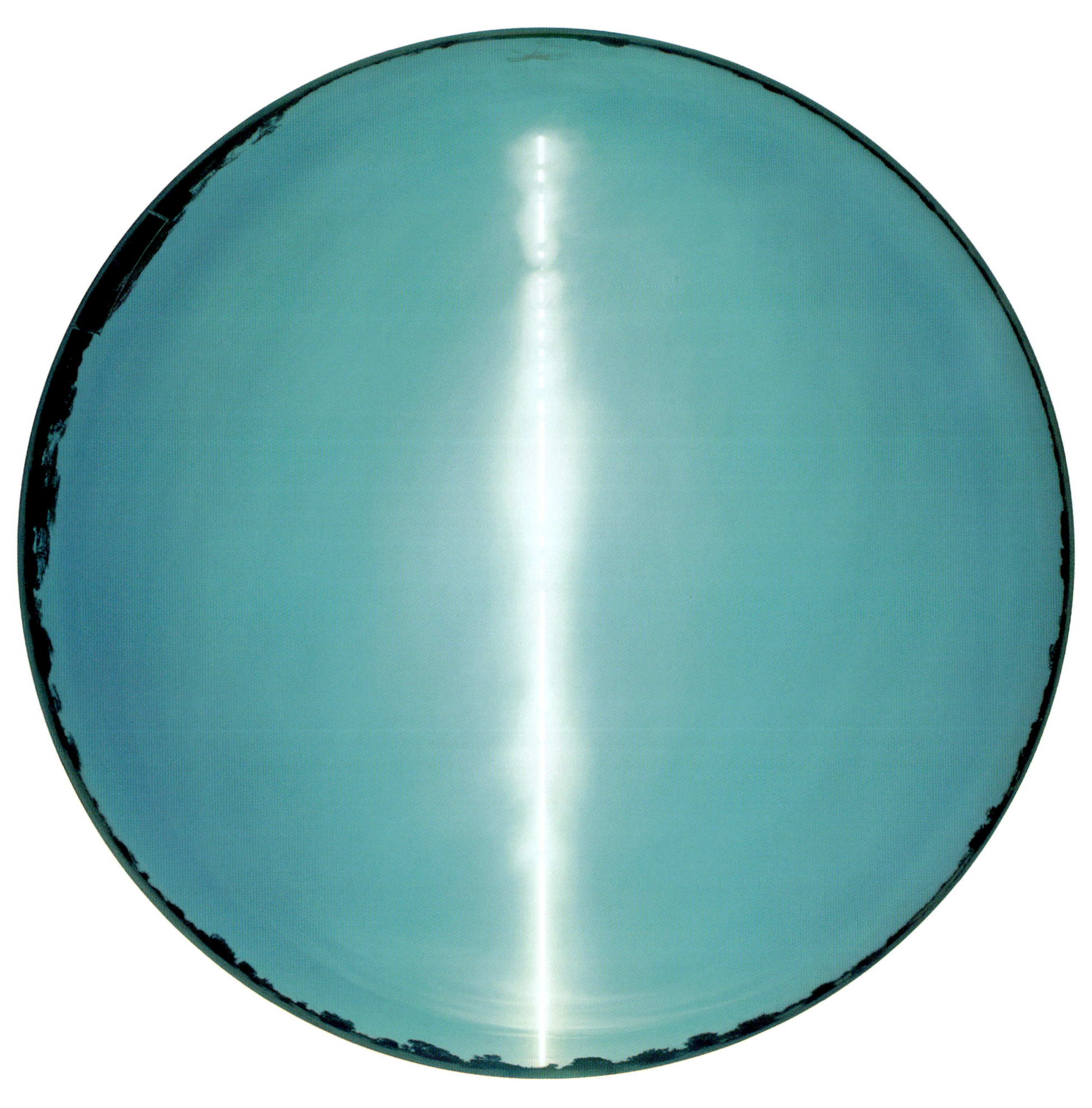

Izima Kaoru, *Nanyuki Kenya*, 2007, *One Sun* series.

Shibata's photographs of deserted landscapes, taken since 2005, suggest a human presence through colours such as the bright red of a bridge, which contrasts with its surroundings in *Okawa Village, Tosa County* (2007) (p. 183). Hatakeyama Naoya's work displays a comparable focus on the relationship between nature and humans. In *Lime Hills*, a series that he began in the late 1980s, he photographed limestone quarries (p. 176). Lime hills exist all over Japan, and limestone is a key ingredient in the production of concrete, steel and glass. After photographing the hills, Hatakeyama became interested in the detonation side of the mining process, starting his *Blast* series in 1995 (p. 176). Using a remote-control camera, he captured the dangerous limestone blasting from point-blank range, creating extremely dynamic, powerful documents of a moment that nobody ever witnesses with their own eyes.[56]

The *Seascapes* photographs by celebrated multimedia artist Sugimoto Hiroshi (b. 1948), who has divided his time between New York and Tokyo since 1974, deserve special mention. The black and white photographs, taken all over the world using a large-format camera, are calm images of the sea, sky and horizon, devoid of any other details (p. 162). Often exhibited, they convey a meditative atmosphere, using the horizon as a motif that transcends space and time. Sugimoto has described his relationship with the sea: 'Every time I view the sea, I feel a calming sense of security, as if visiting my ancestral home; I embark on a voyage of seeing'.[57] He uses photography conceptually, continuously questioning the relationship of the medium with time. In his early *Dioramas* series, he photographed natural history museum displays with stuffed animals, such as *Polar Bear* (1976) (p. 254). What looks like a wildlife snapshot at first sight turns out to be a photograph of a dead polar bear in front of a painted landscape background. The series cleverly raises questions about the photographic medium and reality, time and death.

An interest in the relationship between landscapes and time can also be found in the work of Satō Tokihiro (b. 1957), who studied sculpture before turning to photography. In his *Photo-Respiration* series of long-exposure photographs, begun in the late 1980s, he recorded his own movements with light reflected from a mirror or cast by a penlight as he walked through a landscape (p. 156). The trails and spots of light only came into existence through the encounter with the photographic medium. These mysterious landscape images convey a strong sense of spirituality. Satō has described the photographic process: 'While seeking the sun filtering through the trees, I pursue the slight chance that it will penetrate to the tree I have chosen. The incidental rays shine from the sun to the tree and the light reflects back from me, close beside the tree, and the camera receives both...'.[58] Obata Yūji's black and white photographs convey a comparable aesthetic of mystery. Inspired by Pieter Bruegel's painting *The Hunters in the Snow* (1565), Obata (b. 1962) was compelled to photograph winter scenes, and travelled to northern Japan. He created romantic photographs of the snowy landscapes,

including dynamic shots of ice skaters (p. 161), before becoming fascinated with the challenge of photographing snowflakes. His close-up compositions show the crystals as a phenomenon of natural beauty, without any digital manipulation (p. 160).

Nomura Hitoshi (b. 1945) was one of the first artists to use photography as a conceptual, investigative tool. Using a variety of media, he has often combined his interest in the cosmos with science and art. He has recorded the movements of the moon, and has also examined stars and the sun. *The Analemma '91 – Noon* (1991) exemplifies his interest in repeating photographic shots and prolonging exposure time: it shows the form that emerged from recording the sun at noon from the same place, at the same hour, for a year (p. 157). He has photographed the movement of the sun from dawn to sunset as well, using a fisheye lens. Izima Kaoru (b. 1954) has also photographed the sun using long exposure, in his *One Sun* series (opposite). To Izima, the sun is representative of nature, and linked to his faith that 'God dwells in all nature', a basic belief of Shinto religion. Izima has explained: 'I wanted to create an icon that I could pray to'.[59]

Photography has great potential to look back, and landscapes or interiors can act as vessels for the past. Sugimoto's *Movie Theatres* series, for example, depicts the interiors of old, grand, sometimes abandoned cinemas in the United States (p. 250). He photographed complete film screenings with a long exposure time, leaving empty white screens in the photographs as if to emphasize the passing of time. Inoue Hiroko, who started as a fabric artist before switching to photography and sculpture, has also focused on the relationship between past and present. In a series titled *Inside Out,* begun in 1996, she aimed her camera at windows in historical locations, including a mental hospital in Vienna (p. 186), a Nazi concentration camp and the ruins of a sanatorium, all of which convey invisible 'memories' of past events. A similar approach can be found in the work of London-based photographer Yoneda Tomoko (b. 1965). One of her first solo exhibitions, 'Topographical Analogy', held in 1997 at Zeit-Foto Salon, presented photographs of the visible and invisible traces left behind on interiors and walls in rooms (p. 252). The relationship between past events, and landscapes and people in the present is Yoneda's main theme. For her *After the Thaw* series (2004), she visited Hungary and Estonia, both of which had just joined the EU. A photograph of a couple in a Socialist Realist-style public pool presents traces of the country's political past while focusing on two young individuals, conveying optimism about the future (p. 195).

In 1995, an earthquake with a magnitude of 7.2 struck the city of Kobe and its vicinity. It killed over 5,000 people and destroyed more than 100,000 homes and other buildings. Miyamoto Ryūji photographed the ruins. Yoneda also went back to Japan, to her family, and photographed the aftermath. She did not exhibit the works until 2004, juxtaposing them with photographs of the city ten years later in the series *A Decade After*. The captions explain the specific historical significance of the photographed places, for example *Classroom I, used as a temporary mortuary* (p. 194). Yoneda's calm photographs look different alongside the captions; the titles are important parts of the works, awakening feelings related to past events.

Artists have also dealt with the 2011 Tōhoku earthquake and tsunami, which resulted in a nuclear accident at the Fukushima Daiichi Nuclear Power Plant and the spread of radioactive contamination. Hatakeyama was affected directly: his hometown, Rikuzentakata, was completely destroyed and members of his family died. He decided to exhibit personal photographs of the area before the earthquake, and also to photograph the aftermath and rebuilding (p. 181). He has emphasized how the catastrophe has changed his life and photography.[60] Ōmori Katsumi (b. 1963) created a series titled *Everything happens for the first time* weeks after the event. He experienced the earthquake at his home in Chiba and decided to drive to Fukushima, photographing the blooming cherry trees on the way (pp. 188, 193). He placed a small toy with translucent pink balls between the camera and landscape, creating halations in his images. The mysterious reflections and captions mentioning the date and location convey a feeling of unease; the photographs subtly evoke the invisible problem of radioactivity. Tsuchida Hiromi has visited the radioactive forest in Fukushima regularly since 2011, taking seasonal photographs that convey a subtle, critical message about the unbalanced relationship between humans and nature.

Still Lifes

Still life is an artistic genre defined by compositions of natural or manmade objects, such as cut flowers, fruits, vegetables or game. Kon Michiko (b. 1955), who came to photography from woodblock printing and collage, creates unique still-life photographs in black and white that feature organic matter, such as fish, food and plants. They bring to mind both 17th-century vanitas paintings and surrealist compositions, featuring unexpected 'encounters' between usually unrelated objects. *Yellowtails and Hat* (1986) exemplifies the ambiguous, mysterious style of Kon's work, linking a hat with a dead yellowtail fish and a small rose (opposite). She was the third woman to receive the Kimura Ihei Award, in 1991.

Inose Kou (b. 1960), who studied photography at the University of Osaka with Inoue Seiryu, has taken a small number of highly sought-after black and white photographs. His first series, *Dogra Magra*, presents strange, dark images, some of which could broadly be categorized as still lifes. The photographs are inspired by Yumeno Kyūsaku's science-fiction novel *Dogra Magra* (1935), in which the protagonist wakes up in a hospital with amnesia. The compositions, featuring for example a spider crawling on a tap (p. 256), convey a fascinatingly surreal, uncanny atmosphere.

A still life can be a celebration of pleasures, featuring food, wine or flowers, but at the same time, it warns of ephemerality. Kawauchi Rinko's restrained, calm photographs are quiet celebrations of the circle of life, drawing attention to the beauty of daily scenes and objects. They include symbols of life, like a hen's egg that is just about to open (p. 200), as well as death, including a still life with round dead animal eyes. In his series *musikera*, first exhibited in 2017, Izima Kaoru also concerned himself with dead animals, namely insects such as mosquitos or cockroaches (p. 264). His close-up shots resemble photographs of human corpses – Izima takes a final portrait before throwing the dead insects away.[61]

Araki has enjoyed combining bouquets with small dolls or toys in a playful manner (p. 268). His countless still lifes link sexuality and death: the withering flowers and lifeless dolls (sometimes naked and in bondage, just like his living models) create an atmosphere that oscillates between youthful play and morbid sadism.

Ishiuchi Miyako's oeuvre can be divided into three phases. The first phase, around *Yokosuka Story* (1977), features the surfaces of buildings, cheaply built apartments and former nightclubs (see Chapter 3). The second phase focuses on the human body, revealing a variety of skin textures. *Mother's,* which represented Japan at the 2005 Venice Biennale, marks the beginning of the third phase, in which Ishiuchi has worked with colour photography and objects. The series consists of close-up photographs of Ishiuchi's mother's body in old age, and large still lifes of her now deceased mother's possessions, such as her lipsticks (pp. 260–61). When asked about the change to colour photography, Ishiuchi tends to laugh and say: 'a red lipstick just looks better in colour!' Since *Mother's,* her photography has 'portrayed' personal belongings left behind by people, focusing on fabrics including silk (p. 263).

One of Ishiuchi's most important projects is ひろしま/ *hiroshima* (ongoing since 2007), which features the remnants of clothing, shoes and other possessions from after the atomic bombing. An editor at Shūeisha Publishing commissioned Ishiuchi to create a photobook about the objects at the Hiroshima Peace Memorial Museum, previously also documented by Tsuchida Hiromi (see Chapter 3). Ishiuchi had never been to Hiroshima, and as the theme already had a long history in Japanese photography, she hesitated before accepting.[62] The subjects of her photographs, shot with 35mm film and a handheld camera, were partly on display and partly in storage. The photographs do not show the museum context, often presenting the dresses or shirts on light boxes (p. 262). This emphasis on transparency can be read as a reference to ideas of the photographic medium as a trace of light. Every analogue photograph is indexical, recording reality with light. It shows a trace of something in the past, and is therefore intertwined with memory and death. This relationship between photography and ephemerality has often been discussed: one need only call to mind Susan Sontag's statement in *On Photography* that all photographs are 'memento mori', since they 'testify to time's relentless melt'.[63]

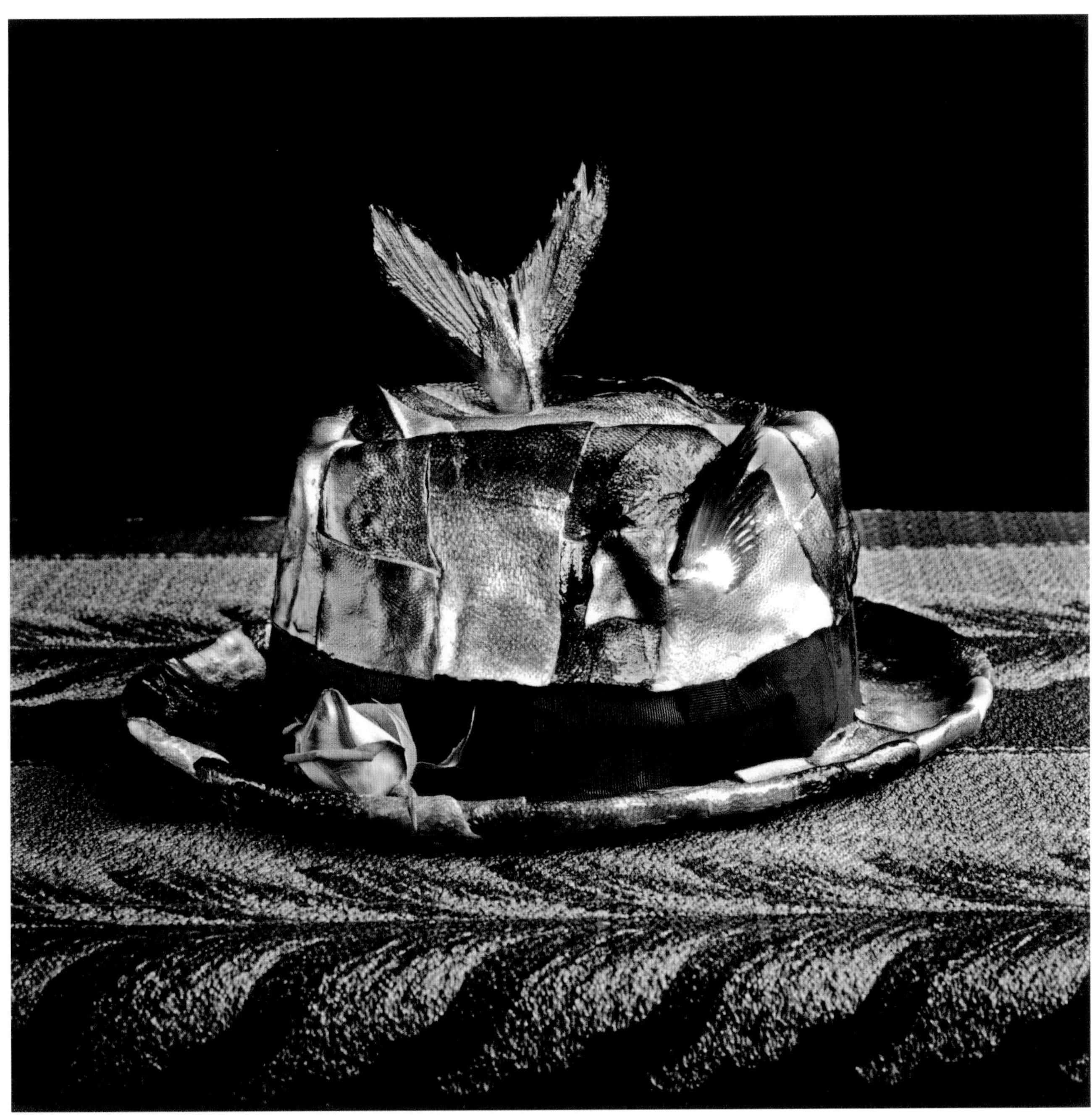

Kon Michiko, *Yellowtails and Hat,* 1986.

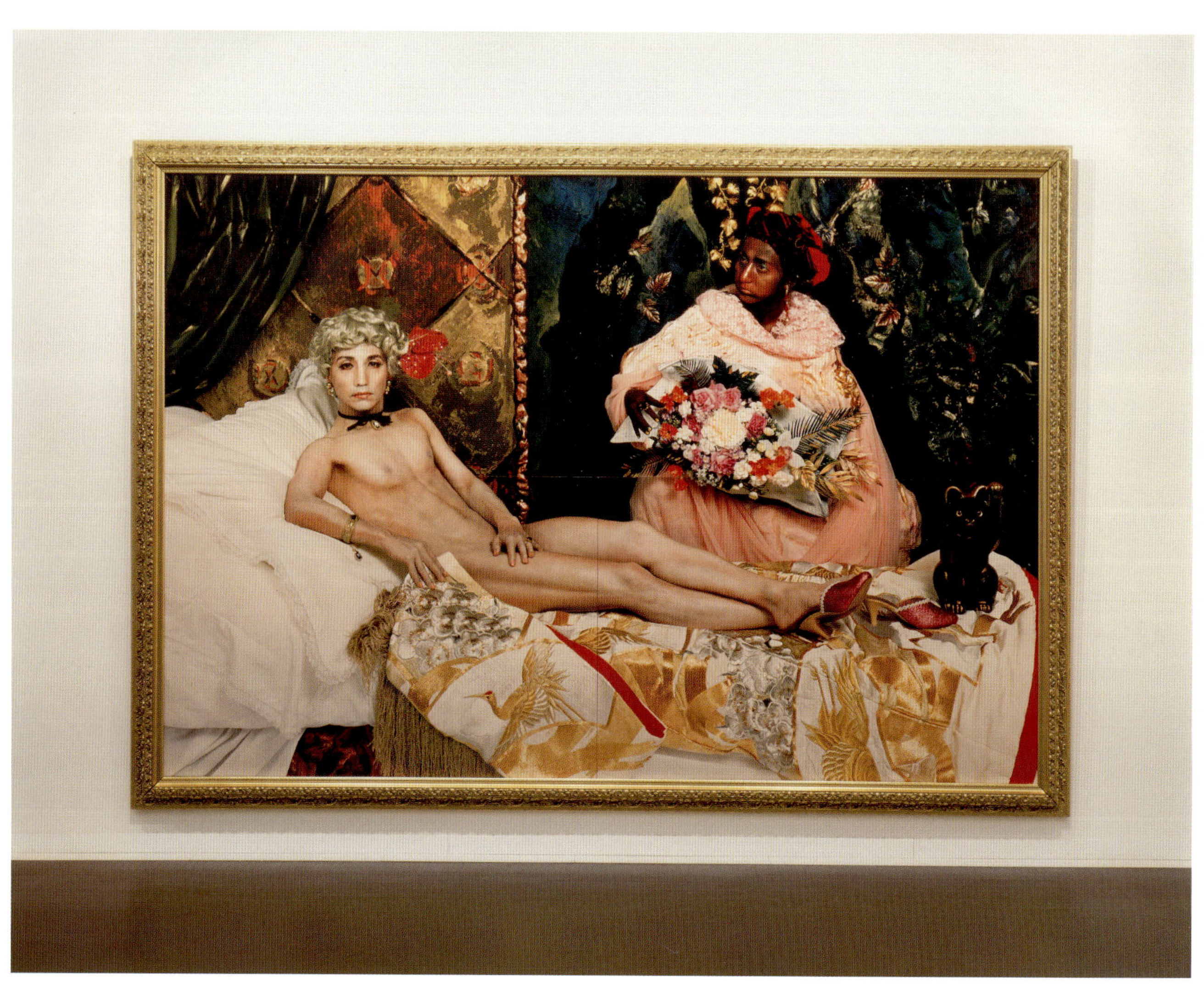

Morimura Yasumasa, *Portrait (Futago)*, 1988–90.

Roland Barthes wrote in *Camera Lucida* that every photograph is 'a kind of *tableau vivant*, a figuration of the motionless and made-up face beneath which we see the dead'.[64] By photographing the relics of the atomic bombing as if they were floating through light and time, Ishiuchi creates a peaceful atmosphere while quietly showing the destructive power of humans. Her still lifes also reflect the traditional Japanese aesthetic of transience.[65] ひろしま/*hiroshima* typifies the calm strength of Ishiuchi's photography; it seduces us with the bittersweet beauty of ephemerality.

Yoneda's ongoing series *Between Visible and Invisible* is also concerned with objects that people have left behind, most of which are kept in museums or archives. It features the original writings of iconic intellectuals of the 20th century, ranging from Sigmund Freud, to Gandhi, to Tanizaki Junichirō (p. 253). Showing these writings through the writers' actual glasses, Yoneda creates fascinating compositions that evoke a journey into the past. She builds a relationship between the visible image and invisible, internal images – historical facts, or the viewers' knowledge of those featured.

The Human

Since the 1990s, questions around 'the human' have become increasingly pertinent. Images of virtual bodies, debates over reproductive technology, the blurring of biological gender boundaries and people's (re)design of their bodies using exercise and cosmetic surgery have made the term ever more complex. Postmodern thought has also altered the concept of a 'person'; it is no longer static and autonomous, but shaped by a range of social factors.[66] As well as being the subject of discourse in the natural sciences, cultural studies and the media, the human body features in countless photographs.

Artists have long used photography to address issues of social and national identity, gender and politics. Morimura Yasumasa (b. 1951), who lives and works in Osaka, has impersonated icons of art history, popular culture and politics in numerous self-portraits. Imitation is the starting point, but in the end there is always a new original. The 1996 exhibition *Self-portrait as Actress* featured photographs of Morimura dressed as female film stars such as Marilyn Monroe (p. 206) and Audrey Hepburn (p. 208). In his *Requiem for the XX Century* series, he appropriated images of influential men from the 20th century, ranging from Albert Einstein to Charlie Chaplin in the role of Adolf Hitler in *The Great Dictator* (p. 209).

The complexity underlying Morimura's entertaining photographs is evident in his early work *Portrait (Futago)* (1988–90) (opposite). It appropriates Édouard Manet's painting *Olympia* (1863), presenting Morimura not only as the naked coquette Olympia, lying outstretched on a bed, but also as the Black servant in a pink dress, holding a bouquet of flowers. It becomes obvious when looking closely that the splendid background is painted. Morimura explained the theatrical process of making the *tableau vivant*: 'I prepared a backdrop…For the servant on the right hand side, I painted

a body, leaving a hole for the head…I applied make-up to my entire body, reclined nude on the divan, and took the first photograph. Then I applied the face make-up for the servant, stuck my head through the hole, and took the second photograph. Afterward, I pieced together the two'.[67] Morimura did not copy Manet's painting but 'japonized' it by inserting a folklore-style bridal kimono and a beckoning cat (*manekineko*),[68] traditionally used as a sexual talisman in geisha houses. He is wearing a blond curly wig instead of copying Olympia's auburn hair. Art historian Norman Bryson has discussed the stereotypes spelled out by the combination of the kimono and *manekineko*: 'geisha, the figuration of Japan-as-woman, and as the predestined object of the West's colonial depredations'.[69] Morimura's choice of *Olympia*, and the changes he has made for his version, can be linked with the tradition of *mitate-e* ('looking at and comparing pictures'). *Mitate-e* is a metaphorical game in poetry and visual art, grounded in shared familiarity with a certain motif. *Portrait (Futago)* highlights the sociopolitical background of *Olympia* in France. Morimura impersonates both a White and a Black person, simultaneously representing the French colonist and the African colonized. By equating the White coquette and the Black servant as 'twins', he compares the subordination of prostitutes with that of Black people.

Set against Japan's historical background, the artwork also juxtaposes two further viewpoints. The first concerns the influence of 'Western' powers in the late 19th century, when Japan was forced to open its borders, around the time that Manet painted *Olympia*. In curator Hasegawa Yōko's words, 'Morimura tells us about a blind longing for the West: about Japanese acting in Western dramas wearing fair-haired wigs, or appearing in oil paintings dressed in Western style.'[70] The second viewpoint is that of Euro-American Orientalism. The cliché of the geisha not only represents a Western fascination with gracious Japanese women, but also highlights how the West has emphasized its superior position by juxtaposing it with the image of a pretty yet childlike female. The influence of Japanese culture on European art is reflected in the definition of the term 'Japonism' in Manet's time, and is evident in *Olympia*.

Portrait (Futago) offers readings connected to the historical background of Manet's time in both France and Japan, but it also draws attention to a contemporary Japanese fascination with the West, and suggests the presence of Neo-Japonism in Europe. The photograph raises questions about gender, too: Morimura provides an ironic critique of conventional gender relations in European art (the male gaze vs. the female body), while re-eroticizing the Japanese male body. Traditionally a common motif in Japanese culture, the beautiful 'adolescent man' (*wakashū*) began to fade as an aesthetic object shortly after Manet painted *Olympia*, mainly due to Western influences. Morimura's discernibly Japanese, slender male body as well as the props used suggest that he did not aim to identify completely with either the female or the Western 'other'.

Instead, the identities in the large photograph are hybrid, confidently staged in bright colours.

By appropriating a French painting of the 1860s, Morimura has, in 1988, presented us with an original new work that offers at least as many readings as *Olympia*.

Yanagi Miwa (b. 1967) made installations before switching to performance and photography. She lives and works in Kyoto, and her debut in the international art world was in 1996, when Morimura introduced her *Elevator Girls* series to curator Peter Weiermair in Frankfurt. The staged, digitally manipulated photographs present similar-looking young women as 'elevator girls' – women who operate elevators in Japanese department stores – in different dreamlike scenarios. Face-mounted onto shiny acrylic, the expansive, panoramic photographs have often been displayed in darkened spaces with dramatic spotlighting. *Elevator Girl House 3F* (1998) shows nine young women standing and sitting on the floor around an octagonal glass hole (p. 234). The shiny hole in the ground is divided into descending shelves, on which white women's shoes are aligned. The women all wear the same neat uniform. Smiling slightly and looking into the hole, they are either not seeing or deliberately ignoring the camera. The viewer gets the feeling of standing in front of an elevator, the doors of which are opening or closing in that very moment.

Mori Mariko (b. 1967) worked as a fashion model and designer before moving to London and then New York. Before switching to elaborate installations, often using fibre optic devices, she featured herself in numerous photographs. In *Tea Ceremony III* (1994), Mori is serving tea in front of a modern glass building in Tokyo (p. 211). She wears typical secretary-style clothes with a blouse, vest and skirt; underneath, however, she wears a shiny silver costume with a cap, to which two protruding ears are attached. Two middle-aged men in suits are walking to the left, ignoring Mori.

Both *Elevator Girl House 3F* and *Tea Ceremony III* are large, colourful photographs featuring pretty young women. Their socio-critical messages can only be understood when analysing the works in the context of Japanese society. Yanagi and Mori both highlight standardized social codes by breaking them: the elevator girls let go of their ritualized body language by sitting on the floor instead of operating the elevator, while the tea-serving secretary wears a strange silver cap with elf-like ears. The silver costume exposes Mori's other garments as nothing but a masquerade that creates the social identity of an 'office lady' (*ōeru*). *Elevator Girl House 3F* points critically at the seductive, dreamscape aesthetic of department stores, including their decorative elevator girls. At the same time, the photograph shows women as consumers who are obsessed with shoes and other goods. *Tea Ceremony III* focuses on disparities within the work system, juxtaposing the two businessmen with Mori as the alien-like secretary. By courteously offering tea and wearing a neat uniform, she reflects the subordinated position of female employees in offices. In 1990s Japan, women were still predominantly supposed to stick to 'feminine' roles, supporting their male colleagues.

Yanagi has continued to examine themes around womanhood. *Fairy Tales* (2004) featured black and white photographs referring to folk tales such as those by the Grimm Brothers and Hans Christian Andersen. However, Yanagi's protagonists are all young girls, and they break away from their passive roles. In *Sleeping Beauty*, a girl confidently fights a witch, as if to defend herself against an endless sleep (p. 235). The series critically emphasizes the fairy tale cliché of innocent girls versus old witches.

The work of Sawada Tomoko (b. 1977) has also been concerned with questions of social identity and gender. It is based on self-portraits, in which Sawada changes her appearance through costumes, hair, make-up and different facial expressions, and even by gaining and losing weight.[71] Her *OMIAI♡* series references the portfolios used for arranged marriages (*omiai*) (pp. 218–19). Sawada was photographed in a professional photography studio in Kobe, visiting as a different type of woman each week. She asked the photographer to imagine that she was a new customer each time. Sawada received the Kimura Ihei Award in 2004; as the first winning artist who did not press the camera's shutter herself, she represented a change in the award's value system.

Other artists who have used self-portraiture in their work include London-based Ōtsuka Chino (b. 1976). *Imagine Finding Me* (2005) presents Ōtsuka as an adult next to herself as a child, in digitally composed photographs (p. 186). The works are based on her personal photo albums, including photographs of travels and other memorable events. Linking the past and present in a journey through time, the series raises questions about identity in relation to time and photography, inviting the viewer to imagine what might have been.

Self-taught Tokyo Rumando (b. 1980) came to photography in 2005 after working as a model for jobs including nude and fetish photographs. Taking control by stepping behind the camera, she has created black and white and polaroid self-portraits that convey a strong female eroticism. In her 2012 *Rest 3000 Stay 5000* series, she went to various love hotels in Tokyo, imagining and presenting herself as different kinds of female visitors (p. 241).[72] In her following series, *Orphée* (2012–14), she undressed and dressed up in front of a circular mirror, confronting her own memories and projections by using the mirror as a tool to link the past and present (p. 236).

Ishiuchi Miyako has been concerned with the human body in a different way, approaching female and male subjects in extreme close-up. *Scars #21* (1996) typifies the artist's interest in the shapes of the human body, its skin patterns and wrinkles (opposite). Scars are featured as natural parts of the skin and the photographic composition, and exist in a tautological relationship with the photographic medium: both the scars and the photographs relate to past events.

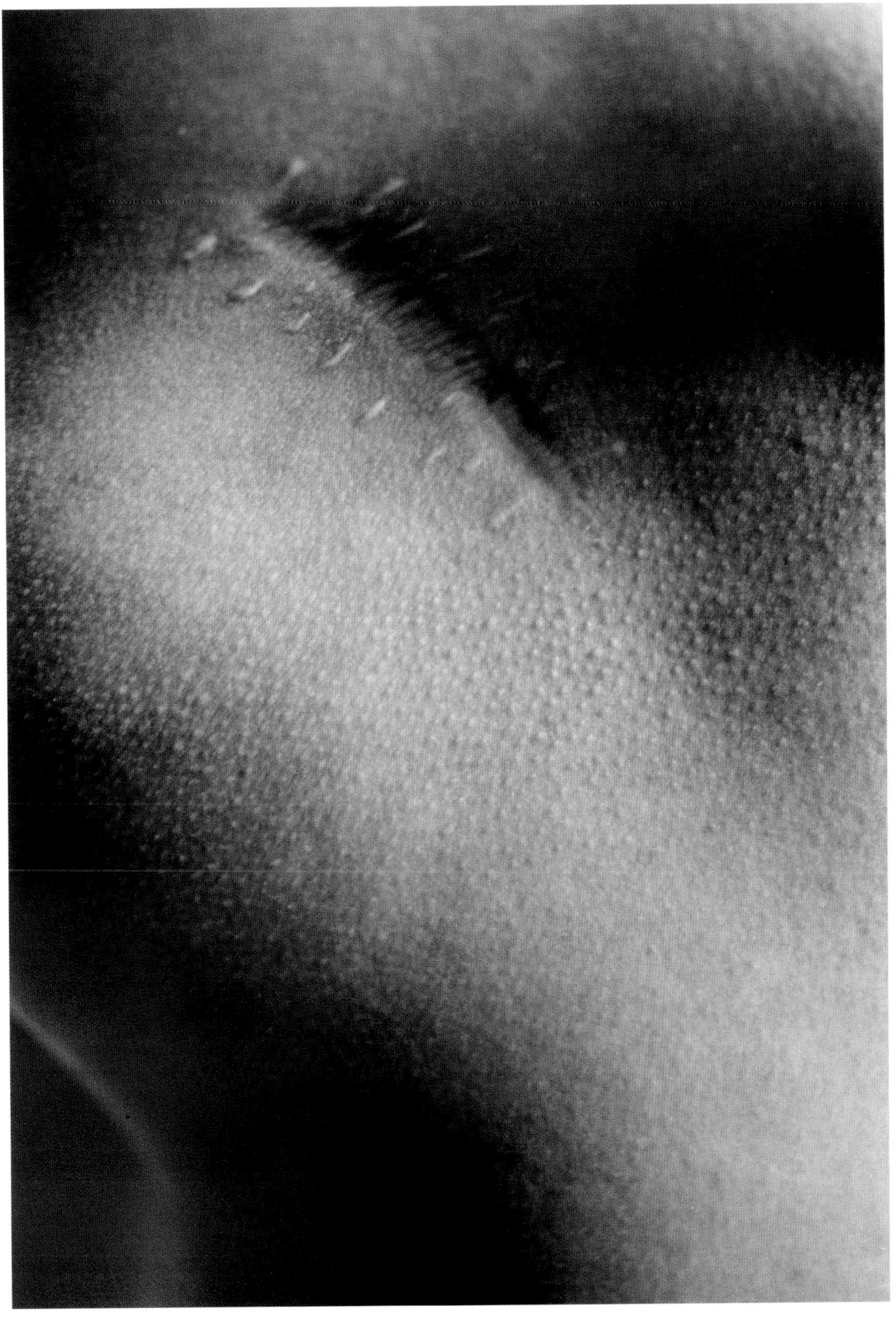

Ishiuchi Miyako, *Scars #21*, 1996.

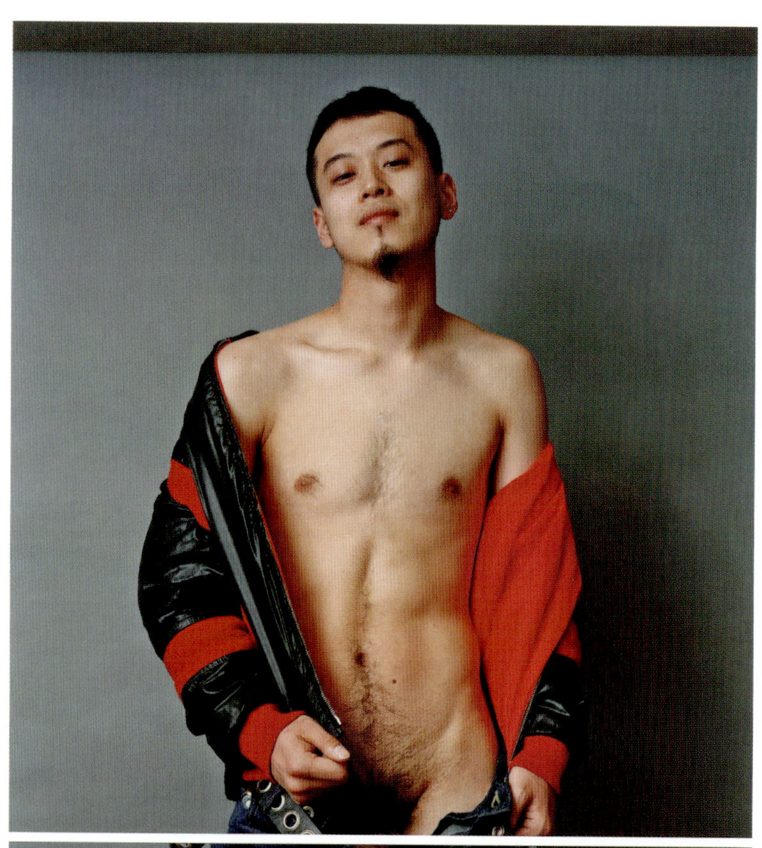
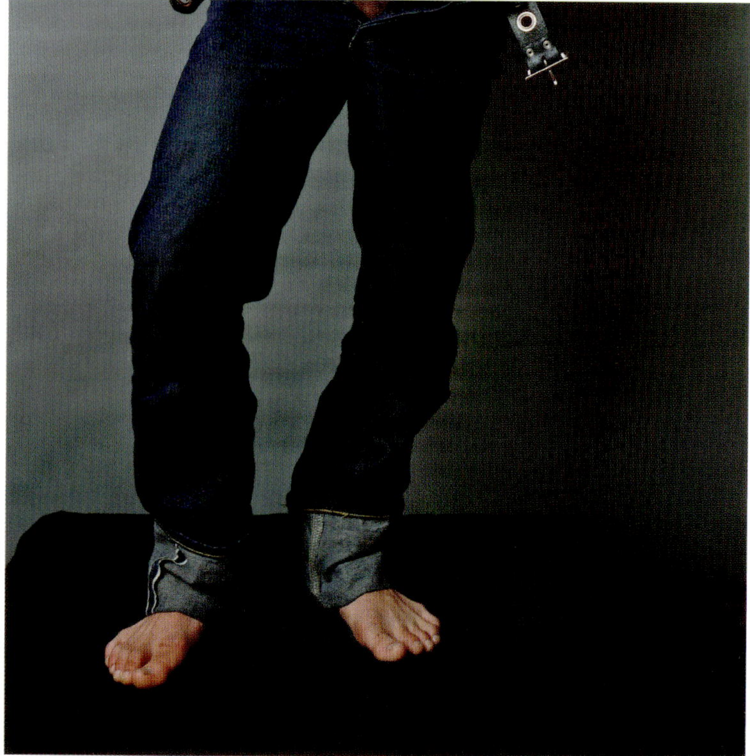

Takano Ryūdai, *TOSHIHISA #3*, 2001, *tender penis* series.

Izima Kaoru, who studied at Tokyo College of Photography, first received attention in the European art world with *Landscapes with a Corpse*. The series began in 1993 and presents elaborately staged, professionally shot 'death' scenes featuring TV and film stars and models, most of whom are young, Japanese and female (pp. 220–23). The photographs were first published in Izima's alternative fashion magazine *Zyappu*, accompanied by tabloid-style articles describing the imaginary cause of death and often quoting 'witnesses'. The photographs are taken from different angles, as if a police officer has recorded a crime scene. Later, the works were also exhibited as prints in galleries and museums. Fashion and tabloid photography, crime scene photography and art history are referenced simultaneously.

Edgar Allan Poe famously stated that 'the death of a beautiful woman is, unquestionably, the most poetical topic in the world.'[73] In 'Western' culture, women's deaths and female corpses have long been popular motifs. The 'death and the maiden' motif originated from dance-of-death cycles in Germany, and has occurred in prints, drawings and paintings since around 1500 – for example, those by Hans Baldung Grien. The images show encounters between attractive young women and a figure that represents their deaths. This is frequently of a sexual nature. Artworks of the 19th and 20th century, such as those by Edvard Munch and Egon Schiele, reflect artists' enduring fascination with this theme. The drowning of Ophelia in Shakespeare's *Hamlet* was another popular motif in literature and art, perhaps most famously presented in Pre-Raphaelite John Everett Millais' painting *Ophelia* (1851–52). In Japanese art history, images of corpses are linked with Buddhist devotional exercises. Since the 5th century there have been Buddhist texts that describe the decay of a corpse in nine stages, and images of a young woman's corpse in *kusōzu* ('images of the nine stages of a decaying corpse'). These images narrate the woman's decomposition, juxtaposing her attractiveness in the first of the nine images with her body's decomposition in the latter. The visualization of decay seeks to help the Buddhist viewer to overcome his sexual desires.

The *Landscapes* photographs place the viewer in a powerful position, looking down at a 'dead' woman and investigating the scene. The series reinforces the stereotypical juxtaposition between the female as an alluring, passive image and the male as an active creator and viewer. It is not surprising that feminist writer Alice Schwarzer criticized the series as misogynistic.[74] However, Izima used the female image as a fantasy – an opportunity to visualize the abstract phenomenon of death. To return to Poe's words, not only does death make a beautiful woman the 'most poetical' motif, the woman also makes death 'poetical' and by extension 'viewable'. The viewpoints reflected are the models' fantasies: Izima asked the women about their death fantasies (a location, designer and story), and interpreted their answers photographically. The models are therefore in an interestingly ambiguous position: they pose as passive, but are active in the process of artistic production. They embody their own fantasies.

Takano Ryūdai (b. 1963), who graduated in politics and economics before becoming a photographer, has frequently aimed his camera at nude men, creating the tender portraits and compositions of the human body that won him the 2006 Kimura Ihei Award. In the history of Japanese photography, the female nude is omnipresent but the male body is rarely depicted. The young, handsome male (*wakashū*) used to be a classic motif in literature and woodblock prints, as an object of desire for both females and males. However, the movement towards 'Western' culture and binary concepts of gender at the end of the 19th century saw this motif fade in most areas of Japanese culture. From the beginning of Japan's period of rapid economic growth in the 1960s, the stereotypical Japanese man had to be a good company worker and citizen, and a family representative. In anthropologist Laura Miller's words, men were evaluated 'primarily on the basis of character, social standing, earning capacity, lineage and other social criteria';[75] attractive appearance was excluded. At the end of the last century, however, a new masculinity began to develop. An increasing number of young men have become concerned with their appearance, going to the gym, plucking their eyebrows or using cosmetic products. In magazines such as *Fine Boys*, men are encouraged to improve their physical appearance. Against this background, Takano's work draws attention to a renewed interest in men as sexually alluring objects. His photographs mirror a new confidence to look at a variety of men from an aesthetic perspective.

Article 175 of the 1907 Japanese Penal Code prohibits the public display of 'obscene' images. Until the 1990s, photographs showing the pubic area in magazines like *Playboy* were censored by airbrushing or manually scratching over them – a popular students' job. Even pubic hair was not publishable. The interpretation of the law has eased, but the police still have to respond to any allegations from the public in a museum. Various Japanese artists, including Araki or Izima, have mocked this censorship by painting over the pubic area or ironically accentuating it. Takano's large portraits of half-naked men in his *Tender Penis* series (1999–2000) are composed of an upper and a lower shot, mounted together (opposite). The penises are cut out and pasted on the back of the photographs, so that they are not visible in an exhibition and the censorship law is cleverly skirted.

The work of Nomura Sakiko (b. 1967) also includes numerous photographs of nude men, presented in photobooks such as *Tsukuyomi* (2005) or *Black Darkness* (2008) (pp. 230–23). Her dark and often grainy black and white photographs convey an intimate atmosphere, approaching the young men tenderly. Nomura began working for Araki in 1991, and despite great stylistic differences, Araki's understanding of photography as a medium to simply record what is close by is visible in her works as well.

The Future of Japanese Photography

Many 'newcomers' have created interesting work over the last years, and it goes beyond the scope of this book to introduce all of them.

Asakai Yōko (b. 1974) has portrayed people watching films at home in her *sight* series (2006–10) (opposite). She draws attention to her subjects' absorption in a fictitious world, as well as to the relationship between looking and being looked at in photography. Shiga Lieko (b. 1980) has created surreal worlds by using simple techniques such as opening holes in photographs, holding them against the light and re-photographing them. Ranging from her early *Piano* series (1998), which shows her little brother 'performing' on an imaginary piano (pp. 242–45), to her *Canary* series (2006) (pp. 247–49), Shiga's photographs are mysterious and uncanny.

Yokota Daisuke (b. 1983) has a similarly otherworldly style, and is celebrated worldwide for his experimental, black and white photographs. Their grainy, blurry style is reminiscent of early *Provoke* images. Shooting on a compact digital camera, Yokota has repeatedly printed and re-photographed his work on medium-format film, using heat and light or applying acid or flames to the end results. His meticulously created images oscillate between photographic records and imaginative scenes, as is evident in his *Back Yard* series (2011) (pp. 266–67). In *Color photographs* (2015), Yokota layered sheets of unused large-format colour film, and experimented with unusual developing methods in the darkroom before scanning the results (p. 265). This focus on the materiality and 'alchemy' of film has resulted in abstract images, full of ecstatic colours and liquescent forms.

Japanese photography today continues to be at the forefront – it moves forward relentlessly in original directions, taking fascinating new forms. At the same time, iconic Japanese photographers of the 20th century are beginning to receive more attention, and they are increasingly present in the global art historical canon. Not only are their works exhibited in large shows, they are included in the permanent collections of a growing number of international museums.

This book has sought to present an introduction to Japanese photography, developing a cultural bridge that connects 'Western' readers with a fascinating photography history. Looking forward, I am convinced that the future of Japanese photography remains exciting and diverse.

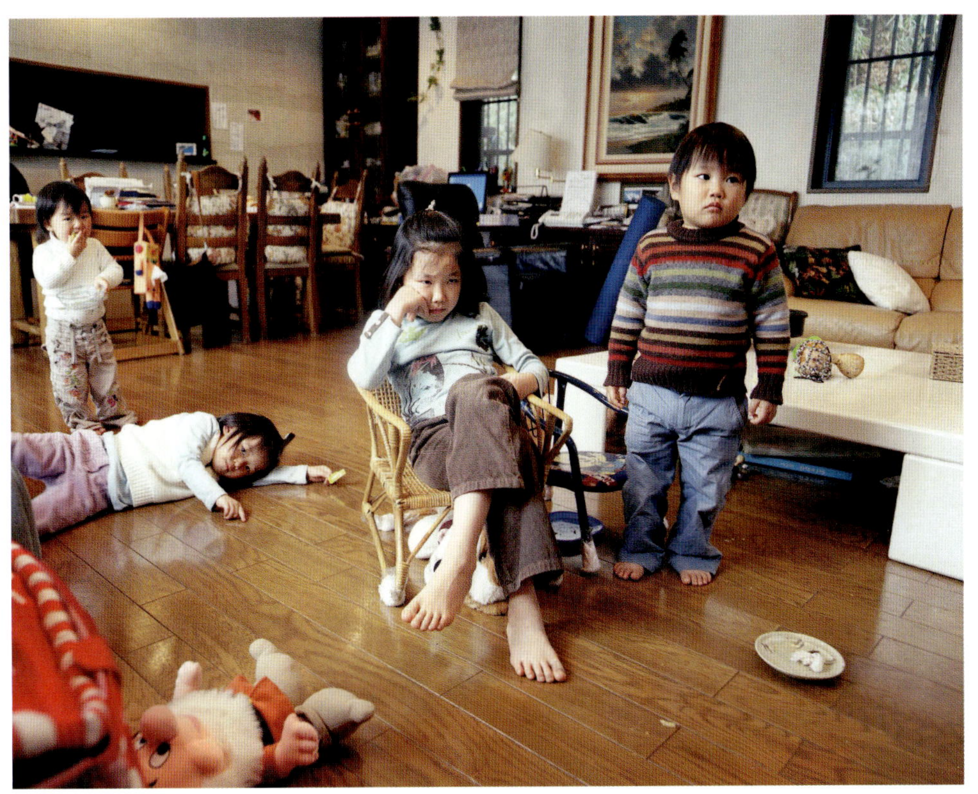

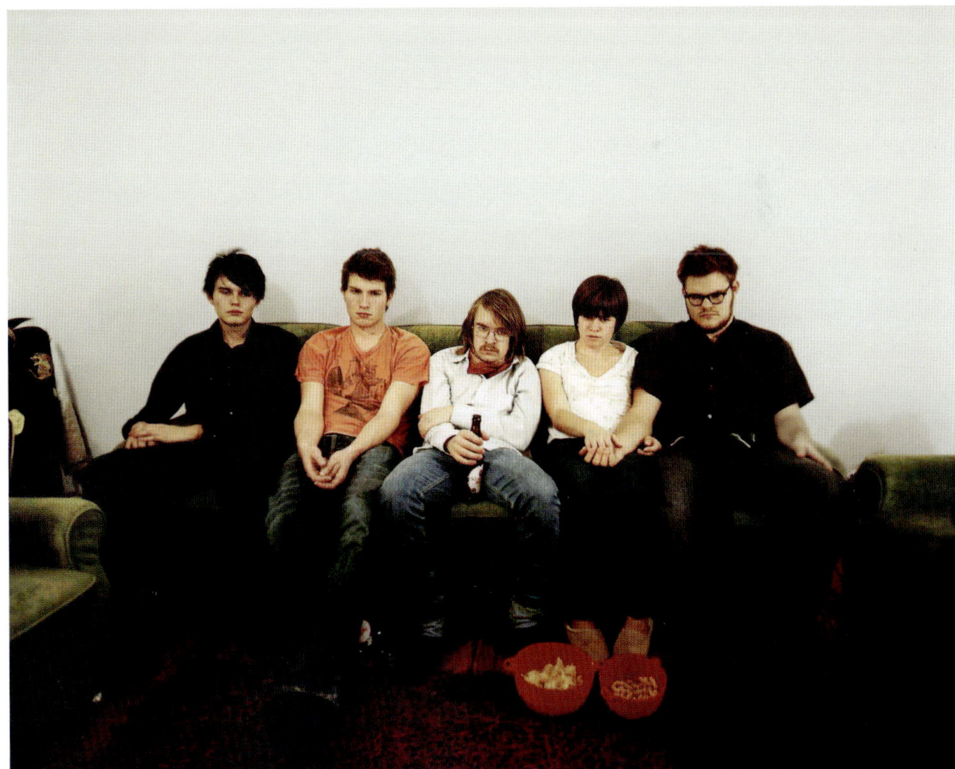

Above: Asakai Yōko, *Home Alone, Tokyo*, 2007, *sight* series.
Right: Asakai Yōko, *The Seventh Seals, Berlin*, 2006, *sight* series.

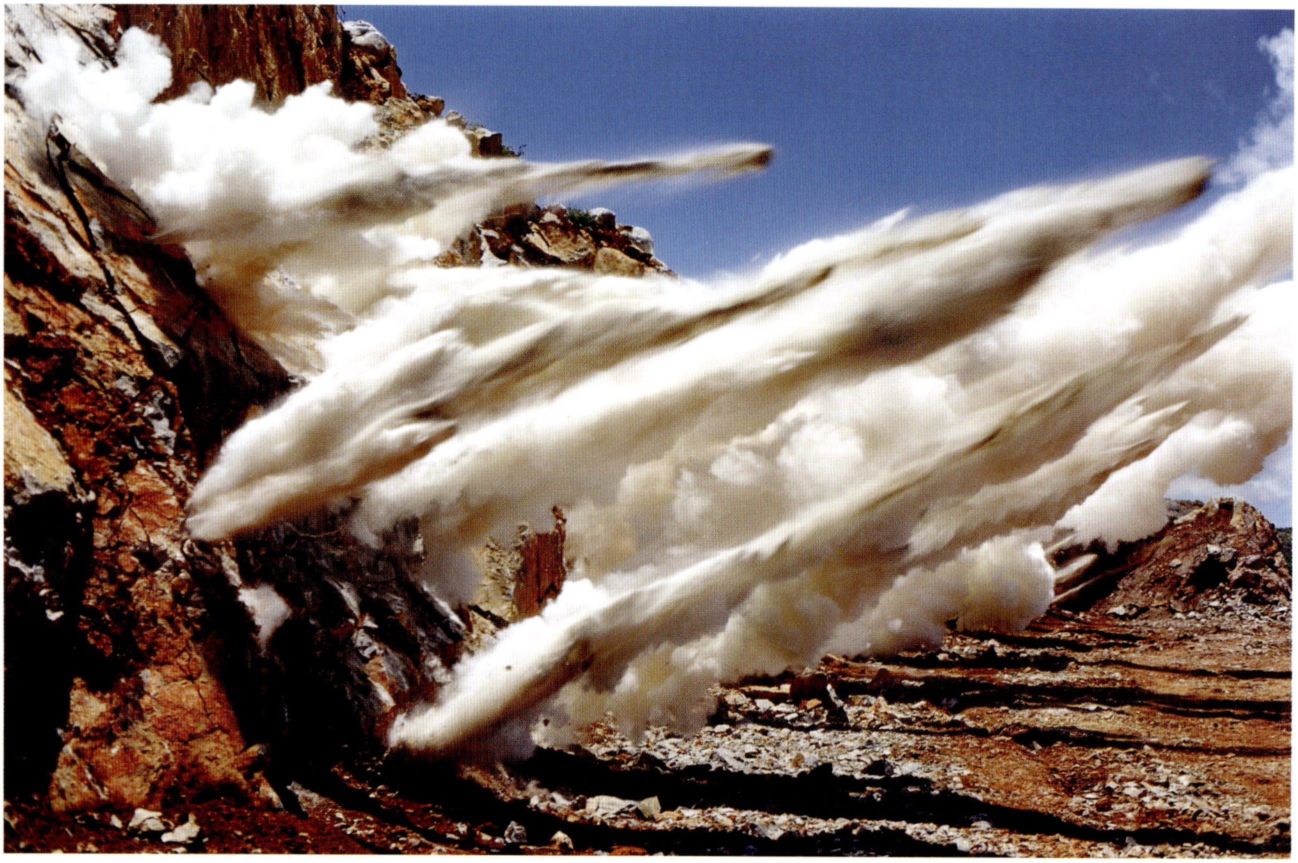

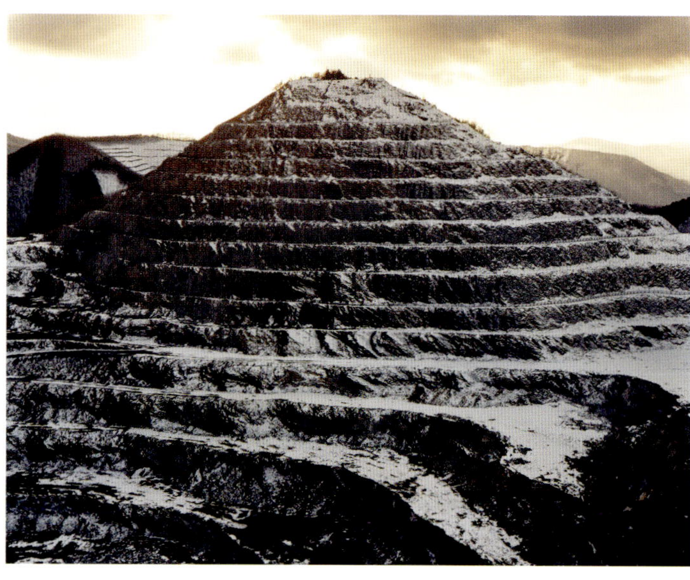

Above: Hatakeyama Naoya, *Blast #05707*, 1998.
Left: Hatakeyama Naoya, *Lime Hills #29214*, 1990.

Lena Fritsch: Let's start at the beginning – what inspired you to take up photography?

Hatakeyama Naoya: I studied at Tsukuba University, and there was a professor who I respected very much: Ōtsuji Kiyoji. As you probably know, he was a member of the Japanese post-war avant-garde group Jikken Kōbō (Experimental Workshop). He gave the kind of explanations that I had never heard before. Encountering him, I began to see how fascinating photography can be. I did not have any particular interest in cameras before this.

When I was twenty-five years old, I was given an opportunity for a solo exhibition at Zeit-Foto Salon. I thought that following the exhibition I could just become a photographer, but it was not that easy [laughs]. For quite a while I did commercial work for magazines, for example in tourist articles or the luxury section, taking photographs of watches and so on.

At the time, were you interested in or inspired by any photographers in particular?

I became interested in photography in around 1980. The movement around *Provoke* was already over, but there was the *konpora* (contemporary) trend: Tamura Shōei, Gochō Shigeo, Yamazaki Hiroshi. They were a decade older than me, and they were my heroes. Moriyama and Araki were not so influential for my work. Of course, Araki has produced photographs for a long time, but it was not until the 1990s that he became so well-known in the international art world. Moriyama has been a star since the 1960s, but his position also reached its current heights in the 1990s or the beginning of the 21st century.

In the mid-1980s you made your photographic series *Lime Hills* [p. 176]. Could you tell me about this work – what was the trigger?

Not far away from my home – just a twenty-minute drive away – there were lime hills. There are many lime hills in Japan and when I found out about this, I started to take photographs of them all over the country, down to Okinawa.

Could you tell me how you took the photographs? It is probably not always easy to shoot at the quarries.

First I called them or sent a fax to get permission to take photographs. There is also the Limestone Industrial Society in Tokyo, and they helped me. I would usually go for a few days. People were helpful, driving me by jeep to the right spots. In other words, there was always someone else next to me when I took these photographs.

Generally speaking, I don't have an assistant; I always work on my own. I use a medium-format camera, a 6x7 camera, which is not too heavy to carry, and a tripod.

In 1996 you compiled the *Lime Hills* photographs in a photobook. When you make a photobook, how do you proceed?

I usually look at the contact sheets and pick out the images that interest me. I print these and put them on the wall so I can look at them. By looking at them for a long time, I gradually realize which ones I remember and which ones I forget. I then create a list of the works that seem important to me.

Could you tell me about your *Blast* series [p. 176]?

When I was taking the *Lime Hills* photographs, every day we were repeatedly asked to take shelter while they were using explosives. Nobody was allowed to go where the stones flew during the explosion. I became interested in taking photographs of these explosions from nearby. I was told that it was not possible, but then I asked if I could put a camera there and use a radio-control method to activate it. It was not easy to get permission. I originally wanted to use a large-format 5x4 camera, but it would have been too difficult to control this wirelessly. Then I got the Nikon F5 camera: you could be 200 metres away and still control the camera. In the 1990s, this was special – it was a sophisticated camera.

Photographing the explosions was really dangerous. Also, I didn't want to go to the quarry all the time, because if I went too often people probably would not have liked me any more [laughs].

How long did you continue the series?

I called them once in a while, 'could I perhaps come again and take photographs'? I took the photographs over a period of more than fifteen years. They became nice memories for the technicians at the hills as well, so I gave them the photographs as presents. They would not be able to see the explosions otherwise – because they also have to take shelter during them. Nobody sees the moment of the explosion.

It must be extremely loud.

It is, and the earth vibrates.

What about the camera – did it ever break during the explosions?

Yes. I would be fine, as I was a bit further away, but the camera fell and broke a few times.

In your work, nature and the relationship between humans and nature seem to be important themes.

This has been an important theme for me since I began photography. In everyday life, particularly in the cities, humans have forgotten that they are mortal animals. However, sometimes there are events and incidents that remind them: for example, when they get hurt or become ill, or when a child is born. These moments that make you feel like your convenient life has been turned completely upside down remind you that you are an animal. In my case, it was when the 2011 tsunami destroyed my hometown. Nature can give you that feeling – it can be threatening and remind you of your mortality. But it can help humans to be a bit more modest, too.

I'm not interested in taking photographs of the 'beauty of nature', like the autumn leaves, Mount Fuji or other conventional forms of expression. Photographers who enjoy that might think that they are recording nature, but actually all they record is culture.

Could you tell me about your series *Underground* [p. 181] and *Rivers*? Have you been to the catacombs in Paris, underneath the city?

No, I have never been.
There is quite a large space underground, and they used a lot of limestone there. I became interested in this when I was working on my *Lime Hills* series, and so I went to Paris. In the 18th century, during the large city planning projects, they required catacombs because there was not enough space at the cemeteries. Close to Place Denfert-Rocherau you can visit the catacombs as a tourist. Underground spaces are quite particular, and I became interested in them. I had made it a task for myself to take photographs in Tokyo, and I went out a lot. One day I discovered a ladder at the river in Shibuya, and I walked down to the riverbed, discovering this interesting view and walking further along the tunnel. There is nobody inside it, but you can hear the cars and people's voices from the streets above. There are bats, mice, small fish and insects.

Looking at this series as well as other series that you have made, beauty is an important part of your work, I think. What is beauty to you?
This is a difficult question, but I have actually been asked to talk about beauty at an aesthetics symposium at Waseda University next Saturday [laughs]. Sometimes the photographs that I took after the tsunami are described as 'beautiful', but of course even the people who say this feel uncomfortable about it. After all, around 20,000 people died. There is a complex link between aesthetics and ethics, between graphics and contents. Therefore, all I can do when people describe my work as 'beautiful' is to ask back 'what do you find beautiful about it?' and then discuss this with them. I also don't think that beauty is the greatest value. I want to include something in my photographs that actively addresses

people's feelings; however, this does not mean that all my photographs have to be beautiful. Maybe we use the word 'beautiful' too much and should differentiate more.

I think that by showing particular motifs (such as tunnels that other people would normally not go into) in an 'art-like' way, you create an aesthetic that people might view as 'beautiful'. Maybe 'art-like' would be a better word?
There are references to art history in my head: European paintings, photographic history since the 19th century and so on. I choose my photographic compositions and colours while carrying these references. Therefore, I can't help the art historical layers in my photographs. My photography is not just about recording something. I spend time, think about it and make artistic choices – just like a chef who makes a dish.

You already mentioned the photographs that you took in your hometown in Iwate, Rikuzentakata, before and after the tsunami [p. 181]. Originally you took them as private photographs for yourself, correct?
Yes. The compositions and the way that I used the light might be similar to some of my works; however, I did not have any concept in mind when taking these photos at all. Originally they were more like snapshots of my hometown. However, after the tsunami happened and the town completely disappeared, the meaning of these photographs suddenly changed. I thought it would be wrong to keep them as a secret, so I showed them. There is a value to these photographs: maybe not artistically, but they carry a primitive photographic value because they are records of things and people that don't exist anymore. This is something that I did not see in my art photography until then. At the moment, I feel that I am breaking new ground.

So photography as a medium has changed for you since 2011?
Yes. I have become aware of the primitive function of photography again. Photographs that I took randomly have suddenly gained some value. It has made me think not just about art but also about life in general. I feel like I'm in a post-historical state of mind – as if history has disappeared.

What do you like best about the medium of photography?
I like the feeling of loveliness when looking at the paper images – they are small and cute. It is a weird answer, but I like that. You can see a number of different places in the world next to each other [pointing at photographs on his studio wall]: Japan, Mexico, France, Poland. Different

fragments come together and create a mosaic. In a photobook it is similar: things from different times and places can come together. I like that.

From the 19th century to modern times there have been many wonderful photographers who have created a fascinating history of photography. It is great to see their diverse work; I enjoy looking at it. If possible, I would like to join this line and be together with all these wonderful people.

*   This is a shortened version of an interview conducted in Japanese on 5 September 2016, at Hatakeyama Naoya's studio, Tokyo.
1   *Konpora* (from the English 'contemporary') is a term used for a photographic style that first became popular around 1966, with an exhibition at George Eastman House entitled *Contemporary Photographers: Towards a Social Landscape*. The images produced by the *konpora* photographers are marked by their neutral 'snapshot' style, photographic composition (generally in landscape format) and their focus on everyday life.

Lena Fritsch: Let's start at the beginning – what inspired you to take up photography?
Shibata Toshio: I started as a painter and studied fine art. Before going to Belgium, I had never thought of taking photographs.

Why Belgium?
There was an opportunity, that's all. Basically, I just wanted to get out of Japan [laughs] I started in 1968 and graduated in 1974. At the time, American Pop Art was very popular, and I wanted to go to the United States. However, $1 was something like ¥360, so I did not get a chance to go. After graduating I worked for a year. I had a friend from Belgium while at university, and when a fellowship came up to go to Belgium and study at the Royal Academy in Ghent, I thought why not?

What inspired you to start photography in Ghent?
A new photography class had just been established at the Academy, and a professor (the principal) asked me if I wanted to join. I originally made oil paintings but had become more interested in silk screens, so in a sense I already used photography. I was also interested in film, and had worked at a film company, Toei Company, after university. So when I was asked, I accepted.

Of course, I had seen photographs in Japan: in the 1970s, for example, Moriyama Daidō and Araki Nobuyoshi were very active. But I wanted to do something different from their direct, political and sometimes violent, grainy aesthetic. I did not know anything about photography in general. When I received an Edward Weston photobook as a birthday present, I really liked it, particularly the photograph of a pepper. I had never seen anything like it: the pepper looked like a nude photograph of a woman and it stimulated one's imagination. I had tried different media until then but suddenly thought, 'photography could be it' [laughs].

At the time, were you interested in or inspired by any photographers in particular?
I didn't even know about large-format cameras [laughs]. I started to research all kinds of photographs. I was particularly interested in photographs that were not grainy and ambiguous but sharp and clear, more 'artwork-like'. For example, I liked Edward Weston. I was in Ghent for four years, until 1980, and during these years I studied a lot, mostly by myself as the other students were a lot younger than me. No art galleries in Japan represented photography, so when I saw galleries that sold photographs, for example Galerie Zabriskie in Paris, it was exciting. They showed me original prints and different photographs, like Joel Meyerowitz's first series *Cape Light*. I saw the 8x10 contact prints. I remember thinking that it is amazing how photography is an art medium that everybody can use – unlike oil painting, for example.

After your return to Japan, you made a series titled *Nihon Tenkei*, which you published in 1992 as a photobook. Could you tell me about this series?
After returning from Belgium I thought I should try and do photography in my own country. I only took photographs at night for quite a while. Then I started travelling throughout the country, always trying to avoid any kind of 'Japonism'. In general, I do not take many photographs, and I also try to take them rather quickly because I don't want to be too influenced by the place and its history, or by any art historical associations that I might have. I used a 5x4 camera, and I needed a tripod. I try to not engage with the place too much, and don't do much research about the locations in advance.

I started photography very late; when I began to publish the *Nihon Tenkei* photobook, I was already over forty years old. It was not easy, and it took me ten years to publish it.

In 2015, you published the photobook *Yodaka* with even earlier works, from the 1980s [p. 251]. Could you tell me more about these photographs?
From 1983 until 1986, I used a 5x4 camera and took photographs around Tokyo at night. 1980s Japan seemed a bit chaotic and disorderly, and returning from Ghent, which is a quiet town, I was not used to it any more [laughs]. I didn't want to take photographs of traditional Japanese subjects. I became interested in the streets and motorways, which look quite similar in all countries. If you look really closely you might see some Japanese writing, but overall the aesthetic of these places is similar everywhere.

I could not publish the photographs as a photobook at the time. I really liked Edward Hopper and his painting *Nighthawks* – this depiction of a world at night. I suggested it as a title to the publisher, but it was not possible because it already exists, so we chose the Japanese *Yodaka*. It is a bit misleading, as this word is associated with prostitution in Japanese [laughs]. But there is also another association: Miyazawa Kenji's short story *Yodaka no hoshi (The Nighthawk Star)* for children, about an ugly bird. I liked the double meaning [laughs].

It is a very quiet series.
It was a peaceful time – sometimes I would set up my tripod on the middle of the street and no cars would come for five minutes.

It would be impossible to take these kinds of photographs now.

Landscapes and the relationship between humans and nature have been important themes in your work since the 1980s. Could you tell me more about your interest in this?
As a painter I spent a lot of time in my room or studio. Since learning photography in Belgium, I have enjoyed going out and working outside. Taking photographs while travelling felt like a dream. The fact that you can be outside and see new things is something that I really like about photography. In that sense, my photography is straight photography. I wanted to travel around Japan to look at this country again, and get a complete picture of it, in my own way. Landscapes and the outside have become my studio.

Your picture of Japan is one with hardly any people in it...
I'm not good with people; I get nervous [laughs]. I don't like people to talk to me when I'm working so I try to go to places where there are no people. But I'm also interested in these landscapes and human infrastructures – not so much in their meaning but just as photographic subjects.

First you only took monochrome photographs [pp. 184–85], but over the last ten years you have mostly taken colour photos [pp. 182–83]. How do you choose which one you are going for?
I have never really taken black and white and colour at the same time. When I first started I took monochrome photographs, and I continued with monochrome photography for twenty-five years. Around 2000, I got fed up [laughs]. I had ignored thoughts inside me that some things could look good in colour, and realized that I should stop ignoring them. Gradually I started taking both monochrome photographs and colour photographs. Then I stopped taking monochrome photographs around 2007, and have been using colour ever since.

Naturally with monochrome photography, the focus is more on the forms than in colour photographs, where a certain colour can gain a viewer's attention as well. Has your photographic approach changed?
The monochrome photographs were mostly taken with a large-format camera, 8x10. There were only four lenses to choose from, and I only took photographs of subjects that I could take with these lenses. There were things that I had to exclude; it was a bit restrictive. Taking colour photographs, I use a 5x4 camera and there are more lenses that I can choose from. I feel freer, and I also take photographs of things that

I felt I could not photograph in monochrome [laughs]. In that sense I really enjoy it.

When you create a photobook, how do you proceed?
I usually make a pre-selection of photographs, but then I let the editor work on it. Of course we talk about it, but if it is an editor that I trust, I let them make most of the decisions. I have made photobooks by myself before, but I find it more interesting to see how another person sees my photographs. To do it all by myself is pretty boring and narrow.

What do you like best about the medium of photography?
I have tried different artistic media, and when I painted as a student I was torn between minimalism and art that focuses more on the image, by artists like Robert Rauschenberg. Well, I have moved more towards the image. With photography I can be carefree and it somehow feels 'light'. Light in different ways: even literally 'light' because photographs are printed on paper. They are things, but also images that can stimulate the viewer's imagination.

*   This is a shortened version of an interview conducted in Japanese on 3 September 2016, at Zeit-Foto Salon, Tokyo.

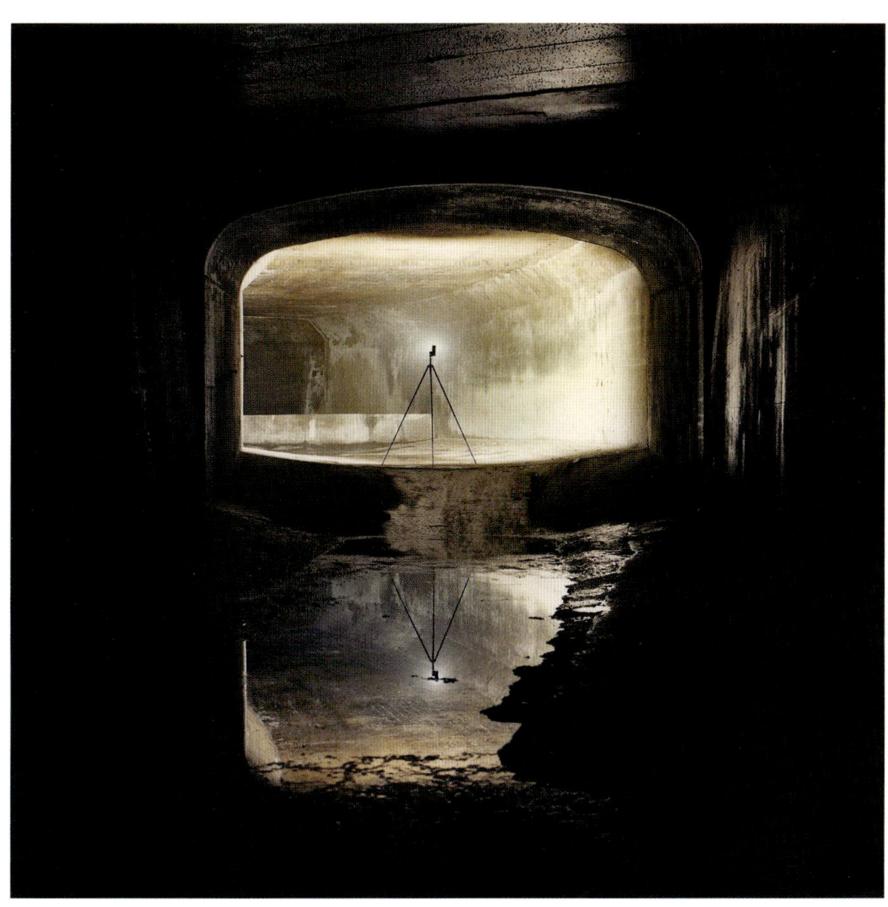

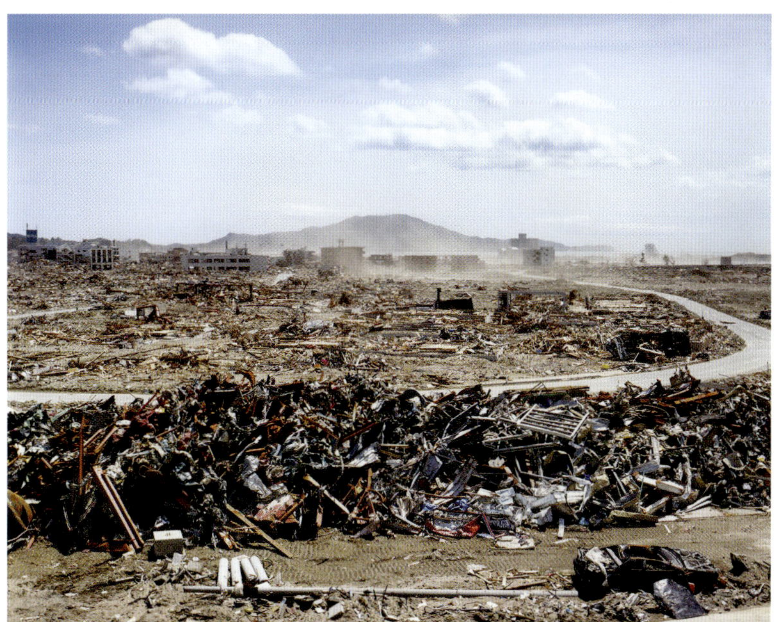

Above: Hatakeyama Naoya,
Underground #6411, 1999.
Right: Hatakeyama Naoya,
Rikuzentakata 2011/05/2, 2011.

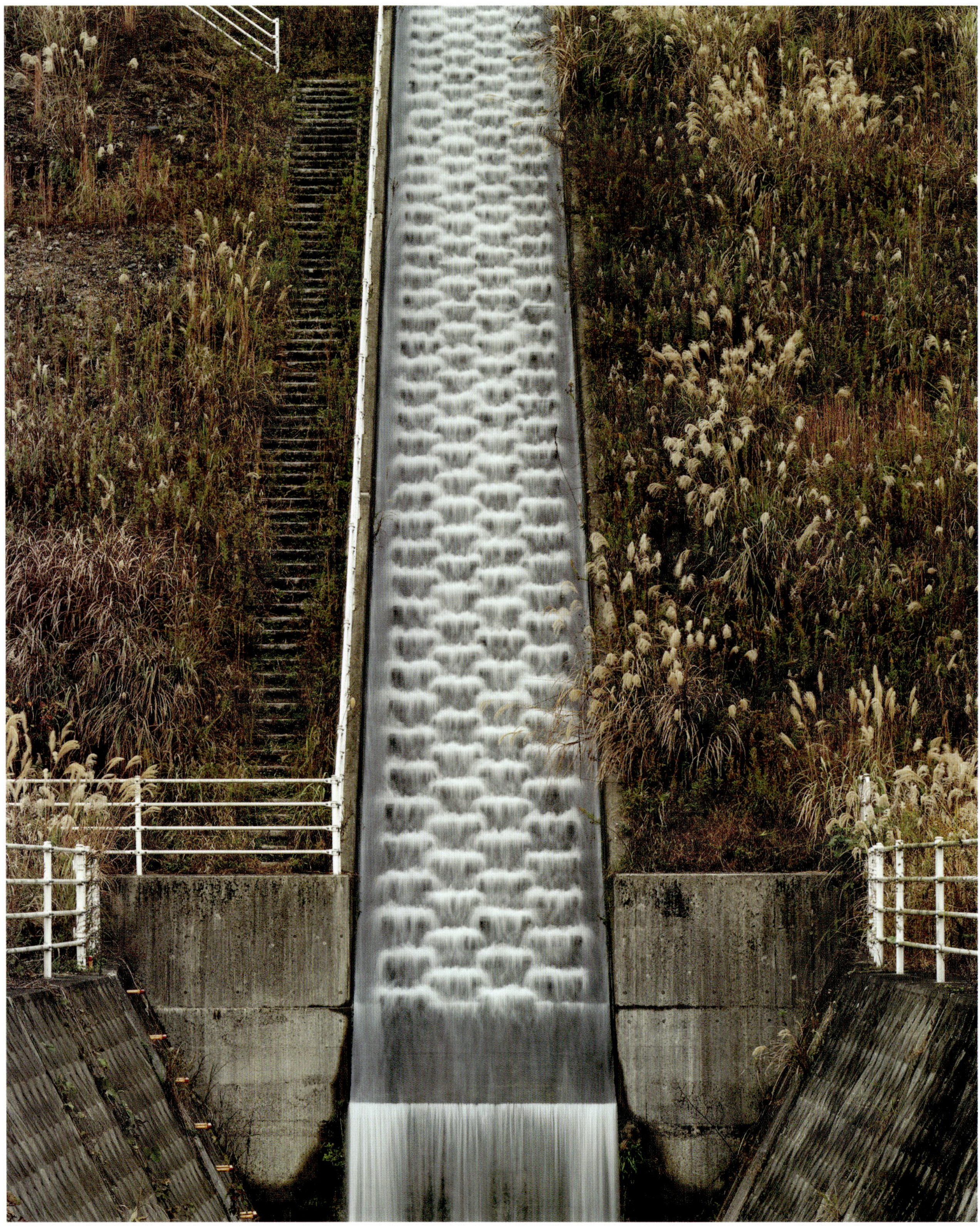

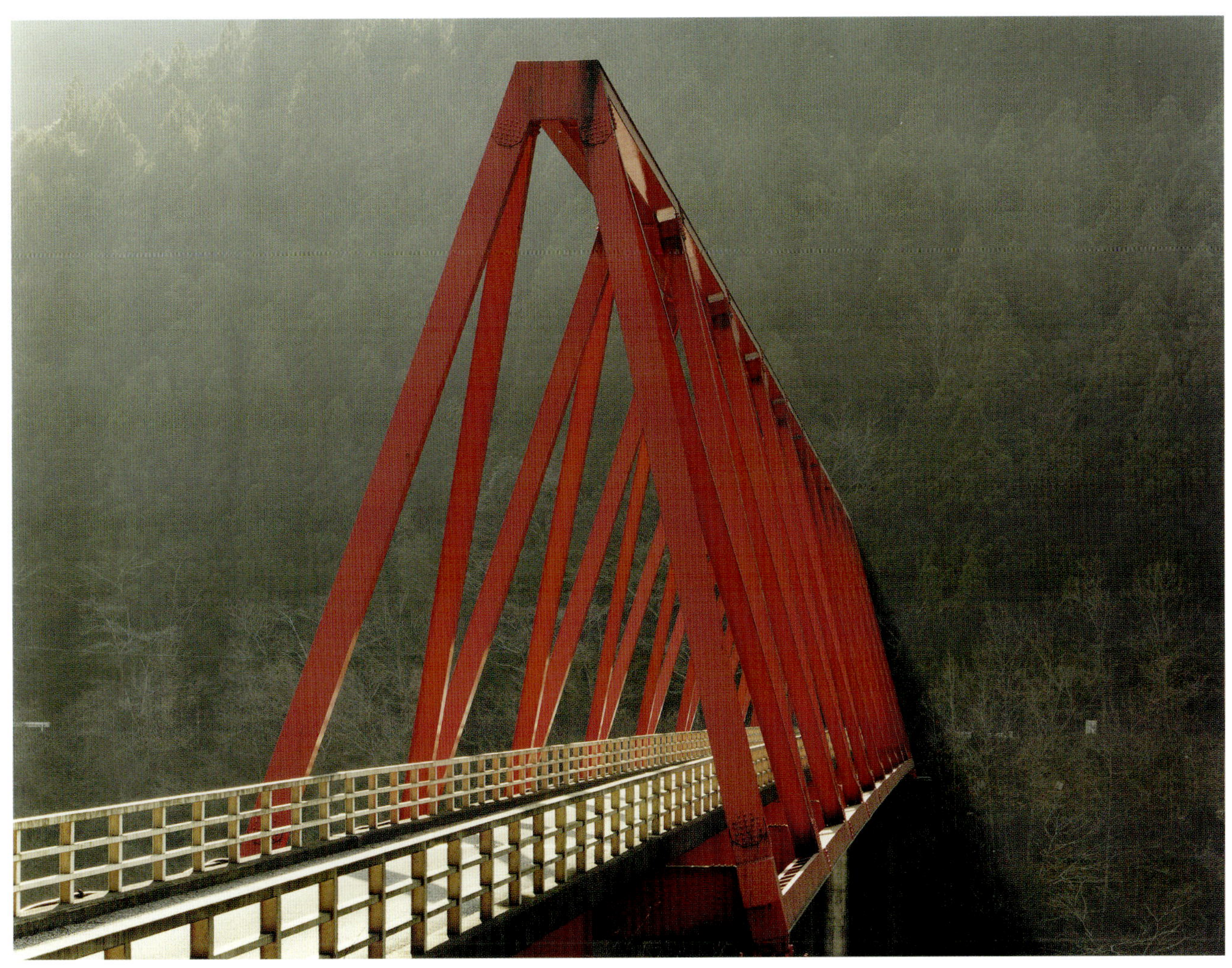

Opposite: Shibata Toshio, *Itsuke Village, Kumamoto Prefecture*, 2015.
Above: Shibata Toshio, *Okawa Village, Tosa County*, 2007.

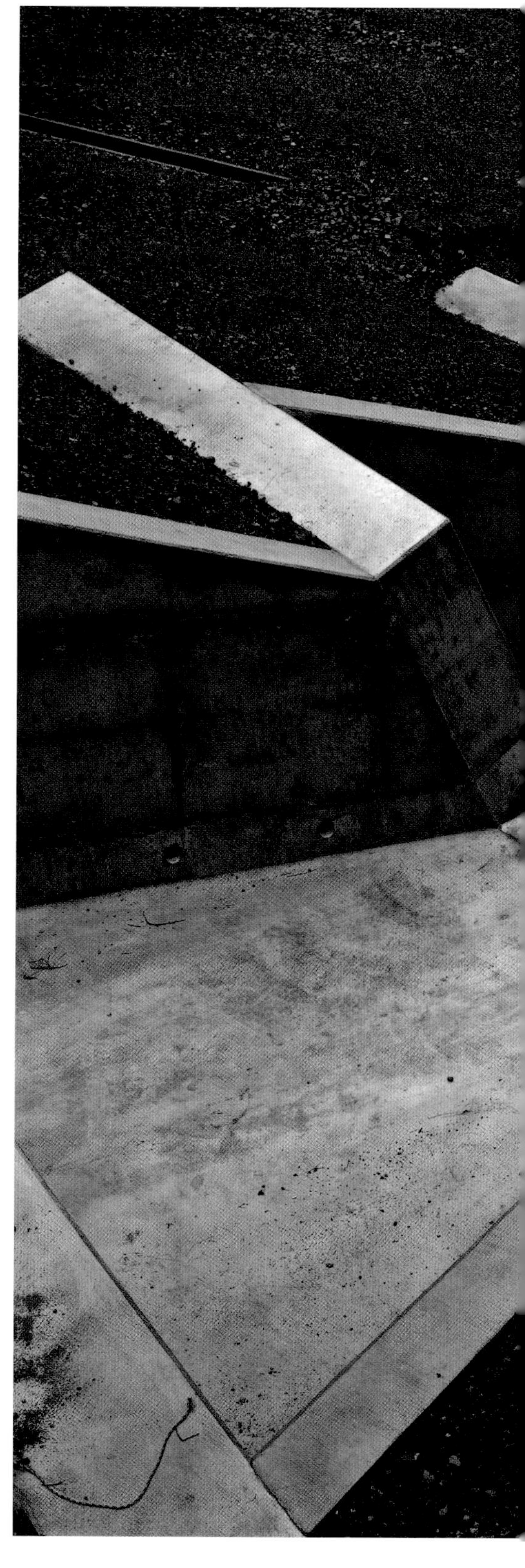

Shibata Toshio, *Honkawane Town, Shizuoka Prefecture*, 1997.

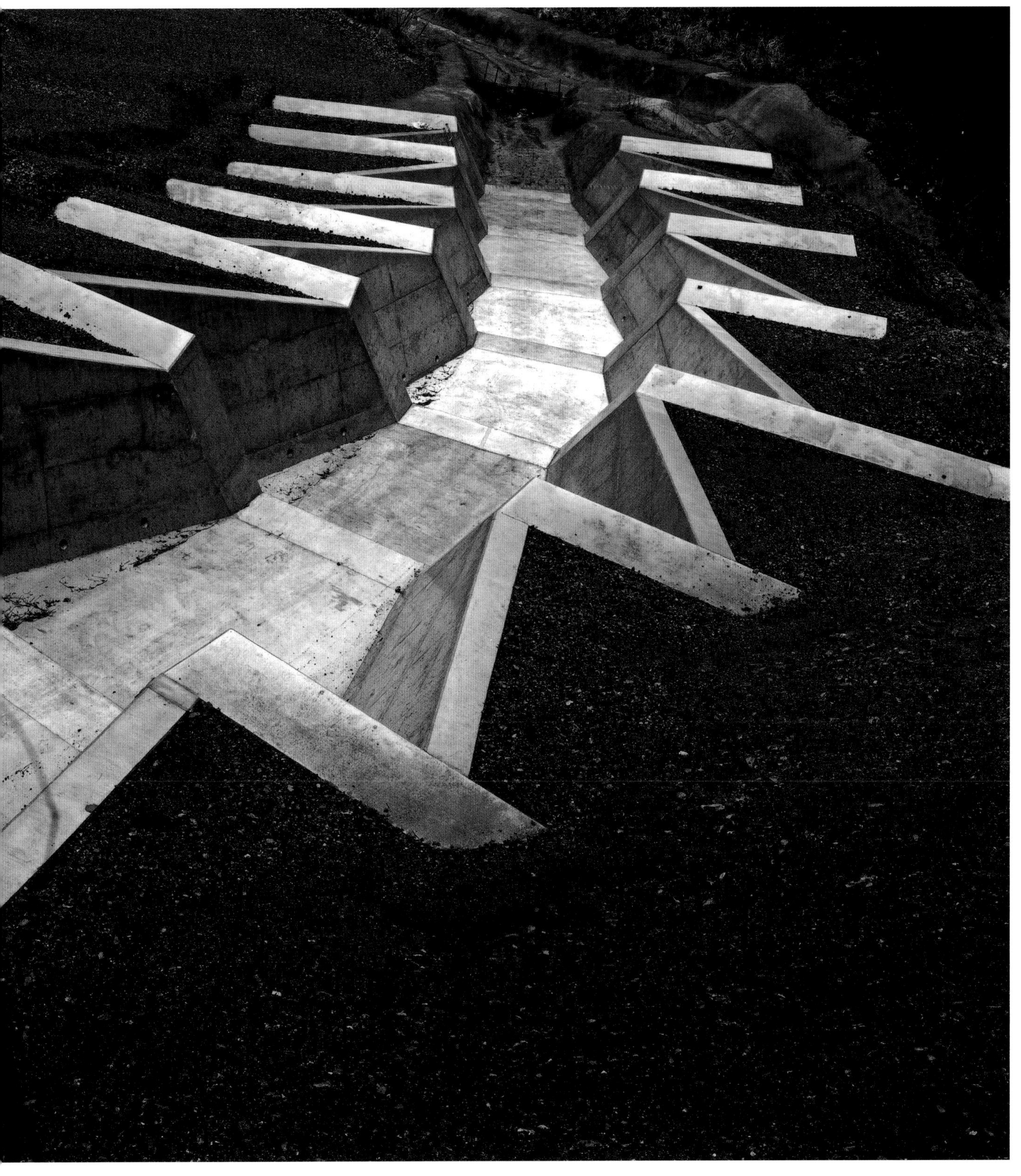

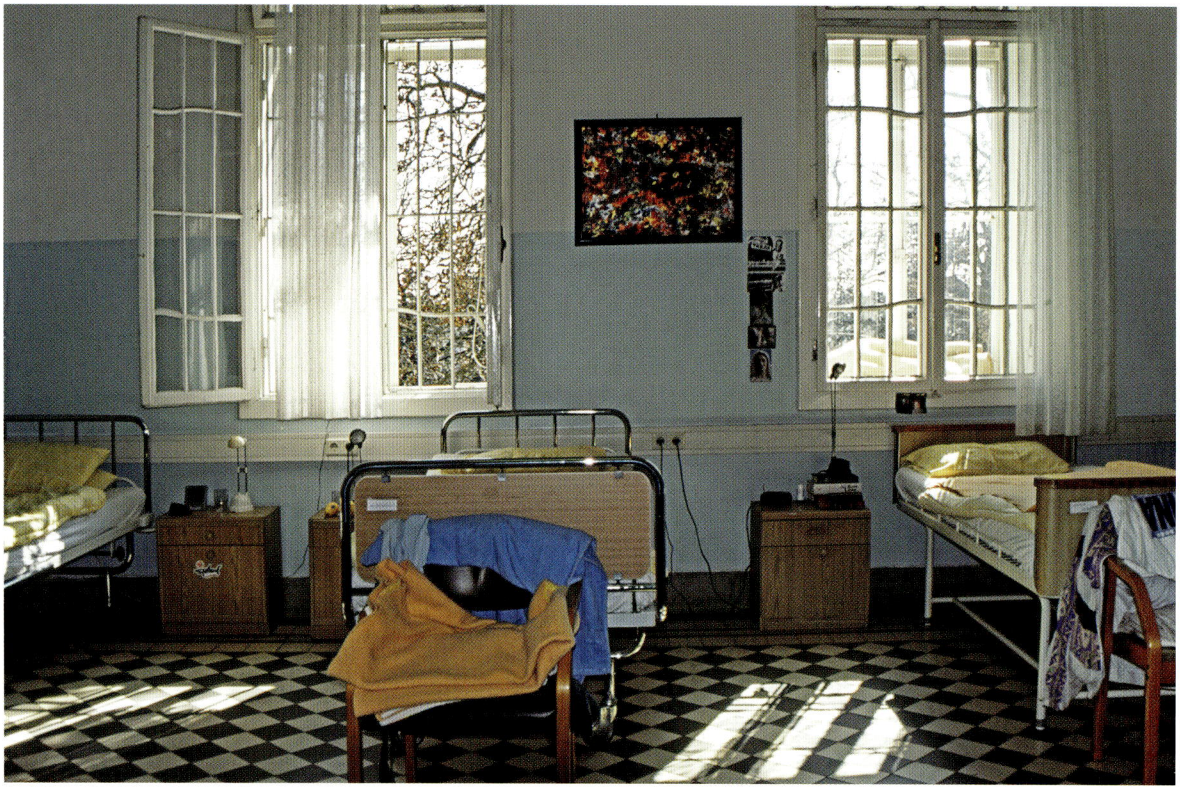

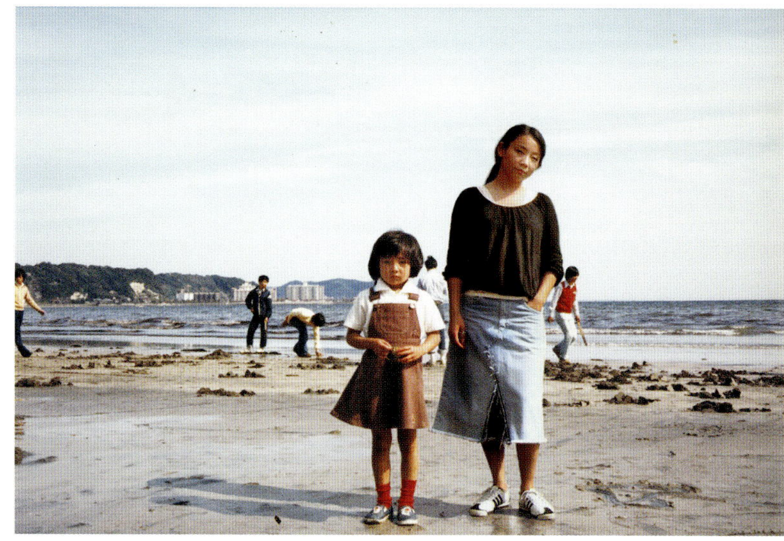

Above: Inoue Hiroko, *Otto Wagner Spital.
Vienna, Austria*, 2005, *Inside Out* series.
Right: Ōtsuka Chino, *1976 and 2005,
Kamakura, Japan*, 2005, *Imagine
Finding Me* series.

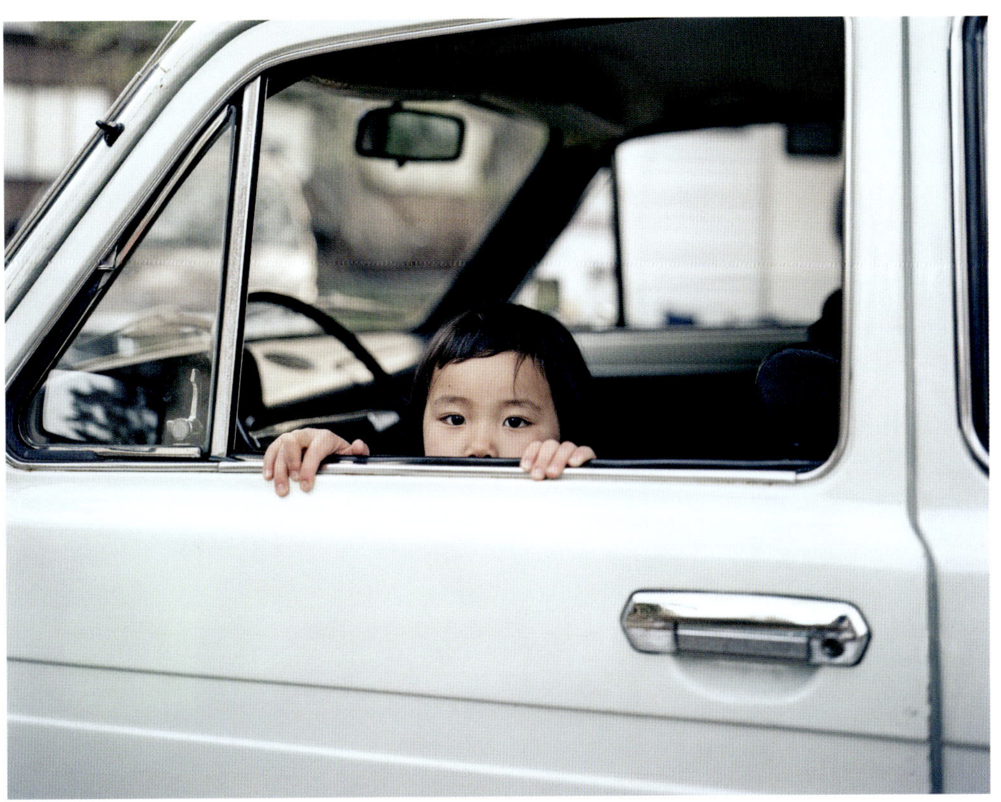

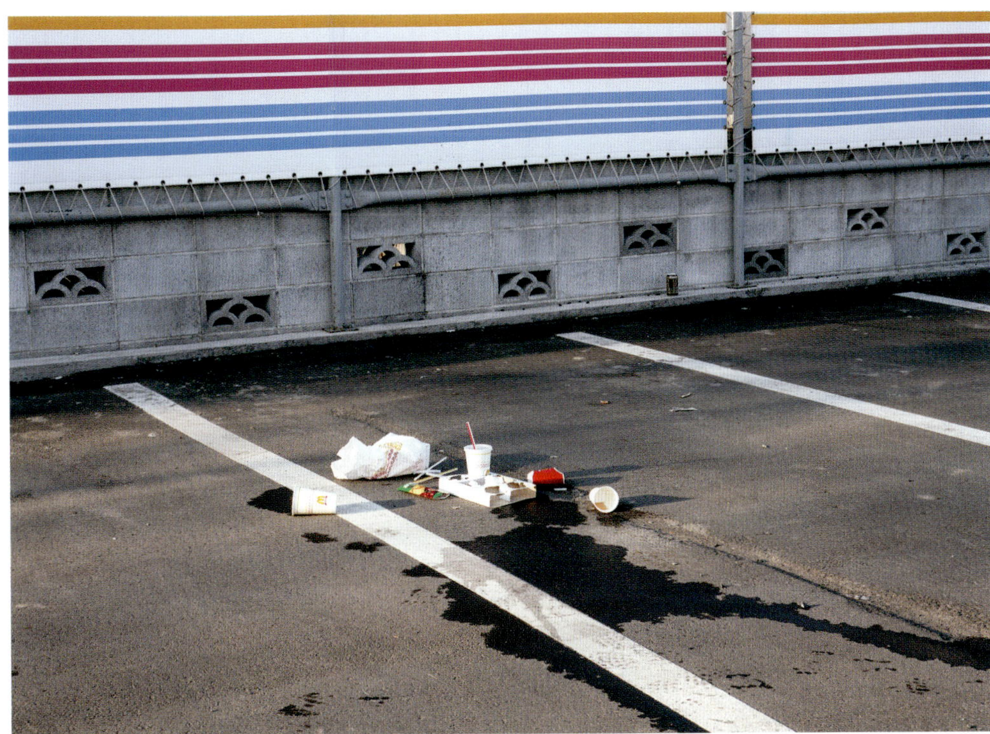

Above: Homma Takashi, *Tokyo and My Daughter*, 1999–2010.
Right: Homma Takashi, *Tokyo Suburbia, Parking Lot*, 1995.

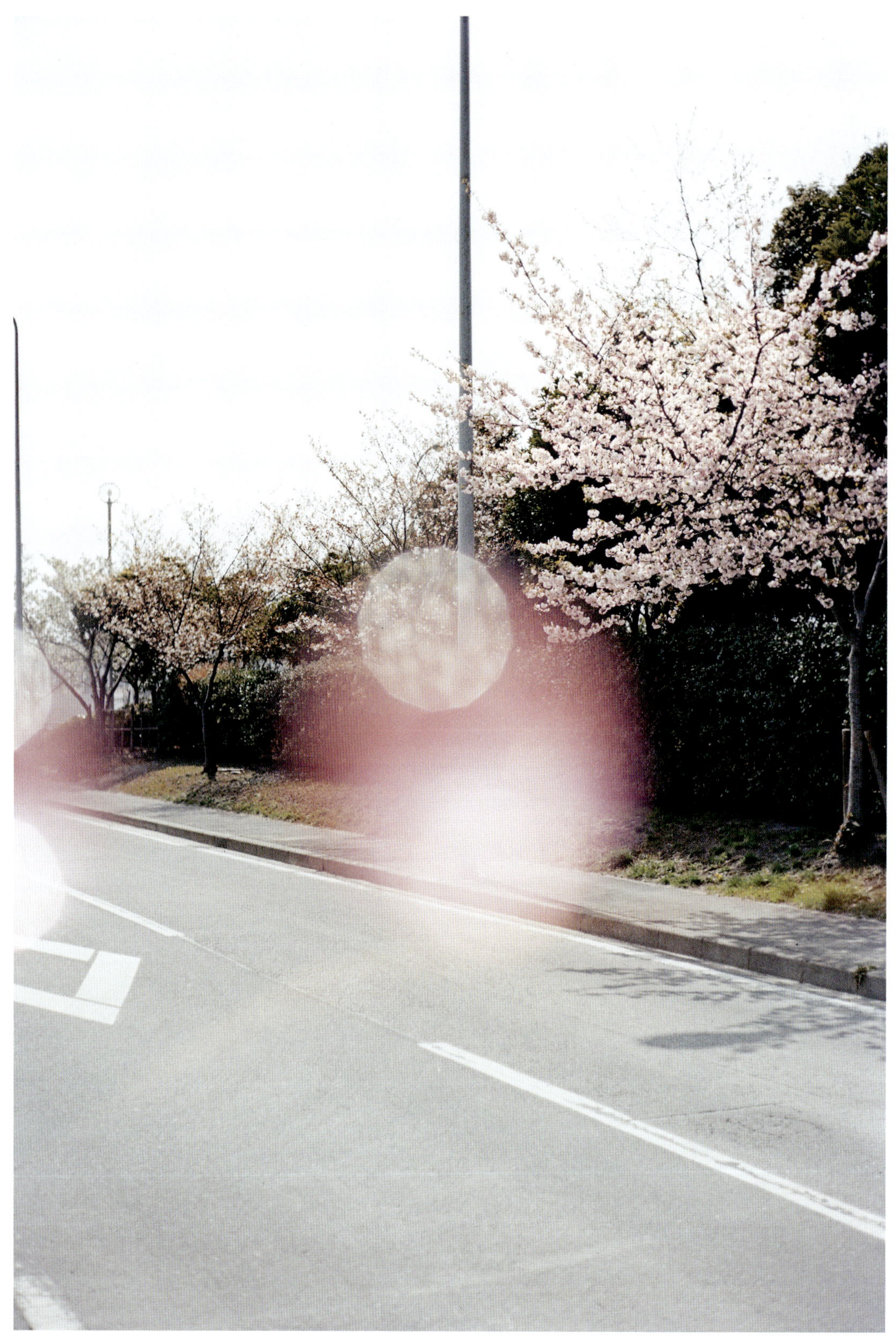

Ōmori Katsumi, *Urayasu-shi, Chiba*, 2011, *Everything happens for the first time* series.

Lena Fritsch: Let's start at the beginning – what inspired you to take up photography?
Ōmori Katsumi: There was an amateur photography boom in Japan, and my father and grandfather both liked taking photographs. I lived in Kobe and often went to my grandfather's, where I used to look through family albums, asking about the people that I didn't know. When I was in my first year of junior high school, I saw a photograph from 1945; after Japan had lost the war, a family photograph had been taken to remember the loss. When I looked at the photo, I noticed that I was older than my father, who had been in elementary school when the photo was taken. It was a weird, serious feeling, as if time had been frozen. Once in a while, I would also borrow my dad's camera and take photographs. To begin with we developed the photos at home: we did not have a darkroom, but used the bathroom and a so-called 'dark bag' that you put the film in to develop. They were quite popular in the 1960s and early 1970s. Many photographs have inspired me – artists' photographs, journalistic photographs, pin-up photographs – but the first were photos in family albums, and the ones that my father took.

When I was at senior high school, I liked rock and punk music. Working in an *okonomiyaki* restaurant,¹ I earned some pocket money that I used to buy records or clothes. I liked the cover of the album *Exile on Main Street* by the Rolling Stones, with the collage of photographs by Robert Frank (*The Americans*), and the cover of *For How Much Longer Do We Tolerate Mass Murder* by The Pop Group, a punk band from the UK, which featured André Kertész's photograph of two gypsy children. I did not know Kertész, but I loved the cover [laughs]. I also liked the photographs on The Clash records – photographs of the band's live concerts. I decided to go to a university that would allow me to study photography, so I came to Tokyo. However, Nihon University was more conservative than I had imagined, and I became bored. They would not teach us about people who were active in Japan at the time, like Araki or Moriyama, only about Ansel Adams and works from the past [laughs]. After two years, I left and started to do commercial work, for example as a lighting assistant at Studio Ebisu. I did not differentiate much between 'commercial photography' and 'serious photography'. I loved photography, but did not really know yet what kind of photographs I should take. It was the late 1980s, the time of the economic bubble; there were many small jobs available. I began taking photographs for magazines, to present in shops or to accompany interviews. I also became friends with a music magazine editor and began to photograph gigs. In 1992, I met the French band Mano Negra and toured with them, taking photographs of their performances and the band backstage, as well as street photographs in Latin America. I created my first portfolio by compiling these photographs, and in 1994 Robert Frank himself chose my work for the Excellence Award of the New Cosmos of Photography.

At the time, were you interested in or inspired by any photographers in particular?
When I started university in 1982 I often went to bookshops with Western books, to look at the work of Robert Frank, Garry Winogrand, William Eggleston and other American street photographers. There were hardly any galleries at the time and not many exhibitions, so I mainly looked at photographs in magazines or photobooks. I saw works by Lee Friedlander, Diane Arbus, Irving Penn, but of course I also looked at European photography: Eugène Atget, Man Ray and so on. I found out about all these works from different times at the same time [laughs]. But I also liked the work of Araki, Moriyama and Fukase.

Many years later, in 2011, you made an interesting series with photographs linked to the earthquake and tsunami in Fukushima: *Everything happens for the first time* [pp. 188, 193]. Could you tell me about this series?
The series was triggered directly by the earthquake and nuclear catastrophe. I live in Chiba, in Urayasu, and the earthquake destroyed quite a lot there. Our house was relatively ok, but the area is built on manmade land, so some buildings were heavily affected. During the first few weeks after the earthquake the water did not run properly and everyday life was difficult. At the same time, news trickled in about the terrible nuclear power plant accident in Fukushima. So the starting point of my series was that I wanted to go to Fukushima to see it with my own eyes. I did not even know what I wanted to see, but I somehow felt that I had to get as close as possible to the nuclear power station. Even now, nobody knows exactly what impact the radioactivity has had because you can't see it directly. But I just wanted to go. Although Urayasu and Tokyo are close, Tokyo was not affected much, and there was a strong feeling of distance. But around my neighbourhood, houses were destroyed, so I felt a closer link to Fukushima. I also felt that I had to take a different photographic approach – not straight photography. I knew that my approach could be wrong, but I just wanted to do something that was different to my usual photography.

I had just finished a small portfolio of ten photographs that I took in Los Angeles in 2010, after doing some work there for a magazine, meeting the novelist Salvador

Plascencia. In a Mexican toy shop, I had bought a small toy with translucent pink plastic balls. It reminded me of my childhood, when I liked to look at the city or various objects through a piece of glass or ice. I took one photograph with this pink toy. When going to Fukushima, I remembered this and thought, 'why not include something in the photographs that has absolutely nothing to do with Fukushima, the earthquake, Tokyo or the year 2011'. I had been thinking about radioactivity and things that you can't see with your eyes. By inserting that layer into the documentary photographs, they become something different – intuitively, I wanted to emphasize that you look at things *through* something. I didn't have any friends in Fukushima and at first I didn't know where to go. But then I thought, why not start at my home and go towards Fukushima, stopping at the cherry blossom trees?

It was April after all.
Exactly: cherry blossom season. So I stopped whenever I saw a cherry blossom tree and took a photograph.

The way you have used the toy differs between your Fukushima photos and the photo that you took in LA in 2010. In the LA photo, the toy appears sharply, whereas in the *Everything happens for the first time* photographs, you use a softer aesthetic. The pink spots are more 'beautiful' and more ambiguous; as a viewer you don't know what they are.
I started the journey in Chiba close to my own home, which is quite important. People in Tokyo differentiated strongly between Tokyo and Fukushima. But for me, living in an area where a lot was destroyed, this seemed weird. After taking the photographs, I thought about whether or not to present them for quite a while.

You then created the *sounds and things* series – are sounds and music important to you?
Yes. Sounds and smells are obviously not recorded in photographs. There are many things that are not recorded in photography. I never thought about sounds, smells or other things that are not visible in relation to photography. But then I realized that I, as a human, connect looking with hearing. I might hear something and as a reaction look at something. In 2011, I took the photographs for *Everything happens for the first time*, and inside me a '2011 issue' developed, realizing that a tsunami might suddenly destroy everything that you can see with your eyes. At the same time, there are also things that you can't see, including the radioactivity in Fukushima. It made me rethink the relationship between visible things and invisible things. Simply put, 'sounds' stand for things that you can't see with your eyes, and 'things' represent the visible things. Through photography, I wanted to reconsider their relationship. Each photograph has a title, which can become a starting point for the viewer to think about the different meanings and photographic layers.

Some photographs would even work without a title. For example, your photograph of *sashimi* looks so delicious, but after Fukushima, I also have another reaction because we don't know if it is safe to eat fish...
Yes, that has changed. I used to think that a title defines the way a photograph is viewed too much, but sometimes it is good to give direction. Of course, the title of the series, *sounds and things*, is quite open; everything is either a sound or a thing [laughs]! I now use this series for all kinds of photographs, and even take them with my iPhone and upload them to Instagram. At the same time, I do other thematic projects, such as a series of cherry blossoms and photographs of the crossing in Shibuya. This helps me to keep a balance.

Do you take photographs every day?
Yes, I usually do.
  I am not sure about Instagram, but I think the links are interesting. For example, I use the hashtag #soundsandthings for all the photographs, and then for some portraits of women I use #everywomanissomeonesdaughter. This way, my photographs sometimes come up in the context of photographs that were taken by someone else. I find it interesting that words can create such categories – it is endless and therefore dangerous, but at the same time, it is very internet-like and I find the classifications interesting. There is a playful element to it as well as a serious element. The year that I live in is 2016 so why not do both – film and digital?

What do you like best about the medium of photography?
This is probably related to time: I like that a photograph of my father when he was younger than me can make me think about time. That is fascinating. It is also interesting how photographic meanings can change: a photograph of *sashimi* can look delicious, but after a nuclear catastrophe, it can suddenly carry a different meaning. The portrait photograph of one's girlfriend can turn into a photograph of your ex-girlfriend or it can become a photograph of your wife. As such, you take a photograph in the present but also plant a seed for the future. These temporal layers are interesting – I probably say this because I have become older. When I was young, I used to just focus on the graphic beauty of photography, not thinking about the future of images.
  I also like the scope and ambiguity of the language of photography – unlike other languages, it has flexible grammar and rules. You can be a complete amateur but you can still take a photograph. My mother can take photographs, there are commercial photographs – oh, there are so many different photographs!

*   This is a shortened version of an interview conducted in Japanese on 28 August 2016, at MEM, Tokyo.
1   *Okonomiyaki* is a pancake made of flour, water, eggs, shredded cabbage and usually also octopus, squid or shrimps and vegetables. It is served with a sauce, bonito flakes, seaweed flakes and mayonnaise. The pancakes are associated with the Kansai area of Japan, particularly Osaka, and mostly sold in small bars or fast-food booths.

Lena Fritsch: Let's start at the beginning – what inspired you to take up photography?

Yoneda Tomoko: I wanted to study at a university in the United States and went to Milwaukee, first learning English and then taking journalism classes. I was interested in journalism and photography, the pen and the camera, text and image. I saw them as two things that are closely linked. I had not studied art or photography in Japan and when I took an art class in Milwaukee, I realized that I was not bad at taking photographs.

My father was an amateur photographer, taking family and snapshot photos, and he loved all new technologies. He had a darkroom at home that he used when I was little. When I went to the United States, I took his camera with me – not speaking much English, I thought it could be useful for my journalism studies. I did not know that the American Midwest had a tradition in photography: Edward Weston, Edward Streichen and so on. Chicago, with the New Bauhaus, was not far either. A friend of mine who was in Chicago recommended that I go to the University of Illinois, saying that Chicago would be the best place for photography. I studied with Joseph Jackna, who recently passed away and who had studied under Aaron Siskind and Harry Callahan. I always thought a camera was something that men had. But when I learnt the basics of photography, I realized that I could do it as well. The whole city conveyed a feel for architecture, design and photography – a sense of design is part of everyday life there.

At the time, were you interested in or inspired by any photographers?

When I was in the United States, I looked at all kinds of photobooks and magazines, studying in libraries. I remember seeing a photobook by Aperture, about post-war photography in Japan.[1] I didn't know much about Japanese photography and its tradition, and it had a strong impact on me. But as it was the 1980s, a different kind of photography was popular: constructed photography, for example, by Sandy Skoglund. Or photographs with a strong sense of narrative.

In 1997, you had your first solo show, 'Topographical Analogy' [p. 252], at Zeit-Foto Salon in Tokyo. Could you tell me about the exhibited works?

After graduating from the University of Illinois, I came to London in 1989 and studied at the Royal College of Art. I thought about staying in Chicago for my MA but my professor recommended that I change my environment; he said that as an artist, it is a good thing to do. At the time there was nothing in London. Of course, there was a tradition of photographers like Bill Brandt, the Victoria and Albert Museum had a small collection of photographs and there was The Photographers Gallery. But in general, you never saw any photographs in fine art galleries. Photography was not part of the fine arts department but of the commercial department; I did not enjoy my studies very much and did not learn much either [laughs]. External critics and artists came, though, including Keith Arnatt. I remember how he encouraged me. Zelda Cheatle, who had one of the first photography galleries in London, also liked my work and included it in two group shows, and later gave me solo shows. But in general, the photography scene was not very developed, so I returned to Japan to show my photographs there. Ishihara-san from Zeit-Foto Salon liked my work, and just before or after this I also met Kasahara Michiko [now chief curator at the Tokyo Photographic Art Museum]. She had actually also been to Chicago, briefly studying at the same university as I and then at Columbia College.

The photographs for the 'Topographical Analogy' exhibition were all taken in East London. I had exhibited them the year before at The Photographers Gallery, receiving the Second Prize in a photography competition – Paul Wombell was the director at the time. I was interested in historical constructions and their layers. They are not typically English but could also exist in Germany or Japan or anywhere – things that are not particular to one place but analogous to other places, all with traces of time.

The theme of invisible historical layers is something that has remained an important part of your photography. I really like your *Between Visible and Invisible* series, that you started a few years later, photographing texts through the eyeglasses of their authors [p. 253]. What was the trigger for this series?

Living in London and also becoming older, I strongly felt the year 2000 approaching. The Berlin Wall had fallen, the Soviet Union was dissolved and not only did I see all this in the media but I was also physically in Europe, in a location where you could feel these changes. That's when I started taking photographs of the eyeglasses of Freud, Hermann Hesse – of the people whose works I had studied and which were around me. It was a time that made me feel that even 'big' historical changes can be based on the 'small' power of many individuals.

How did you research the eyeglasses and documents, for example those of Sigmund Freud?

At the time, the internet was not yet as advanced so I went to the British Library, searching in international museum catalogues. I then sent out requests by phone or fax to different places and met with museum researchers, literary executors and so on before taking the photographs. There are photographs that I have not taken yet; the series is still ongoing. I recently took photographs of Foujita Tsuguharu's eyeglasses – this had been planned for a very long time. Sometimes I ask people and they check for me in the archives and suddenly contact me years later, when they have found something. The first photograph of the series with Freud's glasses was easy: he is well-known and died in London. Tanizaki Junichirō was also not difficult as I'm from the Kansai region originally and when I had an exhibition in the region, I talked to the researcher at the Tanizaki Memorial Museum of Literature. I always get very nervous when I see these original letters and eyeglasses right in front of me. Sometimes the museum curators are worried and stand next to me, thinking that I will take the photographs quickly – but it can take time, not just one hour.

Speaking of the photographic process – do you take a large number of photographs that you then choose from later?

I decide on a case-by-case basis. For the *Between Visible and Invisible* series I used to make appointments for two days. On the first day, I looked at different texts and thought about the angles, and on the second day I took the photographs. It depends on the series but in general, I am prepared and go to a particular place for a particular reason. I'm not the restless type who takes photographs without any reason. But that does not mean that there are no spontaneous photographs within my projects. When I went to Hungary, I wanted to take photographs of a Socialist Realist pool building. At first there was a class of schoolchildren in the pool, but when they left a couple came and I quickly set up my tripod and took a photograph of them [p. 195]. Love within the cold surrounds of the pool, Hungary having just joined the EU in the same year – there was an optimistic feeling that I wanted to show in the photograph.

I often compare myself to an athlete: I prepare, practise and then, when it is 'kick off' time, I'm ready to go and can take photographs!

That is an interesting comparison. Could you tell me about your series

A Decade **After, which you started in 1995 [p. 194]? It again focuses on historical traces – in this case the traces of the big earthquake in Kobe in 1995.**

I was born in Akashi so Kobe is really close. To me, Kobe was part of my hometown and a place that I admired. I was shocked to hear how much of it was destroyed by the earthquake. Akashi was not affected as much, but nevertheless I was worried about my parents. One month after the earthquake, I returned to Japan and to my home. Friends of mine lived in Kobe and asked me if I wanted to go and see how it looked. I went and took monochrome photographs. I developed these but just kept them personally. In 2003, when I had a solo exhibition at Shiseido gallery, I met the curator Yamamoto Atsuo, who was thinking about a ten-year anniversary exhibition in Ashiya [at the Ashiya City Museum of Art and History], on the earthquake. He asked me to be involved because my home is close to Kobe but I was not there when the earthquake happened; unlike other artists from the region, I was able to look at Kobe from a more distant, objective viewpoint. Together with a volunteer from the region I went to different locations. Again, I researched most of the places and then went a second time to shoot, but there are spontaneous photographs as well. We exhibited my photographs from 1995 alongside the new images.

You were not in Japan when the earthquake happened in 1995 and I assume you were not there in March 2011, during the tsunami and nuclear plant catastrophe in Fukushima?

I was not there in March, but I had received a Tokyo Wondersite residency and it had already been decided that I would go to Tokyo in May 2011. So I was there a few months later. I didn't go to Japan because of Fukushima; I was there by coincidence. I wanted to make a series related to the history and modernization of Japan, and to the issues this has caused, even if they are not really visible [*Cumulus* series, p. 196].

The relationship between the visible and invisible, the present and the past is an important motif in your photography, I think.

The relationship between the present and places where something happened historically is important. They are places to contemplate, to reflect on the past. I try to show these places in an objective way. I have continued to photograph landscapes and scenes from the same stance – straight and not dramatic – and from the same height, which is probably the average Japanese height [laughs]. Places, spaces, objects – they all have a certain power themselves. When I came to London in 1989, I wondered

why constructive and staged photography was so popular – there is no need for so much decoration in photography, I thought.

When you look back at these years and the beginning of your photographic career now, how do you think your photographic approach has changed?

I'm not sure if my own photography has changed much, but the art world and the role of photography in the art world has changed a lot. Photographic technologies have changed too – they have become less hands-on, and people manipulate the images endlessly, using Photoshop and such. When I started it was all so much more hands-on! I do wonder what the meaning of photography is these days. Even when going to photo forums, people always suggest that I upload photos online, on Instagram and such [laughs].

I have met some Japanese photographers who do Instagram…

I find it confusing [laughs]. I think these trends will change again at some point. What I like about photography and what is important to me personally is to show the real photograph in an exhibition or similar, and make viewers appreciate the beauty of it. Good photobooks are usually well printed, too, sometimes confusingly even better than the photographic prints. There is craftsmanship involved in the printing. But at the same time, another technology, namely the digital, has developed a lot.

What do you like best about photography?

I like the fact that photography is open, it reflects like a mirror. I think that paintings are very subjective, as they are directly linked to your hands: you paint each brushstroke manually. Paintings come into existence through a process of transformation. And texts are of course subjective as well – again, writing is a process of transformation. I like that photography does not require that. Using a machine is more direct, and can show something that the viewer is already familiar with. Photographs are more objective. At the same time, every human is different and has a different way of thinking: you might be a man or a woman, have a different nationality, different religion. So we are all unique – we see images very differently and contemplate them individually. I find that interesting, and in my photography I always search for something 'in-between' images.

*   This is a shortened version of an interview conducted in Japanese on 6 December 2016, at Tate Modern, London.
1   Mark Holburn, *Black Sun: The Eyes of Four* (New York: Aperture, 1986).

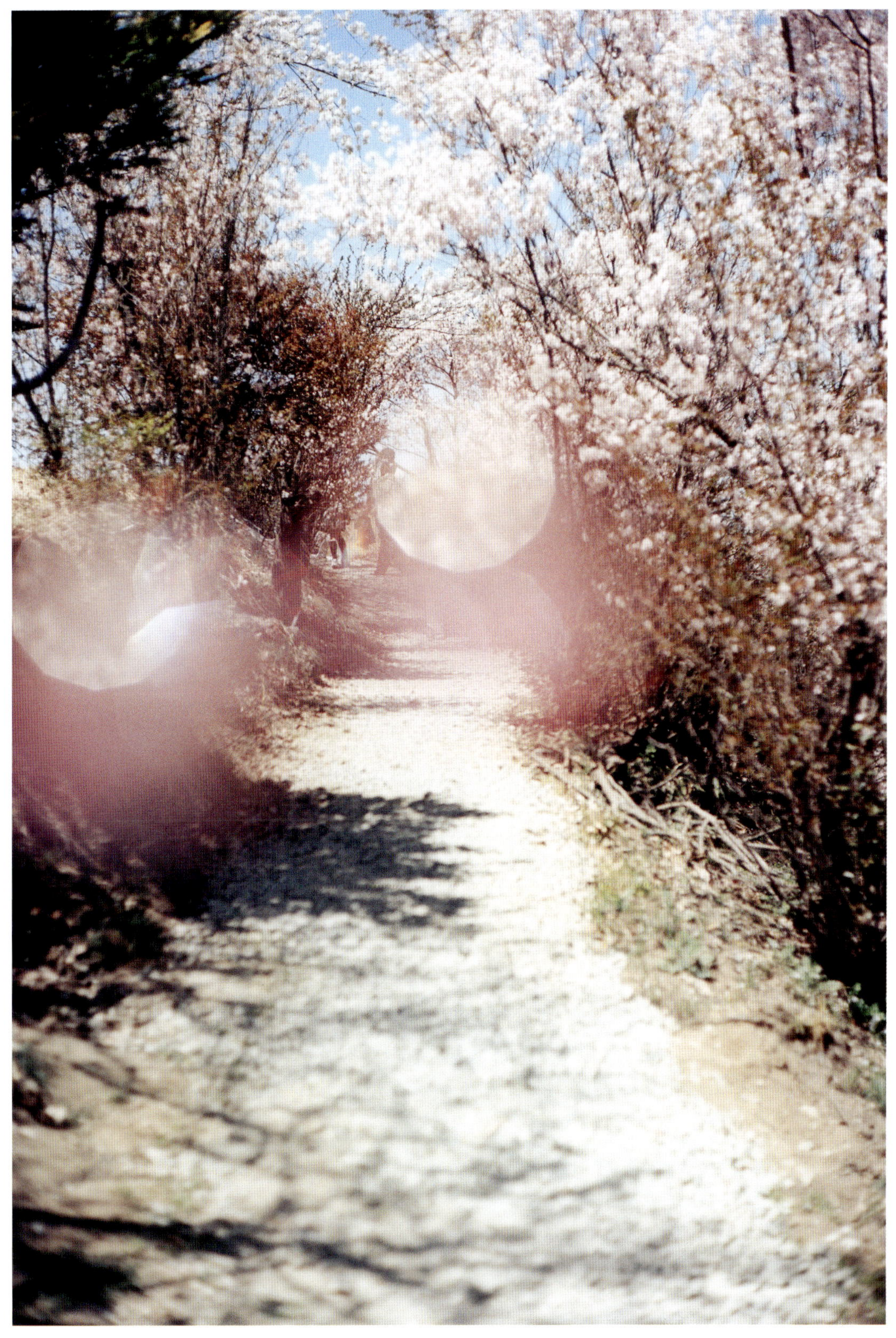

Ōmori Katsumi, *Fukushima-shi, Fukushima*, 2011,
Everything happens for the first time series.

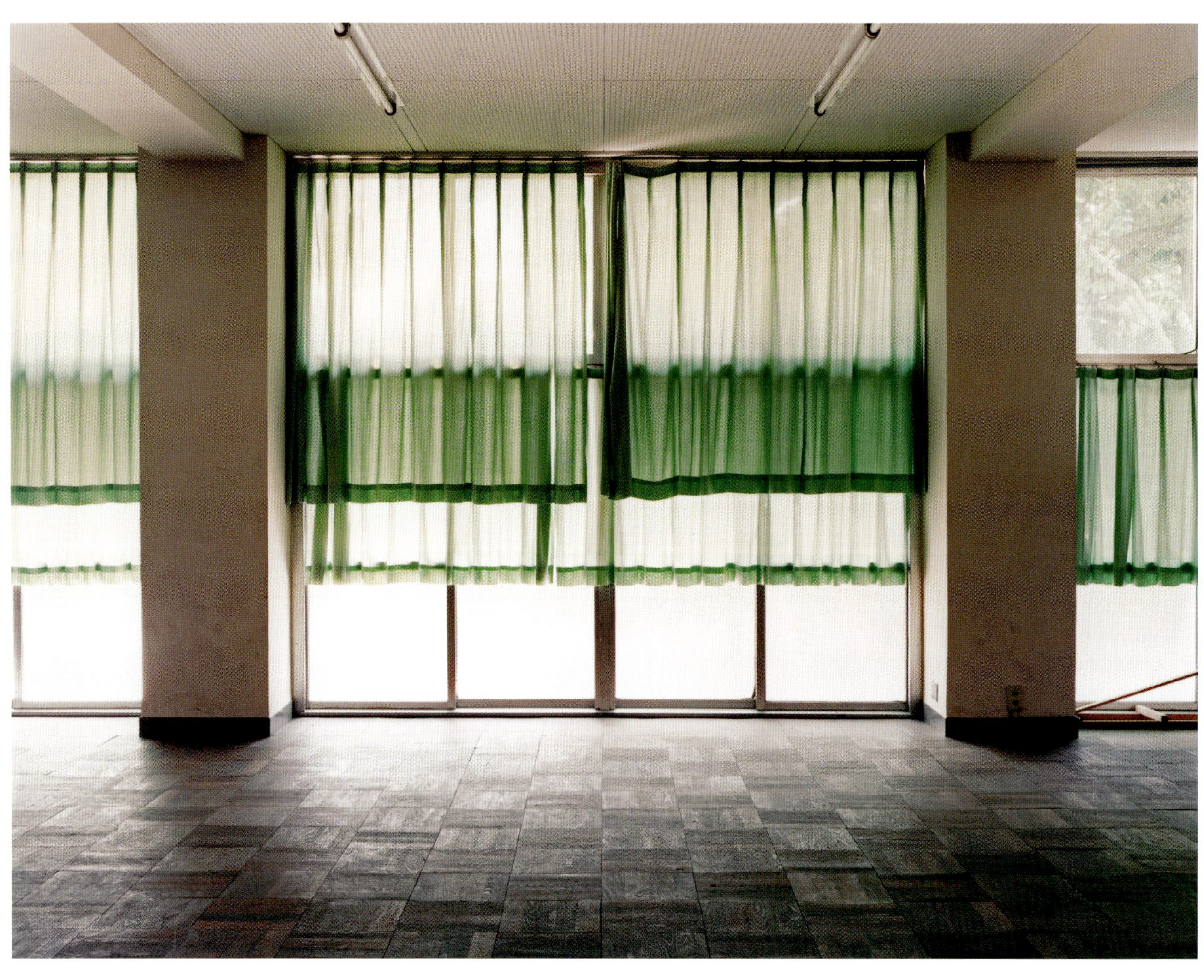

Yoneda Tomoko, *Classroom I, used as a temporary mortuary immediately after the earthquake*, 2005, *A Decade After* series.

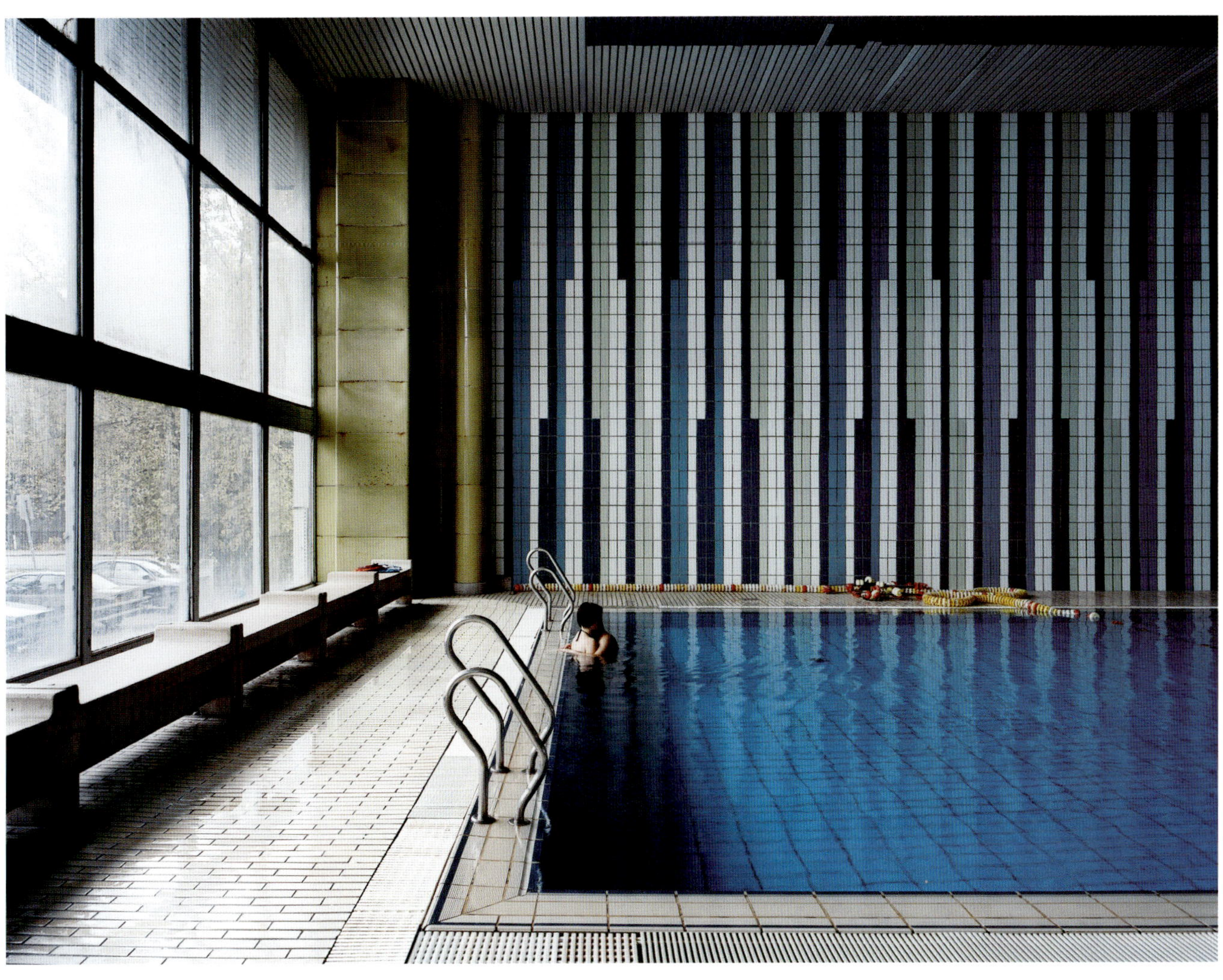

Yoneda Tomoko, *Lovers, Dunaújváros (formerly Stalin City), Hungary*, 2004, *After the Thaw* series.

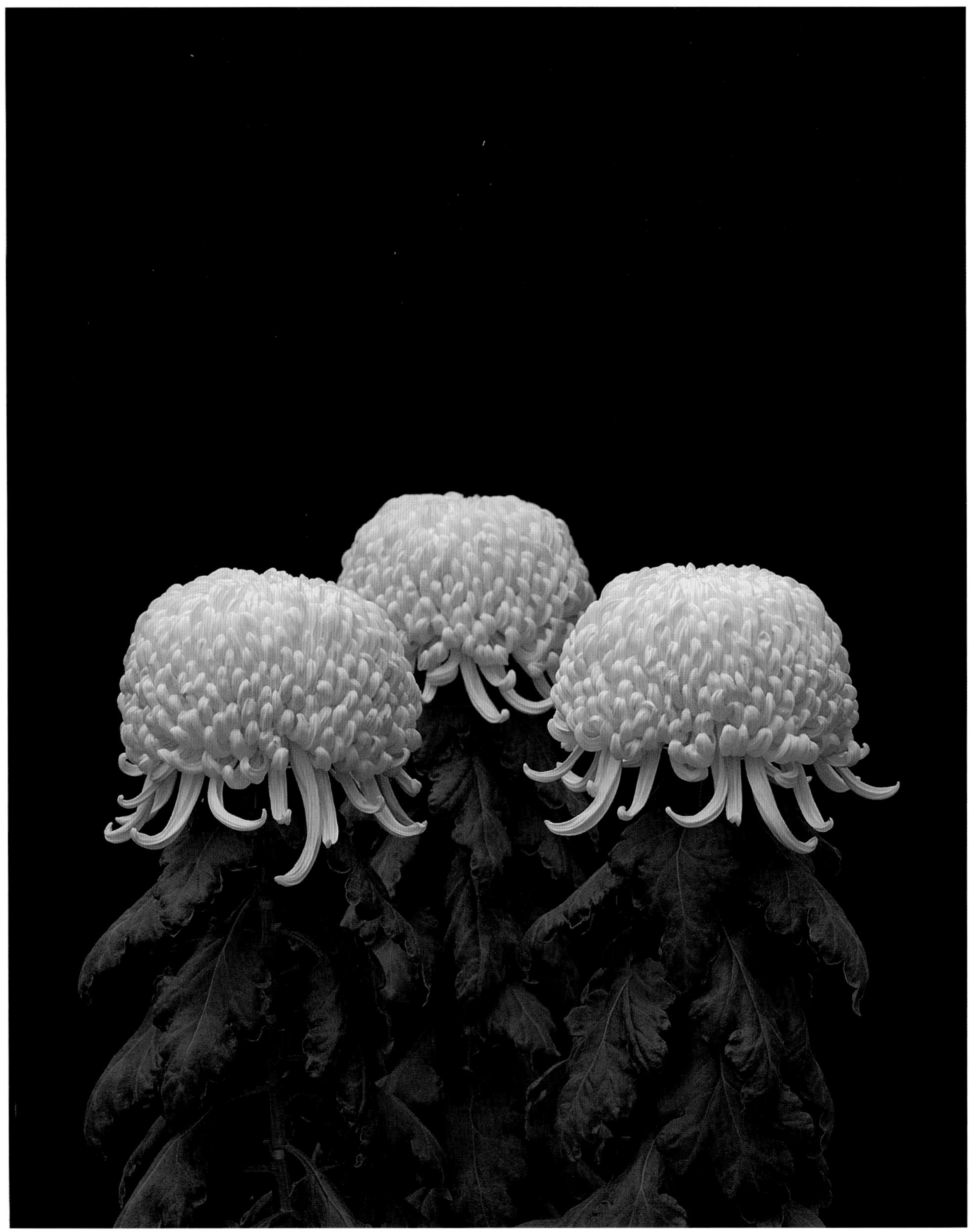

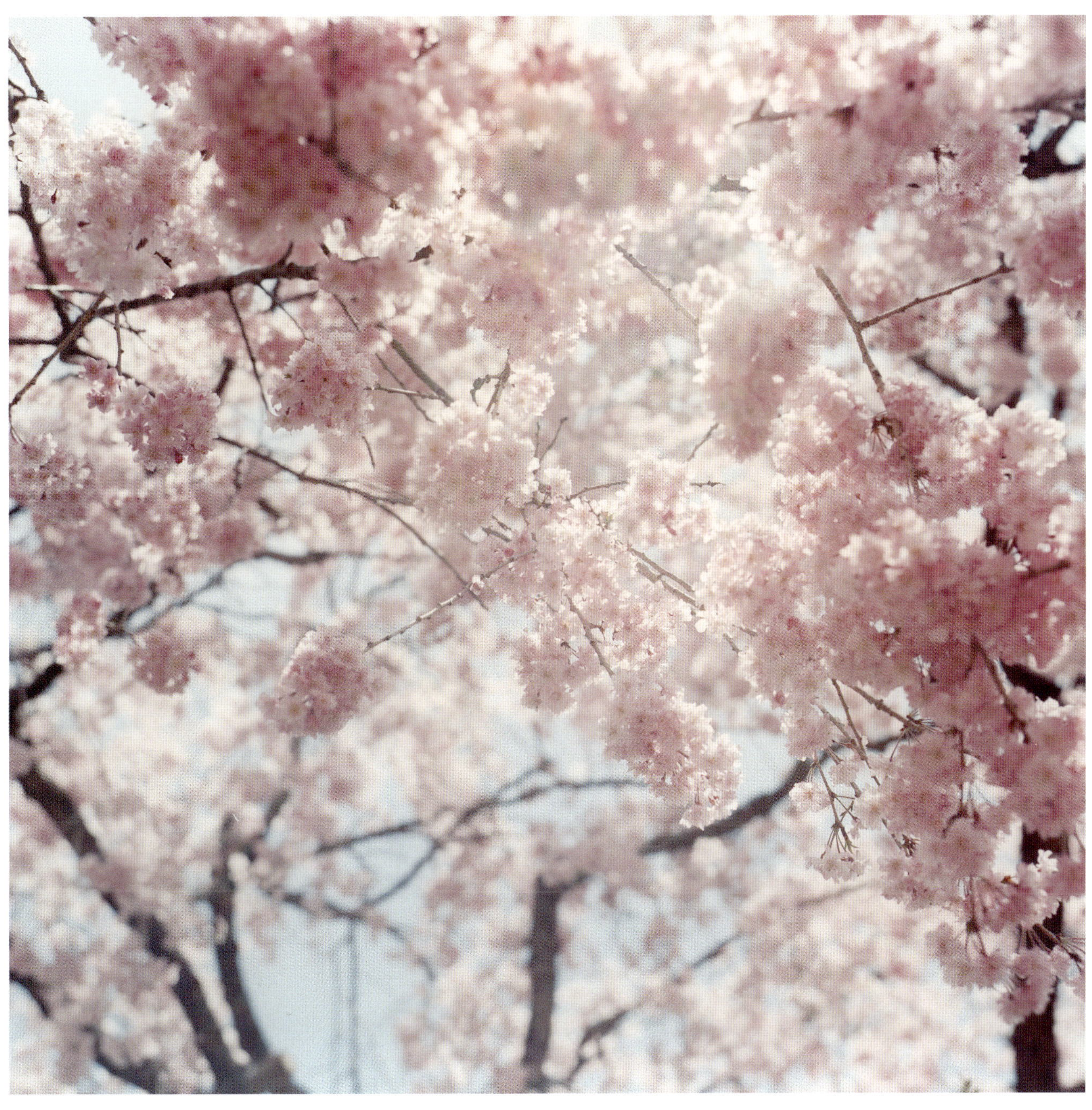

Opposite: Yoneda Tomoko,
Chrysanthemums, 2011, *Cumulus* series.
Above: Kawauchi Rinko, untitled, 2011,
Illuminance series.

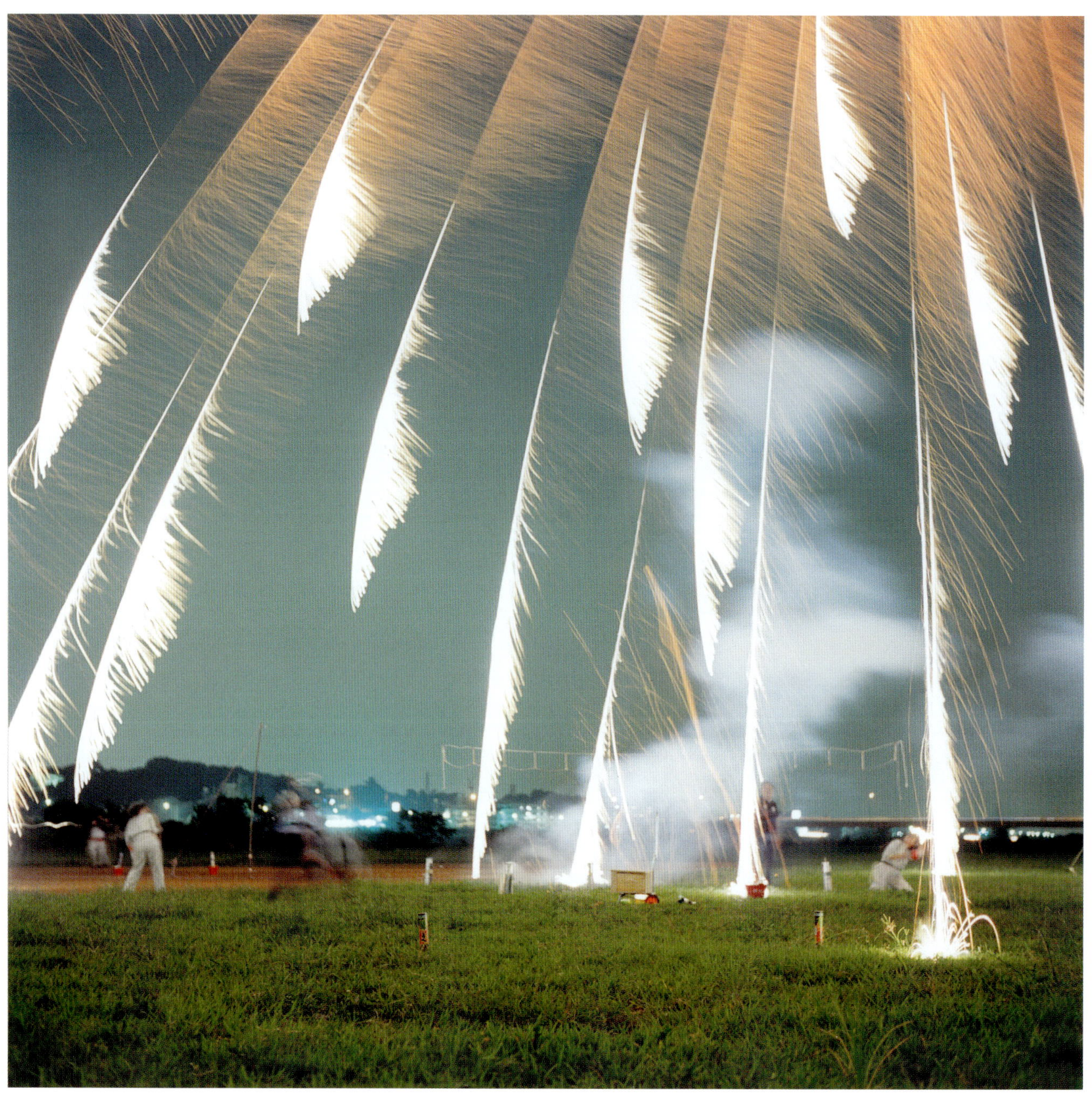

Kawauchi Rinko, untitled, 2001, *Hanabi* series.

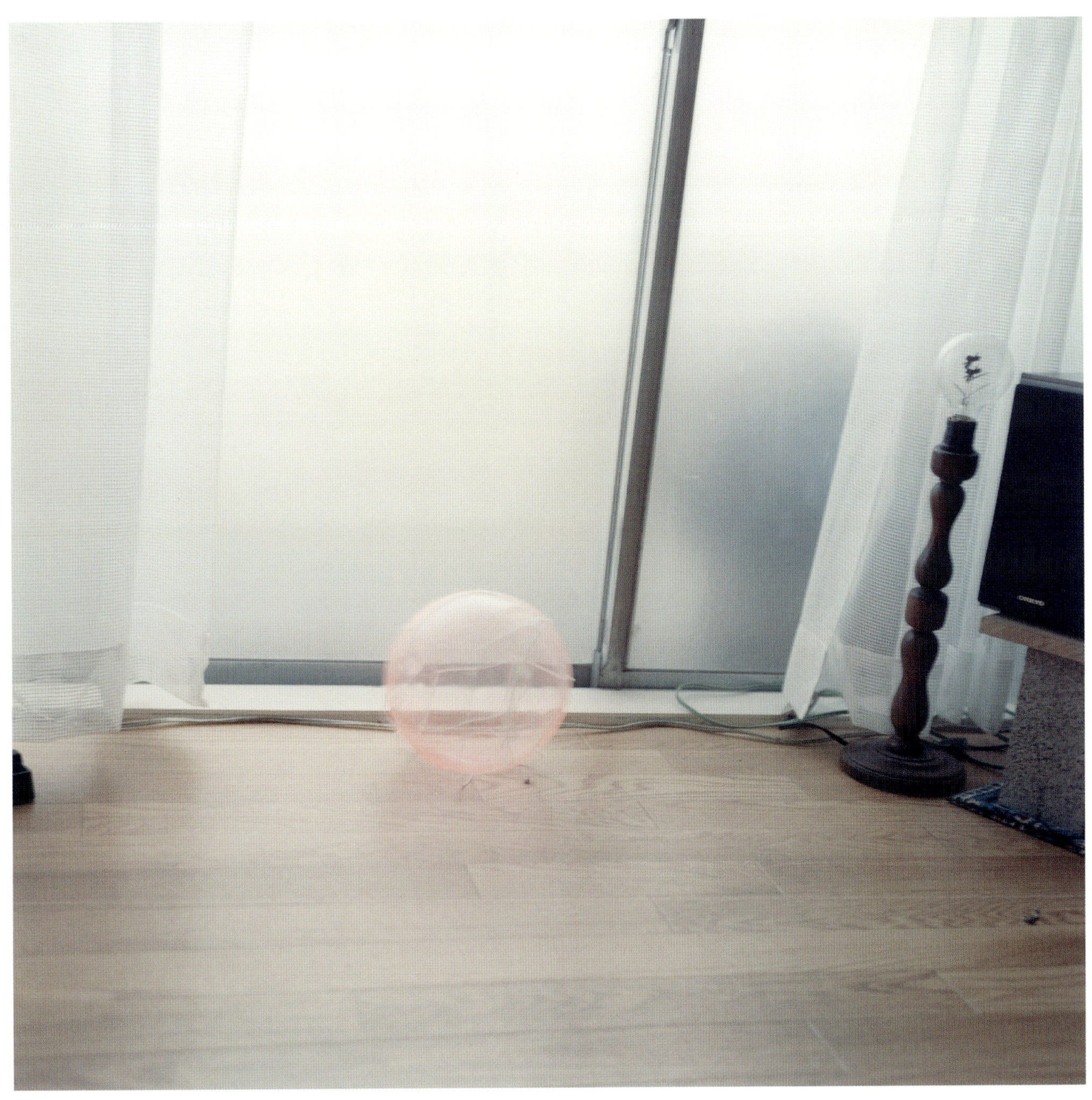

Kawauchi Rinko, untitled, 2001, *Utatane* series.

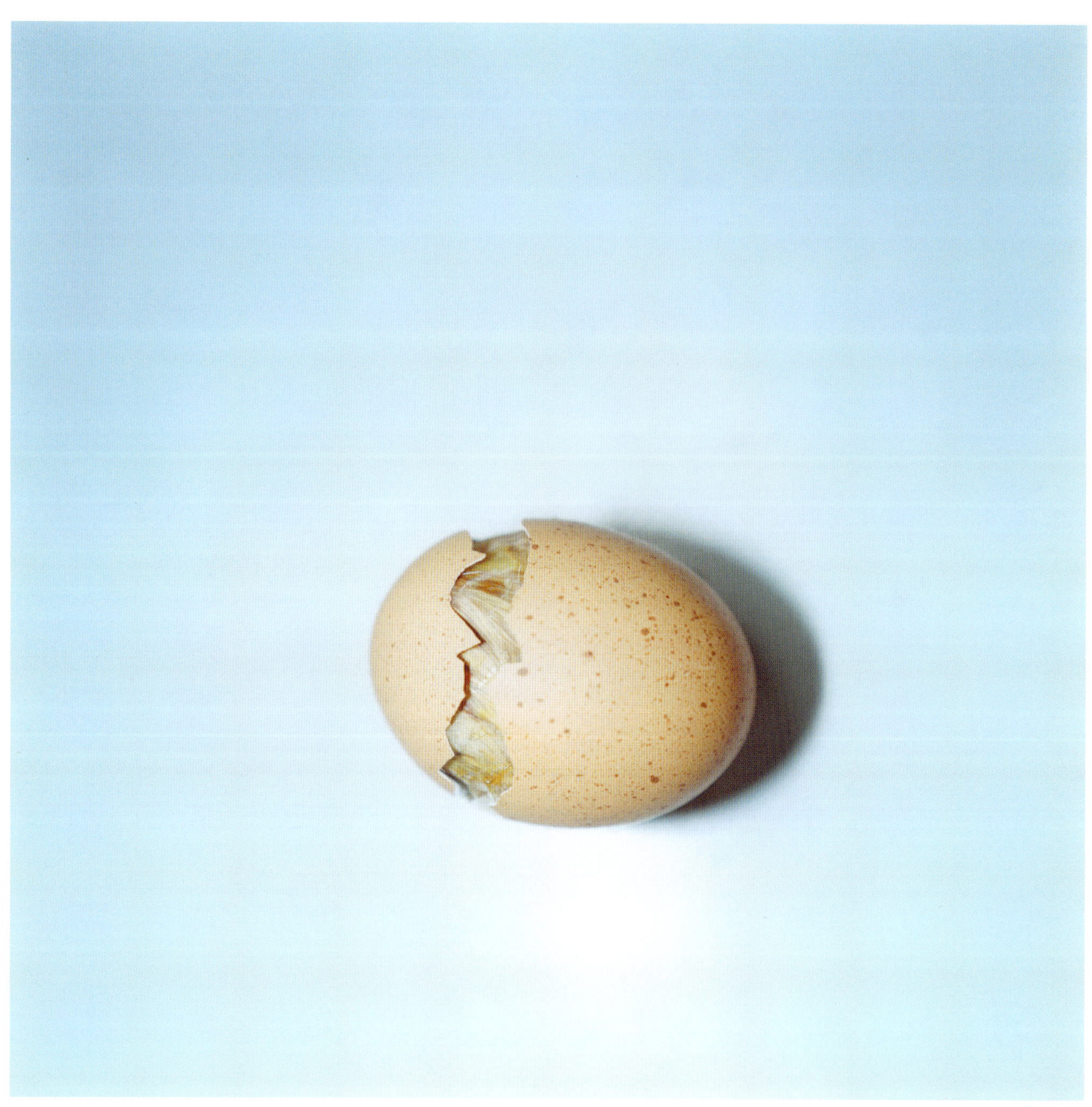

Kawauchi Rinko, untitled, 2004, *AILA* series.

Lena Fritsch: Let's start at the beginning – what inspired you to take up photography?
Kawauchi Rinko: I studied graphic design at the Seian University of Art and Design [in Shiga Prefecture] and they also offered lessons in photography. I ended up enjoying the photography lessons more than graphic design. After graduating, I started working in a photography studio.

Were you interested in photography before going to university?
Yes. During a senior high-school trip, I took snapshot photographs with a compact camera and enjoyed it.

When enrolling in graphic design at university, I knew that they offered lessons in photographic printing and I was looking forward to it. I was interested in art and photography even before university, but did not want to go to a photography school.

When you started photography were you interested in or inspired by any photographers in particular?
Not really – when I started photography I didn't know other photographers' work at all.

Later, I became interested in photobooks. In Japan, this included Araki, Moriyama, Takahashi Kyōji, Homma Takashi, Ōmori Katsumi, but also people of my generation who were active in the 1990s, like Nagashima Yurie for instance. In the 1990s there was a lot going on in photography, and after my lessons I often looked at photobooks.

In 2001, you published three photobooks: *Utatane* [p. 199], *Hanabi* [p. 198] and *Hanako*. Could you tell me about these photobooks?
Utatane featured different photographs in my own style that I had taken over quite a long period of time. The firework photographs from *Hanabi* were taken over a period of around three years. These two books were ready for publication when our conversations about *Hanako* began. So in the end, all three books were published at the same time.

In these photobooks and in your work in general, round forms appear quite often, conveying a very natural atmosphere.
I didn't consciously choose round forms, but I think that the circle is a symbolic motif. A friend of mine has compared the round forms in my photography with traditional *ensō* circles.[1]

Analysing my photographs, I think that while choosing circle forms subconsciously, deep down in my mind there were probably thoughts that

relate to *ensō* and the Buddhist concepts behind it.

Are you inspired by traditional Japanese artworks or concepts?
Not directly, but Buddhist thought definitely has some influence on my work.

Another of your photobooks that I really like is *Illuminance* (2011) [pp. 197, 205] – what inspired you to create these photographs?
This book is the first work that I published with a foreign publisher: Aperture, in the United States. I see *Utatane* as a major early book, the roots of my photography.

When it was decided that I would do a book with Aperture, it was exactly ten years after *Utatane*. I wanted to make a photobook in a similar style, and I compiled many photographs that I had taken over a long period of time.

The title *Illuminance* was chosen by the publisher. Before, I was thinking about 'Iridescence' – the colours of jewel beetles. Depending on the light, their colours change considerably; for example, they appear silver or bluish. The same beetle has different colours, depending on the angle when you look at it. I found that interesting. Something can appear very beautiful to you today when you are happy, but perhaps you will look at the exact same thing tomorrow when you are not feeling well and then you won't react to it at all. That applies to everything, I think – depending on your viewpoint, things look different. That is why I wanted to use the title *Iridescence*. But *Illuminance* is easier to remember.

Light and illumination are motifs that appear often in your work, for example in your photographs of fireworks in *Hanabi* [p. 198].
Fireworks are beautiful, and within just a moment they have already disappeared. As a motif they connect with the photographic medium, trying to keep a moment. The firework is a metaphor for photography that is easy to understand. I also feel that I want to find and pursue beautiful things.

You try to find 'beautiful things' mostly in everyday life. What is beauty to you?
Beauty is inextricably intertwined with living; it is cheerful and makes life more worth living. Without beauty, life would be a lot harder. It is connected to life – and therefore also to death.

Would you say that in the background of your work there are Japanese traditional aesthetics linked to beauty and death, such as *mono no aware* or *wabi sabi*?
Yes, I am influenced by those things.

I think that the passing of time, *mono no aware*, is very beautiful – for example, cherry blossoms are beautiful. In that regard, I'm very Japanese. When my works have been exhibited overseas they have been compared with *haiku* poems. I understand *haiku* a bit differently, but it is an interesting comparison.

Finding beauty in small everyday life situations could be a similarity between *haiku* and your photographs.
Yes, the search for beauty in this world is comparable, and the link with nature is a similarity as well.

Could you tell me about your approach to photography – do you take photographs every day? Do you decide on themes and concepts before making a series?
It is mixed. I take photographs spontaneously in everyday life, but I also go to places deliberately to take photographs. These places can be nearby or even overseas. I think it is interesting to combine images that are set up with spontaneous shots.

When you compile your photographs in a photobook, how do you proceed?
I start by making a pre-selection – either using photographic prints or by moving the photographic images on my computer into a specific folder. I compile these works and then make another selection. I repeat that process of selecting and compiling a few times.

Since your debut photobooks, fifteen years have passed – do you think your approach to photography has changed, and if so how?
I think when I was younger I took more photographs, basically every day, because I was not as used to it. Now I don't take that many photographs any more.

What do you like best about the medium of photography?
I like that photography reflects reality, what you can see – it is different to painting or text.

*   This is a shortened version of an interview conducted in Japanese on 2 September 2016, at Kawauchi Rinko's office, Tokyo.
1   *Ensō* is a circle motif common in traditional Japanese art, particularly calligraphy. It is linked to Zen Buddhism, symbolizing ideas of enlightenment, the universe and the void.

Lena Fritsch: Let's start at the beginning – what inspired you to take up photography?
Morimura Yasumasa: When I was a child in the first or second year of elementary school, my father bought me the Fujipet camera, a compact camera for children produced by Fujifilm. Taking photographs with that camera was my first encounter with photography. My father liked photography; he had a Leica, and he took photographs of the family that still exist, which is very nice. There was a camera shop next to our house, too, and the wife of the owner was a beautiful woman. She was very ill, and died when she was young. I have many early memories of photography. Looking back, I think that these encounters with photography and the camera as a child were important.

My interest in photography as a form of expression developed when I was at university. I studied design, and this included photography lessons. We received a photographic task: the theme was 'bicycles'. I remember that I really enjoyed taking the photographs and printing them in the darkroom, but when I handed in my work, the professor told me that it was not interesting. I realized that there were 'interesting photographs' and 'uninteresting photographs'. Until then, to me photography did not necessarily have to be more than a fun activity. My professor's statement made me wonder what 'interesting photographs' were, and I began looking at photobooks and camera magazines and learning about the history of photography. At our university there was a professor of photography whose lessons I started to attend: Ernest Satow. I began taking photographs as a form of artistic expression. My early works were monochrome photographs: still lifes, cityscapes and self-portraits.

When you started photography at university were you interested in or inspired by any photographers in particular?
There was Ernest Satow's influence, but I was also interested in other photographers, such as Walker Evans, Edward Weston, Ansel Adams and Henri Cartier-Bresson. Another important person was Robert Singer, who later became Head of the Japanese Art Department at the Los Angeles County Museum. He lived in Kyoto at the time and introduced me to original prints, like those by Edward Weston. Until then, photographs to me were images in photobooks or magazines; that was the way they were presented in Japan. But he told me to wear gloves and 'hush!' to be quiet when looking at the photographs [laughs]. He showed me a new world, the world of vintage prints. At the time, there were also photographers like Moriyama

Daidō or Nakahira Takuma, who took dynamic, grainy photographs. I was looking at all these different photographs and wondering what kinds of photographs I myself should take.

When did you become interested in art history as a photographic motif?
I enjoyed painting when I was a child. I was shy, and did not like to interact with others much. Painting is something that you can do alone. In high school I became interested in Western oil paintings. As homework over the summer holidays, we were asked to paint a holiday experience. After the holidays most of the children brought back a watercolour painting on paper. But one classmate brought an oil painting on canvas. It depicted flowers and made the classroom smell of oil paint – a smell that was unknown in Japan at that time. To me, it represented an unknown adult world. I decided that I would join an arts club and do oil painting at senior high school – that dream helped me during my studies for the final exams [laughs].

In senior high school I joined an arts club and enjoyed both painting and photography very much. At the beginning we painted in a colourful, impressionistic style, but in my second year, I realized that I was painting like artists a hundred years ago and became more interested in contemporary art. I learned about contemporary art, but did not study art history very much. To be honest, when I created my *Portrait (Van Gogh)* in 1985 I did not know much about van Gogh [laughs]. A few years later, I made my Rembrandt works – but I did not know anything about Dutch Baroque painting!

You once told me that, in the process of creating photographs that appropriate works of art history, you learn a lot about the paintings.
Yes, I still think so: creating works that are concerned with art history is a form of studying art history for me. It is interesting, as I discover a world that is a bit different to usual art history.

You just mentioned Rembrandt: in 1994, you made a series concerned with Rembrandt's paintings and had a solo exhibition, 'Rembrandt Room', at Hara Museum of Contemporary Art. Could you tell me about your interest in Rembrandt, and about the photograph *White Darkness* [p. 207] from the series?
My interest in Rembrandt came from my interest in self-portraits. I had a big book of Rembrandt paintings, and the whole book was only about his self-portraits. So many Rembrandt faces! I found it fascinating that there existed an artist a long time ago who made so many self-

portraits throughout his life. I wanted
to make works that combined his self-
portraits with my self-portraits.

**In *White Darkness* you present
another important characteristic
of Rembrandt's paintings: he was a
master of light. The work is also typical
of your art, as you appropriate his
painting from your own perspective,
adding more layers to it. Could you tell
me more about it?**
White Darkness is a special work to me.
There is Rembrandt's oil painting, with the
big ox carcass. It is not a self-portrait. He
combines the medium of the oil paint and
the motif of the meat very skilfully, and I find
the painting interesting. There is a woman
in the background, but its main motif is the
meat. I wondered: 'how can I make a self-
portrait connected to this painting?' In the
end, I created a photograph in which I
stand naked next to a big cow carcass.
I have always been really happy with this
work; however, I did not always know why,
and thought about this for many years. Now,
I think that the work is connected with my
self-portraits in a general way. The personal
'I' only exists 'as' somebody. For example,
I 'as a person who was born in 1951', or I 'as
a Japanese person', or I 'as an artist'. Of
course, not everybody agrees with that.
There might be people who think that deep
down there is something like a core identity
or that there is only one main identity. But
I don't believe that. My face is without any
make-up right now, but I can put a mask on
as Rembrandt, or as Marilyn Monroe. There
are many masks. Using different masks,
different personalities appear. I don't exist
without a mask because even my 'pure face'
without make-up is always a mask; I always
exist 'as' someone. However, the moment in
which I change from one mask to another
is interesting.

Returning to *White Darkness*: I saw this
cow and a little later it was killed. When
I took the photograph, I stood next to a
cadaver hanging from the ceiling: it was
not a cow any more but it had not been
processed into meat either. I was interested
in that indescribable in-between stage.
It was difficult to get permission for the
photoshoot, because they have to turn it
into beef really quickly [laughs]. Standing
next to this thing that is not a cow anymore,
but is not meat yet, I wanted to lead an
indescribable in-between existence as well.
I think that this work is at the core of my self-
portraits. I have made a number of works by
turning myself into different people, but in a
way *White Darkness* deals with all of this at
once. It is an important work.

**It is a strong work, I think. It deals with
death in a very intense way as well.**
I saw the cow when it was alive and
again shortly after it was processed into
something edible: probably into beefsteaks

that looked really yummy [laughs].
But I was interested in that very short
moment between the living animal and
the edible thing.

**In Japan, butchers and people who
work with blood were part of the
burakumin group, and were
discriminated against for a long time.
That also shows that the slaughterhouse
is a place that people normally don't
go to and don't (want to) see.**
Yes, it is a world that many people
never see.

**In your series *A Requiem: Theater of
Creativity* you impersonate different
artists. Could you tell me about this
series and your *Self-Portrait as Yves
Klein* [p. 210]?**
The series is concerned with different
artists. I was interested in Yves Klein; for
example in the way he used the elements
of fire or air in his works, and how he
created non-material works of art. There
is also this fake-ish quality, and a way
in which he was a bit romantic in his art
[laughs]. I was interested in the *Leap into
the Void* photograph because it represents
that 'fake-ish' aspect: the viewer does not
know if Klein really jumped or not.

I also noticed that indirectly there are
a number of vehicles in the photograph:
the random man on a bicycle in the
background, Klein as a flying man
referencing an aeroplane and the dream
of flying, and the train tracks. All these
represent speed, but also an element
of uncertainty. I think that in many ways,
Klein's photograph typifies what he
was interested in as an artist and what
I personally like about his work. The
photograph deals with the dream of flying,
the fascination with vehicles and speed.

**I assume you took your photograph
in Osaka. I noticed the old-fashioned
Japanese downtown hairdresser
in the background, offering perms.**
Yes. I searched a while until I found
the right setting, the perfect setting for
'my Yves Klein'.

**Why did you choose photography and
what do you like best about the medium
of photography?**
When I had my debut with *Portrait
(Van Gogh)* in 1985, I used the medium of
photography to make a painting. To me,
there are two important things: art and
the world of art on the one hand, and
photography and photographic expression
on the other. I found a way to link these
two by 'painting with photography'. I
enjoyed painting but I was not good at it;
I was not good at drawing people and
faces. But when I started painting on my
own face, using my face as the canvas,
I naturally got a 'painted face'. Recording

this through photography in a simple and
neutral way, without any special lighting
or anything, the three-dimensional
suddenly became two-dimensional, just
like a painting [laughs]. So the ability of
photography to record something has
been convenient for me. My photographic
self-portraits show that I really became Van
Gogh, Marilyn Monroe and so on. In a way
they both prove and record this – I find that
fascinating, and I use this characteristic of
photography to create my works.

*   This is a shortened version of an interview
conducted in Japanese on 1 September 2016,
at MEM, Tokyo.

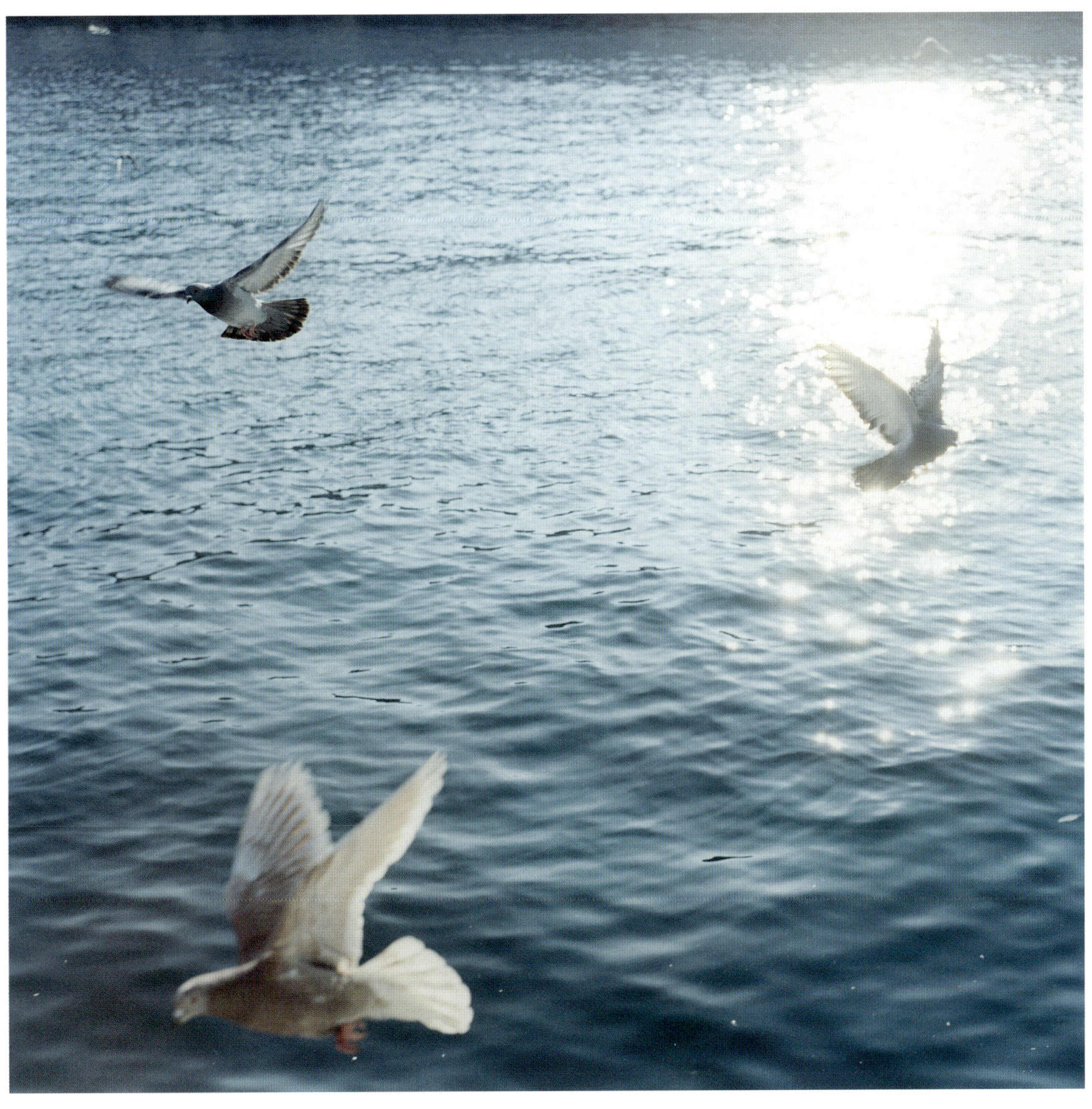

Kawauchi Rinko, untitled, 2011, *Illuminance* series.

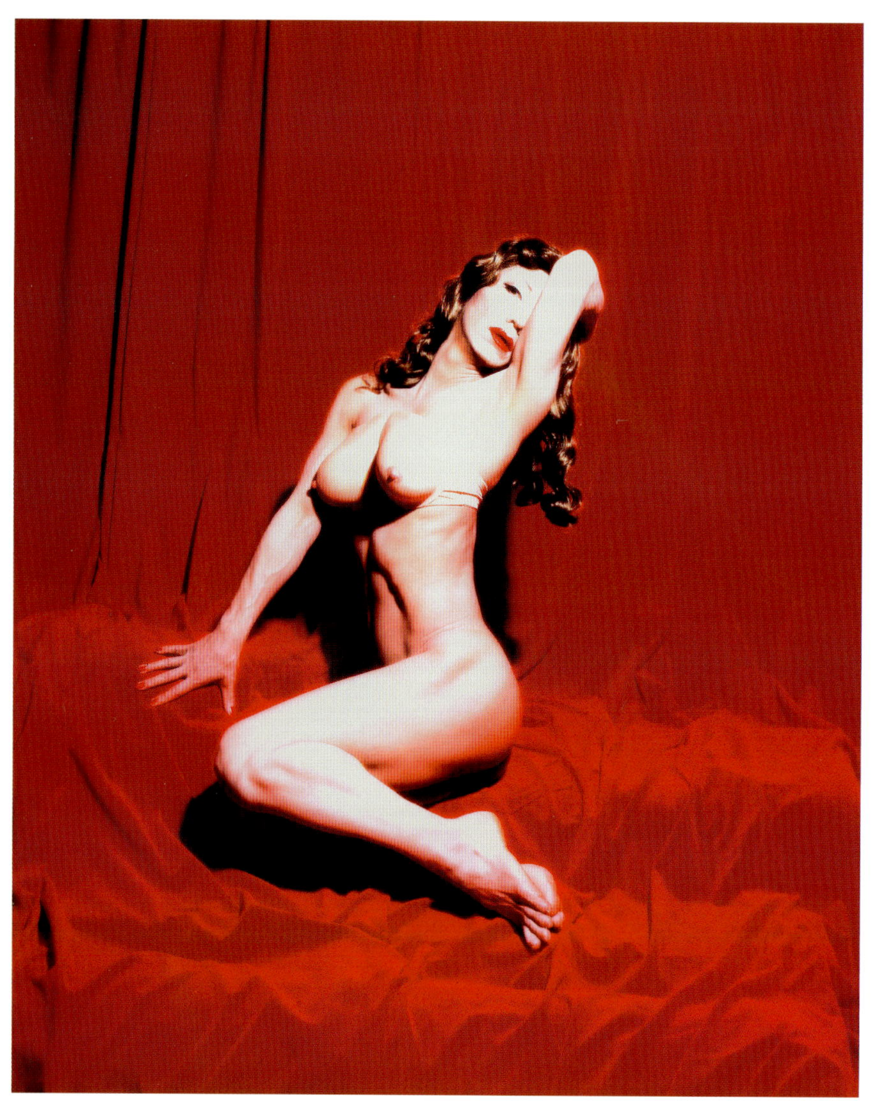

Above: Morimura Yasumasa, *Self-portrait
as Actress/Red Marilyn*, 1996.
Opposite: Morimura Yasumasa,
White Darkness, 1994/2008.

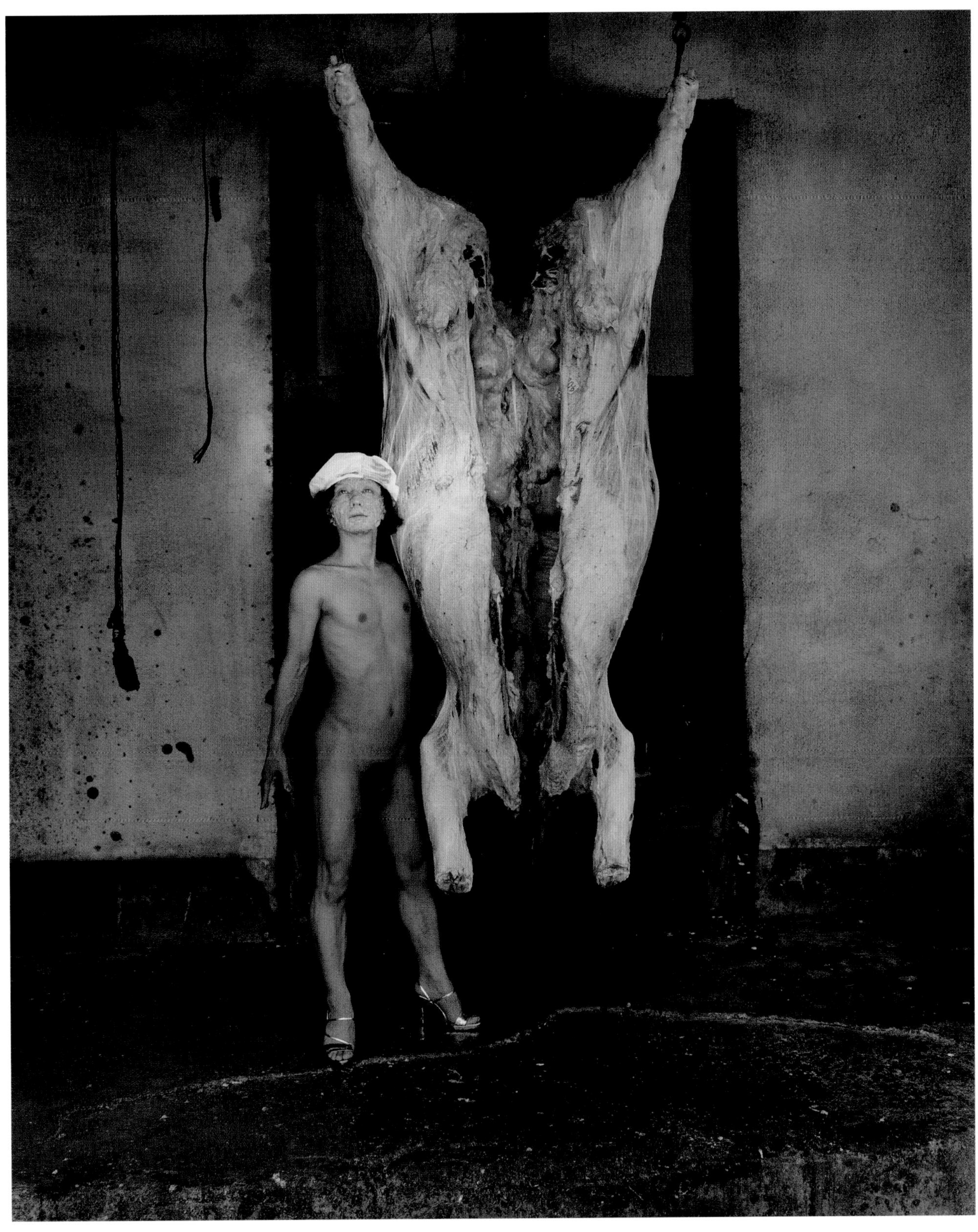

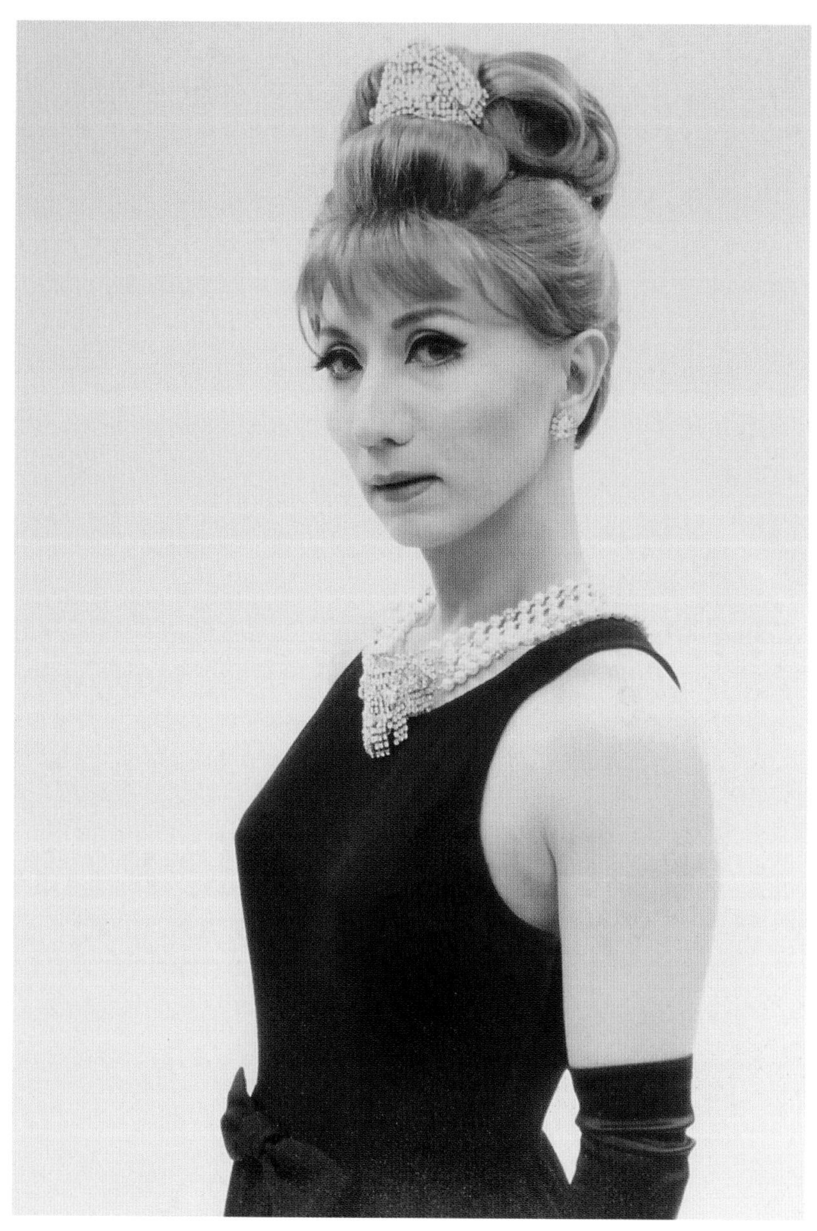

Above: Morimura Yasumasa, *Self-portrait/
After Audrey Hepburn I,* 1996.
Opposite: Morimura Yasumasa
A Requiem: Where is the Dictator? I, 2007.

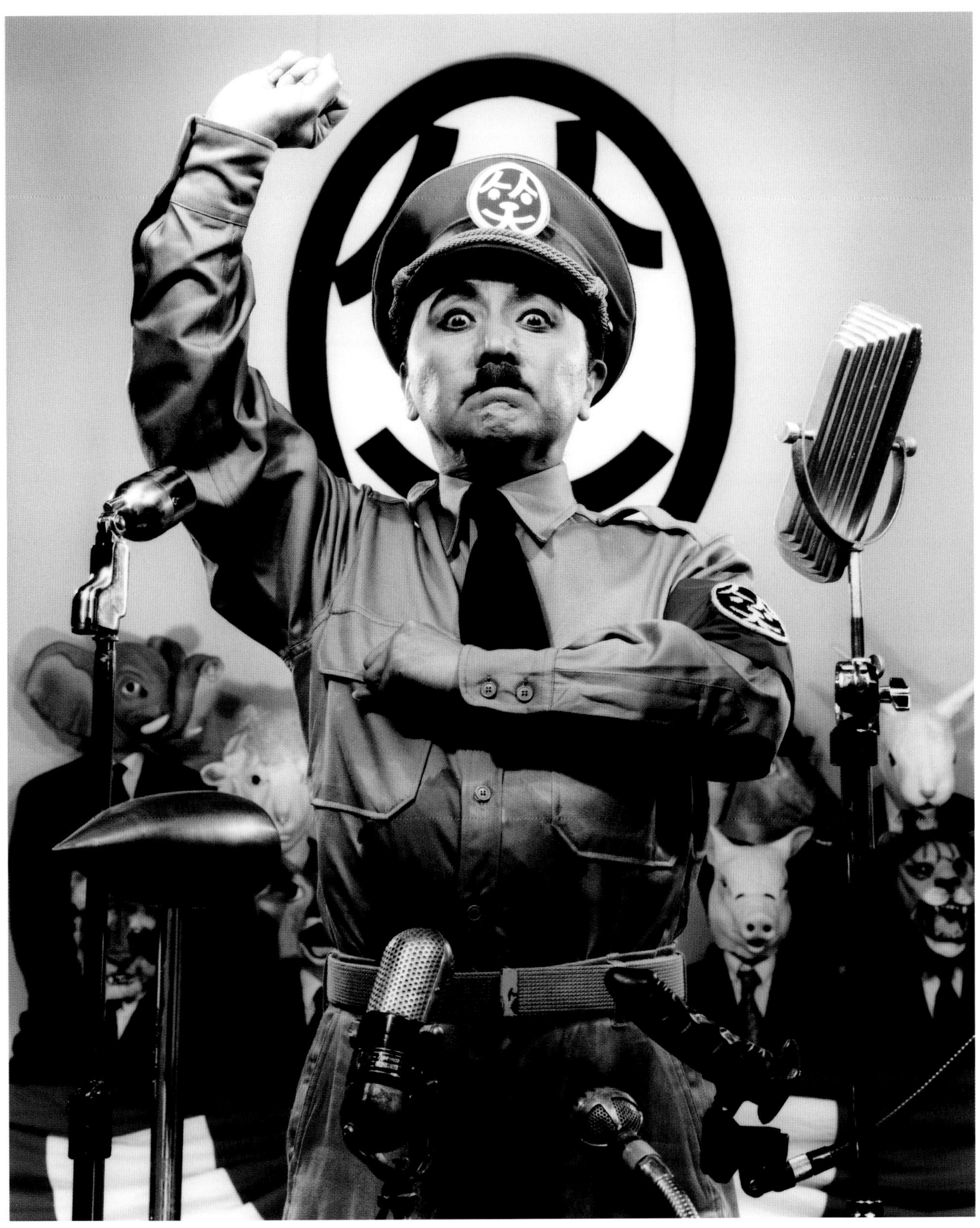

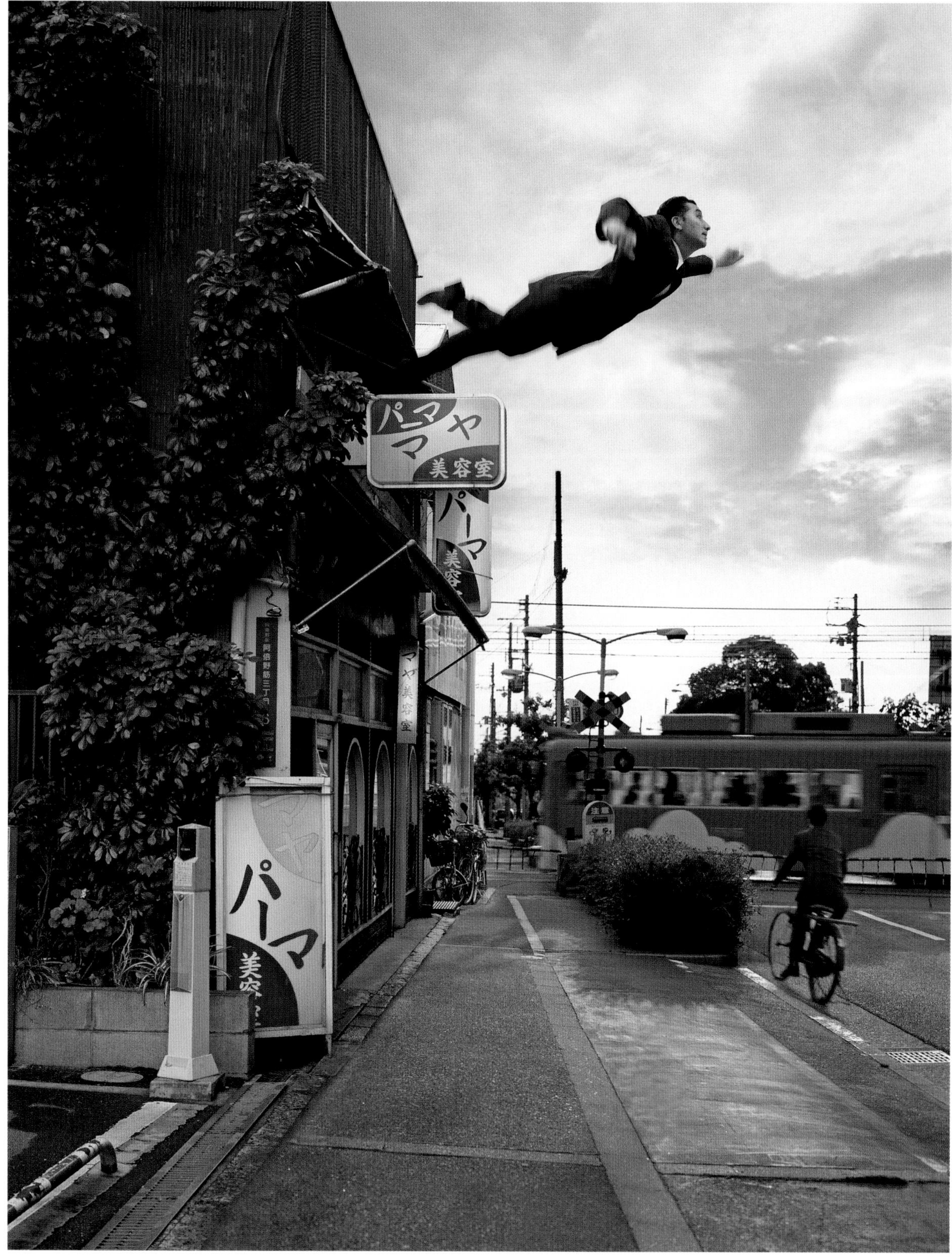
パーマ
ヤマ
美容室
パーマ
美容
パーマ
美容

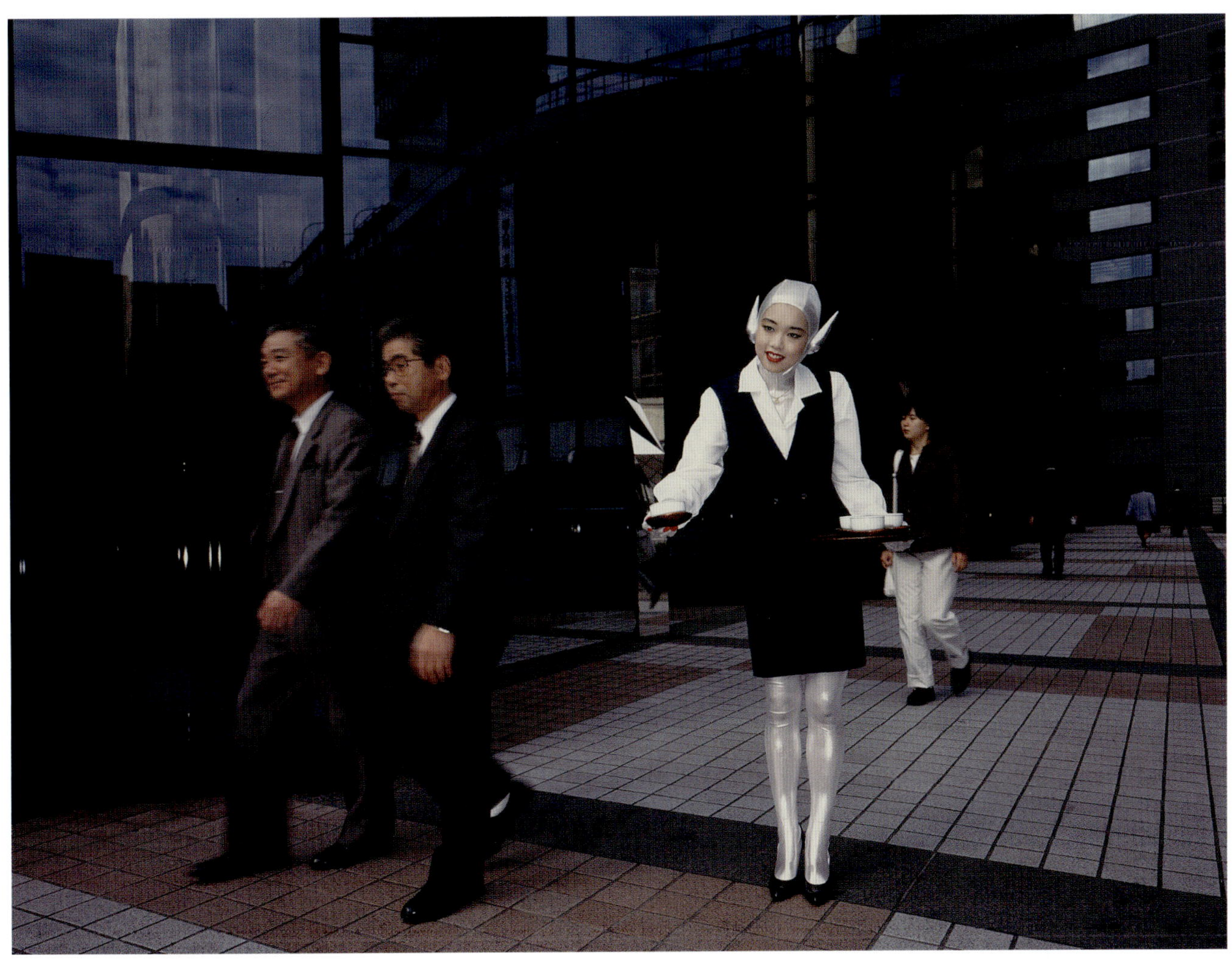

Opposite: Morimura Yasumasa, *A Requiem:*
Theater of Creativity/Yves Klein, 2010.
Above: Mori Mariko, *Tea Ceremony III*, 1994.

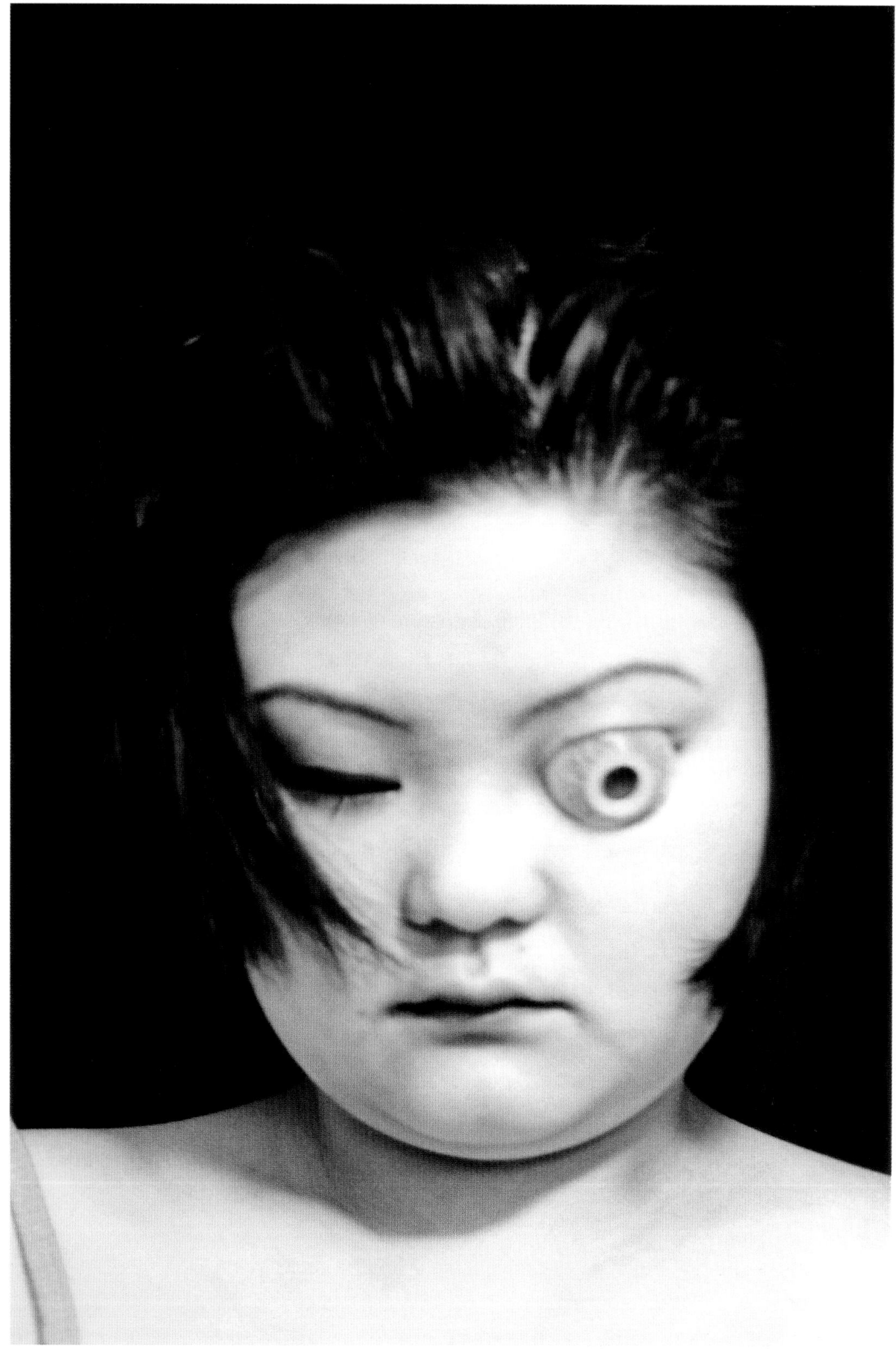

Sawada Tomoko, *Early Days*, 1996.

Lena Fritsch: Let's start at the beginning – what inspired you to take up photography?
Sawada Tomoko: During high school, I met a great teacher of modern art, the artist Tsubaki Noboru. He seemed to really enjoy art and I thought, 'I want to become an artist as well, it seems like fun'. When entering senior high school, I began to think more seriously about what to do after school and decided to become an artist. However, I did not know what suited me best: photography, painting or sculpture, so I decided to go to an art academy where I could try different things. Tsubaki-sensei then advised me to go to a university of art and design, and I joined the media design class at Seian University of Art and Design, where you could do different things. I learned all the basics in photography lessons, including how to print photographs. One day, we received a photographic task: self-portraits. We all watched a Cindy Sherman documentary in class – so more than half of the pupils thought that 'self-portrait' meant the subject is in disguise. They presented works in which they are in some sort of a masquerade [laughs].

That is funny – the opposite of the traditional 'self-portrait' definition. To start with Cindy Sherman instead of Rembrandt or Dürer is funny [laughs].
It is indeed. I also thought, 'ok, let's start with the disguise'! When creating these self-portrait photographs, I intuitively realized that it suited me. That is how I took up photography – and I have continued ever since [laughs].

Are these early photographs that you took as a student part of your *Early Days* series [p. 212]?
Yes.

At the time were you interested in or inspired by any photographers – I guess, Cindy Sherman?
There was not one artist in particular. I looked at all kinds of images, not just art. I also went to the theatre, concerts and such, and saw many things that indirectly influenced my photographs over time.

Your first series, your debut in the art world, was *ID400*, a large number of passport photographs of you. Could you tell me about this series and what triggered it?
Yes, that was my debut – I won an award for it. After my two-year course at Seian College of Art and Design, I realized that I wanted to continue studying photography. I thought about moving to another university, but there was a photography class for the students who did the four-year course at Seian University of Art and Design, and all the required equipment

and materials were there. My professor also advised me to stay, so I changed to the four-year course. I saw many works of art that I had never seen before, and there were also opportunities to do colour printing, which I could not do during the first two years. The course was too much information at once, and it became difficult to differentiate between things that I needed as an artist, and things that were just interesting to me. I even considered quitting university and making works on my own. I thought about photography a lot over the summer months, and wrote down my ideas. One day, when I was on the bus, I suddenly had the idea for *ID400*. It fitted perfectly with my thoughts on photography. The following weekend, I started taking the photographs at the photo booth. Overall, it took me around three months to finish the work. I was still at university and also worked part-time, so I took the photographs mostly on the weekends. I also went during the holidays, bringing a friend with me and various clothes and props.

That sounds like a lot of fun.
It was fun! I wanted a booth where the four photographs are all the same and also monochrome, so I did some research before going. There was no internet at the time so I had to make some phone calls [laughs]. I'm glad I took the photographs then, because there are hardly any photo booths anymore.

Could you tell me about your *OMIAI* ♡ series [pp. 218–19], which you presented a few years later?
After receiving the award for *ID400*, I exhibited the series a few times. Interestingly, most of the people who came to the exhibitions did not notice that it is the same person in all the 400 photographs. Even when I was in the gallery, people would not notice that it was me in the photos. They often wondered whether some of the subjects were the same person, but were always surprised when I told them that all of them were me. I did not expect that reaction, and realized that by changing just a few things about your looks, people would be more or less interested in you. *Omiai* photographs [photographs for arranged marriages] are the ultimate set of photographs in which you are judged very quickly by your appearance. At that time, the first of my friends started marrying, and I also had friends who went on *omiai* dates. I thought, 'if I disguise myself as different women in *omiai* photographs and send a man ten photographs to choose from, he can only choose one'. I liked that concept and the complex relationship that would develop between me and the viewer.

Your photographs were taken in a real *omiai* photo studio, weren't they?
Yes. A friend introduced me to a photo studio in Kobe. I went there with my *ID400* photos and explained my idea. By coincidence, the photographer had worked with artists before and appreciated contemporary art. He agreed, and I arrived there every Saturday in different disguises. I asked him to treat me as if I was a new customer each time [laughs]. We took two different photographs each time: for example, one kimono version (p. 218) and one version in Western clothing (p. 219). I did this over a period of six months. At the beginning I ate a lot and gained five kilos. Then, I lost twenty kilos [laughs].

Wow, twenty kilos is a lot. I noticed that you look quite different in some of the photographs…You have exhibited the photographs in different ways, even in portfolios.
Yes, like a real *omiai*-portfolio, which is exchanged between the two marriage candidates.

A series that presents a different image of women is your *Cover* series [p. 217]. You portray yourself in different youth fashion trends of the late 1990s, for example as *ganguro* with tanned skin, bright colours and extreme eye make-up. I always thought that these trends were fascinating, as they are quite the opposite of any traditional Japanese beauty ideals. Could you tell me about the series?
As a child I enjoyed dressing up, asking my parents to buy me fashionable clothes and trying out different hairstyles. I have always liked these things. After finishing my *OMIAI♡* series, I continued to be interested in people's appearances. I did an opinion poll with the visitors to my exhibition, asking them to put a sticker next to the photograph of me that they liked the most. Women in my age group chose the clothes that they liked best, for example their favourite kimono. Women who were older chose the type of woman that they would like as a partner for their son.

And men chose the type of women that they personally like best?
Yes. But they would not tell me which one it was. They took it rather seriously – despite knowing that the women were all the same person, namely me. I was surprised by how powerful the impact of one's appearance can be on people's feelings. At that time, in 2002, just when I was thinking about people's appearance, the *ganguro* trend began to fade. I thought, 'assuming that I continue my work as an artist until I'm in my seventies or eighties, this is the only time that I can take photographs as *ganguro*.' I could still

buy the shoes, clothes and make-up before the trend was finished.

In Japan, the series is less popular because it is seen in relation to a trend that has ended – overseas, it has been exhibited and written about more. At the time, the *ganguro* look was the most obvious trend that really focused only on people's appearance. They would gather as a group in Shibuya, in front of the 109 shopping centre. But of course, they did not all live there and there must have been girls travelling on their own, from their homes in Saitama or other areas around Tokyo to the city centre to meet their friends. Seeing them on the train on their own, their appearances stood out and they were surely judged by how they looked. It was the perfect motif.

I always thought that in a way, the girls had some courage – to dress up like that and wear such heavy make-up. They stood out from Japanese society quite a lot.
Nevertheless, the *ganguro* trend was quite a Japanese thing, I think. *Ganguro* would often turn up as friends in a group of two, in a 'pair look'. I have never seen these pair looks among friends overseas. Japanese people tend to be a bit scared of doing something that is different from other people; they like to be the same as everybody else, but within that sameness there is often an element of wanting to be slightly individual. *Ganguro* looked similar and felt at ease as members of a group, but nevertheless included small individual features in their style. It was just like adding a little ribbon to your school uniform. That characteristic is the same in different social groups in Japan, and I was interested in that.

Why have you continued to take so many self-portraits until now?
When I started to take self-portraits while at university, it really suited me. The themes and ideas that I have in my head need a concrete form; as a method, I mostly end up using a self-portrait. It seems to be the best method for me to express myself. I'm in control and can change my face just the way I want – it would be more difficult to change another person's face like that. Perhaps I just like myself [laughs].

When you take your self-portraits, how do you usually proceed – do you take a large number of photographs that you choose from later?
I usually decide on a particular pose and then take three photographs – particularly in the past, when using film. Now I sometimes take a few more, working digitally, with an assistant checking the image on the screen right after taking it. But even now, I usually take three

photographs. For the *OMIAI ♡* series we took a few more as the photographer suggested all these possible poses [laughs].

When you create a photobook how do you proceed – do you do all the work yourself?
When making a photographic series I already have a broad image in my mind of how I want the photobook to look. I try to make my photobooks small, so they can fit into a woman's handbag.

That's great – I have your photobooks in my handbag right now and they fit perfectly!
I also try to make photobooks that don't interfere with the interior design in people's homes, so they can put them on their shelves, next to other books. I see a photobook as a work of art in its own right – it is not an exhibition catalogue. You can usually only afford a work of art if you have enough money and space in your home. However, there are people who like my works but can't afford to collect my photographs – I see my photobooks as works that they can collect instead. I tell the designer how I imagine the book and make all the decisions.

Your latest photobook *FACIAL SIGNATURE* has a great design and beautiful paper.
The designer, publisher and printer really worked hard and helped me to create a good book.

What do you like best about photography?
I like photography very much indeed. On the one hand, there are things that appear in photographs by pure coincidence, but on the other hand, there are things that you can set up and control. It is handy that you can control your photographs by learning and polishing your techniques. But there are also cases in which someone who has never taken a photograph before presses the shutter and creates a fantastic photograph. Perhaps I like the openness of photographic expression. You can experiment with photography, but also use it to just take a visual note. I like that freedom.

*   This is a shortened version of an interview conducted in Japanese on 11 September 2016, in the café of ANA Crown Plaza hotel at Shin-Kobe station.

Lena Fritsch: Let's start at the beginning – what inspired you to take up photography?

Izima Kaoru: I was nine years old and in my third year of elementary school when my father bought me an automatic camera: an Olympus Pen EE. It was very new at the time and you just had to press the shutter. The films were new too: instead of thirty-six photographs you got seventy-two photographs. Until then, people thought that only adults could take photographs, but with this new camera, even if you were only nine years old you could press the shutter and take photographs. I started using the camera and 'click, click', enjoyed taking photographs.

Do you still have those photographs?

I probably do. At least the photographs that I took as a teenager in high school. They are not particularly interesting: they depict my friends at school and such [laughs]. But I continued taking photographs, created a small darkroom and developed the photographs at home. I went to photography school for two years. Then I quit and began to work as an assistant for the photographer Kobayashi Akira. He actually asked me if I wanted to work for him, and I agreed and assisted him for one year. Following this, I went to the United States for one year without any particular aim – first to Los Angeles, then along the West Coast by bus and finally to New York, continuously taking photographs. I exhibited the photographs at Ginza Nikon Salon – that was my first exhibition. I was twenty-three years old. At the time, the only galleries for photography were galleries run by photo companies, such as Nikon Salon, Canon Salon, Pentax Gallery...

When did you begin to create your first magazine?

I was twenty-five years old, and it was a collaborative project with a designer/art director. *SALE Magazine* was a free paper and it included many advertisements, for example for clothes designed by friends. I took photographs and the designer made the pages. I worked freelance, and there was hardly any work. I used most of the money that we received from the advertisements to print the magazine. I didn't have much material to promote myself – just the photographs that I had taken in the United States. I needed some photographs that I could show to people; the magazine was a good start, and allowed me to present my photographs.

When did you begin to take fashion photographs?

When I became an independent photographer, I was friends with a music band: the band members were stylists, graphic designers, clothes designers. At the time, punk and new wave were fashionable and everybody looked really weird – the band members were really into their looks, a bit *visual kei*-style [laughs].[1] They asked me to take photographs of their gigs, and when they became more popular, my photographs began to appear in magazines. I began to receive requests from other musicians to take their photographs for music magazines, record covers and so on. I was taking photographs of clothes for designer friends, too, and soon fashion magazines began to contact me. I gradually received more and more work.

I find the music connection interesting – many photographers here in Japan tell me that their first jobs were photographs of gigs, or they say that they became interested in photography through record covers.

Oh, I liked record covers as well. When I started listening to music, records would be quite big: 30 cm or so. The photograph or design of the record jacket definitely had a strong influence on my decisions when I was wondering whether I should buy a record or not.

You became known in the art world with your series *Landscapes with a Corpse* [pp. 220–23]. Could you tell me about the very beginning of this series? Last time we talked, the series was still ongoing – do you still take photographs for the series now as well?

I started the series in 1993, while taking many fashion photographs for work. At first, fashion photography seemed really interesting to me, and I tried different angles and approaches. In the beginning they let me do this freely, but then I noticed that there were many rules and limitations and I got a bit bored of fashion photography. Magazines can exist because of advertisements, and they obviously have to use the brands that they advertise for. One day, when I saw a photo of an accident, I had the idea to present clothes on 'corpses'. There was a fashion magazine titled *Ryūkōtsūshin*, and I went to the editor and told him about my idea. He liked it and agreed to include the photos as 'fashion photography'. I also talked to the weekly journal *Shūkanbunshun*, and they agreed to include them as 'documentary photos'; and the magazine *Takarajima* agreed to include them as 'gossip', because the photographs featured actresses. I thought it would be interesting to look at the same photographs from different angles. They all liked the idea. However, the editor of *Ryukōtsūshin* then had to leave his job, and the other journals did not want to do it anymore either [laughs]. But I really wanted to realize my idea, so I decided to publish my own alternative fashion photography magazine: *Zyappu*.

You then included the series regularly in *Zyappu*. When did you begin to exhibit the photographs in galleries?
That was after I stopped producing *Zyappu* because the main sponsor, a publisher, went bankrupt. A gallery in Cologne and a gallery in Munich both asked me if I would like to do an exhibition. Thanks to them, I was able to continue my series for a long time – but I have done 51 series, and I don't take photos for this project anymore. There are still many people who would like to be models for it, but after so many years I have become a bit tired of it [laughs].

One of the reasons I find the series interesting is that it is so difficult to categorize, because it references so many photographic genres: fashion photography, landscape photography, police photography. You have included it in different magazines but also exhibited it on gallery walls...
I guess I don't really care about genres or categories very much. Last time when you interviewed me [in 2008], you asked me if I saw myself as an artist or a photographer in the Japanese scene, and I said that I was a photographer. But now, I'm not sure anymore – I think I'm in-between, or both, or maybe something completely different. Recently, I don't take so many photographs; I mostly help my wife to promote her jewelry and underwear brand [laughs].

A main theme of your photography – ranging from *New Beauty I* and *New Beauty II*, to *Landscapes with a Corpse*, to your series *You are Beautiful* – is beauty. What is beauty to you?
That is a difficult question to answer. I don't take photographs of something or someone because I think they are beautiful. Rather, the things that I show in my photographs are the things I myself want to see; they turn into something beautiful in my photographs. Beauty is a very individual concept. It is often said that 'people with a beautiful soul look beautiful' or the other way around: 'if your soul is beautiful, you don't have to look beautiful externally'. But I think that if I interact with a person whose ways I like, and who seems to have a beautiful soul, that person looks beautiful to me. I think the personal aspect is very important.

One of your series is quite different to your other work, and very conceptual: *One Sun*. What was the trigger for it?
In Japanese you say 'living under one roof' to mean 'family'. The 'one' in the title 'One Sun' is linked to that: it refers to us, to the fact that we are all living under the same sun. It is like my religion.
I grew up in a non-religious family environment; close to atheism. When taking the photographs for the *Landscapes with a Corpse* series, I began asking myself why I'm so scared of dying and whether other people are as scared as I am. I think all humans have a certain level of fear inside, knowing that they are going to die one day. I realized that one of the main functions of religion is to help with that fear. I thought, 'I need a religion as well', something to believe in.
In Japan, there is Buddhism, Shintoism, Christianity...and then there are these different schools of Buddhism, and there are Catholics and Protestants...I asked myself, why are there all these different subcategories? They call it religion, but there must also be other reasons [laughs]. I realized that I didn't want to choose any of them. The religion that I found it easiest to believe in is 'God dwells in all nature', the basic belief of Shintoism. Basically, it is gratitude towards nature. The sun represents nature and is something that you can always see, so I thought why not pray towards the sun? I wanted to create an icon that I could pray to. For around five years, I took photographs of the sun but didn't manage to create anything interesting. One day, I thought about the way the sun moves and decided to record it through long exposure. I liked the idea that the sun would appear as a straight line, just like the hands when praying [laughs]. I bought a camera with a fisheye lens and began taking photographs of the sun in different places, such as here in Tokyo, Hawaii and Singapore. But it is difficult to get a straight line, particularly here in Japan – which makes sense if you think about it. I then went to Kenya, to the equator on the day of the equinox, and I finally got a photograph of the sun in a straight line [laughs] [p. 164].

You decided to keep the photographs round – just like the form of the sun.
Taking the photographs with a fisheye lens, they are naturally round. I had not really thought about that, but when the photographs developed, I liked the round form and found it interesting.

What do you like best about the medium of photography?
The first camera that I used as a child was so easy to use: you just pressed the shutter and got a photograph. Everybody, including children, can take photographs. I like that simplicity. Today it has become even easier, and there are millions of people who take photographs with their iPhone. But at the same time, there is not one photograph that is exactly the same as another – I find that fascinating.
Recently, after creating the large photographs for the *You are Beautiful* series, I have focused on just taking photographs that I like, for myself. I have even been thinking about just presenting them on Instagram. I opened an account recently and have uploaded all my photographs from *Landscapes with a Corpse* and *One Sun*. Perhaps soon I will also upload the photographs that I have been taking over the last two years. [Pointing at a tiny photobook titled *musikera* with photographs of dead insects; see p. 264.] They are 'corpses' again: the corpses of insects [laughs].

I like this size – after large photographs, it is great to see these tiny images – and it suits the subjects. Did you just take photographs of dead insects whenever you saw one? You didn't kill them, did you?
Yes, I did. When there are mosquitos or a cockroach around, my family all start screaming, so I go 'bam' and kill them. But I do feel a bit sorry for that, and have started thinking that instead of putting them in tissue paper and throwing them away, I should look at the killed insects first. I use a new camera that you can hold very close to the photographic subject.

*   This is a shortened version of an interview conducted in Japanese on 29 August 2016, at Izima Kaoru's studio, Tokyo.
1   *Visual kei* (literally 'visual style') describes a subculture trend in Japanese pop and rock music that was particularly prominent in the 1990s. It is characterized by the use of elaborate costumes, hairstyles and make-up, often resulting in an androgynous look.

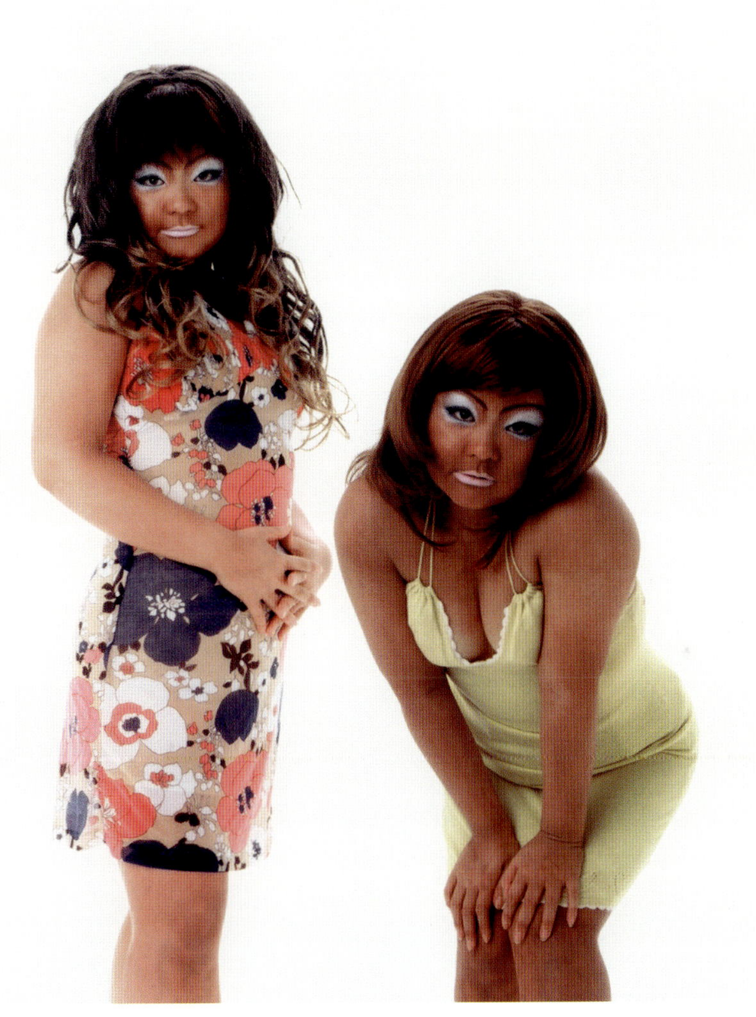

Sawada Tomoko, *Cover,* 2002.

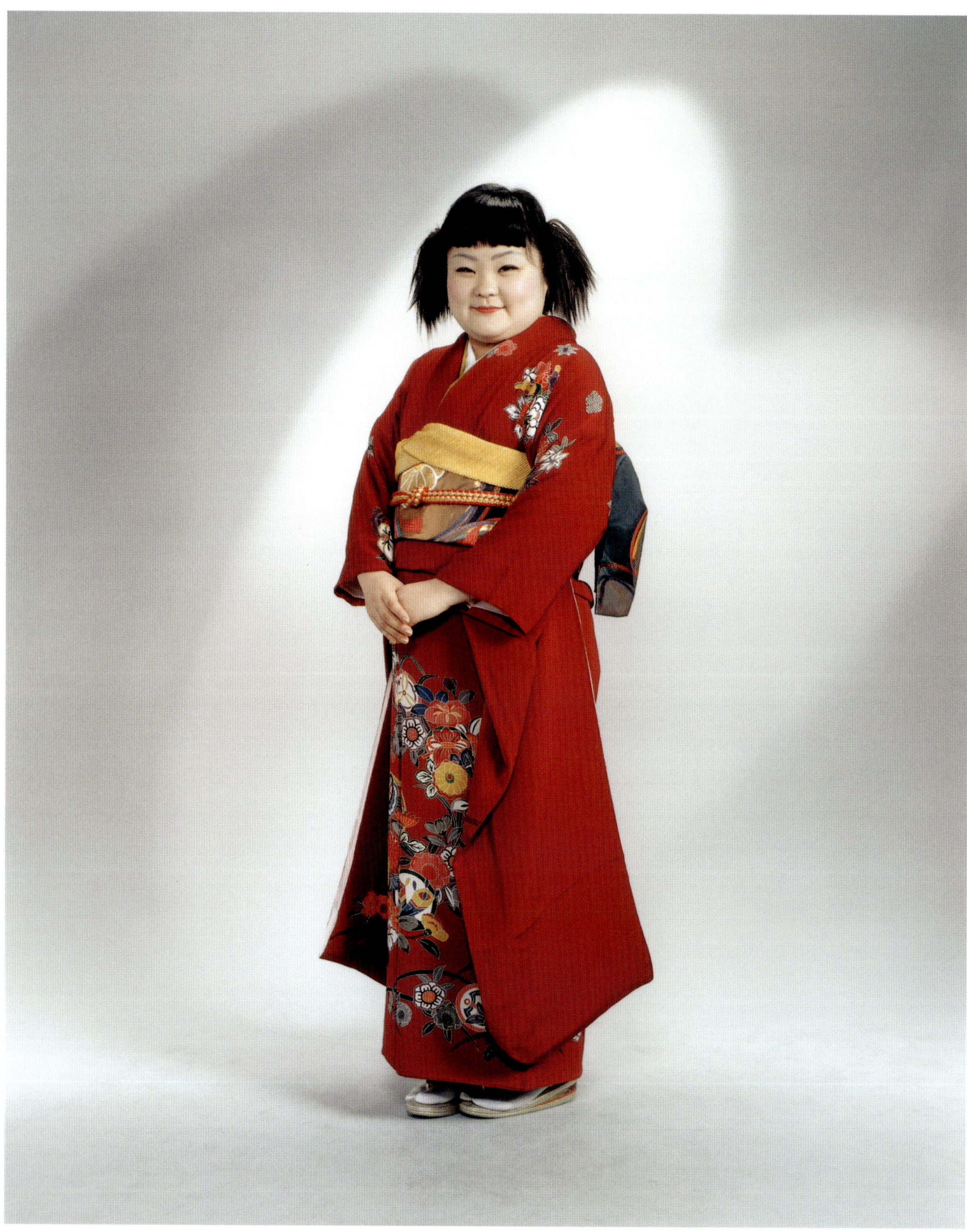

Sawada Tomoko, *OMIAI ♡*, 2001.

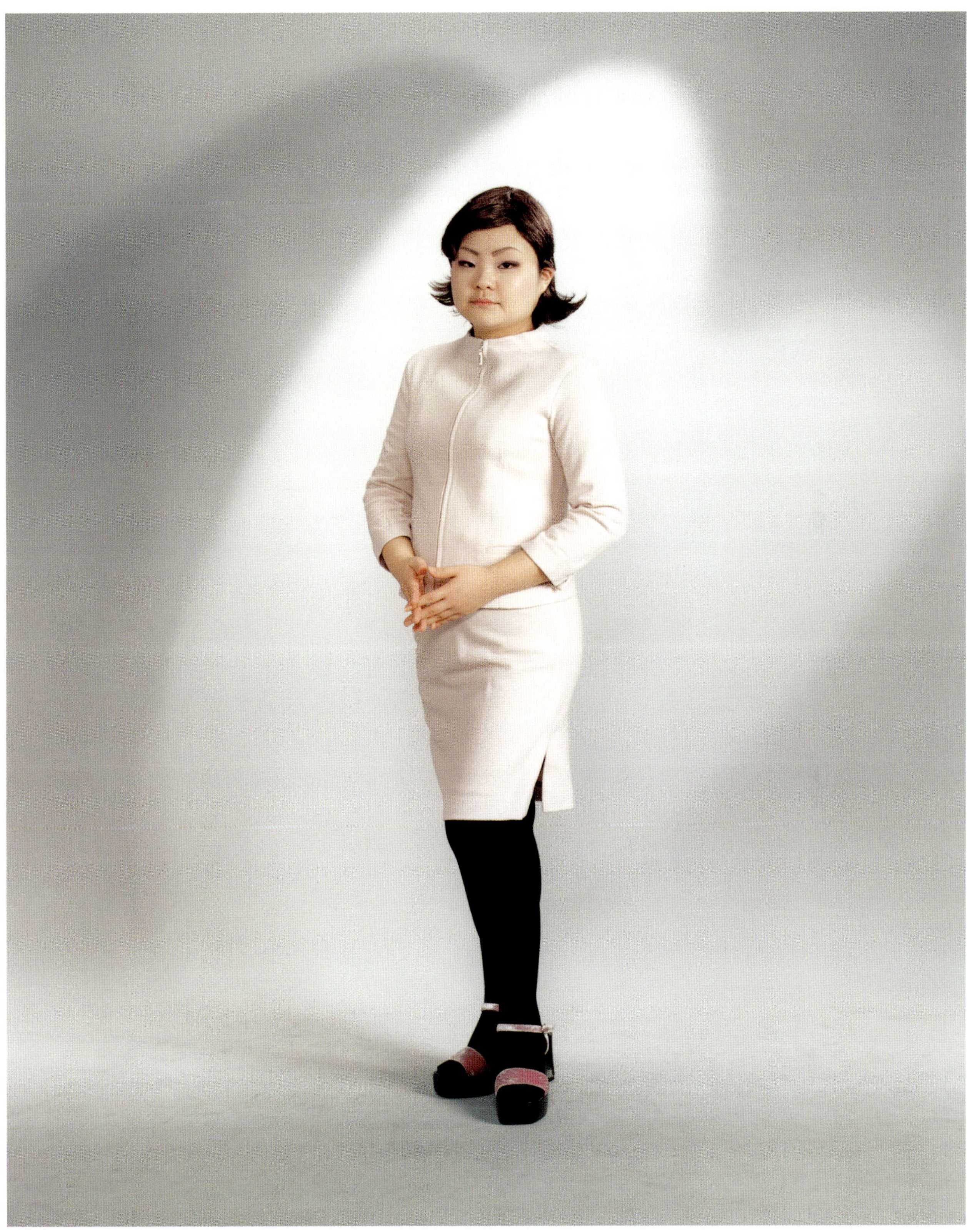

Sawada Tomoko, *OMIAI ♡*, 2001.　　　Contemporary Japanese Photography　　219

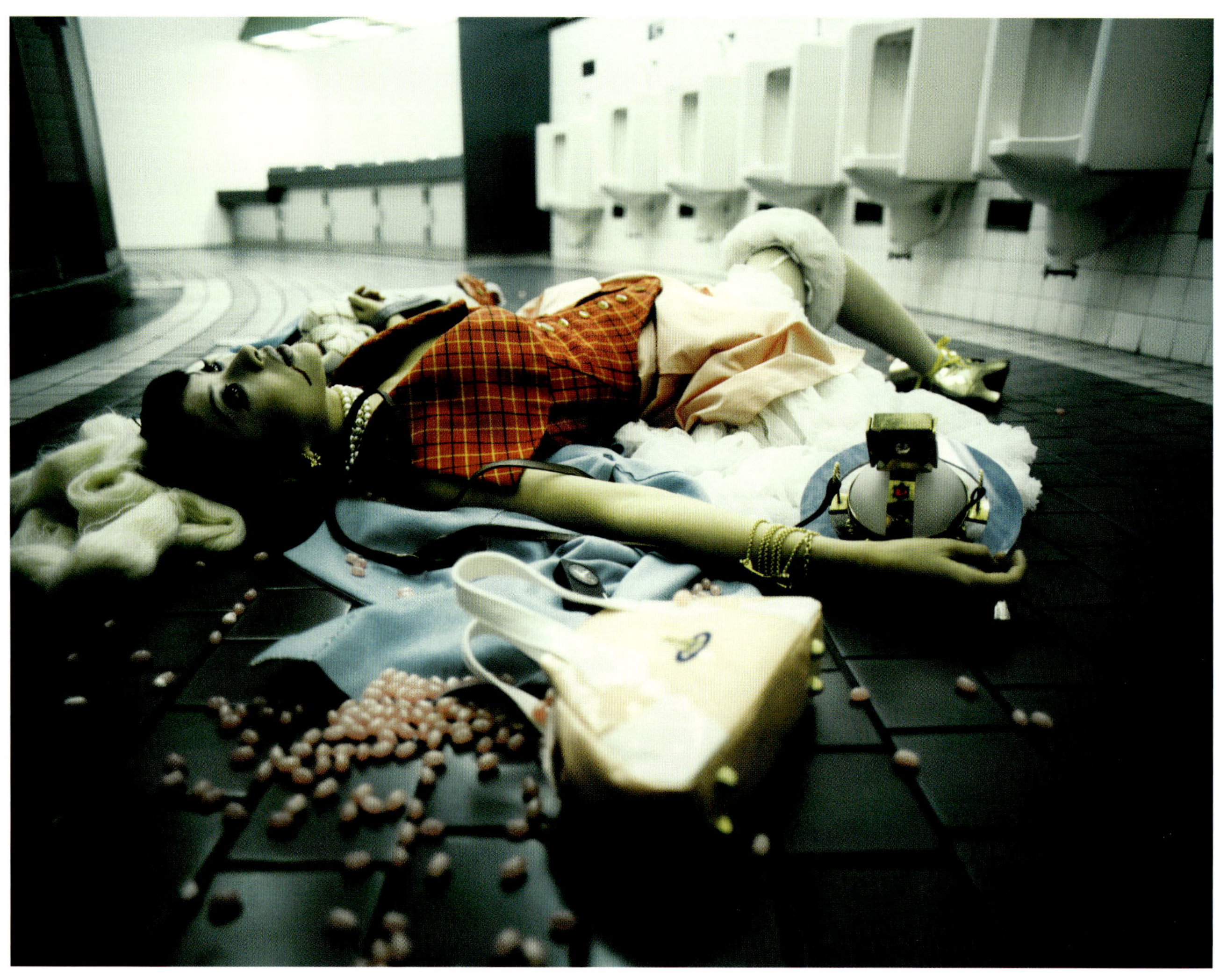

Above: Izima Kaoru, *Shinohara Ryoko wears Vivienne Westwood #91*, 1996, *Landscapes with a Corpse* series.
Opposite: Izima Kaoru, *Shinohara Ryoko wears Vivienne Westwood #94*, 1996, *Landscapes with a Corpse* series.

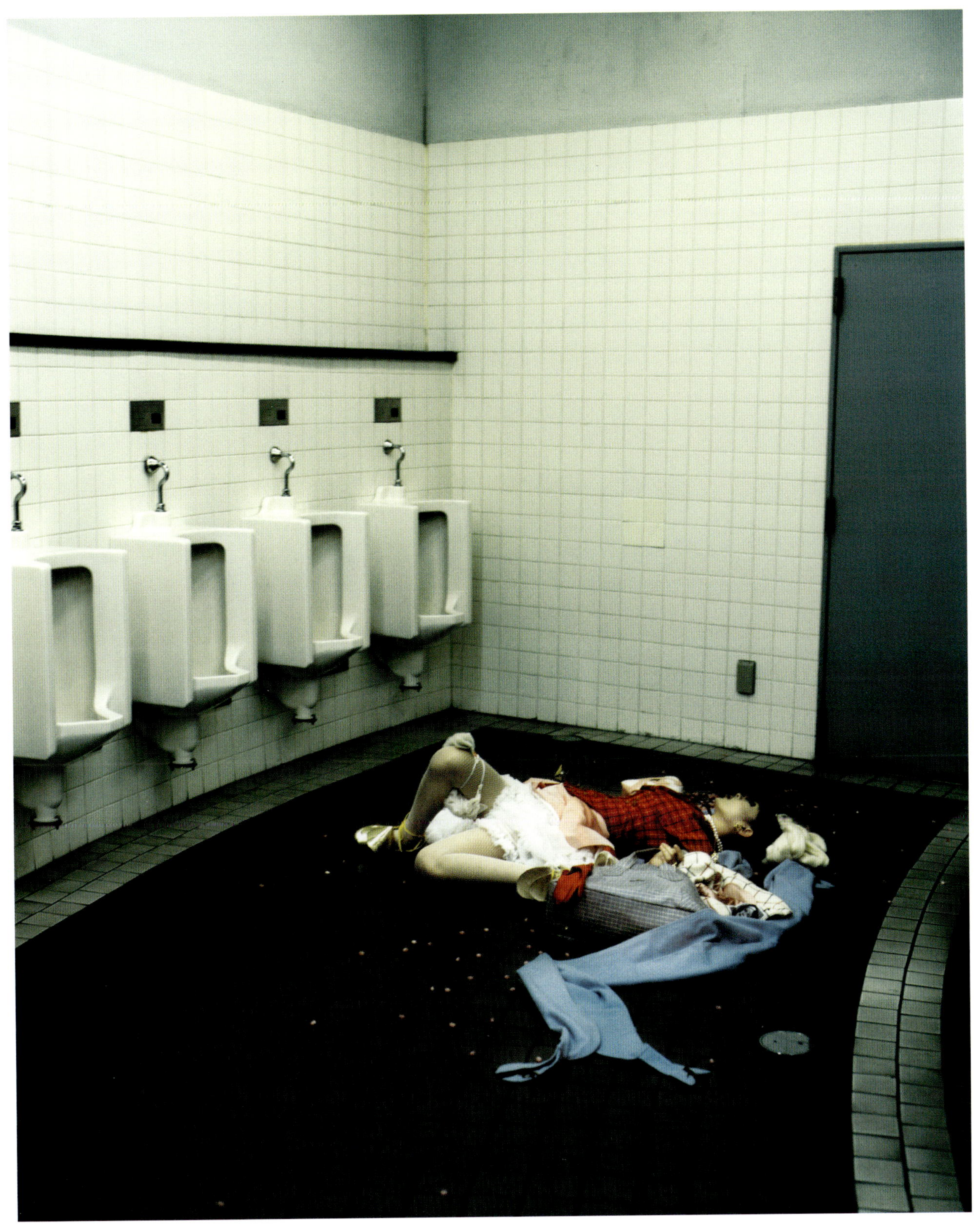

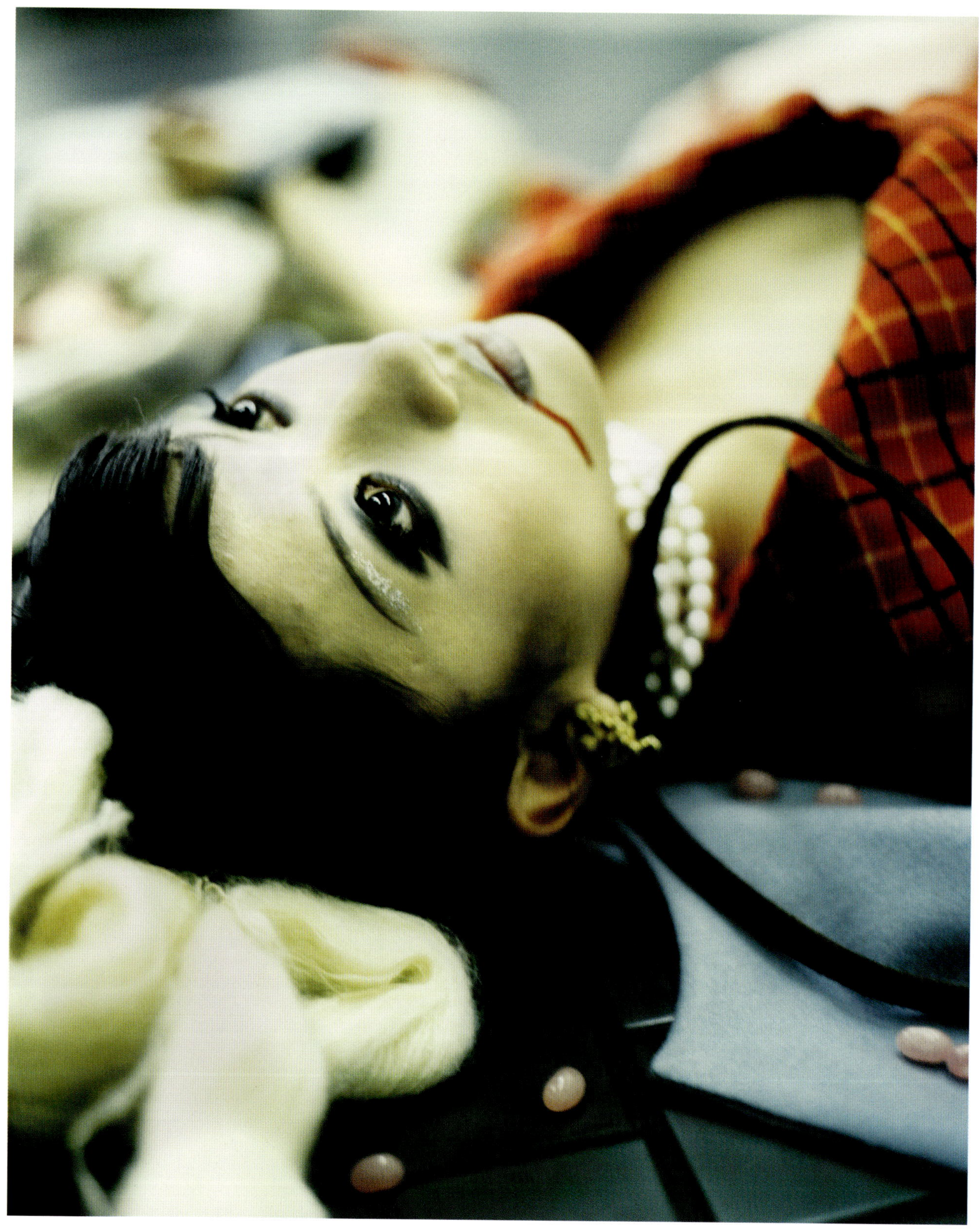

Izima Kaoru, *Shinohara Ryoko wears Vivienne Westwood #95*, 1996, *Landscapes with a Corpse* series.

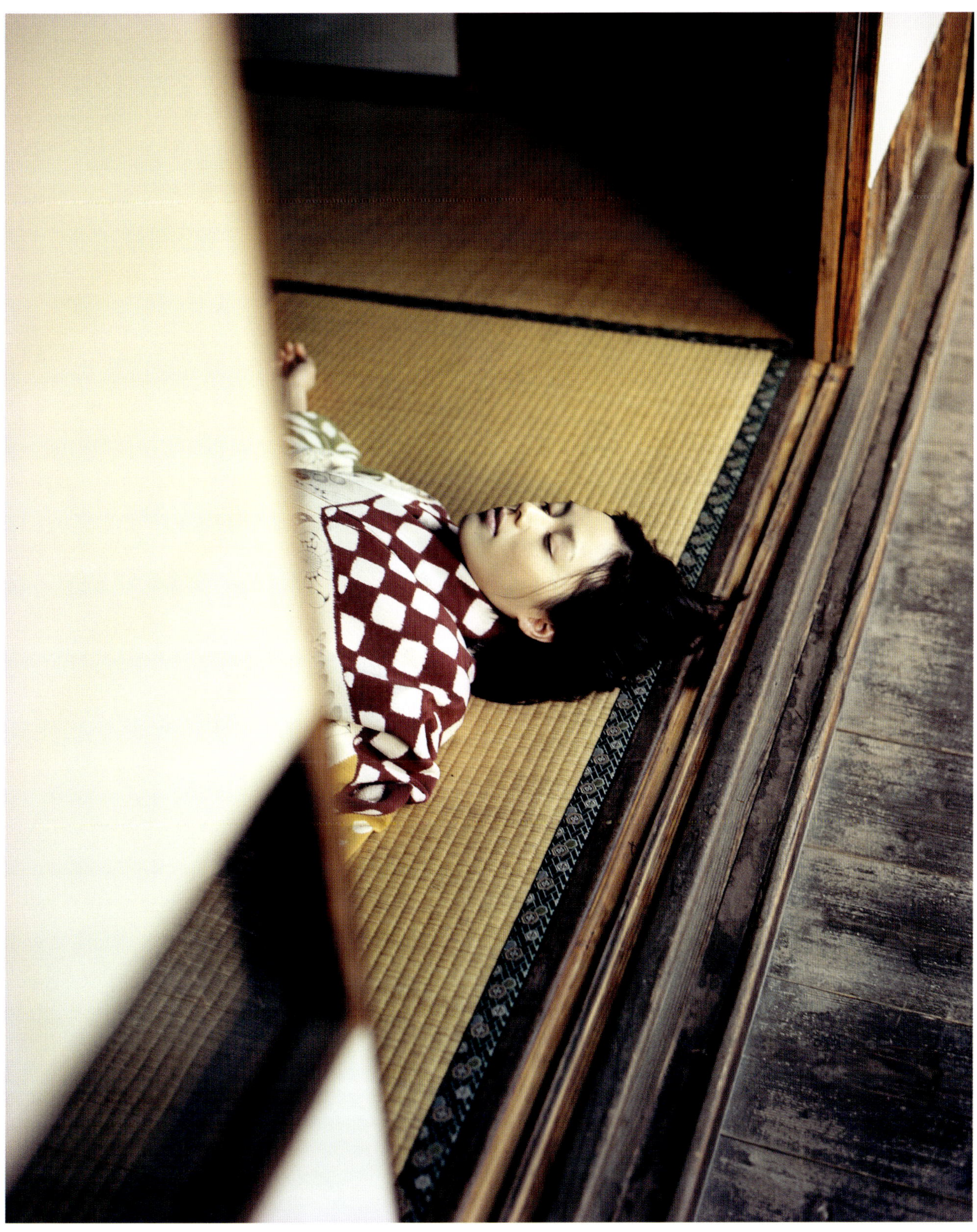

Izima Kaoru, *Otsuka Nene wears Tuzigahana #214,*
1999, *Landscapes with a Corpse* series.

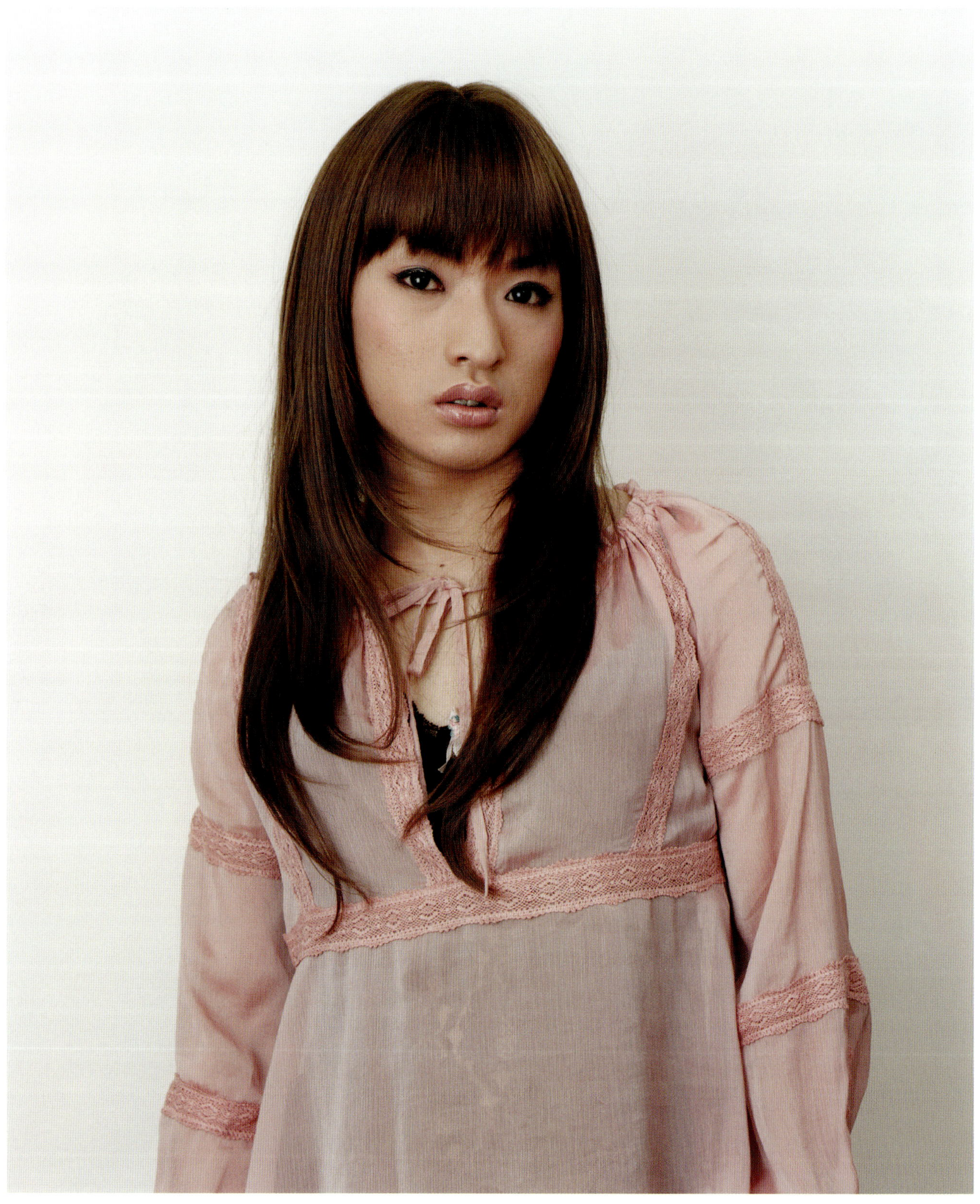

Takano Ryūdai, *Long hair nesting on a pink cloth*, 2002, *In my Room* series.

Lena Fritsch: Let's start at the beginning – what inspired you to take up photography?

Takano Ryūdai: When I was at university, I had an actor friend who asked me to take photographs of him in a theatre performance. This was in the second half of the 1980s and not many people had a camera. My parents randomly had a single-lens reflex camera, so he asked me. I enjoyed taking the photographs. The photographs conveyed a dramatic feeling and my friend said to me 'you're a genius!'. In hindsight, with the stage and all the setup this dramatic atmosphere is not surprising [laughs]. However, being able to pride myself on the photographs was a good start.

You studied at Waseda University – was it politics and economics?

Yes. But I often did not go to lectures, and just did the things I liked best instead. I was interested in paintings but I lacked the technical skills. I wanted to paint everyday life and city scenes, and I was interested in people as well, their movements and such. I took some drawing lessons but it was not that easy. That's when I was asked to photograph my friend and realized that this could be it: 'by just releasing the shutter, I'm able to create an image!' The paintings that I wanted to make were like snapshots, and I was fascinated with the ease and speed of photography. That was the very beginning of photography for me.

At the time, were you interested in or inspired by any photographers?

A friend introduced me to Moriyama Daidō's work, to his photobook *Light and Shadow*, and I liked it. There were also second-hand bookshops around my university, and I found a photography magazine from the late 1960s or 1970s with photographs of the city, people and the student protests. I was fascinated by the fact that the photographs looked like my childhood memories. The photographs recorded the memories of the people who physically experienced that time, and reminded me of the atmosphere of that decade. As a student I had yearned for Western art, but looking at these photographs made me realize for the first time that there is value in taking photographs of subjects in Japan, things that are close by and part of my everyday life. At first I took snapshots, but after a while I realized that they would always come out in a Moriyama-like way. Therefore, I decided I should start expressing myself in a different way, and began to focus on my own sexuality.

I first saw your *tender penis* series in 2001 at the 'kiss in the dark' exhibition at the Tokyo Photographic Art Museum.

Could you tell me about this series? The works are large and have a strong presence...

I always knew that I wanted these photographs to be printed at a large size. As test photographs of the men, I playfully took photographs of the upper and lower parts of their bodies separately. I first took a photo of the lower half of the man's body, with his penis erect. Then, I asked him to keep that pose and took a photograph of the upper half of his body, with the penis down. I realized that the man's penis was mostly cut off and found this interesting.

I see. I only knew that you cut off the penis part and pasted them at the backs of the photographs.

Naturally I had to cut them, because otherwise the lower and upper parts would not have matched. At the beginning I intended to just discard the photos, but it seemed a waste to throw them away so I pasted them at the back.

Could you tell me about your interest in the nude as a photographic object? There are many female nudes but not many male nudes in the history of Japanese photography. The man as a sexual motif used to be a more common theme in the past – in *ukiyoe* woodblock prints and similar – but it hardly exists in photography.

I think I was unhappy about the fact that I could only see female sexual objects in photographs. I did not seek to create particularly erotic images, but there were wonderful boys around me and I wanted to take photographs of them, in my own way. Before this series I took monochrome photographs of a fat, naked, middle-aged man – I wanted to show a type of naked body that has been ignored in images. There are a large number of nude images, but at the same time certain naked bodies are completely absent, and this seemed cruel to me. These kinds of people exist and there should not be any problem with showing their bodies. I wanted to encounter such bodies – but when I exhibited the works from my *Reclining Woo-Man* series at the Ueno Royal Museum, a curator asked me directly: 'why do you take such photographs? I really don't want to see them'. I thought that it might be violent to show things that people don't want to see, but at the same time, it would also be violent to ignore them. Which violence is better? I don't think this question can be answered easily. Anyway, people did not like these works [laughs]. I began to think about motifs that people enjoy a little bit more, and decided to take photographs of wonderful boys.

In Japanese aesthetics the beauty of a young man is a traditional motif – if you think of the *wakashū* (adolescent man) and so on.[1] Or even in manga, young men have a particular beauty. They have been left out of photography, but in other areas of Japanese visual culture there are important motifs of male beauty – maybe even more so than in other countries.

In Japan, images of beautiful men have a long history. I like *ukiyoe* woodblock prints, for example those by Suzuki Harunobu. The Meiji period, the modernization of Japan, was a time of change, and one of the things that was excluded was an awareness of love and sexuality between men – it was basically erased. In Japan, many men have bisexual tendencies and in the Edo period, there was no differentiation between homosexual love and heterosexual love. Both were possible; there was no concept of differentiating between them. Then in the Meiji period, suddenly a line was drawn. This part of Japanese history is usually only told in a very ambiguous way, but it is a fact that there were close friendships between men as well as sexual encounters.

The negative influence of the West and its Christian ideas…Japan used to have more ambiguous and flexible gender concepts.

These ambiguities continued secretly in the 20th century, in literature, music and so on. But by the 1990s when the economic bubble burst they had completely vanished. The LGBT movement in Japan has become quite big now, but this is a very recent development, since maybe two years ago. Suddenly there is a movement to make companies and such aware of sexual minorities, but if you research the history behind it, this is weird [laughs]. Even to call them 'minorities' seems paradoxical – that idea did not exist in Japan.

Looking at, for example, *In my Room*, your work has a very intimate, familiar quality. Could you tell me about the photographic process behind your works?

When working on the *Tender Penis* series, connecting the upper parts of the photographs with the lower parts, I thought it could also be nice to take photographs of the upper or lower parts freely, without connecting them. Therefore, *In my Room* features photographs of men's upper and lower bodies. I set up a 4x5 large-format camera, so I didn't take that many photographs, maybe around ten or twenty of one pose. I usually told the photographic subjects to look to this or that side but otherwise they just stood there, naturally. When they came to my room, we drank tea and chatted for thirty minutes, an hour or even two hours before starting with the

photoshoot. I wanted to create familiarity between the men and I and the space, which might have resulted in a feeling of intimacy.

When you create a photobook, how do you proceed?

It depends on the series, but for example for *In my Room*, I let the publisher decide. I take the photographs, select them and proceed in my own way. I feel that if I also make the book, it can't spread out; it is good to include another viewpoint for the work to develop further. But there are also books that I have done completely myself, such as *How to contact a man*. I made the final selection, decided on the order of the images, cut them and basically designed the book.

In some of your works, I see an element of humour. I find it funny that you cut the penis from the photographs and pasted them on the back of the photographs, showing them in a public exhibition in which the photos would otherwise be censored. Is humour important to you?

I don't intend to create photographic works by colouring the world with my colours and presenting my own sense of beauty. Such works can be a bit pushy, telling the viewers to 'agree with me!' Instead, I make works that say 'this is what I have found, what do you think?' I think humour is vital to keep people interested. However, it is very difficult to include humour in works, and I often fail – it makes me happy that you have felt a sense of humour in my works.

What do you think about censorship? When your works were exhibited in Aichi recently, you had to put fabric in front of the genital areas.

Yes, we hung some white fabric over the parts that showed genitals, after the police came. I think that it would be good if the role of art museums was better recognised in society: they are funded by taxpayers' money and can't just do what they want freely, but there should be room for liberal or even weird works. Art museums are not only spaces that display beauty. I believe that they are also liberated places where people can encounter different worlds, including things that are heterogeneous or discomforting. If more people shared an awareness of this, ugly situations like the one at Aichi Prefectural Museum of Art, where the police walked into the museum, could probably be avoided.

I would not say that your works are weird – they just show naked men.

Yes, but to some people that is weird. There is a law in Japan that you can't show anything that is obscene. It is ambiguous: if the police interpret it as obscene, it

becomes a crime to show it. They can decide freely – that is the scary part about it. I did not expect my photographs to be seen as 'obscene' in Aichi and to cause problems. However, we had to do something and therefore we chose the fabrics.

I like the idea of using fabrics. It reminds me of traditional Christian paintings that were behind fabrics and just shown at special occasions. They are particularly precious works.

If the works are viewed as precious, that is nice [laughs]. Ten years ago when I exhibited the *How to contact a man* photographs at Zeit-Foto Salon, we put white translucent tape on top of the penises. People who wanted to see it had to buy the photograph [laughs]. They could take it off at home. In 2014, at the Aichi Prefectural Museum of Art, when I had to hide them I thought that white fabrics, looking a bit like bed sheets, were a good and slightly erotic way to deal with it.

What do you like best about photography?

This has probably not changed since I started photography: I like that just by releasing the shutter, you can create an image. It is different from painting: you press a button and then mechanically, an image is created instantly. I still find that fascinating. Of course, there is some conscious control, but at the same time, the image comes into existence by itself and I can encounter it later.

I don't take digital photographs and one reason is that I don't like seeing the photographs right away. You take one photograph and then check it on the screen; instead of facing your photographic subjects you look at the screen, consciously creating images. In doing that, I think you lose another aspect that I like about photography: wondering how something has come out in the photograph, and looking forward to finally seeing it.

*   This is a shortened version of an interview conducted in Japanese on 6 September 2016, at Zeit-Foto Salon, Tokyo.

1   Male youthful beauty, personified by the *wakashū* (adolescent man) as an erotic object for both women and men, was a relevant topic in literature as well as visual art in pre-modern Japan, especially between the 16th and 18th centuries.

Lena Fritsch: Let's start at the beginning – what inspired you to take up photography?
Nomura Sakiko: I have been interested in images from an early age, and at university I decided to study in the photography department. At the time, there were very few people who took nude photographs of men. It was a bit of a joke when a superior at university suggested that I take photographs of nude men. There were not many women on the course, maybe fourteen out of around 250 people. I have continued photography ever since.

At the time, were you interested in or inspired by any photographers?
I was not influenced by anybody directly, but it was the time of Cindy Sherman, for example, and I saw a lot of different photographs as a student. Of course, working with Araki has had an influence on me. And I really respect Fukase Masahisa's work.

You began to work for Araki after graduating from university. Could you tell me more about that?
In the Japanese photography world at the time, it was quite common to become a 'disciple' at another photographer's studio. I went to Araki and asked him directly if I could work for him. Of course, he did not have any disciples working for him and he does not today, either. However, he agreed that I could do some work for him. I think it was because I reminded him a bit of his cat [laughs]. This was in 1991, and I still work in his office.

So you take your own photographs while also working in Araki's studio?
Yes, exactly.

You already mentioned the photographs of nude men. In 1994 you had a solo exhibition with nude photographs, and in 1997 you released a photobook titled _Naked Time (Hadaka no jikan)_ [p. 231]. Could you tell me about these?
I photographed a large number of male nudes right from the beginning. When I took photographs in hotels, this meant asking a man to come to the hotel room. When going to his home, it meant entering his private space. So there were different kinds of photographs, but for me it always started from the premise of treating the photographic subject with respect. For the exhibition and books, I just compiled my photographs.

How did the men react when you asked them to model for your nude photographs? Are they mostly friends or acquaintances, or complete strangers?
It was actually pretty easy and normal – just like asking 'shall we go for dinner sometime?' They would mostly agree. Men usually don't care so much about what other people think of them. They were all friends, or friends of friends of friends...

In your 2000 photobook _Time of Love (Ai no jikan)_, you included nude photographs of men but also of women.
I take photographs of everything: male and female nudes, the city, everything that the world provides me with. I decide on themes and titles for an exhibition or photobook later. I think reality gives us so many interesting motifs – that is why I do photography. Not painting or literature, but photography. For the photobook _Time of Love_, I was actually asked by someone to take photographs for a book, and we agreed that I would take photographs of beloved people. These favourite people also include a lesbian couple and a gay couple.

In terms of numbers, your photobooks include quite a high percentage of nude photographs. What do you like about nude photography?
Nudes are fascinating [laughs]. They are all about the relationship between the photographic subject and me. It is not about forms or beauty but, for example, about the moment when he gets out of his clothes. I find that interesting. If I was just looking for beautiful motifs, my photography would probably be very different.

During the photoshoots, how do you work? For example, do you suggest particular poses?
I don't say much – maybe sometimes 'please look to this side', but in general the models move in their own ways and I take photographs of that. Instead of me suggesting poses, I'm more interested in their habits and mannerisms. Of course, I am wearing clothes and he is naked, so it is not an everyday situation, but I'm also interested in the way that the model deals with the unusual circumstances.
I look at their movements and try to take photographs of them just the way they are.

Let's talk about your series _Black Darkness_ [pp. 232–33]. In general you have taken many dark photographs, and seem to be interested in the aesthetics of grainy darkness, even in your colour photographs. Could you tell me about your interest in this dark aesthetic?
I think that light is extremely important, and therefore I pursue darkness. If you don't search for the things that you cannot see, they don't become visible. Just by doing this, my photographs have become

increasingly dark [laughs]. There are things that exist and are visible in the shadows, and these things interest me. Shadows are of course intertwined with light.

Your interest in shadows and the dark can be linked to a traditional Japanese aesthetic. Maybe it is just my foreign viewpoint, but it reminds me of Tanizaki Junichirō, who emphasized the beauty of a dark room or dark miso bowl.
Yes, there might be a connection. Looking for things that are visible in darkness is part of this idea of darkness. My photographs have gradually become darker and darker [laughs].

And now you just released *Another Black Darkness* (2016) [p. 257], a photobook that at first sight looks like it is completely black! Could you tell me more about the technique and your interest in solarization?
I printed all the photographs myself, and for the book I was interested in the idea of light in the darkroom. I wanted to recreate the photographs that I had taken, and look at them again. Through a simple form of solarization, I re-exposed the images to light and 're-encountered' them. Well, and they became even darker [laughs].

That also shows how important your work in the darkroom is for your practice.
Yes, it is. My work in the darkroom is similar to the way that I take photographs: instead of trying to achieve something in a particular style, I choose reality and what reality gives me. Normally, solarization can result in clearer, more beautiful images, but to me that was not the point.

Now that you have pushed the idea of darkness to the limit with *Another Black Darkness*, perhaps the next series will be light and white [laughs]?
Well, darker than this is surely not possible [laughs]. It is nice to see viewers' reactions when exhibiting these works. They look at the photographs closely because otherwise they can't see anything. Normally, if you see a photograph of the Tokyo Tower or the Kinkakuji temple [p. 257] you recognize it and just look at it for a few seconds. But with these photographs, people need time for themselves in order to realize what the image is. As such, they are much more concerned with the images. I find that interesting.

Why did you choose photography and what do you like best about photography?
To me, photography is about what is on the 'other side'. My photography comes into existence because there is something out there and I encounter it. That is more interesting than going out and searching for a particular form or motif. I don't create my works out of emotion, or because I want to express myself. Painting or literature would not have worked – it had to be photography.

* This is a shortened version of an interview conducted in Japanese on 31 August 2016, at Akio Nagasawa Gallery, Tokyo.

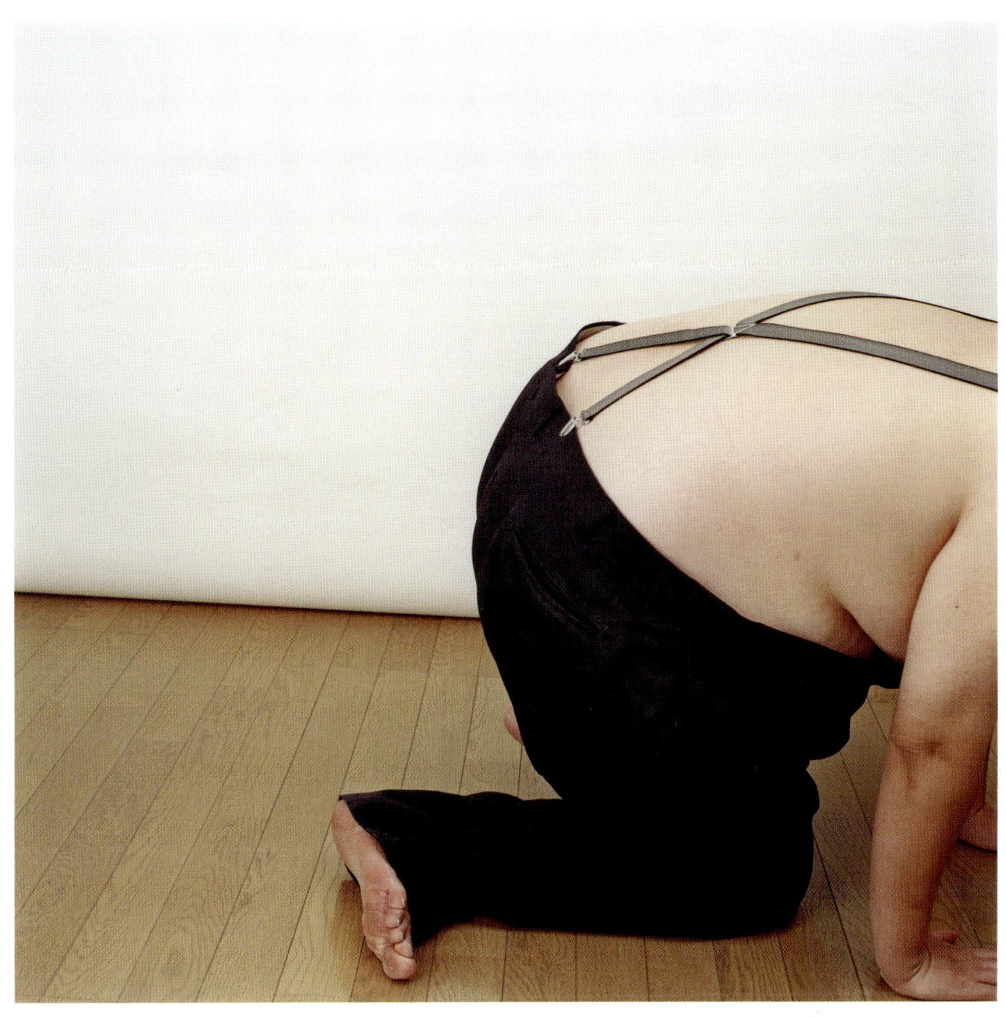

Takano Ryūdai, 2012, *Stand up Kikuo!* series.

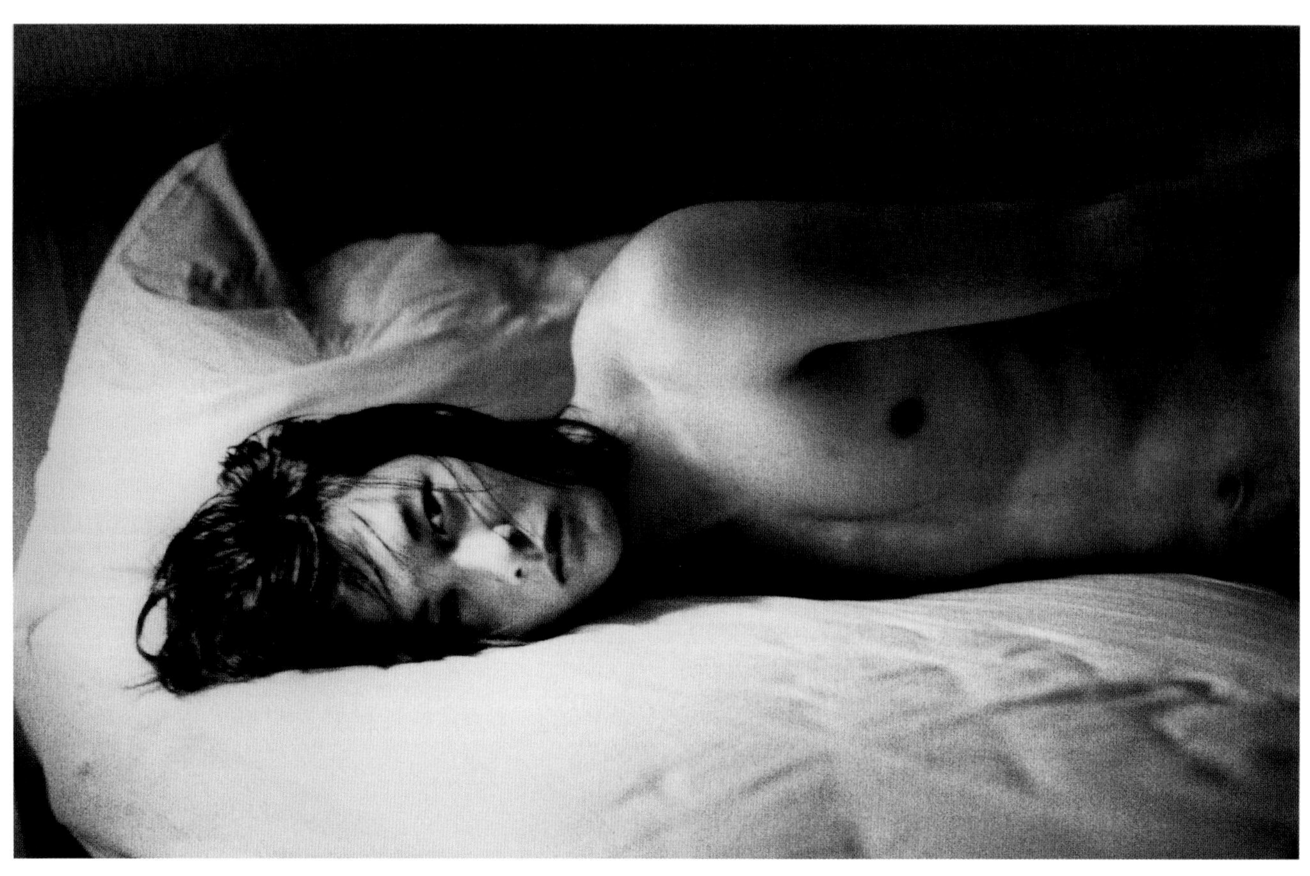

Above: Nomura Sakiko, 2005, *Tsukuyomi* series.
Opposite: Nomura Sakiko, 1997, *Naked
Time (Hadaka no jikan)* series.

230

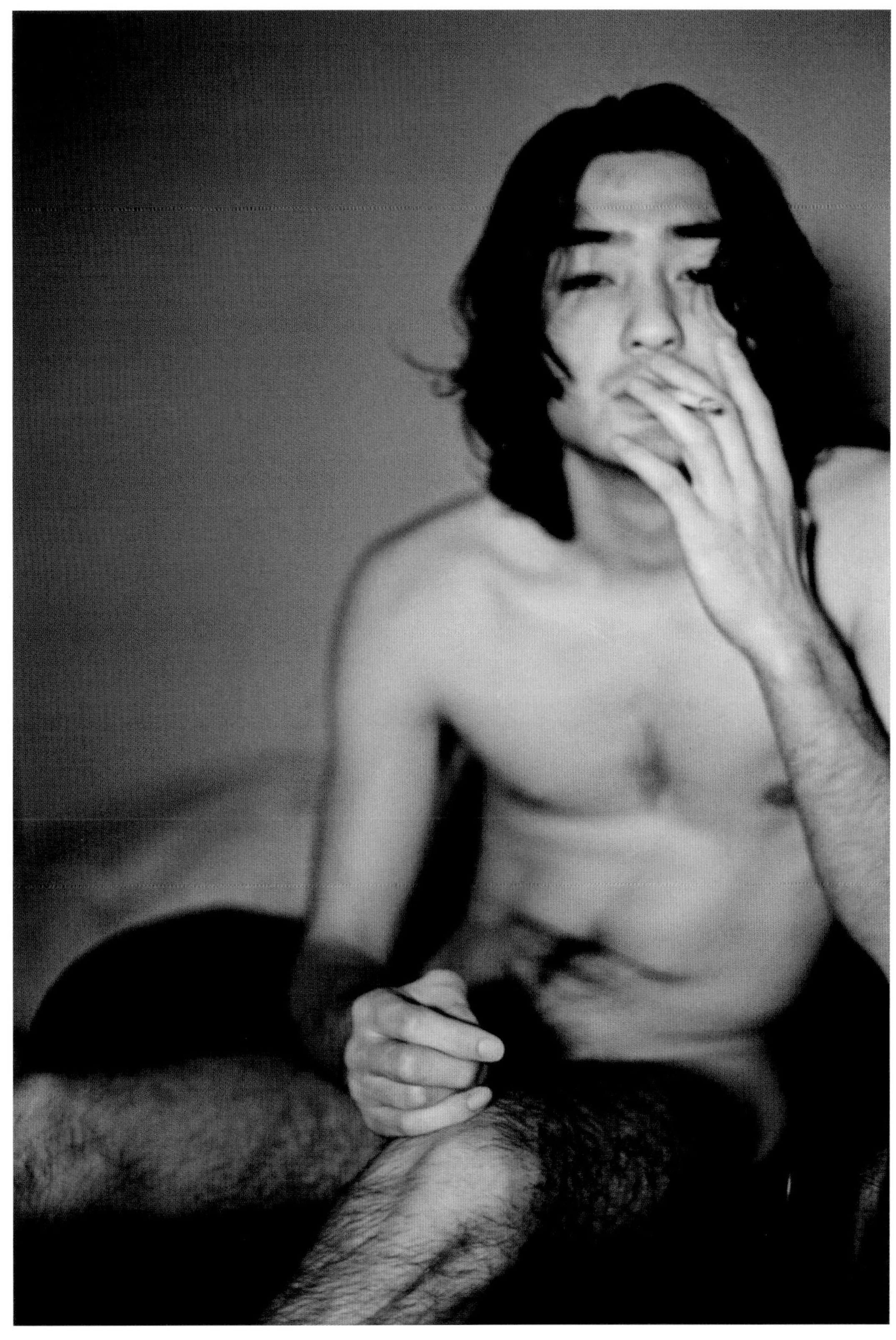

Nomura Sakiko, 2008, *Black Darkness* series.

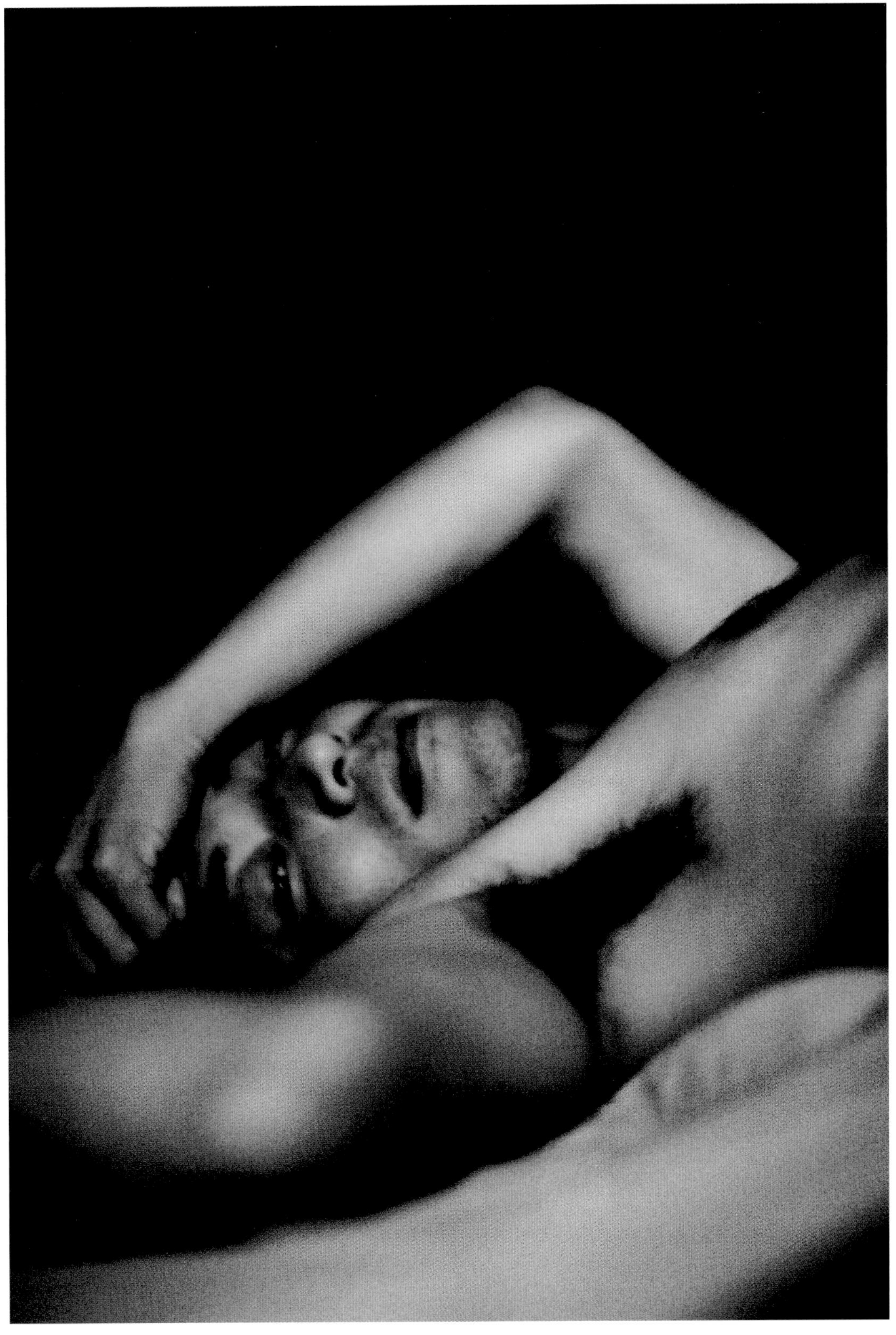

Nomura Sakiko, 2008, *Black Darkness* series.

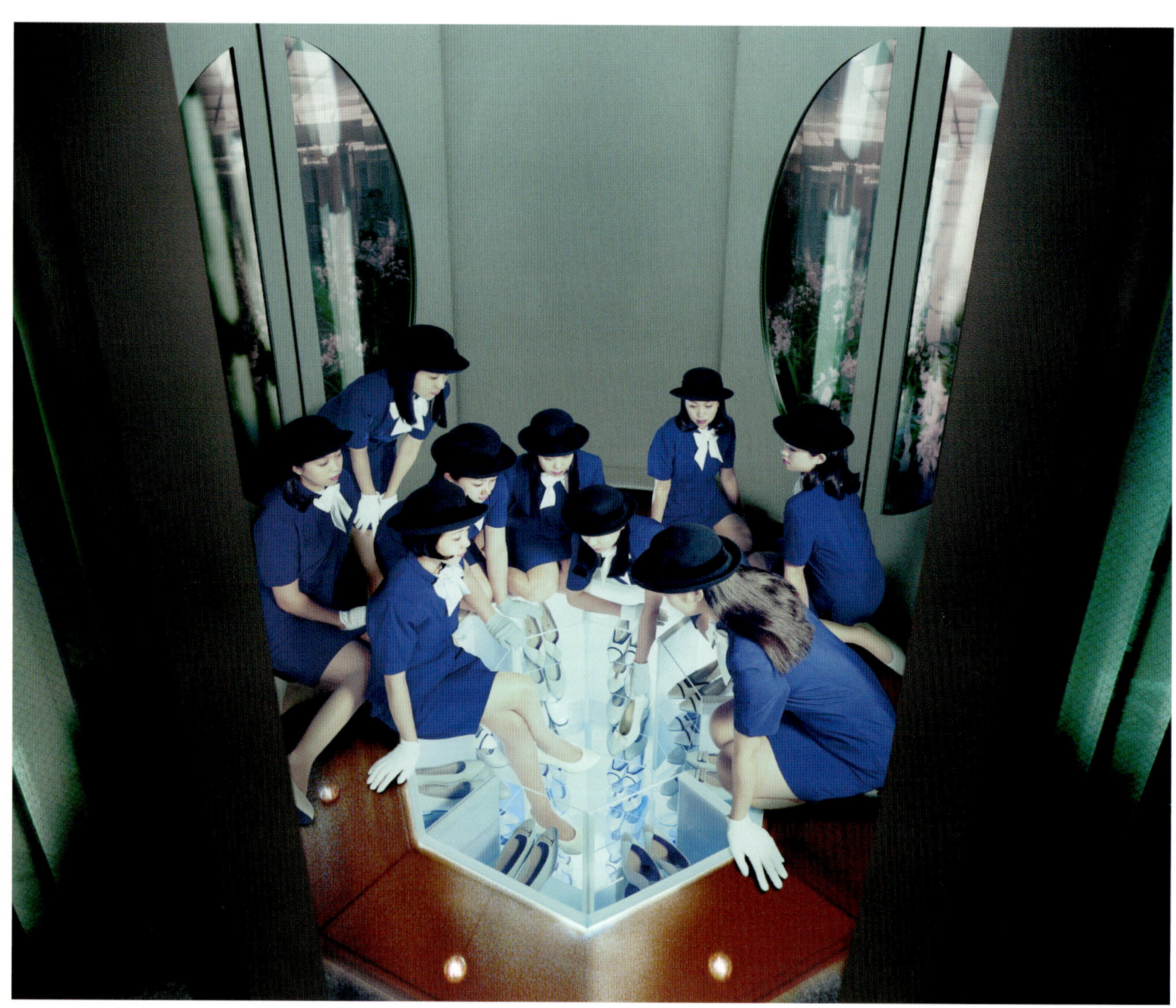

Yanagi Miwa, *Elevator Girl House 3F,* 1998.

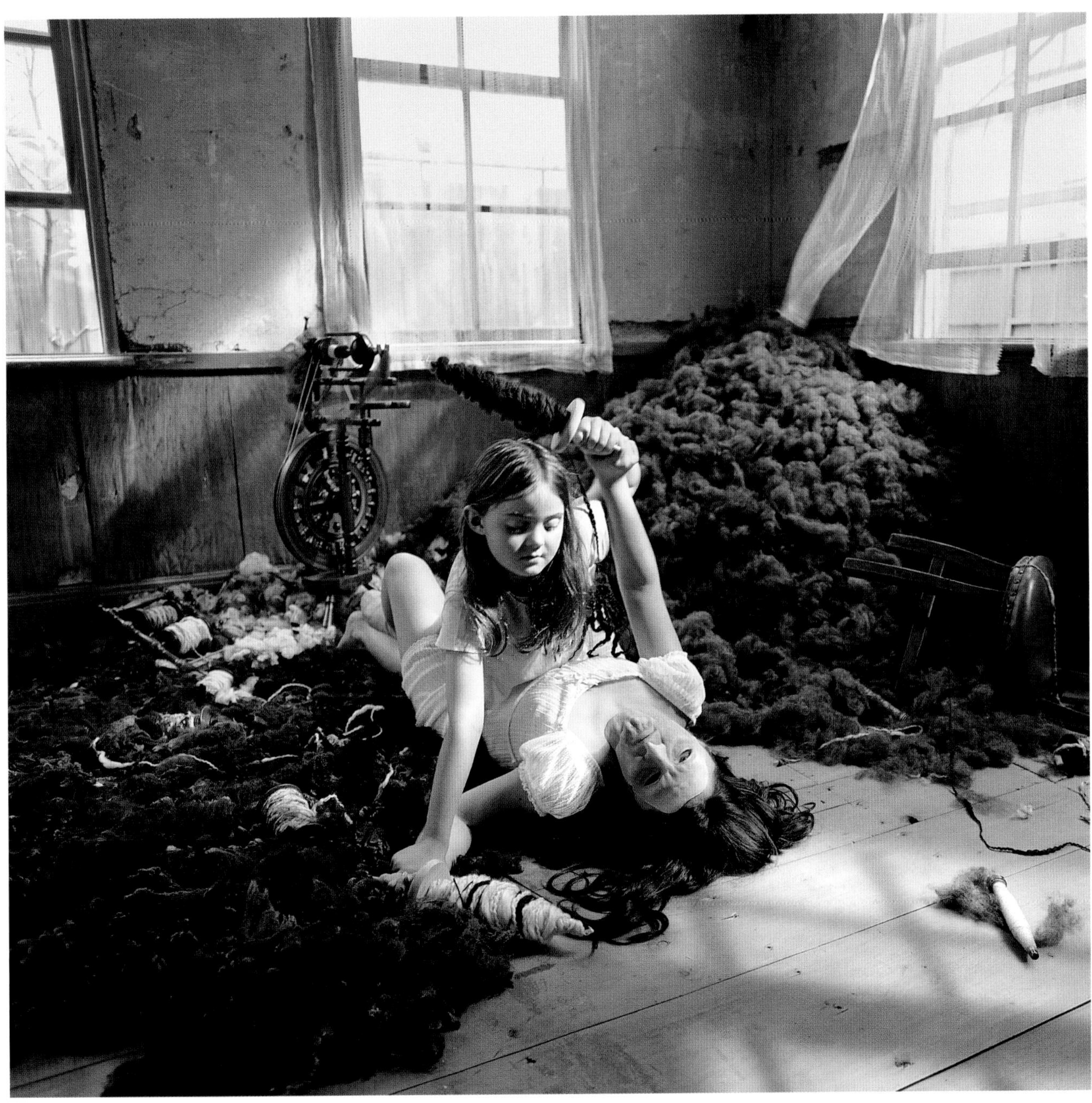

Yanagi Miwa, *Fairy Tale/Sleeping Beauty*, 2004.

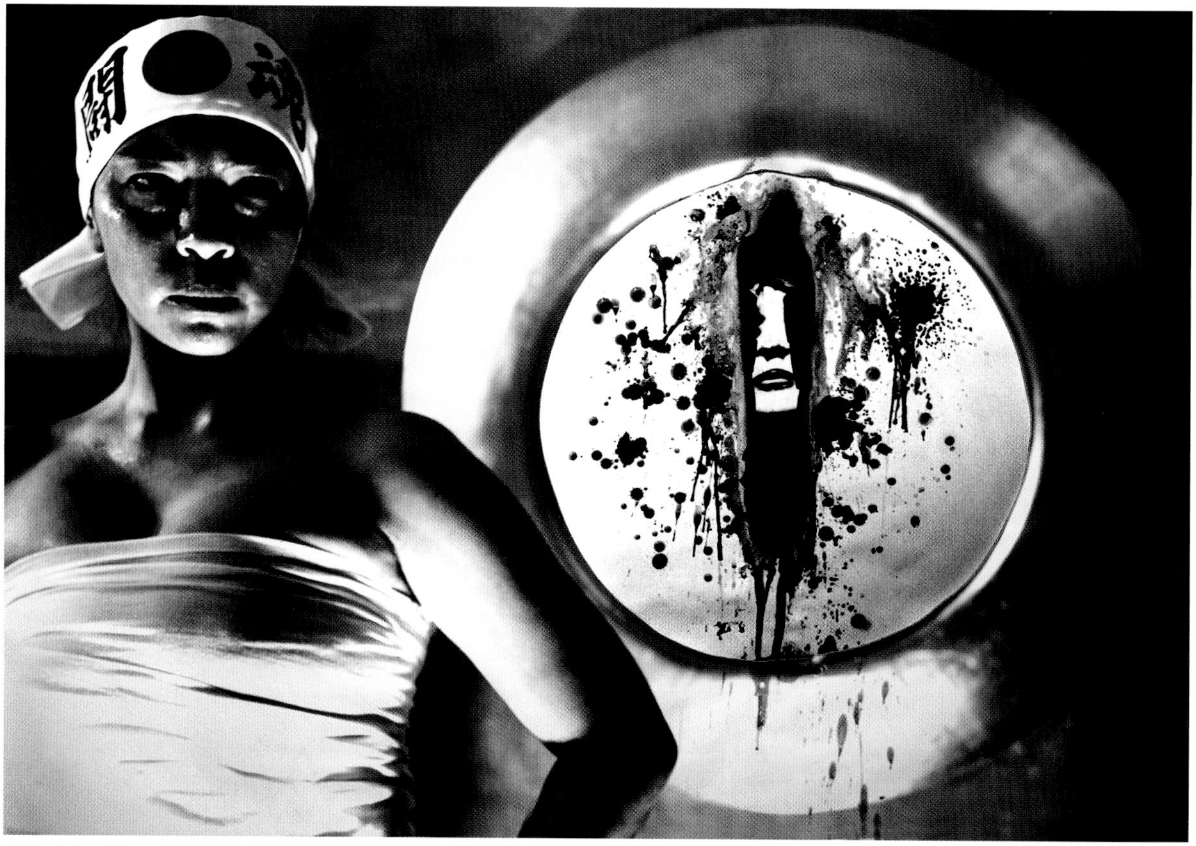

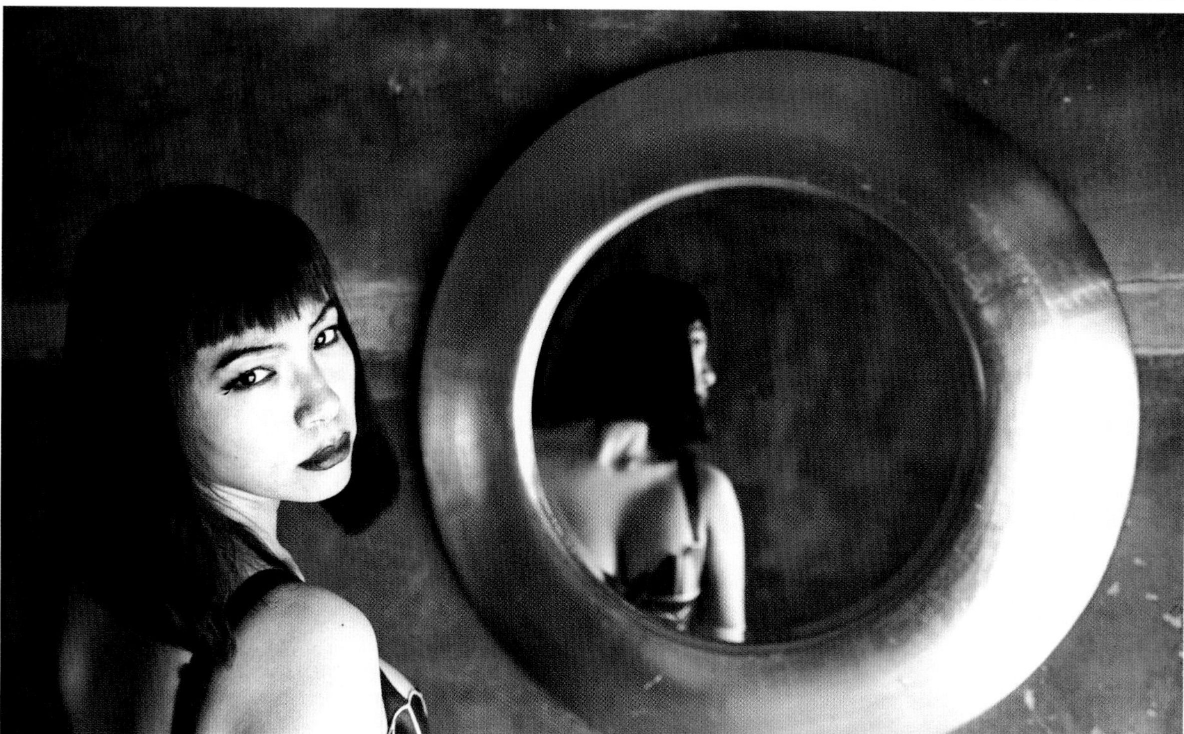

Top: Tokyo Rumando, *Orphée no. Y4*, 2012–14.
Above: Tokyo Rumando, *Orphée no. A1*, 2012–14.

Lena Fritsch: Let's start at the beginning – what inspired you to take up photography?
Tokyo Rumando: At first I was on the other side of the camera. I worked as a model; my jobs included nudes, and fetish images such as bondage. I also worked in a strip bar a few times. I started this kind of work when I was twenty years old and continued until around twenty-five. One day, I was photographed by Araki. I became interested in photography, and wanted to be the person who is releasing the shutter and creating a world, rather than the person whose photograph is taken by someone else.

Were you interested in photography when you were even younger, too?
Yes, I was. I was in senior high school when photography by people like Hiromix was at the peak of popularity. We all had these small disposable cameras and took photos of ourselves together, in the girls' bathroom or wherever [laughs]. I took photographs with my friends all the time.

When did you start to take self-portrait photographs?
I must have been around nineteen years old: I positioned myself in front of a wall that I had decorated with some cute fabrics, and did something like a fashion show. I was in a small dirty apartment and wanted to make it look more elegant [laughs]. I found these negatives just recently.

When you started photography, were you interested in or inspired by any photographers in particular?
Yes, I was interested in photographers from overseas: Cindy Sherman of course, and Irena Ionesco. In terms of photographic atmosphere, I liked Diane Arbus's work. I also liked fashion photography, for example by Helmut Newton. In Japan, there were people like Hiromix, who created her own world, and whose photography seemed like fun. I remember watching a feature about her on TV at the time. Of course, I also like Araki and Moriyama's photography, but I don't think they influenced my work very much.

In 2012, you published your first photobook *Rest 3000 Stay 5000*, featuring photographs in love hotels [p. 241]. Could you tell me about this series? I guess the numbers refer to the prices of the hotel: ¥3,000 if you just 'rest' for a few hours and ¥5,000 if you stay overnight.
Exactly. It is written on signs next to love hotels, advertising the price [laughs].

That's pretty cheap, isn't it? You don't get a love hotel room for such a low price these days.

Yes, it would have to be a very old hotel [laughs]. Living in a city in Japan and at a certain age, women typically go to love hotels with their boyfriends or whoever. When I went in the early 2000s, many rooms were decorated in a particular 'Western' style, often with the walls painted in red, or with red carpets; or they were 'traditionally Japanese' with motifs from *ukiyoe* woodblock prints on the wall. The interior design and atmosphere was fun. There were also round beds that could move around, and games in the room; love hotels had a somewhat amusement park-like character.

When I decided to start taking photographs, I began to think about a 'stage' for myself. I considered cafés, my apartment, rental studios. But I wanted to connect my photography with my nude modelling work, and so I decided to choose a similar context: love hotels. The women that I impersonated in the series are the different types of women who would go to a love hotel: women who only go there with their boyfriend, women who go with someone who is not their boyfriend, women who have an affair, women who sell their bodies. I was interested in impersonating these different women.

You went to a number of different love hotels too.
Yes, I went to around thirty love hotels in Tokyo: in Shibuya, Shinjuku, Uguisudani…

In 2001, I bought a photobook, *Satellite of Love*. It features different love hotel interiors, and I remember that the author wrote that he wanted to record the hotel rooms because the hotels were gradually being closed down.
Yes, that book is by Tsuzuki Kyōichi, with many colour photos. When I took my photographs I hurried too, because I noticed that sometimes just three months after I took my photographs, the hotel had already disappeared. As Tsuzuki wrote in the book, the love hotel is an element of Japanese culture that is gradually dying. The hotels either close completely or they are renovated and reopened in a new, simple style. The law has changed and there are more rules now: for example, carpets on the wall are not possible any more because it is not hygienic and they are flammable. When I took my photographs, I had the feeling that I was recording a part of Japanese culture that is disappearing.

Your series *Orphée* [p. 236] again features self-portraits. Could you tell me more about these works?
Rest and Stay, Orphée and the series that I am currently working on are connected, as a kind of trilogy. *Rest and Stay* was about the outside: the nude female body,

poses, love hotels. Perhaps it is erotic –
a series that is easy to understand right
away. *Orphée* was about the inside: when
I was around thirty years old, I wanted
to look back at my past. I decided to use
a mirror and the motif of reflection – I'm
looking back at different forms of my old
self. When making these collages, cutting,
pasting and layering, I was not sure what I
was actually doing, so I felt really honoured
when the works were displayed in the
'Performing for the Camera' exhibition
at the Tate Modern this year. It gave me
a lot of self-confidence.

**Where did you take the photographs,
is that your own apartment?**
Yes, I used the round mirror in my room.
I bought the mirror cheaply in an online
auction around ten years ago.

How did you decide on the title *Orphée*?
Once the series was finished, I needed
a title. I saw Jean Cocteau's film *Orphée*
and thought that it fit perfectly [laughs].
The motif of the mirror and the idea of
looking at someone that you should not
look at fascinated me: Orpheus' wife
returned from the dead, but he was not
allowed to look at her – of course he
couldn't help himself. In life there are
things or people that you just can't help
looking at, that you should face. For
example, your own past – be it good or
bad. I needed to face my past. How do
you look back at your past?

**I tend to reflect on my past on my
birthdays, usually trying to travel
and get some distance from my
normal everyday life.**
Reflecting from a distance is interesting.
I do think it is very important to look back.

**Tell me about the new series that you
are currently working on – the third
part of your trilogy.**
The photographs are self-portraits as well.
But after showing my external body with
Rest and Stay and my inside with *Orphée*,
I'm now doing performances in which I
try to go back to zero and focus less on
myself...People are probably already tired
of seeing my face [laughs].

**I'm looking forward to seeing your
new works. How do you feel as a
female photographer in the Japanese
'photography world', which is
traditionally a male-dominated scene?
Is it difficult sometimes?**
Yes, it is a fight. There are photographers
like Ishiuchi Miyako, who has been around
for a long time, and later Hiromix and
Nagashima Yurie, but I think they all had
to fight as well. In Japan, photographs
have been viewed as something that men
take; photographers are called *kameraman*
[from the English 'cameraman']. Things
have changed a bit, thanks to the 'girly
photography' trend in the 1990s sending
the message that 'everybody is allowed to
take photographs'.

**Why did you choose photography and
what do you like best about the medium
of photography?**
I can't paint or draw and photography
allows me to visually express what is going
on in my mind. I also like that I'm the judge
of my photography: I can press the shutter
myself and select the photographs myself.

*   This is a shortened version of an
interview conducted in Japanese on
30 August 2016, at Coffee L'ambre, Tokyo.

Lena Fritsch: Let's start at the beginning – what inspired you to take up photography?

Shiga Lieko: It began in high school, with an autofocus compact camera that I used to take photographs at a sports day. After the sports day, there were some exposures left over, and I thought I had to finish the complete film to take it to the photo shop. I took photographs of my desk: first a photo of how it was, then slightly changing the position of a cup on the desk, and then another photo, again changing the arrangement. I continued taking photographs until the film was full, not really thinking about it.

Afterwards, when collecting the prints at the photo shop (Palette Plaza) and looking at the photos of the desk, I was surprised – they depicted the desk in a natural way, despite the fact that in some of the photographs I had intentionally changed the position of the things on the desk. In other words, they showed scenes in which I had controlled reality. What's more, as if to emphasize their 'naturalness', I was standing at the service desk in the photo shop, holding these photographic prints in my hands, as 'proof that this really existed'. It was printed on paper. It felt good that the images had become physical objects that I could hold in my hands. The printed photograph – its adhesive surface was sticky, like something still fresh. It was like a sample image inside a frame. The photographic paper even felt sexual; no matter how I looked at it, it was not like normal paper. These experiences were the beginning: without even thinking about it, I became completely absorbed in taking photographs.

I didn't go out, carrying my camera around to find something to photograph. Instead, simply put, my method was setting up a scene. I went manic in my room, thinking about the fact that I had created a situation using the objects in front of my eyes. It felt like the world was upside down and I was carrying a shocking secret – and I was intoxicated by this.

Why was that? I was born in 1980, in a residential area of Okazaki in Aichi Prefecture. For as long as I can remember, I lived a comfortable life in which the lights would go on in the evening when I flicked the light switch, and my excrements would be flushed away somewhere, to an unknown place. I suddenly felt that with the birth of my primitive body, like 'plop', a sense of discomfort had begun. The fact that I had no life problems became a problem. Intuitive thoughts that I had had as a small child, such as 'it is all a lie', 'dad and mum are both made of papier mâché' or 'this wall is just a wall and perhaps there is nothing behind' began to swell up. It was the feeling that perhaps nothing really existed. Within that, the only things that I could believe in were the feelings of my physical body, like 'agonizing', 'hot', 'painful' when my body was stressed. The feeling of pain when saying 'ha, ha', or 'ouch' when grabbing something were senses that I could trust. They somehow made me feel more at ease, and more psychologically relaxed. I got used to treating my body in a violent way to stay relaxed. I think I was negotiating with the society that I lived in by treating my body this way. But during puberty my body began to change into an adult's, gaining weight and beginning to change shape. Negotiating with it did not work anymore; I became excessively self-conscious, and my body distanced itself from me. The mirror that reflected my body became more important than my actual body. Creating images by using photography felt like a moment in which I could sneak away from this agonizing, painful body and emerge into another reality that my mind had imagined. To me, the photographic images felt like the truth and real life like a lie.

I think it is important that whatever photographic subjects and scenes one creates, in the end one just presses the shutter and 'stays away' from the image, which returns as a proof of reality. In other words, the distance between one's body and the image created is actually extremely large. I liked that distance. Untouched by the photographic subjects, I was able to remain indifferent. I succeeded in sneaking away from my painful, immediate body through the images that were engraved on the photographic paper. By using an autofocus mechanism, I rediscovered my own 'automatic' body. I think that the camera and my body became a unit. It had to be an easy process. It couldn't be a manual camera. It couldn't be 'pictures' painted directly by hand, either – the images would have been too close to me and I can't stand that, it makes me feel sick.

Sometimes I had a guilty conscience, as if I had done something wrong. In the process of growing up, I avoided society and reality and instead gave myself over to a world that I could control. Thinking about it now, these were extremely dangerous ideas, but they were the starting points.

When you started to take photographs, were there any photographers in particular that inspired or interested you?

I was more influenced by dance and theatre. From a young age, I have really liked the work of Pina Bausch.

In 1998 you presented your first photographic series, *Piano* [pp. 242–45]. What was the trigger for this work?

I have a younger brother, and when I started photography I took photographs as though I was playing with him. He was also my very first photographic subject. He knew how to move his body; he was naked and made various gestures that I photographed. He learned the piano, and this series shows him imitating playing the piano.

I put holes into the photographs with needles and held them against the sun so the light shone through the holes beautifully. I re-photographed that.

Could you tell me about *Lilly* [p. 246] – about the idea for this series, and the photographic process?
Lilly is a photographic series that is an extension of my feelings from shooting *Piano*. It was a determined working process of encountering the ferocious feelings within myself. While I was taking portrait photographs of other people, I was doing nothing but encountering my own personal memories. It is a work that could only come into existence through photography.

In the apartment where I lived [in London], I hung a blackout curtain on the walls, fixed a tripod and then asked the people who lived in the same block to come in one after the other to have their photographs taken. In hindsight, I think what I did was cruel: I did not go more than ten metres outside my world; I took photographs of the people around me and then put my hands on these photographs, cutting them, opening holes in them, shining light on them. I changed the photographic subjects into completely different, fictitious characters. I met many people during the photoshoots, but the project was quite one-sided.

Could you tell me about your series *Canary* [pp. 247–49]? I saw the photographs in 2008, in the 'on your body' exhibition at the Tokyo Photographic Art Museum. In the exhibition catalogue you wrote 'I created a device to produce chance events, waiting to be shot by the camera at a moment that is impossible to predict, in order to lose any control over the images'. Could you tell me about this inclusion of coincidence in the photographic process? What does the title *Canary* refer to?
The image in a photograph is always far away, because one can't touch the photographic subject. The camera is a mechanism that reproduces something: no matter how close it gets, it never touches the things that it depicts. However, I felt that to reflect images (photographic subjects) without touching them was also a way of stealing images. It was a way of calming my feelings, by bringing out the violence from within me. In hindsight,

I think it was also a form of healing. I began to reflect on what I had done. I thought I should get out of the vicious circle of images in myself, and create a structure to connect with the outside.

During the journey I took to shoot *Canary*, I met many people and landscapes. I looked at all the things that happened in front of my eyes and, according to them, I decided which attitudes to take and what kinds of relationships to build. I took the photographs as though they were an experiment. Instead of deciding on the content of the photoshoots right from the beginning, I continuously experimented by interacting with the photographic subjects, just like training one's physical body (like in sports). In doing this, the situations always developed in an unpredictable, sometimes last-minute way. Consequently, there were times when I was full of impulsive feelings and actions, or showing an unsightly side of myself, and I got to know my real feelings, deep down in my stomach.

It was important to me to continue the photoshoots until another big reality appeared, progressing into images. I think that because the photographic subjects and I deliberately included elements of coincidence, a new reality came into existence, and created images that couldn't be controlled.

As such, the relationship between the photographic subjects and I was not just one of 'taking and being taken', but was based on an awareness of one another. In the composed photographs, there was room to move around the past, present and future, and to express myself to the outside world. It became like a 'confession' to the society that I live in.

The starting points of the individual photographic images for *Canary* were something thoroughly impulsive. I only became aware of this when starting the photoshoots.

A canary is a bird that miners used to take into the mineshafts because they could sense poison gas. They breathe six times faster than humans; if the canary died, it meant that there was poisonous gas. I think that holding a camera towards reality is similar to this.

When you create a photobook, how do you proceed?
Photographs can show a world that you can't predict and can't see with the naked eye. When I see a photograph that does that, I select it from the large number of photographs that I have taken. The remaining decisions are based on what is necessary.

What do you like best about the medium of photography?
I think I like that photography is a medium that keeps changing.

*   This is a shortened version of an interview conducted by email, in Japanese, in June 2017.

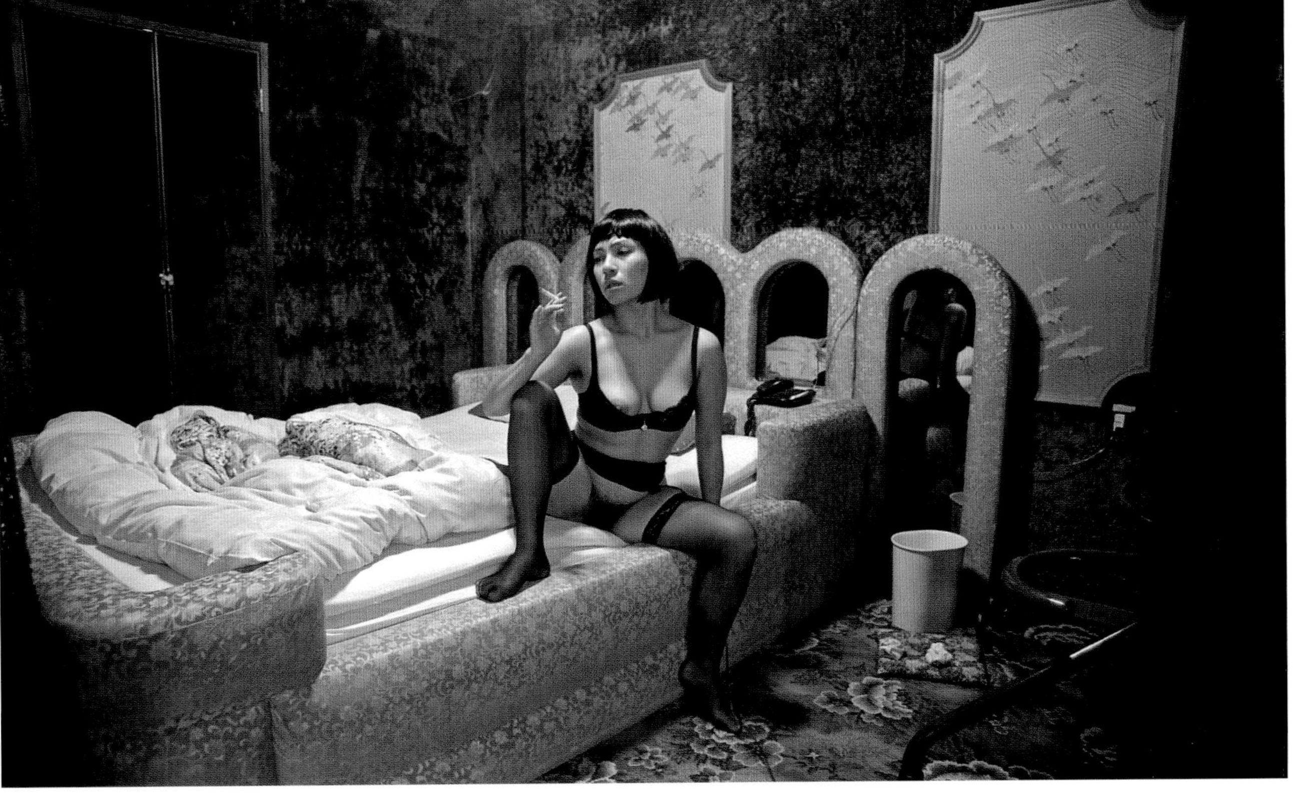

Tokyo Rumando, untitled, 2012, *Rest 3000 Stay 5000* series.

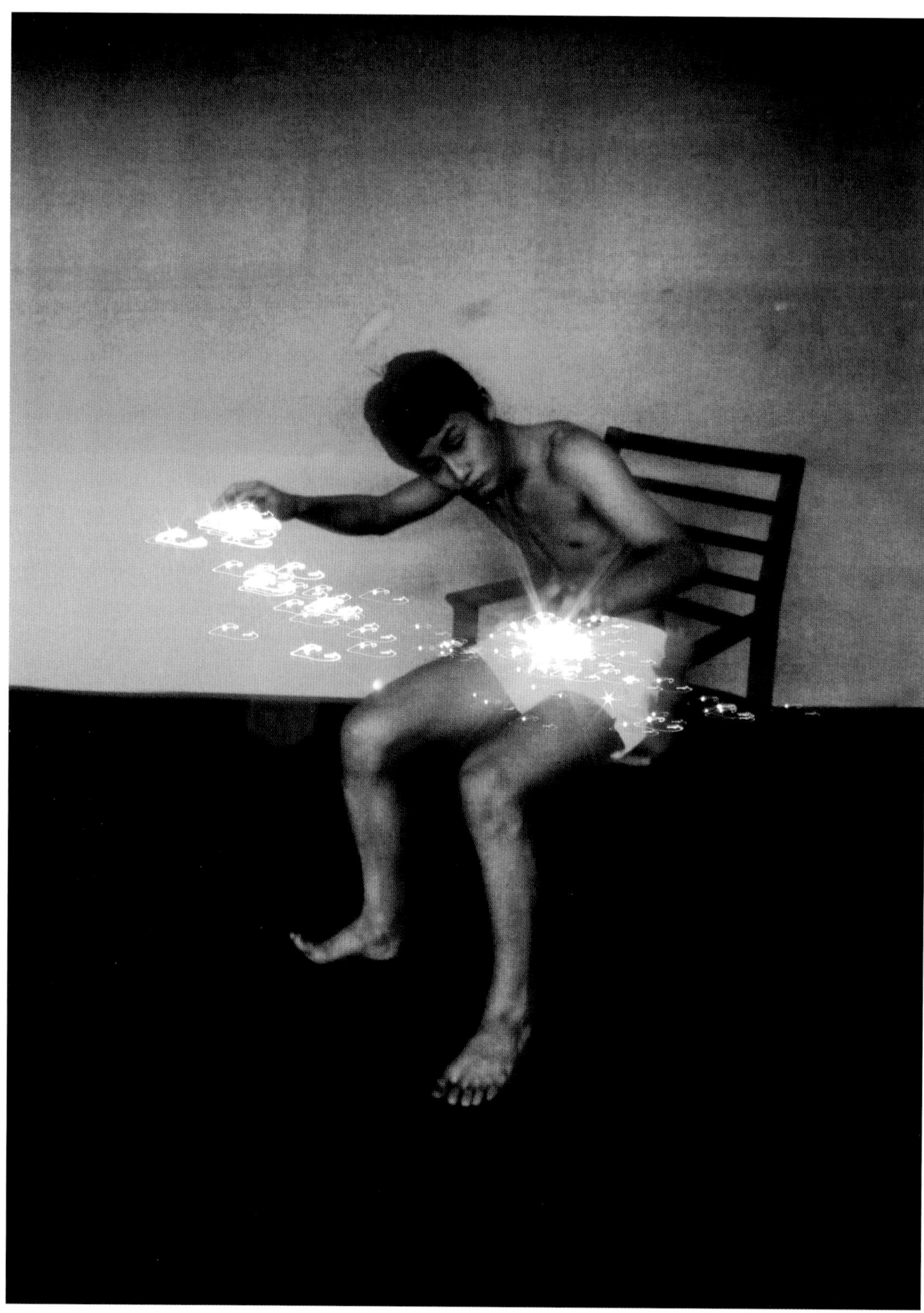

Above and opposite: Shiga Lieko, *Piano* series, 1998.

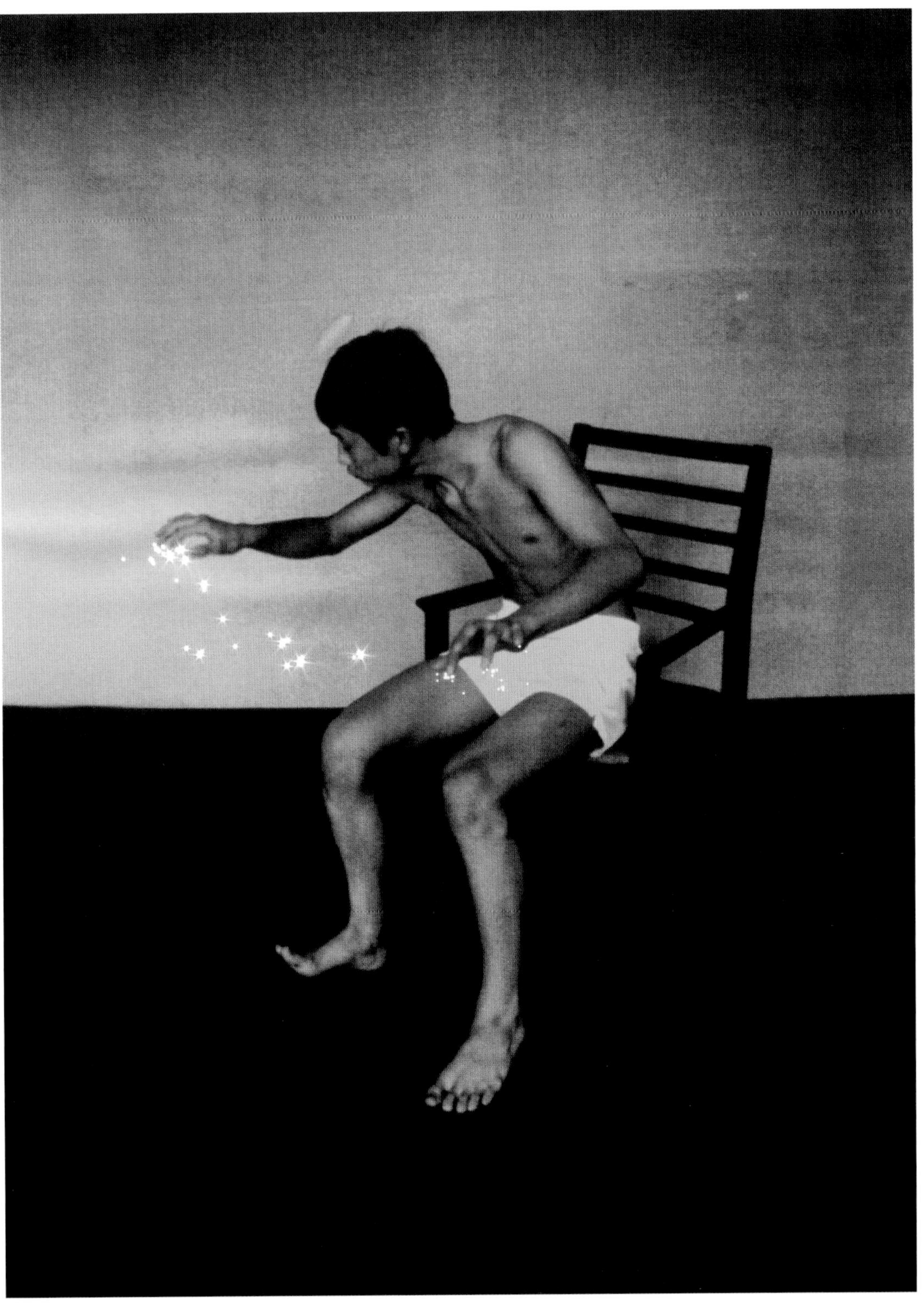

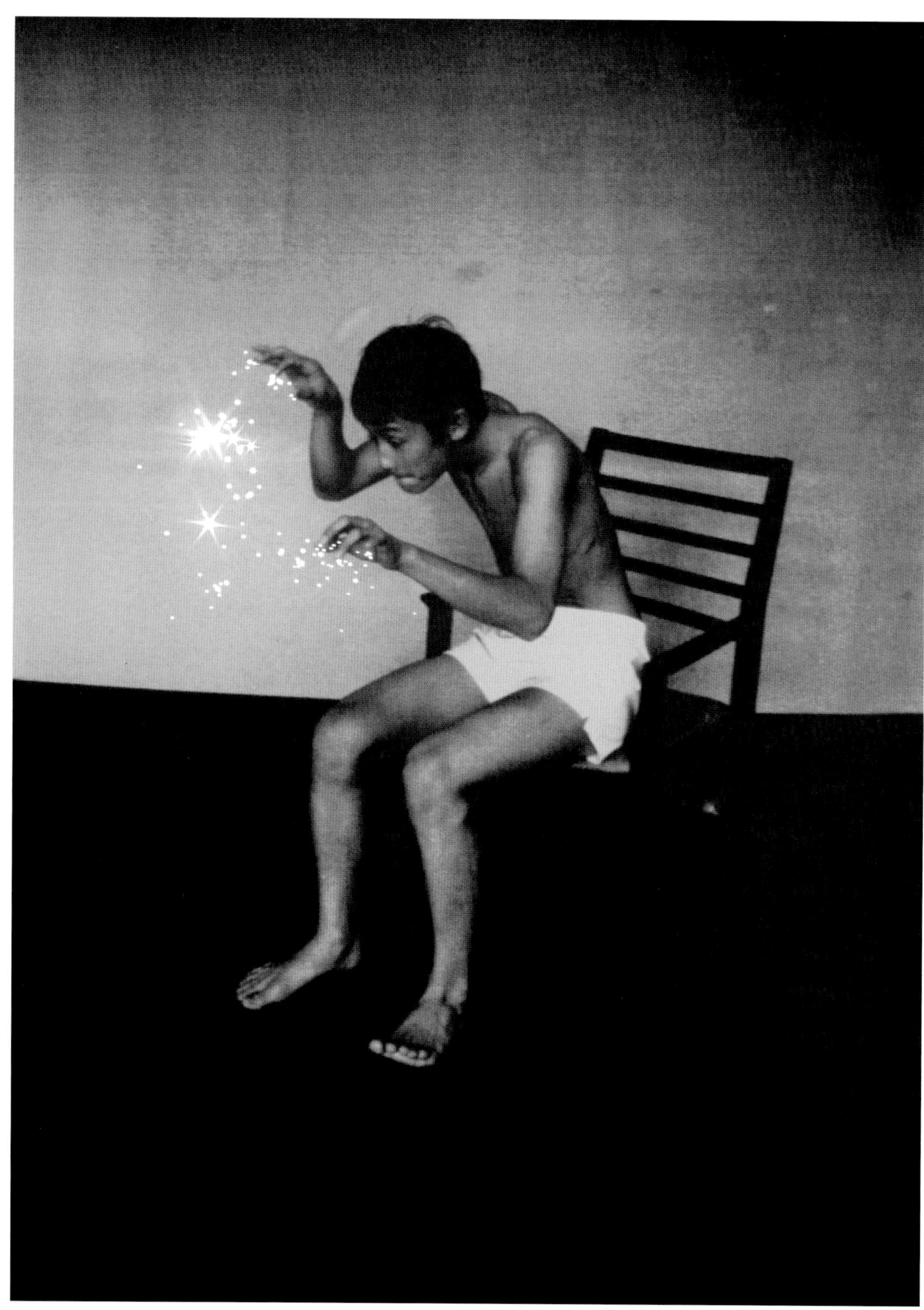

Above and opposite: Shiga Lieko, *Piano* series, 1998.

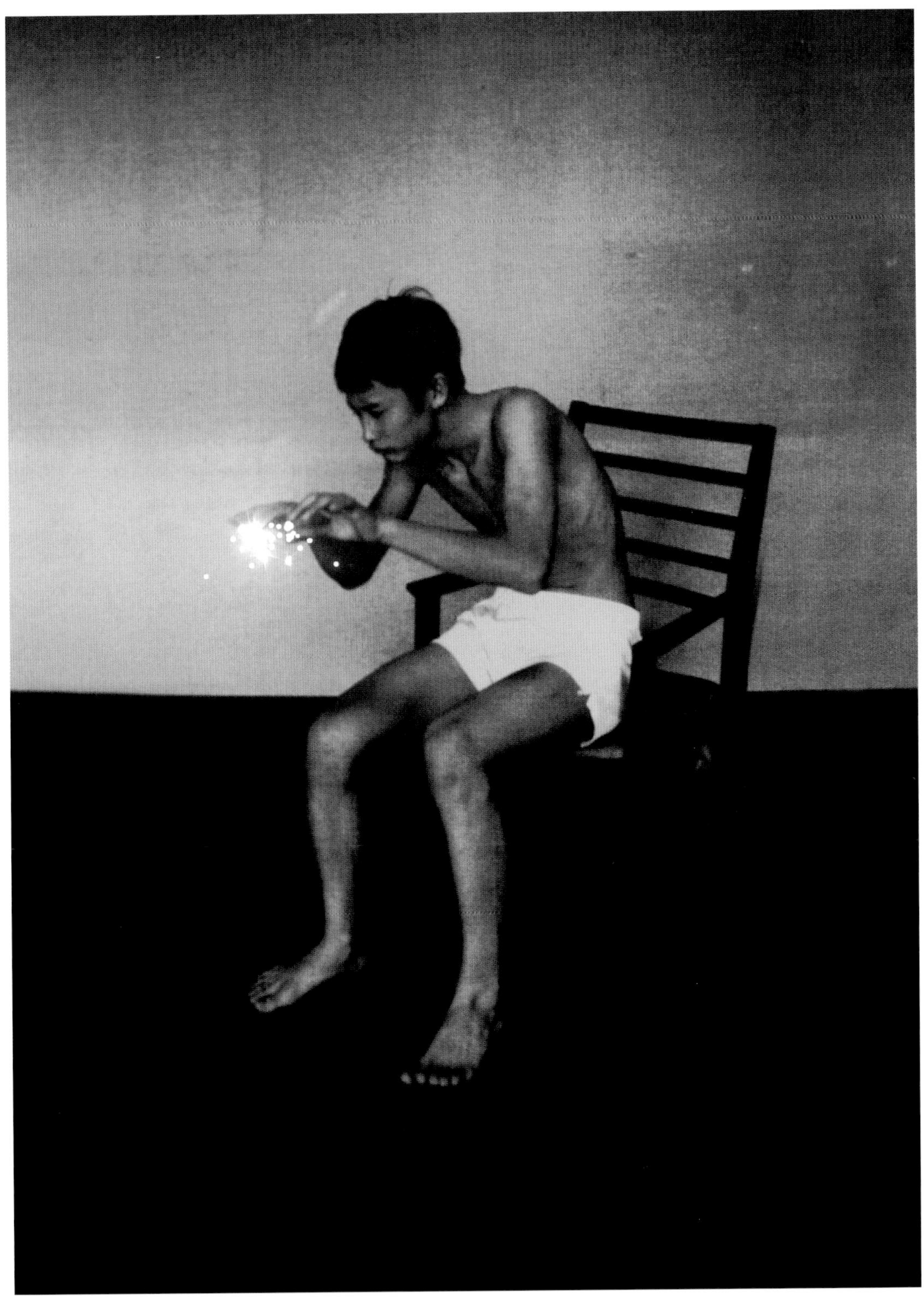

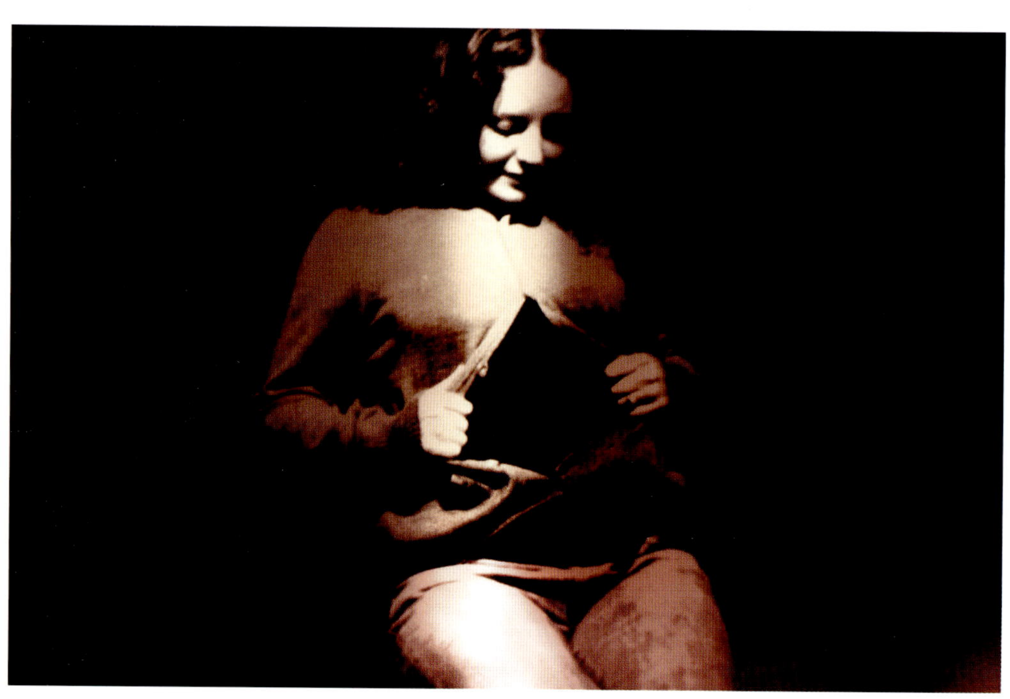

Shiga Lieko, *Bethany*, 2005, *Lilly* series.

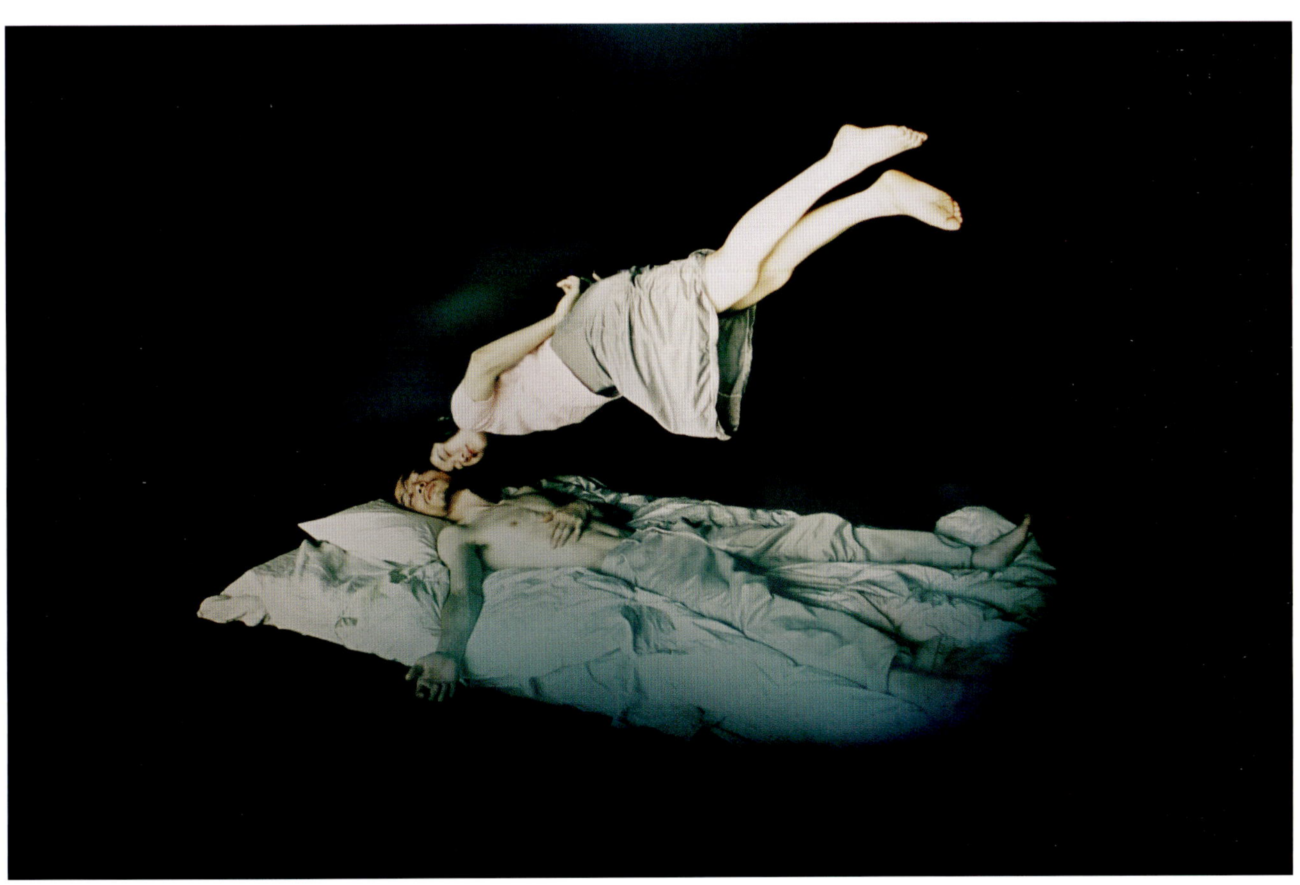

Shiga Lieko, *Chiako,* 2006, *Canary* series.

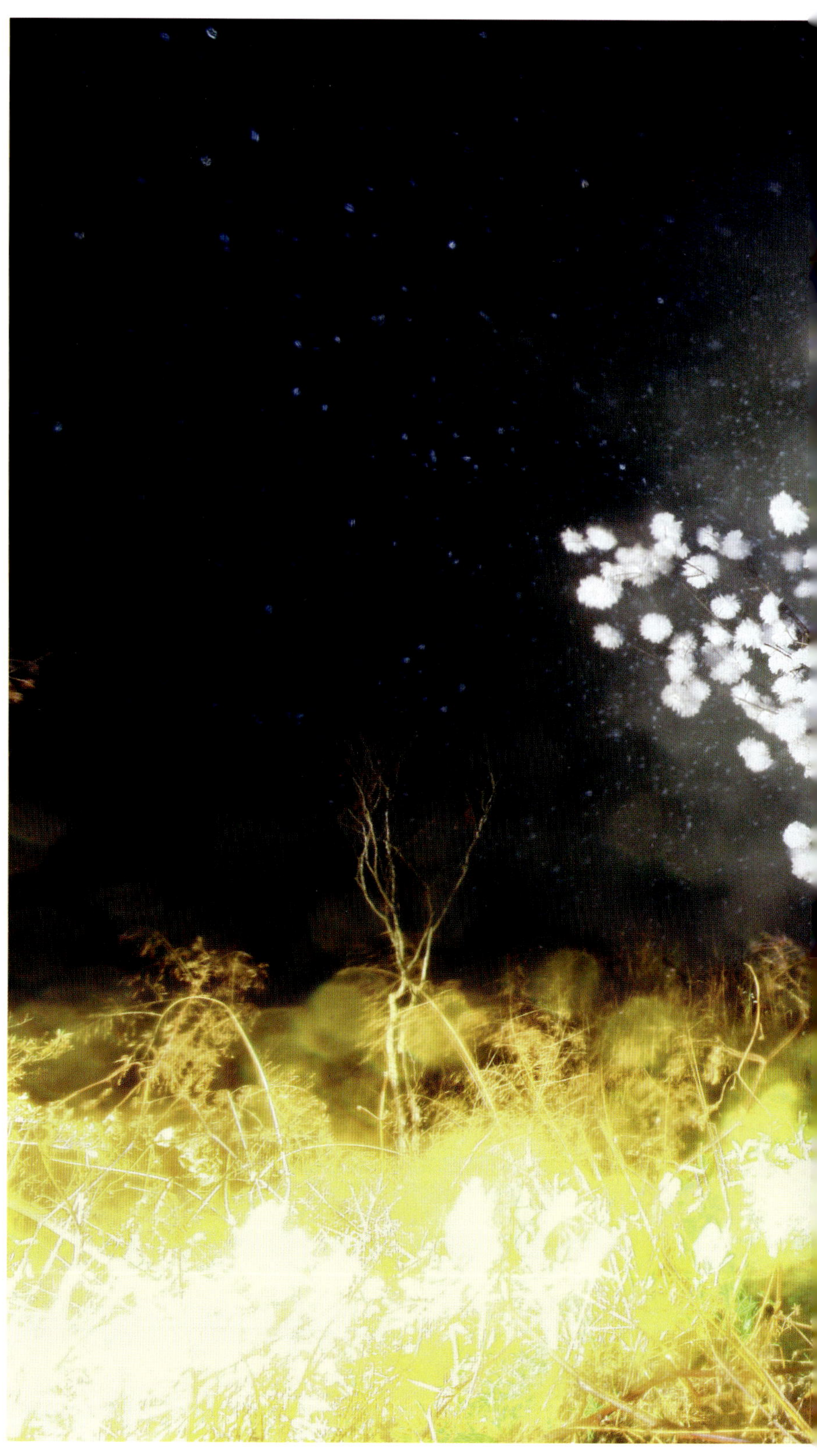

Shiga Lieko, *Wedding Veil*, 2006, *Canary* series.

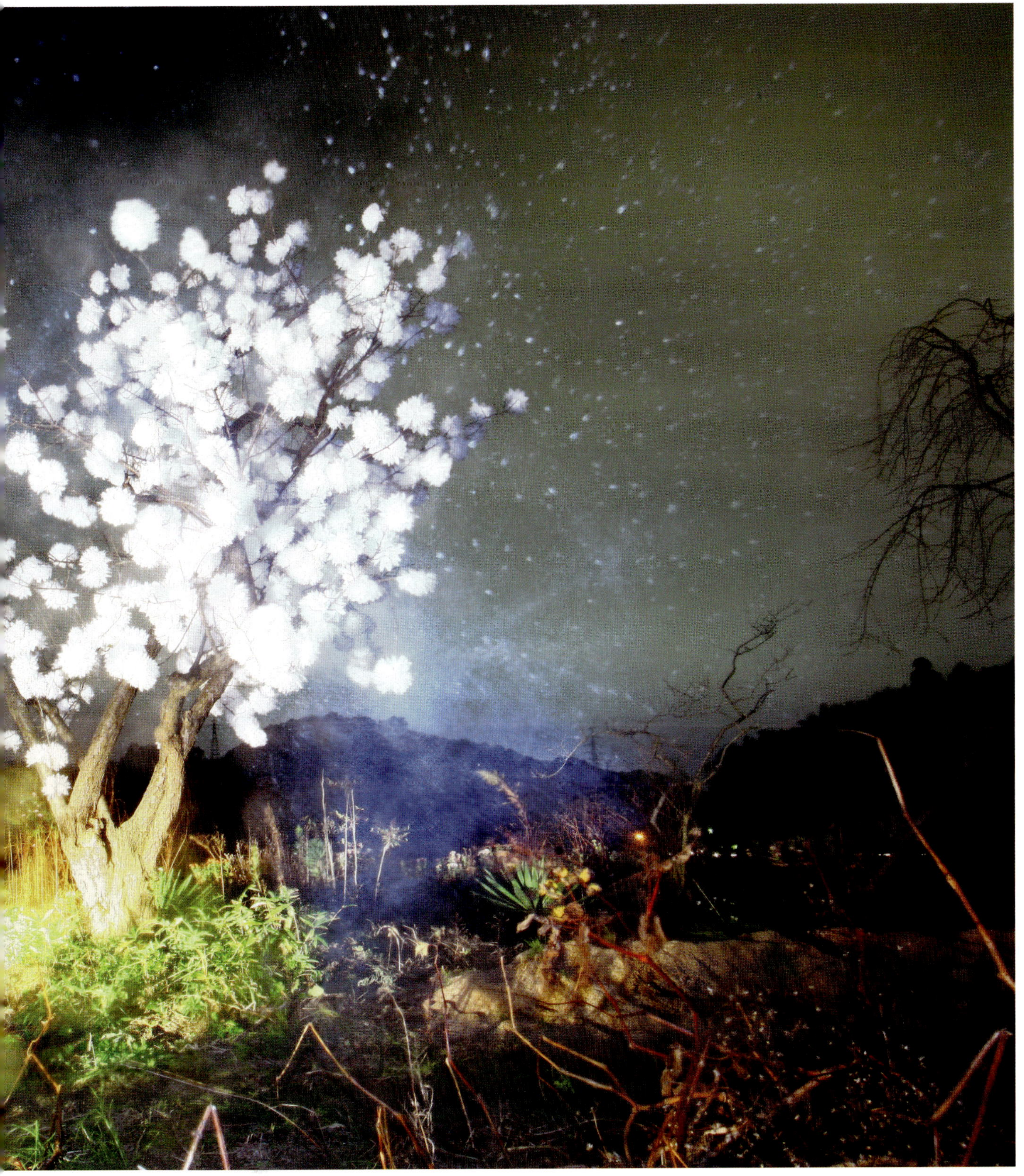

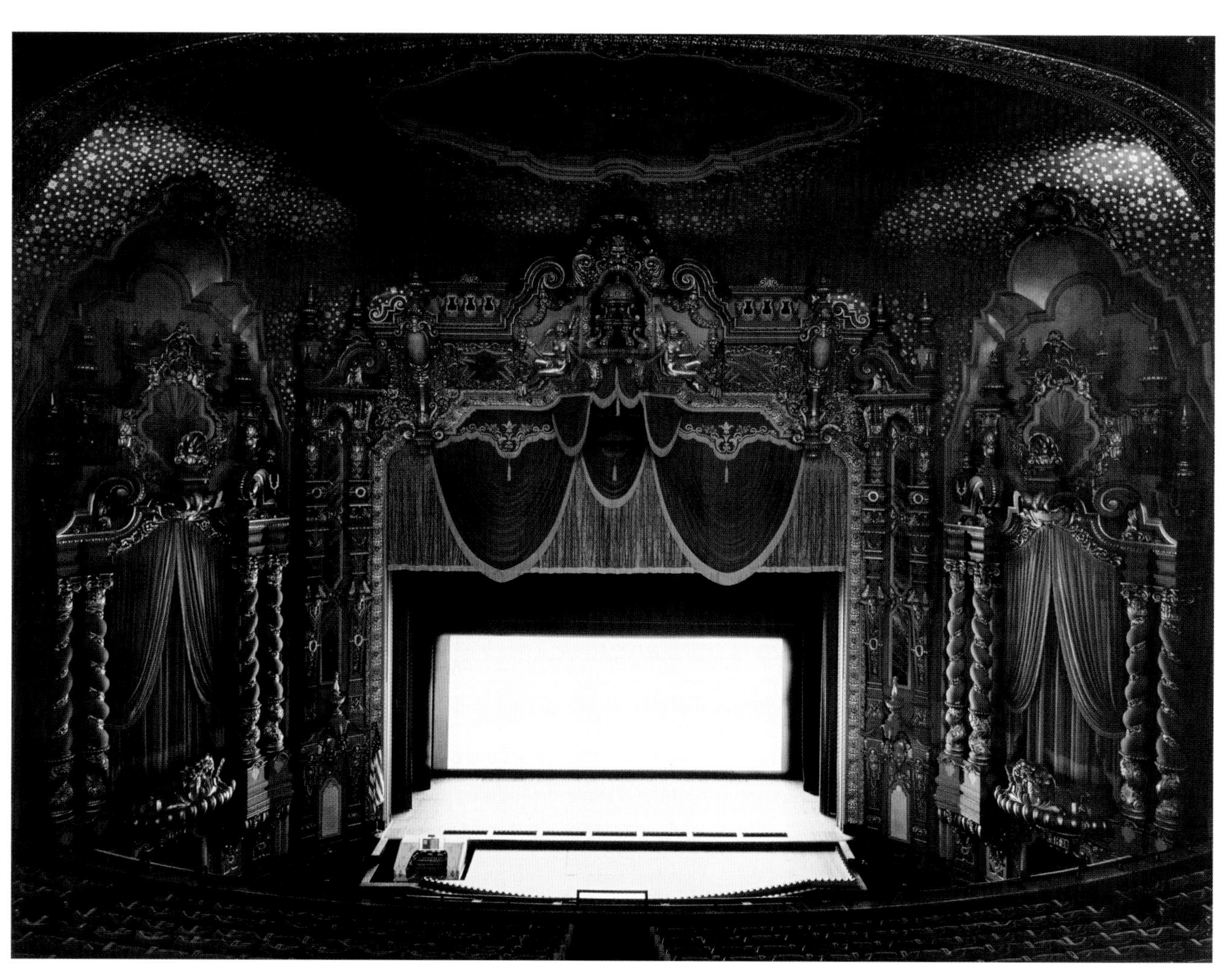

Sugimoto Hiroshi, *Ohio Theatre, Ohio,* 1980.

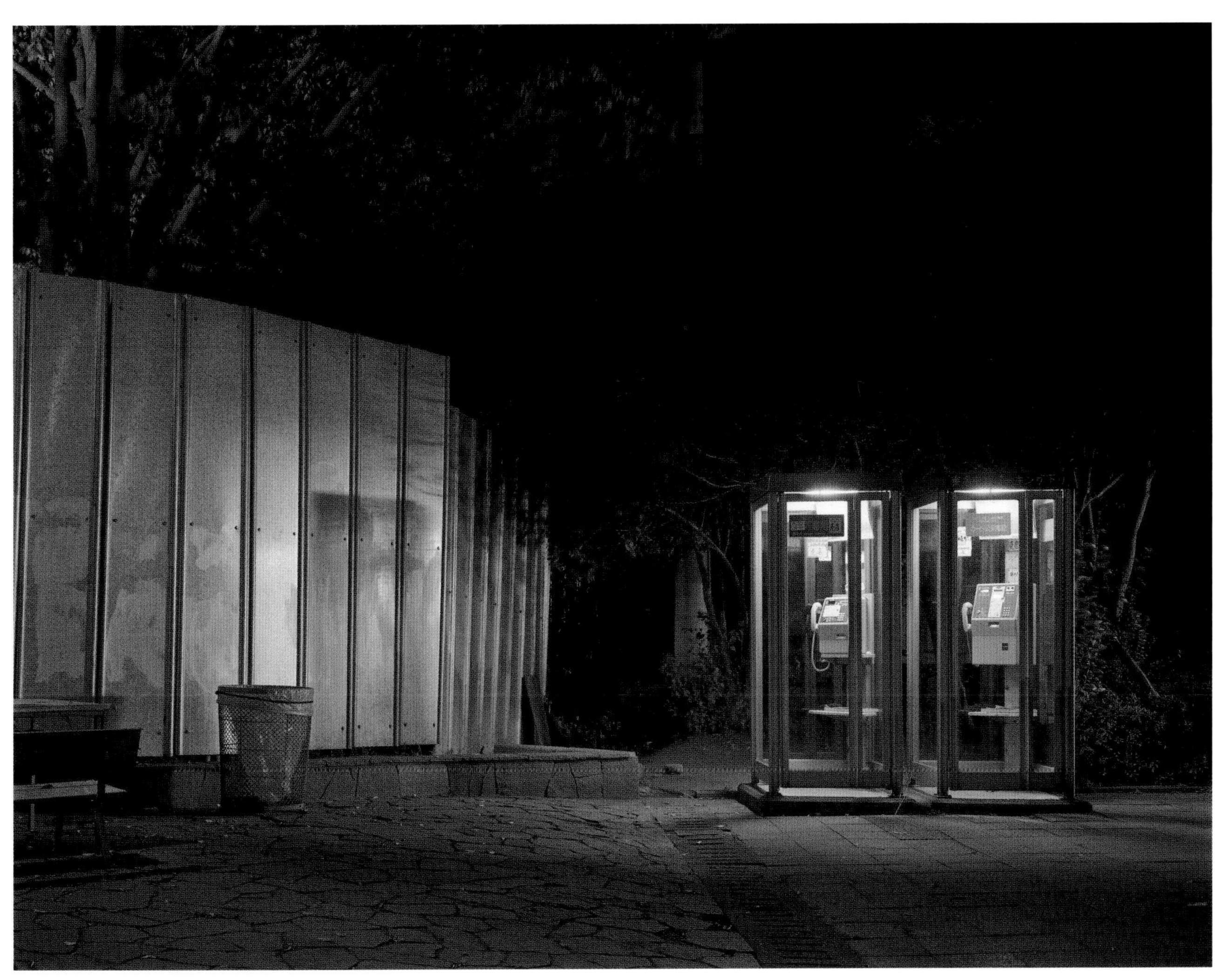

Shibata Toshio, *Nakai Parking Area, Tomei Expressway*, 1986.

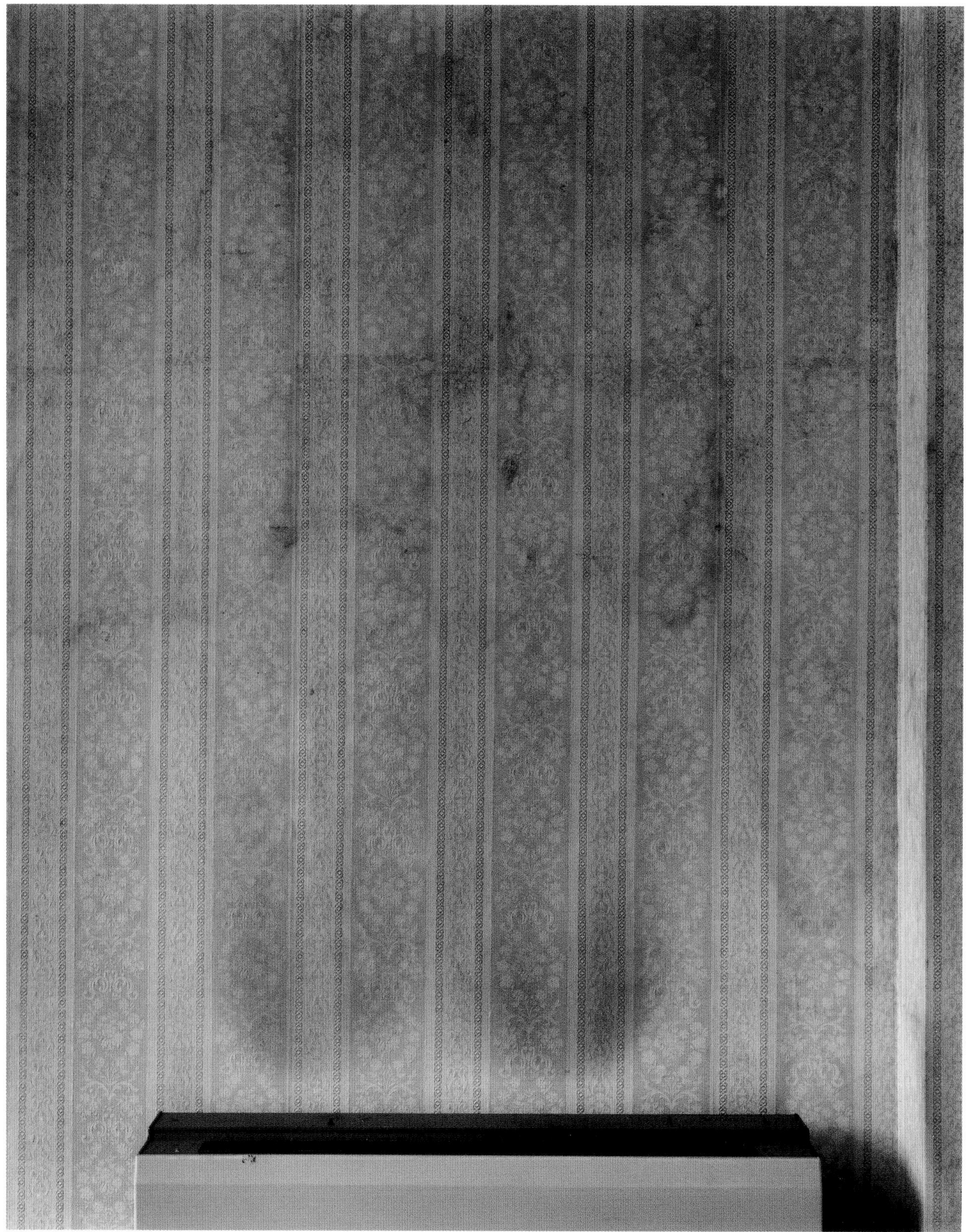

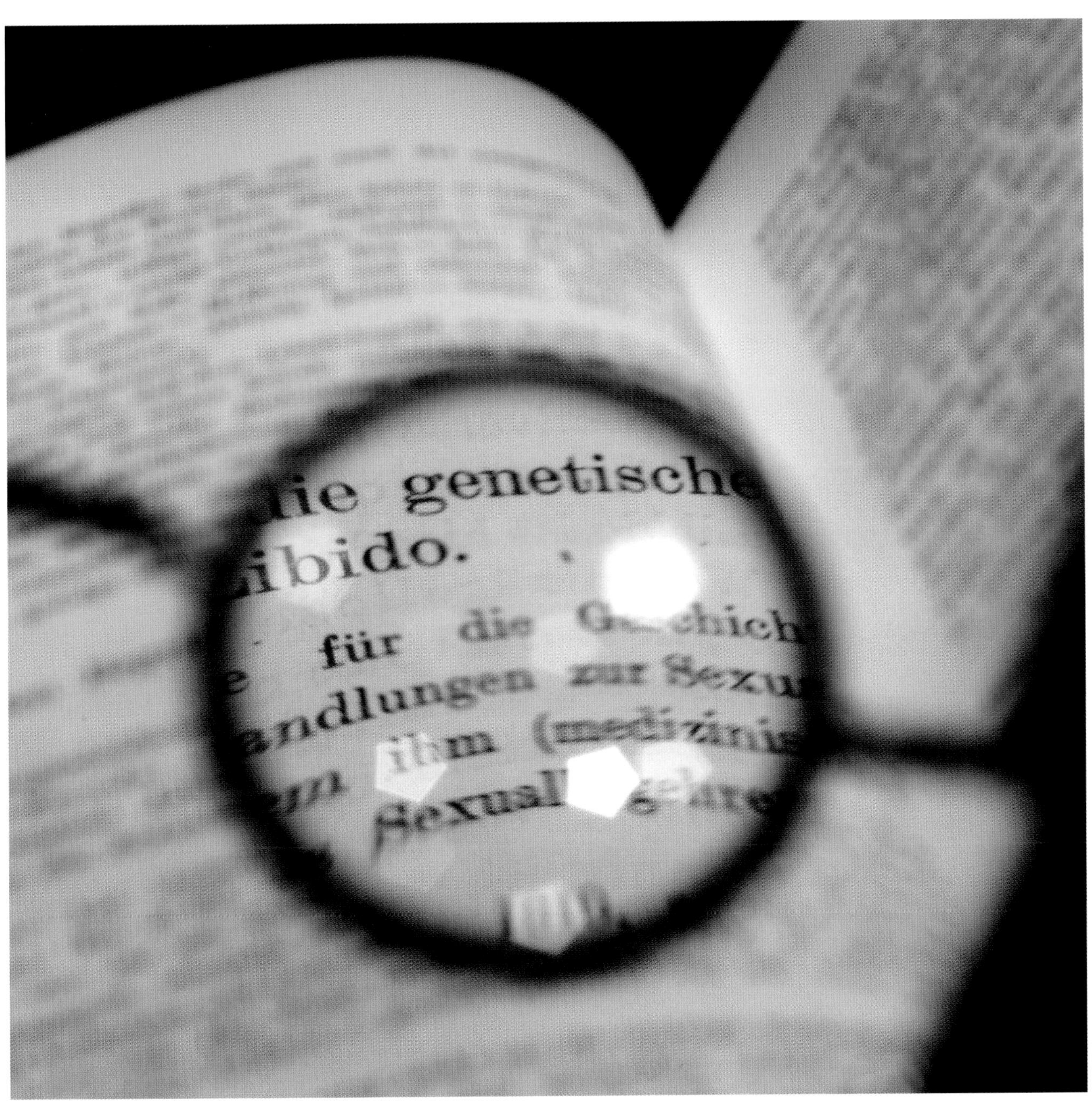

Opposite: Yoneda Tomoko, *Heat I*, 1996,
Topographical Analogy series.
Above: Yoneda Tomoko, *Freud's Glasses – viewing a text
by Jung II*, 1999, *Between Visible and Invisible* series.

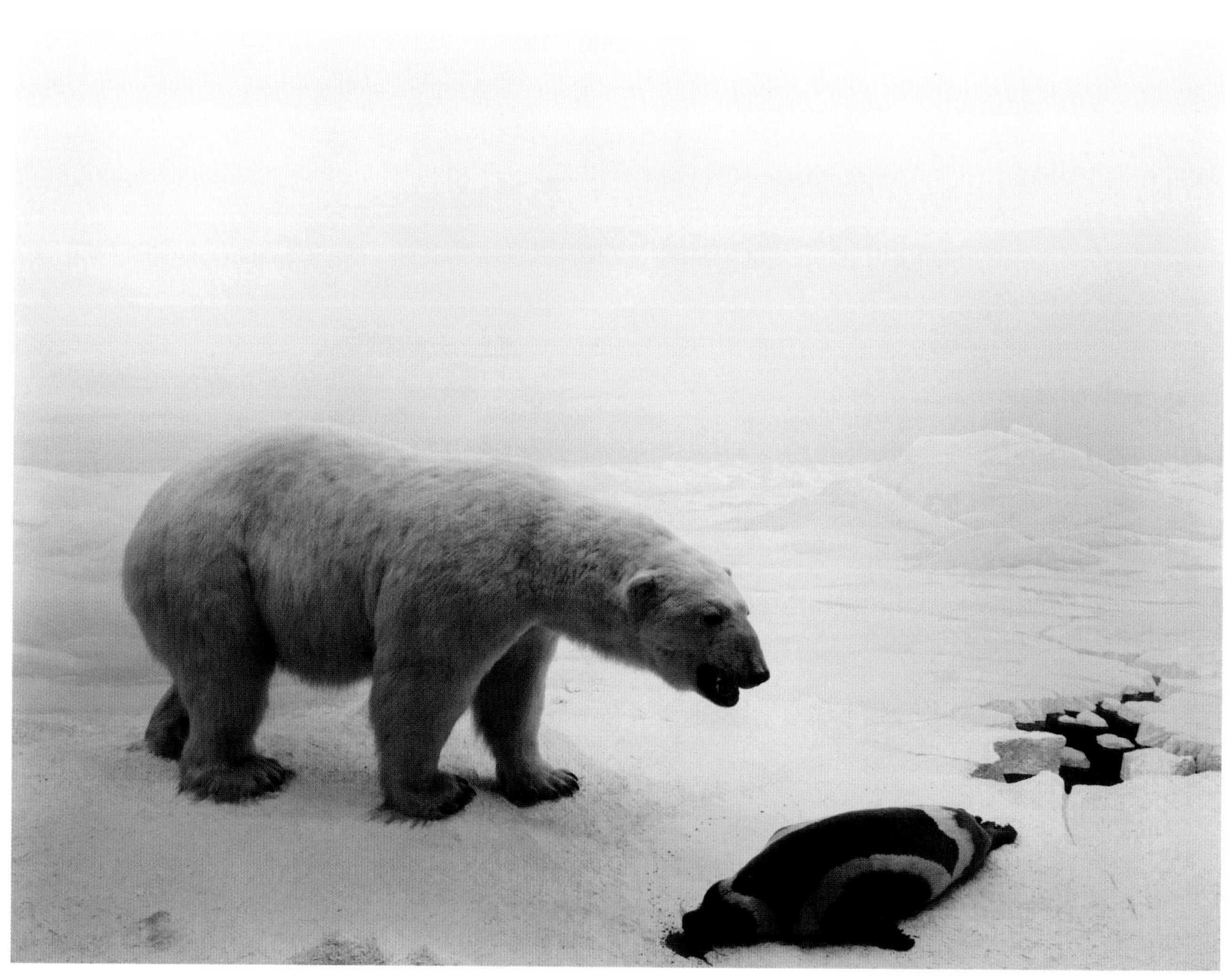

Sugimoto Hiroshi, *Polar Bear,* 1976.

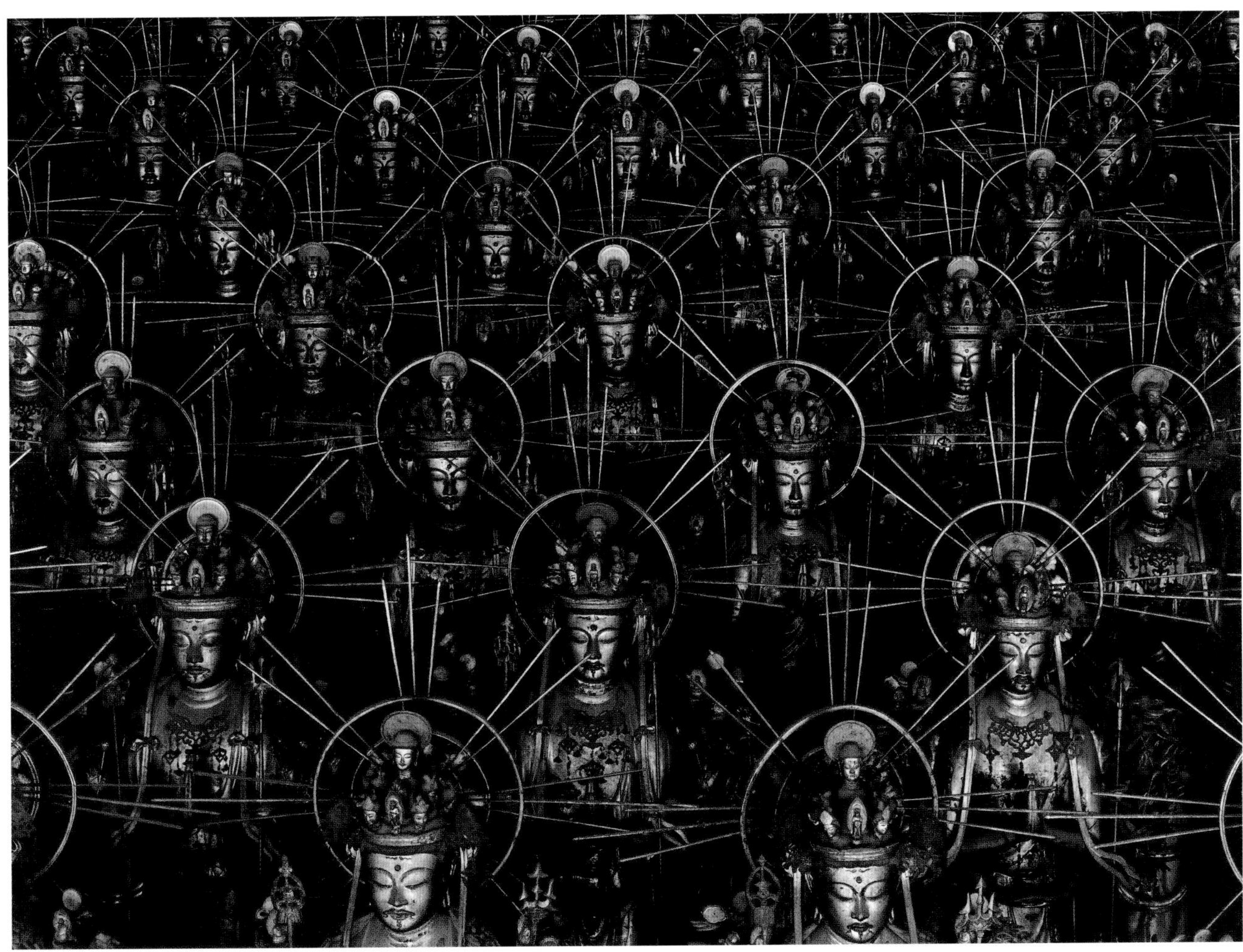

Sugimoto Hiroshi, *Sea of Buddha,* 1995.

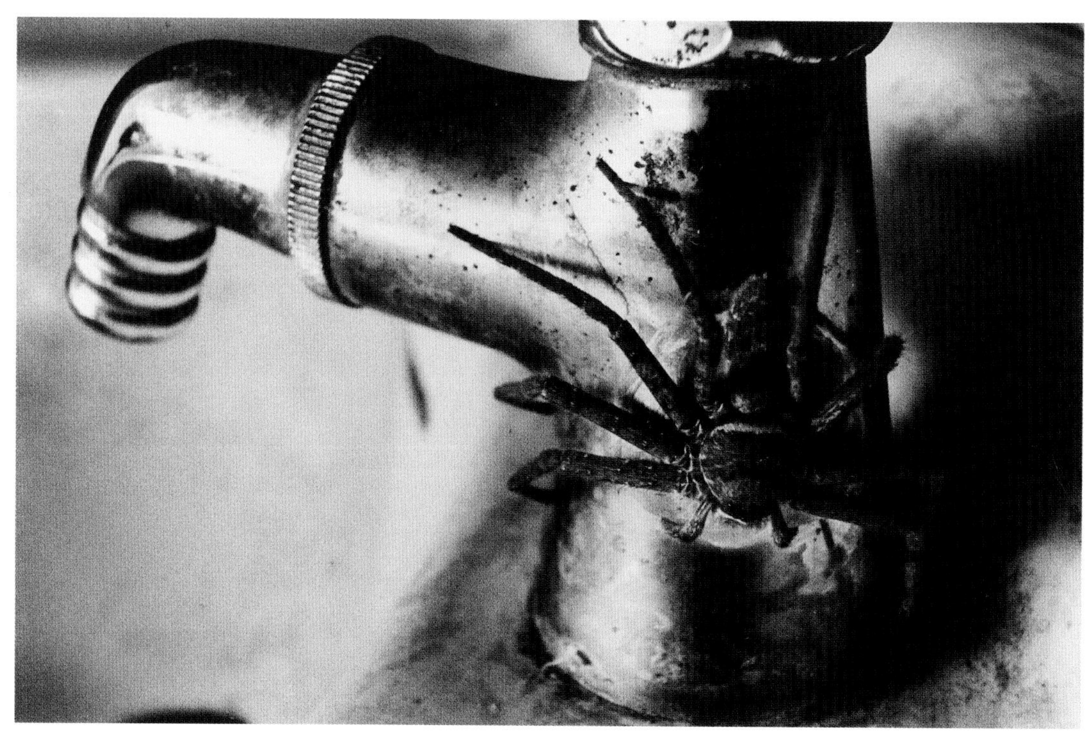

Above: Inose Kou, 1983, *Dogra Magra* series.
Opposite: Nomura Sakiko, 2016, *Another Black Darkness* series.

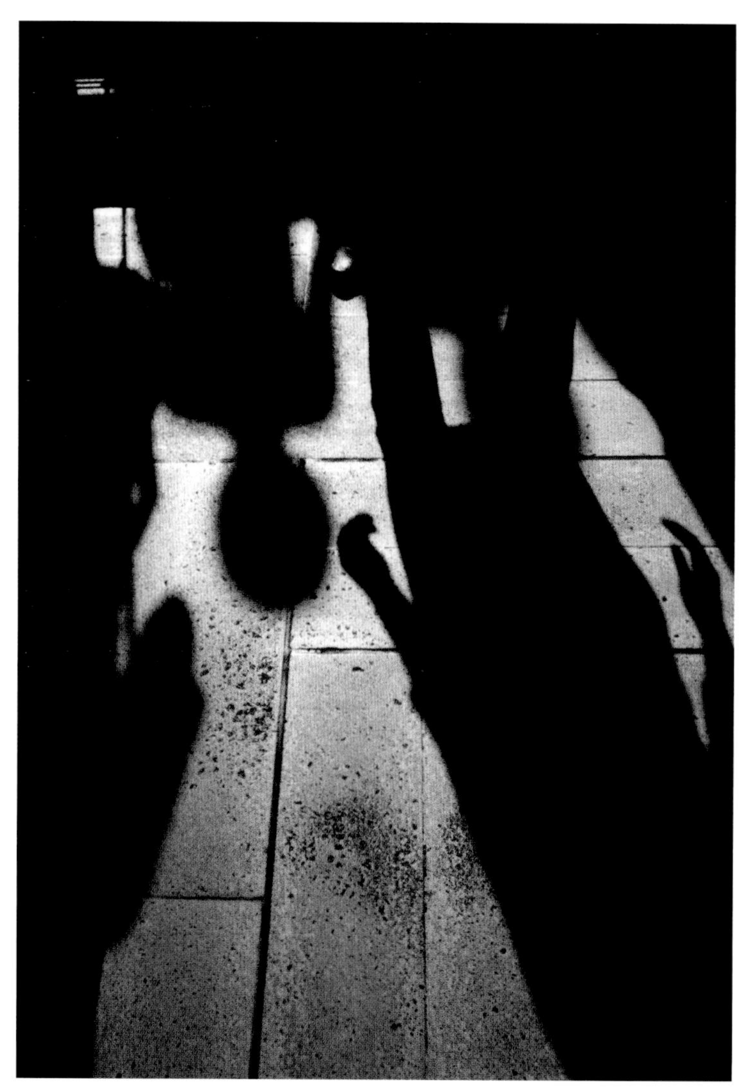

Above: Takano Ryūdai, *16.05.14 #b29*, 2016,
*When the absence of light touches the ground,
Distance is lost and distance created* series.
Opposite: Suda Issei, 2013, *Rei* series.

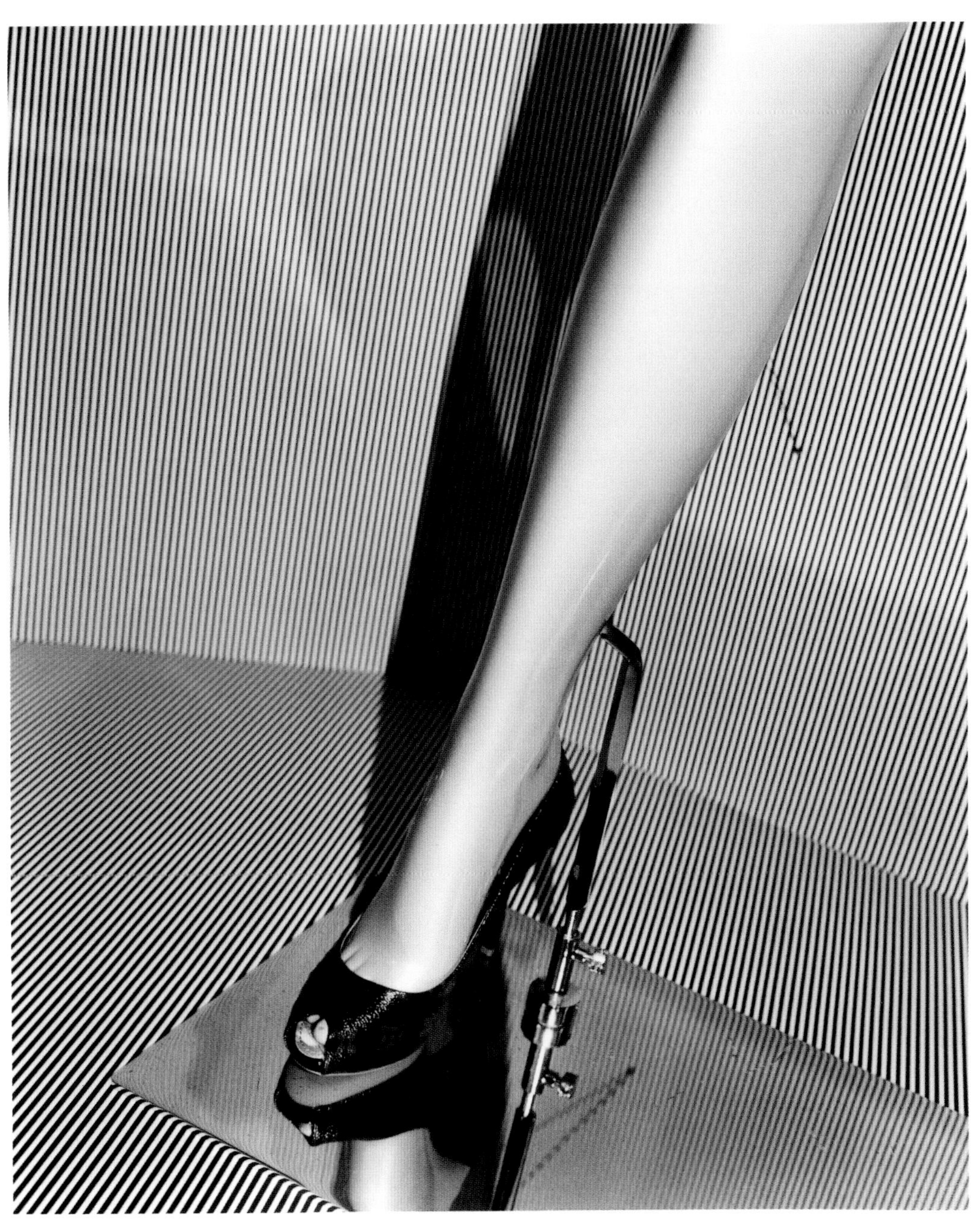

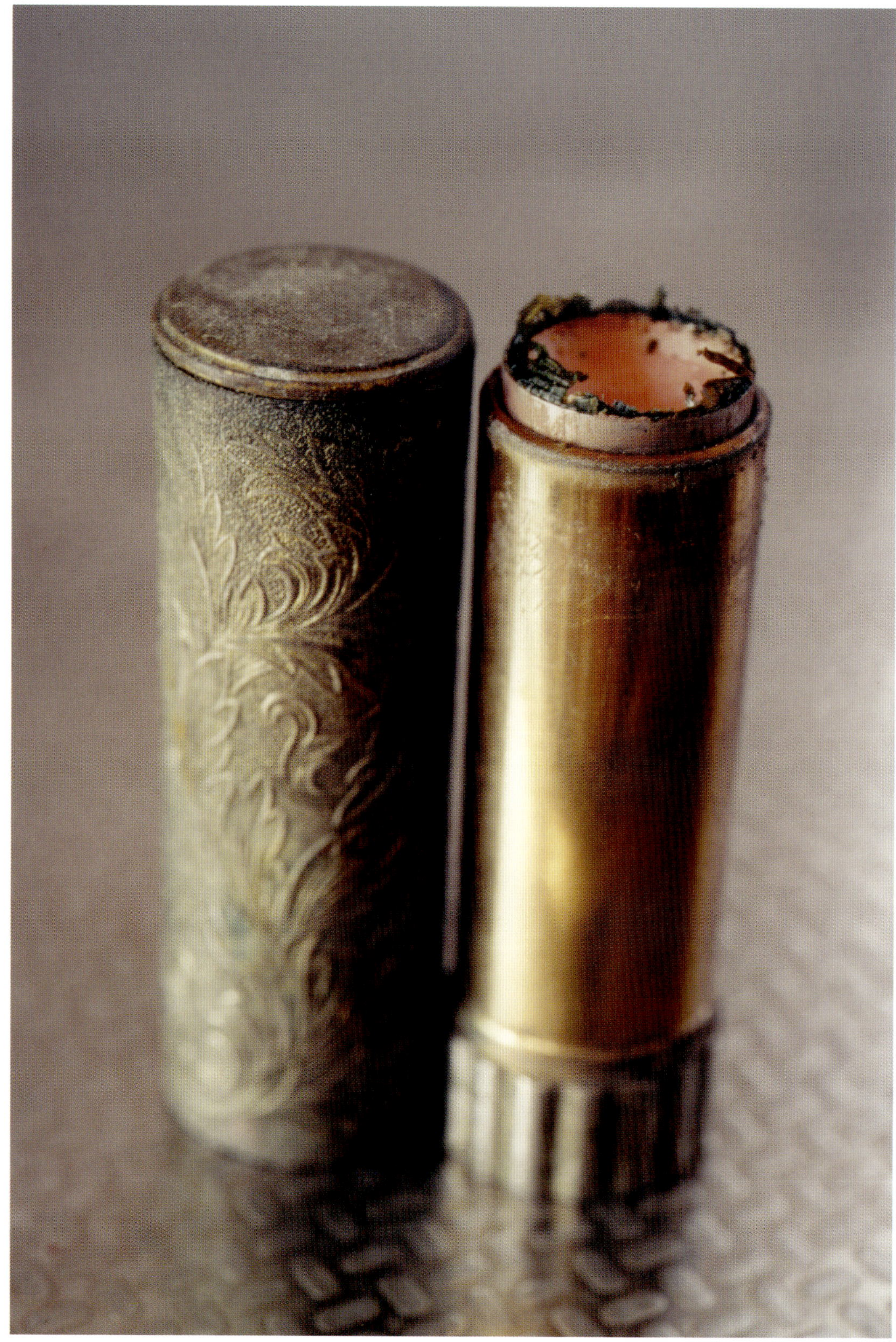

Ishiuchi Miyako, *Mother's #33*, 2002.

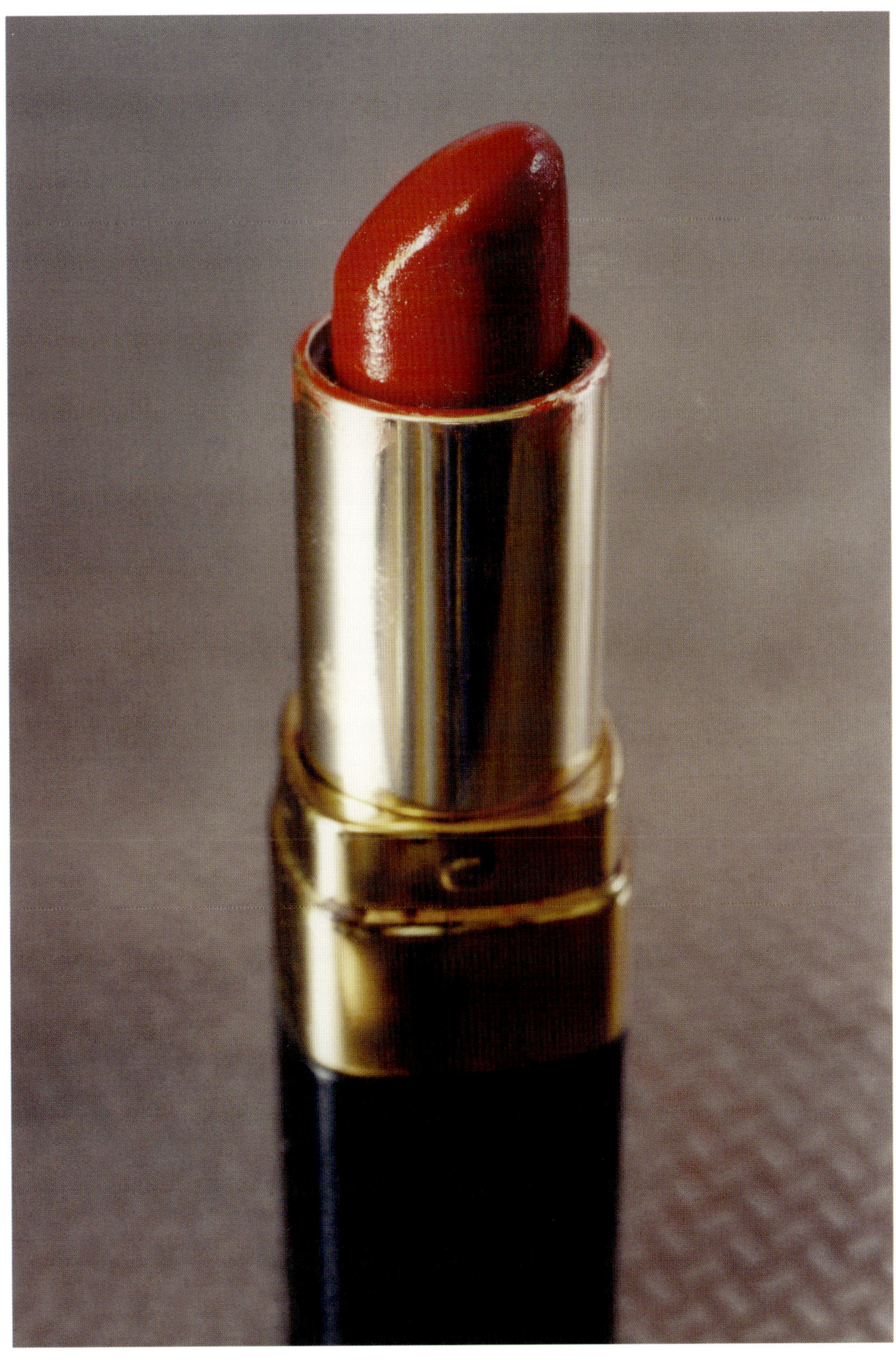

Ishiuchi Miyako, *Mother's #38*, 2002.

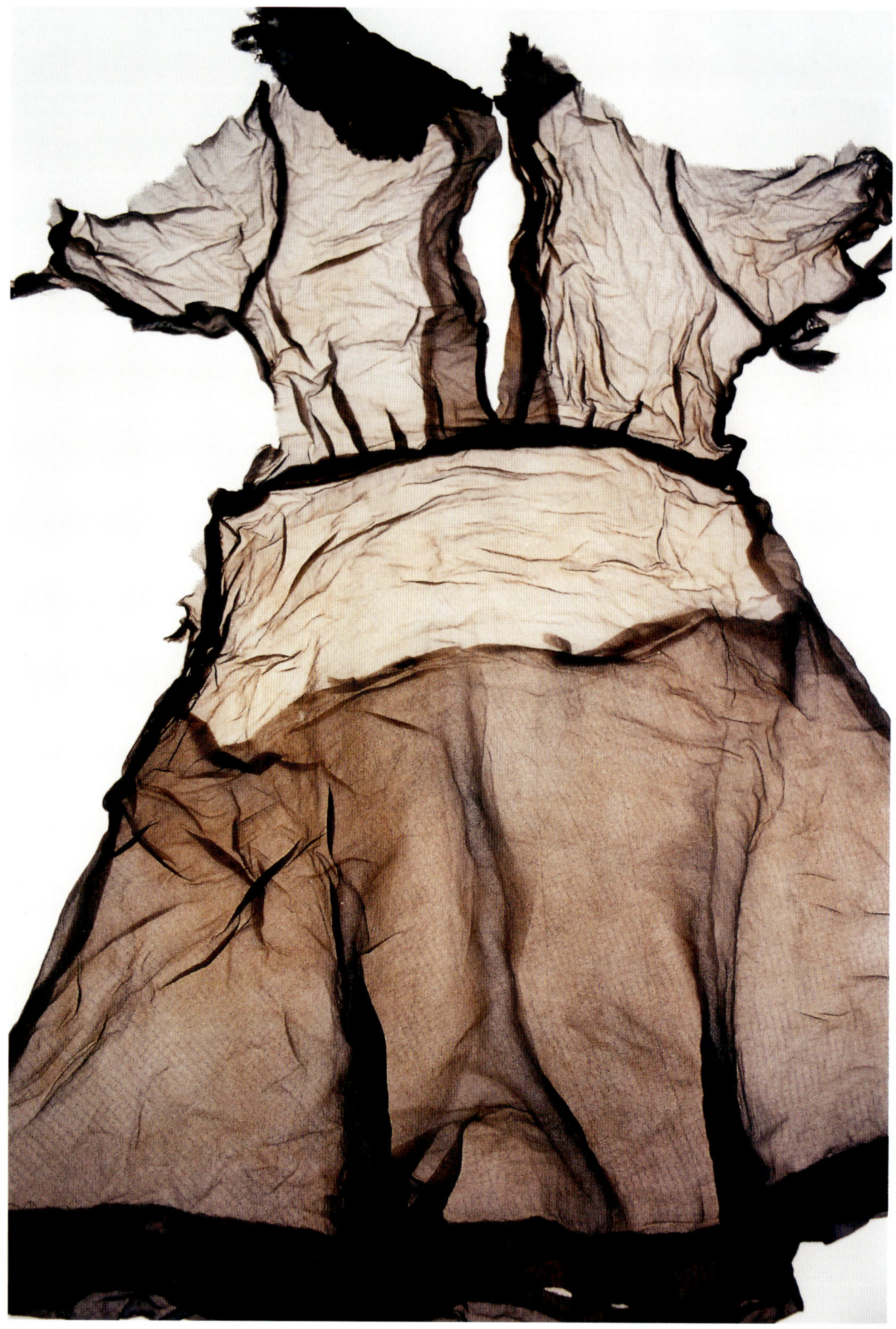

Ishiuchi Miyako, *Donor: Ogawa R., #9*, 2007, ひろしま/*hiroshima* series.

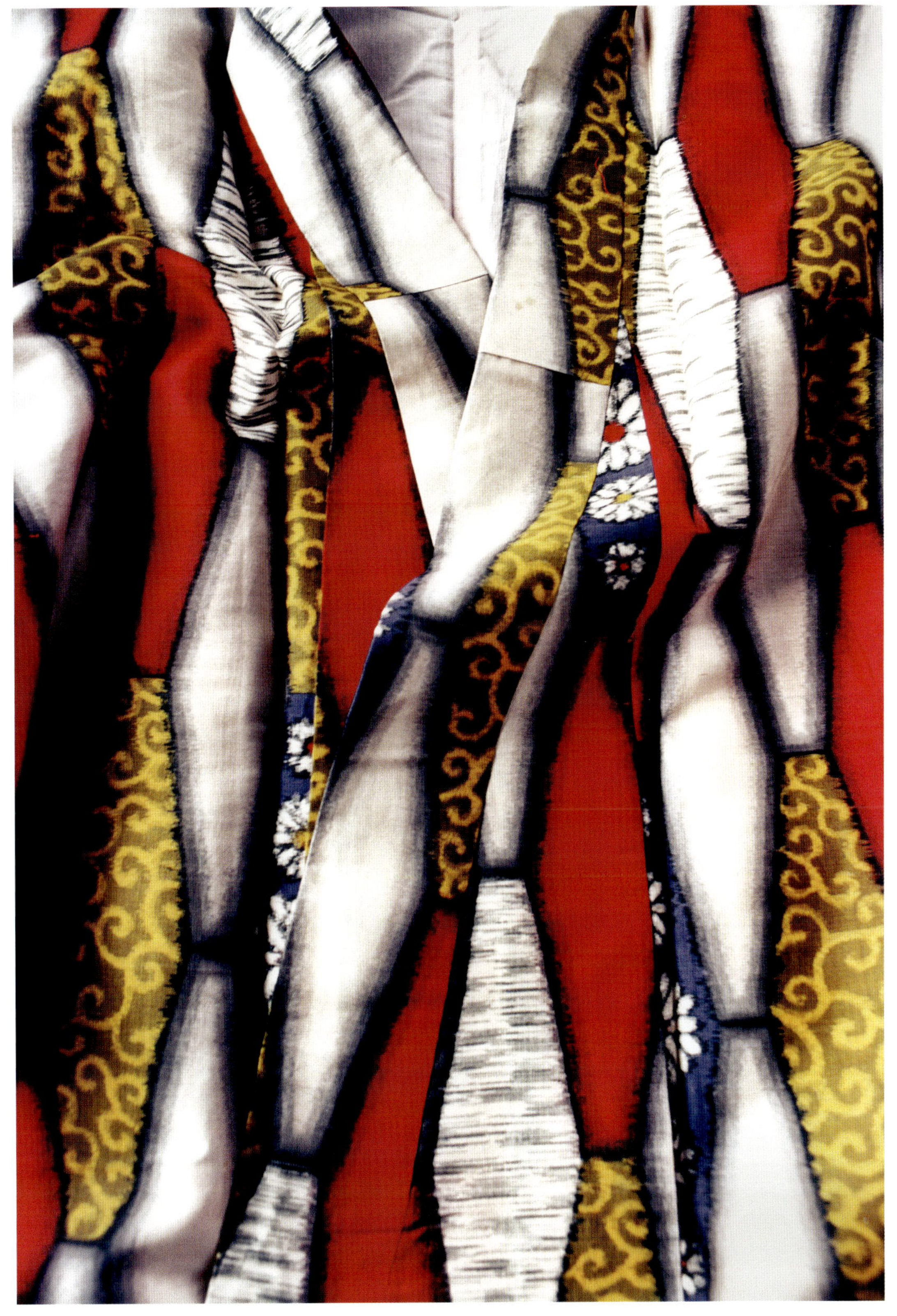

Ishiuchi Miyako, *Silken Dreams #6*, 2009–10.

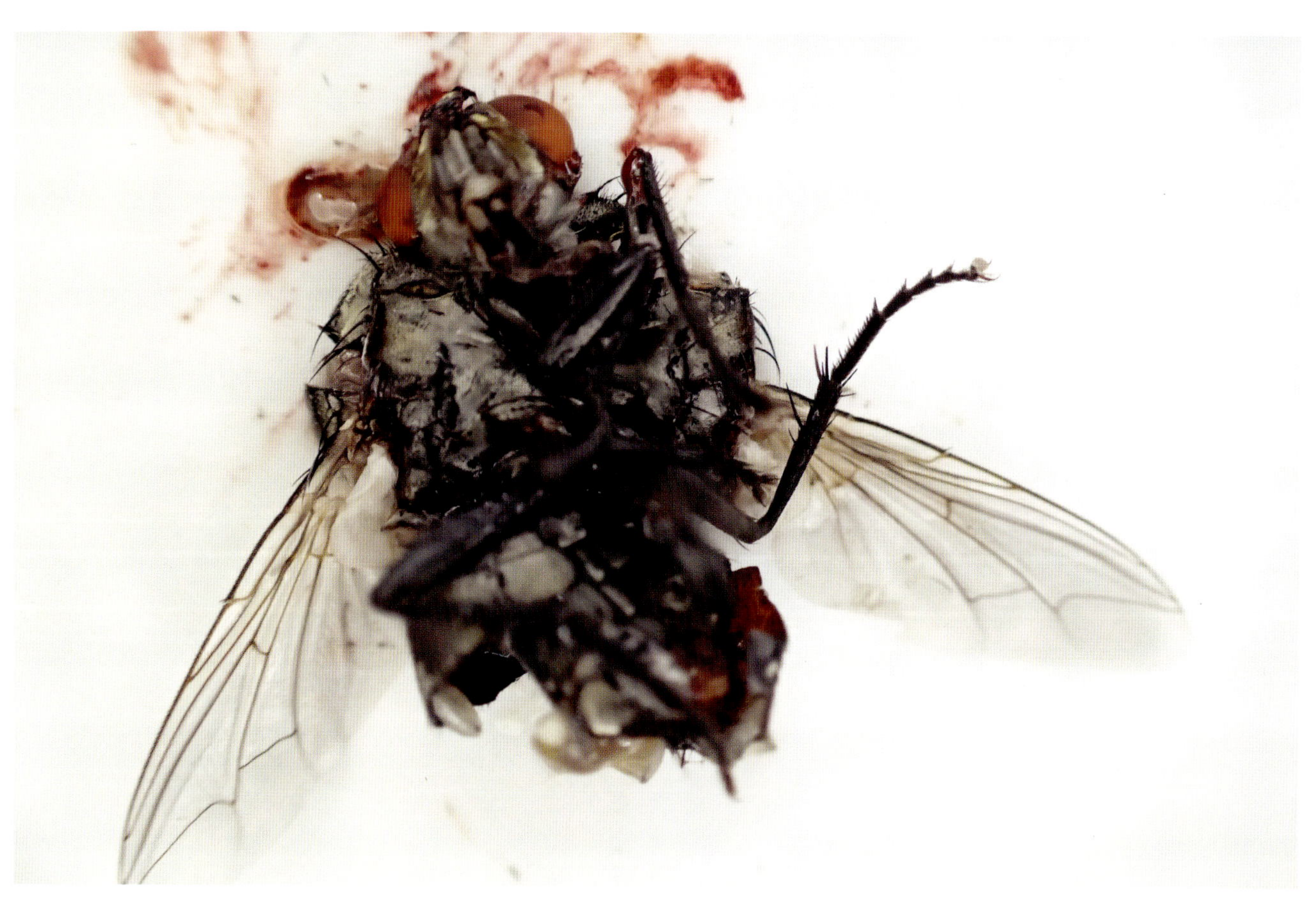

Above: Izima Kaoru, untitled, 2017, *musikera* series.
Opposite: Yokota Daisuke, untitled, 2015, *Color photographs* series.

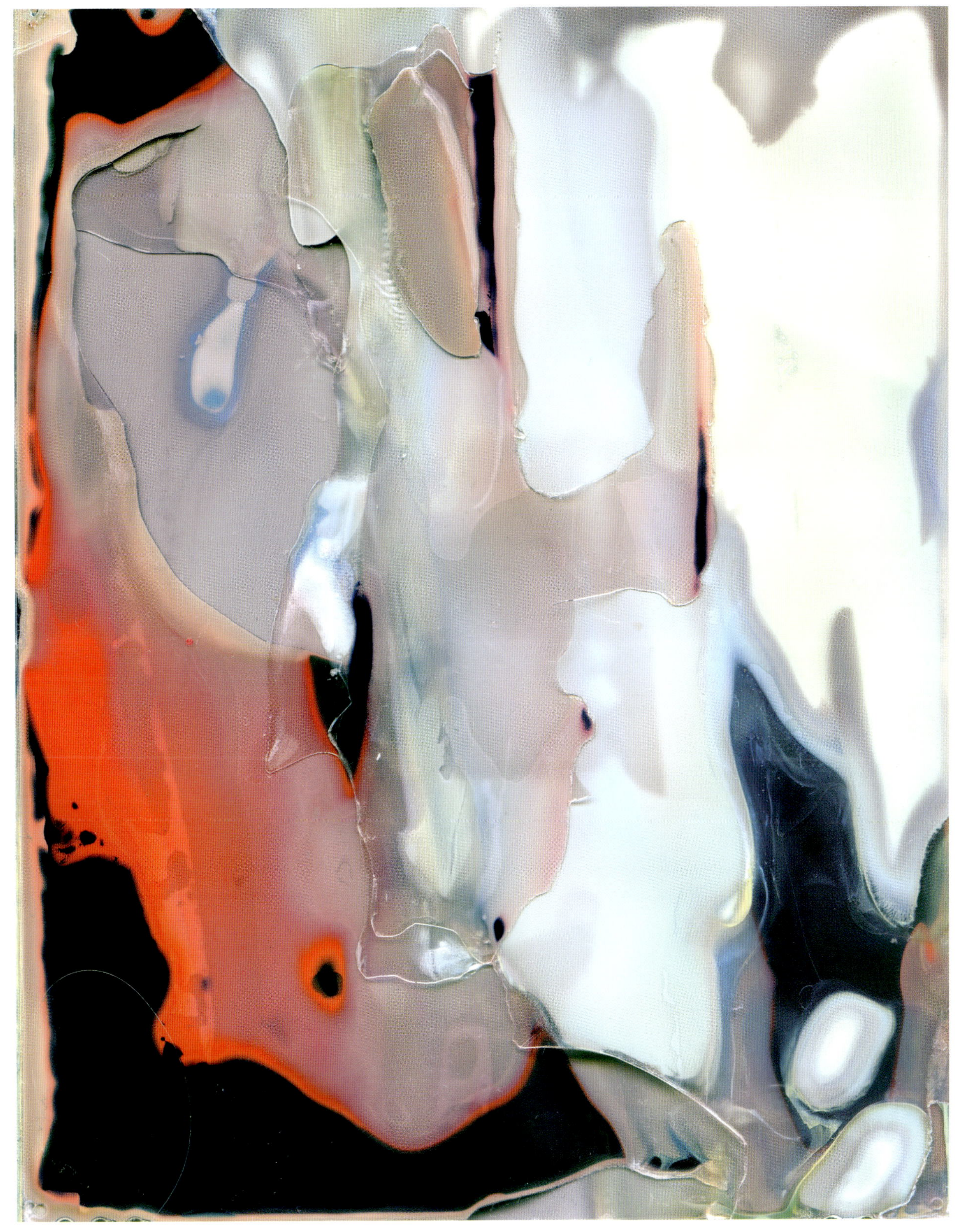

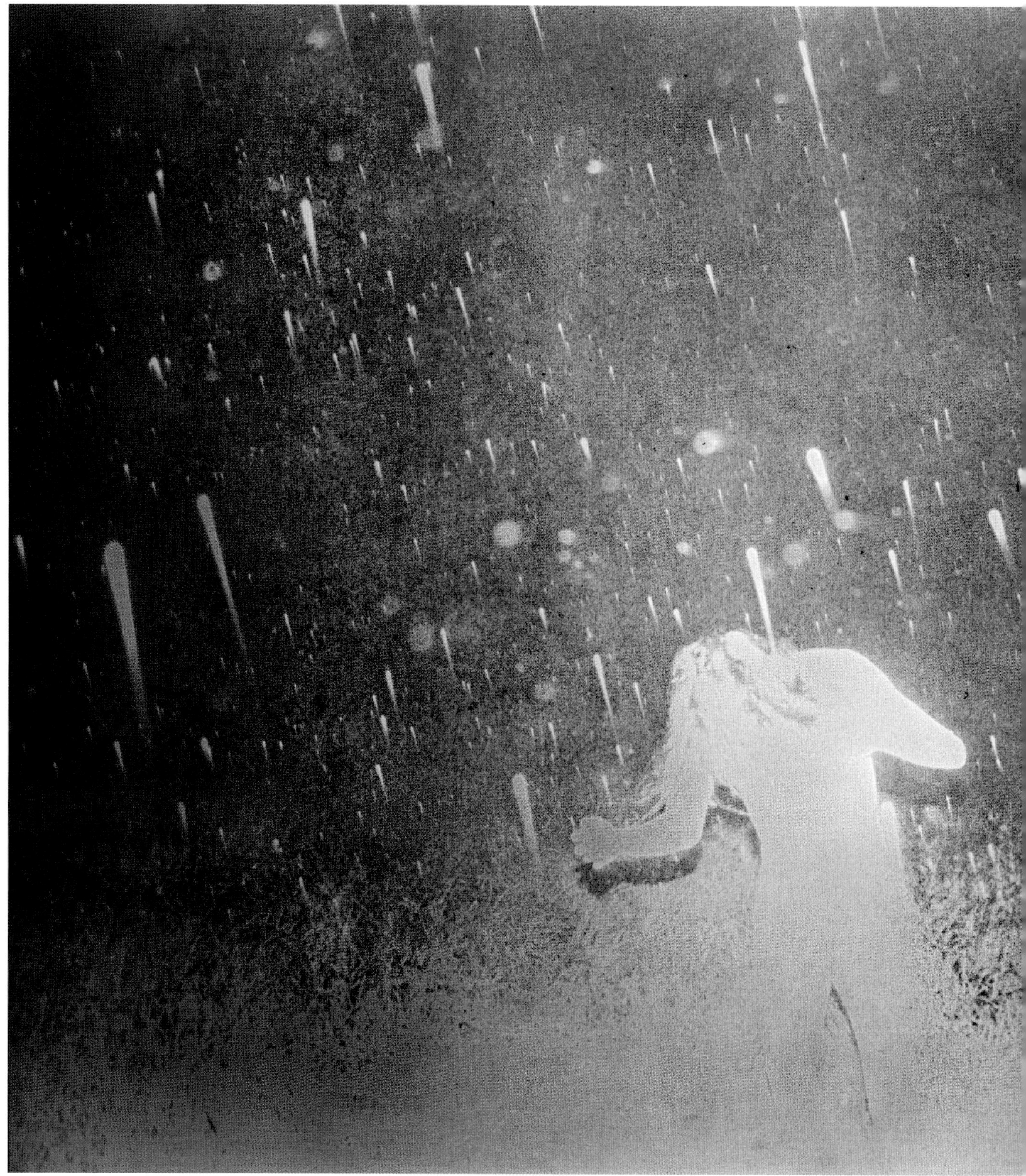

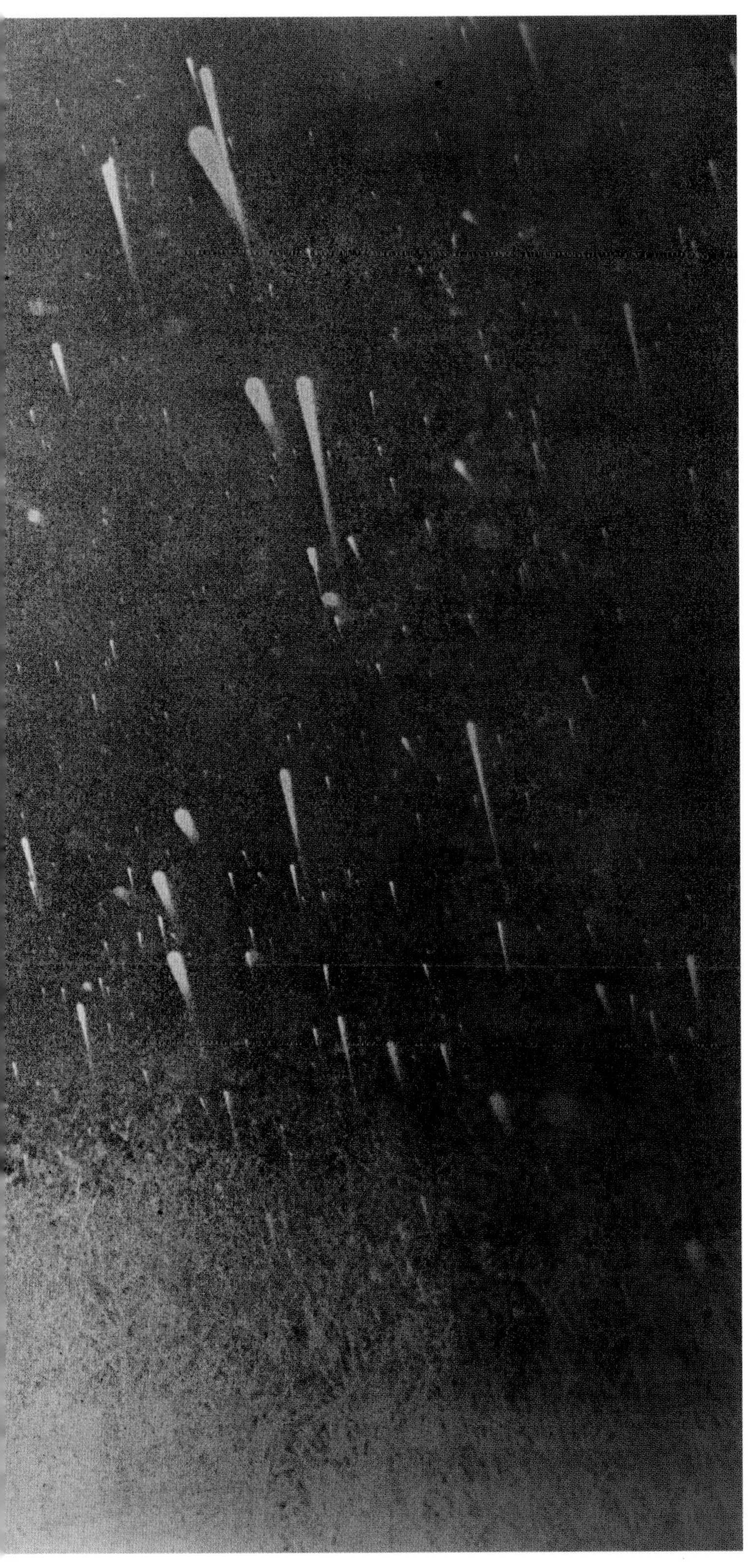

Yokota Daisuke, untitled, 2011, *Back Yard* series.

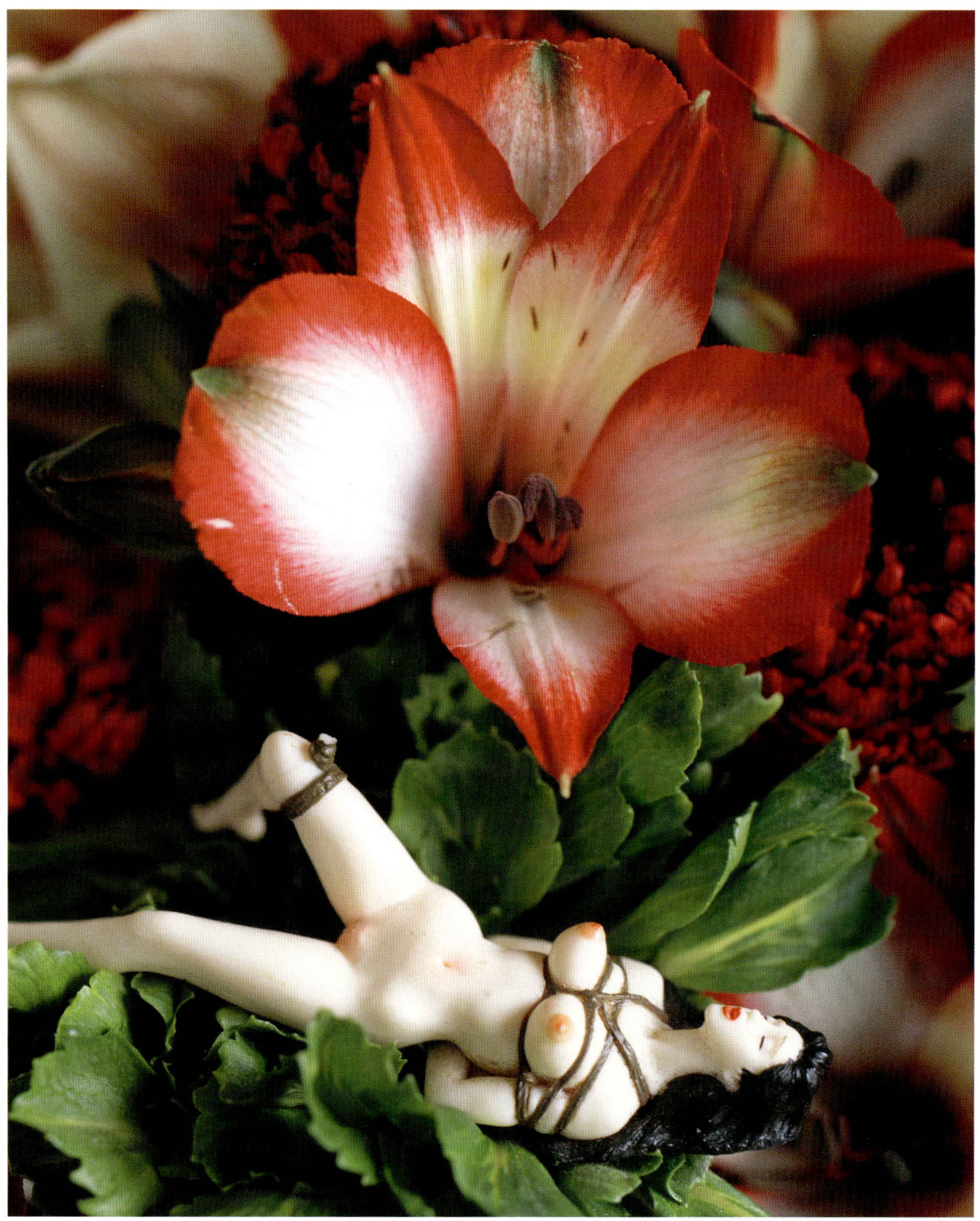

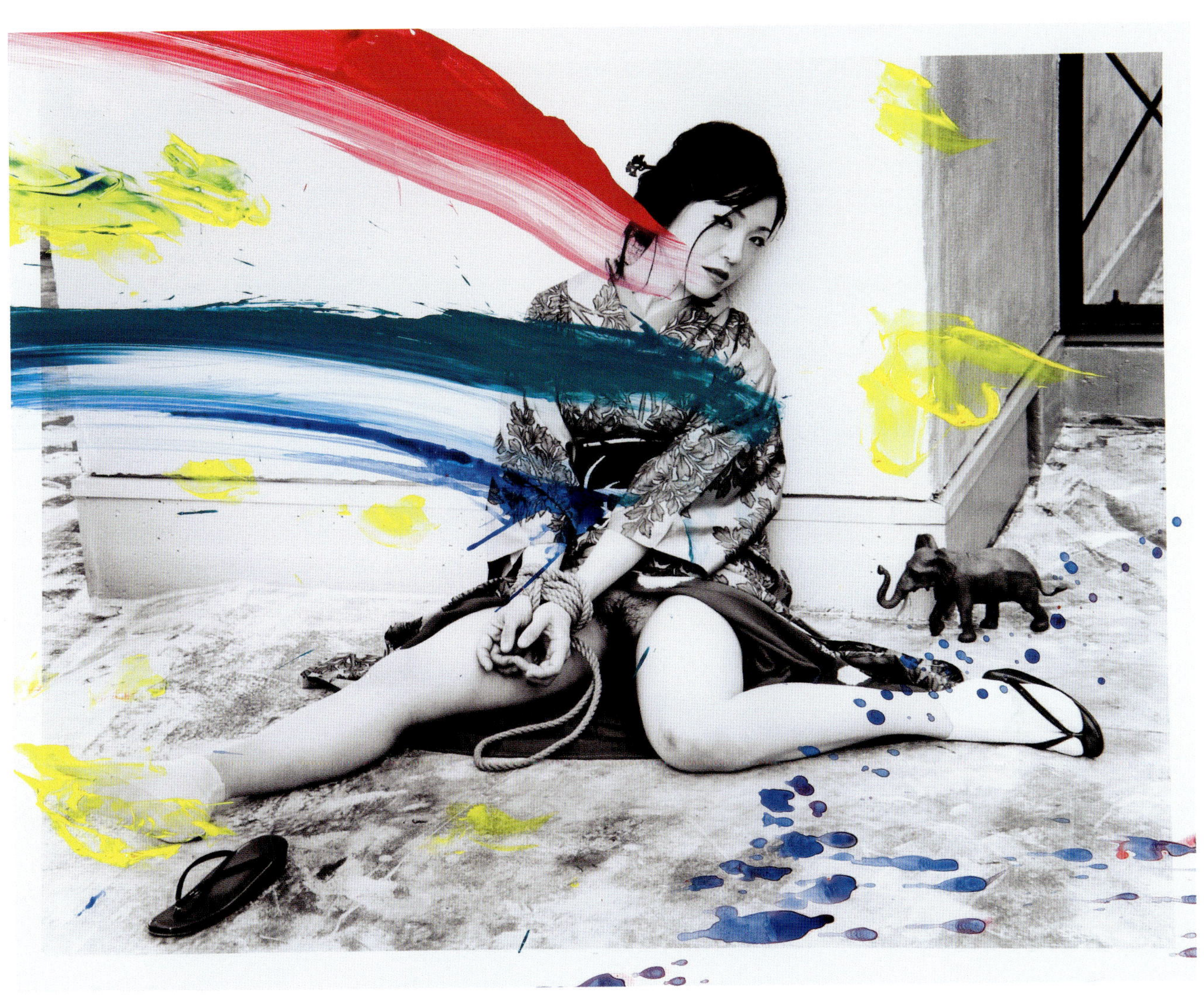

Opposite: Araki Nobuyoshi,
untitled, 2017, *Imshun* series.
Above: Araki Nobuyoshi, untitled,
2010, *Paintings* series.

1850s

Commodore Matthew Perry arrives in Japan with the 'Black Ships' and demands on behalf of the US that Japan open itself to foreign commerce and diplomatic relations.

Photography is introduced to Japan and scholars begin research on the daguerreotype using Dutch texts. Artists Shiba Kōkan and Satake Shōzan use the word *shashin* to describe the realism of Western art, before it becomes associated with photography.

1862–65

One of the first professional photographers, Ueno Hikoma, opens a photo atelier in Nagasaki. Felice Beato, a photojournalist, and Charles Wirgman, a correspondent for the *Illustrated London News,* open a studio in Yokohama.

1868

The Meiji period begins. The new emperor is moved to Edo, which is renamed Tokyo and becomes Japan's capital city. The new government promotes Westernization in all aspects of society.

1871–72

Baron Raimund von Stillfried-Rathenitz establishes a photo studio in Yokohama. When he photographs the emperor without permission, the plates are confiscated. A year later, the Imperial Household commissions Uchida Kuichi to take the first portrait photograph of the emperor.

1878

American professor Ernest Fenollosa begins teaching at the Tokyo Imperial University. Fascinated with Japanese art, he examines private art collections and temples, working closely with Okakura Tenshin. Fenollosa later helps found the Tokyo School of Fine Arts and the Tokyo Imperial Museum. Fenollosa and Okakura influence the development of modern art education, academic art history and Japanese people's appreciation of their traditional arts.

1880s

Through the introduction of the dry plate process, photography is no longer exclusively the preserve of professionals. In 1889, the amateur club Japan Photographic Society (Nihon Shashinkai) is established. The market for souvenir photography grows.

1894–95

The Sino-Japanese War breaks out. Photographers are sent to the front to document it.

1896

The export of souvenir photographs to the US and Europe, depicting 'traditional' Japanese customs and sceneries, reaches its peak.

1904–5

During the Russo-Japanese War photographers are sent to the front. Soldiers receive photo-postcards from their families and friends.

The Naniwa Photography Club is established.

1907

The Mitsukoshi department store in Nihonbashi, Tokyo, opens a photography department.

Article 175 of the Japanese Penal Code prohibits the public display of 'obscene' images. The police have to respond to any allegations from the public in a museum. Until the 1990s, photographs showing the pubic area (including in magazines like *Playboy*) are censored by airbrushing or scratching over them.

1910

The photo company Konishi begins selling the small Minimum Idea camera, which contributes to the popularization of photography among amateurs.

1915

The Tokyo School of Fine Arts establishes the first photography course; it is a three-year programme. After twelve years, it is terminated.

The Eastman Kodak Vest Pocket compact camera is imported to Japan and makes photography more accessible.

1921–22
Asahi Graph begins life as a supplement to the Sunday edition of *Asahi Shinbun* newspaper in Osaka. Photo magazines including *Camera* are also launched.

1923
The Great Kantō Earthquake devastates Tokyo and its surroundings. Photographers document the aftermath, while many magazines are forced to suspend or cease publication.

Konishi founds the Konishi Professional School of Photography (Konishi Shashin Senmon Gakkō), which today is part of Tokyo Polytechnic University.

1926
The All-Japan Association of Photographic Societies (AJAPS, Zennihon Shashin Renmei) is founded, merging the All-Kansai Association of Photographic Societies from Osaka and the surrounding area and the All-Kantō Association from around Tokyo. AJAPS is supported by the Asahi Newspaper Company and sponsors photography competitions.

Asahi Camera, the oldest surviving monthly photography magazine in Japan, is launched. It introduces the work of international photographers, for example László Moholy-Nagy and Man Ray, to Japan.

A group of young experimental photographers found the collective New Photography Research Society (Shinkō Shashin Kenkyūkai).

1931–32
The Manchurian Incident, a staged explosion at a Japanese railway line in Manchuria that is engineered by Japanese military personnel, leads to Japan's invasion of northeastern China.

The photography section of the 'Internationale Ausstellung, "Film und Foto"', organized by Deutscher Werkbund, is exhibited in Tokyo and Osaka.

1933
Natori Yōnosuke (who practised journalistic photography in Germany before returning to Japan), Kimura Ihei, Ina Nobuo and Hara Hiromu co-found the Japan Studio (Nippon Kōbō).

1934
The magazine *Nippon* is launched by Nippon Kōbō, publicizing Japanese culture to other countries and promoting Natori Yōnosuke's photojournalism.

1937-8
The Marco Polo Bridge incident sets off the Sino-Japanese War. The Japanese army overruns Northern China and Nanking falls.

Photography begins to promote surrealism and abstraction. Avant-garde photography becomes popular, with collectives like the Avant-Garde Image Group (Avant-Garde Zōei Shūdan) and the Avant-Garde Photography Association (Zen'ei Shashin Kyōkai).

1941–45
In 1941, Japan bombs Pearl Harbor and declares war on the US and Great Britain. During the Pacific War, the Japanese Home Office bans the English language and Western music, and photography is used for propaganda. In 1945, the US begins to firebomb Japanese cities intensively. The atomic bombing of Hiroshima on 6 August 1945 kills approximately 150,000 people, either instantly or gradually over the following months. The bombing of Nagasaki three days later kills over 75,000 people. Buildings are destroyed or heavily damaged, turning the cities into atomic wastelands. Japan unconditionally surrenders and the war ends. The American occupying forces impose censorship, prohibiting photographs of the bombed cities.

1946
A revival of art exhibitions begins with the first Japan Art Academy (Nitten) exhibition, held by the Ministry of Education. Post-war photography is dominated by realism and photojournalism.

1949
Nihon University opens a Department of Photography in its College of Art. Graduates will later include Watanabe Hiroshi, Takanashi Yutaka, Kitai Kazuo and photography critic Iizawa Kōtarō.

1950
The Korean War begins. Japan provides ample support to the logistics of the US campaign. Mass firearms orders from the US help Japan's economy to increase rapidly.

The Japan Professional Photographers Society (Nihon Shashinka Kyōkai) is founded; Kimura Ihei becomes its first president.

1951
Japan signs the San Francisco Peace Treaty.

Nippon Camera magazine is launched, featuring photographs by established and promising photographers and organizing a monthly contest.

The avant-garde collective Experimental Workshop (Jikken Kōbō) is established; it comprises artists, photographers, designers, composers and choreographers and is based around the fusion of different disciplines. The Democratic Artists' Association, with artists such as Ei Kyū, is also formed.

Large exhibitions organized by the *Yomiuri* newspaper begin to present European art, for example by Henri Matisse.

1952
The San Francisco Peace Treaty officially ends the US post-war occupation of Japan; anti-American sentiment begins to grow.

The Photographic Society of Japan (Nihon Shashin Kyōkai) is founded, supporting competitions, exhibitions and the publication of periodicals.

1953–54
NHK begins TV broadcasting in Japan.

The first 'Nippon-ten' exhibition opens, presenting early works of 'reportage painting'.

Konishiroku Photo Gallery opens its first space, in Ginza, Tokyo.

In the Kansai area, the Gutai Art Association is formed around artists Yoshihara Jirō and Shimamoto Shōzo. Gutai means 'concrete' and represents the artists' direct engagement with materials. Gutai seeks to break down the barriers between art and everyday life, experimenting with new materials, performance and theatrical events.

Subjektive Fotografie, first advocated by German photographer Otto Steinert, is introduced to Japan in journals such as *Camera*.

1956
Japan joins the UN.

The Japan Subjective Photography League (Nihon Shūkanshugi Shashin Renmei) is established. The Takashimaya department store in Nihonbashi, Tokyo, presents the 'First International Subjective Photography Exhibition' with works by eighty photographers.

1957–59
Hosoe Eikoh, Kawada Kikuji, Narahara Ikkō, Satō Akira, Tanno Akira and Tōmatsu Shōmei participate in the 'Eyes of Ten' (*Jūnin no me*) exhibition at Konishiroku Photo Gallery. Two years later, they co-found the photographers' group Vivo. Although dissolved after two years the collective is very influential, representing a newly subjective, expressive style.

1958
The Tokyo College of Photography (Tōkyō Sōgō Shashin Senmon Gakkō) opens in Nakano, Tokyo. A few years later it is moved to Yokohama. It has become one of the most acknowledged photography colleges in Japan, producing graduates such as Shinoyama Kishin, Suda Issei and Tsuchida Hiromi.

1960
Japan experiences political upheaval. After a revised Treaty of Mutual Cooperation and Security (*Sōgo Kyōryoku oyobi Anzen Hoshō Jōyaku*, abbreviated as *Anpo*) is signed with the US, it becomes the subject of heated debate and students' protests. One argument against the treaty is article 6, which allows the US to use military forces and facilities in Japan for combat purposes other than the defence of Japan. This is seen as a threat to Japan's sovereign power. Millions of people participate in *Anpo* demonstrations and strikes; photographers such as Kitai Kazuo document these.

1962–63
Japan becomes the largest producer of cameras worldwide. Tokyo continues to grow and its population breaks 10 million.

1964–65
Tokyo hosts the Olympic Games and the Tōkaidō bullet train line opens.

Araki Nobuyoshi is awarded the first Taiyō Award for his *Sachin* series.

Kawada Kikuji publishes the photobook *The Map* (*Chizu*).

1967
The Japan Photographic Academy (Nihon Shashin Gakuen) opens in Iidabashi, Tokyo. It will teach photography until 2005, when it closes due to a decrease in student enrolment.

Moriyama Daidō receives the Newcomer's Award by the Japan Photo Critics Association for his photographs in *Camera Mainichi*. In the following year, he publishes the photobook

Japan: A Photo Theater (*Nippon Gekijōshashinchō*).

The Pentax Camera Museum opens in Nishi Azabu, Tokyo.

1968–69
Moriyama joins Nakahira Takuma, Takanashi Yutaka, Okada Takahiko and Taki Kōji, who have co-founded the photography magazine *Provoke*. It is subtitled 'provocative materials for thought', and seeks to give experimental photography and photo theory a platform, overriding the conventions of modern photography. The magazine is discontinued in 1969; the name *Provoke*, however, remains associated with the photographers as a collective.

Narahara Ikkō is awarded the Mainichi Art Award for his photobook *Europe: Where Time has Stopped* and is also presented the Award of Arts by the Minister of Education.

Nikon Salon opens at Ginza, Tokyo.

1970
The Osaka World Exposition brings international artists to Japan. The 10th Tokyo Biennale 'Between Man and Matter', at the Tokyo Metropolitan Art Museum, introduces conceptual, post-minimal and performance art to a wider audience. For Japanese artists, the World Exposition and the Biennale provide rare opportunities to exchange ideas and experiences with their Western contemporaries.

Hosoe Eikoh receives the Award of Arts from the Minister of Education for his *Kamaitachi* series.

The Osaka University of the Arts establishes a photography department.

1971
The tenth 'Contemporary Japanese Art Exhibition' opens at the Tokyo Metropolitan Art Museum, exhibiting photographs by Moriyama Daidō, Nakahira Takuma, Naitō Masatoshi

and Takanashi Yutaka. It is the first time photography is included in the exhibition.

1973
The oil embargo proclaimed by the Organization of Arab Petroleum Exporting Countries hits Japan hard. The oil crisis becomes a major factor in shifting Japan's economy away from oil-intensive industries.

The photography gallery Canon Salon opens in Ginza, Tokyo.

1974
John Szarkowski and Yamagishi Shōji co-curate the 'New Japanese Photography' exhibition at the Museum of Modern Art, New York. It features 187 photographs and is the first exhibition dedicated to contemporary Japanese photography outside Japan.

Araki Nobuyoshi, Fukase Masahisa, Moriyama Daidō, Tōmatsu Shōmei and others set up the small avant-garde photography school The Workshop.

1975–77
After Kimura Ihei's death, the Kimura Ihei Award is established, becoming the most prestigious photography award in Japan. The first award is given to Kitai Kazuo in 1975, for *To the Village*.

Minolta Photo Space, Photo Gallery Prism, Image Shop Camp and Photo Gallery Put all open in Tokyo.

Tōmatsu Shōmei receives the Mainichi Art Award and the Award of Arts from the Minister of Education.

In 1976, photographer Shinoyama Kishin represents Japan at the 37th Venice Biennale.

The 'Contemporary Japanese Photography Exhibition' opens at the Graz Municipal Art Museum, featuring works by Hosoe Eikoh, Kawada Kikuji, Moriyama Daidō, Suda Issei and Tōmatsu Shōmei, among others. The exhibition is organized in two parts: the first

exhibition in 1976 is followed by a second show a year later.

1978
Zeit-Foto Salon gallery opens in Nihonbashi, Tokyo. It becomes an important exhibition space for photography and will continue until 2017.

Ishiuchi Miyako receives the Kimura Ihei Award for her *Apartment* series.

1979
Photo Gallery International (PGI), Olympus Gallery and Nagase Photo Salon open in Tokyo.

The International Center of Photography in New York presents the exhibition 'Japan: A Self-Portrait', including photographs by Fukase Masahisa, Kawada Kikuji, Narahara Ikko, Tōmatsu Shōmei and Suda Issei.

1981–83
Hamaya Hiroshi wins the Japan Art Grand Prix. When he is offered the Award of Arts by the Minister of Education in 1982, he declines, arguing that the government should not judge arts.

The Dōmon Ken Award is established after the photographer's death. A Dōmon Ken museum in Yamagata Prefecture follows in 1983; it is Japan's first museum devoted to photography.

1984
The Picture Photo Space gallery, specializing in original prints, opens in Osaka.

1985
Japan's economy grows steadily. At the height of a three-decade long 'economic miracle', new museums and spaces for art and photography are planned throughout the 1980s.

'Black Sun: The Eyes of Four' opens at the Museum of Modern Art, Oxford, featuring works by Hosoe Eikoh, Fukase Masahisa, Moriyama Daidō and Tōmatsu Shōmei. It travels to London and Philadelphia.

Camera Mainichi ceases publication. In the following years, other magazines are also discontinued. Photographers turn to photobooks as a way of disseminating their work and the number of prints on the art market begins to increase.

1986–87
Hamaya Hiroshi is awarded the Master of Photography Award by the International Center of Photography in New York, and the prestigious Hasselblad Award.

1988
The Kawasaki City Museum is established, with the first photography collection in a Japanese art museum.

1989
The Higashikawa Photography Museum is established in Hokkaido. The Yokohama Museum of Art opens, collecting and displaying photographs alongside other art media. A number of gallery and museum exhibitions dedicated to photography are organised all over Japan, celebrating the 150th anniversary of the birth of photography.

Sugimoto Hiroshi wins the Mainichi Art Award.

1990
The Tokyo Metropolitan Museum of Photography opens in a temporary space.

Watanabe Yoshio is the first photographer to be awarded the title 'Man of Cultural Distinction' by the government.

1991
The Japan Society for the Arts and History of Photography (Nihon Shashin Geijutsu Gakkai) is established; it is the first scholarly organization dedicated to research on photography.

1992
The collapse of the economic 'bubble', in which real estate and stock market prices in Japan were greatly inflated, leads to decades of economic stagnation.

The Irie Taikichi Memorial Museum of Photography Nara City and the Midorikawa Yōichi Photography Museum are established.

Araki Nobuyoshi's retrospective 'Akt–Tokyo 1971–1992' opens at Forum Stadtpark in Graz, before travelling through Europe. Numerous exhibitions and photobooks soon make him one of the best-known, most exhibited Japanese photographers in the international art world.

The Photographers Gallery, London, presents 'The Contemporary Japanese Photographers Exhibition', featuring Hatakeyama Naoya, Ishiuchi Miyako, Kon Michiko and others.

1993
Morimura Yasumasa is nominated for the Kimura Ihei Award for his self-portrait photographs, leading to a debate among the jury as to whether his work could be considered 'photography' or not. In the end, the majority argue that his work is fine art and does not qualify. Toyohara Yasuhisa wins the photography award.

1994
Taka Ishii Gallery opens in Tokyo, with an exhibition programme devoted to contemporary photography and representing Japanese photographers internationally.

1995
An earthquake with a magnitude of 7.2 strikes the city of Kobe and its vicinity. It kills over 5,000 people and destroys more than 100,000 homes and buildings. Artists such as Miyamoto Ryūji and Yoneda Tomoko photograph the aftermath.

The Tokyo Metropolitan Museum of Photography inaugurates its permanent building in Ebisu and hosts the first 'Tokyo International Photo-Biennale'. The Kiyosato Museum of Photographic Arts opens in Nagano Prefecture, with photographer Hosoe Eikoh as its founding director. In the same year, a museum dedicated to Ueda Shōji's work

opens in Tottori. Photography becomes more recognized by art museums; exhibitions in and outside Japan and the interaction between Japanese museums and overseas institutions begin to increase. The exhibition 'Photography and Beyond in Japan: Space, Time and Memory', organized by the Hara Museum of Contemporary Art, Tokyo, opens in Tokyo before travelling to Mexico City, Vancouver, Los Angeles, Washington, Denver and Honolulu.

Hiromix wins the 11th New Cosmos of Photography contest, sponsored by Canon. Young women's photography rises to prominence and soon prompts the term 'girls' photography' (*onnanoko shashin*).

1996
The Yokohama International Photo Festival '96 presents exhibitions at different venues in the city.

Ueda Shōji is awarded a French Chevaliers des Arts et des Lettres.

1997
Hamaya Hiroshi is the first Japanese photographer to win honorary membership of the Royal Photographic Society of England.

Kunsthalle Wien organizes the photography exhibition 'Japanische Photographie: Lust und Leere', featuring twelve artists including Araki Nobuyoshi, Hatakeyama Naoya, Mori Mariko, Morimura Yasumasa and Yanagi Miwa.

2001
Hiromix, Nagashima Yurie and Ninagawa Mika share the Kimura Ihei Award.

Sugimoto Hiroshi receives the prestigious Hasselblad Award.

2002
Kawauchi Rinko wins the Kimura Ihei Award.

2003
A large-scale photography exhibition, 'History of Japanese Photography',

opens at the Museum of Fine Arts, Houston, accompanied by an extensive catalogue.

2004
Sawada Tomoko receives the Kimura Ihei Award for her self-portraits in costumes; the jury begins to value artistic concepts as much as photojournalistic qualities.

2005
Ishiuchi Miyako represents Japan at the 51st Venice Biennale with the series *Mother's*, commissioned by Kasahara Michiko, chief curator at the Tokyo Metropolitan Museum of Photography.

Emon Photo Gallery opens in Hiroo, Tokyo.

2006
Takano Ryūdai wins the Kimura Ihei Award for *In my Room*.

Michael Hoppen gallery, which opened in London in 1992, begins to focus on 20th-century Japanese photography, introducing many photographers and estates to the European market.

2007–8
A large retrospective of Sugimoto Hiroshi's work opens at Kunstsammlung Nordrhein-Westfalen, Düsseldorf, before travelling to Museum der Moderne Salzburg, Neue Nationalgalerie, Berlin and Kunstmuseum Luzern.

2009
Yanagi Miwa represents Japan at the Venice Biennale with *Windswept Women: The Old Girls' Troupe*, featuring photographs and a video installation.

Zen Foto Gallery opens in Tokyo, specializing in Chinese and Japanese photography.

2011
The Tōhoku earthquake and tsunami result in a nuclear accident at the Fukushima Daiichi Nuclear Power Plant and the spread of radioactive contamination. Photographers such

as Hatakeyama Naoya, Ōmori Katsumi and Tsuchida Hiromi all produce work concerned with the catastrophe.

'Japan: A Self-Portrait, Photographs 1945–1964', curated by Marc Feustel and the Japan Foundation, begins to travel through North America and Western Europe.

2012
A double retrospective, 'William Klein + Daido Moriyama', opens at Tate Modern, London. The Photographers Gallery dedicates an exhibition to 'Contemporary Japanese Photobooks'.

2013
The Art Institute of Chicago opens the exhibition 'Shomei Tōmatsu: Island Life' shortly after Tōmatsu has passed away.

The annual photography festival Kyotographie, in Kyoto, is organized for the first time.

2014
Ishiuchi Miyako becomes the first female Japanese photographer to be awarded the Hasselblad Award.

In Tokyo, the Daikanyama Photo Fair is organized. Akio Nagasawa Gallery/ Publishing, specializing in Japanese photography and photobooks, opens its first space in Ginza.

2015
The Prix Pictet Japan Award is created to celebrate early to mid-career Japanese photographers whose work carries strong messages on global sustainability.

2015–16
The J. Paul Getty Museum in Los Angeles presents a large-scale retrospective of Ishiuchi's work, 'Ishiuchi Miyako: Postwar Shadows', together with the exhibition 'The Younger Generation: Contemporary Japanese Photography'.

'Pale Pink and Light Blue: Japanese Photography from the Meiji Period' is shown at the Museum für Fotografie,

Staatliche Museen zu Berlin, presenting photographs from different collections of the national museums in Berlin.

The Museum of Fine Art, Boston, exhibits photographs concerned with the tsunami and nuclear accident in Fukushima in 2011, in a show titled 'In the Wake: Japanese Photographers respond to 3/11'.

In Antwerp, IBASHO gallery opens its doors, showing Japanese photography ranging from works by well-known photographers to younger artists.

2016–17
After two years of renovation, the Tokyo Metropolitan Museum of Photography reopens under the new name Tokyo Photographic Art Museum (TOP). The first exhibition is 'Hiroshi Sugimoto: Lost Human Genetic Archive'. Sugimoto is also given an exhibition at Foam Fotografiemuseum, Amsterdam.

The exhibition 'Provoke' opens at the Albertina, Vienna, travelling to Winterthur, Paris and Chicago. The accompanying catalogue presents important Japanese writings on photography in English for the first time, including texts by Hamaya Hiroshi, Nakahira Takuma, Taki Kōji, and Tōmatsu Shōmei.

'Yokohama 1868–1912', at the Museum für Angewandte Kunst, Frankfurt, exhibits photographs from the Meiji era together with woodblock prints.

Young photographer Yokota Daisuke wins the Foam Paul Huf Award in Amsterdam.

2018
The Museum der Moderne Salzburg opens a series of exhibitions dedicated to its large holdings of Japanese photography from the 1960s and '70s. The first show, 'I-Photo', focusses on the depiction of humans.

2019
Moriyama Daidō wins the Hasselblad Award.

2020–22
Following the worldwide spread of the COVID-19 disease, the Government of Japan closes its borders for travellers. The 2020 Tokyo Summer Olympics is postponed to 2021 and mostly held behind closed doors with no public spectators permitted. Due to the pandemic, photography exhibitions and publications are cancelled or postponed worldwide.

In 2021, the Ashmolean Museum Oxford exhibits Japanese photography alongside works in other artistic media in a transhistorical exhibition, 'Tokyo: Art & Photography'. In Paris, the Maison Européene de la Photographie stages the exhibition 'Moriyama – Tomatsu: Tokyo'. In Vienna, the Albertina Modern dedicates a major exhibition to the work of Araki Nobuyoshi.

In 2022, Stills Centre for Photography in Edinburgh hosts the first solo exhibition of Ishiuchi Miyako in the UK.

2023–24
Kawauchi Rinko wins the Sony World Outstanding Contribution Photography Award 2023.

A retrospective exhibition of Moriyama Daidō opens at Instituto Moreira Salles (IMS), Sao Paulo, before travelling to C/O Berlin and to The Photographers Gallery, London.

The Hayward Gallery, London dedicates a major survey exhibition to the work of Sugimoto Hiroshi, titled 'Hiroshi Sugimoto: Time Machine'.

Anzaï Shigeo (b. 1939 in Kanagawa Prefecture, d. 2020) began his artistic practice as a self-taught painter. He moved towards photography in the late 1960s, documenting artworks, exhibitions – including the 10th Tokyo Biennale 1970 – and avant-garde artists in their original contexts. Anzaï established himself as the foremost photographer of the art movement Mono-ha ('The School of Things'), which emerged in the early 1970s. Numerous early Mono-ha installations, including works by Lee Ufan and Suga Kishio, survive today only in Anzaï's photographs. However, his photographs are not only historical documents but also carefully composed artworks in their own right, which have been exhibited regularly since 1968. His work is held in collections such as the Tokyo Photographic Art Museum and M+, Hong Kong.

Araki Nobuyoshi (b. 1940 in Tokyo) graduated from Chiba University, where he studied film and photography, in 1963. While working at the advertising agency Dentsu, he received attention for his photographs of a young boy and his friends, portraying their lives in a run-down apartment block not far from Araki's home in Tokyo. In 1964, Araki was awarded the first Taiyō Award for this series, entitled *Sachin*. His diaristic approach has defined his photography since the 1970s. One of his most important photobooks is *Sentimental Journey* (1971), which records his honeymoon. In *Winter Journey* (1991), the viewer witnesses his last days with his terminally ill wife, her funeral and his lonely return home. Having published over 500 photobooks and exhibited his works worldwide, Araki's photographic practice is inextricably intertwined with his personal life, and he has been a prominent figure in international photography for decades. In 2012, he received the Mainichi Art Award. Araki's work is exhibited internationally and included in collections such as the San Francisco Museum of Modern Art, and Tate, London.

Hatakeyama Naoya (b. 1958 in Iwate Prefecture) studied painting at Tsukuba University and has lived and worked in Tokyo since the late 1970s. In 1978 he met Ōtsuji Kiyoji, a leading figure in the avant-garde collective Jikken Kōbō (Experimental Workshop), who inspired him to take up photography. Hatakeyama completed postgraduate studies under Ōtsuji's tuition in 1984. Since then, his use of photography to explore the relationship of humanity to landscapes and cityscapes has earned him a reputation as one of the most important photographers in Japan. He received the 1996 Kimura Ihei Award and the 2003 Photographer of the Year Award from the Photographic Society of Japan. Together with sound art by Fujimoto Yukio and installations by Nakamura Masato, Hatakeyama's photographs represented Japan at the Venice Biennale in 2001. His works are held in collections internationally, ranging from the Museum of Modern Art, Osaka to Tate, London.

Hiromix (b. 1976 in Tokyo) began photography as a middle-school student. She rose to prominence in 1995, when she won first prize at the 'New Cosmos of Photography' exhibition. Her photographs offered a light-hearted look into her everyday life, and in 1996 she published the photobook *Girls Blue*, followed by *Hiromix* two years later. Her work prompted the term 'girls' photography' (*onnanoko shashin*), which was promoted by magazines, exhibitions and TV programmes. In 2001, she shared the Kimura Ihei Award with Nagashima Yurie and Ninagawa Mika.

Hosoe Eikoh (b. 1933 in Yamagata Prefecture) is one of Japan's most influential photographers. He graduated from the Tokyo College of Photography in 1954 and began his career working for magazines. In 1959, he co-founded the photographers' collective Vivo. His best-known series is probably *Ordeal by Roses (Barakei)* (1961), which features the writer, actor and nationalist Mishima Yukio. Hosoe collaborated with *butoh* dancer Hijikata Tatsumi on an equally striking series, *Kamaitachi* (1968). Both series present his cinematic aesthetic, his interest in the human body and his collaborative practice, linking dance or acting with photography. He co-founded the photography school The Workshop in 1974 and returned to the Tokyo College of Photography as a professor one year later. He has taught international workshops and became founding director of the Kiyosato Museum of Photographic Arts in 1995. In 2003, Hosoe received the Royal Photographic Society's 150th anniversary medal. He has also received multiple other awards, including the title Japanese Person of Cultural Merit (2010). Hosoe's work is represented in collections worldwide, including the Museum of Modern Art, New York, and the Victoria & Albert Museum, London.

Ishiuchi Miyako (b. 1947 in Gunma Prefecture) lives and works in Kanazawa Prefecture. She studied design and weaving at Tama Art University but eventually stopped attending. Ishiuchi took up photography at the age of twenty-eight, and in 1977 she revisited her hometown, Yokosuka, recording the US Navy town with a handheld camera. This *Yokosuka Story* series was the beginning of a long career that led to her winning the Kimura Ihei Award in 1979, the Photographic Society of Japan's Lifetime Achievement Award in 2006 and the Hasselblad Award in 2014. Ishiuchi is one of the few female photographers who has been active in the male-dominated field of Japanese photography since the 1970s. In 2005, her series *Mother's* represented Japan at the Venice Biennale. Ishiuchi's work has been concerned with motifs ranging from deserted bordellos to the belongings of Frida Kahlo, but one topic has stayed relevant: the visual effects of time and decay, intertwined with human memory. Ishiuchi's work is held in collections such as the J. Paul Getty Museum, LA and Yokohama Museum of Art.

Izima Kaoru (b. 1954 in Kyoto) studied at the Tokyo College of Photography; he lives and works in Tokyo. After working as an assistant to photographer Kobayashi Akira, he travelled America, taking photographs that he exhibited at the Ginza Nikon Salon, in 1977. During his twenties and thirties, Izima's income depended on music and fashion photography, film and TV work. He first received attention in the European art world with his *Landscapes with a Corpse* series, begun in 1993. The series presents elaborately staged, professionally shot 'death' scenes featuring (mostly female, Japanese) film stars and models. The photographs were initially published in Izima's alternative fashion magazine *Zyappu*, and simultaneously reference fashion and tabloid photography, crime scene photography and art history. His photographs are held in collections such as the Musée d'Art Moderne Grand-Duc Jean, Luxembourg.

Kawada Kikuji (b. 1933 in Ibaraki Prefecture) is a seminal figure in post-war Japanese photography. He lives and works in Tokyo. After graduating in Economics from Rikkyō University, he began his career as a photographer at Shinchosha Publishing. In 1959 he co-founded the photographers' collective Vivo. Kawada is best known for his first major photobook, *The Map (Chizu)* (1965), which addresses the scars of post-war Japan in symbolic, expressive photographs. It is often cited as the most innovative photobook to come out of Japan. In 1996, Kawada received the Photographic Society of Japan's annual award and in 2011, he was awarded their Lifetime Achievement Award. His work is held in collections worldwide, including the Museum of Modern Art, New York, Tokyo National Museum of Modern Art and Tate, London.

Kawauchi Rinko (b. 1972 in Shiga Prefecture) graduated from Seian University of Art and Design in 1993 before starting work in a photography studio. She lives and works in Tokyo. Kawauchi first received attention when she published the photobooks *Utatane, Hanabi* and *Hanako* in 2001. She won the Kimura Ihei Award in 2002. Since then, her serene, poetic images of ordinary motifs have been compiled into multiple photobooks, which have been popular worldwide. Kawauchi's photography is represented in international collections from the Museu de Arte Moderna de São Paulo to the San Francisco Museum of Modern Art.

Kitai Kazuo (b. 1944 in Anshan, Manchuria) returned to Tokyo with his family at the end of the Second World War. He began documenting student protests while studying photography at the Nihon University College of Art from 1963 to 1965. In 1965, he self-published the photobook *Teikou/Resistance*, which investigated the protests in Yokosuka. In 1968, he photographed the demonstrations at Nihon University from inside the barricades, showing his own political stance. The photographs were published in *Asahi Graph* magazine. A year later, Kitai turned his camera to the village of Sanrizuka, where farmers were demonstrating against the building of Narita airport. Following this, he decided to focus on everyday rural life, and in 1975 his series *To the Village (Mura-e)* won him the first Kimura Ihei award. In 2013, he received the Great Artist Award from the Photographic Society of Japan. Kitai's work is represented in collections such as the Tokyo Photographic Art Museum.

Morimura Yasumasa (b. 1951 in Osaka) graduated from the Kyoto City University of Art in 1978 and has been active as an artist ever since, living and working in Osaka. His practice encompasses a variety of media, focusing on photography, and is often concerned with questions of identity in the contexts of gender and nationality. Appropriating iconic images from art history, popular culture and politics, he draws attention to concepts of originality and imitation. Since showing in the Aperto section of the Venice Biennale in 1988, Morimura has exhibited widely. He has received multiple awards, including the Purple Ribbon Medal of Honour by the Government of Japan in 2011. In 2014, he was artistic director of the Yokohama Triennale. Morimura's work is held in collections such as the Queensland Art Gallery, Brisbane, and Tate, London.

Moriyama Daidō (b. 1938 in Ikeda) was a graphic designer before shifting to photography. He apprenticed in the studio of photographer Iwamiya Takeji and moved to Tokyo in 1961, assisting the Vivo collective. He became Hosoe Eikoh's personal assistant after the dissolution of Vivo. A major member of the *Provoke* journal (1968–69), Moriyama is known for a grainy and subjective style that combines formal innovation with a sense of social awareness, inspired by William Klein's street photography, Andy Warhol's silk screen disasters and the work of his precursor Tōmatsu Shōmei. Since publishing his first photobook *Japan: A Photo Theater* (*Nippon Gekijōshashinchō*). in 1968, which radically eschewed documentary stories or themes, Moriyama has been one of the most prolific photographers in Japan. The idea of 'equivalence' is central to his work: photography does not aim to represent a coherent context, but exists in its own right. Moriyama's work has been exhibited widely and is held in collections worldwide, ranging from the Metropolitan Museum of Art, New York, to Tate, London.

Nagashima Yurie (b. 1973 in Tokyo) rose to prominence while still a student, by winning the 1993 Parco emerging artists Prize for her portraits of herself and her family, naked. The works are concerned with ideas of family, gender and the female body. Two years later, Nagashima graduated from Musashino Art University. Promoted like a celebrity as part of the 'girls' photography' trend, Nagashima decided to leave Japan in 1997. She attended the California Institute of the Arts, graduating with an MFA in photography in 1999. After returning to Tokyo, she shared the 2001 Kimura Ihei Award with Hiromix and Ninagawa Mika. Nagashima has continued to investigate issues of gender and personal conflict in her artistic practice, working with other artistic media as well as photography. Her work can be found in collections such as the Tokyo Photographic Art Museum.

Ninagawa Mika (b. 1972 in Tokyo) began to study graphic design at Tama Art University in 1993. She submitted her photographs to open exhibitions and won first prize at the 'New Cosmos of Photography' exhibition in 1996, graduating from university a year later. In 2001, she received the Kimura Ihei Award for two photobooks: *Sugar and Spice*, which featured her commercial work, and *Pink Rose Suite*, a collection of her art and snapshot photography. She shared the award with Hiromix and Nagashima Yurie. Since then, Ninagawa has been successful in both her commercial and artistic work, focusing on photography and film. Her photographs have been exhibited internationally and are represented in collections such as the Tokyo Photographic Art Museum and Toyota Art Collection.

Nomura Sakiko (b. 1967 in Shimonoseki) graduated from the photography department of Kyushu Sangyo University. She began her career in Tokyo in 1991, as the assistant of Araki Nobuyoshi, and has continued working in his studio ever since. Nomura's practice as a photographer is characterized by a dark, grainy style, focusing on motifs that she encounters in her everyday life, with a repeated interest in the (mostly male) nude. Her photographic subjects are presented in a tender, intimate way. She works in both colour and black and white, and has experimented with photographic and printing techniques in series' such as *Another Black Darkness* (2016). Nomura's works are held in collections including the Tokyo Photographic Art Museum and Tate, London.

Ōmori Katsumi (b. 1963 in Kobe) studied at Nihon University College of Art before doing commercial work, for example as a lighting assistant at Studio Ebisu and a magazine photographer. In 1992, he began touring with the French band Mano Negra, taking photographs of their performances as well as street photographs in Latin America. He created his first portfolio from this work, and in 1994, Robert Frank chose him as winner of the New Cosmos of Photography award. Ōmori currently lives and works in Chiba. He is best known internationally for the conceptual series *Everything happens for the first time*, created after the 2011 Tōhoku earthquake and the resultant nuclear accident at Fukushima Daiichi Nuclear Power Plant. Driving towards Fukushima, Ōmori photographed the blooming cherry trees on the way. His work can be found in collections such as the Tokyo Photographic Art Museum.

Sawada Tomoko (b. 1977 in Kobe) joined the media design class at Seian University in 1996, and graduated in Photography in 2000. Her work is mostly based on self-portraits in which she changes her appearance through costumes, hair, make-up, facial expressions and even by gaining and losing weight, critically raising questions about gender and social identity. She received the Kimura Ihei Award in 2004; as the first winning artist who did not press the camera's shutter herself, she represented a change in the award's value system. Sawada's work is exhibited widely and represented in collections such as the International Center of Photography, New York, and the National Museum of Modern Art, Kyoto.

Shibata Toshio (b. 1949 in Tokyo) studied oil painting at the Tokyo National University of Fine Arts and Music, graduating with an MFA in 1974. He continued his studies at the Royal Academy in Ghent, and changed his focus to photography. After his return to Tokyo, he began to photograph deserted Japanese cityscapes and landscapes. Shibata's work has drawn attention to human interventions across the country, showing dams, bridges and other constructions as part of the landscape, conveying an almost abstract aesthetic. In 1992, he received the Kimura Ihei Award. After working in black and white, he switched to colour photography in 2005–6. He has taught at Tsukuba University and Tokyo College of Photography and his work is exhibited and held in museums worldwide, including the Tokyo Photographic Art Museum.

Shiga Lieko (b. 1980 in Aichi Prefecture) studied at the Chelsea College of Art and Design in London, graduating in 2004 with a BA in New Media. Series like *Lilly* (2002–5) and *Canary* (2006) represent her typically surreal and uncanny worlds, created by using simple photographic techniques. Shiga received the 2008 Kimura Ihei Award and the 2009 Infinity Award (Young Photographer) from the International Center of Photography, New York. She lives and works in Miyagi. Her work has been exhibited internationally and is represented in collections ranging from the Tokyo Photographic Art Museum to San Francisco Museum of Modern Art.

Suda Issei (b. 1940 in Tokyo, d. 2019) graduated from Tokyo College of Photography in 1962. He began his photographic career in 1967, taking photographs for Terayama Shūji's avant-garde film company Tenjō Sajiki for three years. Following this, Suda worked freelance, focusing on festivals across the country for his series *Fūshi Kaden* (1977). In 1997, he received the Dōmon Ken Award for *Human Memory* (*Ningen no kioku*). His photography often combines images of folklore, everyday life or ordinary street scenes with a mysterious, dark atmosphere. He has taught at Osaka University of Fine Arts and now lives in Chiba, continuing his photographic practice. Suda's work is held in collections such as the Tokyo Photographic Art Museum.

Takano Ryūdai (b. 1963 in Fukui Prefecture) graduated in Politics and Economics from Waseda University in 1987 before becoming a photographer. Living and working in Tokyo, he is best known for his tender portraits and compositions of the nude male body, such as the series *In my Room*, which won him the 2006 Kimura Ihei Award. Takano's work looks at a variety of male bodies from an aesthetic perspective. His photographs can be found in collections such as the Kawasaki City Museum and Shanghai Art Museum.

Tokyo Rumando (b. 1980 in Tokyo) had a career in modelling, including work in fetish and nude photography, before becoming a photographer in 2005. Most of her staged photographs are of herself, and raise questions around identity. In *Rest 3000 Stay 5000* (2012), Rumando immersed herself in the world of love hotels, visiting hotels in and around Tokyo to create narrative scenes. In her following project, *Orphée* (2012–14), she transformed herself into different characters linked to her past, using a mirror. The series has been exhibited worldwide, including at Tate Modern, London, in the 'Performing for the Camera' exhibition in 2016. Rumando has also worked with polaroid photography.

Tsuchida Hiromi (b. 1939) studied chemistry at the University of Fukui and worked at a make-up company before enrolling at Tokyo College of Photography in 1965. When Tsuchida turned thirty, he began to focus on photography full time. He travelled through rural areas across Japan to photograph ordinary people, traditional festivals and religious rituals. In 1976, this work was published in the photobook *Zokushin*. Tsuchida is best known for his work recording historic traces of the atomic bombing of Hiroshima, a theme that he has revisited repeatedly in series such as *Hiroshima Collection* (1995). He has taught at Tokyo College of Photography and has received multiple awards, including the 2008 Dōmon Ken Award. His work is represented in collections worldwide, such as the Tokyo Photographic Art Museum and Tate, London.

Yoneda Tomoko (b. 1965 in Hyogo Prefecture) left Japan to study at the University of Illinois, where she discovered her interest in photography and graduated with a BFA and the faculty award in 1989. She then moved to London, graduating from the Royal College of Art with an MA in 1991. Yoneda divides her time between London and Helsinki. Her work is mostly concerned with the history and memories associated with places and things, recording their visible and invisible traces worldwide. Her work has been exhibited widely, and Yoneda has received multiple commissions and awards. Her photographs can be found in collections internationally, including the Museum of Fine Arts, Houston, and Queensland Art Gallery, Brisbane.

Yoshiyuki Kōhei (b. 1946 in Hiroshima Prefecture, d. 2022) studied photography at an evening school, working during the day. After graduating, he moved to Tokyo and worked for a photography shop, printing photographs. Today he lives and works close to Tokyo. Yoshiyuki is best known for his series *The Park (Kōen)* (1972–80), which documents couples in parks in Tokyo at night, often with spectators around them. He mostly used handheld infrared cameras. The series attracted much attention in *Camera Mainichi* and was exhibited at Komai Gallery in 1979. Works from *The Park* are held in collections worldwide, including the Museum of Modern Art, New York, and Swedish Art Council, Stockholm.

Endnotes

1 Recent shows outside of Japan include: 'I-Photo: Japanese Photography 1960s–1970s from the collection', Museum der Moderne, Salzburg (2018)
'Araki. Tokyo', Pinakothek der Moderne, Munich (2017–18)
'Japanorama: New visions on art since 1970', Centre Pompidou-Metz, Paris (2017–18)
'Provoke', Albertina, Vienna; travelled to Winterthur, Paris and Chicago (2016–17)
'Mémoire et Lumière: Photographie Japonaise, 1950–2000', Maison Européenne de la Photographie, Paris (2016–17)
'Ishiuchi Miyako: Postwar Shadows', J. Paul Getty Museum, Los Angeles (2015–16)
'The Younger Generation: Contemporary Japanese Photography', J. Paul Getty Museum (2015–16)
'For a New World to Come: Experiments in Japanese Art and Photography 1968–1979', Museum of Fine Art, Houston (2015–16)
'Pale Pink and Light Blue: Japanese Photography from the Meiji Period', Staatliche Museen zu Berlin (2015–16)
'In the Wake: Japanese Photographers respond to 3/11', Museum of Fine Art, Boston (2015)
'ARAKI', Foam Fotografiemuseum, Amsterdam (2014–15)
'Japan: A Self-Portrait. Photographs 1945–1964', organized by the Japan Foundation; travelled through North America and Western Europe (2011–15)
'Girl with Parasol', National Museum, Denmark (2013–14)
'Shomei Tomatsu: Island Life', Art Institute of Chicago (2013–14)
'Japan's Modern Divide', J. Paul Getty Museum, Los Angeles (2013)
'William Klein + Daido Moriyama', Tate Modern, London (2012–13)
'Contemporary Japanese Photobooks', The Photographers' Gallery, London (2012)
'Rough, Blurred and Out of Focus', Art Institute of Chicago (2012)

2 I use 'West' and 'Western' as geographic terms and as a functional-notional category to refer to North America and Europe. They also reflect my subjective viewpoint as a 'Western European' writer.

3 Spielmann (1984), pp. 125–26.

4 *Ibid.*, p. 10.

5 Streiff (1993), p. 9.

6 Ishiuchi Miyako, interview with the author, 2 December 2008, at Meguro Art Museum, Tokyo.

7 Sawaragi Noi, 'An Anomaly called Bijutsu' (1992), in Munroe (1994), p. 389.

8 See: Bijutsu Techo (1989); Yamamoto (1991); Fuse (1991), p. 165; Mita (1994); Morimura (2001), p. 18; Kasahara (2002), p. 93.

9 See: The Light Factory (1994), p. 8; Bryson (1995), 74–79; Wright Jasinowski (2001); Abby Walton, 'East meets West, with a twist: The art of Morimura Yasumasa', *The Sophian* (published online 30 September 2004) ‹http://www.smithsophian.com/media/paper587/sections/20040930Arts.html› accessed 16 April 2016.

10 Iizawa Kōtarō, 'The Shock of the New: Early Photography in Japan', in Stearns (1994), pp. 39–40.

11 The Japan Photographic Society, originally founded in 1889, ceased to exist at the end of the 19th century, after its main sponsor declared bankruptcy. In 1924, another photographers' club with the same name was founded. This club has continued until today.

12 Quoted in Spielmann (1984), p. 244.

13 Yamamoto (1987), pp. 16–17.

14 Marc Feustel used this photograph as the opening image in his touring exhibition 'Japan: A Self-Portrait, Photographs 1945–1964'. See also Feustel (2009), pp. 10–23.

15 Fraser (2011), pp. 66–68.

16 Wilkes-Tucker et al (2003), pp. 211–12.

17 Fukagawa (2012), p. 466.

18 *Ibid.*

19 'In conversation with Kawada Kikuji', pp. 49–50.

20 Iizawa Kōtarō, 'The Evolution of Post-War Photography', in Wilkes-Tucker et al (2003), p. 217.

21 Tōmatsu Shōmei, 'I Am a King' (1972), tr. Lena Fritsch, in Dufour et al (2016), pp. 72–75.

22 Kawada (2005), unpaginated.

23 Mishima Yukio is also famed for his theatrical death at the Self-Defence Forces' headquarters in Tokyo. In 1970, after Mishima and other members of his right-wing militia had failed to inspire a coup to restore the Emperor's pre-war powers, the writer committed *seppuku* (suicide by disembowelment).

24 *Butoh* is an expressive dance form founded by Hijikata Tatsumi and Ohno Kazuo in 1959, as a reaction against the rigid contemporary dance scene. Incorporating both Western and Japanese elements, it is traditionally performed in white body make-up. It often features grotesque imagery, slow, controlled motion and taboo topics.

25 Baker and Moran (2016), p. 18.

26 Feustel (2010), unpaginated.

27 Rubinfien et al (2004), p. 53.

28 Quoted in Iizawa, in Wilkes-Tucker et al (2003), p. 216.

29 *Ibid.*, p. 217.

30 'In conversation with Kitai Kazuo', pp. 87–88.

31 Taki (2012), p. 67.

32 Nakahira Takuma, 'William Klein' (1967), tr. Lena Fritsch, in Dufour et al (2016), p. 365.

33 Shimizu (2012), p. 55.

34 *Ibid.*

35 Moriyama (1984), p. 227.

36 Fukagawa (2012), p. 465.

37 'Interview with Moriyama' (1972), p. 147.

38 Takanashi and Badger (2010), unpaginated.

39 'In conversation with Moriyama Daidō', pp. 85–86.

40 Quoted in Fukagawa (2012), 467.

41 Araki (1993), pp. 86–88.

42 'In conversation with Araki Nobuyoshi', pp. 97–98.

43 Fukase (2017), p. 143.

44 'In conversation with Ishiuchi Miyako', pp. 111–12.

45 Ishiuchi Miyako, 'Ningen to interia' [People and interiors] (1976), in Ishiuchi (2008), p. 267.

46 'In conversation with Yoshiyuki Kōhei', pp. 99–100.

47 'In conversation with Tsuchida Hiromi', pp. 123–24.

48 *Ibid.*

49 Iizawa (1999), p. 16.

50 Dana Friis-Hansen, 'Internationalization, Individualism, and the Institutionalization of Photography', in Wilkes-Tucker et al (2003), p. 272.

51 'In conversation with Hiromix', p. 144.

52 Yamamoto (1987), p. 17.

53 Kasahara (2001), pp. iii–iv.

54 Fukagawa Masafumi, interview, 26 December 2008, Kawasaki City Museum.

55 'In conversation with Shibata Toshio', pp. 179–80.

56 'In conversation with Hatakeyama Naoya', pp. 177–79.

57 Sugimoto Hiroshi, 'Seascapes' homepage ‹https://www.sugimotohiroshi.com/seascapes-1› accessed 14 August 2017.

58 Quoted in Tokyo Metropolitan Museum of Photography (2014), p. 51.

59 'In conversation with Izima Kaoru', pp. 215–16.

60 'In conversation with Hatakeyama Naoya', pp. 177–79.

61 See also work by Yamanaka Manabu or Itozaki Kimio, concerned with small dead animals.

62 'In conversation with Ishiuchi Miyako', pp. 111–12.

63 Sontag (1979), p. 15.

64 Barthes (1981), pp. 31–32.

65 See Fritsch (2014), pp. 137–41.

66 This is evident in Michel Foucault's analyses, which deal with the 'person' as a subject that constantly enters into new social and political relations. See *The Birth of the Clinic* (1963) or *Discipline and Punish* (1975).

67 Morimura (2003), p. 123.

68 The *manekineko* (beckoning cat) is a popular sign of good luck and fortune, and can be seen in the entrances of shops and restaurants.

69 Bryson (1995), p. 75.

70 Hasegawa (1997), p. 18.

71 'In conversation with Sawada Tomoko', pp. 213–14.

72 'In conversation with Tokyo Rumando', pp. 237–38.

73 Thompson (1984), p. 19.

74 Alice Schwarzer used Izima's *Shinohara Ryoko Wears Vivienne Westwood* (1996) as an example of 'misogynistic photography', reading the photographs of Shinohara lying 'dead' before the long row of urinals in a men's restroom as 'pornographic' in a manner similar to work by Helmut Newton and Araki Nobuyoshi. Schwarzer (2000), pp. 22–28.

75 Miller (2006), p. 37.

Further Reading

Araki, Nobuyoshi, 'Interviews: Purovōku ni shigeki sareta 'hitoridake no nanajūnen anpo' [Interviews: My solitary 1970 protest against the US-Japan Security Treaty provoked by *Provoke*], *déjà-vu*, 14 (1993), 86–88

Asai, Toshihiro (ed.), *Private Room II: Photographs by a New Generation of Women in Japan* (Mito, 1999)

Baker, Simon and Moran, Fiontán (eds), *Performing or the Camera* (London, 2016)

Barthes, Roland, *Camera Lucida: Reflections on Photography* (New York, 1981)

Bijutsu Techo, 'Topics. Itte tanoshii, mite tanoshii, sankashite tanoshii' [Topics. It is fun to go there, to see it, and to participate.], *Bijutsu Techo*, 50/754 (1989), 199

Bryson, Norman: 'Morimura: 3 Readings', *Art and Text*, 52 (1995), 74–9

Dufour, Diane and Matthew Witkovsky (eds), *Provoke: Between Protest and Performance – Photography in Japan 1960–75* (Göttingen, 2016)

Favell, Adrian, *Before and After Superflat: A Short History of Japanese Contemporary Art 1990–2011* (Hong Kong, 2011)

Feustel, Marc, *Japan: A Self-Portrait, Photographs 1945–1964* (Tokyo, 2009)

—— *Eikoh Hosoe: Theatre of Memory* (Cologne, 2010)

Fraser, Karen M., *Photography and Japan: Exposures* (London, 2011)

Fritsch, Lena, 'The Bittersweet Beauty of Ephemerality – Ishiuchi Miyako's Photography', in *Ishiuchi Miyako: Hasselblad Award 2014* (Heidelberg, 2014), pp. 137–41

—— *The Body as a Screen* (Hildesheim, 2011)

Fritsch, Lena and Clare Pollard (eds), *Tokyo: Art & Photography* (Oxford, 2021)

Fukagawa, Masafumi, 'Is the World Beautiful? Moriyama Daidō's Provocation of the History of Photography' (2007), tr. Lena Fritsch, *Art in Translation*, 4 (2012), 459–73

Fukase, Masahisa, *Ravens* (London, 2017)

Fuse, Hideto, 'Art of Arts Man Among Men, Morimura Yasumasa', *Taiyo*, 357 (1991), 159–65

Hara Museum (ed.), *Mika Ninagawa: Self-Image* (Tokyo, 2015)

Hasegawa, Yūko, 'Pachinko, Mandala and Merry Amnesia', in Peter Noever (ed.), *Japan today: Kunst, Fotografie, Design* (Vienna, 1997), pp. 16–21

Iizawa, Kōtarō, *Nihon shashinshi wo aruku* [Walking through the history of Japanese photography] (Shinchōsha, 1992)

'Interview with Moriyama Daidō', *Asahi Camera* (April 1972), p. 147

Ishiuchi, Miyako, *Hiroshima/Yokosuka: Ishiuchi Miyako* (Tokyo, 2008)

Kaneko, Ryūichi and Ivan Vartanian (eds), *Japanese Photobooks of the 1960s and '70s* (Tokyo, 2009)
Kaneko, Ryūichi, Masako Toda and Ivan Vartanian (eds), *Japanese Photography Magazines 1880s-1980s* (Tokyo, 2022)

Kasahara Michiko, *Gender shashinron 1991-2017 [Gender and Photography Discourses]* (Tokyo, 2018)

—— *On Your Body: Contemporary Japanese Photography* (Tokyo, 2008)

—— *Shashin, jidai ni kō suru mono* [Photography, something that resists history] (Tokyo, 2002)

—— *Kiss in the Dark: Contemporary Japanese Photography* (Tokyo, 2001)

Kawada, Kikuji, *The Map (Chizu)* (Tokyo, 2005)

Mackie, Vera, '"Understanding through the Body": The Masquerades of Mishima Yukio and Morimura Yasumasa', in Mark Mcleland and Romit Dasgupta (eds), *Genders, Transgenders and Sexualities in Japan* (Oxford and New York, 2005), pp. 126–44

Maddox, Amanda (ed.), *Ishiuchi Miyako: Postwar Shadows* (Los Angeles, 2016)

Matt, Gerhard and Peter Weiermair (eds), *Japanische Photographie: Lust und Leere* (Vienna, 1997)

Michael Hoppen Gallery (ed.), *Eyes of an Island: Japanese Photography 1945–2007* (London, 2007)

Miller, Laura, *Beauty Up: Exploring Contemporary Japanese Body Aesthetics* (Berkeley and London, 2006)

Mita, Haruo, 'Morimura Yasumasa – Renburando no heyaten: Kowareyuku jiga wo yūmoresu ni' [Morimura Yasumasa – the Rembrandt's Room exhibition: don't take the breaking down of the ego too seriously], *Mainichi Shinbun (Tokyo) Evening Edition*, (26 September 1994), 6

Morimura, Yasumasa, *Daughter of Art History* (New York, 2003)

—— *Mā, eeqana' no kokoro* [The 'well, it'll be fine' mindset] (Tokyo, 2001)

Moriyama, Daidō, *Inu no kioku* [Memories of a dog] (Tokyo, 1984)

Mostow, Joshua S., Norman Bryson and Maribeth Graybill (eds), *Gender and Power in the Japanese Visual Field* (Honolulu, 2003)

Munroe, Alexandra (ed.), *Japanese Art After 1945: Scream Against the Sky* (New York, 1994)

Nakamori Yasufumi (ed.), *Eikoh Hosoe* (London, 2021)

Phillips, Sandra, John W. Dower and Leo Rubinfien (eds), *Shomei Tomatsu: Skin of the Nation* (London and New Haven, 2004)

Sawaragi, Noi, *Nihon – Gendai – Bijutsu* [Japan – Contemporary – Art] (Tokyo, 1998)

Schwarzer, Alice, 'Pornografie: Der sexualisierte Menschenhass', *Emma* (November/December 2000), 22–28

Shimizu, Minoru, '"Grainy, Blurry, Out-of-Focus": Daido Moriyama's *Farewell Photography*', tr. Lena Fritsch, in Simon Baker (ed.) *Daido Moriyama* (London, 2012), pp. 51–64

Sontag, Susan, *On Photography* (Harmondsworth, 1979), p. 15

Spielmann, Heinz, *Die japanische Photographie* (Cologne, 1984), pp. 125–6

Stearns, Robert (ed.), *Photography and Beyond in Japan: Space, Time and Memory* (Tokyo, 1994)

Streiff, David, 'Einführung und Dank', in *In die Felsen bohren sich Zikadenstimmen* (Zürich, 1993), pp. 7–21

Takanashi, Yutaka and Gerry Badger, *Toshi-e (Towards the City)* (New York, 2010)

Taki, Kōji, 'The Myth of the City', tr. Lena Fritsch, in Simon Baker (ed.), *Daido Moriyama* (London, 2012), pp. 67–77

The Light Factory Photographic Arts Centre (ed.), *Inside/Out: Contemporary Japanese Photography* (Charlotte, 1994).

Thompson, G. R. (ed.), *Edgar Allan Poe: Essays and Reviews* (New York, 1984)

Tokyo Metropolitan Culture Foundation (eds), *The Half-Life of Awareness: Photographs of Hiroshima and Nagasaki* (Tokyo, 1995)

Tokyo Metropolitan Museum of Photography (ed.), *Satō Tokihiro: Presence of Absence* (Tokyo, 2014)

—— *1968 – Japanese Photography* (Tokyo, 2013)

—— *The Founding and Development of Modern Photography in Japan* (Japan, 1995)

Tokyo Photographic Art Museum (ed.), *Naito Masatoshi: Another World Unveiled* (Tokyo, 2018)

—— *Nagashima Yurie. And a Pinch of Irony with a Hint of Love* (Tokyo, 2017)

Wilkes-Tucker, Anne, Dana Friis-Hansen and Ryūichi Kaneko (eds), *The History of Japanese Photography* (London and New Haven, 2003)

Wright Jasinowski, Rosemary, *Morimura Yasumasa: A Cross Cultural Study in the Self-Portrait, Self-Definition and the Creative Process* (New York, 2001)

Yamamoto, Kazuhiro, 'Kettai na amari ni kettai na kachi no tenpuku' [A crazy, absolutely crazy, yet valuable turning point], *Art & Critique*, 15/2 (1991), 17

—— *Gendaibijutsu ni natta shashin* [Photography that has become contemporary art] (Utsunomiya, 1987)

Picture List

a = above, b = below, c = centre, l = left, r = right

2 Courtesy Fukase Masahisa Archives. © Fukase Masahisa Archives

6 Tate, London 2018

9a Courtesy the Estate of Nakayama Iwata and MEM, Tokyo. © The Estate of Nakayama Iwata

9b Courtesy Taka Ishii Gallery Photography/Film, Tokyo

10–11 Courtesy Tokyo Photographic Art Museum. © The Estate of Koishi Kiyoshi

12 Courtesy the Estate of Shiihara Osamu and MEM, Tokyo. © The Estate of Shiihara Osamu

15 Courtesy Tokyo Photographic Art Museum. © The Estate of Yamawaki Iwao

16–17 ullstein bild/Getty Images

18 © Dōmon Ken Museum of Photography, Sakata-city, Yamagata

20 Courtesy Tokyo Photographic Art Museum

23 Courtesy Keisuke Katano, Estate of Hamaya Hiroshi. © Keisuke Katano, Estate of Hamaya Hiroshi

24 United States Army. Photo Lt. Gaetano Faillace

25 Courtesy the Estate of Kimura Ihei. © Estate of Kimura Ihei

26–27 Courtesy the Hayashi Tadahiko Archive. © Hayashi Tadahiko Archive

28 Courtesy the artist. © Tanuma Takeyoshi

29, 30 Courtesy the Estate of Kimura Ihei. © Estate of Kimura Ihei

31 Courtesy Keisuke Katano, Estate of Hamaya Hiroshi. © Keisuke Katano, Estate of Hamaya Hiroshi

32 Courtesy Tokyo Photographic Art Museum. © The Estate of Midorikawa Yōichi

33–36 © Dōmon Ken Museum of Photography, Sakata-city, Yamagata

37 Courtesy the artist. © Tanuma Takeyoshi

38–39 © Ueda Shōji Office

40 Courtesy the artist and Akio Nagasawa Gallery/Publishing, Tokyo. © Hosoe Eikoh

42 Collection of the Museum of Art, Kochi. Courtesy Kochi Prefecture, Ishimoto Yasuhiro Photo Center. © Ishimoto Yasuhiro

45a Collection Société française de photographie (coll. SFP)

45b Courtesy the Estate of Sakurai Shū and Zen Foto Gallery. © The Estate of Sakurai Shū

46 Courtesy Inoue Haruko and Rat Hole Gallery, Tokyo. © Inoue Seiryu

48–55 Courtesy the artist and PGI, Tokyo. © Kawada Kikuji

56–61 Courtesy the artist and Akio Nagasawa Gallery/Publishing, Tokyo. © Hosoe Eikoh

63–63 Courtesy the Estate of Tanno Akira and Zen Foto Gallery, Tokyo. © The Estate of Tanno Akira

64 Courtesy Satō Ema and Michael Hoppen Gallery, London. © Satō Ema

65 Courtesy Michael Hoppen Gallery, London. © Tōmatsu Shōmei – INTERFACE

66a, b © Tōmatsu Shōmei – INTERFACE

66c Courtesy Taka Ishii Gallery Photography/Film, Tokyo. © Tōmatsu Shōmei – INTERFACE

67 Courtesy Taka Ishii Gallery Photography/Film, Tokyo. © Tōmatsu Shōmei – INTERFACE

68 Courtesy the artist and Akio Nagasawa Gallery/Publishing, Tokyo. © Hosoe Eikoh

69, 70–71 Courtesy Taka Ishii Gallery Photography/Film, Tokyo. © Narahara Ikkō

72 Courtesy Osiris. © Nakahira Gen

74 Courtesy the artist and Yumiko Chiba Associates, Tokyo. © Kitai Kazuo

77a Courtesy the artist and Taka Ishii Gallery, Photography/Film, Tokyo. © Takanashi Yutaka

79 Courtesy the Estate of Yanagisawa Shin. © The Estate of Yanagisawa Shin

81–84 Courtesy Moriyama Daidō Photo Foundation. © Moriyama Daidō Photo Foundation

89 Courtesy the artist and Yumiko Chiba Associates, Tokyo. © Kitai Kazuo

90–91 Courtesy Osiris. © Nakahira Gen

92–93 Courtesy the artist and Akio Nagasawa Gallery/Publishing, Tokyo. © Naitō Masatoshi

94–96, 101 Courtesy the artist and Yoshiko Isshiki Office, Tokyo. © Araki Nobuyoshi

102–103 Courtesy the artist and Akio Nagasawa Gallery/Publishing, Tokyo. © Yoshiyuki Kōhei

104–106 Courtesy the Estate of Shin Yanagisawa and Only Photography, Berlin. © The Estate of Shin Yanagisawa

107, 108, 113 Courtesy the artist and Akio Nagasawa Gallery/Publishing, Tokyo. © Suda Issei

114–115 Courtesy the artist and Third Gallery Aya, Osaka. © Ishiuchi Miyako

116–117 Courtesy Fukase Masahisa Archives. © Fukase Masahisa Archives and Yoko Works

118–119 Courtesy Masahisa Fukase Archives. © Masahisa Fukase Archives

120 Courtesy the artist and Zeit-Foto, Tokyo, Japan. © Anzaï Shigeo

125, 126, 127 Courtesy the artist. © Tsuchida Hiromi

128–129 Courtesy the artist and Yumiko Chiba Associates, Tokyo. © Uematsu Keiji

130 Courtesy Taka Ishii Gallery Photography/Film, Tokyo. © Ōtsuji Seiko, Musashino Art University Museum & Library

131 Courtesy the artist and Yumiko Chiba Associates, Tokyo. © Wakae Kanji

132–133 Courtesy Moriyama Daidō Photo Foundation. © Moriyama Daidō Photo Foundation

134 Courtesy the artist and Tomio Koyama Gallery, Tokyo. © Ninagawa Mika

136 Courtesy the artist and Maho Kubota Gallery, Tokyo. © Nagashima Yurie

139 Courtesy the artist and Tomio Koyama Gallery, Tokyo. © Ninagawa Mika

140, 145 Courtesy the artist and Maho Kubota Gallery, Tokyo. © Nagashima Yurie

146–147 Courtesy the artist and Tomio Koyama Gallery, Tokyo. © Ninagawa Mika

148–151 Courtesy the artist. © Hiromix

152 Courtesy the artist and Yoshiko Isshiki Office, Tokyo. © Araki Nobuyoshi

154 Courtesy the artist and MEM, Tokyo. © Sawada Tomoko

156 Courtesy Leslie Tonkonow Artworks + Projects, New York. © Tokihiro Satō

157 Courtesy the artist and ARTCOURT Gallery, Osaka. © Nomura Hitoshi

158 Courtesy Taka Ishii Gallery, Photography/Film, Tokyo. © Miyamoto Ryūji

160, 161a Courtesy Danziger Gallery, New York. © Yūji Obata

161b Courtesy Leslie Tonkonow Artworks + Projects, New York. © Tokihiro Satō

162 Courtesy the artist and Marian Goodman Gallery, New York. © Sugimoto Hiroshi

163 Courtesy the artist. © Narahashi Asako

164 Courtesy the artist. © Izima Kaoru

167 Courtesy Robert Mann Gallery, New York and PGI, Tokyo. © Michiko Kon

168 Courtesy the artist and Yoshiko Isshiki Office, Tokyo. © Morimura Yasumasa

171 Courtesy the artist and Third Gallery Aya, Osaka. © Ishiuchi Miyako

172 Courtesy the artist and Yumiko Chiba Associates, Tokyo. © Takano Ryūdai

175 Courtesy the artist and MUJIN-TO production, Tokyo. © Asakai Yoko

176, 181 Courtesy the artist. © Hatakeyama Naoya

182–183, 184–185 Courtesy the artist and Zeit-Foto Salon, Tokyo. © Toshio Shibata

186a Courtesy the artist. © Inoue Hiroko

186b Courtesy the artist. © Ōtsuka Chino

187 Courtesy the artist and TARONASU, Tokyo. © Homma Takashi

188, 193 Courtesy the artist and MEM, Tokyo. © Ōmori Katsumi

194–195, 196 Courtesy the artist. © Yoneda Tomoko

197–200, 205 Courtesy the artist. © Kawauchi Rinko

206–210 Courtesy the artist and Yoshiko Isshiki Office, Tokyo. © Morimura Yasumasa

211 Courtesy the artist. © Mori Mariko

212, 217–219 Courtesy the artist and MEM, Tokyo. © Sawada Tomoko

220–223 Courtesy the artist. © Izima Kaoru

224, 229 Courtesy the artist and Yumiko Chiba Associates, Tokyo. © Takano Ryūdai

230–233 Courtesy the artist and Akio Nagasawa Gallery/Publishing, Tokyo. © Nomura Sakiko

234–235 Courtesy the artist and Yoshiko Isshiki Office, Tokyo. © Yanagi Miwa

236, 241 Courtesy the artist. © Tokyo Rumando

242–249 Courtesy the artist. © Shiga Lieko

250 Courtesy the artist and Marian Goodman Gallery, New York. © Sugimoto Hiroshi

251 Courtesy the artist and Zeit-Foto Salon, Tokyo. © Toshio Shibata

252–253 Courtesy the artist. © Yoneda Tomoko

254–255 Courtesy the artist and Marian Goodman Gallery, New York. © Sugimoto Hiroshi

256 Courtesy the artist and Akio Nagasawa Gallery/Publishing, Tokyo. © Inose Kou

257 Courtesy the artist and Akio Nagasawa Gallery/Publishing, Tokyo. © Nomura Sakiko

258 Courtesy the artist and Yumiko Chiba Associates, Tokyo. © Takano Ryūdai

259 Courtesy the artist and Akio Nagasawa Gallery/Publishing, Tokyo. © Suda Issei

260–263 Courtesy the artist and Third Gallery Aya, Osaka. © Ishiuchi Miyako

264 Courtesy the artist. © Izima Kaoru

265–267 Courtesy the artist and G/P gallery, Tokyo. © Yokota Daisuke

268 Courtesy the artist and Yoshiko Isshiki Office, Tokyo. © Araki Nobuyoshi

269 Courtesy the artist and Yoshiko Isshiki Office, Tokyo, and Bob van Orsouw, Zurich. © Araki Nobuyoshi

Acknowledgments

This book depended on the generous support of many individuals and institutions. It is impossible to name all of those to whom I owe a debt of gratitude. However, above all, I would like to thank the photographers and artists who have shared their precious time in my interviews: Anzaï Shigeo, Araki Nobuyoshi, Hatakeyama Naoya, Hiromix, Hosoe Eikoh, Ishiuchi Miyako, Izima Kaoru, Kawada Kikuji, Kawauchi Rinko, Kitai Kazuo, Morimura Yasumasa, Moriyama Daidō, Nagashima Yurie, Ninagawa Mika, Nomura Sakiko, Ōmori Katsumi, Sawada Tomoko, Shibata Toshio, Shiga Lieko, Suda Issei, Takano Ryūdai, Tokyo Rumando, Tsuchida Hiromi, Yoneda Tomoko, Yoshiyuki Kōhei.

I am indebted to artists, estates, galleries, and museums for generously sharing photographs and information. Some of the people listed below have sadly passed away since the first edition of this book was published in 2018; I am truly grateful for the time I got to spend with them: Anzaï Shigeo; Araki Nobuyoshi; ARTCOURT Gallery; Asakai Yōko; Akio Nagasawa Gallery | Publishing; Daido Moriyama Photo Foundation; Dōmon Ken Museum of Photography; Getty Images; G/P Gallery; Hatakeyama Naoya; Hayashi Tadahiko Office; Hiromix; Homma Takashi; Hosoe Eikoh; Inoue Hiroko; INOSE Kou; Ishiuchi Miyako; Izima Kaoru; Kawada Kikuji; Kawauchi Rinko; Estate of Kimura Ihei; Katano Keisuke and the Estate of Hamaya Hiroshi; Kitai Kazuo; Maho Kubota Gallery; Marian Goodman Gallery; Masahisa Fukase Archives and Yoko Works; Estate of Matsumoto Eiichi; Michael Hoppen Gallery; Miyamoto Ryūji; Mori Mariko; Morimura Yasumasa; MUJIN-TO production; Nagashima Yurie; Naitō Masatoshi; Estate of Nakahira Takuma; Estate of Nakayama Iwata; Narahashi Asako; Narahara Ikkō; Ninagawa Mika; Nomura Hitoshi; Ōmori Katsumi; Osiris; Ōtsuka Chino; Roland Angst and Only Photography; Photography Museum of Koichi; Estate of Sakurai Shū; Estate of Satō Akira; Satō Tokihiro; Sawada Tomoko; Shibata Toshio; Shiga Lieko; Estate of Shiihara Osamu; Shoji Ueda Office; Shomei Tomatsu Office INTERFACE; Suda Issei; Sugimoto Hiroshi; Taka Ishii Gallery; Takahashi Sayaka and PGI; Takanashi Yutaka; Takano Ryūdai; The Estate of Tanno Akira; Tanuma Takeyoshi; TARONASU; Tate Gallery; The Third Gallery Aya; Tokyo Photographic Art Museum; Tokyo Rumando; Tsuchida Hiromi; Uematsu Keiji; Wakae Kanji; Watanabe Yoshio; White Rainbow Gallery; Estate of Yamawaki Iwao; Yanagi Miwa; Estate of Yanagisawa Shin; Yoshiko Isshiki Office; Yokota Daisuke; Yoneda Tomoko; Yoshiyuki Kōhei; Yumiko Chiba Associates; Zeit-Foto; Zen Foto Gallery.

For providing diverse help, such as introductions or intellectual input, I am thankful to Kasahara Michiko and her team at Tokyo Museum of Photographic Art; Nagasawa Akio and his gallery; Odate Natsuko from Yoshiko Isshiki Office; Ishida Katsuya and MEM; Tsuzuki Rika at Zeit-Foto; Chiba Yumiko and colleagues; Marc Feustel; Masaki Hiroshi; Roland Angst; Simon Baker; Michael Hoppen.

At Thames & Hudson, special thanks go to editorial director Roger Thorp for believing in this project and supporting it right from the beginning. I would also like to thank project editor Kate Edwards and editorial assistant Amber Husain for their tireless editorial and organizational work, and Ginny Liggitt for her work on the production of the book. The elegant book design is the work of Sarah Boris. Jo Walton has provided great support in the field of picture research.

Without a travel grant by the Great Britain Sasakawa Foundation, it would have been more difficult to conduct the interviews. I am truly grateful for their support.

Last but not least, I would like to deeply thank my partner Anish Shonpal for patiently bearing with me in stressful times and my mother Ingrid Fritsch for her helpful advice in Japanese studies.

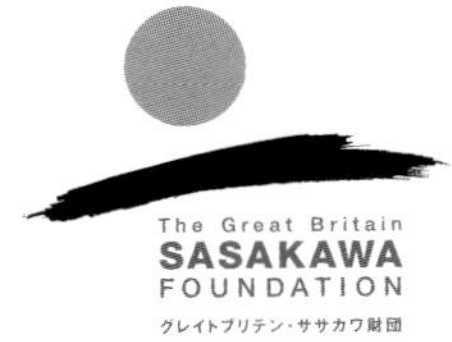

Index